ENCYCLOPEDIA OF
LITERATURE AND
SCIENCE

ENCYCLOPEDIA OF
LITERATURE AND SCIENCE

Edited by
PAMELA GOSSIN

EDITORIAL BOARD
Stephen D. Bernstein
Shelly Jarrett Bromberg
David N. Cassuto
Paul A. Harris
Dale J. Pratt

GREENWOOD PRESS
Westport, Connecticut   •   London

Library of Congress Cataloging-in-Publication Data

Encyclopedia of literature and science / edited by Pamela Gossin.
    p. cm.
  Includes bibliographical references and index.
  ISBN 0–313–30538–2 (alk. paper)
    1. Literature and science—Encyclopedias. I. Gossin, Pamela.
  PN55.E53   2002
  809'.93356—dc21   2001040552

British Library Cataloguing in Publication Data is available.

Library of Congress Catalog Card Number: 2001040552
ISBN: 0–313–30538–2

First published in 2002

Greenwood Press, 88 Post Road West, Westport, CT 06881
An imprint of Greenwood Publishing Group, Inc.
www.greenwood.com

Printed in the United States of America

The paper used in this book complies with the
Permanent Paper Standard issued by the National
Information Standards Organization (Z39.48–1984).

10 9 8 7 6 5 4 3 2 1

CONTENTS

PREFACE

The mission of the *Encyclopedia of Literature and Science* is to introduce the emergent field of interdisciplinary literature and science (LS) studies to those just discovering it and provide a ready reference tool for those already working in a specific area of LS. We have intended this volume to be of most use to undergraduate college and university students and their instructors, especially those exploring together in the classroom some area of the interrelations of the humanities and sciences. We hope the *Encyclopedia* will also interest and serve the broad and diverse community of interdisciplinary scholars working within literary and language studies, the creative and performing arts, history, the social sciences, and computer science and engineering as well as historians of science and technology, health professionals, medical humanists and ethicists, and teaching and research scientists.

Although the *Encyclopedia* aims to represent the concerns of LS in as many manifestations as possible, the editor and editorial board acknowledge that it is *impossible* to refer to every topic, approach, or theme that has ever arisen within, or could be construed as relevant to, "literature and science" per se. The present volume contains over 650 entries, varying from 50 to 3,500 words in length. These entries provide introductory information about a wide range of topics, themes, writers, scientists, their works, theories, and methodologies. The entries order and allude to both major and minor, current and historical, classic and controversial areas, with a central goal of providing a starting point for further research, always keeping in mind that most readers will be new to the material in some way. The primary purpose of each entry is to define *literary* topics in terms of their *scientific* relations and the *scientific* topics in terms of the *literary* and/or to describe the topic's general relation to interdisciplinary LS studies. For individual subject entries, only biographical information not readily available in standard discipline-specific and general reference sources and/or those points of information that are especially relevant to the figure's interdisciplinary contributions are included.

Thematic, contextual, and survey entries provide basic historiographical and interpretative frameworks and discussion of the various relations of each topic to and within LS, both past and current. Such entries introduce problems, describe challenges and late-breaking approaches, and suggest prospects for future directions. In some cases, contributors have exercised their own discretion in choosing whether to treat the interdisciplinary relations of a particular topic or to emphasize discipline-specific concerns (this has been especially true of entries in which the contributor has felt it was important to clarify the meaning of technical concepts or ideas in a specific literary/humanistic or scientific area that he or she believes have been poorly or incompletely understood within LS in the past). Throughout the volume, "literature" and "science" have been broadly defined, and contributors have been asked to utilize those definitions and connotations that are of greatest relevance to their individual approaches and subject matter. Thus, from entry to entry, "literature" might variously mean belles lettres and creative writing, essays and articles, linguistics, nonverbal communication, signs and other symbolic forms of information transfer, or in general, humanistic, artistic, and cultural endeavors and artifacts. Similarly, "science" might refer to specialized knowledge about nature, scientific theories, practices, products, institutions, concepts, discoveries, methods, technology, engineering, or medical research.

Bibliographic references appear at the end of most entries, with differing purposes. Some citations document works cited or discussed within the entry. Others serve as lists for further reading, especially noting books or articles that lead across disciplinary boundaries in various ways. Some contributors have devoted particular entries to discipline-specific information and have then used the works listed to suggest interdisciplinary relations with "the other." Contributors were asked to list book-length studies preferentially to articles or other documents, whenever possible.

The initial pool of items considered for possible inclusion numbered over 2,000. These suggestions were made by the general editor, editorial board members, and contributors, as well as by members of the LS community at large. Many ideas were submitted as the result of appeals issued through conferences, newsletters, journal announcements, email, and electronic listserv postings. Generally, topics were selected according to their currency, ongoing importance, range of relevance, and potential usefulness to all levels of LS readership. We considered such factors as whether any (and how many) scholars are currently working in the area (measured by the item's presence as a panel topic and in journal citations); how long the topic has been important and how wide its influence seems to have been; how representative or typical the topic is within LS and how likely it is to become or remain important; how many readers would be likely to need or value the information in the entry; how many other topics the item is related to, illustrates, or explains; the availability of a qualified scholar to write the entry; and space considerations. Sometimes topics new to, or little known within, LS were given greater consideration in this volume than "high-profile" topics for which additional information could easily be found in scholarly monographs, articles, standard references, and bibliographies. For instance, there is no survey of LS in Great Britain here (because that material receives strong coverage throughout the volume and elsewhere), but there is such an entry for "Ireland, Scotland, Wales," as well as for "Italy" and the "Hispanic World," among others. Some planned entries, regrettably, do not appear in this edition (e.g., mathematics, India, and Asia), because contributors could not be recruited to write them or the contributors who agreed to do so did not provide the content in time for inclusion.

Contributors and editorial board members were invited to participate in this project according to identical criteria: professional expertise and demonstrated activity (publications and public presentations) in LS studies and wide-ranging knowledge of and/or specialized work in particular areas pertaining to LS. Efforts were made to make the selection process as democratic as possible, not only to ensure a broad representation of a range of topics, interests, methodological perspectives, professional positions, and disciplines (in the sciences as well as humanities) but to provide diversity in the cultural backgrounds, national origins, gender, and generational membership of the contributors themselves. Contributors were given creative control over the content of their entries and were asked to freely include discussion of controversies and contentions in their fields. They were cautioned, however, to consider the long-term value of such material, suggesting that descriptive guidance through contested terrain might be more appropriate here than providing additional examples of grandstanding, axe-grinding, and backstabbing (among other less exalted academic activities). Each contributor was responsible for the factual accuracy of his or her own entries as well as for their interpretative content. The general editor and editorial board members made every effort to preserve the unique voices and inflections of the nearly 100 contributors while attending to typos and infelicities of style and syntax and making occasional emendations or additions. Unfortunately, some evidence of global diversity was sacrificed to matters of uniformity and continuity (concessions were made, e.g., to the publisher's house style in preferring American spelling to British). Contributors are identified at the end of each entry.

In designing the taxonomy for the *Encyclopedia*, we have intended the volume to address as broad an array of readers' needs as possible and, simultaneously, to suggest the breadth of LS studies—all within the length restrictions set by the publisher. Anticipating the information-seeking needs of prospective users, the volume is organized according to a conventional (and easy-to-use) A to Z format. The longest entries provide chronological and national surveys of their subject matter; midlength entries provide a variety of contextual, thematic, and topical studies; the briefest provide specialized "ready-reference" information. Cross-references (in **boldface**) direct readers to other related entries within the volume. An index provides additional access to the *Encyclopedia*'s contents. By consulting the index and/or following the internal cross-references, readers will be able to work their way "up" or "down" the scale of topics from specific to general, or vice versa, traveling, for instance, from a chronological survey of literature and medicine to entries on individual physician–writers and literary representations of particular diseases to a definition of illness narratives.

While our chief concern was to design a taxonomy that provided an educational service and research resource to LS scholars and students (primarily at the undergraduate level), the general editor and editorial board were also interested in creatively exploring the representational possibilities of encyclopedias as experimental, nonnarrative forms of history. David Perkins's *Is Literary History Possible?* (Johns Hopkins, 1992) was especially useful in encouraging the general editor to give careful consideration to matters of form in addition to problems of content. In thinking about how the formal structure of an encyclopedia might relate to its entries, she found it helpful to visualize the table of contents in terms of a fractal model—a set of geometric shapes that displays symmetry ("self-similarity" or "regular irregularity") across scales, from large to small and vice versa. This model invested the alphabetical arrangement with a meaningful underlying framework for representing the professional, methodological, and philosophical concerns as well as the "content" of LS—an emergent nondiscipline that merely purports to investigate the interaction of two of the most extensive and influential intellectual modes of expression and knowledge production in human history. The use of fractal branching as an organizing principle allowed the editor to identify and track the interrelationships of individual entries within the taxonomy as well as to develop and emphasize those interconnections. LS itself, then, is "represented" by a general introduction to the "discipline" and an overview of the "two cultures" debate; by national and chronological surveys; by topical treatments of the interrelations of literature and individual sciences such as literature and astronomy, literature and chemistry, literature and technology; by "form and genre" entries on literary and scientific relations in, for example, the essay, poetry, popularization; and by particular (particulate) entries on AIDS, alterity, Aratus of Soli, Aristotle, utopias, virtuoso, Vitruvius, Voltaire, X-rays, and Zola. For more background on the making of this encyclopedia, see Pamela Gossin, "An Encyclopedia of Literature and Science: Experimental History or Experimental Community?" (originally presented at the Society for Literature and Science, November 1998) posted at <http://www.utdallas.edu/~psgossin>.

More than is usual in most projects of this kind, the contributors have had a strong, ongoing influence in shaping the overall taxonomy as well as the internal content of the volume. Yet to whatever extent our collective efforts may have succeeded in "representing" LS—in carrying a slice of the life of literature and science studies within it—we are all aware of the ultimate impossibility of the task. In recognition of the unavoidable fact that readers will find expected topics missing or underrepresented, and in general acknowledgment of the open-ended nature of the encyclopedic enterprise, we are formulating plans to post an electronic supplement. Readers are encouraged to participate in its construction by sending corrections and comments as well as suggestions for topics or texts of new entries you would like to see included to psgossin@utdallas.edu.

ACKNOWLEDGMENTS

Special thanks are due to the members of this project's original advisory board: David Perkins, N. Katherine Hayles, Stuart Peterfreund, Ronald Schleifer, John Neu, Gregg Mitman, Stephen Bernstein, Margot Kelley, and Robert Kelley. Your ideas, suggestions, and critiques were taken to heart. We gratefully received professional support and advice at critical junctures from especially loyal contributors: Doug Russell, Liam Heaney, Roslynn Haynes, Jacob Korg, Dennis R. Dean, Joseph Duemer, James Paradis, Stephen Weininger, and Jay Labinger. We also benefited from the voices of experience proffered by fellow encyclopedia editors: Wilbur Applebaum, John Lankford, and Marc Rothenberg and biographical dictionary editors Marilyn Ogilvie and Joy Harvey. The success you all demonstrated in taking on the "impossible" gave us hope. Thank you, too, to our special colleagues in LS and the History of Science who have taught us so much by example: James J. Bono, Kenneth Knoespel, Judith Yaross Lee, Joseph W. Slade, Mary Jo Nye, and Robert Nye. The general editor is also sincerely grateful for the friendship and collegiality of Patricia Howell Michaelson, Gerald Soliday, and Michael Wilson—you understand that "real" scholarship does include scholarly editing.

Especially heartfelt thanks is owed to all of the editorial board members: Stephen D. Bernstein (who survived both incarnations), Shelly Jarrett Bromberg, David N. Cassuto, Paul A. Harris, and Dale J. Pratt. Your critical eye, collective good sense, and generous contributions all helped tremendously. In addition to fulfilling her general editorial board responsibilities, Shelly unselfishly provided no end of special editorial assistance, reading and critiquing numerous drafts of entries of all shapes and sizes and topics, as well as fact-checking and rechecking. The project would have been both practically and theoretically "impossible" without *you*.

Finally, I wish to express personal appreciation to the National Endowment for the Humanities, the Pollock Foundation of the Dudley Observatory, and the George A. and Eliza Gardner Howard Foundation Fellowship in the History of Science (Brown University) for support that enabled me to research and write a number of entries for this volume as well as make good progress on two related monographs.

BIBLIOGRAPHIC NOTE

This volume concludes with a selected, general bibliography of the most important broad works on the study of literature and science.

INTRODUCTION: LITERATURE AND SCIENCE AS DISCIPLINE AND PROFESSION

Lance Schachterle

Nothing in that ghostly realm called "the objective physical world" compels anyone to worry about the relations of literature and science. Unlike the pursuit of science or technology, nothing in literature and science studies is likely to predict or control the phenomenal world. Unlike the pursuit of literature, literature and science studies have never been strongly determined by a received corpus of artifacts such as the canonical "Great Books" with their accumulated generations of cultural baggage.

More so than most intellectual pursuits, literature and science studies are entirely a social construction consciously or unconsciously articulated by self-identified practitioners. Or perhaps more accurately, a series of constructions highly variegated and diverse both synchronously and diachronically.

The diversity of views of what constitutes the practice of literature and science studies is well illustrated by the one institution, the Society for Literature and Science (SLS), created in the words of the Society blurb to

foster the multi-disciplinary study of the relations among literature and language, the arts, science, medicine, and technology. SLS was inaugurated at the 17th International Congress of the History of Science, Berkeley, CA, in August 1985. Since then membership in SLS has grown rapidly. Each year the annual SLS convention attracts hundreds of participants from many different disciplines, including the history, sociology, anthropology, rhetoric, and philosophy of science, technology, and medicine; literary history and criticism; art history and media studies; the cognitive sciences; and all areas of science, technology, engineering, and medicine. In addition to [its journal] *Configurations* SLS sponsors a book series, maintains an active Speakers' Bureau, publishes a newsletter, *Decodings*, and distributes a membership directory, which lists members' interests. The Society also produces an annual bibliography of scholarship, which will be published in *Configurations*.

By any standards, the scholarly apparatus presented here by SLS—annual conferences, a membership directory and speakers' bureau, a newsletter, a journal, a book series—constitutes significant institutionalization. Yet with respect to an even stronger characteristic of institutionalization—a significant number of homes at or within disciplinary or interdisciplinary programs—literature and science lacks the credentials of other professional interest categories with which it is sometimes compared such as the history or philosophy of science.

The vigorous conversations conducted within an international society like SLS—but the paucity of official niches within the world of academic departments—point to a distinctive characteristic of literature and science at the present moment: the absence of a fundamental definition to which even a significant plurality of its self-confessed practitioners might subscribe. Literature and science studies are energized by their embrace of whatever anyone wishes to bring to the table as an appropriate topic, rather than by their pursuit of a well-defined, shared agenda. This diversity is well illustrated by a review of the topics offered at recent programs of the SLS annual conference, where presentations were offered in at least the following different topics: the influences of science on literature; rhetorical/linguistic analyses of scientific texts; literature as a science or technology; sciencepoetry (a genre that purports to collapse the usual distinctions between science and poetry); literary and scientific artifacts as exemplars of underlying cultural force fields; the evolution of rhetorical strategies to legitimize and empower science; literature and science as a cultural criticism of science; the competing claims for knowing of literature and science; the history of literature as seen in science; the history of specific forms of scientific literature, such as alchemy, scientific explorations, evolution, or various forms of popular writing; scientific journalism and essays; the adoption by specific imaginative writers of ideas, strategies, or modes of communication first developed in science; literature as the technology of communications; science fiction; the historical evolution, within a societal context, of the rhetoric developed to present science and its claims to authority.

While one might hazard the view that this diversity of approaches could all be set down under three or four focal areas of study such as historical, language and linguistic, theoretical, and societal and political, any attempt to rationalize the current heuristics risks marginalizing one or more topics of interest to someone active in literature and science studies.

This extraordinary multiplicity of discourses results from literature and science studies constituting neither a disciplinary nor interdisciplinary field but rather naming a broad range of description and analysis hovering over the distinctive claims for authority made by both science and by literature. Literature and science studies are not simply the study of one discipline through the lens of another, as are fields like history of science or philosophy of science. Instead, practitioners from all the areas named in the SLS description attempt to reach out from the discipline closest to them to try to comprehend areas of discourse new to them. For example, a distinctive tactic adopted by both students of science and literature is to explicate in broad cultural terms scientific ideas in texts they admire or to apply rhetorical or other literary theories to scientific texts.

For most contemporary students, literature and science became an interesting discourse only when the tension on the conjunction "and" linking the two nouns increased almost to the breaking point. Only in the last several decades when "literature" and "science" separately laid significant claim to interpretive authority did "literature and science" become more than either a scholarly pastime dedicated to showing the influence of science on specific authors or a fuzzy pairing used to compare or contrast the competing claims of either to a cultural role within a partisan debate like the "two cultures."

This tension began when modern science as we now know it began. The individual contributions of people like Isaac Newton and Galileo Galilei, along with new kinds of corporate collaboration embodied in national organizations like the Royal Society, unmistakably marked to contemporaries the rise of modern science in seventeenth-century Europe. Recognition of and unease with the "new philosophy [that] calls all in doubt" may be found not only in John Donne (*An Anatomy of the World*) but in the various debates between the Ancients and the Moderns and over a Universal Language, in the best-known works of the latter-day Christian Humanist Jonathan Swift, among the Encyclopedists, and still later with the High Romantics (one of whom, Johann Wolfgang von Goethe, contributed original work of merit to both literature and science).

The first well-known public conjunction of "literature and science" was Matthew Arnold's 1882 Rede Lecture of that title, best known in the form read during his American tour of that year. Arnold wrote in direct opposition to the claims made two years earlier in Thomas Henry Huxley's "Science and Culture," in which the prominent scientist spoke in favor of barring "mere literary instruction and education" from a new scientific school founded in Birmingham. By stating flatly that "for the purpose of attaining real culture, an exclusively scientific education is at least as effectual as an exclusively literary education" (141), Huxley directly confronted the Victorian high priest of literary culture with a radical formulation of the importance of science—not only to providing material comforts and satisfying human curiosity but to sustaining "a criticism of life" (143).

Arnold's "Literature and Science" thus conjoins the two substantives that occasion this encyclopedia precisely because "science" now claims parity with, if not dominance over, literature; the conjunction in his title—as will be often the case later—really signals disjunction and conflict. Arnold's response to Huxley is twofold: Literature includes written texts in all fields including mathematics and science, not just mere belles lettres; and more important, literature alone—not science—ministers to "our sense for conduct, our sense for beauty" (Arnold 62). To know the culture of the Romans and Greeks is to know their science, mathematics, and technology as well as their plays, and such knowledge of the whole culture fulfills the Arnoldian touchstone rephrased in this essay as the capacity "to know ourselves and the world" through being able "to know the best which has been thought and said in the world" (Arnold 56).

This gentlemanly exchange between the two preeminent Victorian advocates of literature and of science occurred just when both discourses were becoming academically institutionalized: literature, especially in Great Britain, and science, especially in Germany. The study separately of literature and science increasingly plays out within the arena of universities and learned societies. Some benchmarks: The American Association for the Advancement of Science was founded in 1848, whereas the American Philological Association came into existence in 1869 and the Modern Language Association in 1883.

In the twentieth century, writers from outside literary scholarship have strongly shaped literature and science studies, especially in terms of addressing broader cultural issues. Writing as a practicing scientist, J. Bronowski published several books and essays on the importance of science within cultural history and in 1953 gave three lectures at the Massachusetts Institute of Technology (published in 1956 as *Science and Human Values*) arguing that science and literature were more similar than different with respect to creative processes, empirical referentiality, and the formation of values. Even better known is C.P. Snow's 1959 Rede Lecture on the "Two Cultures," perhaps best consulted in the full form printed in his book *Public Affairs* (Scribner's, 1971) and titled "The Two Cultures and the Scientific Revolution."

Snow confessed in a later essay that his ideas might have been better received had he used a title he considered but rejected: "The Rich and the Poor," which better articulated his underlying plea for social activism. Despite this and other failures to focus his argument sharply, Snow's contrast between the two cultures—"Literary intellectuals at one pole—at the other scientists, and as the most representative, the physical scientists" (15)—captured much attention. Snow's basic distinction between literary scholars and scientists proceeded along a few simple axes: backward versus forward looking, pessimistic versus optimistic, contemplative versus active, respectively. These simple polarities aroused much pointed rebuttal. But Snow's basic thesis remains unambiguous: The Scientific and Industrial Revolutions offer the world's swelling masses a greater chance of ameliorating their physical conditions than does literary criticism. In one form or another, reference to the "Two Cultures," with its suggestive but inconclusive allusions as to how differing upbringings, languages, and values differentiate professional cultures, continues to inform much subsequent thinking about the relations of literature and science.

What quickly became the "two cultures" debate became institutionalized—at least for a decade or so and at least in England and North America—in both academic and semipopular discourses. The English critic F.R. Leavis reacted with an intensity many thought excessively personalized against Snow. Much of Leavis's bile flowed from Snow's incessant name-dropping and embracing of the mantle of the Oxbridge power structure, a maneuver that made clear that if to Snow literature no longer was knowledge, science was still very much power. Other, more temperate responses to Snow and Leavis include the novelist and essayist Aldous Huxley's *Literature and Science* (Harper and Row, 1963), which sought to distinguish between the two pursuits by contrasting private (literary) and public (scientific) discourses, and the biologist Sir Peter Medawar's 1968 lecture "Science and Literature," which argued that "imagination is the energizing force of science as well as poetry, but in science imagination and a critical evaluation of its products are integrally combined. To adopt a conciliatory attitude, let us say that science is that form of poetry (going back now to its classical and more general sense) in which reason and imagination act together synergistically" (18).

However, with the exception of the now largely quiescent "two cultures" debate, the authors named above did not create a body of scholarly activity (both printed and human in terms of graduate students) that could be regarded as an institution. Bronowski, Snow, Medawar, and others who helped make the relations of literature and science a topic of concern in intellectual circles wrote as members of the scientific confraternity essaying broader societal issues about the role and impact of science. Their work was largely tangential to their scientific or administrative professions. As such, they did not write primarily for or as part of an ongoing academic community.

The beginnings of the institutionalization of literature and science occurred as a result of the work of literary scholars, not scientists. The earliest example given in the literature is Carson Duncan's 1913 *New Science and English Literature*. Another early instance is I.A. Richard's *Science and Poetry* (1926; almost entirely on poetry and its superiority to science). The first substantial body of scholarship we would recognize as some form of "literature and science" was the work on seventeenth- and eighteenth-century British poets by Marjorie Hope Nicolson. Nicolson worked early in her career with Arthur O. Lovejoy (founder of the "history of ideas" school) and taught first at Smith College before removing to Columbia University and a later career largely with graduate students. Beginning in the mid-1930s, Nicolson developed a scholarly strategy of compiling and explicating references to contemporary science throughout a wide range of poetry. Perhaps the strongest example of her work was the 1946 *Newton Demands the Muse: Newton's "Opticks" and the Eighteenth Century Poets*, which begins characteristically by explaining how numerous passages of English poetry in the half century after Newton's death in 1727 can only be fully understood as versifications of concepts from *The Opticks* (1704). After much literary history, leading up to the Romantics, the study concludes by arguing that the early-eighteenth-century shift toward topographical poetry and away from the Metaphysicals was motivated in part by exploiting for poetry Newton's valorization through his prism experiments of the colorful palette of the natural world.

Nicolson's work was influential in lending credibility to similar projects on behalf of other authors, from Chaucer through the English Romantics to Thomas Hardy. A late manifestation of this genre is Douglas Bush's historically arranged influence study published in 1950 as *Science and English Poetry: A Historical Sketch, 1590–1959*. This body of scholarship demonstrated that for many writers and their audiences some familiarity with contemporary science was a given within their discourse communities. But in the scholarship of Nicolson and her immediate successors, the traffic is generally one-way. Science influences literature by supplying images and ideas, with literature always deriving from science.

As the Modern Language Association (MLA) responded to increasing specialization among its membership, specific interest groups or "divisions" were formed. Nicolson's work helped ensure that literature and science was recognized as one of the first MLA divisions as early as 1939. With respect to relating science to the humanities, literature thus was behind both history and philosophy institutionally: The History of Science Society was formed earlier in 1924, and the Philosophy of Science Association in 1933. Other disciplinary groups outside of science also responded to the growing importance science (and technology) had throughout Western culture by forming similar "Science and . . ." groups: the American Association for the History of Medicine, 1925; the Society for the History of Technology (SHOT), 1958; the Society for the Social Studies of Science (4S), 1975; and the Society for Philosophy and Technology, 1980. Each of these cross-disciplinary groups soon produced a journal and an annual convention as a means to promoting self-defining communications and achieving legitimacy within the general community of scholars.

From the 1970s on, interest in literature and science as measured by the scholarly metrics of publications, conferences, and new societies clearly increased, while—paradoxically—major scholars like G.S. Rousseau who identified themselves as professors within this new field expressed concern about its legitimacy and vitality. Rousseau, one of the last graduate students of Nicolson, was eager both to continue her historical erudition and to come to grips with the new challenges to such conventional scholarship arising from the suffusion into literary studies of continental cultural theories in the forms of linguistic, Marxist/political neo-Freudianism and structural/poststructural interpretive strategies. In a series of papers in *ISIS*, Rousseau issued the challenge to himself and his colleagues to define a balance between historical and theoretical analysis in literature and science that would make such studies of interest to a younger generation of theory-oriented students. In a series of sessions at MLA meetings in the mid-1980s, Rousseau brought together several panels who debated these issues.

The MLA recognized the increasing interest its members had in literature and science studies by publishing two major scholarly works in the 1980s. In 1982, Jean-Pierre Barricelli and Joseph Gibaldi edited for MLA the *Interrelations of Literature*, a series of essays reviewing scholarly and critical activity in thirteen fields where literature was one of a pairing of disciplines. George Slusser and George Guffey wrote the chapter on "Literature and Science," which followed Aldous Huxley in distinguishing between the two in terms of concept versus percept; subsequent sections review the history of commentary of the relations including a review of science fiction. In 1987 Walter Schatzberg, who for many years had edited the annual MLA-division sponsored bibliography in literature and science, published *The Relations of Literature and Science: An Annotated Bibliography of Scholarship, 1880–1980*; several essays originally intended as prefatory context appeared separately in the same year in volume 19 of *The University of Hartford Studies in Literature* (edited by G.S. Rousseau). These essays, by Rousseau, Stuart Peterfreund, E.S. Shaffer, and John Neubauer, are especially valuable for recording perceptions of where literature and science studies presently were and which directions these pursuits might take. Of special concern was preserving a sense of historicity within the nascent field as more practitioners (including some of these authors) also pursued new theoretical models.

In addition to this increase in activity in scholarly publications, the 1980s witnessed a string of conferences on literature, science, technology, and culture. At least five drew some attention: 1981—the Library of Congress offered an invitational conference centered around papers by the chemist George Wald and Shakespearean scholar O.B. Hardison; 1981—Clark University, under the guidance of Walter Schatzberg, sponsored a conference in Luxembourg; 1982—Long Island University mounted a conference attended by several hundred on Science, Technology and Literature, organized by Joseph W. Slade and Judith Yaross Lee; 1984—the University of Virginia organized a conference on "Philosophy of Science and Literary Theory," with selected invited speakers and colloquia, and an invited audience, intended to celebrate the influence of their colleague Richard Rorty in a multitude of fields; and 1989—the Center for the Critical Analysis of Contemporary Culture at Rutgers offered a seminar on "Reality and Representation," chaired by George Levine.

The most recent large-scale indicator of institutionalization was the establishment in 1985 of the Society for Literature and Science—the organization referenced at the beginning of this introduction. SLS emerged directly from the MLA Literature and Science Division, whose leadership in the early 1980s had become increasingly concerned that students of science rarely became engaged in MLA discussions. Contacts with members of cognate groups in the physical and social sciences, and to some degree the visual arts, indicated that an audience existed for a society independent of a parent body in either literature or science. SLS hoped to attract both literary and scientific scholars; its success with the latter has always remained problematic in that the institutional rewards for presentation or publication in SLS venues accrue more favorably to literary scholars than to scientists.

The broad base of support solicited by SLS acknowledged that much of the current ferment on literature and science studies originated largely outside the MLA. French thinkers such as Michel Foucault, Bruno Latour, and Michel Serres pressed very hard on claims science made to accessing privileged truths about the external world, often viewing such assertions at best as politics rather than epistemology. In the social sciences, "social constructionism" in various flavors presented new ways of conceptualizing the relations between thinkers, audiences, and social constructs that strongly energized literature and science studies. Scientific texts could be examined the same way any other document was scrutinized, in terms of the positions designed rhetorically to win assent and thus claim authority.

Science increasingly is viewed as yet another social artifact to be discussed in seminars in literature, philosophy, and sociology, using investigative tools drawn from these and other disciplines. Contemporary scholars seek to define ways of viewing science and literature as epiphenomena characterized by deeper, underlying cultural pressures. Employing a sophisticated grasp of science, literature, and the concept of influence, N. Katherine Hayles precipitated the study of literature and science as a form of cultural studies in her *The Cosmic Web: Scientific Field Models and Literary Strategies in the Twentieth Century* (1984). Hayles is one of an increasing number of scholar–critics within literature and science studies whose work appears in forums devoted to the broad and most rigorous inquiries about the engagement of science in our society.

Where, then, may we say the literature and science studies are currently institutionalized? No departments exist solely to promote the relations of literature and science. At the same time, its strongest practitioners (like Hayles) are widely recognized throughout both the literary and scientific communities. (Enough so in her case both to bring graduate students to the University of California at Los Angeles (UCLA) and to attract the deprecations of Paul R. Gross and Norman Levitt in *Higher Superstition: The Academic Left and Its Quarrels with Science*, 1994). A distinctly small but increasing number of institutions report some program activity in literature and science.

In 1989, as a project for SLS, Lance Schachterle published a collection of some fifty-seven course syllabi "on the Relationships of Literature and Science." These syllabi came from thirty-seven institutions large and small, with both broad liberal arts and more narrow professional specializations (often in engineering and science). The large majority of syllabi represented singular undergraduate courses offered as part of a curricular smorgasbord; only three institutions—UCLA, Rensselaer Polytechnic Institute, and the Georgia Institute of Technology—indicated that their offerings were part of a larger program. These three institutions also indicated that programs involving literature and science studies were also available at the graduate level.

A survey of SLS members in spring 1996 confirmed that these three programs continue and provided some additional information: (1) UCLA is starting a "Cultural Studies of Science" program drawing upon faculty from history, literature, and philosophy. The program will include undergraduate and graduate course offerings, a lecture series, graduate and faculty colloquia, and workshops. The objective is a graduate certification program with a concentration in literature and science. (2) The Georgia Institute of Technology School of Literature,

Communication and Culture offers a B.S. degree in Science, Technology, and Culture and a Master's in Information Design and Technology. (3) Carnegie Mellon University has an undergraduate program in literary and cultural studies and Master's and Ph.D. programs in Literary and Cultural Theory. Of the areas of several areas of study, culture and science is the largest in terms of faculty. (4) Other institutions that the survey disclosed with programs at some stage of development in literature and science studies include the University of California at San Diego, the City University of New York, Michigan State University, Massachusetts Institute of Technology, New York University (Medical Humanities), Rutgers, Virginia Polytechnic Institute and State University, and West Virginia University.

As these programs suggest, the number of graduate students in various fields who write on literature and science topics or offer talks grows steadily and probably can be counted in the hundreds. However, the distribution among disciplines is skewed away from the sciences (especially the physical sciences). Institutionalization of literature and science studies is often regarded within scientific cultures, at best, as a questionable use of time and resources or, at worst, consorting with irrational critics of science who challenge notions of scientific objectivity (and thus authority and funding). Even senior scientists interested in literature and science topics must consider whether explicit contributions to forums outside their field will help or hinder their careers.

The wide range of activities that practitioners collect within "literature and science" continues to mean that agreement about, or parity among, programs is not easily obtained or perhaps much sought. From Matthew Arnold to the present, "literature and science" declares itself disjunctively and disparately. In one way or another, literature and science studies provide yet another tool for those trying to characterize our present culture, in which science and technology play a large, complex but rarely transparent role. Many of the strategies and structures its practitioners employ lend themselves well to a plethora of cultural critiques and are grafted readily into diverse inter- or multidisciplinary enterprises, as often within social science as within humanities programs. Thus literature and science studies may proceed at many sites without formal institutional sanction or recognition. Its practitioners may even choose to "go underground" into a variety of programs addressing broad critical and cultural topics, without benefit of a "literature and science" label.

For these reasons, literature and science studies are likely to remain largely unhoused and uninstitutionalized, by definition. It is increasingly clear that this freedom from institutional constraint contributes significantly to the growing complexity of discourse, as literature and science studies continue to explore various configurations of each entity separately, conjointly, and in marked contradistinction. In much of the most interesting work, assumptions and patterns of analysis in either discipline are fruitfully challenged, modulated, and energized by contact with the other.

REFERENCES

Arnold, Matthew. *The Complete Prose Works of Matthew Arnold.* Vol. 10. *Philistinism in England and America.* Ed. R.H. Super. Ann Arbor: U of Michigan P, 1974.

Graff, Gerald. *Professing Literature: An Institutional History.* Chicago: U of Chicago P, 1987.

Hayles, N. Katherine. *The Cosmic Web: Scientific Field Models and Literary Strategy in the Twentieth Century.* Ithaca, NY: Cornell UP, 1984.

Huxley, Aldous. *Literature and Science.* New York: Harper and Row, 1963.

Huxley, Thomas. *Science and Education.* New York: A.L. Fowle, 1880.

Medawar, Peter. "Science and Literature." *Pluto's Republic: Incorporating the Art of the Soluble and Induction and Intuition.* Oxford: Oxford UP, 1982. 42–61.

Rousseau, G.S. "Literature and Science: The State of the Field." *ISIS* 69 (1978): 583–91.

———, ed. "Science and the Imagination." *Annals of Scholarship: Metastudies of the Humanities and Social Sciences* 4.1 (1986).
[Contents: " 'Till We Have Built Jerusalem': The Berkeley Symposium and the Future of Literature and Science" by G.S. Rousseau; "The Re-Emergence of Energy in the Discourse of Literature and Science" by Stuart Peterfreund; "Blake and the Perception of Science" by Nelson Hilton; "Blake's Marriage of Heaven and Hell: Technology and Artistic Form" by Mark L. Greenberg; "What Really Distinguishes the 'Two Cultures'?" by Lance Schachterle; "Sciences of the Mind in French Science Fiction" by George Slusser.]

Schatzberg, Walter, R.A. Waite, and J.K. Johnson, eds. *The Relations of Literature and Science: An Annotated Bibliography of Scholarship, 1880–1980.* New York: MLA, 1987.

———. Special issue. *University of Hartford: Studies in Literature* 19.1 (1987).
[Contents: Preface by G.S. Rousseau; "The Discourse of Literature and Science" by G.S. Rousseau; "Literature and Science: The Present State of the Field" by Stuart Peterfreund; "Literature and Science: Towards a New Literary History" by Elinor S. Shaffer; "Literature and Science: Future Possibilities" by John Neubauer.]

Slusser, George, and George Guffey. "Literature and Science." *Interrelations of Literature.* Ed. Jean-Pierre Barricelli and Joseph Gibaldi. New York: MLA, 1982.

Snow, C.P. "The Two Cultures and the Scientific Revolution." *Public Affairs.* New York: Scribner's, 1971.

A

Abbey, Edward (1927–1989). Author of *Desert Solitaire: A Season in the Wilderness* (1968) and six other volumes of essays on environmental (see Environment) topics as well as five novels including *The Monkey Wrench Gang* (1975). Abbey has a close association with the desert Southwest and is known for controversial views expressed in defense of the American West. His ideological roots are in theoretical anarchism, and his most admired writers include the anarchist B. Traven as well as **Jack London** and **Robinson Jeffers**.

While he does not turn to the details of ecological information and concept that other nature essayists have and he forswears any expertise in natural history, Abbey is indebted to science for his basic outlook. "Democritus, **Galileo, Copernicus, Kepler, Newton, Lyell, Darwin**, and **Einstein**," he writes, are "liberators of the human consciousness" because they have expanded knowledge and awareness more than "all the pronouncements of all the shamans, gurus, seers, and mystics of the earth, East and West, combined" (*Abbey's Road* 125). Any good writer, he argues, must begin with a scientific view of the world. But he also argues that "any scientist worth listening to must be something of a poet, must possess the ability to communicate to the rest of us his sense of love and wonder at what his work discovers" (*Journey* 87).

References

Abbey, Edward. *Abbey's Road*. New York: E.P. Dutton, 1979.
———. *The Journey Home: Some Works in Defense of the American West*. New York: E.P. Dutton, 1977.
Ronald, Ann. *The New West of Edward Abbey*. Albuquerque: U of New Mexico P, 1982.
James I. McClintock

Acker, Kathy (1948–1997). Avant-garde novelist. In the essay "Models of Our Present" (1984), Acker uses mathematical models of time based on Newtonian and quantum mechanics to explore artistic activity. In novels like *Empire of the Senseless* (1988), Acker uses Freudian theory (*see* Freud) (theories of schizophrenia especially) to explore postmodern identity.

Elizabeth J. Donaldson

Ackerman, Diane (1948–   ). Poet and nature writer who has sought deep integration of literature and science in her life and work. Her Cornell dissertation on **Metaphysical poets** was produced under the direction of a doctoral committee that included poet **A.R. Ammons** and astrophysicist **Carl Sagan**, the latter of whom also served as the "technical adviser" for her volume of astronomical poetry entitled *The Planets: A Cosmic Pastoral* (1976). A self-described "sensuist," Ackerman draws upon deep, physical, firsthand experience of nature, as in her best-selling *A Natural History of the Senses* (1990) and *The Moon by Whalelight* (1991), the former of which was televised as a five-part Nova series. The author of dozens of science and nature essays published in popular periodicals, Ackerman has been especially successful in encouraging her female readers to seek direct knowledge of nature and science. She has recently extended her literary engagement with nature to the writing of children's books on bats and seals, to an examination of human nature as encountered while volunteering as a counselor on a local suicide prevention hotline (*A Slender Thread*, 1997), and to an exploration of human creativity (*see* Imagination and Creativity) (*Deep Play*, 1999). As the title character, she is the subject of Paul West's natural history of their longtime relationship in *Life with Swan* (1999).

Pamela Gossin

Acosta, José de (1539–1600). Jesuit theologian, missionary to the New World, natural historian, and author of *Natural and Moral History of the Indies* (1590). He wrote on the **natural history** of Mexico and Peru. His works contain useful descriptions of New World plants and animals.

Rafael Chabrán

Adams, Douglas [Noel] (1952–2001). Creator of the British Broadcasting Corporation radio and television series *Hitchhiker's Guide to the Galaxy* (1978), Adams went on to novelize *The Hitchhiker's Guide* (1979) and produce several sequels, the most recent being *The Ultimate Hitchhiker's Guide* (1996). Adams's satire of more serious **science fiction** and his farcical presentation of science and **technology** gone awry are further explored in his detective novels beginning with *Dirk Gently's Holistic Detective Agency* (1987).

Shelly Jarrett Bromberg

Adams, Henry (1838–1918). Historian whose insistence that the Second Law of **Thermodynamics** explained social change demonstrated that metaphor could bridge the "two cultures." *Mont-Saint-Michel and Chartres* (1904) and *The Education of Henry Adams* (1907) contrasted thirteenth-century faith in a unified cosmic purpose (symbolized by the Virgin) with modern bewilderment at the proliferation of electromechanical energies (symbolized by the Dynamo). Adams's "A Letter to American Teachers of History" (1910) summed up his reflections on **entropy**.

Reference

Martin, Ronald E. *American Literature and the Universe of Force*. Durham, NC: Duke UP, 1981.

Joseph W. Slade

Addison, Joseph (1672–1719). Essayist, dramatist, poet. In his essay periodicals Addison popularized contemporary science by promoting its pursuit; emphasizing its religious utility (especially its contributions to a "scientific" **natural theology**); celebrating its greatest exemplars—**Isaac Newton**, **Robert Boyle**, and **John Locke**; urging its usefulness as a source of poetic imagery; and parodying its discourse (in dreamed dissections of a "Beau's Head" and a "Coquet's Heart"). In his influential "Pleasures of the Imagination" *Spectator* essays (1712) he articulated an empirical, Lockean, affective theory of the imagination founded on the individual's perception of and psychological response to the "great," the "uncommon" (or new), and the "beautiful" in nature.

Reference

Bloom, Edward A., and Lillian D. Bloom. *Joseph Addison's Sociable Animal*. Providence, RI: Brown UP, 1971.

Lisa Zeitz

Aeronautics/Aviation. The science and technology of flying, a fascination for humankind throughout history. African (*see* Africa) and African American folk legends, the classical myths (*see* Mythology (Greco-Roman)) of Daedalus and Icarus, the Arabian tales of flying carpets, **Leonardo's** drawings of flying machines, and **Jonathan Swift's** Flying Island of Laputa all attest to the imaginative allure of the idea of human flight.

The science of modern aeronautics began with the work of George Cayley (1773–1857), who first studied bird flight as the basis for mechanized flight. In his writings, he began the effort to translate natural forces, including the shape and motion of wings, into language humans could understand and master. These efforts included both word pictures and mathematical representations of the forces at work in flight. Otto Lilienthal's *Bird Flight as the Basis for Aviation*, published shortly after his death in a gliding accident (1896), was especially influential. *Bird Flight* owed its genesis to the work of Cayley and to the influence of German poet–scientist **Johann W. von Goethe**, who was respected in Europe as much for his scientific theories as for his **poetry** and prose. Lilienthal borrowed the Goethian impulse to examine nature intensely, which would release its secrets to benefit human life to the sensitive and knowing student. Most experimenters, seeing little practical success in the ideas of Lilienthal and others, chose to develop the balloon as a means of flight. While the balloon had a number of short-term successes, it could never provide the sense of accomplishment and mastery of the air that humans desired.

Chicago engineer Octave Chanute encouraged Wilbur and Orville Wright to follow Lilienthal's line of reasoning and experimentation. The Wright brothers discovered weaknesses in Lilienthal's methods and experimented on wing designs in wind tunnels, leading to their eventual success as the first humans to fly (Kitty Hawk, North Carolina, December 17, 1903). Contemporary aeronauts, convinced of the truth of the Lilienthal method, produced little subsequent success until more mechanical-minded students, like Glen Curtiss, Tommy Sopwith, and Louis Bleriot, showed how to design aircraft based on sound mathematical principles. After World War I, the airplane gained significantly in its performance characteristics, load-carrying capability, and range. These characteristics had been presaged in a pre–World War I work by **H.G. Wells**, *The War in the Air*. The powered aircraft quickly became a weapon of destruction, widely feared, especially after the aerial bombing attacks on Spanish cities during the Spanish Civil War (1935–1938). Although commercial air travel was rapidly growing, due to the success of the British-built Handley Page, the Boeing Clipper, and the DC-3, World War II intervened with further examples of destructiveness brought on by flying machines.

In the first half of the twentieth century, the possibilities of flight filled the pages of children's books such as the dime and nickel novel series "Airship Boys" and "Silver Fox Farm." The impulse to merge insight into nature with aeronautical achievement received more serious treatment by the British-Australian author **Nevil Shute**, whose novels described members of society working to develop a natural sympathy with the ideal characteristics of the aircraft, an impulse shown most directly in *Around the Bend* (1950). Other aviation writers who have combined an interest in science and technology with social and aesthetic themes include the American writer Richard Bach and the French writer Antoine de Saint-Exupéry. Beginning with writings based directly on the flying experience (*Stranger to the Ground*, 1963), Bach also explored paranormal themes in *Jonathan Livingston Seagull* (1970) and *Illusions: The Adventures of a Reluctant Messiah* (1977). Perhaps understanding the strange symbiosis of the human and technological better than any other pilot, Saint-Exupéry encapsulated his existential philosophy of flying in *Wind, Sand and Stars* (1939), *Night Flight* (1931), *Airman's Odyssey* (1943), and *The Little Prince* (1943). In *On Extended Wings: An Adventure in Flight* (1985), poet and science popularizer **Diane Ackerman** recounted her encounter with flying lessons, adding her voice to those of earlier female pilots who found new freedom in the skies.

Other interdisciplinary relations of flight include popular **representations** in film and literature of ultramasculine "right stuff" test pilots (Tom Wolfe), the recurrent motifs of "flying girls" in Japanese **anime** and African American and

Chicano literature, as well as recent applications of discourse analysis to "black box" miscommunications.

References

Bell, Elizabeth S. "A Place in the Sky: Women Writing about Aviation, 1920–40." *Proteus: A Journal of Ideas* 10.2 (1993): 43–48.

McCurdy, Howard E. *Space and the American Imagination.* Washington: Smithsonian Institute, 1997.

Pratt, John Clark. "Writing about Flying: A Pilot's View." *War, Literature and the Arts* 5.2 (1993): 77–83.

David Kirk Vaughan and Pamela Gossin

Africa (LS in). Characterized not only by considerable variety, among a great wealth of highly idiomatic traditions, but fraught with great divergence and controversy as well. Contemporary African writers have so often criticized the deleterious effects of Western science and **technology** on African life and thought that their protests have frequently seemed to sound the dominant note of twentieth-century African letters. It would be a grave mistake, however, to confuse this very particular and quite recent form of protest with the broadly considered—and long-enduring—attitudes toward science and technology informing African literature and thought.

In the early centuries of the Common Era, North African scholars helped to preserve and advance scientific knowledge at a time when such activities were quite moribund in Europe. The archaeological record confirms, moreover, the assertions traditionally made by West African griots—and in the story-songs linking the Shona to their ancient forebears in Zimbabwe—of the existence of technologically flourishing, advanced cultures in Africa during the European "Dark Ages." Scholars have, in fact, shown that African blacksmiths were forging implements from iron long before such materials were made and used in Europe (see Berliner). More recently, Zulu singers have celebrated not only Chaka's fearlessness in battle but also the development of a technologically and tactically superior assegai as well.

Commentary on the role played by science and technology during the colonial era came largely from Europeans, who described Africa as a kind of negatively empowered maelstrom where science and technology essentially failed to ameliorate the condition of a humanity largely overwhelmed by, and subservient to, the powers of nature. The work of Edgar Rice Burroughs is exemplary in this regard. In *Tarzan of the Apes* (1914), a European expedition, tricked out with the latest technological gimmicks, ends in disastrous failure, leaving a male infant to be raised through the kindness of a band of great apes. Growing into powerful manhood without the assistance of, or interference from Western science, but rather through the powerfully chthonic agency of the African air and soil, Tarzan emerges as the living repudiation of any ideology that deems science and technology crucial to human life. Thus, Tarzan cannot thrive in heavily industrialized England, even with all the privileges adhering to Lord Greystoke. He must and can only return to a world where science and technology are considered to have little force, an Africa that is, in Burroughs's rendering, the romanticized counterpart to the world envisioned by scientistic ideologies.

In *Heart of Darkness* (1899; 1902), **Joseph Conrad** interpolated his own fevered journey up the Congo—a journey in which he scarcely set foot on African soil—into an idiomatic account of the failure of Western science and technology to adequately confront the African wilderness. Marlow expects to encounter, in the heroic figure of Kurtz, an exemplar of the progressive ethos of European scientific **culture**, but the actual meeting undercuts this expectation decisively. Having become as wildly articulate and unfathomably incomprehensible as the wilderness he sought to tame, Kurtz embodies the inadequacy of science to overcome human weakness, especially inasmuch as the latter is confirmed by the vast African wilderness. Returning to Europe a desiccated, yellowed "idol" of a man, Marlow cannot bring himself to speak this truth to the person who needs to hear it most—Kurtz's "Intended," who he visits in Brussels—only to an audience of his benighted peers, sitting in darkness adrift on the Thames.

African writers have held no such illusions about the power of Western science and technology to subdue their lands. In *Things Fall Apart* (1958), the Nigerian novelist Chinua Achebe depicts how the **chaos** caused by the actions of one powerful man, Okonkwo, is absorbed and righted through the essentially orderly structures of Igbo life, only to show how fragile such lifeways can be when confronted by the overwhelming power of British colonial rule.

While Achebe has continued to write critically of the impact of Western science and technology on African life and thought, writers as diverse as Ngugi wa Thiong'o (*Petals of Blood*, 1991), Nadine Gordimer (*July's People*, 1981), Sembene Ousmane (*God's Bits of Wood*, 1960), and perhaps above all, Ken Saro-Wiwa (*A Month and a Day: A Detention Diary*, 1996; *A Forest of Flowers*, 1997) have written movingly of the failure of Western science and technology to bring much comfort to an Africa faced with the loss of vital cultural, political, and social lifeways and with the dire destruction and loss of what had previously seemed unassailable ecosystems. As the philosopher V.Y. Mudimbe has pointed out, an idiomatically African approach to reconciling science and technology with the interests of indigenous people and ecosystems is only now just beginning to take shape.

References

Berliner, Paul. *The Soul of Mbira*. Chicago: U of Chicago P, 1993.
Mudimbe, V.Y. *The Invention of Africa: Gnosis, Philosophy and the Order of Knowledge*. Bloomington: Indiana UP, 1988.

Michael B. McDonald

Agassiz, Elizabeth Cary (1822–1907). A founder and the first president (1894–1903) of Radcliffe College and the wife of natural historian **Louis Ag-**

assiz and popularizer of his work. As "Actea," Agassiz wrote *First Lesson in Natural History* (1859) for children and, with her stepson Alexander Agassiz, *Seaside Studies in Natural History* (1865). A member of the Thayer expedition to Brazil (April 1865–July 1866) led by Louis Agassiz, she wrote its expedition narrative, *A Journey in Brazil* (1868), and later produced *Louis Agassiz: His Life and Correspondence* (1885).

Reference

Bergmann, Linda S. "A Troubled Marriage of Discourses: Science Writing and Travel Narrative in Louis and Elizabeth Agassiz's *A Journey in Brazil*." *Journal of American Culture* 18 (1995): 83–88.

Linda S. Bergmann

Agassiz, Louis (1807–1873). Natural historian, founder of Harvard's Museum of Comparative Zoology (*see* Biology/Zoology) (1859), and chief American scientific opponent of **Darwin's** theory of evolution. This prominent Swiss ichthyologist and glacial theorist immigrated to the United States in 1846, arousing wide public interest in his never-completed *Contributions to the Natural History of the United States*. Active in the Lazzaroni scientific circle and dedicated to the professionalization of American science, Agassiz was also a member of the Saturday Club and friend of **Emerson** and Longfellow.

Reference

Lurie, Edward. *Louis Agassiz: A Life in Science*. 1969. Baltimore: Johns Hopkins UP, 1988.

Linda S. Bergmann

Agee, James Rufus (1909–1955). American journalist, novelist, screenwriter, and critic who, with Walker Evans, melded anger, guilt, aesthetic sensibility, and humanity into a new form of documentary fiction in the phototext *Let Us Now Praise Famous Men* (1941). Inspired by the righteous poetic, spiritual, political, and social furies of **Swift** and **Blake**, among others, Agee saw writing and photography as equally powerful technologies for the **representation** of the awful beauty and fragility of the actual and, potentially, as a vehicle for personal and social change. Sought after as a screenwriter following his work on *The African Queen*, he died of heart disease exacerbated by **alcoholism**, not living long enough to learn if he could live with success. *A Death in the Family*, published posthumously, won the Pulitzer Prize. Reissues of *Let Us Now Praise . . .* made it a best-seller during the Vietnam War and it became a bible of the civil rights movement. Agee and Evans's work also influenced the development of the "empathetic observer" in cultural **anthropology**.

Pamela Gossin

Agriculture. Perhaps the most influential factor in the evolution of human civilization. The great and small civilizations that populate history are defined by their agricultural methods and their relationships to their local **environments**. Agriculture's literary influence is often felt indirectly. For example, in the United States, American culture was shaped by and continues to feel the influence of the Jeffersonian (*see* Jefferson, Thomas) ideal of the yeoman farmer who lived off the land and knew it intimately. Thomas Jefferson's *Notes on the State of Virginia* (1785) may well be the most influential text in American literature that almost no Americans have read.

References

Leslie, Michael, and Timothy Raylor, eds. *Culture and Cultivation in Early Modern England: Writing and the Land.* Leicester: Leicester UP, 1992.
Nelson, Stephanie A., et al. *God and the Land: The Metaphysics of Farming in Hesiod and Vergil with a Translation of Hesiod's* Works and Days *by David Grene.* Oxford: Oxford UP, 1998.
Sarver, Stephanie. *Uneven Land: Nature and Agriculture in American Nature Writing.* Lincoln: U Nebraska P, 1999.

David N. Cassuto

AIDS. Acronym for "acquired immunodeficiency syndrome," the last stage of infection by human immunodeficiency virus, or HIV. AIDS is not a disease but a syndrome, a collection of somatically destructive effects that are enabled by immune system compromise; one does not die of AIDS but of the opportunistic infections and diseases against which one's body can no longer defend.

Over the last twenty years, AIDS has been the subject of a tremendous amount of cultural, political, and theoretical activity, in part because of the devastation suffered by the intellectual and artistic communities of the United States, Britain, Canada, and elsewhere, and in part because of the arrival of AIDS as a new international medical phenomenon at the end of the twentieth century. While much can be said about the governmental and media ineptitude regarding AIDS, the challenge of AIDS to prevailing notions of body, health, and self, and so on, the difficulty in characterizing the meaning of AIDS as a medical, human, national, or geopolitical event is its most important aspect for LS studies.

Cultural critic Susan Sontag and others have argued that the inability of the medical community to understand and treat AIDS has produced other meanings in **culture** and society (which, of course, also have effects on **medicine** and science). Cultural studies scholars such as Paula Treichler and **Donna Haraway** have delineated the traffic of meanings—many of them sexist, racist, homophobic, militaristic, and xenophobic—that continue to circulate powerful understandings of AIDS in response to scientific and popular ignorance.

So too have myriad authors, playwrights, filmmakers, artists, and poets grappled with the meaning of AIDS: Hervé Guibert and Paul Monette wrote acclaimed memoirs of their illness before they died; Tony Kushner's *Angels in America* won the Pulitzer Prize for Drama in 1993. Finally, AIDS has produced a revolution in cultural politics. Groups such as the AIDS Coalition to Unleash

Power (ACT-UP), Queer Nation, and Gay Men's Health Crisis staged die-ins, wrote and distributed safe-sex pamphlets, handed out clean IV (intravenous) drug works, and stormed scientific conferences in direct attempts to transform the politics, cultures, and discourses of AIDS.

Chris Amirault

Alchemy. Medieval protochemistry with strong links to the magical worldview. Alchemy has inspired the sciences and literature alike. In its exoteric tradition oriented toward making gold and discovering the elixir of life, it has been heavily criticized for its materialism and its actual and potential abuses by charlatans. **Dante Alighieri, Geoffrey Chaucer**, and **Ben Jonson** represent the literary satire directed against the alchemist as puffer and fraud who deceives others and often himself about his ultimately vain and fruitless quest. In the seventeenth century, alchemy begins to be taken more seriously by **metaphysical poets** in its spiritual dimensions, while its empirical elements turn into **chemistry**. Alchemy reappears in Romantic and **Symbolist** literature from **Johann W. von Goethe** and **Ernst Theodor Amadeus Hoffmann** to August Strindberg and **William Butler Yeats**. It regained a place in twentieth-century thought through Carl Gustav Jung's studies on the **psychology** of alchemical symbols. Writers have been inspired by alchemy because they believe that the transformations alchemy studies and produces are related to the act of literary and artistic creation.

References

Linden, S.J. *Darke Hieroglyphicks. Alchemy in English Literature from Chaucer to the Restoration.* Lexington: U of Kentucky P, 1996.
Meakin, D. *Hermetic Fictions. Alchemy and Irony in the Novel.* Keele, United Kingdom: Keele UP, 1995.

Elmar Schenkel

Alcoholism. Excessive use of, often leading to a pathological dependence upon, alcohol. The relationship of alcoholism to literature comprises three main categories in nineteenth-century and twentieth-century literature. First, intoxication through alcohol provides thematic avenues to explore complex developments among individuals, as well as between individuals and society. Second, biographies on authors noted for alcoholic tendencies increasingly examine the effects of this now-recognized disease on their creative legacies. Third, writings of such authors provide unique insights into the psychology (*see* Anthropology/ Psychology/Sociology) underlying their works. Some critics postulate a relationship between alcoholism or similar dependencies and the creative literary mind.

References

Crowley, John W. *Drunkard's Progress: Narrative of Addiction, Despair and Recovery.* Baltimore: Johns Hopkins UP, 1999.

Lilienfeld, Jane and Jeffrey Oxford, eds. *The Languages of Addiction*. New York: St. Martin's, 1999.

Robert J. Bonk

Allman, John (1935–   ). American poet and novelist. His *Curve away from Stillness: Science Poems* (1989) constitutes one of the most fully sustained meditations on science in contemporary American **poetry**. Consisting of five sections, "Principles," "**Physics**," "**Chemistry**," "Planets," and "**Biology**," the book represents a passionate, personal attempt to reunite the domains of poetry and science. "It may only be in recent times that we separate the poetic experience from the world of measurable facts, believing that there's something so neutral, so unpretty, so abstract in the laws of the physical world," Allman writes in his *Prolegomenon*, "that poets must withdraw from scientific views as from harsh and prosaic metals." Allman's project in *Curve* is to set this misconception to rights, bringing poetry and science together as twin speculative modes of intelligence.

Reference

Allman, John. *Inhabited World: New and Selected Poems 1970–1995*. Potsdam, NY: Wallace Stevens Society, 1995.

Joseph Duemer

Alterity. The concept of duality or otherness pervades literature and literary theory. The creator/created aspect of alterity extends back through literature to the Bible, Judaic tradition, early myths (*see* Mythology (Greco-Roman)), legends, and sagas. **Jorge Luis Borges**, **James Joyce**, **Virginia Woolf**, and many other authors problematize the author/narrator, narrator/character relations and decenter their self-reflexive universes. Are they one or plural, different or together in times and spaces? A kind of "otherness" or present absence is found. Alterity itself seems to perform what is magic yet "literal" about literature: its ability to depict the natural elevation in language as one moves from the materiality of reading to the figural levels of meaning. Alterity, especially in modernist **fiction**, operates through representations of internally and externally observed differences and from operational failure of the Aristotelian (*see* Aristotle) principle of noncontradiction. It also is shown in doubling character and motif traits as they structurally determine meaning and action, as shown in Vladimir Prop's *Morphology of the Folktale*. The identity principle is shown false not only with the individual but also with **culture** and society. Julia Kristeva, Luce Irigaray, Jacques Derrida, Jacques Lacan, Homni Bhabha, Gloria Anzaldua, and many other theorists use the concept of alterity to illustrate intersubjectivity, discuss postcolonialism, and establish the "différence" in deconstruction.

Mary Libertin

Ammons, A[rchie] R[andolph] (1926–2001). American poet and teacher. Though trained as a biologist, and certainly a philosophical materialist, A.R. Ammons is profoundly distrustful of analysis and reductionism. His use of organic form is probably the most accomplished in twentieth-century American **poetry**. Always interested in the larger picture, his watershed poem "Corson's Inlet" was written before the advent of **chaos theory**, yet it seems in some ways to prefigure that science. As with **Wallace Stevens**, Ammons's central concern is the relation between forms of mind and forms of the world.

References

Ammons, A.R. *Selected Poems*. New York: Knopf, 1987.
Bloom, Harold. "A.R. Ammons: The Breaking of the Vessels." *Figures of Capable Imag-
    ination*. New York: Seabury, 1976.

Joseph Duemer

Analogy. From a Greek root that means "proportionate," in general usage, denoting similarity in some aspects between entities that are otherwise dissimilar. Analogies are essential to literature, enlivening writing and making it concrete, as in the example "Money is like muck, not good unless it be spread" (Fowler 26). Analogy is widely used in logical inference; Fowler comments that it is "perhaps the basis of most human conclusions, its liability to error being compensated by the frequency with which it is the only form of reasoning available" (Fowler 26).

Analogy has specific meanings in science. In **biology**, it means similarity in function or location of organs that come from different evolutionary roots (*see* Evolutionary Theory). In linguistics, it means the process whereby words are created or extended by following existing patterns of grammar. In computational science, an analog computer represents a set of physical quantities with a corresponding set of different physical quantities; for instance, mechanical properties such as velocity and mass can be represented by voltages and other electrical parameters, which are then manipulated electronically to solve a problem in mechanics. (In contrast, in a digital computer, numbers are represented directly, in coded form.)

Equally important is the power that analogy has in creative scientific thought. Analogy led the great nineteenth-century mathematical physicist James Clerk Maxwell to realize that light is a traveling electromagnetic disturbance. In 1864, Maxwell published the equations he had derived to represent **electricity** and magnetism and noted that they resembled an earlier mathematical result. In the eighteenth century, physicists had developed an equation to describe the traveling wave that results when a taut string is plucked, the basis for the production of musical tones. That equation predicted the speed of the wave along the cord. Maxwell's analogous result implied that electromagnetic effects could travel as waves and showed that they would do so at the speed of light—in short, that light was an electromagnetic wave, as was confirmed by experiment in 1888.

Analogy can also make scientific abstraction concrete and illuminate parts of nature remote from human perception. It has been applied to the wave-particle duality, the quantum paradox (*see* Quantum Physics) that light and matter are extended waves and well-defined particles at the same time, which has never been resolved. One view, held by **Niels Bohr** in the 1920s, takes waves and particles as different faces of reality. Depending on the experiment, we see one or the other but never both. In 1925 J.J. Thomson, discoverer of the electron, caught the idea with a powerful analogy. He likened waves and particles to tigers and sharks, each "supreme in his own element but helpless in that of the other" (Wheaton 306). A second example is the unforgettable image **Ernest Rutherford** gave for his experiment that uncovered the atomic nucleus (*see* Atomic Theory). In 1911, Rutherford bombarded a thin gold foil with subatomic particles. Most penetrated the foil or were slightly deflected, but some were repelled by the nuclei of the gold atoms to return along their original path. Rutherford made this microscopic interaction vividly real when he likened it to blasting a sheet of tissue paper with enormous artillery shells, only to find that some shells bounced off the paper directly back at the cannon.

References

Fowler, H.W. *A Dictionary of Modern English Usage*. New York: Oxford UP, 1985.
Wheaton, Bruce R. *The Tiger and the Shark: Empirical Roots of Wave-Particle Dualism*. Cambridge: Cambridge UP, 1983.

Sidney Perkowitz

Anime. Japanese animation, frequently concerned with the interrelations of science, **technology**, and the human, often with strong apocalyptic elements. Intended primarily for mature audiences rather than the young children targeted by much of American animation, such features as Hayao Miyazaki's *Nausicaa* and *Princess Mononoke* offer complex fictional possibilities for individual human lives and societies in situations where good and evil are not clearly defined or separated (in the former case, after environmental holocaust and, in the latter, within medieval **culture**). The lush, detailed depictions of nature, sophisticated representations of animals (more wild and less anthropomorphic than Disney's), and the nuanced characterizations of this form (often testing conventional **gender** roles) are having a strong influence on **representation** through animation worldwide. Like the popular **manga** (graphic novels, cheap pulp "comic" books) that often inspire it, a vast array of different anime genres appeal to a wide variety of audiences, from the well-known children's programs *Sailor Moon* and *Dragon Ball Z* to cyberpunk stories and soft- and hard-core pornography. While a vast network of anime fans have long exchanged analyses and interpretations in local clubs, regional and national conventions, and even more extensively online, the form is now attracting increasing scholarly attention, especially within LS, Asian, and cultural studies. *Nausicaa*, in both anime and manga forms, was first taught as part of a required college-level course in the United

States in 1998 where the work served as the centerpiece of an experimental pedagogical collaboration in interdisciplinary humanities between historian of science Pamela Gossin and space science research physicist Marc Hairston at the University of Texas, Dallas. Recognizing the importance of anime as cultural export, the Japanese Consulate recently began to sponsor visits and intellectual exchange between U.S. students and scholars and Japanese anime artists and producers.

References

<http://utd500.utdallas.edu/~hairston/ah3300.html>.
Napier, Susan J. *Anime from Akira to Princess Mononoke*. New York: St. Martin's, 2001.

Pamela Gossin

Anthropology/Psychology/Sociology. Interdisciplinary social sciences, linked (particularly in the last thirty years) with literature and LS, both academically and through a growing body of publications. Defying a strict compartmentalization and often converging simultaneously in many aspects (cf. Poyatos, "New Perspectives"), their most fruitful catalytic avenue of interdisciplinarity has been the extremely rich field broadly identified as nonverbal communication studies, the weaving element for this discussion.

The definition of nonverbal communication, and of the two other terms that follow—**culture** and interaction—must be carefully pondered in their every word, for they suggest the presence of the disciplines here discussed as well as others closely related to them. "Nonverbal communication" should be understood as the emissions of signs by all the nonlexical, artifactual, and environmental sensible sign systems contained in the realm of a culture, whether individually or in mutual costructuration and whether or not those emissions constitute behavior or generate personal interaction. As for "culture," we must view it as a series of habits shared by members of a group living in a geographic area, learned but biologically conditioned, such as the means of communication (language being the basis of them all), social relationships at different levels, the various activities of daily life, the products of that group and how they are utilized, the peculiar manifestations of both individual and national personalities, and their ideas concerning their own existence and their fellow people. Thus, particularly narrative literature, from the national epics to the modern novel or theater, reflects, both synchronically and diachronically, a conspicuous or veiled cultural locus in which not only is a society reflected but many sociopsychological aspects of its members' interactions among themselves and with their cultural **environment**. The third cross-disciplinary area is "interaction," here defined as the conscious or unconscious exchange of behavioral or nonbehavioral, sensible, and intelligible signs from the whole arsenal of somatic and extrasomatic systems (independently of whether they are activities or nonactivities) and the rest of the surrounding cultural systems, as they all act as sign emitting components (and as potential elicitors of further emissions) that determine the specific characteristics of the exchange.

As words are the stuff of literature, the cornerstone of its relationship with the other three fields is people's basic triple structure of speech, that is, language (words), paralanguage (voice modifications and wordlike utterances), and kinesics (gestures, manners, postures), as in: "He [Ethan] kept his eyes at the way her face changed with each turn of their talk" (Wharton, *Ethan Frome* 67). Speech is also surrounded by other nonverbal somatic signs—chemical (tears, emotional sweat, natural body odors); dermal (gooseflesh, blushing or palling, clinical reddening or blanching); thermal (emotional rises and falls in body temperature, consistency and strength, color), as in: "I heard her breath [Laura's] quickening—I felt her hand growing cold" (Collins 191) and "He still held her hand. . . . A sense of his strength came with the warm pressure, and comforted her" (Grey 69). The intimate interrelated bodily signs and texture of clothes, artificial odors like perfume, also function in similar ways—"the feeling of her smooth, round arm, through the thinness of her sleeve, pressing against his cheek" (Norris, *Octopus* 221)—as do our subtle psychological-emotional links with environmental elements, as in the following examples: "[T]he harmony of soft hangings and old dim pictures, wove about them a spell of security" (Wharton, *Reef* 324) and "the mingled odours of flowers, perfume, upholstery, and gas, enveloped her . . . the unmistakable, entrancing aroma of the theater" (Norris, *The Pit* 19). Given the expressive limitations of words, we must recognize that the nonverbal elements of speech, and even those other concomitant elements, often allow us to express what with words alone would be simply ineffable. And this does not occur in a semiotic vacuum (*see* Semiotics) but associated to people's universal as well as culture-specific social behaviors and attitudes and their artifactual and natural environmental elements, whether static or dynamic, all sensibly and intellectually apprehended and obviously related to the cointeractant's personality and mood.

All the signs identified so far form together the universal or culture-specific fabric of daily human interactions, a perspective that affords literature, anthropology, sociology, and social psychology a joint and much deeper sounding and pondering of interpersonal and person-environment interactive relations. As this organic, living concept of culturally based interpersonal and person-environment encounters is depicted in literature, we are led to a deep analysis of the literary work itself, especially narrative literature, as it can describe and evoke an awesome array of sensory and person-environment exchanges. And this becomes even more complex through synesthesial perception (e.g., smoothness through vision, vision through sound, softness or hardness through audition of physical contacts) that may affect our interactive behaviors and attitudes; for instance: "Maggie could hear ["see"] soda-water squirting into a tumbler" (Woolf 118). A novel can evoke people's permanent (static appearance), changing (e.g., through suffering, exertion), and dynamic (e.g., while talking) facial features, speech audible repertoires, and the rest of the person-related element just illustrated—all brought forth by virtue of the reader's intellectual-psychological sensory-channel amplification of what the writer left only as a visual printed text containing precisely that writer's reduction of his or her real-life multisensory perceptions into that text.

There are two prominent theoretical and methodological models for the orderly observation and data gathering in any interdisciplinary and systematic study of interpersonal communication and of our interaction with the built, modified, or natural environments. One is an interdisciplinary morphological and functional classification (*see* Classification Systems) of nonverbal categories (e.g., Poyatos, *Nonverbal Communication*, vol. I, ch. 6). The other, as a complement, is a structural model of the fascinatingly complex phenomenon of everyday conversation (e.g., Poyatos, *Nonverbal Communication*, vol. I, ch. 7) that enables the detailed analysis of our conversational exchanges with people of the same or mixed cultures, backgrounds, and personalities, all richly illustrated by literature. Both models (at times combined) help immensely in seeking and analyzing the deeper levels of our conversational or nonconversational interactions and, from a sociological and even clinical point of view, the eloquent presence or absence of specific behavior types.

Take as one case the example of a multidisciplinary approach to the "speaking faces" in a woman-man encounter. Such an approach would suggest the engagement of all four disciplines, based on the richness of the twosome's personal sensory and intelligible sign emissions and perceptions:

1. Their personal features: "[T]he formation of a particular face could work this spell . . . the curl of a lock of hair, the whiteness or roundness of a forehead, the shapeliness of a nose or ear, the arched redness of full-blown petal lips. The cheek, the chin, the eye—in combination with these things— . . . Tendencies are subtle things . . . deeper than human will" (Dreiser, *Genius* 274–75).

2. Paralanguage (Poyatos, *Advances*): As the voices of the two people expressed through their audible-visual "speaking faces" (with multi- and interdisciplinary implications) can even travel through time to later become alive in their **imagination** and even elicit their acting upon that whole communicative complex. Paralanguage includes four categories: basic "primary qualities," such as his specific voice resonance and rhythm; her lively pitch and intonation features translated into equally lively facial and manual speech markers; the drawling of her syllables coinciding sometimes with her long gazing; the smooth rhythm of both her voice and gestures of face, hands, and body. All these components they judge according to her and his own personal and cultural esthetic values and thus are also important in first encounters as first-impression-forming and rapport-eliciting elements that will condition further interactions, as in: "[S]he asked, in a toneless voice, persisting in appearing casual and unaffected" (Lawrence 489).

To these basic features of the paralinguistic are added any of the many voice "qualifiers" or voice-type controls, such as laryngeal or pharyngeal (creakiness, breathiness, huskiness, harshness, whisperiness), labial (French lip-rounding sounds), mandibular (muttering), and artifactual (while eating). For example:

"Are you crazy?" he [Yossarian] hissed frantically. "Put it away and keep your idiot voice down" (Heller 308) or "She had hairpins in her mouth and spoke through them" (Dos Passos, *42nd Parallel* 213). Further, within paralinguistic "differentiators," literature describes, for instance, interactive or noninteractive, normal or pathological forms of laughter and crying that reveal the profound psychological, social, and cultural relevance of these physiological or emotional reactions, as in: "Stephen heard his father's voice break into a laugh which was almost a sob" (Joyce, *Portrait* 92). To these should be added shouting, spitting, and reflexes like sighing, gasping, yawning, and sneezing, managed differently across many cultures ("Now and then he [Mohammed Latif] belched, in compliment to the richness of the food" [Forster 16]).

Finally, "alternants" (hesitation clicks, inhalations and exhalations, hisses, moans, groans, grunts, sniffs, snorts, smacks, blows, slurps, shudders, gasps, pants, yells, etc.) identify culturally differentiated repertoires and cross-cultural differences (e.g., in hesitations, animal-calling utterances). Paralinguistic speech components, besides serving to gauge the literary writer's ability to individualize characters and convey psychological **realism** (beyond their stylistic and technical functions), identify also aspects of socioeconomic and educational backgrounds (refinement, uncouthness) and normal or pathological psychological behaviors (manic-depressive speech and body behavior changes), as in: "the variety of articulated noises, which cousin Holman made while I read, to show her sympathy, wonder, or horror" (Gaskell 39).

But, beyond paralanguage, literature evokes many engaging and truly quasi-paralinguistic sounds from the artifactual and natural environments, which must be approached also at a psychological perceptual level closely related to personality configuration. For instance, "a nondescript clatter and chatter—of china partly; . . . sound of rain falling, and the gutters chuckling and burbling as they sucked up the water" (Woolf 43) and "[Mary] on the train . . . too excited to sleep . . . listening to the rumble of the wheels over the rails, the clatter of crossings, the faraway spooky wails of the locomotive" (Dos Passos, *Big Money* 125).

The third speech communication channel, kinesics, rooted in cultural anthropology and ethology (e.g., Eible-Eibesfeldt; Ekman), has seen many fruitful applications in social psychology and the behavioral and clinical sciences (e.g., Kendon; Scheflen; Scherer and Ekman) and in literary analysis (e.g., Korte; Portch; Poyatos, *Advances*; Poyatos, *Nonverbal Communication*, vol. III). We must acknowledge the perception of kinesics as visual (e.g., a posture), audible (e.g., finger snapping), and kinesthetic (e.g., embracing) and its transmission through space and time not only as a component of the triple structure of speech but also totally independently as an eloquent anthropokinesic system. Kinesics involves our entire external anatomy (with obvious interdisciplinary implications), and like language, it is subject to an ontogenetic maturational curve (e.g., von Raffler-Engel), social stratification (unlike language, still poorly studied), geographical and cultural distribution (dealt with by a growing body of interculturally oriented cultural inventories), and historical development (e.g., in social manners, which are related to furniture, clothes, moral values, etc. [Wildeblood]). Besides a research and fieldwork classification into gestures, manners, and postures, we must acknowledge the "parakinesic qualities" of intensity, range, pressure, speed, and duration—equally basic for any cultural, sociological, psychological, clinical, historical, artistic, or literary study, as in: "She held out her hand . . . and when I took it gave mine a warm and hearty pressure" (Maugham 59–60). But narrative literature contains even more implicit kinesic behaviors than we read descriptions of, which particularly the native reader of the original language would recognize as co-occurrent or alternating with the rest of the verbal and nonverbal behaviors and attitudes ("And Winfield, picking his teeth with a splinter in a very adult manner, said, 'I knowed it all the time' " [Steinbeck 400]). We also find that many of the movements through which we contact other people and the surrounding artifactual or natural environments are differently perceived by people and betray specific cultures, social attitudes, and historical periods ("The rustle of her pretty skirt was like music to him" [Dreiser, *Carrie* 204]).

As the absence of what does not happen can be as eloquent as its presence, silence (e.g., Poyatos, *Nonverbal Communication*, vol. II, ch. 7; Tannen and Saville-Troike), and stillness, as opposites to sound and movement (life's basic sensory dimensions), differ cross-culturally (e.g., between East and West) and occur quite eloquently also in the animal kingdom ("The silence of the birds betokened a message" [Grey 136]), in the natural environment ("They [Brian and Joan] walked on hand in hand; and between them was the silence of the wood and at the same time the deeper, denser, more secret silence of their own unexpressed emotions" [Huxley 176]), and in the general cultural environment, carrying even the total message and enhancing certain sounds ("[T]he only sounds in the room were the ticking of the clock and the subdued shrillness of his quill [Dr. Kemp's, restless], hurrying" [Wells 120]).

As for interaction itself, the study of its deeper levels (Poyatos, *Nonverbal Communication*, vol. II, ch. 7) clearly cuts across cultural anthropology, sociology, and several branches of psychology (e.g., perception, persuasion, development) and reveals the less obvious interactive components, as in these further examples from Wharton: "In some undefinable way she had become aware, without turning her head, that he was steeped in the sense of her nearness, absorbed in contemplating the details of her face and dress; and the discovery made the words throng to her lips. She felt herself speak with ease, authority, conviction" (*Reef* 117). Those deeper levels include, first, those that seem more personal ("judging that one of the charms of tea is the fact of drinking it together, she proceeded to give the last touch to Mr. Gryce's enjoyment by smiling at him across her lifted cup" [Wharton, *House* 22]); but also the environmental ones, among which light and sounds should not be neglected ("the lamp. The dark discreet room, their isolation, the music that still vibrated in their ears united them" [Joyce, *Dubliners*, "Painful Case" 122]). Furthermore, one should not neglect, through a traditional cause-effect approach, the interactive effect of even things that have not yet happened or may never happen, as with the frequent occurrence of advanced hidden feedback ("Waythorn felt himself reddening in anticipation of the other's smile" [Wharton, "Other Two" 463]). Another seemingly trivial aspect of interaction that is nonetheless sociopsychologically relevant and incisively illustrated by literature are daily miniencounters that can contain many subtle elements ("good-looking young women [at a tubercular sanitarium] . . . who smiled at him . . . and let their warm soft hands touch his slightly as they paid him [for a magazine delivered as a young boy]" [Wolfe 122]).

As for our literary experience itself, even what can be called the reading act engages not only the other three disciplines but the physiological dimension of reading, since we are mostly aware of the whole printed page through macular vision (12°–15° horizontally, 3° vertically), peripherally (90° on each side of the sagittal plane [i.e., 180° total], and 150° vertically—so important also in personal and environmental interaction and in environmental design). Hence the crucial importance of our perception of punctuation and the differences (within the physiopsychology of the intellectual-semiotic-communicative process of our literary recreation) determined, for instance, by the often misleading phrase-end location of [!] and [?], against more realistic Spanish [¡ !] and [¿ ?]. At any rate, the explicit and implicit nonverbal components of a text must be identified beyond paralanguage and kinesics, for they are perceived differently according to the reader's skills and sensitiveness. But the multiple psychological-communicative processes undergone by both the characters and their environment, from the writer's creation to the reader's recreation, depend largely on the latter's previous storage of multisystemic sensory perception, in turn conditioned by his or her own personality, culture, and historical time—to the extent that the character unavoidably splits between author's character and (each) reader's character, subject to an also unavoidable plurality that nevertheless should preserve a certain behavioral and attitudinal coherence (i.e., personality and temperament).

One specific relationship between literature and anthropology constitutes the foundation of literary anthropology, defined in the early 1980s (Poyatos, *Literary*) as "the systematic diachronic or synchronic study of the documentary and historical values of the cultural signs contained in the different manifestations of each national literature, particularly narrative literatures," for which the different literary genres are unique sources.

Finally, there is so much else in the literary text, apart from what the writer intended, that we truly run the risk of missing much invaluable material and not being able to fathom it more deeply, seeing that the characters and their world, what lives organically as well as what we vivify and even humanize, acquire a greater reality, which obviously includes (when based on interdisciplinary intercultural communication and interaction studies) the responsibility of literary translators in their very difficult interlinguistic-intercultural task (Poyatos, "Aspects").

References

Ashley, Kathleen M. *Victor Turner and the Construction of Cultural Criticism: Between Literature and Anthropology*. Bloomington: U of Indiana P, 1990.

Collins, Wilkie. *The Woman in White*. 1860. London: Penguin Books, 1974.

Dos Passos, John. *The Big Money*. New York: Washington Square, 1961.

———. *The 42nd Parallel*. 1930. New York: Washington Square, 1961.

Dreiser, Theodore. *The Genius*. 1915. Toronto: Signet Books, 1967.

———. *Sister Carrie*. 1900. New York: Dell, 1960.

Eibl-Eibesfeldt, Irenäus. "Social Interaction in an Ethological, Cross-Cultural Perspective." *Cross-Cultural Perspectives in Nonverbal Communication*. Ed. F. Poyatos. Lewiston, NY, and Toronto: C.J. Hogrefe, 1988. 107–30.

Ekman, Paul, ed. *Darwin and Facial Expression: A Century of Research in Review*. New York: Academic, 1973.

Forster, E.M. *A Passage to India*. 1924. Harmondsworth: Penguin, 1970.

Gaskell, Elizabeth. *Cousin Phillis*. 1864. London: Penguin, 1995.

Grey, Zane. *The Last Trail*. 1909. Philadelphia: Blakiston, 1945.

Heller, Joseph. *Catch-22*. 1962. New York: Dell, 1962.

Howells, William Dean. *A Hazard of New Fortunes*. 1890. New York: Bantam Books, 1960.

Huxley, Aldous. *Eyeless in Gaza*. 1936. New York: Bantam Books, 1961.

Iser, Wolfgang. "What Is Literary Anthropology? The Difference between Explanatory and Exploratory Fictions." *Revenge of the Aesthetic: The Place of Literature in Theory Today*. Ed. Michael P. Clark. Berkeley: U of California P, 2000.

Joyce, James. *Dubliners*. 1914. The Portable James Joyce. New York: Viking, 1947.

———. *A Portrait of the Artist as a Young Man*. 1916. Harmondsworth: Penguin, 1976.

Kendon, Adam, ed. *Nonverbal Communication, Interaction, and Gesture*. The Hague: Mouton, 1981.

Korte, Barbara. *Body Language in Literature*. 1993 (German orig.). Toronto: U of Toronto P, 1997.

Lawrence, D.H. *Women in Love*. 1921. New York: Random House, 1950.

Maugham, W. Somserset. *Cakes and Ales*. 1930. Harmondsworth: Penguin, 1960.

Norris, Frank. *The Octopus*. 1901. New York: Bantam Books, 1971.

———. *The Pit*. 1903. New York: Grove; London: Evergreen Books, 1956.

Portch, Stephen R. *Literature's Silent Language*. New York and Frankfurt: Peter Lang, 1985.

Poyatos, Fernando. "Aspects, Problems and Challenges of Nonverbal Communication in Literary Translation." *Nonverbal Communication and Translation: New Perspectives and Challenges in Literature, Interpretation and the Media*. Ed. F. Poyatos. Amsterdam and Philadelphia: John Benjamins, 1997. 17–47.

———. "New Perspectives on Intercultural Interaction through Nonverbal Communication Studies." *Intercultural Communication Studies* 12 (2000): 1–41.

———. *Nonverbal Communication Across Disciplines*. 3 vols. Amsterdam and Philadelphia: John Benjamins, 2002.

———, ed. *Advances in Nonverbal Communication: Sociocultural, Clinical, Esthetic and Literary Perspectives*. Amsterdam and Philadelphia: John Benjamins, 1992.

———. *Literary Anthropology: A New Interdisciplinary Approach to Signs and Literature*. Amsterdam and Philadelphia: John Benjamins, 1988.

Scheflen, Albert E. 1969. *Stream and Structure of Communicational Behavior*. Commonwealth of Pennsylvania: Eastern Pennsylvania Psychiatric Institute; Bloomington: Indiana UP, 1969.

Scherer, K., and P. Ekman, eds. *Approaches to Emotion*. Hillside, NJ: Lawrence Erlbaum, 1984.

Steinbeck, John. *The Grapes of Wrath*. 1931. New York: Bantam Books, 1964.

Tannen, Deborah, and Muriel Saville-Troike. *Perspectives on Silence*. Norwood, NJ: Ablex, 1985.

von Raffler-Engel, Walburga. "Developmental Kinesics: The Acquisition and Maturation of Conversational Nonverbal Behavior." *Developmental Kinesics*. Ed. B.L. Hoffer and R.N. St. Clair. Baltimore: University Park, 1981. 5–27.

Wells, H.G. *The Invisible Man*. 1897. Glasgow: Fontana Collins, 1974.

Wharton, Edith. *Ethan Frome*. 1911. New York: Dover, 1991.

———. *The House of Mirth*. 1905. New York: New American Library, Signet Classic, 1964.

———. "The Other Two." 1904. *Great Short Works of American Realism*. Ed. W. Thorp. New York: Harper and Row, 1968.

———. *The Reef*. 1912. London: Penguin, 1993.

Wildeblood, Joan. *The Polite World*. 1965. London: Oxford UP.

Wolfe, Thomas. *Look Homeward, Angel*. 1929. New York: Modern Library, Random House.

Woolf, Virginia. *The Years*. 1937. Harmondsworth: Penguin, 1973.

Fernando Poyatos

Anthroposophy. Spiritual and philosophical school established by Rudolf Steiner (1861–1925) that attracted writers and artists (Andrei Belyi, Wassilij Kandinsky, Joseph Beuys, Saul Bellow) since it seeks to overcome scientific materialism and overspecialization. **Johann W. von Goethe's** scientific practice is used as a model for the way it relates subjectivity to **empiricism**. The English-speaking world was made familiar with anthroposophy by Owen Barfield.

Reference

Barfield, Owen. *Romanticism Comes of Age*. Middletown, CT: Wesleyan UP, 1966.

Elmar Schenkel

Aratus of Soli (315–245 B.C.E.). Greek poet, best known for his long astronomical-astrological-meteorological poem *Phaenomena* in which he describes the constellations and motions of the planets and explains their influences here below. Translated into Latin verse by **Cicero** and **Vergil**, among others, his description of the relationship of the terrestrial and celestial realms influenced St. Paul's conception of the Holy Spirit and **Milton's** poetic discussion of **astronomy** in *Paradise Lost*.

Pamela Gossin

Argument from Design. An ancient proof for the existence of God based upon the evidences of order and purposive function in the natural world, design arguments were reinvigorated in support of science in the seventeenth and eighteenth centuries. Empirical, probabilistic, and teleological, the argument appears most influentially in the natural theologies (*see* Natural Theology) of **John Ray**, **William Derham**, and William Paley. Based upon an aesthetic **analogy**—only a divine artificer could create an artifact (Nature) evincing such order and contrivance—and employing both mechanical (clockwork) and organic images, design arguments were popularized in Augustan nature **poetry** and appropriated (for varying purposes) by novelists like Henry Fielding and **Laurence Sterne**.

References

Hurlbutt, Robert H., III. *Hume, Newton, and the Design Argument*. Rev. ed. Lincoln: U of Nebraska P, 1985.
Loveridge, Mark. *Laurence Sterne and the Argument about Design*. London: Macmillan, 1982.
Olson, Richard. "On the Nature of God's Existence, Wisdom and Power: The Interplay between Organic and Mechanistic Imagery in Anglican Natural Theology—1640–1740." *Approaches to Organic Form: Permutations in Science and Culture*. Ed. Frederick Burwick. Norwell, MA: Kluwer Academic Publishers, 1987. 1–48.

Lisa Zeitz

Aristophanes (c. 445–380 B.C.E.). Greek comic playwright whose works provide the only surviving example of Old Comedy, a fantastic and ribald genre that includes elements of political and social **satire**. In *The Clouds*, Aristophanes attacks Socrates and his fellow Sophists (philosophers) by portraying Socrates's school as a place where students measure the size of flea feet and learn to make the weaker argument prevail.

Jacqui Sadashige

Aristotle (384–322 B.C.E.). Greek polymath especially known for his extensive writings on **natural philosophy** and **natural history**, poetics and **rhetoric**, logic, and analysis. The most famous student of **Plato**, he served as tutor to Alexander the Great, who sent him scientific specimens during his expeditions across central Asia. Seeing reality in the particular and individual rather than in a Platonic ideal or type, his *Historia animalium* contains encyclopedic information on animal life of all kinds, ordered according to a **classification system** that would influence virtually every natural history for over 2,000 years, including **Darwin's**. Founder of his own interdisciplinary academy, the Lyceum, his extant works deal with topics still of keen interest to scholars working in literature and science studies today, such as: the nature of reality, **time** and causation, change, generation and decay, the relative reliability of the senses and reason, the nature of thought and **imagination**, metaphysics, ethics, **politics**, poetics, and rhetoric.

Reference

Gross, Alan G. "Renewing Aristotelian Theory: The Cold Fusion Controversy as a Test
    Case." *Quarterly Journal of Speech* 81 (Feb. 1995): 48–62.
                                                                Pamela Gossin

Arnold, Matthew (1822–1888). Poet, critic, and cultural theorist. Arnold
wrote essays on a vast variety of topics—literary, social, philosophical, political,
pedagogical, and religious. While affirming classical literary standards and can-
onizing Romantic sentiment, he also agitated for liberal political reform and
insisted that all traditional beliefs be subordinated to the modern critical intelligence. In his campaigns for the modern spirit, he frequently invoked "science"
as a general authority, but he interpreted this term loosely as a synonym for
realism, **objectivity**, and rationalism. In a famous exchange about the curriculum with **Thomas Henry Huxley**, Arnold maintained the primacy of literary
education.

References

Arnold, Matthew. *The Complete Prose Works of Matthew Arnold*. Ed. R.H. Super. 11
    vols. Ann Arbor: U of Michigan P, 1960–1977.
Dudley, Fred A. "Matthew Arnold and Science." *PMLA* 57 (1942): 275–94.
                                                                Joseph Carroll

Art and Aesthetics. The practice and theory of beauty, in most times and
places with a scientific basis of some kind. Chinese **poetry**, painting, ceramics,
sculpture, dance, and **music** have been founded on Taoist theories of nature at
least since the composition of the *I Ching* (c. 150 B.C.E.). Traditional Hindu arts
are likewise founded on such physical theories as that of the three Gunas (darkness, fire, and light) as expounded in the Vedic literature. **Plato** regarded beauty
as the resemblance of an object, natural or artificial, to the ideal form of which
it was the shadow; **Aristotle** as the extent to which such an object had satisfied
its final cause; Plotinus as its participation in the realm of the divine and the
eternal.

   With the rise of rationalism and empirical science in the late Renaissance,
however, material reality was divested of most of its qualitative attributes, leaving only such measurable characteristics as mass and extension. Beauty, and the
art that created it, could no longer be predicated of an object in itself but now
required psychological explanations. Aesthetics moved from the realm of ontology to the realm of **epistemology**. Kant gave this approach its decisive formulation in his *Critique of Judgment*. The deterministic and predictable universe
pictured by the followers of **Newton** and Laplace provided no place for aesthetic
creativity and the "freedom of the beautiful" in the physical world. Artists and
poets thus found it necessary either to reject the scientific view altogether (e.g.,
William Blake's hostile portrayal of Urizen, the god of scientific reason) or
severely and dualistically to divide the realms of *Naturwissenschaft* (natural

knowledge or science) and *Geisteswissenschaft* (spiritual/introspective knowledge, or the humanities). Accordingly, those forms of aesthetic creation and appreciation that celebrated unity, harmony, and the immanence of meaning within material expression fell out of fashion, and those forms in which meaning violently transcends or contradicts its embodiment became dominant. Thus the sublime replaced the beautiful as the goal of artistic practice; originality and novelty replaced decorum and excellence of classical form.

The results of the division between arts and sciences worked themselves out in the twentieth century in the movements known as **modernism** and postmodernism. During this time most of the traditional forms and genres of the arts were undermined or discarded by avant-garde artists: narrative structure, figurative and representational images, musical melody and tonality, poetic meter, dramatic identification, and so on. Many late-twentieth-century humanities theorists espouse the notion of the social construction of reality, which, like Platonism or idealism, tends to reject the objective reality of the physical world and, like Christian fundamentalism, to deny the relevance of scientific fields such as evolution, **sociobiology**, and **neuroscience** to human behavior. Scientific explanations are replaced by cultural **politics** and the concept of the world as text.

Modernity can be usefully defined as that period in which politics came to be polarized into left and right. **Thomas Carlyle**, writing about the French Revolution, was the first major writer in the English language to use the term "left" in its political sense, in 1837 (though *gauche* and *droite* had been in political use in France since before the turn of the century, deriving from the factional seating arrangements of the prerevolutionary parliaments). By 1887 the left-right distinction was a regular and recognizable description of the two wings of the British Parliament. At almost the same time the word "beauty" was replaced in intellectual circles by "the aesthetic"—a term that came into English from Kant's German just seven years before the first known English use of "left" in its political sense. It has been precisely since politics divided itself into left and right that beauty began to be rejected by artists and critics, or euphemized as aesthetics. These events may be connected by the decline in the nineteenth and twentieth centuries of traditional institutions designed to accept the shame of human physical existence and the consequent impoverishment of literature and the arts. Without traditional rituals and arts to situate one's consciousness within a bodily presence and a context of social needs and natural processes, it is possible that artists and intellectuals developed the political categories of left and right as ways to deflect their free-floating shame. "The aesthetic" carries with it a large vocabulary of technical terms whose possession protects the user from the embarrassment of "beauty," with its freight of involuntary and emotional responses. Once the aesthetic was detached from its humanity, its shame, and its mystery, it could then be turned to political uses, and political orthodoxy could become the fundamental principle of aesthetics.

There are signs, however, that a large intellectual reversal is currently under way. The science that the arts rejected is not the science of today. **Chaos theory** has undermined the old scientistic assumption that the world is predictable, and complexity theory, based on the work of Ilya Prigogine, Benoit Mandelbrot, Murray Gell-Mann, and others, has shown that the world need not be deterministic to be scientifically understandable, nor radically fragmented to be capable of producing novelty. "Emergentism," the notion that genuinely new forms of organization can intelligibly arise out of far-from-equilibrium situations, has challenged older scientific philosophies in which **time** was considered to be reversible, or the world was seen thermodynamically as drawing down a limited stock of order in a way that could in theory be predicted if all the variables were known (see the work of N. Katherine Hayles). **Evolutionary theory** has taken on a new lease of life as an exploration of the results of nonlinear iterative processes in the biological realm. In a wide range of fields, including comparative cultural **anthropology**, linguistics, sociobiology, psychopharmacology, human evolution, psychophysics, behavioral genetics, neuroscience, human development, psychology (*see* Anthropology/Psychology/Sociology), and **cognitive science**, the connection between human subjective states and human biology has been clearly demonstrated. If the physical and mental worlds can no longer be so clearly distinguished, and if at the same time the physical world is increasingly showing itself to be free and capable of novel creation, the old split between *Geisteswissenschaft* and *Naturwissenschaft* would seem to be no longer necessary. The dismissal of science as cultural politics would no longer be morally required if the natural world as it exists at any moment were no longer seen as deterministic and thus normative for human social arrangements.

Meanwhile there has been a renewed interest in ritual as a creative and transformative activity, rather than as a conservative and traditional one. The work of Victor W. Turner has been especially influential in popularizing such terms as "rites of passage," "liminality," and "communitas," in suggesting culturally universal patterns in ritual, in showing how ritual connects the "orectic" (biological and affective) with the "ideological" (mental and moral) sides of human experience, and in rooting the whole process of ritual in the structure and function of the human brain and endocrine system. The implication, that it might not have been altogether wise to take the **enlightenment** and modernist step of rejecting the old rituals as obscurantist and politically conservative, has begun to be appreciated by artists, writers, and critics.

Art and aesthetics are thus beginning to experience a profound change, which some believe to be the beginning of the new cultural era that will succeed modernism and its postmodern postscript. Strong critiques of poststructuralist theories of the world as text, the social construction of reality, and the foundational role of cultural politics have been advanced within the humanities by such thinkers as Alexander Argyros, Joseph Carroll, and Frederick Turner. A "biopoetics" or evolutionary aesthetics, based on neo-Darwinism and neuroscience, is being developed by the above writers and by such scholars as Brett Cooke, Ellen Dissanayake, Nancy Easterlin, Kathryn Coe, Koen dePryck, Jean

Baptist Bedaux, Jerre Levy, Ingo Rentschler, Irenaeus Eibl-Eibesfeldt, Richard Dawkins, Ernst Pöppel, David Epstein, Robin Fox, Edward O. Wilson, Melvin Konner, Eric Rabkin, Desmond Morris, John Pfeiffer, Daniel Rancour-Laferrière, Kapila Vatsyayan, Jan Brogger, and others. New aesthetic theories, including Coe's of art as attracting attention, Dissanayake's of art as "making special," Argyros's and dePryck's as evolutionary emergence, Cooke's as genetic cautionary tale, Dawkins's as meme, Rentschler's as maximal sensory information, Wilson's as "**biophilia**," and many others, have emerged; many of these are included and reconciled in Turner's **natural classicism**.

Beauty in this view is a real property of the universe, its creative potential; and the capacity to recognize it, selected for by human genetic and cultural evolution, is the highest integrative level of understanding and the most comprehensive capacity for effective action. The guidance of beauty enables its appreciators to go with, rather than against, the deepest tendencies or themes of the universe, to be able to model what will happen and adapt to or change it.

In the arts and literature a major set of changes are taking place in the light of the revised picture of the physical world and the radical alteration in the perceived relationships between nature and **culture**, heredity and **environment**. In serious music, traditional forms of melody and tonality—no longer seen merely as arbitrary cultural inventions but as founded upon the human ear and nervous system and at bottom culturally universal—are making a strong comeback. In the visual arts, various movements proudly claiming the once-despised title of **realism** are demonstrating the return of the figurative and the representational. If objects in physical reality are no longer seen as inert beneath the human gaze, but as actively helping to construct the universe of which they are a part, indeed representing and picturing in their own way the world around them, the human artist need no longer cling to abstraction as the assurance that no dishonesty be introduced into the art object in itself. If all objects picture their world, and gain their own authenticity in doing so, to picture is not to offer a secondary reality but a primary one. In poetry, the New Formalism, New Narrative, and Expansive movements have recovered the ancient forms of meter and storytelling, once banished by modernist aesthetics as elitist artifices but now shown to be pan-human practices based on the information-processing capacities of the brain. There has been a return to traditional irreversible nonlinear narrative technique in fiction, supported by the theorizing of writers like John Gardner and Tom Wolfe, and a turn away from the highly linear and reversible arrangement of scenes as practiced in the New Novel. Ethnodrama assumes fundamental nonlinear human constants beneath linear cultural differences. Even in landscape architecture and landscape gardening (*see* Landscapes), until recently dominated by a sharp theoretical division between wilderness and the built environment, there is an abandonment of the idea that the artificial is by definition unnatural and an exploration by such writers as William R. Jordan III of a new restorationist environmentalism in which humans can be active participants within the ecosystem.

References

Argyros, Alexander. *A Blessed Rage for Order: Deconstruction, Evolution, and Chaos.* Ann Arbor: U of Michigan P, 1991.

dePryck, Koen. *Knowledge, Evolution, and Paradox.* Albany: State UP of New York, 1993.

Dissanayake, Ellen. *Homo Aestheticus: Where Art Comes From and Why.* New York: Free Press, 1992.

Hayles, N. Katherine, ed. *Chaos and Order: Complex Dynamics in Literature and Science.* Chicago: U of Chicago P, 1991.

Mandelbrot, Benoit. *The Fractal Geometry of Nature.* New York: Freeman, 1977.

Prigogine, Ilya, and Isabelle Stengers. *Order out of Chaos: Man's New Dialogue with Nature.* New York: Bantam, 1984.

Rentschler, Ingo, David Epstein, and Barbara Herzberger, eds. *Beauty and the Brain: Biological Aspects of Aesthetics.* Basel, Boston, and Berlin: Birkhauser, 1988.

Turner, Frederick. *Beauty: The Value of Values.* Charlottesville: U of Virginia P, 1991.

Wechsler, Judith, ed. *On Aesthetics in Science.* Cambridge: MIT P, 1978.

Frederick Turner

Ashbery, John Lawrence (1927–   ). Author of *Self-Portrait in a Convex Mirror, A Wave,* and *Flow Chart,* among many volumes of **poetry** in which he seeks to register in language the diffuse physical expressions of "the new spirit." Ashbery was raised on a farm in upstate New York, where his grandfather, whom he credits with having provided the foundation for his education, was chair of the Physics Department at the University of Rochester.

Steven Meyer

Asimov, Isaac (1920–1992). U.S. biochemist who popularized science in a prolific output of both nonfiction and hard **science fiction**. As a whole, Asimov's fiction moves extrapolatively and speculatively toward a future history, a grand yet plausible, intricately detailed yet simply crafted narrative projecting a landscape of cosmic spatiotemporal proportions. As a scientist–storyteller, Asimov first creates, then observes, theorizes, experiments with, and records (*Encyclopedia Galactica*) a future where humanity's biosocial evolution is shaped by advances in robotics, **cognitive science**, artificial intelligence (*see* Virtual Reality and Artificial Intelligence), **space travel**, and interplanetary colonization. Particularly memorable are his *Three Laws of Robotics,* his story "Nightfall," and his *Robot* and *Foundation* series of tales.

Robert C. Goldbort

ASLE. Association for the Study of Literature and Environment, founded in October 1992 to promote the exchange of ideas and literature that considers the relationship between human beings and the natural world. ASLE's purview includes but is not limited to **nature writing**, literary nonfiction, **poetry**, environmental fiction ("ecofiction"), and other forms of literature that illuminate both human and nonhuman nature. These concepts are explored in the journal *ISLE* (*Interdisciplinary Studies in Literature and the Environment*), published semi-annually by the University of Nevada Press. ASLE encourages traditional as well as innovative scholarly approaches to environmental literature and interdisciplinary environmental research, including discussion between literary scholars and environmental economists, historians, journalists, philosophers, psychologists, art historians, natural scientists, and scholars in other relevant disciplines. ASLE's homepage on the **Internet** may be found at <http://www. asle.umn.edu/>.

David N. Cassuto

Astronomy. Throughout history, human beings have believed that life on earth is influenced by the drama unfolding in the solar system and the vast reaches of space beyond it. This conviction took many forms over the centuries. It expressed itself in astrology, in the fear that the sun might burn itself out, in the idea that comets and eclipses signaled death or disaster, or as in modern times, in the theory that the stars and planets offer clues about the origins of the earth. English literature abundantly reflects the many forms that this astronomical consciousness has taken.

Up to the seventeenth century and even later, when writers alluded to the stars, the moon, and other features of the sky, they did so within the context of a Ptolemaic or geocentric universe. Specific conceptions varied, but in the general picture, a stable and spherical earth was the center of a cosmos consisting of revolving concentric spheres that were both solid and transparent. The outermost sphere was studded with the stars, and its daily revolution imparted motion to the inner spheres, so that it was called the *primum mobile*, or first mover. There were a number of spheres between this shell and the earth in each of which the planets, including the sun and moon, were embedded. Early observers realized that the stars occupied fixed positions with relation to each other but that the positions of the planets changed, and this movement was explained in a variety of ways.

Various moral or qualitative values were attached to the features of this universe. Each planet was identified with a deity and was thought to control certain virtues or attributes. The universe within the *primum mobile* was fallen and changing, and as some thought, in the process of decay, but beyond it lay the empyrean, a region of unalterable perfection. Perhaps the two features of this image that had the profoundest influence on people's thinking were the centrality of the earth and the circularity of the spheres. The first seemed to declare that the universe was essentially a stage for human life, the second that it was an image of perfection.

Imposed on this physical picture was the ancient but purely imaginary concept of the zodiac, a belt of twelve links, each enclosing a group of stars identified with the familiar zodiacal signs, which revolved around the earth in the path of the sun as it traversed the sky. The science of astrology consisted of interpreting the movements of the zodiac as its individual signs reached particular regions of the sky or coincided with stars or planets. These celestial events could determine, or at least strongly influence, both human behavior and such natural events as floods or earthquakes.

In the medieval world, ordinary people were familiar with astrology, casually employing its concepts in identifying the **time** of day and the season of the year, in explaining temperament, treating illness, and accounting for natural disasters. Medieval universities taught astronomy as one of the four subjects forming the higher course of study called the quadrivium, and it had a role in the study of **medicine**, **music**, and mathematics. The close attention paid to it for purposes of divination produced many discoveries of genuine scientific value, and up to the nineteenth century, it was the most prominent field of study that could be called a science.

Geoffrey Chaucer (1343–1400) had a special interest in astrology and became something of an expert on the subject. He naturally accepted the **cosmology** of his time, and the geocentric universe appears in his translation of Boethius's *Consolation of Philosophy* and in the conclusion of *Troilus and Criseyde* where the ghost of the slain Troilus travels to the sphere of the stars and looks back at a small and oppressive earth. The astrological formula at the opening of the *Canterbury Tales*, identifying the season as the time when "the yonge sonne/ liath in the Ram his halve course yronne," is no more than a common rhetorical device, but Chaucer's *Treatise on the Astrolabe* shows that he paid special attention to astrology, consulting many authorities on the subject, and his works are permeated with astrological lore. To give a few examples from the *Canterbury Tales*: In the *Knight's Tale*, the two deities to whom the knights pray, Venus and Mars, are associated with their planets, and the quarrel between the two is settled astrologically, as Saturn claims dominance over the two planetary deities on the ground that his sphere or orbit is larger than theirs. The clerk, Nicholas, in the *Miller's Tale* possesses a copy of Ptolemy's work the *Almagest* as well as an astrolabe, and this enables him to predict the flood that occurs in the story. The Wife of Bath attributes her personal characteristics of lust and aggressiveness to the fact that Mars and Venus were in conjunction at the time of her birth.

Although **Nicholas Copernicus's** *De Revolutionibus Orbium Caelestium* appeared in 1543, the heliocentric theory it proposed did not at once supersede the Ptolemaic conception of the cosmos. For example, the form of the universe described by Mephistophilis in *Dr. Faustus* by **Christopher Marlowe** is the geocentric one still accepted through the Renaissance and beyond. Renaissance **poetry** makes rich use of this image of the cosmos. **William Shakespeare** has it in mind when he has Hamlet praise "this brave o'er hanging firmament, this majestical roof fretted with golden fire." The stars, because they held fixed positions, were regarded as emblems of stability and transcendence, as in Richard Barnfield's lyric that begins, "Bright star of beauty, fairest fair alive, /Rare president of peerless chastity." The changeable moon, on the other hand, meant fickleness, as when Juliet asks Romeo not to swear by the moon "th'inconstant moon,/ That monthly changes in her circle orb," and the reference in the prologue of the play to "star-crossed lovers" employs astrological ideas that had become an integral part of the poetic idiom.

While Shakespeare did not seem to have more than an ordinary knowledge of astrology, his dialogue shows that his people have thoroughly assimilated it into their worldview, for they can be heard attributing their fates to their horoscopes and blaming celestial influences for their fates. However, skepticism about astrology also appears in Shakespeare's plays, and in two cases it is assigned, significantly, to unsympathetic characters. In *Julius Caesar*, Cassius encourages the hesitating Brutus with the modern-sounding, "The fault, dear Brutus, is not in our stars,/ But in ourselves that we are underlings." And in *King Lear*, the illegitimate Edmund expresses contempt for astrology, saying he would have been what he was regardless of the state of the sky at his birth.

In the seventeenth century, as Copernicus's theory became better known, and as **Galileo** made remarkable discoveries by means of his **telescope**, the facts of astronomy aroused much excitement and began to replace the superstitions of astrology as a basis for literary tropes. The new discoveries also inspired a line of authors who narrated fanciful voyages to the moon and in space, ranging from **John Wilkins** in the seventeenth century through **William Blake** and **Jules Verne** to **H.G. Wells**. In time, the rotation of the earth, heliocentrism, the discovery of new bodies in the solar system, and the open, apparently infinite extent of the universe led writers to pay fresh attention to astronomy as they hovered between belief in the old and new cosmologies.

John Donne was familiar with these controversies, as is evident from his antipapist satire *Ignatius His Conclave* (1611), where astronomy's role as a religious issue is underlined. Donne employed the Ptolemaic cosmology in the analogy he proposes at the opening of "Good Friday, 1613, Riding Westward," where the inconstancy of the soul is paralleled with the irregularity of the planet-bearing spheres, whose motions are controlled by the "intelligences" or spirits that were thought to inhabit them and by the influence of the outer sphere, or "first mover." Geocentrism seems to prevail here (for a different interpretation, see Gossin). But in other contexts, Donne displays a confused and even fearful awareness that the cosmic image is changing. Famous lines from his *First Anniversary* declare that "new philosophy calls all in doubt" and that because of the new astronomical discoveries, the old universe "Is crumbled out again to his Atomies./ 'Tis all in peeces, all cohaerance gone." From this time on, astronomical ideas came into conflict with Christian and biblical doctrines on such issues as the centrality and age of the earth, the infinite extent of the universe, and the plurality of worlds.

Paradise Lost (1667) by **John Milton** reflects both rival theories of the universe. Milton met Galileo, one of the pioneers of heliocentrism, and mentions the astronomer and his telescope several times in *Paradise Lost*. But his great epic is set in a cosmos that corresponds to the traditional Ptolemaic one. In it,

Satan flies to the outer firmament of a newly created universe and lands on the sun, forming "a spot like which perhaps/ Astronomer in the Sun's lucent Orbe/ Through his glaz'd Optic Tube yet never saw." In Book 8, the angel Raphael implies that the universe consists of concentric spheres but then describes a heliocentric cosmos, asking, hypothetically whether the sun is the center of the world and whether the earth does indeed have three motions.

By the end of the seventeenth century, astronomy became a leading activity of the **Royal Society** (chartered in 1662), and the Greenwich Observatory was founded in 1672. The Royal Society advocated the newer Copernican system, but Oxford and Cambridge clung to the Aristotelian theories, which included geocentrism and perfection, until nearly the end of the century. Isaac Newton's (*see* Newtonianism) revolutionary contributions, the invention of the reflecting telescope and the discovery that **gravity** controlled the movements of the planets, ignited a new interest in astronomy, and Newton himself was the subject of such poetic encomia as **Alexander Pope's** intended epitaph, "God said, Let Newton be, and all was light!"

Newton's insight that the solar system was controlled by mathematical laws suited the neoclassic taste for rules and regularity and was enthusiastically mentioned in philosophical and meditative poems of the eighteenth century by Alexander Pope, **James Thomson**, John Gay, and others. The popular enthusiasm for astronomy also generated some characteristic satires of the period, of which the most famous is the passage about the astronomers of Laputa in *Gulliver's Travels* by **Jonathan Swift**, where the catalog of stars and comets and the discovery of planetary satellites are treated as follies.

Celestial imagery expressive of awe and wonder is a major element in the nature imagery of early nineteenth-century Romantic poetry. Such allusions as "Bright star, would I were stedfast as thou art" by **John Keats** and "The soul of Adonais, like a star/ Beacons from the abode where the eternal are" by **Percy Bysshe Shelley** owe nothing to scientific astronomy. Traditional notions survived in such images as "sphere'd skies" and "the orb of the Moon." William Blake made the heavenly bodies and the constellations integral parts of his elaborate **mythology**. While he integrated some scientific astronomy, he condemned scientific investigation in general and included Newton among the rationalistic enemies of the **imagination**.

However, two of the major poets of the nineteenth century were responsive to the advances in astronomical knowledge. **William Wordsworth**, in spite of his opposition to science, was fascinated by astronomy and in some famous lines of *The Prelude* describes the statue of Newton at Trinity College, Cambridge, as "The marble index of a mind for ever/ Voyaging through strange seas of Thought alone." Shelley's poetry, which often takes the cosmos as its setting, reflects his knowledge of post-Newtonian astronomy. "Ode to Liberty" envisions "The daedal earth,/That island in the ocean of the world," and the notes to *Queen Mab* discuss the vast dimensions of the universe. The lines "those wandering isles that gem/ The sapphire space of interstellar air" from "Hellas" appear to refer to the nebulae or clouds of stars observed by **William Herschel** with his improved telescope. Herschel, the leading astronomer of his time, came to fame with the sensational sighting of a new planet, Uranus, in 1781, an event commemorated by John Keats's lines in "On First Looking into Chapman's Homer": "Then felt I like some watcher of the skies/When a new planet swims into his ken."

Astronomical progress made many Victorians uncomfortable because it revealed vast tracts of the universe that were unknown and because it often conflicted with biblical teaching. In *Daniel Deronda* by **George Eliot**, the heroine is disturbed by the astronomy she learns at school. *Two on a Tower* by **Thomas Hardy** has as its hero an astronomer who is appalled as he learns of the terrifying spaces of the sky. But **George Meredith** could use the heavens envisioned by science to confirm divine authority. In his sonnet "Lucifer in Starlight" the fallen angel retreats before the stars, whose regular movements seem to embody the morality he has transgressed: "Around the ancient track marched rank on rank/ The army of unalterable law." **Alfred Tennyson**, one of the poetic heroes of the Victorian age, was captivated by astronomy. Herschel's nebulae, the rings of Saturn, the constellations, the multiplicity of stars, and concern about the endurance of the solar system are among the many astronomical themes that appear in his poems.

If **science fiction** is set aside, the major works of modern literature rarely directly reflect the twentieth century's exciting advances in astronomical knowledge and space exploration. There is an exception, perhaps in *Ulysses* by **James Joyce**, where sight of "The heaventree of stars hung with humid nightblue fruit" leads Leopold Bloom to a long meditation, larded with astronomical detail, on the night sky and its constellations. The lunar and stellar imagery in the poetry and plays of **William Butler Yeats** owes nothing to astronomy but much to occult traditions. A passage in "Burnt Norton" by **T.S. Eliot** asserts that nature's conflicts are "reconciled among the stars." On the other hand, "A Walk after Dark" by W.H. Auden laments the gap between the eternal stars and limited human fates, and in "Moon Landing" and "Ode to Terminus," Auden treats astronomical exploration with cynicism. But these are nearly exceptional instances, for the moderns did not respond to astronomy as earlier English writers had.

References

Abetti, Giorgio. *The History of Astronomy*. Trans. Betty Burr Abetti. New York: Henry Schuman, 1952.

Gossin, Pamela. "Poetic Resolutions of Scientific Revolutions: Astronomy and the Literary Imaginations of Donne, Swift, and Hardy." Diss. U of Wisconsin, 1989.

Korg, Jacob. "Astronomical Imagery in Victorian Poetry." *Victorian Science and Victorian Values: Literary Perspectives*. Ed. James Paradis and Thomas Postlewait. New Brunswick, NJ: Rutgers UP, 1985.

Meadows, A.J. *The High Firmament*. Leicester: Leicester UP, 1969.

Nicolson, Marjorie Hope. *The Breaking of the Circle: Studies in the Effect of the "New Science" upon Seventeenth-Century Poetry*. Rev. ed. New York: Columbia UP, 1960.

———. "The New Astronomy and English Literary Imagination." *Studies in Philology* 32 (July 1935): 428–62.

———. *Science and Imagination*. Ithaca, NY: Great Seal Books, 1956.

Orchard, Thomas N. *The Astronomy of Milton's Paradise Lost*. New York: Haskell House, 1966.

Toulmin, Stephen, and June Goodfield. *Fabric of the Heavens*. New York: Harper, 1961.

Wedel, T.O. *The Medieval Attitude toward Astrology*. New Haven, CT: Yale UP, 1920.

Wood, Chauncey. *Chaucer and the Country of the Stars: Poetic Uses of Astrological Imagery*. Princeton, NJ: Princeton UP, 1970.

Jacob Korg

Astrotheology. Belief system employing the **argument from design** and focusing on celestial order and "heavenly law" (including planetary motions and **gravity**). Astrotheology provided, in the words of its most influential spokesperson **William Derham**, "a demonstration of the being and attributes of God, from a survey of the heavens" (*Astro-theology*, 1715). In popularizing Newton's (*see* Newtonianism) work in the *Principia* (1687), astrotheology contributed both argument and sublime imagery to contemporary **poetry** and prose (e.g., James Hervey's *Meditations*) and helped to make Newton a symbol of science who (as **James Thomson** wrote) "from *Motion's* simple Laws/Could trace the boundless Hand of PROVIDENCE,/Wide-working thro' this universal Frame" (McKillop 30).

References

Macklem, Michael. *The Anatomy of the World: Relations between Natural and Moral Law from Donne to Pope*. Minneapolis: U of Minnesota P, 1958.

McKillop, Alan Dugald. *The Background of Thomson's "Seasons."* 1942. Hamden, CT: Archon, 1961.

Lisa Zeitz

Atomic Theory. Study of the fundamental units of a chemical element. It is perhaps a unique topic in literature and science studies, in that the core message—that matter consists of discrete, subdiscernible particles rather than being continuous—owes its earliest expression much more to literary than scientific endeavors, particularly to **Lucretius** and his Greek predecessors (Democritus, Epicurus). Over time it has entered the province of experimental scientific consideration—in seventeenth-century explanations of the properties of gases; with John Dalton's nineteenth-century laws of chemical proportions; and a host of twentieth-century techniques that purport to examine individual atoms. Through all of this evolution, though, the fundamental literary/philosophical aspect of atomic theory remains the issue of how (if at all) we justify invoking invisible entities to account for macroscopic observable behavior and the connections to associated concepts such as **realism** and reductionism.

Jay A. Labinger

Atwood, Margaret (1939–   ). Canadian novelist, poet, and literary critic who has enjoyed both critical and popular success. Born into a family of scientists, Atwood invokes scientific ideas in her fiction and suggests new ways of writing about women's experiences in scientific terms. The dystopian *The Handmaid's Tale* (1985) (*see* Dystopias), which depicts a futuristic conservative theocracy suffering the effects of industrial pollution after a twentieth-century nuclear war, links technological irresponsibility and an antifeminist backlash. The novel *Cat's Eye* (1989) makes explicit references to **relativity** theory and quantum mechanics. More implicit allusions to **physics** appear in *The Robber Bride* (1993). In these two works, Atwood applies scientific ideas about **time**, space, energy, and matter to significant aspects of human experience, particularly women's experience under patriarchy. For example, one can see in these novels' content and formal arrangements illustrations of the interchangeability of both physical and emotional energy and mass, the interconnectedness of space and time, and the probability and uncertainty of postmodern culture. Atwood underscores the demystification of **scientific method** performed by recent philosophers and sociologists of science. Her writing also links science, imperialism, and patriarchy in their attempt to control the female body.

References

Bouson, J. Brooks. *Brutal Choreographies: Oppositional Strategies and Narrative Design in the Novels of Margaret Atwood.* Amherst: U of Massachusetts P, 1993.
Strehle, Susan. *Fiction in the Quantum Universe.* Chapel Hill: U of North Carolina P, 1992. See esp. ch. 6.

June Deery

Australia (LS in). May be best understood by reading popular science, exploration narratives, and scientists' cultural critiques, which reveal the contribution of **paleontology**, archeology, geology, ecology (*see* Environment and Natural History), and other natural sciences to the cross-fertilizations, conflicts, and tensions that characterize Australians' senses of place, history, and society.

Australia's largest city Sydney stands where the first non-Aboriginal settlement, a British penal colony, was established in 1788. Since that time, exploration and the dispossession of Aboriginal landholders in the name of **agriculture**, **mining**, and tourism have produced conflicting views of indigenous history, **culture**, and ecology and a struggle to understand the unique flora, fauna, and geology of a continent the size of the United States. The brute facts and simple narratives of colonization obscure the complex role the natural sciences have played in the changing rhetorical and ideological responses to the land and its people, particularly in Australian variants of the British and American traditions of **nature writing** and commentary on the impact of science on society.

Paleontologist John Long's accessible and richly illustrated *Dinosaurs of Australia and New Zealand* (1998) is exposition at its most attractive. Long and Ken McNamara's more complex work *The Evolution Revolution* (1998) discusses the implications of the latest additions to the **fossil record** and puts Australia on the paleontological map. Essential reading for cultural and literary studies of science, their book demonstrates that popular science is a cultural conduit for up-to-the-minute knowledge and **theory**.

The political legitimacy of indigenous history, culture, and claims to ownership of land is grounded in archeological proof, initially by D.J. Mulvaney's radiocarbon dating in the 1960s, of Aboriginal occupation of the continent for a period exceeding 40,000 years. A keen sense of his science's capacity to shake up the orthodox view of history infuses the opening sentence of Mulvaney's landmark *The Prehistory of Australia* (1969): "The discoverers, explorers and colonists of the three million square miles which are Australia, were its Aborigines." In *Man Makes Himself* (1936), Mulvaney's predecessor V. Gordon Childe had made a similar challenge to concepts of the ancient world when he wrote of prehistoric "revolutions" in modes of production, economic and social structure, and scientific knowledge. Representing another strand of politically reflexive archeology, Rhys Jones's "Ordering the Landscape" (in Ian and Tamsin Donaldson's *Seeing the First Australians* [1985]) is a richly informative essay on the contradictions between European concepts of wilderness (or *terra nullius*) and the Gidjigali people's seasonal management of their land. Important ideological shifts effected by Australian archeology warrant further literary-historical study.

Paul Carter's *The Road to Botany Bay* (1987) and Simon Ryan's *The Cartographic Eye* (1996) offer stimulating readings of science, **politics**, and culture in explorers' journals. Irony, ambiguity, and subversion of preexistent tropes and knowledge by a strange land and encounters with Aborigines are the focuses of readings of exploration offered by James Cook (1770), Matthew Flinders (1802–1803), Edward John Eyre (1841), Thomas Livingston Mitchell (1830s and 1840s), and Charles Sturt (1844). Carter's fascinating interpretation of strategies of naming pits **botany's** fixed grid of Linnaean **classification** against the particularizing, provisional, and dynamic science of exploration. Carter's and Ryan's valuable analyses of the tension between scientific accuracy and generic conventions are asymmetrically literary in focus, leaving the way open for studies that give more weight to the matrix of scientific practices (**astronomy**, surveying, geology, and others) that exploration encompasses.

Since the early twentieth century, ecologists have addressed the problems encountered applying European farming methods to a non-European natural environment. Historian Libby Robin credits Francis Ratcliffe's *Flying Fox and Drifting Sand* (1938) with raising public consciousness of the environmental limits of agriculture in Australia. A student of eminent biologist-popularizer

Julian Huxley, Ratcliffe offers an engaging account of his study of the native fruit bat problem in tropical Queensland and soil erosion on inland South Australian pastoral leases. His book warrants close reading for its adaptation of British and American science, and the Huxleyan popular genre, to new conditions. Naturalist Crosbie Morrison's extraordinarily popular radio broadcasts from the late 1930s to the 1950s (*Along the Track with Crosbie Morrison* [1961]) promoted awareness of the value, from local and international perspectives, of preserving Australia's remarkable wildlife, including the monotremes (platypus and echidna) and the marsupials (kangaroo and koala).

Since the 1970s, George Seddon has played a key role in maintaining the tradition of **nature writing** in Australia. Literary critic, geologist, polymath, Seddon has articulated, first in *Sense of Place* (1972), the transition from a European disappointment with the dryness and seeming featurelessness of much of the landscape toward a recognition of the land on its own terms. *Landprints* (1997) brings together three decades of essays that document redefinitions of place and critique the language and concepts Australians use to represent their land. A similar disciplinary crossing—from literary studies to earth sciences to zoology (*see* Biology/Zoology)—underpins Tim Flannery's *The Future Eaters* (1994), a provocative interpretation of geological history, biological evolution, and the impact of human occupation. An invaluable contribution to popular consciousness of the way the land has shaped its people, Flannery's book invites debate from literary and scientific fields alike. From cultural studies, Stephen Muecke's *Textual Spaces* (1992) proposes a "nomadological" aesthetic that enables Aborigines to speak their history and knowledge of the country.

Geological and evolutionary time frames have reduced the significance of social history in much of the popular literature of science. Nevertheless, the science and society discourse has played a significant part in Australian culture. During the 1930s and 1940s, eminent British botanist Eric Ashby and colleagues, concerned by the misuse of science in war, developed a local hybrid of the popular commentary by British activist scientists J.D. Bernal, J.B.S. Haldane, and others. Today, scientist–critic Ian Lowe leads the revival of the discourse and acknowledges his 1930s British forebears, Bernal in particular. His analysis of public scientific policy is spelled out in Martin Bridgstock and others' *Science, Technology and Society: An Introduction* (1998). Lowe can be described as Australia's Haldane: He has his predecessor's facility with irony and analogy in popular commentary—for instance, the 1991 radio lectures *Changing Australia*.

Reference

Seddon, George. *Landprints: Reflections on Place and Landscape*. Cambridge: Cambridge UP, 1997.

Doug Russell

Australian Science Fiction. In the 1840s Australia offered one of the few large areas of uncharted land where **Jules Verne**–style adventures could still plausibly take place, and much early science fiction in Australia was associated with the exploration of the interior of the continent and the quest for a national history and identity. A popular theme was the discovery in central Australia of a lost civilization, usually technologically advanced but ethically questionable, allowing discussion of the Australian dream of a utopian society (*see* Utopias). One of the earliest such stories was the anonymous " 'Oo-a-deen' or the Mysteries of the Interior Unveiled" (1847), but the lost civilization theme blossomed with the spread, during the 1880s and 1890s, of the legend of Lemuria, allegedly a lost, prehistoric continent joining Africa, Australia, and Malaysia. Basic ingredients of the Lemurian romance as it developed in Australia included European explorers, inland desert, gold, and a technologically advanced society. G. Firth Scott's *The Last Lemurian* (1898), which owes much to Rider Haggard's *She*, revolves around the discovery by two English adventurers of a technologically advanced Lemuria ruled by a yellow giantess, in the Australian desert. Also prevalent during the same time was a strand of fiction focusing on contemporary social issues but involving a utopian counterpart located on another planet or in a future time. Joseph Fraser's *Melbourne and Mars: My Mysterious Life on Two Planets* (1889), the first major work of utopian science fiction set in Australia, recapitulates the life story of Jacob Adams who discovers that he is concurrently living a new life on Mars, in a technologically and morally superior civilization that points up the deficiencies of Australian society. *Anno Domini 2000: or, Woman's Destiny* (1889), a utopian novel by Sir Julius Vogel, unusual for its time in its feminist stance, enunciates as its premises equality of the sexes (the U.S. president is a thirty-five-year-old woman), the formation of a powerful and beneficent United British empire, and the relief of poverty and social oppression. *A Woman of Mars; or, Australia's Enfranchised Woman* (1901) by Mary-Ann Moore-Bentley also champions women's rights through the example of a Martian society of emancipated women. In G. Read Murphy's *Beyond the Ice: Being the Story of the Newly Discovered Region Round the North Pole* (1894), Dr. Frank Farleigh, the only survivor of an expedition to the North Pole, is saved by a technologically advanced polar society and is converted to their "scientific" social values. By the 1920s, however, there was increased skepticism about technologically based utopias and more discussion of the human cost involved. In Erle Cox's *Out of the Silence* (1925), for example, an advanced, subterranean race has achieved mastery over Nature and perfection of the race through such technological marvels as death rays and light without heat, but the price (eugenic control and the genocide of the colored races) is rejected.

After these early forays into what may loosely be called science fiction, there was a long hiatus occasioned by the trade embargoes on American goods and the consequent relative isolation of Australian writers from the prolific output of their American counterparts. Exceptions were provided by James Morgan Walsh, Frank Bryning, and A. Bertram Chandler. Walsh, a prolific author of mystery stories, published a space thriller *Vandals of the Void* (1931) that introduced many of the elements that were to become standard ingredients in space operas such as *Star Wars*—intergalactic alliances and power politics and an "interplanetary James Bond figure" as hero (Ikin, 1982 xxvi). During the 1950s Bryning produced a series of stories set in the twenty-first century and based on a Commonwealth Satellite Space Station with a central female scientist, Dr. Vivien Gale, the counterpart of **Asimov's** Dr. Susan Calvin. Chandler, who had published prolifically from the 1940s, also focused on interplanetary politics in his Galactic Rim novels, most featuring Commander Grimes. The 1950s also saw the publication of two "mainstream" novels with strong science fiction elements, **Nevil Shute's** *In the Wet* (1953), about an idealized future Australia in A.D. 2000, and *On the Beach* (1957), which, with its graphic picture of a world dying from nuclear fallout, became a cult novel and film of the Cold War.

In 1975 the 33rd Annual World Science Fiction (SF) Convention (AussieCon) was held in Melbourne, presided over by **Ursula K. Le Guin**, who also ran a writers' workshop (Harding 1976). This provided a significant impetus for the writing and publishing of SF in Australia. Paul Collins launched a science fiction magazine, *Void*, and went on to publish a series of anthologies—*Envisaged Worlds* (1978), *Other Worlds* (1978), *Alien Worlds* (1979), *Distant Worlds* (1981), and *Frontier Worlds* (1983)—featuring mostly Australian writers, while Bruce Gillespie and Carey Handfield founded the Norstrilia Press with a particular commitment to publishing SF. By the 1970s the scientific optimism that had characterized the pulp stories of the golden age of American science fiction had given way to a strong element of skepticism about science; fueled by the Cold War and fears about genetic engineering, catastrophe (usually environmental) emerged as the dominant theme and remained so for a decade. George Turner's trilogy *Beloved Son* (1978), *Vaneglory* (1981), and *Yesterday's Men* (1982), set in the twenty-first century after a nuclear war, explored the dangers and social implications of biogenetic research in warfare, agriculture, ecology, cloning, and genetic engineering, which, Turner argued, would always be commandeered by those in power.

The decades since AussieCon have also seen the emergence of a more literary, witty, and allusive treatment of science fiction. The work of three authors exemplifies three different strands of this neomythic rewriting of standard science fiction themes as a mode of exploring sociological and psychological issues. Damien Broderick's *The Dreaming Dragons* (Norstrilia, 1980) (runner-up for the John W. Campbell Memorial Prize for the best science fiction novel in the world) plays with alternate versions of human ancestry, and his other science fiction novels *Sorcerer's World* (1970), *The Judas Mandala* (1982), and *Transmitters* (1984) are characterized by their intellectual and verbal playfulness, a quality rare in the genre. A similar blurring of boundaries marks the novels of Lee Harding, who employs the reality-fantasy interface to explore psychological states in *A World of Shadows* (1975), *Future Sanctuary* (1976), *The Weeping Sky* (1977), *Displaced Person* (1979), and *The Web of Time* (1980). A different kind of wit in the form of metafictional allusiveness is found in the novels of

David J. Lake, which revisit the worlds of earlier science fiction. His *The Gods of Xuma, or, Barsoom Revisited* (1978) reconstructs the Mars of Edgar Rice Burroughs's John Carter stories, while *The Man Who Loved Morlocks* (1981) revises and extends the possibilities of the world of **H.G. Wells's** *Time Machine*.

Younger writers directly inspired by the Le Guin writers' workshop include Philippa C. Maddern, Leanne Frahm, Petrina Smith, and Rosaleen Love, who have revised the stereotypical minor role of women in traditional science fiction.

References

Harding, Lee. *The Altered I.* Melbourne: Norstrilia Press, 1976.

Ikin, Van, ed. *Australian Science Fiction.* St. Lucia: U of Queensland P, 1982.

———. *The Glass Reptile Breakout, and Other Australian Speculative Stories.* Nedlands, Western Australia: Centre for Studies in Australian Literature, 1990.

McNamara, Peter, and Mary Winch, eds. *Alien Shores: An Anthology of Australian Science Fiction.* Adelaide, Australia: Aphelion Press, 1994.

Stone, Graham. *Australian Science Fiction Index 1925–1967.* Canberra, Australia: Australian Science Fiction Association, 1968.

Turner, George. "Australian SF, 1950–1980." *Science Fiction* (Sydney) 5 (1983): 4–11.

———, ed. *The View from the Edge: A Workshop of Science Fiction Stories.* Melbourne, Australia: Norstrilia Press, 1977.

Roslynn D. Haynes

Autopoiesis. Term coined by Humberto R. Maturana, **Francisco J. Varela**, and Ricardo Uribe, in a now-classic 1974 critique of classical **cybernetics**, to designate the self-productive interactions that constitute living organisms. Subsequently, Niklas Luhmann generalized the term to apply to social systems, and more recently Richard Halpern has suggested that it might fruitfully be extended, or returned, to works of **poetry**.

Reference

Halpern, Richard. "The Lyric in the Field of Information: Autopoiesis and History in Donne's Songs and Sonnets." *Yale Journal of Criticism* 6.1 (Spring 1993): 185–216.

Steven Meyer

B

Bacon, Sir Francis (1561–1626). Philosopher and essayist who rose to become Lord Chancellor of England (1618) and First Viscount St. Albans (1621) before being imprisoned on grounds of corruption. Fearing that the current ill repute of learning would result in a second Dark Age, Bacon proposed a program for intellectual and scientific reform, his "Great Instauration," set out in his philosophical works *The Advancement of Learning* (1605), *Novum Organum* (1620), and *Sylva Sylvarum: or, a Natural History* (1627). By locating the basis of scientific knowledge in God's laws, he contended that the study of Nature was theologically respectable, while simultaneously arguing for the autonomy of secular knowledge. His famous dictum "Knowledge is power" was to have long-term implications for the rise of **technology** and scientific materialism.

In addition to his philosophical works on the subject, Bacon wrote the (unfinished) fictional *New Atlantis* (1627) to popularize his new methodology of science and the role of **scientists in society**. On the utopian Pacific island of Bensalem (*see* Utopias), the members of the college of **natural philosophy**, Salomon's House, constitute a ruling elite "dedicated to the study of the works and creatures of God." Bacon's model society had far-reaching effects on the development of science. Rejecting the traditional dependence on earlier authorities, usually **Aristotle**, it stressed inductive method based on experiment and direct observation, and by emphasizing investigation of natural phenomena over a wide range of conditions, it initiated the preoccupation with scientific equipment that characterized the early years of the **Royal Society** and contributed to the **Industrial Revolution** in England. Bacon also introduced the notion of the international community of science (his "merchants of light" transcend political boundaries to collect and share knowledge) and the altruistic ideal of scientists laboring for the social good.

New Atlantis had a major influence on the course of science. It was the philosophical inspiration for the establishment of the Royal Society of London for the Improving of Natural Knowledge, which obtained its royal charters in 1662 and 1663. The frontispiece of **Thomas Sprat's** *History of the Royal Society of London* (1667) depicted Sir Francis Bacon as "Artium Instaurator" in company with Charles II as "Author et Patronus" and William, Viscount Bruckner, president of the Royal Society. The physicist **Robert Hooke**, a founding member, described the aims of the Royal Society in terms that effectively summarize the premises of *New Atlantis*.

Objections to Bacon's philosophy of science focus on his neglect of the role of measurement and mathematics, leading to an almost wholly qualitative view of science, and his unquestioning faith in inductive method, which leads to the assumption that general laws would inevitably emerge from vast collections of observations. Bacon has also been criticized for his naive belief in the necessary ethical superiority of scientists. Possibly his most important contribution to the philosophy of science was his assertion of two independent truths—sacred and secular—that paved the way for the future divergence of science from **religion** and for the autonomy of the former.

References

Faulkner, Robert K. *Francis Bacon and the Project of Progress*. Lanham, MD: Rowman and Littlefield, 1993.

Leary, John E. *Francis Bacon and the Politics of Science*. Ames: Iowa State UP, 1994.

Martin, Julian. *Knowledge Is Power: Francis Bacon, the State and the Reform of Natural Philosophy*. Cambridge: Cambridge UP, 1988.

Perez-Ramos, Antonio. *Francis Bacon's Idea of Science and the Maker's Knowledge Tradition*. Oxford: Clarendon, 1988.

Rossi, Paolo. *Francis Bacon: From Magic to Science*. Trans. Sacha Rabinovitch. London: Routledge and Kegan Paul, 1968.

Solomon, Julie Robin. *Objectivity in the Making: Francis Bacon and the Politics of Inquiry*. Baltimore: Johns Hopkins UP, 1999.

Roslynn D. Haynes

Ballard, J(ames)G(raham) (1930–   ). **Science fiction** writer who, after writing such planetary disaster novels as *The Drowned World* (1962) and *The Drought* (1965), took the genre in new directions. Works such as *The Atrocity Exhibition* (1970) and *Crash!* (1973) deploy surreal machine metaphors to explore the extreme psychopathologies of "inner space."

Reference

Ballard, J.G. "Which Way to Inner Space?" *A User's Guide to the Millennium*. London: HarperCollins, 1996. 195–98.

Noel Gough

Balzac, Honoré de (1799–1850). French novelist who placed his works under the common title "La Comédie humaine" (The Human Comedy). Some share characteristics of the Romantic period and the genre of the fantastic (*La Peau* *de chagrin*). Balzac's Realist novels reflect his genius for minute descriptions of French bourgeois and aristocratic life. Money and economic power are the driving forces behind the stories, which critics have read as parallel to the new theories of **thermodynamics** (*Le Père Goriot, La Recherche de l'absolu, Le Chef-d'oeuvre inconnu*). "The idea that kills" is the Balzacian theme of artistic, scientific, and psychological obsession that lends itself to readings along concepts of dynamical systems and complexity theories.

Maria L. Assad

Banville, John (1945–   ). Irish novelist and journalist and author of a trio of fictional biographies deeply engaged with crucial moments from the history of science: *Doctor Copernicus* (1976), *Kepler* (1981), and *The Newton Letter: An Interlude* (1982). In these novels, Banville artfully juxtaposes the order and rigor of scientific inquiry with the vagaries and chaotic tendencies of everyday life. This narrative structure is still present, though in a subtler, more implicit form, in Banville's later fiction, especially *The Book of Evidence* (1989), *Ghosts* (1993), and *Athena* (1994).

Michael B. McDonald

Baroja y Nessi, Pío (1872–1956). Major Spanish novelist. Baroja studied and practiced medicine before taking up writing. Baroja's medical training and his readings in Nietzsche and Schopenhauer deeply influence his sixty-six novels. *El árbol de la ciencia* (The Tree of Knowledge) (1911) is a transparently autobiographical account of a medical student's education that traces various positions regarding science's place in the modern world. The conclusion that humans cannot render the world intelligible overwhelms the scientific optimism of the protagonist, who commits suicide. Baroja called scientists modern tragic heroes because they resemble Sisyphus in their endless quest for knowledge.

Reference

Templin, E.H. "Pío Baroja and Science." *Hispanic Review* 15 (1947): 165–92.

Dale J. Pratt

Barth, John [Simmons] (1930–   ). American writer, an early, premier practitioner and theorist of postmodern fiction, professor emeritus, Johns Hopkins University, since 1990. His award-winning short stories, novellas, novels, and essays explore the possibilities and impossibilities of perception, identity, intellect, and spirit in a comic-absurdist relativistic cosmos. Like the works of **James Joyce**, **Vladimir Nabokov**, and **Jorge Luis Borges**, Barth's stories are replete with eclectic word-play, labyrinthine narratives, doublings, and mirrorings. *The Floating Opera* (1956), *The Sot-Weed Factor* (1960), *Lost in the Funhouse* (1968), and *Giles, Goat-Boy* (1966) all experiment with—and challenge—the relationship of reader and text and the perversity of authority. Deliberately disorienting, philosophically nihilistic, combining pity, terror, parody, and irreality, Barth's genre-bending writings directly contributed to the early definition and development of the postmodern in fiction and **culture**.

Pamela Gossin

Barthelme, Donald (1931–1989). American writer of novels, short stories, fantasy, and children's fiction. In his collected stories (*Come Back Dr. Caligari*, 1964; *Unspeakable Practices, Unnatural Acts*, 1968; *City Life*, 1972) and novels (*Snow White*, 1967; *The Dead Father*, 1975), Barthelme made sophisticated, highly self-conscious use of language in the attempt to reinvent **fiction**. In these early postmodern texts, he experimented with narrative **time**, space, and dramatic structure, notions of the chance and absurd, as well as the ironic power and powerlessness of the artist in postindustrial society.

Reference

McCaffrey, Larry. *The Metafictional Muse: The Works of Robert Coover, Donald Bartheleme and William H. Gass*. Pittsburgh: U of Pennsylvania P, 1982.

Pamela Gossin

Bartram, William (1739–1823). Son of John Bartram and author of *Travels through North and South Carolina, Georgia, East and West Florida* (1791). His ornate lyricism and romantic observations of the beauty and violence of nature made natural science into art. His tale delighted the English Romantic poets, especially **Coleridge**.

Raymond F. Dolle

Bateson, Gregory (1904–1980). A pioneering transdisciplinary thinker whose work spanned many fields including **anthropology**, psychiatry, evolution, **genetics**, **cybernetics**, and ecology. His primary dictum was that the unit of survival for an organism, species, or planet is the system in its **environment**. This emphasis on a contextual analysis of phenomena informed all his work and his understanding of thought itself. He developed an "ecology of mind" that diagnosed pathologies at all levels: He understood schizophrenia as a problem of double binds; he analyzed communication in terms of "levels of logical typing," leading to a theory that play—human or animal—is metacommunication; he laid bare the destructive drives in Western culture in terms of the "epistemological errors" on which mistaken premises are founded. He believed that many such errors stem from Cartesian dualism, which separated mind from nature and enabled science to part company with **philosophy** and the arts, leading to a devastating "loss of aesthetic unity" among these domains. For Bateson, "mind" has nothing to do with consciousness, but with relationship, because mental function results from the interactions of differentiated "parts." Mind is a specific kind of "Wholes constituted by such interactions." Minds are not only part of nature; nature is a vast interconnected mind, made up of "patterns that connect."

Reference

Harries Jones, Peter. *A Recursive Vision: Ecological Understanding and Gregory Bateson*. Toronto: U of Toronto P, 1995.

Paul A. Harris

Baudelaire, Charles (1821–1867). French poet and author of *Les Fleurs du Mal* (The Flowers of Evil), a collection of 132 poems. Regarded as the "archetypal modern poet" (de Man 73), his poems express reality as the space of unsolvable and open-ended processes. Disorder is the underlying trope that knits together his rich imagery. His work lends itself to readings along concepts of complexity theory and thereby reveals emergent properties, which explains the enduring power of his metaphors.

Reference

De Man, Paul. "Process and Poetry." *Critical Writings, 1953–1978*. Minneapolis: U of Minnesota P, 1989.

Maria L. Assad

Beckett, Samuel [Barclay] (1906–1989). Irish-born dramatist, poet, novelist, and critic who lived much of his life in France and wrote primarily in French. He won the Nobel Prize for Literature in 1969. His most famous works, *Waiting for Godot* (1953), *Endgame* (1954) and *Krapp's Last Tape* (1958) explore existential dilemmas, nihilism, and hopelessness within the "theater of the absurd," an experimental style of **drama** also engaged by Jean Genet and Eugene Ionesco, among others. By deliberately disorienting stage **time** and employing disengaged monologue and dialogue, Beckett queries the unreality of **reality**, the meaninglessness of human existence, and the futility of human action. Giving voice to the myriad thoughts and feelings of individual minds and hearts (including those employing the naming power of scientific terminology, such as the character "Lucky" in *Godot*), all human speech is uttered into the sheer emptiness of cosmic space. Critical analyses of Beckett's rich conceptualization of nothingness have noted his understanding of mathematics and early-twentieth-century **physics**, especially **entropy** and quantum mechanics, and have employed psychoanalytic and linguistic approaches.

References

Baker, Phil. *Beckett and the Mythology of Psychoanalysis*. New York: St. Martin's, 1997.
Davies, Paul. *The Ideal Real: Beckett's Fiction and Imagination*. Cranbury, NJ: Association of University Presses, 1994.
Montgomery, Angela. "Beckett and Science: Watt and the Quantum Universe." *Comparative Criticism: A Yearbook* 13 (1991): 171–81.
Wolosky, Shira. *Language Mysticism: The Negative Way of Language in Eliot, Beckett and Celan*. Stanford, CA: Stanford UP, 1995.

Pamela Gossin

Behn, Aphra (1640–1689). Dramatist, poet, novelist, translator, and professional spy, often described as the first professional woman author in England. Her firsthand experiences with the people and culture of Surinam inspired the setting, plot, and characters of her antislavery novel *Oronooko* (1688), which is an important early fictional treatment of the **noble savage**. Best known to her contemporaries as the writer of popular "bawdy" comedies that often ridiculed marriage customs and **gender** roles, she also offered cutting satires against the **medicine** and **astronomy** of her day in *Sir Patient Fancy* (1678) and *Emperor of the Moon* (1687), respectively. She further participated in popular scientific discourse by writing "A Pindaric Poem to the Rev. Dr. Burnet" (1689) and by making an influential translation of **Fontenelle's** *Conversations on the Plurality of Worlds* under the title *A Discovery of New Worlds* (1688).

Reference

Goodfellow, Sarah. " 'Such Masculine Strokes': Aphra Behn as Translator of *A Discovery of New Worlds.*" *Albion* 28 (1996): 229–50.

Pamela Gossin

Berry, Wendell (1934–). Essayist, poet, and environmental advocate. Although Berry has adopted a simple agrarian existence and has often eschewed the conveniences of modern **technology** (most notably the **computer**), his connections to the modern scientific discipline of ecology run deep. In essays such as "Discipline and Hope" from the 1972 collection *A Continuous Harmony*, Berry presents an attack on what he calls the "linear vision" of technological progress and embraces instead the "cyclic vision" of ecology. **Poetry** is, for Berry, a means of both describing and understanding ecological interconnections; as he says in his essay "A Secular Pilgrimage," poetry can become "a power to apprehend the unity, the sacred tie, that holds life together" (15). One of America's most well-known poets, Berry's writings on ecology and organic farming have in recent years proven to be influential among agricultural theorists such as Wes Jackson, as well as bioregional advocates such as **Gary Snyder** and Kirkpatrick Sale.

References

Berry, Wendell. *Collected Poems: 1957–1982.* San Francisco: North Point, 1984.
———. *Home Economics.* San Francisco: North Point, 1987.

Rod Phillips

Bicycle. Engine with the optimal ratio of **energy** to output has intrigued writers for more than a century. Around 1900, it became a symbol of spatial liberation for women and the lower classes, an aspect explored by writers, feminists, and philosophers from **H.G. Wells** to Frances E. Willard. Speed, circular movement, and the need to adapt bodily functions to a machine made the bicycle a ready symbol of fantasy, absurdity, and nonsense from Dada to Flann O'Brien and **Samuel Beckett**.

Reference

Schenkel, Elmar. "The Word and the Wheel. Bicycles and Literature." *Moving the Borders*. Ed. M. Bignami and C. Patey. Milano: Edizioni Unicopli, 1996. 213–20.

Elmar Schenkel

Biodiversity. The variety and interdependence of life on earth. "Biological diversity" or "biodiversity" came into popular environmental thought in the late 1980s as biologists became concerned about species and habitat loss in the tropics and throughout the world's major ecosystems. Prominent scientists like **Edward O. Wilson** and environmental groups like The Nature Conservancy and World Wildlife Fund began warning, in Wilson's words, of "the sixth great extinction spasm of geological time" in an effort to gain support for new, global conservation initiatives, such as ecosystem protection (*Diversity* 351).

Unlike American conservation efforts in the past that focused on charismatic species or scenic wonders, the biodiversity conservation movement addresses "the whole, all of life, the microscopic creepy crawlies" (Meadows 150). In other words, conservation biologists and other biodiversity advocates stress the ecological importance of native plants, insects, fungi, swamps, and such, as well as grizzly bears, elephants, and mountain ranges.

In part, the biodiversity cause is the most serious attempt to date to realize **Aldo Leopold's** "The Land Ethic" by enlarging ethical consideration, and thus protection, to the "soils, waters, plants, and animals, or collectively: the land" (211). While experts quibble over the precise definition of the word, the concept of "the diversity of life" is gaining cachet in environmental, intellectual, and political spheres as a potent new defense of nature.

References

Leopold, Aldo. "The Land Ethic." *A Sand County Almanac*. 1949. New York: Oxford UP, 1987. 201–26.
Meadows, Donella. "What Is Biodiversity and Why Should We Care About It?" *Reading the Environment*. Ed. Melissa Walker. New York: Norton, 1994. 149–51.
Wilson, Edward O. *The Diversity of Life*. New York: Norton, 1992.
———, ed. *BioDiversity*. Washington: National Academy, 1988.

John A. Kinch

Biology/Zoology. Broadly defined as the study of life, biology emerged as a dynamic and process-oriented science in the early nineteenth century. Gottfried Treviranus, Jean-Baptiste Lamarck, and others sought to distinguish the study of physiological processes such as respiration and development from the classifying and descriptive work of **natural history**. Zoology denotes the study of animals and with **botany** formed the two main branches of early biological study. Currently, biologists recognize and study five different kingdoms of life: monerans (bacteria and viruses), protoctists (amoebas, algae, and slime molds), fungi, plants, and animals. Consequently, modern biology encompasses a wide variety of subdisciplines—including microbiology, cytology, **genetics**, developmental biology, and evolution—and intersects with other major scientific disciplines, notably **chemistry** and ecology. LS studies focus on biological/ zoological themes within literature; use the tools of literary analysis to critique biological texts, metaphors, and institutions; and educate specialized and general audiences about biological issues, controversies, and trends.

With the advent and growth of **biotechnology** in the 1980s and 1990s—a diverse and growing industry that encompasses genetic engineering, the development of reproductive technologies, and the Human Genome Project—biology has taken center stage as the vital science of the twenty-first century. Given the ethical, legal, and political challenges these burgeoning technologies create, as well as global environmental problems such as threats to **biodiversity**, loss of species habitat, and ecosystem decay, critical literacy in biology is an important skill and knowledge base for the general citizenry to possess in order to make informed decisions on biotechnology and environmentally related public policy issues. To this end, literature and biology studies can help create an informed and critically savvy public as well as sound science policy.

Several key instrumental and theoretical developments have profoundly affected the study of organisms. The development and use of the **microscope** gave nineteenth-century biologists interested in processes of growth, differentiation, **reproduction**, and physiology a powerful tool for exploring the minute structures of organisms. This new microscopic perspective laid the groundwork for the cell theory of biology, in which cells are considered to be the fundamental units of life's organization and functions. Cell theory underpins our notions of life's patterns of development, unity, reproduction, and evolution and thus is a controlling metaphor of modern biology.

Arguably, the two most important biological disciplines are genetics, the study of the patterns and causal mechanisms of inheritance, and evolutionary biology, the study of how life has diversified and changed over time. Both strands of inquiry began in the mid-nineteenth century: Gregor Mendel quietly published his treatise on the patterns of inherited traits in pea plants in 1865; through quantitative experiments Mendel suggested that certain physical traits were determined by discrete factors (later called genes). Six years earlier, **Charles Darwin** and Alfred Russel Wallace proposed a mechanism (natural selection) for the evolution of life's diversity. Though the relationship between these two insights was far from clear for many decades, biology since the early twentieth century has sought to synthesize evolutionary and genetic theory. In the 1950s, molecular biology has helped characterize and explain evolutionary processes as they occur on the level of the genetic material.

Within the interdisciplinary field of literature and science studies, the study of biological themes, characters, and controversies is as rich and diverse as the science of life. Subjects and approaches range from the rhetorical analysis of biological discourse; to the reevaluation of the writings and scientific contributions of women in biology; to the elucidation of how biology and **medicine** have been influenced by, as well as shaped, ideologies of **gender**, race, and class; to the interpretation of biological themes, tropes, and characters in literary texts; to the biological basis of language acquisition. Three influential examples of biology-centered scholarship in literature and science are Gillian Beer's *Darwin's Plots* (1983), **Donna Haraway's** *Primate Visions* (1989), and Greg Myers's *Writing Biology* (1990).

Beer explores Darwin's evolutionary discourse in the context of key nineteenth-century writers such as **George Eliot** and **Thomas Hardy**; examines and analyzes narrative strategies, themes, and metaphors within the *Origin of Species*; and argues how these elements constitute Darwin's theory of natural selection. She suggests ways in which **evolutionary theory** functioned as a powerful trope in a range of other contexts—particularly, how Victorian writers responded to, assimilated, and/or resisted evolutionary theory in their writings.

Haraway's history of twentieth-century primatology combines Marxist and feminist analysis, cultural studies, **history of science**, and literary criticism to identify and analyze the narratives, metaphors, and controversies within the study of primates. Biology is appropriate to examine from this perspective, Haraway contends, for it is fundamentally a historical science that expresses itself through narratives. *Primate Visions* critiques the notion of scientific **objectivity** and analyzes how primatology is fashioned by ideologies of sex, race, and class. For Haraway, primates are interesting because they occupy contested territory and expose our tacit beliefs about nature and **culture**.

By combining rhetorical analysis with insights from the sociological study of science, Myers explains how different biological texts—proposals, formal articles, and popular accounts—produce scientific knowledge and reflect and reinscribe the cultural authority of science. *Writing Biology* examines how various discourses appeal to different communities; how texts persuade, create consensus, or spark dissension; how they construct a notion of scientific expertise; and how the revision and evolving reception of texts affect the status of truth claims.

Lastly, the sizable and heterogeneous body of writings by literary biologists and zoologists—professional scientists who publish literary works and/or write for a wide audience—constitutes both a fruitful synthesis of literary and biological knowledge and a rich source of primary material for literature and science scholars. Scientists-writers such as **Rachel Carson**, Richard Dawkins, **Loren Eiseley**, Jane Goodall, **Stephen Jay Gould**, and **Edward O. Wilson** have produced works of popular science, autobiography, history of science, and **poetry** and have contributed to the critical analysis of how biology affects and is shaped by culture.

References

Beer, Gillian. *Darwin's Plots: Evolutionary Narratives in Darwin, George Eliot and Nineteenth-Century Fiction.* 1983. London: Ark, 1985.
Haraway, Donna. *Primate Visions: Gender, Race, and Nature in the World of Modern Science.* New York: Routledge, 1989.
Myers, Greg. *Writing Biology: Texts in the Social Construction of Scientific Knowledge.* Madison: U of Wisconsin P, 1990.

Michael A. Bryson

Biophilia. "The innately emotional affiliation of human beings to other living organisms" (Wilson, *Biophilia* 1). A term coined by Harvard biologist **Edward O. Wilson** and used as the title of his 1984 book to describe a philosophical and biological **hypothesis** espoused by Wilson and environmental thinkers that suggests **genetics** and evolutionary history predispose contemporary humans to identify with nonhuman life. "The brain evolved in a biocentric world, not a machine-regulated world," writes Wilson in the 1993 *The Biophilia Hypothesis*, a compilation of essays by scientists, philosophers, and others (32). Wilson argues, as do others, that in terms of evolutionary history, contemporary humans are only recently estranged from nature by modern technological living. Thus, modern humans yearn for reconnection to nature, in part, because of their evolutionary past.

Related to "ecopsychology," proponents of biophilia believe that further explication and scientific inquiry could lead to a deeper environmental ethic, based less on human self-interests and more on evolutionary biology. "We are literally kin to other organisms," as Wilson has said (*Biophilia* 131).

References

Wilson, Edward O. *Biophilia: The Human Bond with Other Species.* Cambridge: Harvard UP, 1984.
Wilson, Edward, O., and Stephen R. Kellert, eds. *The Biophilia Hypothesis.* Washington: Island, 1993.

John A. Kinch

Biotechnology/Genetic Engineering. Harnessing **biology** and related sciences for practical applications, such as large-scale production of genes or enzymes for medical, agricultural, or industrial uses. Both fields expanded with the development of recombinant DNA (deoxyribonucleic acid) techniques since the late 1970s, after its nascency with elucidation of DNA's double-helical structure by **James Watson** and **Francis Crick** in 1953. As a primary unit of heredity, the gene, as being mapped in the Human Genome Project, may now be commercially exploitable for intended benefits, such as new medical treatments or prenatal screening.

Wider understanding of biotechnology, particularly among lay society, however, reshapes our understanding of human nature. **Genetics** underpinned by biotechnological knowledge strengthens preprogrammed attribution, potentially undermining the alternative view of personal responsibility for actions and consequences. Moreover, biotechnological parameters redefine our concept of the individual. Genetic manipulation through eugenics, or the selective breeding of humans, further introduces ethical issues from the unintended risks associated with these futuristic technological applications.

Advances in biotechnology, such as the Human Genome Project, identify eugenics and related topics in genetic engineering as themes for rhetorical discourse. Rhetoricians no longer stand distinct from scientists; instead, the **symbolism**, myth, and narrative of literature on ethical and societal issues influence the conduct of scientific inquiry, just as the proliferation of biotechnology and genetic engineering fuels new literary topics. Creative writing, particularly **science fiction**, imaginatively explores the linkage between literature and the fields of biotechnology and genetic engineering.

Reference

Hasian, M.A., Jr. *The Rhetoric of Eugenics in Anglo-American Thought*. Athens: U of Georgia P, 1996.

Robert J. Bonk

Black Box. A device, system, or physical process described by giving its effect on an input to produce a known output or result, without specifying its internal details, either by choice or because the information is unavailable. The idea originated in electronic circuit diagrams, in which standard symbols denote elements such as resistors and transistors that are joined to process signals in a specified manner. An example is a diagram that shows how electronic components are linked to perform the functions of a radio, or of a **computer**. A designer who wished to indicate a subsystem within the larger design—for instance, the part of the radio circuit devoted to tuning among different stations—without giving details, would show it in the diagram as a featureless "black box," described only by its function. In recent usage, the phrase has appeared to describe aspects of human **genetics**, computational theory, and the design of human-machine interfaces.

Sidney Perkowitz

Blake, William (1757–1827). English visionary poet, painter, and engraver whose illustrated ("illuminated") texts combine art and **technology** in both form and content. Throughout his life, Blake's work called for a revolution of artistic and spiritual **imagination** over the servitude and oppression of rationalism, **mechanism**, and materialism (embodied, for him, by such figures as Newton [*see* Newtonianism], **Locke**, and Joshua Reynolds). "An Island in the Moon" (c. 1784–1785), an early satiric medley against science utilizing the cosmic voyage motif, was followed by lyric declamations against the human cost of the "progress" of the **Industrial Revolution** in *Songs of Innocence and Experience*

(1789–1794). The brief "Mock on, Mock on, Voltaire, Rousseau" (1800–1803) encapsulates Blake's antirational, antideist, anti–"action/reaction" **philosophy**, describing "light" as a spiritual, redemptive phenomenon, not just particulate matter in motion, and celebrating the value of infinite, divine vision and revelation over limited, physical perception and ratiocination. Professionally thwarted by contemporary aesthetic values, Blake's work embodied his rebellion against the restrictive, unnatural formalist concerns of the neoclassical period. He invented his own combination of poetic and artistic expression, melding illustration, emblem, interlinear design, and cadenced verse into a single powerful image or "vision" on each page. Inspired by the spiritual energy of Swedenborg, the political energy of the French Revolution, and the poetic energy of **Milton**, Blake offered his own cosmic **mythology** on a still grander scale envisioning the essential tensions of existential oppositions before and through all **time** and space (*The Book of Thel*, 1789–1793; *The Marriage of Heaven and Hell*, 1790–1793; *Visions of the Daughters of Albion*, 1793; *The Book of Urizen*, 1794; *Milton*, 1804–1808; and his last great poem, *Jerusalem*, (1804–1820). His poetic vision inspired the Pre-Raphaelites' painting and the **poetry** and prose of such diverse writers as **Algernon Swinburne** and **James Agee** and has attracted a wide range of critical studies from literature and science perspectives, including Freudian (*see* Freud) and Jungian analyses. Reading Blake's prophetic verse in black and white printed text can in no way reproduce the kind of artistic experience he hoped his creations would generate, so serious readers have long recognized the importance of making a pilgrimage to see his luminous originals in the Tate Gallery.

References

Ault, Donald. *Visionary Physics: Blake's Response to Newton*. Chicago: U of Chicago P, 1974.

Bronowski, Jacob. *William Blake and the Age of Revolution*. New York: Harper, 1969.

Peterfreund, Stuart. *William Blake in a Newtonian World: Essays on Literature as Art and Science*. Norman, OK: U of Oklahoma P, 1998.

Pamela Gossin

Bohr, Niels (1885–1962). Danish physicist, awarded a Nobel Prize for his solar system model of atomic structure (the "Bohr atom"). Bohr's significance for relations between science and literature rests on two outgrowths of his **atomic theory**: his stress on metaphor as an instrument for visualizing the invisible and his development of complementarity—diverse points of view—as a way of resolving apparent paradoxes in quantum behavior.

When referring to atoms, Bohr asserted that "language can be used only as in poetry" and that, like poets, physicists are concerned less "with describing facts [than] with establishing mental connectedness" (qtd. in Heisenberg 41). Concern to establish mental connectedness led him to another literary strategy: manifesting wholeness by multiplying perspectives. Greek tragedy and the fiction of Poul Martin Møller had suggested to Bohr the impossibility of acting simultaneously on such ethical imperatives as charity and justice (Bohr 3: 15). And this wisdom, gleaned from literature, was confirmed in life when he found himself obliged to punish his son for shoplifting. He was thus well prepared to recognize, as complements rather than contraries, classical and quantum perspectives as vehicles for characterizing the microscopic world.

References

Bohr, Niels. *The Philosophical Writings of Niels Bohr.* 3 vols. Woodbridge, CT: Ox Bow, 1987.

Heisenberg, Werner. *Physics and Beyond: Encounters and Conversations.* Trans. Arnold J. Pomerans. New York: Harper and Row, 1977.

Pais, Abraham. *Niels Bohr's Times, in Physics, Philosophy, and Polity.* Oxford: Clarendon, 1991.

Petruccioli, Sandro. *Atoms, Metaphors and Paradoxes: Niels Bohr and the Construction of a New Physics.* Trans. Ian McGilvray. Oxford: Clarendon, 1993.

Barton Friedman

Borges, Jorge Luis (1899–1986). Argentine poet and writer. As a young man he spent most of his time reading books in his family library in Buenos Aires. Ironically, he had poor eyesight, which eventually deteriorated into blindness. Borges wrote his first short story at the age of seven and his first poems at fifteen. He spent much time writing **poetry** until the 1930s, when his attention turned to writing short stories. It is at this point that the Borges we know today was born. In *The Western Canon* (1994), Harold Bloom writes: "Twentieth-century Hispanic American literature, possibly more vital than North American, has three founders: the Argentine fabulist Jorge Luis Borges; the Chilean Pablo Neruda, and the Cuban Alejo Carpentier" (463). Borges is one of a few writers who can make scientific principles emerge as literature. Many times scientists cite his short stories as examples in their own work. Steven Rose, for instance, in his book *The Conscious Brain* (1973), uses Borges's "Funes, the Memorious" as an example of a young man who could remember everything by some sort of eidetic process (267). Interestingly enough the author parallels this example with a real case story reported by the Russian neurologist **A.R. Luria** (268). The work of Borges can be interpreted through modern **physics**. Some critics have found the concept of space-time in physics very useful to the understanding of the story "Garden of Forking Paths" (Capobianco). Symmetry is also important in the work of Borges, "Death and the Compass" and "The Library in Babylon" (Fayen). N. Katherine Hayles has studied infinite series and transfinite numbers in his short stories. Borges is one of the masters of the synthesis of literature and science, because in the few pages of a short story science and literature become one.

References

Bloom, Harold. *The Western Canon: The Book and School of the Ages.* New York: Harcourt Brace, 1994.

Capobianco, Michael. "Quantum Theory, Spacetime, and Borges's Bifurcations." *Ometeca* 1(1989): 27–38.

Catalá, Rafael. "Para una teoría latinoamericana de las relaciones de la ciencia con la literatura: La cienciapoesía." *Revista de Filosofía* 28 (1990): 67–68.

Fayen, George. "Ambiguities in Symmetry-Seeking: Borges and Others." *Patterns of Symmetry*. Ed. Marjorie Senechal and George Fleck. Amherst: U of Massachusetts P, 1977.

Hayles, Katherine N. *The Cosmic Web*. Ithaca, NY: Cornell UP, 1984.

Rose, Steven P.R. *The Conscious Brain*. New York: Knopf, 1973.

Rafael Catalá

Botany. The classification, anatomy, and physiology of plants, with deep roots in folk tradition and links to the literary metaphor of organicism. Carl Linnaeus systematized botany into a science central to the exploration and naming of New World nature. The artificiality of Linnaeus's "sexual" system (based on the number of flower parts) provoked the search for a "natural" system based on plants' true relationships, leading to the professionalization of botany during the nineteenth century. Yet the Linnaean system's accessibility made botany a popular science, encouraged as a healthful intellectual pursuit suited for women and children, in a tradition closely tied to **nature writing** and to environmental education.

Reference

Shteir, Ann B. *Cultivating Women, Cultivating Science: Flora's Daughters and Botany in England 1760–1860*. Baltimore: Johns Hopkins UP, 1999.

Laura Dassow Walls

Boyle, Robert (1627–1691). Anglo-Irish chemist and natural philosopher, founding member of the **Royal Society**, known for his corpuscular notions of matter and for establishing the modern theory of chemical elements. Boyle demonstrated with the air pump the necessary role of air in the transmission of sound, respiration, and combustion (*New Experiments Physio-Mechanicall, Touching the Spring of the Air and Its Effects*, 1660, 1662). In *The Christian Virtuoso*, Boyle claimed the study of nature as a prime religious duty, dedicated to showing how the clocklike mechanism set in motion by the Creator functioned according to secondary scientific laws. In literary terms, Boyle was willing to make himself a character in his own writings, fashioning the public image of the gentleman scientist. Otherwise, Boyle was notorious for his distrust of the romantic literary **imagination** and publicly spoke against the emerging form, the novel.

References

Harwood, John T. "Science Writing and Writing Science: Boyle and Rhetorical Theory." *Robert Boyle Reconsidered*. Ed. Michael Hunter. Cambridge: Cambridge UP, 1994.

Sargent, Rose-Mary. *The Diffident Naturalist: Robert Boyle and the Philosophy of Experiment.* Chicago: Chicago UP, 1995.

Shapin, Steven, and Simon Schaffer. *Leviathan and the Air-Pump: Hobbes, Boyle, and the Experimental Life.* Princeton, NJ: Princeton UP, 1985.

Diana B. Altegoer

Brahe, Tycho (1546–1601). Flamboyant Danish nobleman, greatest observational astronomer of his time, denied the reality of the celestial spheres, presented a compromise model between the Ptolemaic and Copernican systems. He was an uneasy collaborator with theorist **Johannes Kepler**. Tycho wrote elaborate baroque prose. He was the subject of Max Brod's drama *The Redemption of Tycho Brahe.*

Reference

Christianson, John Robert. *On Tycho's Island: Tycho Brahe and His Assistants, 1570–1601.* Cambridge: Cambridge UP, 1999.

Val Dusek

Brecht, Bertolt (1898–1956). Political dramatist, deeply concerned about the humanizing potential of science and how it could work as a powerful force against the corruption spawned by a market economy. His *Life of Galileo* (1940), substantially revised and translated into English by Charles Laughton (who had portrayed **Galileo** on the American stage), is the principal work in which this important issue is explored.

Galileo, for Brecht, represented the ideal citizen: a truth-seeker who possessed a zeal for sharing his ideas and discoveries with a populace ruled by superstition and Church dogma and preoccupied with materialistic gain. Brecht wished to convey the notion that scientific demonstration, perhaps more than anything else in this drama, could topple revered authority if the latter conflicted with demonstrable results. In other words, empirical science was one of the most effective weapons against tyranny and injustice ever conceived because anyone, not just a scientific "priesthood," could participate in its revelations. In a scene that is at once comic and chilling, Galileo disproves **Aristotle's** hitherto unquestioned claim that objects with a density heavier than **water** always sank when placed in water; he performed a simple experiment that anyone in the audience could perform: floating a needle by placing it on a piece of paper, laying paper with needle gently on the water's surface inside a bowl, then carefully moving away the paper. As Galileo and his friends laugh heartily (and haughtily), his housekeeper Mrs. Sarti shudders, understanding instinctively what could happen when revered authority gets cavalierly tossed out the window. This foreshadows the central crisis of the play: Galileo's arrest and forced recantation for having presented new astronomical evidence that the earth was not the center of the universe, just as **Copernicus** had argued.

Galileo in Brecht's eyes was not just a brilliant scientist but an engaging personality. The most influential scientists, far from being pale eccentrics detached from the mundane affairs of society, are robust lovers of life, are teachers at heart, who wish to spread the spirit of scientific inquiry to the people, thereby empowering them.

Fred D. White

Brin, David (1950–   ). A physicist as well as a Hugo and Nebula award-winning **science fiction** writer who manages to combine mythic quest adventure with carefully extrapolated "hard" science. In addition to a trilogy of novels (*Sundiver*, 1980; *Startide Rising*, 1983; *The Uplift War*, 1987) in which humanity discovers its anomalous place in a complex intergalactic society, Brin has written an important "ecospeculation" novel, *Earth* (1990), set in the mid-twenty-first century, when several environmental crises are occurring simultaneously, including what could be termed the worst possible crisis: the escape from magnetic containment of an artificially produced, microscopic black hole, which falls to earth and begins devouring the planet from the inside out. Each of the several story lines corresponds to a particular "sphere" of the planet—mantle, lithosphere, biosphere, hydrosphere, ionosphere, exosphere (i.e., in earth orbit), and core. From the perspective of the whole novel, Brin is giving the question "What is a world?" a contemporary futuristic answer: A world is a highly interactive realm of subsystems, the corruption of any one of which can profoundly affect the whole.

Fred D. White

Brontë, Emily Jane (1818–1848). English novelist and poet whose work habitually features meteorological (*see* Meteorology) and astronomical (*see* Astronomy) motifs, abounding in references to wind, storms, and stars. Brontë locates a transcendent sphere beyond earthly existence; her poems "No coward soul is mine" (1850) and "Julian M. and A.G. Rochelle" (1938) rely on celestial imagery to accomplish this task. Her novel *Wuthering Heights* (1847) features a pre-Darwinian (*see* Darwin), adversarial natural world while it poses questions about heredity and atavism.

Reference

Barker, Juliet. *The Brontës*. New York: St. Martin's, 1995.

Stephen D. Bernstein

Browne, Sir Thomas (1605–1682). English physician. Through an esoteric prose style and elaborate systems of correspondence, Browne unified scientific reason with religious faith (*Religio Medici*, 1642), catalogued "vulgar errors" exposed by science (*Pseudodoxia Epidemica*, 1646), and assessed the metaphysical significance of geometrical order in nature (*The Garden of Cyrus*, 1658).

Nicholas Spencer

Browning, Robert (1812–1889). A poet of strong religious convictions whose belief that the soul progresses through successive stages of knowledge had a strong affinity with the evolutionary doctrines of his time. His poetic drama *Paracelsus* deals with the spiritual struggle of a Renaissance scientist. Browning occasionally uses extended science-inspired imagery. For example, admitting that the sun is not under man's control, he recalls that Prometheus nevertheless made use of it by capturing its fire in a device like a magnifying glass. Hence, men should be content to remain ignorant about the ultimate mysteries of the universe and to use them for practical purposes. Particularly striking is his use of recent astronomical discoveries to express traditional moral views. But he also turns to pre-Copernican (*see* Copernicus) ideas, as when he speaks of the "perfect round" of heaven compared with the "broken arcs" of earth, ignoring **Johannes Kepler's** discovery that the planetary orbits are elliptical rather than round.

Reference

Smith, Willard C. *Browning's Star Imagery*. Princeton, NJ: Princeton UP, 1941.

Jacob Korg

Bruno, Giordano (1548–1600). Natural philosopher and religious reformer, burned at the stake for advocating hermetic, Egyptian religion, Copernican (*see* Copernicus) astronomy, and an infinite universe. He was the first modern to take **Lucretius's cosmology** seriously. His Italian dialogues, written in the circle of Sir Philip Sidney, are his best. Critics have noted connections with Rabelais, **Shakespeare**, and **Christopher Marlowe**.

Reference

Yanow, Morton Leonard. *The Nolan: Prisoner of the Inquisition: A Novel*. New York: Crossroad, 1998.

Val Dusek

Buck, Pearl S(ydenstricker) (1892–1973). American novelist who also wrote five novels under the pseudonym John Sedges. She is best known for her novels set in China, including *The Good Earth* (1932), for which she won the Nobel Prize for Literature in 1938. In her later novel *Command the Morning* (1959), written in the ambivalent climate of response to the Cold War, Buck explores the possible motivation of the scientists who worked on the Los Alamos project, and having spent weeks studying the site and interviewing the scientists and their families, she integrated real and fictitious characters in her novel. Her characterization of physicist Enrico Fermi typifies the scientist who repudiates social responsibility for his research and restates his much-quoted statement, "Don't bother me with your conscientious scruples. After all, the thing is superb physics."

Although many of Buck's scientists begin with moral scruples concerning the project, these are dissolved by the Japanese attack on Pearl Harbor, when the decision to make the bomb becomes one involving American lives. This, combined with the belief that the Germans have almost perfected an atomic bomb, produces a sense of ethical inevitability about the research. Buck portrays the American scientists as avoiding individual responsibility for the decisions, resorting to opinion polls among the scientific fraternity, seeking safety in numbers, and ultimately assigning to the military the decision of whether or not to use the bomb.

Buck indicates that such avoidance of responsibility is not, as is frequently claimed, a position of moral neutrality but a positive evil and implies that the traditional claims for a value-free science will inevitably issue in scientific arrogance. The novel ends with the ambivalent view of the project leader, Burton Hall, who is both fascinated and repelled by the arrogance and moral simplicity of a younger generation of scientists.

Reference

Doyle, Paul A. *Pearl S. Buck*. Boston: Twaynes, 1980.

Roslynn D. Haynes

Buffon, G.L. Leclerc de (1707–1788). French geological theorist, censored by the Sorbonne, published a comprehensive *Natural History* (1749 ff.) beginning with a view of the earth's history that ignored Genesis. Translated and revised by Oliver Goldsmith as *A History of the Earth and Animated Nature* (1774; many editions), it became a popular source of nature lore for Romantic and Victorian writers. Buffon's first geological theory, involving a recreating universal ocean, was succeeded by a second (*Epochs of Nature*) in 1778 that divided the history of the earth (and life upon it) into six eras prior to our own. A superb writer, Buffon popularized natural history, secularized understanding of it, and greatly furthered its assimilation into both literature and **art**. Among the European writers influenced by him, besides Goldsmith, are **Rousseau, Voltaire**, **Stendhal**, Herder, **Goethe**, **Samuel Johnson**, **Erasmus Darwin**, **Blake**, **Wordsworth**, **Coleridge**, **Moore**, **Byron**, **Percy Bysshe Shelley**, and **Keats**. Because Buffon characterized nature in America as degenerate, he was vigorously opposed by American writers, particularly **Thomas Jefferson**.

Dennis R. Dean

Burroughs, William S[eward] (1914–1997). Core member of the "Beat Generation" (with Jack Kerouac and Allen Ginsburg) and "Grandfather of punk" who wrote **experimental novels**, plays, screenplays, and **essays** (*The Naked Lunch*, 1959; *The Soft Machine*, 1961; *BladeRunner: A Movie*, 1979). He attended medical school in Vienna, studied **anthropology** at Harvard, and documented his own morphine addiction in *Confessions of an Unredeemed Drug Addict* (1953, under the pseudonym William Lee). Expanding and exploiting "pulp fiction" as literary form, Burroughs's "cut-up" method put nonlinear plot sequences and chaotic structure to the purpose of social **satire**. Drawing upon his own experiences, he explored the surrealism of homosexuality and altered consciousness in *The Wild Boys: A Book of the Dead* (1971) and *Queer* (1986). His self-conscious experimentation with literary form and protopostmodern sense of space/**time** have been of wide influence within popular culture, directly inspiring the work of avant-garde artists such as David Bowie and Patti Smith.

Pamela Gossin

Burton, Richard Francis (1821–1890). Victorian linguist, explorer, and author known for his translations, ranging from *The Arabian Nights* to the *Kama Sutra*, and travels, particularly his quest for the source of the Nile and his haj to Mecca. By turns bigoted and startlingly broad-minded, his work popularized Near Eastern and African (*see* Africa) cultural studies, both furthering anthropological research and serving British imperialist ambitions. In 1989, William Harrison's biographical *Burton and Speke* (1982) inspired the critically acclaimed film *Mountains of the Moon*.

References

Lovell, Mary S. *A Rage to Live: A Biography of Richard and Isabel Burton.* New York: W.W. Norton, 1998.

Rice, Edward. *Captain Sir Richard Francis Burton.* New York: Charles Scribner and Sons, 1990.

Alison E. Bright

Burton, Robert (1577–1640). Author of *Anatomy of Melancholy* (1621), an encyclopedic treatise on the human body and soul that not only synthesized classical and medieval thinking but shaped later imaginative and scientific discourse on **melancholy** and other cognitive disorders. *Anatomy* influenced writers such as **Laurence Sterne**, **John Locke**, and the Romantics.

Kristine Swenson

Butler, Octavia E[stelle] (1947–　). **Science fiction** writer who, in novels such as *Dawn* (1987), *Adulthood Rites* (1988), and *Imago* (1989)—the XENOGENESIS trilogy—deploys many thematic conventions of her genre (including catastrophe, survival, and metamorphosis) to imagine alternative stories of human origins and future evolution informed by feminist and African American perspectives.

Reference

Peppers, Cathy. "Dialogic Origins and Alien Identities in Butler's XENOGENESIS." *Science-Fiction Studies* 22.1 (1995): 47–62.

Noel Gough

Butler, Samuel (1612/1613–1680). Author of the burlesque epic *Hudibras* (1663), perhaps the most popular poem of the age, which satirized contemporary **religion** and the misuse of the intellect as directed toward metaphysics and esoteric knowledge of all kinds, including many endeavors of the early modern sciences. He refined his scientific **satire** by targeting the fledgling **Royal Society** in "The Elephant in the Moon," contrasting the Fellows' credulity and far-fetched interpretations of the astronomical phenomena as revealed by enormous instruments of observation against the simple and powerful explanations provided by direct vision exercised in concert with common sense.

Pamela Gossin

Butler, Samuel (1835–1902). English novelist who incorporated evolutionary ideas into his novels as well as writing nonfiction works promoting his own views of evolution (*see* Evolutionary Theory), which were heavily dependent on the work of **Buffon**, **Erasmus Darwin**, and Lamarck. The son of a clergyman, Butler prepared for a career in the church, but after graduating from Cambridge, he refused to take orders on the grounds of religious doubt. After making a small fortune in sheep farming in New Zealand, Butler devoted the rest of his life to writing, painting, composing **music**, and following the intellectual currents of his day. He was particularly interested in the theory of evolution and was an ardent admirer and defender of *The Origin of Species* when it was first published. Delving further into other evolutionary writing, however, he came to believe that **Charles Darwin** had not given adequate credit to earlier theorists like George Buffon, Erasmus Darwin, and Jean Baptiste Lamarck and that Darwin was basically dishonest in presenting his theories and discoveries as radically new. Furthermore, he felt that Darwin's theory of evolution by natural selection was too mechanistic, that it emptied mind out of the universe. In a satirical fantasy *Darwin among the Machines*, Butler suggested that a new species of life—machinery—was evolving and that it would eventually make people dependent on itself and thus enslave them. Although he could not accept the Christian God as the creator of the universe, Butler could not accept a blind and purposeless evolution either. Like Buffon, Butler adopted the theory that personal identity is transmitted through the ages, that people transmit their thoughts to their posterity, becoming, in a sense, one with their descendants. Butler shared Lamarck's belief that the acquisition of advantageous characteristics is due to an organism's determination and desire to survive, as much as to mere luck or chance.

Butler himself wrote four books on evolution: *Life and Habit* (1878), *Evolution Old and New* (1879), *Unconscious Memory* (1880), and *Luck or Cunning?* (1887). He insisted that natural selection is not an adequate explanation of variation and argued for purposefulness in evolutionary development, not emanating from a divine creator but inherent within the organism itself. He assumed that there is an intelligence residing inside organisms themselves that gives direction to the changes of evolution.

Four important principles emerge from Butler's writings on evolution: (1) The oneness of personality between parents and offspring; (2) memory on the part of offspring of certain actions that it did when in the person of its forefathers; (3) the latency of that memory until it is rekindled by a recurrence of the associated ideas; (4) the unconsciousness with which habitual actions come to be performed. These ideas found expression in Butler's two most popular books: the satirical fantasy novel *Erewhon* and the autobiographical novel *The Way of All Flesh*. *Erewhon* critiques the Darwinian mechanistic universe by describing a land where the use of machines is forbidden because they are considered an incipient and rival form of intelligence. Satirizing the principle of "the survival of the fittest," Butler has his Erewhonians approve of and reward bodily strength and health and severely punish physical frailty and disease as a crime. In *The Way of All Flesh*, the hero succeeds by a mixture of luck and cunning. He inherits, or "remembers," his great-grandfather's capacity to appreciate music and art. He has an aptitude for culling and assimilating the good instincts from all the bad ones he has inherited. Butler's theories of unconscious memory and willed adaptation were the philosophical foundation for his view of life, in which tolerance, forbearance, and the cultivation of one's best qualities create the best possibilities for human life.

Reference

DeLange, Petronella Jacoba. *Samuel Butler: Critic and Philosopher.* New York: Haskell House, 1966.
Raby, Peter. *Samuel Butler: A Biography.* Iowa City: U of Iowa P, 1991.

Marian Elizabeth Crowe

Byron, George Gordon (Lord Byron) (1788–1824). British poet influenced by Cuvier's geologic notion that the earth undergoes periodic convulsions in the process of creating a succession of new worlds. This model underlies the organization of *Don Juan* (1818–1824). In that poem Byron suggests that **technology** gives the convulsions an upward boost, but this attitude is not consistent in such lyrics as *Song for the Luddites* (1816). Across his narrative poems, Byron suggests a near Lucretian atomism of colliding events with no teleological direction.

William Crisman

C

Calvino, Italo (1923–1985). Italian novelist and essayist. Spurred by his father, a doctor, he read widely in the sciences from childhood on. He tapped science for both inspiring ideas and rhetorical riches; **Lucretius** and **Galileo** were important stylistic influences. The role of science in Calvino's writings might be described as enactive. The twin collections of stories *Cosmicomics* (1966; 1968 tr.) and *t zero* (1967; 1969 tr.) carry out literary Gedanken-experiments that translate ideas from **cosmology**, evolution, and **information theory** into deliberately anthropomorphic language. As driven to formalize **fiction** with mathematical precision as he was to humanize scientific thought, Calvino pursued theoretical investigations into the nature of literature. Informed by structuralist and poststructuralist thought—he befriended Roland Barthes and **Michel Serres**—Calvino treated literature as a "combinatoric game" in **essays** and novels alike. He used a range of mechanisms as algorithmic devices for generating texts, from tarot cards (*The Castle of Crossed Destinies*, 1973; 1977 tr.) to contemporary writers and theorists (*If on a Winter Night a Traveler*, 1979; 1981 tr.); as a member of **OuLiPo**, he experimented with computer-generated texts.

Calvino sought to distill the syntax of literature, through sources and genres from fables (*Italian Folktales*, 1959; 1975 tr.) to fantasy (*The Baron in the Trees*, 1957; 1959 tr.). His persistent concern for **epistemology**, and the irreducibly central role of language in shaping knowledge, is seen in *Mr. Palomar* (1983; 1985 tr.). Arguably, his masterpiece is *Invisible Cities* (1972; 1974 tr.), a metafictional recasting of *The Travels of Marco Polo*, which Calvino felt most effectively expressed his desire to combine, he said, "geometric rationality and the entanglements of human lives." His vision of literature (and the influence science had on it) may best be seen in *Six Memos for the Next Millennium* (1988), a series of lectures he was writing when he died of a brain hemorrhage.

The operating surgeon asserted that Calvino's brain was the most elegant he had ever seen.

Paul A. Harris

Canada (LS in). Everywhere subject to ongoing incremental change in definition, though perhaps the more so in Canada on account of a long-standing lack of exact equivalence between the meanings of the terms "literature" and "science" in the two official languages. Particularly with regard to "science," the French usage retains a closer link to its Latin ancestor *scientia*, knowledge or learning in general (akin to German *Wissenschaft*). Nevertheless, both science and *la science* convey the dual sense of the acquisition of knowledge and of an accumulating repository of systematic knowledge. "Nature" is the other key term in this context, for science grew out of **natural philosophy**; and Canada, perhaps more than any other modern society, has grown out of, or within, a relationship with nature.

Although **nature writing**, in Canada as elsewhere in the West, has occasionally lain on the margins of "canonical" literature, it has gained inspiration from both Romantic feeling and religious conviction. In the nineteenth century, Catharine Parr Traill, writing in the tradition of British **natural theology**, traced the creativity of God in the mystery and abundance of nature. Her best-known book, *The Backwoods of Canada* (1836), is a factual and scientific account of her first three years in the Canadian bush. Almost half a century later she published *Studies of Plant Life in Canada* (1885). Other examples from this period and genre include Philip Henry Gosse's dialogue *The Canadian Naturalist* (1840) and two works by William Dawson, *Acadian Geology* (1855) and *Archaia: or, Studies of the Cosmogony and Natural History of the Hebrew Scriptures* (1860). The theme of the harmony of science and faith recurs in the first part of the twentieth century in the botanist and Québecois nationalist Frère Marie-Victorin's *Flore laurentienne* (1935), a work dedicated by the author to the youth of his "pays" and promoting a reading of God's "other" scripture, the book of nature.

Other traditions of nature and science writing in Canada appear in different genres and with varying subject matter. Following in the tradition of Izaak Walton's *The Compleat Angler*—blending self-aware artistic expressiveness, meditation, and concern for technical detail—are Roderick Haig-Brown's numerous influential books, including novels but particularly the nonfictional *A River Never Sleeps* (1946); and David Adams Richards's *Lines on the Water: A Fisherman's Life on the Miramachi* (1998). **Poetry**, too, claims a place in this general category: Don McKay's *Birding, or Desire* (1983); Diana Hartog's *Polite to Bees: A Bestiary* (1992); Bruce Whiteman's *Visible Stars* (1995); and Jan Zwicky's *Songs for Relinquishing the Earth* (1996). These poets may fit more properly under the heading of nature poetry rather than "**sciencepoetry**"; but if the latter is a genre at all, it might well include some of the poems of Christopher

Dewdney (e.g., *A Paleozoic Geologic of London, Ontario*, 1973) and E.J. Pratt ("Erosion," "Sea-Gulls," and many others from the 1920s and 1930s).

Science both in- and outside of literature engages the issue of nature's dominion—or of human dominion *over* nature. Until recently, indeed, the standard phrase denoting the country was (by contrast with republics and kingdoms) the *Dominion* of Canada, with this term carrying both theistic and royalist connotations. Yet the immensity of the land and the frequent hostility of its climate repeatedly raise the question of humankind's place, efficacy, or legitimacy. Hugh MacLennan, writing in *Seven Rivers of Canada* (1961) of his journey down the Mackenzie, confesses to a "moment of panic" in which he wonders "if human beings are necessary to this earth." This question about the status of human dominion may relate also to that of its effects. Haig-Brown, already mentioned, was a pioneering conservationist. More recent ecologically attuned writing includes the **fiction** of Fredrick Bodsworth (*The Last of the Curlews*, 1954) and the powerful polemical chronicles of Farley Mowat, from *People of the Deer* (1952) to *Sea of Slaughter* (1984), which describes and protests the destruction of species in the North Atlantic.

Both Bodsworth's and Mowat's works provide links to the cultures and oral "literatures" of indigenous peoples, whose imagined or actual harmony with nature (if not necessarily with each other) provide a contrast to the dominion of "scientific" Europeans. Much early Canadian writing indeed takes these peoples as its subject matter and may accordingly be seen as scientific in the descriptive and anthropological sense (Jacques Cartier, David Thompson). But, increasingly, translations or rediscoveries of Aboriginal oral literatures themselves are gaining recognition, also under the heading of "other ways of knowing." English-language tellings or retellings of significant myths can be found in such works as Mohawk E. Pauline Johnson's renderings of *Legends of Vancouver* (1911), George Clutesi's Tse-Shaht *Son of Raven, Son of Deer* (1967), and Harry Robinson's *Nature Power* (1992). The anthology *First Fish, First People: Salmon Tales of the North Pacific Rim* (1998) likewise draws attention to neglected or disparaged knowledge.

Ongoing study of this breadth of traditions of literature and knowledge in Canada will continue to extend and complement such landmark academic writings as **Margaret Atwood's** *Survival* (1972) and Northrop Frye's *The Bush Garden* (1971). And the creatively literary character of science writing may itself increasingly gain recognition, especially when it engages realms of science, such as **cosmology**, which transcend the human senses. Examples of this genre include works such as Hubert Reeves's *Patience dans l'azur: L'evolution cosmique* (1981), translated as *Atoms of Silence: An Exploration of Cosmic Evolution* (1984).

Dennis Danielson
with special acknowledgment of the assistance of Iain Higgins

Capek, Karel (1890–1938). Czech novelist and playwright, best remembered for his play *R.U.R.* (1921), "set on a remote island in 1950–1960." One of the first "modern" warnings about science out of control, *R.U.R.* prophetically introduced the concept of mechanical robots (from the Czech *robota*, meaning "drudgery") and explored their impact on society. Capek outlines the dehumanizing effects of scientific materialism in the scientist stereotypes of the Rossums, owners of the title firm R.U.R.—Rossum's Universal Robots. Rossum Senior, a physiologist who has discovered a substance like protoplasm, exemplifies scientific hubris, believing reason is sufficient to create anything; he is eventually killed by one of his monstrous creatures. Rossum Junior, an engineer intent only on producing commercially viable robots, omits all aesthetic and emotional elements. However, the robots, having developed human emotions, destroy their former masters. *R.U.R.* quickly became the prototype for a succession of **science fiction** stories featuring robots.

Capek also wrote utopian romances about the Damoclean sword of science. In *Krakatit* (1925), an engineer Prokop, excited at his discovery of a powerful explosive, krakatit, at first refuses to consider the consequences but is converted to social responsibility. In *The Manufacture of the Absolute* (1923), Capek postulates an "atomic boiler" to turn matter into **energy**, but once the matter is destroyed, the metaphysical Absolute remains behind. The apocalyptic finale suggests that such powerful inventions are best left alone since they lead only to global **chaos**.

Reference

Harkins, W.E. *Karel Capek*. New York: Columbia UP, 1962.

Roslynn D. Haynes

Capra, Fritjof (1939–). Austrian-born popularizer of science. In *The Tao of Physics* (1975) Capra argues that several recent discoveries of Western science are to be found in ancient Eastern **philosophy** and that Eastern ideas are a suitable philosophical foundation for modern **physics**. His approach has been influential in the so-called New Age movement.

June Deery

Cardenal, Ernesto (1925–). Nicaraguan poet and writer. In 1989 he wrote *Cántico cósmico* (Cosmic Canticle). It is a 581-page poetry book divided into forty-three canticles. In his poetry cosmological theories, **quantum physics**, ethics, **religion**, and ecology are masterfully knitted. The critic Enrique Lamadrid called this book "a Song of Songs to the Creation of the Universe, a Cantata to the evolution of Consciousness, a bardic synthesis of scientific theory and poetry" (147).

References

Chabrán, Rafael. "Cienciapoesía, Science Poems and The Cosmic Canticle: Catalá, López-Montenegro, and Cardenal." *Rafael Catalá: Del "Círculo cuadrado" a la "Cienciapoesía."* Ed. Luis A. Jiménez. New Brunswick, NJ: Ometeca Institute, 1994.
Lamadrid, Enrique. "The Quantum Poetics of Ernesto Cardenal." *Ometeca* 2.2 (1991): 147.

Rafael Catalá

Carlyle, Thomas (1795–1881). Scottish essayist and historian. A correspondent of **Johann W. von Goethe's**, Carlyle echoes Romantic interest in nature science through frequent use of biological metaphor, particularly in *Sartor Resartus* (1833–1834). His **philosophy** prioritizes the organic over the mechanistic (with **mechanism** encompassing aspects of industrialism and scientific system-building). A friendship with empiricist **John Stuart Mill** deteriorated as Carlyle's **politics** grew more stridently elitist.

Reference

Clubbe, John, ed. *Carlyle and His Contemporaries*. Durham: Duke UP, 1976.

Alison E. Bright

Carson, Rachel (1907–1964). A trained scientist with the sensitivity of a poet whose legacy redounds in both literature and science. Her landmark work *Silent Spring* (1962) offered a calm but impassioned account of the far-reaching destruction wrought on plants and animals including humans by the pesticide DDT. The book almost single-handedly changed public opinion regarding the prevalence of chemicals in modern society. It also spurred revolutionary changes in government policy while inspiring a generation of writers to tackle what once would have been labeled quixotic environmental causes. After *Silent Spring*, neither the government nor the populace could ignore the increasingly pernicious effects of industrialized and technological society on the natural world.

For most of her professional life, Carson was a marine biologist and a writer for the United States Fish and Wildlife Service. Before *Silent Spring*, she had gained literary fame with *The Sea around Us* (1951) and *The Edge of the Sea* (1955). After the publication of *Silent Spring*, Carson endured vicious ad hominem attacks by the chemical industry, which sought to depict her as an ignorant, hysterical woman eager to turn the world over to the insects. Nevertheless, a report issued by President John F. Kennedy's Science Advisory Committee completely vindicated Carson's thesis. Today, Carson is a revered figure in both the literary and scientific communities.

David N. Cassuto

Catalá, Rafael (1942–   ). Literary critic and professor of Spanish and Latin American literature and director of the **Ometeca** Institute and journal. Author of *Cienciapoesía* (1986) in which he develops a unified theory of poetry and science (*see* Sciencepoetry). In this work he posits an integrated vision of the universe where literature and science are subsystems of a greater sociocultural system.

Rafael Chabrán

Cavendish, Margaret (1623–1673). Eccentric English author of poetry, plays, prose medleys, philosophical treatises, an autobiography, and a biography that display eclectic influences from contemporary literature and **natural philosophy**. Once dismissed as as "mad" as their author, her writings are increasingly regarded as interesting and important examples of early modern women's writing on science. In *Philosophical Fancies* (1653) (the form of which combines fantasy and popular science), she displays her understanding of **chemistry** and natural philosophy. *Observations upon Experimental Philosophy* (1666) includes a scientific romance entitled "The Description of a New Blazing World" in which Cavendish envisions a **utopia** where a "new woman" (very like herself) can effectively exercise her mind and personal and political power. Her flamboyant visit to the **Royal Society** is chronicled in **Pepys's** diary, and her use of a prose medley of **politics**, science, and travel romance was later perfected by **Jonathan Swift** in *Gulliver's Travels*.

Reference

Margaret Cavendish: New Blazing World and Other Writings. Ed. Kate Lilly. New York: New York UP, 1992.

Pamela Gossin

CD-ROM. Compact Disk Read-Only Memory, a **technology** for storing and presenting large amounts of digitized information. CD-ROMs and their successors such as DVD (Digital Versatile Disk or Digital Video Disk) make it possible for personal **computer** users to view multimedia presentations, static graphics, animations, video, and audio. The technology has helped to promote our culture's understanding of the computer as an audiovisual medium and has challenged our concepts of "reading," "writing," and "text." Literary research and pedagogy are being transformed by CD-ROM versions in which texts and their contexts are packaged together, allowing manuscript facsimiles and variants, biographical, historical, and critical background, photographs, videoclips, and audio readings to be easily accessed outside of archives.

Jay David Bolter

Center for the Study of Science and the Arts (CSSA). An informal interdisciplinary research group based at the University of Texas at Dallas. Made up of researchers from local universities and high-tech corporations in a wide range of fields—natural science, psychology, the history of ideas, **philosophy**, literary studies, management, social science, **computer science**, and the arts, it was founded in 1993 by Frederick Turner, David Camacho, David Channell, and others. The Center supports scientific research into the arts and artistic understanding of the sciences and seeks to improve the quality of teaching with the results. It addresses three major research questions: Is there a naturally based aesthetics? Is there an aesthetic element in science? What models and metaphors are appropriate for research combining science and the arts? The Center's participants have addressed such topics as neurobiological roots of aesthetic experience; ecopoetics—the economy and ecology of **art**; animal aesthetics; aesthetics of organism and mechanism; critical **theory** in the light of natural science theory of order and process; cross-cultural studies of arts and aesthetics; **time** and space in the arts; oral tradition, folklore, anthropological study of the arts; theory of artificial intelligence (*see* Virtual Reality and Artificial Intelligence) and literary/dramatic characterization; general systems theory and aesthetics; models, metaphors, and translation in scientific discourse; and **science fiction**.

Frederick Turner

Central Europe—Primarily France, Germany, Italy (LS in). Three countries that (along with the United Kingdom) were instrumental in the inception and development of modern science. Accordingly, French, Italian, and German (or Austrian) writers and artists have, down through the ages, repeatedly turned to science for themes, models, and protocols. Aside from such borrowings, the three countries under consideration here offer a wide historical span for the study of the institutional, intellectual, and rhetorical dimensions both of scientific activity and of the propagation of knowledge. Thinkers and writers from each of these countries have, from before the Renaissance and up to the present day, explored and complexified the connections between scientific knowledge, **philosophy**, and literature. The eminent role of recent French thought in the establishment of **theory** as a literary discipline in the 1970s and 1980s depended essentially on borrowings from the human and social sciences but was not always averse to appealing to the mythological authority vested in the practice of science. However, various efforts toward developing a new alliance between scientific and humanistic culture are currently taking shape in Europe.

In the field of the visual arts, the adoption of linear perspective in Italian Renaissance painting from Alberti and Brunelleschi onward, followed by its triumphant spread throughout Western **art**, provides perhaps the most massively obvious and long-lasting debt owed by painting to science, on both a theoretical and (as evidenced by the wide array of tools devised or adopted by artists down the ages) a technological plane. This question has been thoroughly researched, as has the impact on art of scientific theories of color (for example, by **Johann W. von Goethe** in early-nineteenth-century Germany and, slightly later, by the French chemist Chevreul). Scholars have also investigated the cross-influences of painting and the part played by the invention of photography in French art's break with the Academy, along with a whole range of similar topics, up to and including the cultural and practical effects of the technological explosion of the twentieth century on the exponential diversification of artistic genres and media in avant-garde movements and postmodernism. Other, equally eclectic cross-hybridizations include the role of exploration and ethnography in eighteenth-century "Chinese" **landscape** gardens and the inception of **Cubism**.

In the realm of literature, popular fiction has played a leading part in the dissemination of scientific knowledge and the delineation of imaginative visions and/or ideological descriptions of both scientific practice and possible future developments in the fields of science and technology. The novels of **Jules Verne** at the turn of the century and the *Tintin* comic books of Hergé constitute perhaps the most universally disseminated instances of this phenomenon. More deep-rooted evidence of interchange between science and literature is provided by the philosophical Orientalism of eighteenth-century France, the epistemological am-bitions of German **Romanticism**, and the naturalist novel (**Émile Zola**, 1840–1902). Individual instances of influence could also be multiplied indefinitely. The work of Ernst Mach and Ludwig Bolzmann inspired Robert Musil's *Man without Qualities* (1930, 1933), an epistemological novel that raises issues that continue to inspire debate among German and French academics. Conversely, **Sigmund Freud's** creation of psychoanalysis depended heavily on his readings of the works of individual writers and artists, while literature was not slow to return the compliment, via both surrealism and the psychoanalytical novel, of which Italo Svevo's *The Conscience of Zeno* (1923) provides an early example. At least insofar as they belong to the history of ideas, all such issues have long been explored in France, Germany, and Italy.

The figure of the universal man of letters and science, bridging what would later be known as the "**two cultures**," was perhaps an ideological creation of the Renaissance. Nevertheless, it continued to impress the European imagination long after the demise of Renaissance **humanism**. Consideration of a few ex-emplary instances suggests that much research remains to be conducted on this subject. The name of Goethe (1749–1832), poet, dramatist, and novelist but also the author of scientific works on color, geology, and **mineralogy**, looms large in contemporary bibliographies of literature and science studies. However, a few rare occurrences aside, the slightly earlier figure of **Diderot** (1713–1784) is almost as conspicuously absent, despite his obvious sensitivity to the science of his day (experiments with blind subjects, voyages of discovery, **meteorology**, etc.). Nor does the scientific culture of Italy's foremost early-nineteenth-century poet Giacomo Leopardi (1798–1837), who at the age of thirteen was working at a verse translation of **Horace's** *Art of Poetry* and two years later composed an erudite history of **astronomy** from the origins to the year 1811, seem to have stimulated the scholarly interest it warrants. It is true that **Italo Calvino** has insisted that Leopardi's lunar **poetry** testifies to his assimilation of the Newto-nian (*see* Newtonianism) revolution, while Antonio Negri—who has also, among other subjects, revived forgotten aspects of the relation of nineteenth-century political materialism to the **biology** of the age—devotes some attention to Leopardi's science. Nevertheless, when the Italian Cultural Institute in Paris organized a conference on "Leopardi and Infinity" in 1988, the poetry was treated in parallel to modern science and mathematics, rather than interactively with them. Goethe, in fact, seems to mark the end of an age, with the journal of his 1786–1788 trip to Italy perhaps constituting the most distinguished late example of a truly universal culture in its mingling of the knowledgeable observation of natural phenomena with expressions of a classical sensibility. Significantly, although he would himself have liked to be remembered as a scientist, Goethe has chiefly been seen by posterity as a literary figure, while **Alexander von Humboldt** (1763–1859), a second paradigmatic figure of German learning in the nineteenth century, could no longer aspire to the same sort of dual career.

The case of **Galileo** has long served to illustrate the complexity of the relations between literature and science that the notion of a universal culture involves. In the 1950s, the Italian scientist and man of letters was the subject of a small but significant episode in intellectual history, which can serve as a point of departure for a survey of recent developments in the field of cultural studies of science. The episode in question brought together figures from each of the other nations under consideration here.

The prewar flight to America of German and French writers, artists, and academics constitutes an important aspect of intellectual life in the twentieth century. In 1954, the German-born art historian Erwin Panofsky published a little book on *Galileo as a Critic of the Arts* that, the following year, drew an admiring response from the historian of science Alexandre Koyré, in the form of an article entitled "Aesthetic Attitude and Scientific Thought." Panofsky and Koyré illustrate a swerve away from the popular vision of Galileo, whose tribulations have commonly been taken, both by studies in the **history of science** and by works of art (e.g., **Bertolt Brecht's** 1947 *Life of Galileo*), to epitomize the painful struggle of modern science against the institutional power of **religion**. The paradigmatic role played by Galileo in this extended drama was underlined yet again in the early 1990s by the pope's long-delayed official recognition of the Catholic Church's faults in its treatment of the Italian astronomer. It was, however, to his writings on art (championing painting as against sculpture) and literature (singing the praises of Ariosto and dismissing Tasso) that Panosky paid close attention, suggesting that these provided a clue for his failure to acknowledge **Kepler's** discovery of the elliptical orbits of the planets. Koyré for his part concluded that this paradoxical blindness demonstrated the curious, unpredictable, and illogical course of human thought.

The demonstration that Galileo's progressive humanistic culture contributed to an apparently retrograde scientific blindness still has an appealingly complex feel, even if Panofsky's position has been contested by more recent scholars. Over the past decades, the history of thought has made room for an increasingly sophisticated cultural history of science, leading to (to stay with the examples of Galileo and Kepler) Fernand Hallyn's work on the rhetorical structure of the scientific **imagination**. Europe has also seen numerous studies of the role played in the development of modern science by, for instance, the social and cultural practices of Renaissance courts or by the culture of collecting, from the cabinets of curiosities (which, among other functions, served to incorporate the marvels of the new world into European culture) to the creation of **museums** (such as the French Natural History Museum in the wake of the 1789 Revolution). However, the more contentious political dimension of such topics (in terms of **gender, race**, etc.) has received less systematic attention in France, Germany, and Italy than in Britain or America. One obvious and highly influential exception to this situation is provided by Michel Foucault's histories of the social sciences. However, Foucault's example—and more particularly the role played by technological practices and science in his micropolitics of knowledge/power—has lately proved more influential in England or America than France.

The history of science also has political implications on a macroscopic scale. In the domain of philosophy, Foucault (once again) suggested that epistemological studies in France filled a similar role to that performed in German thought by historical and political reflection on society. According to Foucault, then, in spite of manifest differences of style and subject matter, the most obvious philosophical parallel for the work conducted since the 1930s by Jean Cavaillès (on mathematics), Alexandre Koyré (chiefly on classical **physics**), Georges Canguilhem (on biology) or Gaston Bachelard (on the conditions of scientific knowledge) is the critical philosophy of the Frankfurt School. Both of these traditions are concerned with questioning the limits of the principle of autonomous reason on which the **Enlightenment** had placed its hopes and which, in the interwar years, continued to inspire the rationalism of the Vienna Circle in its efforts to provide philosophy with a scientific foundation based on modern logic. There has been a recent attempt (1991) to revive the Vienna Circle in the form of the Institut Wiener Kreis, whose program to combat all forms of **irrationality**, dogmatism, and fundamentalism by the democratization of science is openly inspired by Enlightenment ideals. Such a project would, however, seem to belong to a bygone age—along with the scientific rationalism of the *Bauhaus* or the Modern Movement in architecture. The ambitions of such schools went beyond the arts (pure and applied) to take in society; the significance of the fact that they were near contemporaries of the technological delirium that led Italian Futurism into the arms of Mussolini has been the object of some debate.

When Koyré and Panofsky defined Galileo's classicism as, respectively, an aesthetic attitude and the manifestation of controlling tendencies that could explain his scientific theories, they continued to read it in fairly narrowly historicist terms, in spite of intriguingly suggesting an element of nonlinear flow. The subtext of such a position is still determined by the tradition of critical philosophy, or what **Bruno Latour**, more generally, calls critique and that he associates with the myth of modernity. Latour's own work, which is at the forefront of the strongly antireductionist slant of the most interesting contemporary trends in the sociology and **anthropology** of science, feeds on an interaction with fiction, using *War and Peace, Robinson Crusoe* (including its contemporary rewriting by the French novelist Michel Tournier), *Frankenstein*, among others, as references in a concerted effort to break down the dichotomy between the social and natural sciences.

Throughout much of the century, in Europe as elsewhere, the split between the "two cultures" has also been undermined from within scientific practice. Witness the epistemological fortunes of **relativity**, the **uncertainty principle** of **quantum physics**, or of Kurt Gödel's incompleteness theorem. Following the publication in 1979 of the emblematically entitled *La Nouvelle Alliance*, coauthored with the philosopher Isabelle Stengers, the challenge to **determinism** represented by Ilya Prigogine's work on dynamical systems far from equilibrium exerted increasing influence in the 1980s. Interestingly, whereas the title of translations of this book into other languages (English, Russian, Italian) focused on its thematic field of **chaos** and order, the French title underlined the epistemological premise of a new alliance between science and the humanities.

Until very recently, appeals to science on the part of writers and literary theorists were characteristically marked by a questionable notion of scientific authority. The distance traveled over the last decades by a literary theorist like **Umberto Eco** can, however, be gauged by setting an early statement explaining the role attributed to art as an intermediary between culture and science by the supposition that the intelligence was always one step ahead of sensibility (*Opera Aperta*, 1962) alongside Eco's later suggestion that analysis of **detective fiction** may serve to cast light on the conjectural procedures employed by scientists. Eco demonstrates an ability to move from a technocratic version of literary theory, based on an appeal to **cybernetics** that involved a reductive model of communication, to something approaching the sophisticated rhetorical understanding of science prevalent today. In contrast, the claim of radical French theory in the 1960s to institute simultaneously a science and a nonrepresentational practice of literature soon ran its course, perhaps because of a misplaced confidence in scientific authority that was particularly vulnerable in the domain of the social sciences.

With the assimilation of Prigogine, of Henri Atlan's application of the notions of information and noise (*see* Information Theory) in theoretical biology, of the brand of cognitivism associated with **Francisco Varela** and most lately of chaos and complexity theory, nondogmatic interchange between literature and science is currently on the upswing in Europe. In Italy, for, example, Guiseppe O. Longo combines research in the field of artificial intelligence (*see* Virtual Reality and Artificial Intelligence) with theoretical reflections on the relations between science, art, and philosophy and with his work as a novelist. In Austria, the quantum physicist Gerhard Grössing, founder of a research center on nonlinear dynamical systems, is developing a principle of "echo-logy" in which science, philosophy, and the arts can be made to resonate. It would be possible to multiply current examples of interchange between writers and scientists in each of these countries. In France, the experimentation stimulated by **OuLiPo**, with the intention of generating new narrative and poetic genres by the injection of mathematical models into literary practice, has in the long run proved more fruitful than the highly politicized recourse to the social sciences and psychoanalysis associated with *Tel Quel*. OuLiPo was founded in the early 1960s; its members have included **Georges Perec** and Jacques Roubaud, as well as the American Harry Mathews and the Italian Calvino. The ethos of such developments in science and literature can perhaps best be illustrated by **Michel Serres's** recent survey of French philosophy: Insisting on the interconnections between science, philosophy, and literature, Serres has recourse to chaos theory as a heuristic tool and to **fractals** as a rhetorical instrument for the organization of his text, in what is a practical exercise in furthering the coevolution of science and the humanities.

References

Le Dimensioni dell'Ifinito/Les Dimensions de l'infini. 50 rue de Varenne, Supplemento italo-francese di Nuovi Argomenti 29 (1989).

Hallyn, Fernand. *La Structure poétique du monde: Copernic, Kepler*. Paris: Seuil, 1987.

Kemp, Martin. *The Science of Art: Optical Themes in Western Art from Brunelleschi to Seurat*. New Haven, CT: Yale UP, 1990.

Prigogine, Ilya, and Isabelle Stengers. *La Nouvelle Alliance: Métamorphose de la science*. Paris: Gallimard, 1979.

Serres, Michel. *Eloge de la philosophie en langue française*. Paris: Fayard, 1995.

Yves Abrioux

Cervantes, Miguel de (1547–1616). Most celebrated of Spanish writers who wrote novels, short stories, plays, and poetry. Best known for his novel *Don Quixote* (Part I, 1605; Part II, 1616), which contains countless references to psychology (*see* Anthropology/Psychology/Sociology), madness, contemporary **medicine**, health practitioners, humoral pathology, and physiology.

Rafael Chabrán

Chambers, Robert (1802–1871). Author of *Vestiges of the Natural History of Creation* (1844), which asserted a basically Lamarckian theory of evolution. *Vestiges* was a controversial and scientifically faulty text. Nevertheless, it was read widely by Victorians including **Charles Darwin, Alfred Tennyson**, and Elizabeth Barrett Browning.

Kristine Swenson

Chaos/Chaotic Systems. Systems whose random behavior is not the result of human error or ignorance but is an ineradicable feature of even the perfectly smooth functioning of the system itself. Chaotic systems are generated by iteration that includes the key feature of feedback. A repeating algorithm that includes positive feedback can behave nonlinearly; that is, it can produce effects that are not proportional to their causes. As such, systems under the influence of nonlinearity can appear to behave in a wild and unpredictable manner and are therefore called chaotic.

One way to understand chaotic behavior is through the notion of extreme sensitivity to initial conditions. Chaotic systems are based on nonlinear equations in which feedback tends to magnify even the smallest differences in initial input into global divergences after only a small number of iterations. The famous butterfly effect, in which the atmospheric disturbance occasioned by the flapping of a butterfly's wings is said to be able to alter the weather pattern halfway around the world, is a perhaps hyperbolic metaphor for the normal behavior of chaotic systems, their ability to explode minor fluctuations into global transformations.

Chaotic systems are so sensitive to initial conditions that they appear to behave in a totally discontinuous and unpredictable manner. However, chaos only gives the appearance of **randomness**. In fact, the science of chaos has arisen because of the discovery of a hidden order within the apparent randomness of chaotic systems. This order is perhaps best visualized by the shape of a **strange attractor**. Although a strange attractor is nonperiodic, and although it is produced by a series of points that are generated in a seemingly random fashion, it nevertheless assumes a perdurable form; that is, although while generating a strange attractor it is in principle impossible to predict where the next dot will fall, it soon becomes possible to predict where it will not fall and to have a good sense of the regions that are likely to continue receiving dots.

Alex Argyros

Chaos Sciences/Chaos Theory. A set of interrelated mathematical and scientific practices that became immensely popular in the 1980s and were generalized and applied by scholars across a range of fields in the social sciences and humanities. Many literary critics and theorists explored—and continue to explore—ways in which chaos theory could be deployed in analyzing language and literature. To map the terrain of chaos theory and/in literature entails a brief historical overview of chaos theory and the ways in which "chaos" has manifested itself in literature, followed by an examination of methods with which relations between chaos theory and literature have been established to date.

Chaos theory is an umbrella term that encompasses a series of interrelated developments in mathematics and many branches of the natural sciences. Its historical roots lie in the late nineteenth century, from the French mathematician Henri Poincaré's study of how three bodies interact. But while chaos was uncovered at this time, the detailed study of chaotic systems (*see* Chaos/Chaotic Systems) became possible only with the development of the **computer**. A seminal moment in this respect was the Fermi-Pasta-Ulam experiment in 1954, when this physicist–computer scientist–mathematician team utilized a MANIAC-I computer developed at Los Alamos to test a **hypothesis** derived from Poincaré and were confounded by a strange result that overturned all expectations about nonlinear behavior, while revealing a new form of orderly dynamical behavior.

Chaotic systems are intriguing across a broad disciplinary spectrum precisely because they combine disorder and order in counterintuitive ways. Chaotic systems form a subclass of classical systems, in that they are deterministic: A complete description of a system and the natural laws that apply to it can predict its future behavior. But complete descriptions of chaotic systems cannot be given, because: (1) their behavior is described by nonlinear differential equations, which means that solutions are given by numerical approximations represented by computer methods; and (2) chaotic systems display "sensitive dependence to initial conditions"—for example, minute inaccuracies in specifying the initial description of the system will amplify quickly, rendering middle- or long-term prediction impossible. Finally, many chaotic systems display self-similarity: that is, their evolutionary path as plotted by computer yields a mathematical model with similar properties across different scales. Mathematical models or "objects" displaying this property were grouped under the name of **fractals** by Benoit Mandelbrot.

The terrain of chaos science and/in literature exemplifies broader methodological questions surrounding the study of literature and science. Scholarship in this area reveals a spectrum of approaches that includes the presence of chaos theory in texts or its influence on writers; an attempt to generalize literary and scientific manifestations of chaos as part of an encompassing paradigm; discovering analogies between chaos theory concepts and literary texts; using chaos theory as a language to describe literary texts; and treating literary texts as chaotic systems proper. Finally, methods from literary theory such as **semiotics** can be brought to bear on chaos theory.

Chaos science has impacted the **imagination** of literary writers in various ways. Some philosophers and scientists see chaos theory as the resurfacing of a **physics** founded on subtle deviations from **determinism**, such as propounded in Epicurean **atomic theory**. In this light, **Lucretius's** *De Rerum Natura* stands out because it elucidates a chaos science in a poetic text whose structural devices reflect the physics it teaches (see Serres, *Hermes* and *La naissance*). In the contemporary era, the popular usage enjoyed by terms from chaos science is reflected in their ubiquitous presence in literature—writers such as **Thomas Pynchon**, **Richard Powers**, and a host of **science fiction** authors allude to fractals, chaos, the butterfly effect, and so on. Perhaps the best-known—and among the most notorious—uses of chaos theory is in **Michael Crichton's** *Jurassic Park*, where a scientist recognizes the potential dangers in a badly hatched plan to incubate dinosaur DNA. A more rigorous, sustained creative reflection on the literary and philosophical implications/extrapolations of chaos science in fiction is Botho Strauss's *Der junge Mann* (1992), at this time as yet untranslated.

As chaos theory rose to extraordinary popularity in the 1980s, critics began to wonder whether it expressed a larger cultural ethos or was part of an encompassing paradigm shift. Critics who seek to historicize chaos science in this way align chaos theory with deconstruction, **poststructuralism**, and/or postmodernism, as well as some contemporaneous **fiction**. All these areas are concerned with forms of orderly disorder; they mark a move from complete, objective descriptions or closed theories to an emphasis on local, fractured accounts (*see* Hayles, *Chaos Bound*). Linguistic signs, literary texts, and chaotic systems are all seen as being driven by an irreducible "noise" or ambiguity, even as they yield certain forms of information (*see* Information Theory). Yet many critics also scrutinized some of these analogies (*see* Analogy) and emphasized that the underlying difference between chaos science and humanistic endeavors foregrounding disorder is that chaos science does not surrender the deterministic view of the world, nor does it simply give up "totalizing" accounts of the world.

The most frequent use of chaos theory in literary criticism involves drawing a metaphoric comparison of some kind between specific aspects of the two domains (see several essays in Hayles, *Chaos and Order*). The general concept of orderly disorder or "order in chaos" finds ready literary analogues in writers who push the limits of language and sense (e.g., **James Joyce**) or emphasize the elusive nature of order and form (e.g., **Herman Melville**). However, such comparisons often remained too general to prove of lasting value, for there is little of inherent interest in showing significant similarities between chaos science and literature if the comparisons are not then put to further use or submitted to critical reflection.

A more radical mode of metaphoric connection between chaos science and literature is to use chaos theory to define and analyze fictional texts. Here the claim that literary texts *are* chaotic systems appears in several guises. The chaos science model of self-organization or "order out of chaos" may be used as a basis to understand how the ambiguities of literature nonetheless give rise to a sense and order at a "higher" level of interpretation (Paulson). These strategies reflect the stature that science enjoys in contemporary culture, for all grant chaos science the status of a metalanguage or privileged description of the world. Chaos science assumes the proportions of an accepted and therefore authoritative scientific theory, and literary texts are seen as examples that express or enact these larger truths about the nature of things. In part, the effectiveness of chaos science as a language for describing phenomena in other fields lies in the generic or ubiquitous nature of its key terms, such as *order, disorder, dynamics* and of course *chaos* itself. Critics can there speak of narrative in terms of a "dynamics" that balances disorder and order in ways that it renders maximal information, or of a self-organizing process by which narratives create and occupy cultural "attractors."

The ultimate question that metaphoric comparisons between scientific theories and literary texts must answer is, What knowledge is produced as a result? That is, if literary texts are described in terms of chaos theory, what insight is gained into literature that could not be obtained without the **scientific model**? One area in which chaos theory offers a "new" way to understand old literary questions is the problem of form. The formalist and New Critical treatments of the spatial form of poems and novels sought to fix a stable structure or pattern that organizes a text, but such attempts faced the simple fact that texts are composed linearly, that language is a temporal medium. By contrast, the geometric forms of fractals and the property of self-similarity across scale evoke a conceptual image of structure as always in process, revealing only qualitative similarities across scale, without freezing into a final form. Thus critics could treat texts that replicated themselves across different scales as being open wholes composed of self-similar parts, whatever one's chosen level of scrutiny happened to be—"self-similarity" gave a technical-sounding name and, as fractals, powerful visual images for an aspect of literature long recognized by critics (see Harris). Also, fractals and self-similarity differ from other literary critical ways of understanding how parts reflect wholes (such as synecdoche), in that they do not assign stability to either—parts can be wholes, wholes can become parts; the scaling process includes both.

Analogies between scientific theories and literary texts depend in large part for their appeal or force on historical context. Academic fashion that makes one set of terms popular for a time gives way to the next whim, and only then, perhaps, does it become possible to discern the substantial claim from the superficial comparison. A skeptical intellectual climate in which such cross-disciplinary connections are often regarded with suspicion or hostility might lead one to think that parallels drawn between chaos science and literature will soon seem dated. But another line of development is also possible, one that follows from the common "platform" that undergirds and largely shapes our views certainly of chaos theory and, increasingly, of language and literature—the **computer**. Just as the computer has made possible new understandings of nonlinear behavior and revealed mathematical models, so too is it refashioning our use of, and relationship to, language and texts. It is possible to envision a mode of understanding scientific models and literary texts alike in terms of parameters or constraints or initial values or conditions that give rise to different kinds of structure, form, and information. From that standpoint, the conceptual analogies and metaphoric comparisons between chaos science and literature of the 1980s will seem not wrongheaded but clumsy.

References

Harris, Paul A. "Fractal Faulkner: Scaling Time in Go Down, Moses." *Poetics Today* 14.4 (Winter 1993): 625–51.

Hayles, N. Katherine. *Chaos Bound: Orderly Disorder in Contemporary Literature and Science*. Ithaca, NY: Cornell UP, 1990.

———, ed. *Chaos and Order: Complex Dynamics in Literature and Science*. Chicago: U of Chicago P, 1991.

Paulson, William. *The Noise of Culture: Literary Texts in a World of Information*. Ithaca, NY: Cornell UP, 1988.

Serres, Michel. *Hermes: Literature, Science, Philosophy*. Ed. and Trans. Josue Harari and David F. Bell. Baltimore: Johns Hopkins UP, 1982. [Includes translations of two chapters of Serres 1977.]

————. *La naissance de la physique dans le texte de Lucrece.* Paris: Minuit, 1977.

Paul A. Harris

Châtelet, Gabrielle-Émilie Le Tonnelier de Breteuil, Marquise du

(1706–1749). French mathematician and physicist. Châtelet established an intellectual alliance with **Voltaire** in 1733, pursued in her château at Circy in Champagne. In 1738, she competed for a prize by the Academy of Sciences, submitting an essay on the nature of fire. While she did not win the award, her *Dissertation sur la nature et la propagation du feu* (1744) was published by the Academy. Châtelet's translation of Isaac Newton's (*see* Newtonianism) *Principia Mathematica* (the only version available for years) was published posthumously in 1756 and 1759, with a preface by Voltaire.

Reference

Schiebinger, Londa. *The Mind Has No Sex?: Women in the Origins of Modern Science.* Cambridge: Harvard UP, 1989.

Diana B. Altegoer

Chaucer, Geoffrey (c. 1340–1400). English poet who shows understanding of medieval science, **technology**, and **philosophy** in his realistic characterizations of the **physician**, the clerk, the priest and prioress, and others in *The Canterbury Tales* and other works. Competent in Latin and Italian and fluent in French, he studied many significant books of contemporaries and ancients, including **Aristotle.** *Consolation of Philosophy* by Boethius was influential upon Chaucer, as was Vincent of Beauvais's *Speculum majus*, the greatest European encyclopedia until the eighteenth century. He received a courtly education and studied law, and he wrote *Treatise on the Astrolabe* for his younger son. The frame structure used in the pilgrimage *Tales* allowed persons from all walks of life to dialogue and make reference to herbal healing, astrology and **astronomy**, and various aspects of **natural history** and philosophy. Praised for his innovations in **poetry** and his understanding of the science of nature and **art**, he is considered the greatest Western writer before **Shakespeare**.

Reference

North, J.D. *Chaucer's Universe.* Oxford: Clarendon, 1988.

Mary Libertin

Chekhov, Anton Pavlovich (1860–1904). Russian dramatist and short story writer, trained as a **physician**. Knowing his own life would be cut short by tuberculosis, he often depicted his middle-class heroes' struggle against unbeatable universal forces. Insensitive physicians are recurrent characters in his works (*Ivanov*, 1887; *Uncle Vanya*, 1899). "A Letter from the Don Landowner

Stepan Vladimirovich N." (1880) parodies the gentry's pretensions to popular scientific knowledge. His use of psychological **realism** and a combination of sentiment with **naturalism** brought some of the concerns of the mid- to late-nineteenth-century's social and **experimental novels** to the stage.

Pamela Gossin

Chemistry. Frequently described as "the science of transformation of substances." These transformations often seem marvelous, even uncanny, and thus inescapably charged with metaphorical potential, which initially found expression in the worldview of **alchemy**. That collection of prescientific practices metamorphosed into the science of chemistry during the sixteenth and seventeenth centuries. The unflattering portrait of the title character in **Ben Jonson's** 1610 play *The Alchemist* mirrors the lowly status to which alchemy had sunk by then. The contrasting ascent of chemistry coincided with the rise of the modern novel, and the subsequent interactions of chemistry and literature seemed to wax and wane as a function of the prevailing spirit of the age.

The first modern scientist to capture the literary **imagination** was Isaac Newton (*see* Newtonianism), whose effects on English poets have been detailed by **Marjorie Hope Nicolson**. However, the end of the eighteenth century saw a reaction against the Newtonian paradigm of a universe divided by Cartesian dualism and occupied only by inert and passive matter. As it happened, attempts to explain chemical phenomena within the Newtonian framework had been conspicuously unsuccessful, so chemistry held special appeal for the anti-Newtonians. One of the first of these was the poet, essayist, and naturalist **Johann W. von Goethe**. While his great poem *Faust* (1808, 1832) reached back to alchemical sources, his novel *Die Wahlverwandtschaften* (Elective Affinities, 1809) drew upon contemporary chemical theory. One striking characteristic of chemical reactions is their dependence upon the identity and not merely the quantity of the reacting substances. Goethe saw in these "elective affinities" the manifestations of a power that extended throughout Nature, embracing both the inanimate and the animate, while denying the possibility of a straightforward extrapolation from one realm to the other. Goethe's novel inspired a successor, *Su Único Hijo* (His Only Son, 1890) by Leopoldo Alas (Clarín).

In Germany, Romantic science reached its apogee in *Naturphilosophie*, whose reign was subsequently characterized by the chemist Justus von Liebig as a "pestilence." Romantic chemistry had a more productive run in England, where its greatest exponent was **Humphry Davy**, who also achieved recognition as a poet and memorist. Davy was the first to isolate nitrous oxide (laughing gas) and personally explored its vision-inducing properties. His indisputable chemical credentials rest principally on his pioneering research in electrochemistry, which reinforced his belief in an active Nature animated by "powers." **Samuel Coleridge** and **William Wordsworth** were both friends of Davy's; Coleridge even attended the chemist's lectures. Davy's concept of "powers" certainly accorded with their vision of an active, organic Nature. Dr. **Frankenstein's** obsession with the life-awakening potential of **electricity** was very likely due at least in part to **Mary Shelley's** having read Davy's work. French writers were also not immune to the pull of Romantic chemistry; its commitment to an underlying unity in nature propels the plot of **Balzac's** *La Recherche de l'Absolu* (Search for the Absolute, 1834).

After *Naturphilosophie* had been repudiated and the path of "positive" science regained, chemistry seems to have lost much of its literary luster. It is a curious fact that while chemistry became increasingly indispensable to daily life and to the conduct of war in the industrialized world, neither its concepts nor its practitioners inspired much imaginative literature. It is not the case that contemporaneous figures and events lacked dramatic possibility; Tony Harrison's 1992 play *Square Rounds* refutes that idea. The play introduces several major nineteenth- and twentieth-century chemists such as Liebig, William Crookes, and most especially Fritz Haber. Haber's ammonia synthesis both provided the fertilizer that staved off potential famine in Europe and fueled the huge munitions output that sustained the slaughter of World War I. Haber also introduced poison gas as a weapon during that war in the futile hope of shortening it. Harrison's play does justice to the many ironies embedded in this history.

However, even when not associated with great issues, chemistry continued to lead an underground existence in literature. Its growing prowess ensured that it would find a place in **science fiction** and crime stories. Growing chemical sophistication encouraged growing literary sophistication and prompted serious forays into the technical literature by mystery writers such as **Conan Doyle**, Agatha Christie (*The Pale Horse*, 1961), and Dorothy L. Sayer (*The Documents in the Case*, 1930). Joseph Wambaugh's crime novel *The Delta Star* (1983) is set partly at the California Institute of Technology; the author spent three months there, gaining background information that included much leading-edge science.

Chemistry gained substantial literary attention again only after World War II, elbowing its way into the phalanx of books looking back at the war. Thomas McMahon's *Principles of American Nuclear Chemistry: A Novel* (1970) takes us into the life of Los Alamos via the son of a thermodynamicist working there. **Thermodynamics**, and especially **entropy**, amount almost to idées fixes for **Thomas Pynchon**, whose encyclopedic novel of the war, *Gravity's Rainbow* (1973), celebrates Kekulé's famous dream of the *uroboros* and the fecundity of the chemistry that flowed from his work.

In recent decades, chemistry's alliance with the life sciences, particularly molecular **biology** and molecular **medicine**, has enhanced its literary appeal. The capacity of those disciplines to alter permanently the genetic characteristics of living beings, including humans, provides ample scope for the imagination. Since the consequences will be economic as well as biological there is no shortage of ethical mazes, which often lead back to the human interactions of chemists themselves. The prominent research scientist **Carl Djerassi** has written a novelistic tetralogy whose action is located at this chemistry/biology interface.

In *Cantor's Dilemma* (1989) and *The Bourbaki Gambit* (1994) the science is detailed and plausible, but the focus is on the "tribal culture" of chemistry and the conflicting desires for professional recognition, scientific insight, and worldly reward.

Only a relative handful of chemists have attained recognition as authors. One of the more visible is **Roald Hoffmann** (Nobel Prize, 1981). Two volumes of his poetry (*The Metamict State*, 1987; *Gaps and Verges*, 1990) draw heavily on his chemical experiences for themes, images, and metaphors. The chemist–author who has gained the widest audience is the novelist, essayist, and Holocaust witness Primo Levi. In *L'altrui Mestiere* (Other People's Trades, 1985) he undertakes a witty comparison of his vocations as chemist and writer. With *La Sistema Periodica* (The Periodic Table, 1975) Levi accomplishes a unique traversal of chemistry that merges empirical practice and organic metaphor into a convincing and moving whole.

References

Cunningham, Andrew, and Nicholas Jardine. *Romanticism and the Sciences*. Cambridge: Cambridge UP, 1990.
Stocker, Jack H. *Chemistry and Science Fiction*. Washington: American Chemical Society, 1998.

Stephen J. Weininger

Chesterton, G[ilbert] K[eith] (1874–1936). Essayist and writer of detective and fantasy fiction who attacks utopian and modern thinkers such as **H. G. Wells**, Friedrich Nietzsche, and **Charles Darwin** in his philosophical essays *Heretics* and *Orthodoxy*. As a Catholic and Rationalist he criticizes superstitions and pseudoscience, taking his detective–priest Father Brown as a mouthpiece.

Reference

Jaki, S.L. *Chesterton: A Seer of Science*. Urbana/Chicago: U of Illinois P, 1983.

Elmar Schenkel

Cicero, Marcus Tullius (106–43 B.C.E.). Roman statesman and author of *De Oratore* (55 B.C.E.) and other works central to the tradition of **rhetoric**. Cicero argued that the orator must understand all branches of knowledge, including science. His emphasis on the discovery of **truth** rather than reliance on norms led to the formation of curiosity as a scientific attitude. Significant fragments of his translation of **Aratus's** *Phaenomena* are extant. In *Somnium Scipionis* (Scipio's Dream), he describes a cosmic voyage as the apt reward for virtuous public servants.

Charles A. Baldwin and Pamela Gossin

Clarke, Arthur C[harles] (1917–). Speculative science writer who shifted the principles of satellite communication in "Extra-terrestrial Relays" (*Wireless World* [Oct. 1945]: 305–8). Clarke's cosmologically oriented **science fiction** includes the novel *Childhood's End* (1954) and the screenplay (with Stanley Kubrick) for the *2001: A Space Odyssey* (1967).

Noel Gough

Classification Systems. Different modes of naming the world. Each system offers a unique "handle"—hence a particular vision of how the world is organized and the place of humanity within it. Historically, controversies have centered on whether categories of classification are "natural" or merely "artificial," human constructions having no real existence in nature. **Realism** holds the former is possible, whereas nominalism asserts that no category transcends the limitations of language. Carl Linnaeus established the scientific convention of binomial naming, but his system's obvious artificiality generated a long search for the one "natural" system, a question rendered moot by **Charles Darwin's** theory of evolution.

References

Foucault, Michel. *The Order of Things.* New York: Random House/Vintage Books, 1970.
Ritvo, Harriet. *The Platypus and the Mermaid and Other Figments of the Classifying Imagination.* Cambridge: Harvard UP, 1997.

Laura Dassow Walls

Clock. A symbol of the ordered cosmos from at least as early as the time of **Cicero**, but was most popular in the seventeenth and eighteenth centuries when familiar metaphors like "the clockwork universe" and "the watchmaker God" described the orderly, predictable, and rational mechanisms of the world. The most famous of the great medieval and Renaissance monumental astronomical clocks, the Strasbourg clock—itself a cultural artifact that was both a technological wonder and a model of the creation—became a favorite vehicle (employed most prominently by **Robert Boyle**) for design arguments utilizing the cosmological clock metaphor.

Reference

Encyclopedia of Time. Ed. Samuel L. Macey. New York: Garland, 1994.

Lisa Zeitz

Cognitive Science. The study of the processes of perception and knowing. The psychology (*see* Anthropology/Psychology/Sociology) of writing has proven to be an exceptionally fruitful area for exploration by cognitive scientists. Clearly, writing is an activity that relies on the deployment of multiple cognitive processes in tandem. While isolated cognitive processes such as perception and memory are often amenable to research that relies solely on objective measurements, studies of complex cognitive activities such as the production of written compositions frequently rely on data in the form of think-aloud protocols by subjects. The verbal facility of writers enables informative accounts of the cognitive activities that underpin their construction of literature.

The study of literature construction by cognitive psychologists has generally consisted of comparisons between novice and expert writers engaged in completing the same writing task or in-depth studies of individuals with established literary reputations. Generally, studies that have focused on writing **problem solving** suggest that the process of constructing literature relies on the same skills that typically contribute to successful problem solving in various fields: observational ability, which permits the detection of informative patterns in the germane data; in-depth knowledge of the methods of the field; sophisticated organization of accumulated knowledge in memory such that the problem solver can search and retrieve pertinent information with facility; and the ability to combine or reconstruct the retrieved information in response to the constraints of a preconceived design. In fact, a number of novelists (e.g., **Émile Zola, Virginia Woolf, Henry James**, Anaïs Nin, **Thomas Hardy**) have characterized their work as extracting factual information from nature, studying the dynamic interrelations of these facts, and then modifying the factual information to arrive at a **representation** of some universal feature of human experience. Thus, in many respects, writing problem solving is indistinguishable from expertise in other domains with expertise generally characterized as following upon a decade or more of dedicated practice within a domain.

There are, however, features of literature construction that are particular to writing expertise. While expertise is generally considered to be domain specific, writing necessarily bridges domains; writers must be knowledgeable about writing strategies as well as the field they are writing about. A number of creative writers including Woolf and **T.S. Eliot** devised extensive writing apprenticeships for themselves that included exercises intended to hone their reading, writing, and critical skills. Furthermore, many novelists (e.g., Guy de Maupassant, **Gustave Flaubert**, Hardy) purposefully engaged in the careful observation of the aspects of human experience they wished to represent in their novels with some (e.g., Fyodor Dostoevsky, Woolf, Nin, André Gide) carefully preserving these observations in journals. Since writing problem solving is, by definition, the utilization of the skills of one domain to discuss another, an examination of writing practices sheds light on the cognitive strategies involved in shuttling between domains during problem solving.

The bridging of domains during problem solving becomes an important issue given the long-standing finding that entrenchment (the tendency to consider only typical, familiar solutions and ignore new approaches while solving a problem) is frequently an obstacle to successful problem solving by experts. That is, experts regularly fail to solve problems within their domains because their attempts to reach a solution are constrained by their past experience solving problems in their field. It may be that the heuristics (guiding principles or general strategies) writers regularly employ to overcome intradomain constraints can be deployed by experts in other fields to safeguard them from succumbing to entrenchment.

An additional feature of writing expertise that distinguishes it from expertise in other domains is the extensive effort expert writers devote to problem representation. It is, almost without exception, the case that, for example, a chess or **physics** problem that a novice finds challenging or unsolvable is solved with ease by the expert. In contrast, expert writers often spend more time than novices in prewriting planning. Even writing problems that are solvable by novices elicit extensive effort from experts. In fact, novelists like Ernest Hemingway and Woolf as well as the expert writers who participated in various psychological studies of writing have reported that writing problem solving remains effortful despite extensive experience successfully producing publications. Given that both psychological research studies and eminent problem solvers (e.g., **Albert Einstein**) have stressed the critical role of problem representation in arriving at successful problem solutions, the fact that writing problem solving regularly entails representational effort identifies it as a unique and promising area of study. That is, the study of writing problem solving may well provide details as to the cognitive strategies that cooperate in problem representation that are not as readily available via the study of experts in other knowledge domains.

As a result of their numerous studies contrasting novice and expert writers engaged in solving the same writing problems, Bereiter and Scardamalia have identified a number of heuristics regularly employed by expert writers, including learning to generate text without the respondent who is available when one engages in conversation; learning to efficiently search memory for germane content; developing the ability to appropriately shift between local and overall text planning; and developing revision techniques, which require the writer to critique his/her own work from a hypothetical reader's point of view and have at his/her fingertips language expertise such that the improvement of grammar, word choice, sentence structure, and organization is possible. An interesting research enterprise would be to teach these strategies to a group of experts in a domain other than writing and see if experts who receive the special training excel over similarly qualified individuals who do not receive such instruction. For example, one group of individuals could be instructed to, while solving an assigned problem(s), imagine they were defending their problem-solving process and the resolution arrived at to a hypothetical person, periodically reconsider their overall plan to reach a solution, and critique their problem-solving progress and solution.

References

Bereiter, Carl, and Marlene Scardamalia. *The Psychology of Written Composition*. Hillsdale, NJ: Erlbaum, 1987.
John-Steiner, Vera. *Notebooks of the Mind*. New York: Oxford UP, 1997.

Sternberg, Robert J., and Peter A. Frensch, eds. *Complex Problem Solving*. Hillsdale, NJ: Erlbaum, 1991.

Maria F. Ippolito

Coleridge, Samuel Taylor (1772–1834). British Romantic poet, critic, and philosopher who had a lifelong interest in science. In *Biographia Literaria* he defended a Platonic (*see* Plato), idealist **philosophy** presenting ideas of Immanuel Kant and translating digested (or plagiarized) passages from Friedrich Schelling, thus introducing German transcendental philosophy of nature to British readers. A close friend of the chemist **Humphry Davy**, he attended Davy's lectures for poetic inspiration and criticized Davy's poetry. In *Hints towards a More Comprehensive Theory of Life* Coleridge presented his romantic philosophy of nature, life, and **medicine**.

Reference

Levere, Trevor H. *Poetry Realized in Nature*. Cambridge: Cambridge UP, 1981.

Val Dusek

Collins, Wilkie (1824–1889). British novelist. In his extraordinarily popular "sensation" novels Collins employed (and sometimes resisted) the ideas and discourses of nineteenth-century psychology (*see* Anthropology/Psychology/Sociology) and physiology. *The Woman in White* (1860) treats issues of mental illness, **gender**, and identity; the institution of the asylum; and through the amateur chemist Fosco, the "physiological determinism of pharmacology" (Taylor 124). *The Moonstone* (1868), Collins's famous detective novel, displays an interest in "the unconscious" and uses the pivotal plot device of a physiological experiment involving opium. More minor engagements with scientific themes include the antivivisection propaganda novel *Heart and Science* (1883), and Collins's parody of the clockwork universe in *Armadale* (1866).

References

Taylor, Jenny Bourne. *In the Secret Theatre of Home: Wilkie Collins, Sensation Narrative, and Nineteenth-Century Psychology*. London: Routledge, 1988.
Zeitz, Lisa M., and Peter Thoms. "Collins's Use of the Strasbourg Clock in *Armadale*." *Nineteenth-Century Literature* 45 (1991): 495–503.

Lisa Zeitz

Colonialism. The subjugation and creation of colony states, usually for the purpose of closed trade (mercantilism) and extraction of resources beneficial to the colonizing partner. **John Locke's** observation in *Two Treatises of Government* (1690) that "in the beginning all the world was *America*" (II: 39) recalls the myth of a golden age, untouched land rich in resources and awaiting exploitation. The American (new world) colonial states of the British Empire were especially important both as profitable tobacco and cotton producers and as a source of wood for sailing boats, following the serious deforestation of much of the English countryside in favor of settled agriculture.

Reference

Locke, John. *Two Treatises of Government*. Cambridge: Cambridge UP, 1997.

Helen J. Burgess

Complexity. A quality or property between simplicity and **chaos**; a pattern that balances variation with repetition. Complexity measures what is irreducible or incompressible; it is often synonymous with our uncertainty regarding something—a message, text, or system. Complex systems are composed of parts that interact in nonlinear fashion: The whole is more than the sum of its parts because small perturbations or changes can make significant differences. In informational terms, the complexity of a message corresponds to how long a set of instructions it would take to build a copy of the message. (This idea is also known as algorithmic complexity.) This quality becomes elusive with respect to literature, since the "content" of literature is ostensibly irreducible to paraphrase. Because information is equated with the content of a message, or its meaning, linguists and communications and literary theorists have differentiated "aesthetic" information from "semantic information." In mathematics, science, and literature alike, complexity connotes a productive ambiguity, a possibility that noise and uncertainty are integral sources of new information and can generate unforeseen forms of order.

Paul A. Harris

Computer Games. Games combining computer-interfacing motor skills with increasingly complex narratives. Early examples that tested reflexes and eye-hand coordination (like the tennis game *Pong* and the simple grid of *Ms. Pac-man*) have now been succeeded by intricate, simulated worlds with complex characters (such as Lara Croft) with identifiable connections to literary genres. Often computer games are electronic epics: The heroic quests of computer surrogates (characters whose identities the player assumes) mimic the plots of westerns or adventure stories for boys. Although some games simulate real activities, like golf, many offer entrance to a purely fictional world through role-playing. Despite the popularity of Lara Croft, these computer roles are predominantly male-identified and entail activities, usually simulated battles, that may reinforce traditional **gender** roles. In their depictions of future world orders and new technologies, fictional worlds of computer games often have much in common with **science fiction** literature.

Elizabeth J. Donaldson

Computer Graphics. Visually displayed **computer** output. Any image that can be coded can be graphically displayed, marking a fundamental change in the relation of image and **reality**. Graphical interfaces developed since the 1970s enable hypermedial or nonlinear linking of elements, whether graphical or textual. These **cyberspaces** provide a new theme for literature, as well as a new form of writing.

Charles A. Baldwin

Computer Network. A configuration of hardware and software that permits individual machines to exchange data very rapidly without direct user intervention. So-called local areas networks can be joined into wide-area networks, which are in turn connected to form the **Internet**, which joins millions of "host" machines in the developed world. Networking has redefined the role of the **computer** in the past twenty years. Through email and the **World Wide Web**, the computer has become a medium for interpersonal and mass communication.

Jay David Bolter

Computers/Computer Science. May be traced historically from the abacus, the earliest computing device used in Babylonia around 3000 B.C.E. The next significant advance in numerical calculation occurred in 1614 in Europe when John Napier introduced logarithms and invented multiplication tables as well as movable columns. In 1642 Blaise Pascal invented a mechanical calculating machine. Coding information using punched cards was done for the first time by Joseph Marie Jacquard in the early 1800s with his invention of a device for controlling the operations of a loom. Charles Babbage in 1823 brought together the idea of a mechanical calculator and punched cards in his "difference engine," which was capable, in principle, of performing recursive computations. Augusta Ada Lovelace, daughter of the English poet **Lord Byron**, assisted Babbage extensively with another computing machine, the "analytical engine," which was never finished. She created the instruction routines for the machine, which makes her the world's first computer programmer.

In 1890, Herman Hollerith developed an electrical tabulator and sorter that used punch cards to process U.S. census data. Important work was done on the foundations of computer science in the 1930s by Alan Turing and Claude E. Shannon. In particular, Alan Turing proposed a model, named after him, that became the conceptual prototype for a general-purpose computer. The first electromechanical computer, Mark I, was developed by Howard Aiken in 1944. Instructions were fed on punched paper tape, and data was input by punched cards. The results were recorded on cards by electric typewriters. Soon after, the first "Electronic Numerical Integrator and Computer" (ENIAC) was assembled. It used 18,000 vacuum tubes and had to be operated by physical manipulation of thousands of wires and switches. As integrated circuit technology was developed and vacuum tubes were replaced by transistors, followed by silicon chips, the size of computers became smaller and their computing abilities magnified. With Intel's development of Random Access Memory (RAM) and microprocessors, the personal computer industry took off in the 1970s. The research and development of the networking potential of computers started as a project of the Department of Defense Advanced Research Projects Agency (ARPA), which led to the creation of ARPANET that was transformed into the government-sponsored **Internet** in the 1980s. In late 1990, Tim Berners-Lee of CERN (the European Particle Physics Laboratory in Geneva) developed the **World Wide Web** project. The extension of computers into the field of communication through the Internet and the World Wide Web has opened it up for new literary forms that make use of the multiuser or multimedia potential of the Web, which has resulted in Web-based **hypertext** fiction or text-based **virtual realities**.

Reference

Shurkin, Joel. *Engines of the Mind: A History of the Computer.* New York: W.W. Norton, 1984.

Jaishree K. Odin

Conrad, Joseph (1857–1924). Polish-born author who wrote in precise English. His main works are *The Nigger of the Narcissus* (1897), *Under Western Eyes* (1911), *Heart of Darkness* (1899; 1902), and *Lord Jim* (1900). Conrad spent eighteen years at sea in the British merchant marine during which time he earned the rank of Ordinary Master. This sea experience gave him, literally, a world culture and a technical vocabulary. He adopted the emerging sciences of geological and biological gradualism to urge political behavior of a higher order. Conrad wrote mainly of themes that dealt with human rights such as natural freedom versus forced government action that limited those freedoms. Some of his themes are less obviously political than others. For example, in *Heart of Darkness*, Conrad criticizes the European imperialists in **Africa**, and he lets Nature swallow their machines *and* their delicate morality in the darkness of the verdant floor. Africa then reverts naturally to its presumably better primordial state.

In a scientific sense Conrad's political writing mimics **Darwin's** evolutionary gradualism (Levine 224). Further, in a philosophical sense he follows **Herbert Spencer's** view that morality comes from feeling others' pain, which itself is the precursor to civilization. That is, a human that does not imagine the pain he inflicts on another stays a savage. To Conrad a savage is simply an utterly selfish human, intent on carnal needs. Conrad sees empathy as man's sense of justice, pity, conscience, tenderness, and altruism, implying that a civilization that will validate these virtues will progress toward the gradual evolution of civil behavior. To Conrad revolution was disruptive, and he denied that abruptness occurs in any evolutionary process; whereas Darwin readily accepted biological anarchy in evolution.

Conrad explains the conflict between primitive survival and civilization as an evolutionary war of morality. Unambiguous morality, not present in savages, is the force creating higher civilization. Conrad writes that although man cannot control nature, he can abide within its rules and survive as a higher order. But he, unlike Spencer and Darwin, denies the brutal reality of nature's amorality, preferring instead to blame the randomness of **chaos** for bad luck.

References

Karl, Frederick R. *Joseph Conrad: The Three Lives.* New York: Farrar, Straus and Giroux, 1979.
Levine, George Lewis. "The Novel as Scientific Discourse: The Example of Conrad." *Novel* (Winter–Spring 1989): 220–27.
Roussel, Royal. *The Metaphysics of Darkness.* Baltimore: Johns Hopkins UP, 1971.

Joseph C. Groseclose

Conservation Biology. "Scientific study of the phenomena that affect the maintenance, loss, and restoration of biological diversity" (*Conservation Biology*). Defined as a "crisis discipline" by its practitioners, conservation biology emerged as a scientific and management approach to combat mass extinction of species first discovered in the 1970s (Noss and Cooperrider 84). Conjoining wildlife **biology**, ecology, and other disciplines, conservation biology is a holistic attempt to protect the world's endangered **biodiversity** and ecosystems. Using satellite imagery of ecosystems and inventories of biological diversity, among other tools, conservation biologists are formulating the most comprehensive models of nature ever in the **history of science**.

In turn, conservation biologists are using this new data in their roles as environmental activists, spurring policymakers and environmental organizations to adopt legislation and plans to protect whole ecosystems instead of fragmented nature preserves. So popular is the mission and method of conservation biology that it is the fastest-growing discipline in the applied sciences, prompting the establishment of academic programs, associations, and publication of numerous books and articles.

References

Conservation Biology: The Journal of the Society for Conservation Biology. Boston, MA: Blackwell Scientific Publications. May 1987–present.
Noss, Reed, and Allen Y. Cooperrider. *Saving Nature's Legacy: Protecting and Restoring Biodiversity.* Washington: Island, 1994.
Soule, Michael E., ed. *Conservation Biology: The Science of Scarcity and Diversity.* Sunderland, MA: Sinauer Associates, 1986.

John A. Kinch

Cook, Robin (1940–   ). American physician and author of novels on biomedical themes. Cook's novels, some of which have been made into films, are case studies in biomedical ethics. Examples of the professional dilemmas that typify his fiction are organ transplantation (*Coma*, 1977) and human genetic engineering (*see* Biotechnology/Genetic Engineering) (*Mutation*, 1989; *Chromosome 6*, 1997). His plot structures are based on the structural metaphor of scientific research, from observed problem to **hypothesis** and solution from gathered evidence. Cook's preoccupation with the abuse of technological power parallels the fiction of **Michael Crichton**.

Robert C. Goldbort

Cooper, James Fenimore (1789–1851). Best known for his Leatherstocking Tales, also wrote further novels and works of other kinds in which science plays a part. There are astronomical references in his novels *Satanstoe* (1845) and *The Crater* (1847). *Mercedes of Castile* (1840) attributes knowledgeable astronomical thinking to Columbus. In *Gleanings from Europe*, Cooper became an enthusiastic supporter of Laplace, whose *Celestial Mechanics* extended and reinforced the astrophysics of Newton (*see* Newtonianism). Even so, Cooper chose elsewhere to satirize some of the pretensions of science. He did so most notably in *The Prairie* (1827), wherein a Dr. Battius full of **Buffon** and Linnaeus is yet unable to recognize his own donkey in the dark. Cooper's *Monikins* (1835) makes extensive if satirical use of Monboddo's pre-Darwinian theory of evolution (*see* Evolutionary Theory). *The Crater*, based on the rapid appearance and disappearance of a submarine **volcano**, apparently derives from the account of Graham Island in **Lyell's** *Principles of Geology*.

References

Clark, Harry Hayden. "Fenimore Cooper and Science." *Transactions of the Wisconsin Academy* 48 (1959): 179–204; 49 (1960): 249–82.
Dean, Dennis R. "Graham Island, Charles Lyell, and the Craters of Elevation Controversy." *ISIS* 71 (1980): 571–88 and front cover.
Scudder, Harold H. "Cooper's *The Crater*." *American Literature* 19 (1947): 109–26.

Dennis R. Dean

Coover, Robert [Lowell] (1932–   ). A major postmodern American writer (along with **Barth, Barthelme, Pynchon**, and others). His unique style constantly experiments with all levels of formal structure as well as generic expectations and the tensions between history and fiction, the real and surreal. In *the Universal Baseball Association, Inc., J. Henry Waugh, Prop.* (1968), Coover creates a baseball commissioner-God who (in anti-Einsteinian [*see* Einstein] fashion) *does* play dice with his imaginary players' fates. When chance introduces evil into his utopian world, he abandons his creation. Recently Coover has explored the horrific and fantastic in fairy tales (*Pinocchio in Venice*, 1991; *Briar Rose*, 1996). His long interest in "novel" relationships of form and content has led him to a deep involvement in **hypertext's** potential for publishing and pedagogy.

References

Gordon, Lois G. *Robert Coover: The Universal Fictionmaking Process*. Carbondale: South Illinois UP, 1983.
Spencer, Nicholas. "Utopia and Zone: Politics and Technology in the Fiction of Upton,

Sinclair, John Dos Passos, Thomas Pynchon, Robert Coover, William Gibson and Bruce Sterling." Diss. Emory U, 1996.

Pamela Gossin

Copernicus, Nicholas (1473–1543). Polish astronomer who postulated a heliocentric theory of the universe—perhaps the single most provocative revolution in science and the paradigm shift sine qua non. Copernicus did more than usher in modern **astronomy** and modern science; his theories represented such a radically new manner in which society viewed the world that it radically changed society's view of itself. An allegory for the Renaissance, its rebirths and transformations, the heliocentric theory represents Copernicus's mathematical rigor, as well as his artistic creativity, all against the background of thirty years of research and study.

Born in the wealthy Polish merchant town of Torun, Copernicus studied in Cracow but also spent eight years of study and travel in Italy. In 1515 he returned to Poland, to the city of Frombork, and dedicated the remainder of his life to his magnum opus *De Revolutionibus*, published in the year of his death in 1543.

Copernicus's overthrow of Ptolemy's geocentric comprehension of the cosmos (*see* Cosmos/Cosmology) transpired against the backdrop of an ever-increasing scientific discomfort with the thirteen-centuries-old system. Yet the heliocentric system stood at odds, not only with prevailing authority and the Church but also with the daily experience of the senses. Copernicus's work is all the more astounding in that he had no telescope at his disposal but only the naked-eye instruments already available to Ptolemy. **Kepler**, **Galileo**, and Newton (*see* Newtonianism) each contributed important refinements that added intelligibility to the basic model of the Copernican solar system.

References

Hallyn, Fernand. *The Poetic Structure of the World: Copernicus and Kepler*. Trans. Donald Leslie. New York: Zone Books, 1990.
Kuhn, Thomas S. *The Copernican Revolution: Planetary Astronomy in the Development of Western Thought*. 2d ed. New York: Vintage, 1959.
Moss, Jean Dietz. *Novelties in the Heavens: Rhetoric and Science in the Copernican Controversy*. Chicago: U of Chicago P, 1993.

Ralph W. Buechler

Corporeality/Body. Focus on the human body as a trope, symbolic figure, or material substance. Studies in corporeality have been pervasive among historians, philosophers, and literary critics since the late 1960s. Scholars and critics interested in the body seek to examine culture and society in the light of such questions as **gender and sexuality**, **race**, class, power, disease, **technology**, materialism, subjectivity, and the mind/body problem. With wide-ranging methodological sources that include phenomenology, Marxism, feminism, psychoanalysis, and deconstruction, the current fascination with corporeality has often produced interpretations that treat the body in chiefly metaphorical terms—that is, as a rhetorical *topos* whose signification is more textual, psychological, or political than organic. This critical trend has, however, also helped to reinvigorate the study of literature and science, in that it has provided a concrete focal point for investigating how biomedical and anthropological theories have interacted with the body's cultural meanings during particular historical periods.

The rhetorical and psychological approach to corporeality predominant in contemporary scholarship can be traced to **Sigmund Freud**, whose theory of the unconscious emphasized language and relegated the physiological body to a supporting role in psychic processes. Michel Foucault also did much to popularize the notion of the body as a discursive, psychosocial construct while also emphasizing the body's rich but often tortuous history in Western thought.

Reference

Hillman, David, and Carla Mazzio, eds. *The Body in Parts: Fantasies of Corporeality in Early Modern Europe*. New York and London: Routledge, 1997.

Anne C. Vila

Cortázar, Julio (1914–1984). Born in Brussels, Belgium, raised and educated in Buenos Aires, became professor of French literature at the University of Cuyo. With the election of Juan Peron, he resigned and in 1951 left Argentina for Paris, where he lived till his death in 1984 working as a translator for the United Nations Educational, Scientific, and Cultural Organization (UNESCO). Cortázar's fame as a writer comes mainly from his use of experimental narrative in his fiction. An avid reader of the science news in Paris's *Le Monde*, Cortázar often discusses principles of **quantum physics** in his essays, novels, and short fiction. One critic has noted a "new physics realism" in Cortázar's work where his narrative occupies a world in which visible reality operates according to the rules of quantum physics. In his most famous novel, *Hopscotch* (1963), Cortázar incorporates references to **Werner Heisenberg**, using them as part of his attack on Cartesian thought.

Reference

Capello, Jean. "Science as Story: Julio Cortázar and Schrödinger's Cat." *Revista de Estudios Hispanicos* 31.1 (Jan. 1997): 41–60.

J. Andrew Brown

Cosmos/Cosmology. A comprehensive account of the nature and origin of the physical universe (including humanity's place within it), often imbued historically with philosophical, cultural, scientific, and religious meanings. Changes in conceptual traditions, disciplinary categories, literary genres, and modes of expression have shaped the depiction of the cosmos in literature. As with the case of scholarly work on **astronomy** in literature, studies of cosmology in literature often emphasize the scientific content of literary works. Classic as well as more recent studies examine (1) the cosmological background of the works of canonical figures such as **Chaucer, Dante, Milton,** and **Shakespeare** and (2) the English literary response in **poetry** and prose to the achievements of the Copernican (*see* Copernicus) and Scientific Revolutions. Exceptions to this focus on the scientific content of literary works are Mark McCulloh's 1983 literary critique and semantic analysis of nineteenth-century German cosmological prose (**Kant, Humboldt,** and **Einstein**) and Eric Charles White's 1990 exploration of contemporary cosmology and narrative theory. The influence of post-Einsteinian **physics** and cosmology on twentieth-century poetry, prose, and **fiction** is one area of continuing interest to scholars. Literary and rhetorical analysis of works by cosmologists (past and present) remains a promising field of inquiry.

References

Encyclopedia of Cosmology: Historical, Philosophical, and Scientific Foundations of Modern Cosmology. Ed. Norriss S. Hetherington. New York: Garland, 1993.
Palmeri, JoAnn. "An Astronomer Beyond the Observatory: Harlow Shapley as Prophet of Science." Diss. University of Oklahoma, 2000.

JoAnn Palmeri

Cowley, Abraham (1618–1667). Poet and essayist who achieved prominence with *The Mistress* (1647). Imprisoned by Oliver Cromwell, Cowley later retired to study **medicine** and **botany.** Founding member of the **Royal Society,** Cowley eulogized that body in *Essays in Verse and Prose* and was a leading intellectual until his death.

Diana B. Altegoer

Creationism. In its broadest sense, the view that the earth was created by divine fiat. Not to be identified necessarily as biblical literalism, a creationist position was held by most scientists (as a fundamental presupposition of their investigations) up to the nineteenth century. It has been argued that creationist views operating *within* seventeenth-century science contributed the idea of the uniformity of nature (its intelligibility, orderliness, and predictability) so essential to the development of the new **philosophy.** The central metaphor of the "laws of nature," for example, is intimately linked to voluntarist notions of the imposition of divine will at Creation. The greatest epic poem in English, **John Milton's** *Paradise Lost* (1667, 1674), exemplifies the important hexameral (God's six days of creation) literary tradition. Indeed, Books 7 and 8 were read as a system of **natural philosophy.** A more "current" science than Milton's was combined with the old hexameral theme in eighteenth-century physicotheological poems like Richard Blackmore's *Creation* (1712).

Recently the term "creationism" has been co-opted by the adherents of "scientific creationism" (or "creation science" or "flood geology")—a fundamentalist American antievolutionary Protestant movement of biblical literalism that claims scientific credentials; the prevailing meaning of the term, then, has shifted from theologically orthodox theories to a populist doctrine that compresses earth history into 10,000 years (Numbers xi) and that has commanded increased public and political attention since the 1960s (especially within the context of legal battles over the teaching of creation science in American schools).

References

Gillespie, Neal C. *Charles Darwin and the Problem of Creation.* Chicago: U of Chicago P, 1979.
Marjara, Harinder Singh. *Contemplation of Created Things: Science in* Paradise Lost. Toronto: U of Toronto P, 1992.
Numbers, Ronald L. *The Creationists.* New York: Knopf, 1992.

Lisa Zeitz

Crichton, Michael (1942–   ). American physician, film director, and author of hard **science fiction**. Crichton's novels deal largely with biomedical and technological advances and their applications and particularly with ethical conflicts between the interests and modus operandi of the cultures of science, business, and **politics**. Several of his novels also have been made into films, including *The Andromeda Strain* (1969), *Terminal Man* (1972), *Sphere* (1987), and *Jurassic Park* (1990).

Robert C. Goldbort

Crick, Francis (1916–   ). British biologist, neurologist, and codiscoverer of the DNA structure (with **James Watson**). Crick and others elucidated the genetic code, that is, how DNA directs protein synthesis. His most recent popular works include the autobiographical *What Mad Pursuit: A Personal View of Scientific Discovery* (1988) and *The Astonishing Hypothesis: The Scientific Search for the Soul* (1994), both of which recount his important ongoing work in neuroscientific studies of the mind/brain.

Michael A. Bryson

Cubism. Western painting style originating with Pablo Picasso's *Les Demoiselles d'Avignon* (1906–1907), named around 1908, and systematized by Picasso, Georges Braque, and others by 1913. Often associated with **relativity** theory and later applied to literature, among other arts, Cubism is an imaginative use of projective geometry that projects all dimensions, including the fourth dimension of **time**, onto two, representing all aspects of the subject in the foreground of the picture plane.

Reference

Golding, John. *Cubism: A History and an Analysis, 1907–1914.* 1968. 3rd ed. Cambridge: Harvard UP (Belknap), 1988.

William R. Everdell

Culture. Includes the lifeways, artifacts, beliefs, attitudes, activities, styles and modes of communication, information production, and transmission of human groups or societies. Although it is intuitively obvious that literature is part of culture, some critics seek to study the literary text in isolation and eschew explanations in terms of the influences on the author or treatment of the text in terms of its times or social, ideological, or historical forces that might have played a part in evoking or constituting the text. To many, including most scientists, science (broadly defined as science, **technology**, and **medicine**) is definitely not a part of culture, and it makes them very cross, indeed, to see it suggested that the sciences of a period are integral to the values, priorities, and beliefs of their time. They believe that thinking of science in these terms is relativistic and seeks to undermine the objectivity and neutrality of science, features that they hold to lie at the heart of what distinguishes science from culture. Treating science as literature is therefore equally an anathema to them. Science, they maintain, is "above the battle" of contending forces in society, a claim they conveniently forget when lobbying for research grants. Most advocates of the cultural perspective on science are untroubled by these fears and purport to leave the truth claims of science where they found them—no more and no less questionable. Many, of course, also want the claims of other forms of insight into nature and human nature to be less subject to patronizing slurs from scientists.

"Culture" is a broad term denoting the way of life of a people. It includes its symbolic order as expressed in its structured social relations, customs, rules of conduct, belief system, values, and worldview or **cosmology**, and of course, its artifacts, including material culture of implements and furnishings and, especially, its **art** and literature. Culture is the place where these things are husbanded, celebrated, questioned, and maintained—not just in official or "high" culture but also in its forms of fun, **music**, fashion, clubs, institutions. Culture is transmitted within and between generations by learning and not by biological inheritance. The recent emergence of the academic discipline of Cultural Studies has widened the definition of culture, so that there are now studies of, for example, the culture of a factory, a street gang, an old people's home, a football team and its supporters. Cultural studies is a discipline the writ of which extends from the highest cultural phenomenon to the lowest, that is, from the most formal and abstruse knowledge, including science, to the most populist expressions of entertainment for ordinary people, for example, television soap operas.

The rise of cultural analyses of science has made some members of the scientific community so cross that they have sought to cut off the funding of research in the history, **philosophy**, and social studies of science and have succeeded in bringing this about in some quarters. They have gone further in some settings and attacked the funding of humanities research. These advocates of science as the only trustworthy form of knowledge have not only campaigned against cultural approaches to science but have also succeeded in raising substantial funds for promoting "the public understanding of science," the point being that if only the public understood science better they would stop doubting science and would cease to place so much emphasis on other approaches to understanding (and manipulating) nature and human nature.

And yet it is easy to make out a case for treating science in cultural terms. Scientific writings are texts; they have arguments and structures; they employ **rhetoric**. All of these are available for examination in ways that other, including literary, texts are analyzed. The science of a period shares the assumptive characteristics of a period, which is why we comfortably speak of Ancient, Medieval, Renaissance, Victorian, and Twentieth-Century science, implying that they are of their time in ways that are not merely chronological; they partake of the cultural preoccupations of the period. For example, in all periods up until the seventeenth century it was important that other planets circled around the earth. When it was shown that, on the contrary, the earth and other planets move around the sun in elliptical orbits, the whole sense of humanity's place in nature was fundamentally changed. Similarly, in the world view of "The Great Chain of Being," celebrated, among many others, by **Alexander Pope** in his *An Essay on Man* (1733), which provided the ruling view of the order of nature from ancient times until the mid-nineteenth century, humanity was "of a middle state," divinely created and situated as the middle link of the chain, halfway between nonbeing and the deity. In the wake of the writings of **Darwin** and others in the middle quarters of the nineteenth century, humanity was seen to have evolved very gradually from lower forms by purely natural processes—random variation and natural selection. "Man's place in nature" changed dramatically in poetry, novels, and even eventually in most theology.

In both of the examples given above—of a new planetary theory and the theory of evolution—developments in science and in the rest of culture were intimately interrelated. Indeed, in those periods there was a common culture of scientific and literary writings. Since the late nineteenth century the division of labor and the proliferation of a specialist periodical literature in science and in the arts has made the interrelations among disciplines less apparent on the surface. Both scientists and literati can easily see those who seek to investigate those interrelations as enemies. This cuts both ways. Scholars increasingly use scientific methods on literary and other cultural artifacts for dating, for establishing authorship, for quantitative analysis of forms of expression and modes of discourse. On the other side, literary and conceptual studies are made of scientific writings, for example, the study of plot or the philosophical use of metaphor in Darwin's writings. Some of the most interesting studies trace the rise of scientific theories and disciplines in cultural and ideological terms and examine the culture of particular disciplines and scientific institutions, for example, a **laboratory**.

In some ways, the controversies around these mutual influences in methodologies from the arts and sciences and their interdisciplinary findings are quite surprising. These interrelations are not new. The influence of science on literature and the presence of science and scientists in literature has been commonplace through the ages. Where is the divide in **Plato's** *Dialogues*, in **Christopher Marlowe's** *Dr. Faustus*, in **Mary Shelly's** *Frankenstein*, in the writings of **Jules Verne** and **H.G. Wells**, in the great Victorian periodicals, the *Edinburgh, Quarterly* and *Westminster Reviews*? How are we to classify Robert Pirsig's *Zen and the Art of Motorcycle Maintenance* or **James Watson's** *The Double Helix*? Both are at the same time literary and scientific.

The result of these developments is the rise of a growing number of hybrid approaches and disciplines: social studies of science, sociology of science, **anthropology** of science, literary studies of science, quantitative literary studies, ideological analyses of both science and literature, cultural studies of science and of literature. There is a danger in each of these that the centrality of the text will get lost in focusing on the analytical apparatus and the terminology of the methodology being cranked up to the scientific or literary work under scrutiny. It has to be granted that some practitioners of these disciplines that purport to illuminate have the effect of obfuscating as a result of disappearing into metaconsiderations. However, that is no reason not to avail ourselves of these illuminating new perspectives. The more light we can shed on a text, the better we are able to comprehend it.

References

Haraway, Donna. *Primate Visions: Gender, Race, and Nature in the World of Modern Science*. New York: Routledge, 1989.

Jordanova, Ludmilla, ed. *Languages of Nature: Critical Essays on Science and Nature*. London: Free Association Books, 1986.

Young, Robert M. *Darwin's Metaphor: Nature's Place in Victorian Culture*. Cambridge UP, 1985.

Robert M. Young

Cybernetics. Also referred to as **information theory** or communication theory. A term coined by Norbert Wiener (from the Greek for governor or helmsman) in the 1940s for the interdisciplinary science of information exchange within and among communication systems he helped develop. The cybernetic practice of using mechanistic models to examine all systems, natural and synthetic, to describe the flow of information has produced and incorporated such concepts as positive and negative feedback, the feedback loop, robotics, artificial intelligence (*see* Virtual Reality and Artificial Intelligence), and the **cyborg**. Authors and critics have incorporated references to cybernetics in literature on both structural and thematic levels. On a structural level, some view the reading of literature as a cybernetic relationship between text and reader and have incorporated that idea within their **fiction** or criticism. On a thematic level, various authors have used references to cybernetics and the mechanization of life as either a positive or negative image in their works. David Porush in his excellent study of cybernetic fiction has noted both the technophobic use of cybernetics as well as the growing interest in the image of the living machine, or the machine metaphor as he calls it, in twentieth-century fiction.

Reference

Porush, David. *The Soft Machine: Cybernetic Fiction.* New York: Methuen, 1985.
                                                                J. Andrew Brown

Cyberpunk. A brand of **science fiction** writing in the 1980s and 1990s that describes future high-tech developments with the nihilistic and cynical attitude of punk rock music. **William Gibson's** *Neuromancer* (1984) is regarded as the quintessential cyberpunk novel. The term is also applied to the works of **Bruce Sterling**, John Shirley, Lewis Shiner, Rudy Rucker, Norman Spinrad, **Kathy Acker**, Pat Cadigan, Greg Bear, and others. Typically, these novels focus on human-machine or organic-technological interfaces and their implications for human, or posthuman, identities. Texts commonly refer to **cyberspace**, **cyborgs**, artificial intelligence (*see* Virtual Reality and Artificial Intelligence), genetic engineering (*see* Biotechnology/Genetic Engineering), and designer drugs in a multinational, late capitalist, popular culture.

References

Csicsery-Ronay, Istvan. "Cyberpunk and Neuromanticism." *Mississippi Review* 47–48 (1988): 266–78.
McCaffery, Larry, ed. *Storming the Reality Studio: A Casebook of Cyberpunk and Postmodern Fiction.* Durham: Duke UP, 1991.
Sterling, Bruce, ed. *Mirrorshades: The Cyberpunk Anthology.* New York: Arbor House, 1986.
                                                                      June Deery

Cyberspace. A term coined by **William Gibson** in the futuristic novel *Neuromancer* (1984) to describe a **computer**-generated, multidimensional, multinational, interactive environment. Gibson was projecting a **technology** that does not yet exist, but soon afterward the term entered high and popular discussions of new communication technologies and may have influenced their actual design. Currently, cyberspace is often invoked in descriptions of the **Internet** and the **World Wide Web**, electronic forums created by globally linked personal computers. However, these are only limited versions of the environment Gibson imagined. The term is also commonly used as a synonym for **virtual reality**, though the latter is still more specifically associated with technology that allows a subject to walk through a computer-generated environment with body gear, such as HMDs (head-mounted displays) and gloves, to give the effect of a three-dimensional sensory experience. Gibson has continued to write about cyberspace in the novels *Count Zero* (1986), *Mona Lisa Overdrive* (1988), and *Virtual Light* (1993). Prominent among recent works that also fictionally explore cyberspace are **Marge Piercy's** *He, She and It* (1991) as well as **Neal Stephenson's** two recent novels, *Snow Crash* (1992) and *The Diamond Age* (1995).

References

Benedikt, Michael, ed. *Cyberspace: First Steps*. Cambridge: MIT, 1991.
Bukatman, Scott. *Terminal Identity: The Virtual Subject in Postmodern Science Fiction*. Durham: Duke UP, 1993.
Heim, Michael. *The Metaphysics of Virtual Reality*. New York: Oxford UP, 1993.
Markley, Robert, ed. *Virtual Realities and Their Discontents*. Baltimore: Johns Hopkins UP, 1996.
Rheingold, Howard. *Virtual Reality*. New York: Touchstone, 1991.

June Deery

Cyborgs. Cybernetic organisms, creatures who/that are part human and part machine, with organic and technological components. Cyborgs have featured as future projections in **science fiction** and might be said to exist in actuality when human beings possess prosthetic devices or develop a symbiotic relationship with **computers**. The notion of a cyborg has been used to highlight the increasingly intimate relations between human beings and **technology** in the late twentieth century. Writers of **fiction** and nonfiction have used the cyborg image to explore changing definitions of being human. Very influential is **Donna Haraway's** essay "A Cyborg Manifesto: Science, Technology, and Socialist-Feminism in the Late Twentieth Century" (in *Simians, Cyborgs, and Women*, 1991), which views cyborgs as useful border creatures that dismantle traditional Western dualisms such as natural/artificial, mind/body, human/animal, self/other, male/female, nature/culture, and maker/made. Some of these ideas have been embodied in the fiction of, for example, **Marge Piercy** in her novel *He, She and It* (1991). Popular representations of cyborgs since the 1970s include "the Six-Million Dollar Man," Darth Vader (*Star Wars*), the Terminator, and the Borg (*Star Trek: The Next Generation*).

Reference

Porush, David. *The Soft Machine: Cybernetic Fiction*. New York: Methuen, 1985.

June Deery

D

Dante Alighieri (1265–1321). Author of one of the greatest works of epic and didactic **poetry** of all times. His *Divine Comedy* (1306–1320) offers an extraordinary glimpse into medieval scientific knowledge. Along the steps of this allegorical journey, Dante demonstrates an impressive mastery of the currents in **astronomy**, **cosmology**, **physics**, mathematics, **optics**, geology, and **biology**, as well as theories of light and of the soul. Having as his main sources such philosophers as **Aristotle**, **Galen**, Albertus Magnus, Avicebron, and Avicenna, the *Comedy* shows Dante's predominantly scholastic view of the world. We can find Platonic (*see* Plato) **natural philosophy**, however, in such notions as the physics of love, as expressed in his *Vita nuova* (1292–1300).

Reference

Boyd, Patrick, and Vittorio Russo. *Dante e la scienza.* Ravenna, Italy: Longo Editore, 1995.

Arielle Saiber

Darwin, Charles Robert (1809–1882). English naturalist and chief originator of the theory of evolution (*see* Evolutionary Theory) through natural selection. After graduating from Cambridge, Darwin accepted a position as naturalist on the H.M.S. *Beagle.* In a voyage that lasted nearly five years, he engaged in intensive researches into the geology and **biology** of South America and other parts of the world. For the next several years, he analyzed and published the results of his researches, and in 1859 he published his masterwork, *On the Origin of Species by Means of Natural Selection.* By identifying natural selection as the causal mechanism through which species evolve, Darwin provided a central principle of order through which the historical development and systematic relations of all living things could be explained. *Origin* is closely reasoned and dense with factual reference, but it also displays much rhetorical skill, is accessible to the general reader, and has extraordinary imaginative power. Darwin assimilated **Charles Lyell's** conception of geological time and envisioned all biological relations as complex ecological systems. Along with many technical volumes on various branches of geology and biology, Darwin published two works that locate human **psychology** within the general field of **natural history**: *The Descent of Man, and Selection in Relation to Sex* (1871)— a deeply meditated essay in moral psychology and precursor to evolutionary psychology—and *The Expression of the Emotions in Man and Animals* (1872). Darwin's more specifically literary works include the journal of his voyage on the *Beagle* and his autobiography.

References

Appleman, Philip, ed. *Darwin: Texts, Backgrounds, and Contemporary Opinion*. 2nd ed. New York: Norton, 1979.

Bowlby, John. *Charles Darwin: A New Life*. New York: Norton, 1990.

Joseph Carroll

Darwin, Erasmus (1731–1802). The most popular poet in England during the 1790s and the best example since **Lucretius** of a poet influenced by his contemporary science. Professionally a **physician**, he was the grandfather of **Charles Darwin** and preceded him in synthesizing an **evolutionary theory** of nature. Erasmus Darwin's interests were even more far-reaching than his grandson's, encompassing virtually the entire science of his day and much of its **technology**. The work for which he is best known today is an attractively illustrated folio volume (including plates by **William Blake**), *The Botanic Garden* (1789–1791). The first part to be published, called "The Loves of the Plants," is an amusingly salacious versification of the Linnaean system of botanic classification. In the other part, "The Economy Vegetation," a Goddess of Botany addresses in turn the four elemental sprites associated with fire, earth, water, and air, incorporating relevant scientific information appropriate to each. The poem's text includes numerous incidental notes on all such topics, and there are more than 200 pages of additional notes at its end, constituting a virtual encyclopedia of contemporary science. Darwin's use of current science in verse was immensely influential on the poets who followed him, including Blake, **Wordsworth**, **Coleridge**, **Shelley**, and **Tennyson** primarily. Darwin's other major poem, *The Temple of Nature* (1803), appeared posthumously and was criticized for its inopportune scepticism. His major prose work, *Zoonomia, the Laws of Organic Life* (1796), describes his evolution theory most fully; it was the acknowledged source of Wordsworth's "Goody-Blake and Harry Gill." **Mary Shelley** also acknowledged Darwin as the source of her **Frankenstein** idea. Charles Darwin wrote a short book about his grandfather, but the extent to which Erasmus influenced Charles scientifically is a subject of continuing debate.

References

Darwin, Charles. *The Life of Erasmus Darwin* (together with an essay on his scientific
    works by Ernest Krause). London: J. Murray, 1879.
King-Hele, Desmond. *Erasmus Darwin*. New York: Scribner's, 1963.

Dennis R. Dean

Darwinism. A theoretical orientation in **biology**, the human sciences, and the
humanities. Darwinism derives from the work of **Charles Darwin** and is characterized by adherence to the central organizing principle of modern biology:
the idea that complex functional structures in living things have evolved by
means of natural selection. Organisms that display favorable variations in innate
structures enjoy greater reproductive success. Heritable variations enable organisms to adapt to environmental change, and the accumulation of heritable variations over time produces distinct species. Darwin's mechanistic causal
hypothesis distinguishes his theory of evolution (*see* Evolutionary Theory) from
formalistic and teleological theories of development, for instance, from those of
Aristotle and of Darwin's contemporaries Karl Marx and **Matthew Arnold**.

Because Darwin's theory of evolution is mechanical and nonprogressive, it
has sometimes been associated with despairing visions of an inhuman cosmic
futility. **Thomas Hardy**, **Joseph Conrad**, and **H.G. Wells** offer signal instances. Because it explicitly stipulates the interaction of **environment** and organism as one of its largest organizing principles, it provides a scientific
framework for the minutely detailed social and psychological analyses of naturalistic **fiction**.

Darwinism, or the emphasis on the evolution of adaptive structures by means
of natural selection, is now sometimes referred to as "the adaptationist program."
Within biology itself, this program stands in opposition to arguments, associated
with the work of Richard Lewontin and **Stephen Jay Gould**, that seek to minimize the importance of adaptation and to maximize the element of **randomness**
or chance within evolutionary change.

Literary scholars affiliated with **poststructuralism** have sometimes interpreted Darwin's work as a precursor to deconstructive theories of indeterminacy.
From the poststructuralist perspective, the import of Darwin's theories would
be incompatible with the determinate causal argument that characterizes Darwinism.

Darwinists regard all behavior as the product of an interaction between innate
biological characteristics and environmental circumstances. Darwinism can thus
be set in opposition to theories—like those both of traditional social science and
of poststructuralism—that discount innate characteristics and attribute autonomy
or exclusive causal force to **culture** or language.

In the human sciences, Darwinism is now most closely identified with two
schools of thought: **sociobiology** and evolutionary psychology. Sociobiologists
focus on "fitness maximization" or the drive for reproductive success as the

ultimate regulator of human behavior. Evolutionary psychologists acknowledge differential reproductive success or "inclusive fitness" as the ultimate regulator of adaptive change, but they also insist that inclusive fitness is mediated by "proximate mechanisms" that can be decoupled from direct reproductive motives. They argue that living things should be conceived not primarily as fitness maximizers but rather as "adaptation executors."

Both Darwin's contemporary Hippolyte Taine and the naturalists of the later nineteenth century demonstrated the power of Darwinian thinking in literary theory and criticism, but from the last decade of the nineteenth century to the last decade of the twentieth, literary theory developed along non-Darwinian lines. In the 1980s and 1990s, major advances in understanding the biological basis of human behavior began to generate a renewed interest in the implications of Darwinism for literary study. Proponents of Darwinism in literary studies believe that the form and content of literary works are constrained by the evolved cognitive and motivational structures of human beings, and in this belief they affiliate themselves with pre-Darwinian literary theorists who regard human nature as a major causal force in culture and literature. Sociobiological readings of literary texts focus on **representations** of mating and kinship relations that reflect evolved patterns of reproductive behavior. Literary scholars who synthesize sociobiology with evolutionary psychology and with cognitive psychology acknowledge the importance of mating and kinship but also seek to analyze the cognitive structures of literary texts—sensory, emotional, and intellective.

Darwinian literary theorists have formulated various speculative hypotheses about the adaptive functions of protoliterary behavior. Proposed functions include sexual display, social manipulation, social bonding, emotional and aesthetic development, emotional and aesthetic therapy, and cognitive mapping or model building.

References

Storey, Robert. *Mimesis and the Human Animal: On the Biogenetic Foundations of Literary Representation.* Evanston, IL: Northwestern UP, 1996.
Wilson, Edward O. *On Human Nature.* Cambridge: Harvard UP, 1978.

Joseph Carroll

Darwinism in Spain. Arrival of **Darwin's** thought here is associated with the social and political events of the Revolution of 1868. *The Origin of Species* was translated into Spanish in 1876. However, most Spaniards read Darwin in French translation. One of the earliest defenders of Darwin's ideas in Spain was Antonio Machado Nuñez, grandfather of the noted Spanish poet of the same name. Spanish followers of **naturalism** also used Darwinian images in their writing. The most important of these was **Emilia Pardo Bazán** and her novel *The Mansions of Ulloa* (1886). Darwinian themes also appear in the novels of **Benito Pérez Galdós** and "Clarín."

Rafael Chabrán

Davy, Humphry (1778–1829). English chemist, discoverer of chlorine and potassium, inventor of the miner's safety lamp. The youthful Davy was an intimate friend of **Samuel Taylor Coleridge** and a friend of Robert Southey and helped edit **William Wordsworth's** "Lyrical Ballads." Davy wrote **poetry** that was taken seriously by Coleridge and Wordsworth. Coleridge attended Davy's spectacular lectures at the Royal Institution for poetic inspiration. In his last prose works, Davy returned to a Romantic philosophy of the world as process.

Reference

Levere, Trevor H. *Poetry Realized in Nature*. Cambridge: Cambridge UP, 1981.
                                                                          Val Dusek

Deep Ecology. Arose as a reaction to the "shallow" environmentalism of the 1970s, calling for fundamental changes in humans' relationship to nature. Deep ecology eschews the methodology of modern science, calling instead for biocentric equality and transformation of consciousness. It aims at a spiritual/animistic approach that merges individual consciousness or "self" into the larger collective "Self." Deep ecologists advocate an organismic democracy that resituates humanity on the same level as all other living things. From this call for drastic shifts in legitimating worldviews have sprung several "radical" environmental movements including EarthFirst!, which supports acts of environmental sabotage or "monkey wrenching" in defense of nature. Deep ecology has been criticized for Luddism, antihumanism, and scientific naïveté. Ecofeminists (*see* Ecofeminism) also cite a failure to acknowledge the relationship between the domination of nature by Man and the domination of women by men.

References

Devall, Bill, and William Sessions. *Deep Ecology: Living as If Nature Mattered*. Salt
    Lake City, UT: Gibbs Smith, 1985.
Foreman, Dave. *Confessions of an Eco-Warrior*. New York: Harmony, 1991.
Snyder, Gary. *Turtle Island*. New York: New Directions, 1974.
Tobias, Michael, ed. *Deep Ecology*. San Marcos, CA: Avant, 1985.
                                                                     David N. Cassuto

Defoe, Daniel (c. 1660–1731). Prolific journalist and novelist. Defoe wrote in many genres including fantastic voyage literature exemplified by *The Consolidator* (1705), **supernatural** writings such as *The Apparition of One Mrs. Veal* (1706), *Political History of the Devil* (1726), and *History and Reality of Apparitions* (1727), and historical fiction like *Journal of the Plague Year* (1721). *Robinson Crusoe* (1720) draws upon his love of travel, exotic natural settings, and adventure and includes an important literary depiction of the **noble savage**.

Reference

Backsheider, P.B. *Daniel Defoe: His Life.* Baltimore: Johns Hopkins UP, 1989.

Philip K. Wilson

De la Beche, Henry (1796–1855). Founder of the Geological Survey of England who wrote influential manuals on how to observe geological phenomena. A talented artist, he expressed his opinions on numerous topics in privately circulated cartoons that have since become popular among historians. One particular target was **Charles Lyell**, author of the highly influential *Principles of Geology* (1830–1875; twelve editions), whom De la Beche accused of seeing natural phenomena through the myopia of **theory**. The best known of his cartoons, "Awful Changes" (1830), parodies Lyell's just-published volume one and includes a quotation from **Byron**. De la Beche's "Duria Antiquior" (Ancient Dorsetshire, also 1830) was a serious attempt by him to reconstruct the fauna of the Liassic period, including plesiosaurs, ichthyosaurs, and pterodactyls, and its **environment**. A significant tradition of such restorations followed: first prehistoric reptiles (as with "Duria Antiquior"), then **dinosaurs**, then prehistoric humans, usually as book illustrations but sometimes as independent works of art.

Reference

McCartney, Paul J. *Henry De la Beche: Observations on an Observer.* Cardiff: Friends of the National Museum, 1977.

Dennis R. Dean

DeLillo, Don (1936–   ). American novelist whose work shows a consistent fascination with science and **technology.** *Ratner's Star* (1976) is structured around the history of mathematics, *White Noise* (1985) addresses the dangers of industrial chemical processes and modern pharmacology, and *Underworld* (1997) concerns the ways that awareness of a Soviet nuclear threat shaped American consciousness throughout the Cold War. The interrelatedness of scientific development, information-gathering technologies, and such organizations as the CIA (Central Intelligence Agency) and KGB (Committee for State Security, USSR) accounts for much of DeLillo's vision of contemporary life, which he most frequently approaches by studying the effects of science and technology on bemused, sometimes paranoid, groups of nonscientists.

Reference

LeClair, Tom. *In The Loop: Don DeLillo and the Systems Novel.* Urbana: U of Illinois P, 1987.

Stephen D. Bernstein

Deming, Alison H. (1946–   ). Winner of the Walt Whitman Award for Poetry in 1994; director of the Poetry Center at the University of Arizona. The title poem of her first book *Science and Other Poems* (1994) makes use of a school science fair to develop the theme of coming of age. Other poems in the book also use scientific themes and subjects.

Joseph Duemer

De Quincey, Thomas (1785–1859). Romantic essayist whose autobiography *Confessions of an English Opium Eater* (1821) is a major contribution to the psychology (*see* Anthropology/Psychology/Sociology) of narcotics influencing such writers as **Charles Baudelaire**, **Edgar Allan Poe**, and Ernst Jünger. His **theory** of the psyche as palimpsest anticipates psychoanalysis; and his essay "The English Mail Coach" (1849) is a meditation on the different types of speed, death, and modernity.

Reference

Hayter, A. *Opium and the Romantic Imagination*. Berkeley: U of California P, 1968.

Elmar Schenkel

Derham, William (1657–1735). Divine, Fellow of the **Royal Society**, a regular contributor to the Royal Society's *Philosophical Transactions*, the friend and editor of **John Ray**, and the author of a notable horological text (an early example of technological writing), *The Artificial Clockmaker* (1696). Derham is most important for his immensely popular, widely translated, and influential encyclopedic **natural theologies** employing the empirical **argument from design** for the existence of God. The frequently reprinted *Physico-theology* (the Boyle Lectures of 1711–1712), first published in 1713 and expanded several times, and its companion *Astro-theology* (1715) not only traced the order and purposiveness discernible in nature and the heavens but also served as "science handbooks" (Jones 21) for writers like **James Thomson**, Oliver Goldsmith, and **Samuel Johnson** (who drew many quotations from Derham for his *Dictionary*). Derham's (and physico-theology's) procedures of comparative taxonomy and teleological argument were brilliantly satirized by **Jonathan Swift** in *Gulliver's Travels* (1726).

References

Jones, William Powell. *The Rhetoric of Science: A Study of Scientific Ideas and Imagery in Eighteenth-Century English Poetry*. Berkeley: U of California P, 1966.
Rothstein, Eric. "In Brobdingnag: Captain Gulliver, Dr. Derham, and Master Tom Thumb." *Études Anglaises* 37 (1984): 129–41.

Lisa Zeitz

Descartes, René (1596–1650). French philosopher, mathematician, and scientist, author of *Discourse on Method* (1637), *Meditations on First Philosophy* (1641), *Principles of Philosophy* (1644), and *Passions of the Soul* (1649). He developed a dualistic system that distinguished thinking mind from extended matter. Descartes's influence on modern Western consciousness stems from his **theory** of knowing by ways of representative ideas and by his notion of the *cogito*, which finds certainty in the intuition of the thinking self. In his stress on **rationality**, Descartes demonstrated a desire to control mind and matter, and underpins the secular goals of contemporary science and society. Cartesian thinking also dichotomized the world, opposing spiritual to material existence. This opposition buttressed the representational movement in artistic and literary expression, so that poetic practices would increasingly be limited to *mimesis* or imitation of concrete reality, thereby further severing the tie between *poesis* and *scientia* that had existed in the Renaissance.

Diana B. Altegoer

Detective Fiction. A literary genre with apparently strong affinities to science. The classic detective, descended from **Edgar Allan Poe's** Dupin and **Arthur Conan Doyle's** Sherlock Holmes, is an exemplary practitioner of the hallmarks—careful observation, logical deduction—of the idealized **scientific method**. In complementary fashion, detection is widely invoked as a metaphor in accounts of scientific research. With the displacement of traditional detective fiction by the "hard-boiled" style, the connections to science become much more tenuous. In any case, explicit incorporation of scientific themes and concepts in detective fiction is not all that common, with some notable exceptions (e.g., Dorothy Sayers).

Jay A. Labinger

Determinism. A nineteenth-century term describing the view that events are determined by causes external to the will. During the eighteenth century nature came to be viewed as "a self-sufficient deterministic mechanism" (Barbour 57) that operated by predictable laws of matter in motion. Not until the nineteenth century, however, did scientific theory underwrite (1) biological (genetic and physiological) determinism—heredity determines destiny—and (2) cultural determinism—**environment** and education determine destiny (included here is "social determinism": the application of **evolutionary theory** to society, generating ideas such as social adaptation and a societal "survival of the fittest" [to use **Herbert Spencer's** phrase]). In the late nineteenth and early twentieth centuries the international literary movement of **naturalism** (most closely associated with **Émile Zola**) depicted humanity operating within the limits dictated by heredity and environment. Perhaps nowhere is determinism more compellingly (but complexly) represented than in **Thomas Hardy's** *Tess of the D'Urbervilles* (1891) with its "adoption of neo-Darwinian inheritance theory" (Morton 207).

The most important recent example of a reductionist biological determinism ("biologism") is **Edward O. Wilson's** controversial *Sociobiology* (1975), which announces its subject as the "systematic study of the biological basis of all social behavior." Like virtually all varieties of scientific determinism, the project of **sociobiology** is colored by "social, cultural, and political biases" (Lewontin,

Rose, and Kamin 8). In its legitimation of the status quo, Wilson's work has been described by its critics as "Pangloss" (**Voltaire's** "best of all possible worlds" philosopher) made scientific through the agency of **Charles Darwin** (Lewontin 237).

References

Barbour, Ian G. *Issues in Science and Religion*. Englewood Cliffs, NJ: Prentice-Hall, 1966.
Beer, Gillian. *Darwin's Plots: Evolutionary Narrative in Darwin, George Eliot and Nineteenth-Century Fiction*. 1983. London: Ark, 1985.
Lewontin, Richard C., Steven Rose, and Leon J. Kamin. *Not in Our Genes: Biology, Ideology, and Human Nature*. New York: Pantheon, 1984.
Mitchell, Lee Clark. "Naturalism and the Languages of Determinism." *Columbia Literary History of the United States*. New York: Columbia UP, 1988. 525–45.
Morton, Peter. *The Vital Science: Biology and the Literary Imagination, 1860–1900*. London: George Allen and Unwin, 1984.

Lisa Zeitz

Dick, Philip K[indred] (1928–1982). Author of numerous science fiction stories, including *Do Androids Dream of Electric Sheep?* (1968) and *Flow My Tears, the Policeman Said* (1974), in which ordinary humans confront the radical epistemological and ontological uncertainties arising from the technological mediation of **reality** and their own identities.

Noel Gough

Dickens, Charles (1812–1870). English novelist and publisher known for his interest in psychology (*see* Anthropology/Psychology/Sociology), **entropy**, contagious disease, human physiology, and recurrent critiques of the negative effects of technological "progress" and industrialization upon the social conditions of the working class. Dickens frequently portrays the scientific mind as being attended by atrophied emotions, most memorably in his novel *Hard Times* (1854), where the materialist educational philosophy of Gradgrind leads to the ruthless and amoral development of his pupil Bitzer. Even more biting is Dickens's parody of the British Association for the Advancement of Science in his 1837 essay *Full Report of the First Meeting of the Mudfog Association for the Advancement of Everything*. As a periodical editor, Dickens assisted in the publication of such reformist authors as Elizabeth Gaskell.

Reference

Ackroyd, Peter. *Dickens*. New York: HarperCollins, 1990.

Alison E. Bright and Stephen D. Bernstein

Dickinson, Emily (1830–1886). American poet. Her works reveal an intellectual fascination with—but mixed feelings about—science. Sometimes the poems are playful and satirical as in #70, "I pull a flower from the woods," in which a "monster" scientist with a magnifying glass analyzes the flower parts, or in #108, "Surgeons Must Be Very Careful," in which the speaker admonishes surgeons to watch out for "the Culprit—Life!" underneath their scalpels.

More often, though, Dickinson is pitting a scientific (i.e., objective, analytical) perception of experience and nature against a spiritual or aesthetic one, not so much to resolve the issue of which is the more "authentic" perception but to heighten awareness of the tensions existing between the two modes of perception that are essentially unresolvable. No matter how much we learn about nature, we can never "decode the mystery" underlying the measurable phenomena. As she asserts in one of her most famous poems (#501), "This World Is Not Conclusion."

What are the limits of human understanding and experience? Human beings apply analytical techniques to achieve holistic understanding (the aims of scientific inquiry), but analysis can itself be nonholistic, as Dickinson implies in #1484, "We Shall Find the Cube of the Rainbow." In this poem Dickinson suggests that even when scientific analysis is used successfully, it distorts the essence of what is observed: The more you analyze a rainbow, the farther you get from its essential nature.

It is important to stress that Dickinson never denigrated science. She had enthusiastically studied geology, chemistry, astronomy, and especially botany. She maintained a herbarium and a conservatory. Even when she writes that the "Logarithm" she had for drink was "a dry Wine" (#728), we need to remember that a dry wine is still wine!

Scientific language and observation permeate her poems, even when she is not writing "about" science, as in her famous "Snake" poem, "A Narrow Fellow in the Grass (#986), and poem #786 in which she refers to death as "Nature's only Pharmacy" for the "malady" of existence.

Reference

White, Fred D. " 'Sweet Skepticism of the Heart': Science in the Poetry of Emily Dickinson." *College Literature* 19 (Feb. 1992): 121–28.

Fred D. White

Diderot, Denis (1713–1784). French philosopher, novelist, dramatist, and chief architect of the *Encyclopédie* (1751–1772). One of the most powerful and creative minds of the **Enlightenment**, Diderot drew from a vast range of scientific fields, all of which were integral to his dynamic, humanistic theory of materialism. He was harassed by the authorities for the *Encyclopédie* and for his own writings; many of his most original works were thus published posthumously.

Diderot was keenly interested in the epistemological and sociomoral significance of eighteenth-century psychology (*see* Anthropology/Psychology/Sociology), **biology**, **physics**, **chemistry**, and **natural history**. In his *Lettre sur les aveugles* (Letter on the Blind, 1749)—a work for which he was imprisoned for three months—he intertwined scientific observations on blindness with reflections on atheism. He examined the methods used by experimental physicists and other natural philosophers in *De l'Interprétation de la nature* (On The Interpretation of Nature, 1753). The most striking expression of Diderot's scientific and philosophical theories was *Le Rêve de d'Alembert* (D'Alembert's Dream, written in 1769), a fictional dialogue based on his extensive readings in biomedical theory, where he used real, contemporary characters to explain his materialistic, monistic views on life, sensibility, intelligence, and human nature.

Diderot's ideas about **natural philosophy** were closely linked to the aesthetic theory he propounded in works like *Le Paradoxe sur le comédien* (The Paradox of Acting, wr. 1773, pub. 1830): He attributed the same perspicacity and instinctive feel for nature's hidden operations to all great observers of nature, whether scientists, **physicians**, poets, or actors. Diderot's conception of **art** as a means of getting the reader-spectator directly engaged with nature also informed his *Salons* (1759–1781), one of the earliest works in art criticism, and his philosophical novels, like *La Religieuse* (wr. 1760, pub. 1796).

Reference

Anderson, Wilda. *Diderot's Dream*. Baltimore: Johns Hopkins UP, 1990.

Anne C. Vila

Dillard, Annie (1945–   ). An accomplished writer of **poetry**, **fiction**, and **essays**, probably best known for her Pulitzer Prize–winning work, *Pilgrim at Tinker Creek* (1974), a Thoreauvian (*see* Thoreau) account of the natural world and its spiritual symbology. Ostensibly a natural history of Tinker Creek in Virginia, the book invokes such diverse sources as the Koran, Thomas Merton, Moses, **Goethe**, and **Kepler** to probe the intricacies of natural phenomena in search of lessons for living and growing.

Dillard groups writing into two opposing categories that she calls "Shooting the Agate" and "Calling a Spade a Spade." She, herself, leans more to the latter style. As in the often reprinted essay "Living Like Weasels" (from the collection *Teaching a Stone to Talk*, 1982), she often takes a fact or event (in this case, a brief staring match with a startled weasel) and teases out in precise, lapidary prose its spiritual and moral significance. In her other work, the subject matter can be by turns beautiful and horrifying. "The Deer at Providencia" deals with our varying reactions to physical pain and suffering, both in animals and humans, and the mystery of how brutality can seem to be both meaningless and profound. The short story "The Living" (which became the basis of the novel by the same name, 1992) also wrestles with the enigma of death and how life is perhaps only meaningful when we keep in mind the certainty of death. Dillard has also produced several volumes of poetry and reminiscences. An excellent introduction to her work is *The Annie Dillard Reader* (New York: Harper-Collins, 1994).

David N. Cassuto

Dinosaurs. Not prehistoric beasts in general, nor even prehistoric reptiles in toto, but rather two fairly distinct groups of either bird-hipped or lizard-hipped creatures—possibly not reptiles at all—that flourished throughout the Mesozoic era and became totally extinct at its end, some 65 million years ago. That there had been an Age of Reptiles preceding the Age of Mammals was not recognized until the nineteenth century. The first dinosaurs to be named were "Megalosaurus" in 1824 (by William Buckland) and "Iguanodon" in 1825 (by **Gideon Mantell**). They, their era, and further new kinds were then popularized by Mantell and others. The Great Exhibition of 1851 included life-sized models (still extant) of Megalosaurus, Iguanodon, and "Hylaeosaurus," which had been grouped into a new category of animal called "Dinosauria" by Richard Owen in 1842. In literature, dinosaurs appear most famously in **Tennyson's** *In Memoriam* (1850), **Dickens's** *Bleak House* (1852, the Megalosaurus at the beginning), and **Arthur Conan Doyle's** *The Lost World* (1912), from which they graduated into film. Longfellow's "Footprints on the sands of time" were made by birdlike creatures later identified as dinosaurs.

References

Dean, Dennis R. *Gideon Mantell, Discoverer of Dinosaurs*. New York and London: Cambridge UP, 1997.
———. "Hitchcock's Dinosaur Tracks." *American Quarterly* 21 (1969): 639–44.

Dennis R. Dean

Discontinuity. Concept arising in mathematics as a condition of the integers, in which there is "space" "between" consecutive numbers. The real number sequence is, by contrast, continuous (Richard Dedekind defined a real number as a "cut") and of a higher order of infinity. Otherwise continuous functions with occasional discontinuities and functions that are wholly discontinuous led Carl Weierstrass to "arithmetize" calculus, which Leibniz had once founded on continuity. By analogy, nonmathematical relationships can be discontinuous, and the concept appears in definitions of molecule, gene, quantum, atomic and subatomic particle, pointillist dot, fictional "moment of being" and "montage," information bit, and pixel, beginning in the late nineteenth century. **James Joyce's** *Finnegans Wake* is said to be composed of discontinuous fragments of the dreams of a character name Earwicker.

References

Bochner, Salomon. "Continuity and Discontinuity in Nature and Knowledge." *Dictionary of the History of Ideas*. Vol. 1. New York: Scribner's, 1973. 492–504.
Kretzmann, Norman, ed. *Infinity and Continuity in Ancient and Medieval Thought*. Ithaca, NY: Cornell UP, 1982

William R. Everdell

Djerassi, Carl (1923–   ). Writer and distinguished chemistry professor at Stanford University who synthesized the first steroid oral contraceptive. Djerassi's public writings include **essays**, autobiographies, **poetry**, hard **science fiction**, and science-in-theater. With *Cantor's Dilemma* (1989), his first of a planned tetrad of novels, he turned to writing "verifiction" as a didactic tool to illuminate scientific culture, ideas, and advances. He also founded the Djerassi Resident Artists Program in California to support promising work in choreography, literature, **music**, and the visual arts. Djerassi's unusually comprehensive homepage <www.djerassi.com> includes his international lecture calendar.

Robert C. Goldbort

Donne, John (1572–1631). Celebrated rake, poet, and dean of St. Paul's. His long poems the *Anniversaries* (1611, 1612) provide perhaps the most complex contemporary poetic response to developments in early modern **astronomy** and **natural philosophy**, including Baconian (*see* Bacon) natural philosophy, Copernican (*see* Copernicus) heliocentrism, and **Kepler's** repudiation of the Aristotelian (*see* Aristotle) "element of fire" and of the circular revolution of the planets. Recent criticism has variously represented the *Anniversaries* as a defense of scholastic **epistemology**, as strongly informed by the skeptical fideism of Agrippa von Nettesheim and **Montaigne**, and as an ideological critique of the "New Philosophy." While critics have generally treated the "New Philosophy" and the politics of Jacobean court patronage as unrelated concerns, more recent criticism represents the poems as exploring the role that patronage played in defining the claims, goals, and methodologies of natural philosophy and astronomy in early modern Europe. The trope of anatomy and dissection, central to the *Anniversaries*, also recurs in Donne's *Songs and Sonnets*. The poet's manipulation of spatial dimensions in poems such as "The Flea" and "The Good Morrow" may be seen, as Thomas Docherty has argued in *John Donne Undone*, as responding to developments in early modern **optics**. Donne's *Devotions upon Emergent Occasions*, meditations written during a lengthy period of illness, provide insights into medical care and doctor–patient relationships in the period.

References

Coffin, Charles. *John Donne and the New Philosophy*. New York: Humanities Press, 1958.

Docherty, Thomas. *John Donne Undone*. London/New York: Metheun, 1986.

Gossin, Pamela. "Poetic Resolutions of Scientific Revolutions: Astronomy and the Literary Imaginations of Donne, Swift, and Hardy." Diss. U of Wisconsin, 1989. *DAI* 51 (1990): 273A.

Hellegers, Desiree. *Handmaid to Divinity: Science, Politics and the Gendered Poetics of Resistance*. Norman: U of Oklahoma P, 1999.

Nicolson, Marjorie Hope. *The Breaking of the Circle: Studies in the Effect of the "New Science" upon Seventeenth-Century Poetry*. Rev. ed. New York: Columbia UP, 1960.

Tayler, Edward. *Donne's Idea of a Woman: Structure and Meaning in* The Anniversaries. New York: Columbia UP, 1991.

Desiree Hellegers

Dos Passos, John [Roderigo] (1896–1970). Modernist author of *Manhattan Transfer* (1925) and a trilogy of novels, *U.S.A.* (1938). In *U.S.A.*, Dos Passos's representation of fictional and nonfictional scientists and engineers is deeply indebted to Thorstein Veblen's belief that social change should be led by a class of engineers rather than left-wing political parties. Scholars have often remarked that his fictional vision rivals the "camera's eye" in its intensity and clarity.

Nicholas Spencer

Doyle, Arthur Conan (1859–1930). Best known as the creator of the amateur detective character Sherlock Holmes. Doyle first acquired an interest in science when studying physiology at Edinburgh University. Holmes, the first forensic scientist in literature, is a problematic hero, embodying in his analytical coolness and social noninvolvement many aspects of the Romantic villain. Significantly, the only person whose intellect Holmes admires is the evil Professor Moriarty.

Doyle also produced a series of **science fiction** novels centered on the character of Professor Challenger, a biologist of towering stature, impressive scientific reputation, and colossal arrogance, who was allegedly modeled on William Rutherford, Doyle's former professor at Edinburgh. In the first of the Challenger stories, *The Lost World* (1912), Doyle used a comic combination of bravery and intellectual arrogance to satirize scientific pretension, while in *The Poison Belt* (1913), which reflected the rampant speculation attending the 1910 appearance of Halley's comet, Challenger dispassionately predicts universal death as earth passes through a belt of poisonous ether. The popularity of his character soon suggested to Doyle a way to promote the cause of spiritualism, in which he had become passionately interested. In *The Land of Mist* (1926) Challenger refuses to examine the claims of spiritualism until, after witnessing an instance of psychic empathy between his daughter and his dead wife, Challenger enrolls in the ranks of spiritualism. Doyle argues that such a response to the empirical evidence is more scientific than the entrenched rejection of the scientific community at large.

In *The Maracot Deep* (1928) Doyle returned to the theme of a scientist's conversion to spiritualism. His marine biologist Dr. Maracot, marooned on the floor of the Atlantic, faces certain death with serenity and scientific integrity until, converted to a spiritualist perception by the good spirit Warda, he faces the evil Lord of the Dark Face and destroys him.

References

Brown, Ivor. *Conan Doyle: A Biography of the Creator of Sherlock Holmes.* London: Hamilton, 1972.

Keating, H.R.F. *Sherlock Holmes: The Man and His World*. London: Thames and Hudson, 1979.
Rauber, D.F. "Sherlock Holmes and Nero Wolfe: The Role of the 'Great Detective' in Intellectual History." *Journal of Popular Culture* 6: (1972) 483–95.

Roslynn D. Haynes

Drama. Literary composition in verse or prose, usually intended to be acted on the stage. From its origins in Greek tragedy to contemporary theater, Western drama has been profoundly influenced by scientific developments in numerous ways. Perhaps the most common intersection of science and drama has been the representation of the individual scientist within playwrights' work. As the forerunners of modern scientists, alchemists and astrologers are frequently depicted in Renaissance drama. Robert Greene's *Friar Bacon and Friar Bungay* (c. 1589) celebrates the alchemist's skill, whereas **Ben Jonson's** *The Alchemist* (1610), his *Mercury Vindicated from the Alchemists* (1615), and **Giordano Bruno's** *The Candle Bearer* (1582) enact the dubious scientific practices of the alchemist. Likewise, Giambattista Della Porta's *The Astrologer* (1570) exposes the astrologer Albumazar as a confidence trickster.

In *The Tragedy of Man* (1860), Imré Madach investigates the Renaissance conflict between innovative science and unscientific authority, as **Johannes Kepler** can continue his scientific research only by providing bogus horoscopes. The enduring significance of this conflict is evidenced in **Bertolt Brecht's** *Galileo* (1938–1939) and László Németh's *Galileo* (1956). In Brecht's play, **Galileo** responds to the Church's threats of torture by renouncing his scientific discoveries about the earth's place in the universe; however, in doing so he has enough time to complete his work in physics, the *Discorsi*. A related struggle between scientific method and the desire for occult and **supernatural** power informs the Faust tale. This legend has been the subject of many dramatic pieces, including **Christopher Marlowe's** *Dr. Faustus* (c. 1588), **Johann W. von Goethe's** *Faust I* (1791–1806) and *Faust II* (1832), and **George Gordon Byron's** *Manfred* (1817, 1834).

Faust represents the desire for nonscientific power in a world that will become increasingly dependent upon the power of science. Through the characterizations of many different types of scientists, dramatists have investigated the ethics of science in modern industrial society. Quite frequently, science is evoked as a destructive force, and scientists are often responsible for technologies that destroy humans. In **Karel Capek's** *R.U.R.: Rossum's Universal Robots* (1921), the robots created by Dr. Goll take over the island factory, kill all humans but one, Alquist, and propagate themselves. Similarly, in Alfredo Testoni's *I Had More Respect for Hydrogen* (1955) scientists are at the mercy of their inventions, and universal destruction ensues. The most common version of this theme is, of course, the story of **Frankenstein**, which has been reworked for the theater on many occasions, such as Barbara Field's *Playing with Fire* (after *Frankenstein*) (1988) and Libby Larsen's *Frankenstein: The Modern Prometheus* (1990).

A more ambivalent and less humanist rendering of the motif of the empowered robot can be found in Filippo Tommaso Marinetti's *Electric Dolls* (1909).

The mentality of the scientist is sometimes presented as inhumane. In François de Curel's *The New Idol* (1895), a scientist injects himself with a lethal inoculation after realizing his experiments caused the death of a young girl. The scientist's concern with objective methods and results is equated with immorality in Silvio Giovaninetti's *Green Blood* (1953), Stanislaw Ignacy Witkiewicz's *Metaphysics of a Two-Headed Calf* (1921) and *Tumor Brainard* (1928), and Maxim Gorky's *The Children of the Sun* (1905). Whereas Gorky's play opposes scientific abstraction with the unscientific will of the people, Aleksander Afinogenov's *Fear* (1930) contrasts the counterrevolutionary science of Professor Borodin with the true science of Soviet **determinism**.

As well as causing harm, the scientist in drama can also be more ethical than his or her society. In Henrik Ibsen's *An Enemy of the People* (1883), a public health officer determines to remedy a town's unhealthy water supply, but he is branded an enemy when the townspeople find out the financial cost of the project; when a scientist invents a time machine to accelerate the development of communism in Vladimir Mayakovsky's *The Bathhouse* (1930), Soviet authorities ignore and then claim credit for the invention and are left behind when the machine proves successful; the doctor in Luigi Capuana's *The White Plague* (1937) hopes to use his discovery of a cure to a horrific disease for beneficial social ends, but he is ultimately killed and his cure is lost; and **Friedrich Dürrenmatt's** *The Physicists* (1962) features a physicist who discovers a formula unifying all scientific knowledge, believes society is unprepared for it, and hides in an insane asylum where he feigns madness.

In addition to the express dramatic content of scientists and technological devices, the less visible presence of scientific theories can be detected in the work of many playwrights. Naturalist theater was greatly influenced by biological theories of heredity, instinct, and **Darwinism**. For example, the theater of Gerhart Hauptmann was informed by Darwinian ideas as popularized by Ernst Haeckel, and August Strindberg's plays enacted naturalist ideas of deterministic decline. Unlike Darwinism, vitalism proposed a theory of creative or psychological human evolution, and the influence of such ideas is apparent in **George Bernard Shaw's** *Man and Superman* (1905) and *Back to Methuselah* (1922). A variety of psychological models have influenced the theater. Menander's comedies were based on the psychological theories of his teacher Theophrastus, and Seneca's dramatic conception of morbid psychology and revenge influenced Renaissance drama. In modern drama, theories of psychology continue to inspire playwrights, as is apparent in the Freudianism of Henri-René Lenormand's *Time Is a Dream* (1919) and the work of former psychiatrist Carlo Terron. The impact of sociological theories on modern drama is evident, as the example of the "unanimism" of Jules Romains's *Doctor Knock, or The Triumph of Medicine* (1923) readily shows.

Many recent and contemporary issues in science have been addressed by dramatists. Environmental concerns are voiced in Frederick Bailey's *Gringo Planet* (1987) and Y. York's *Rain, Some Fish, No Elephants* (1989); the science of AIDS is dealt with in Jim Grimsley's *Man with a Gun* (1989) and Tony Kushner's *Angels in America* (1994); and the consequences of nuclear power and nuclear weapons are dramatized in Dave Carley's *First Strike* (1982), Edward Bond's *The War Plays* (1985), Bruce Graham's *Early One Evening at the Rainbow Bar and Grill* (1986), Jane Liddiard's *Nuclear Family* (1987), and Tom Stoppard's *Arcadia* (1993).

References

Nicholl, Charles. *The Chemical Theater*. Boston: Routledge and Kegan Paul, 1980.
Russell, Robert. *Russian Drama of the Revolutionary Period*. Basingstoke, United Kingdom: Macmillan, 1988.
Willingham, Ralph. *Science Fiction and the Stage*. Westport, CT: Greenwood, 1994.

Nicholas Spencer

Dreiser, Theodore (1871–1945). Influential American naturalist writer who read **Darwin**, Wallace, Tyndall, **Kingsley**, and **Huxley** and claimed that **Spencer's** *First Principles* most altered his views. His novel *Sister Carrie*, two articles on American naturalist John Burroughs, an essay that describes the fossils and paleontological work in the New York Museum of Natural History, a series of articles about plant life and cultivation of crops, articles about advances in **technology**, and "The Shining Slave Makers" all reveal scientific roots.

Reference

Zanine, Louis J. *Mechanism and Mysticism: The Influence of Science on the Thought and Work of Theodore Dreiser*. Philadelphia: U of Pennsylvania P, 1993.

Sandra J. Chrystal

Dryden, John (1631–1700). Poet and dramatist of the English Restoration. His poem *To Dr. Charleton* earned him a fellowship in the **Royal Society** in 1662, which he lost for nonpayment of dues in 1666. Especially in that poem, but elsewhere as well, Dryden helped popularize the "new science" as a "restoration" in the realm of knowledge analogous to the political triumph of Charles II.

References

Harth, Phillip. *Contexts of Dryden's Thought*. Chicago: U of Chicago P, 1968.
Kroll, Richard W.F. *The Material Word*. Baltimore: Johns Hopkins UP, 1991.

Richard Nash

Durrell, Lawrence (1912–1990). Anglo-Irish novelist, poet, travel writer, and author of *The Alexandria Quartet* (1957–1960). Preferring Alexandria's poverty, decay, and sense of adventurous possibility to the wealth, sterile cleanliness, and predictability of life in western Europe, Durrell's bohemian expatriates eschew both the strong sense of triumphalism—and subsequent despair—attending twentieth-century science and **technology**.

Michael B. McDonald

Dürrenmatt, Friedrich (1921–1990). Swiss playwright and novelist who wrote in German. He is known for his ironic and absurdist style, as in the novels *The Quarry* (1953) and *The Pledge* (1958) and the plays *The Visit* (1956) and *The Physicists* (1962). The "physicists" in the last are three inmates of a private sanitarium. One believes himself to be Isaac Newton (*see* Newtonianism), the genius of classical physics. One announces himself as **Albert Einstein**, whose theory of **relativity** changed science and underlies the atomic bomb. The third, called Möbius (the name of the nineteenth-century mathematician who first studied the fourth dimension), is said to have made the greatest scientific discoveries of all. Drawing on the supposed madness of the three, the play combines comic elements with an investigation of how these "physicists" committed murder among their attendants. With this mixture of absurdity and brute reality, *The Physicists* explores what science means in the era of the atomic bomb.

Sidney Perkowitz

Dystopias. A derivation of **utopia**, meaning literally "bad places" or unattractive societies. Like utopias, dystopias are didactic fictional narratives that describe particular, alternative societies and usually take the form of realistic novels set in a place distant in **time** or space from the author's own society. In the case of dystopias, the intent is to shock and warn the reader against what the author considers to be undesirable future trends. In this capacity dystopias have been a significant form of protest against scientific or technological mechanization and reductionism. The form became popular in the early twentieth century, the most commonly cited examples being Evgenii Zamiatin's *We* (1920–1921), **Aldous Huxley's** *Brave New World* (1932), and **George Orwell's** *1984* (1949). Each text expresses a fear of scientific hegemony, of scientific principles being applied to social organization and expectations. They decry behaviorism and other forms of scientific conditioning. They object to humans being treated as cogs in a social machinery. Huxley, for instance, alerts readers to the dangers of applying the principles of mass production and standardization to the human populace. Orwell and Zamyatin are concerned about technological surveillance and social control. All three novelists link scientific **positivism** or reductionism to totalitarian regimes.

Some of the technologies featured in these novels have come into existence, though they may not be used in the manner their authors feared; for example, the surveillance equipment in *1984* and the helicopters, designer drugs, **genetic engineering**, and **reproduction technology** (in vitro fertilization, cloning) of *Brave New World*.

In recent decades, authors have produced more ambiguous works, neither wholly dystopian nor wholly positive. A significant number of feminist writers who began writing utopias in the 1970s and 1980s have found these more open or critical forms more useful; for example, **Margaret Atwood**, **Ursula K. Le Guin**, **Marge Piercy**, and Joanna Russ.

References

Booker, M. Keith. *Dystopian Literature: A Theory and Research Guide*. Westport, CT: Greenwood, 1994.
Krishnan, Kumar. *Utopia and Anti-Utopia in Modern Times*. Oxford: Blackwell, 1987.

June Deery

E

Earthquakes. Seismic activity, in various forms, has appeared frequently in literature, particularly that of southern Europe. **Vergil** (*Georgics*), Seneca, Ammianus, and Augustine all wrote of them in a protoscientific manner. **Aristotle's** theory of their origin in his *Meterologica* remained current into the eighteenth century and would be echoed by **Shakespeare** (I *Henry* IV, III, i). The Nurse, in *Romeo and Juliet*, refers to the earthquake of 1580, which generated a large and pessimistic literature. Modern study of earthquakes began in the mid-eighteenth century with the London-felt tremors of 1750, reported at length in the *Philosophical Transactions of the Royal Society*, and with the Lisbon earthquakes of November 1, 1755. **Voltaire** responded to the latter, first with a poem (criticizing **Alexander Pope**) and then with *Candide* (1750), both of which did much to dissociate natural disasters like the Lisbon earthquake from any kind of divine providence. The Calabrian earthquake of February 1783, as described in the *Philosophical Transactions* by Sir William Hamilton, influenced William Cowper's poems "The Time-Piece" and *The Task* (book II) and would require an entire chapter in **Lyell's** *Principles of Geology* later on. During the American and French Revolutions, earthquakes were often used metaphorically. **Byron**, who personally experienced a number of earthquakes while in Italy and Greece, added them to *Manfred* (1817). The second part of **Goethe's** *Faust* (1832) includes a character named Seismos and scientifically inspired earthquake passages. The 1936 film *San Francisco* culminates in a scientifically correct dramatization of the 1906 disaster.

Reference

Heninger, S.K., Jr. *A Handbook of Renaissance Meteorology, with Particular Reference to Elizabethan and Jacobean Literature*. Durham, NC: Duke UP, 1960.

Dennis R. Dean

Eco, Umberto (1932–   ). A professor of semiotics and author of numerous scholarly studies of language structures and systems. Eco has also written regularly (since the late 1950s) for newspapers and magazines in his native country as a commentator on diverse aspects of everyday life and popular culture. In English-speaking countries, both his academic and popular writings became better known following the publication of his first novel, *The Name of the Rose* (1980; trans. 1983), a multilayered metafiction that uses the conventions of **detective fiction** to explore the physical and metaphysical spaces of conjecture—the materials and meanings that structure investigation as such, be it scientific research or philosophical inquiry (see also his *Postscript*). His similarly multileveled second novel, *Foucault's Pendulum* (1988), is emplotted as thriller set in the world of contemporary publishing but with narrative threads reaching into the esoteric histories of Kabbalah and the occult (and their complex interreferences in the development of European science, **philosophy**, and **politics**) and current intellectual movements in **physics**, information technology, and literary theory. In *The Island of the Day Before* (1994), a quasi-epistolary novel recounting the seventeenth-century adventures of a young nobleman stranded on a deserted ship near an island straddling what we now call the international dateline, Eco again juxtaposes significant problems in the **history of science** (including the determination of longitude and other conceptual and empirical issues in the study of **time** and temporality) with critical questions about **representation** and signification in contemporary cultural debate.

Reference

Eco, Umberto. *Postscript to The Name of the Rose*. Trans. William Weaver. New York: Harcourt Brace Jovanovich, 1984.

Noel Gough

Ecocriticism. Umbrella term covering the growing disciplines of ecologically based **philosophy** and literary and social criticism. Broadly defined, ecocriticism adds place to the categories of **race**, class, and **gender** commonly used in literary analysis. For some, that means looking at how texts represent the physical world; for others, at how literature raises moral questions about human interactions with nature. Ecocriticism includes such subdisciplines as **ecofeminism, deep ecology**, **social ecology**, ecophilosophy, environmental history, and others.

The diversity of views and philosophies within the ecocritical rubric has led to factionalization among the different groups. Nevertheless, as the discipline has matured, feuding among the factions has tapered in recognition of the common goal of increased ecological awareness and a sensitivity to humanity's role in the biosphere.

References

Glotfelty, Cheryll, and Harold Fromm, eds. *The Ecocriticism Reader: Landmarks in Literary Ecology*. Athens: U of Georgia P, 1996.

Merchant, Carolyn. *Radical Ecology: The Search for a Livable World*. New York: Routledge, 1994.

David N. Cassuto

Ecofeminism. Coined by Françoise d'Eaubonne in 1974 as a call to women to lead an ecological revolution to save the planet. Since then, ecofeminism has branched in different philosophical directions, but the overarching theme remains that women and nature must be liberated together. Ecofeminist theory confronts the essential conflict between production and **reproduction** and patriarchy's manipulation of the market economy to increase the wage-based and domestic servitude of women. Ecofeminism shares many ideological concepts with **social ecology**. Both believe that environmentalism starts with societal reform and that environmental ethics take shape through remedying social inequalities.

Among the ideological differences within ecofeminism is a split between those whose ethic is based on women's traditional close links to the land versus those who believe that such a view reinforces a culturally mandated role of women as nurturers.

References

Biehl, Janet. *Rethinking Ecofeminist Poetics*. Boston: South End, 1991.
Kolodny, Annette. *The Lay of the Land: Metaphor as Experience and History in American Lives and Letters*. Chapel Hill: U of North Carolina P, 1975.
Merchant, Carolyn. *The Death of Nature: Women, Ecology, and the Scientific Revolution*. San Francisco: Harper and Row, 1980.

David. N. Cassuto

Ecomachia. Term coined by Robert Markley and Molly Rothenberg to describe the implications of Richard Lewontin's observation that all organisms are irrevocably destroying the conditions that sustain them. Intended to counter idealist descriptions of Nature as inherently harmonious, ecomachia emphasizes the coimplications of complex ecosystems: No organism exists independently of its **environment**; the environment does not exist independently of the organisms that continually reshape it. Ecomachia shares similarities with the work of **Francisco Varela**, **Bruno Latour**, and others; it deconstructs oppositions such as organism/environment, nature/**culture**, production/pollution, and subject/object to foster a dynamic view of humankind's implication in complex systems.

References

Markley, Robert, and Molly Rothenberg. "The Contestations of Nature: Aphra Behn and the Sexualizing of Politics." *Rereading Aphra Behn: History, Theory, and Criticism*. Ed. Heidi Hutner. Charlottesville: U of Virginia P, 1993. 301–21.
Rothenberg, Molly. "Mirabilis Excrementum and the Logic of Ecomachia." *New Orleans Review* 18 (1991): 19–26.

Robert Markley

Economic Value. The meaning of the word "good" in a market context. Some critics and theorists find a new urgency in the creation of value by the market and the relationship of **art** and literature to commerce and the corporation. An ongoing study group organized by Michael Benedikt at the University of Texas at Austin has been examining such issues as natural profit, market ecology, desire, life satisfaction, and the moral basis of market exchange.

Reference

Turner, Frederick. *Love and Money: The Twenty-First Century Economics of William Shakespeare.* New York: Currency Doubleday, 1996.

Frederick Turner

Edelman, Gerald Maurice (1929–   ). Recipient of the 1972 Nobel Prize for Physiology or Medicine and, subsequently, author of a series of volumes outlining a **theory** of consciousness on the basis of "neuronal group selection" or "neural Darwinism." Kroeber has proposed that, with his "biologically materialistic understanding of mind," Edelman fulfills one goal of Romantic thought, and more recently, Michael G. Miller has suggested that **Wordsworth's poetry** anticipated neural Darwinism in emphasizing the unique, hence not entirely genetically determined, development of individual human mind/brains.

References

Kroeber, Karl. *Ecological Literary Criticism: Romantic Imagining and the Biology of Mind.* New York: Columbia UP, 1994.
Miller, Michael G. "Theories of the Mind: Wordworth's Anticipation of Neural Darwinism." *Mosaic: A Journal for the Interdisciplinary Study of Literature* 28.2 (1995): 63–78.

Steven Meyer

Edgeworth, Maria (1767–1849). Anglo-Irish novelist. Growing up in a household controlled by a scientist/inventor father, Edgeworth was enlisted often to help in educational psychology projects. Her closest link to independent scientific reflection is medical, in her presentation of breast cancer, its treatment, and the psychological effects in *Belinda* (1801).

William Crisman

Edison, Thomas Alva (1847–1931). American inventor of the practical incandescent lamp, the **phonograph**, the quadruplex telegraph, and other devices. With little formal schooling, Edison began his career as an itinerant telegrapher. After his first successes at inventing telegraph machinery and related devices, he built laboratories consecutively at Menlo Park (1876) and West Orange, New Jersey (1887), where he assembled groups of skilled workers and pioneered modern practices of programmatic R&D (research and development). His work on textual duplication, telegraphy, telephony, recorded sound, and motion pictures involved him in repeated interrogations of reading, inscription, and communication as modern and variously technological activities. After his invention of the phonograph in 1877, Edison became world famous and was hailed in the newspapers as the "Wizard of Menlo Park." His work perfecting electric light and power lent him further renown, and he became enrolled within a powerful mythos of masculine American individualism, ingenuity, and technocratic ascendance. He first appeared in literature in Villiers de l'Isle-Adam's novel *L'Eve future* (1886), as the creator of a woman android. Later literary incarnations include **John Dos Passos's** *U.S.A.* trilogy (1936) and Harte Crane's *The Bridge* (1930), while the character of Tom Swift, boy inventor, testifies to the potency and longevity of Tom Edison as an American icon.

References

Edison, Thomas A. *Thomas A. Edison Papers, A Selective Microfilm Edition*. Ed. Thomas E. Jeffrey et al. Bethesda, MD: University Publications of America, 1993.
Wachhorst, Wyn. *Thomas Alva Edison: An American Myth*. Cambridge: MIT P, 1981.

Lisa Gitelman

Edwards, Jonathan (1703–1758). Theologian whose reactionary Puritanism prevented him from fulfilling his precocious promise as a scientist. His early writings on the mind and natural science, especially his famous observations of flying spiders, evidence the influence of **Bacon**, **Locke**, and Newton (*see* Newtonianism). Though the New Science influenced his metaphysics, he subordinated science to theology.

Raymond F. Dolle

Einstein, Albert (1879–1955). German and naturalized American physicist. Einstein became the twentieth-century paradigm of scientist and genius. Both as sage of space and **time** and as pacifist whose **theory** is claimed to be behind the atom bomb, and whose letter stimulated its construction, Einstein has been a central figure in literature about science. Einstein created not only the special and general theories of **relativity** but made important contributions to quantum theory and the proof of the existence of atoms. Einstein later criticized the indeterminism and strange connections of quantum theory. Einstein's revolutionary reconception of the relations of space and time influenced or at least were appealed to by many modernist writers in their experiments on new ways of presenting time in literature and by critics in describing those innovations. **Science fiction** is, of course, full of tales that utilize notions of the relativity of time and the possibilities of time travel speculated about or even suggested by Kurt Gödel's later solutions of Einstein's general relativistic equations, as well as transformations of mass into energy, and vice versa, based on Einstein's famous $E = mc^2$. Einstein himself has been portrayed in several plays.

Einstein's favorite literature included **Honoré de Balzac**, **Bertolt Brecht**,

Hermann Broch, **Charles Dickens**, Fyodor Dostoevsky, Anatole France, Maxim Gorky, Gerhart Hauptmann, Heinrich Heine, Robert Musil, and Leo Tolstoy. Einstein's interest in Dostoevsky's *The Brothers Karamazov* has been related by some to a perspectivism of relativistic frameworks. Einstein himself occasionally wrote German quatrains of no great quality.

Einstein's own prose has some of the striking and deceptive simplicity of his mathematical equations. He often formulated deep insights about method, science, and **reality**, as well as social issues, in the form of extraordinarily simple aphorisms and koanlike statements.

Modernist writers, experimenting with stream of consciousness, alternative time orders, and parallel narratives, have referred to Einstein's relativity theory as a justification. Though modernist poems and novels were contemporary with Einstein's work and share experimentation with concepts of time, space, and simultaneity, as in the case of Cubist (*see* Cubism) painting, it is doubtful that the two are conceptually isomorphic, or that there were literal conceptual importations of Einstein's ideas of time into such works of early **modernism**, as **James Joyce's** *Ulysses* or **William Faulkner's** works.

Poets, including **William Carlos Williams**, Archibald MacLeish, and Louis Zukofsky, have created poems about Einstein and relativity. **T.S. Eliot**, **Ezra Pound**, and e.e. cummings, despite their experimentation with time perspectives, were less favorable to drawing positive implications from Einstein's theories. Many other writers have alluded to the relativity and interweaving of space and time. Pirandello is thought to have been influenced by Einsteinian relativity. **Virginia Woolf** combined perspectivism and Cubism with some Einsteinian ideas from Roger Fry and works of Bertrand Russell and James Jeans. The later James Joyce of *Finnegans Wake* makes explicit references to Einsteinian **physics**, and **Lawrence Durrell** and **Vladimir Nabokov** have referred to the influence of Einstein's theories.

Reference

Friedman, A.J., and C.C. Donley. *Einstein as Myth and Muse*. Cambridge: Cambridge UP, 1985.

Val Dusek

Eiseley, Loren Corey (1907–1977). Nebraska-born scientist, poet, and nature essayist. Longtime professor of anthropology and history of science at the University of Pennsylvania, he was tempered by his depression-era childhood, the mental illness of his mother, and personal bouts with tuberculosis and melancholia, producing some of the twentieth century's most poignant reckonings of the human and the natural (*The Immense Journey*, 1957; *The Unexpected Universe*, 1969; *All the Strange Hours: The Excavation of a Life*, 1975). Drawing upon his firsthand experiences as a **fossil** hunter, Eiseley's **poetry** and prose transcribe the personal and philosophical insights he gained from his research in anthropology and **paleontology**, **natural history**, and the history of science

(*The Invisible Pyramid*, 1970; *The Innocent Assassins*, 1973; *Darwin's Century*, 1958; *The Man Who Saw Through Time*, 1973). Acutely sensitive to the fragile miracle of his own existence as a collection of living chemicals, Eiseley brought poetic sensibility to popular science writing as he sought meaning for human life under post-Darwinian conditions, beneath a post-Sputnik sky.

Reference

Christianson, Gale E. *Fox at the Wood's Edge: A Biography of Loren Eiseley*. New York: Henry Holt, 1990.

Pamela Gossin

Electricity. Fundamental property of moving particles, manifested in electrical changes. Widespread use of electrical technologies began in the eighteenth century. **Romanticism**, under the influence of the experimental work of Galvani, saw electricity as a life force of mysterious origin. With the proliferation of cheap electrical power, this "flow" came to figure the circulation and communication of social and economic networks.

Charles A. Baldwin

Electronic Bulletin Boards and Journals. The former have existed for decades. In the 1980s they constituted an electronic samizdat through which hackers and other technologically sophisticated groups could share ideas and resources. The cultural functions of bulletin boards have been largely superseded by the **World Wide Web**, newsgroups, and listservs on the **Internet**. Electronic journals are beginning to rival the printed publication of technical and scholarly information, as print journals become prohibitively expensive, especially for esoteric academic subjects. These online publications, usually mediated by the **World Wide Web**, can provide the traditional functions of both communication and scholarly validation.

References

SLS listserv, LITSCT-L, see: <https//www.law.duke.edu/sls>.
<http://muse.jhu.edu/journals/configurations>.
<http://sls.press.jhu.edu> (includes links to SLS listserv, LITSCI-L).

Jay David Bolter

Elevator. Mechanical lift. The modern safety elevator was invented by Elisha Graves Otis in 1853. A prerequisite for the skyscraper age, the elevator has been largely unnoticed by the authors of modern literature. One notable exception is William Dean Howells, for whom the elevator became a symbol of the new and tenuous parameters of social status. Howells wrote a one-act play entitled *The Elevator* in 1884, and in his *Hazard of New Fortunes* (1889), Mr. and Mrs. March wander the streets of New York seeking to rent an apartment in an "elevator building." The elevator was a central element in **Einstein's visualizations** of **relativity**.

Lisa Gitelman

Eliot, George (1819–1880). Pseudonym of Mary Ann Evans, British novelist whose works frequently engaged the scientific issues of her day. Eliot had a lifelong interest in science and kept current with contemporary theories and discoveries. She read and discussed the works of George Henry Lewes, **Herbert Spencer**, **Darwin**, Comte, and others. None of her works, however, is an apology for any **theory**. She consistently utilizes the world of science to enrich her novels through imagery and metaphor. Further, her novels participate in scientific debate. Through metaphor, narrative comment, dialogue, and plot she examines the possible interconnections of **evolutionary theory** and organicism with individual character and development, **gender** relations, social responsibility, and societal change. Her views of science also influenced her methodology.

Eliot's relation to the exceedingly varied scientific theories of her day was in continual flux. Each novel reflects a reevaluation of scientific matters. By the end of her career, science appealed to her most in its opening of possibilities for human beings, its experimentation, and sense of discovery. She saw it as problematic whenever it narrowed possibilities for growth or sought to champion certainty and closure over openness and exploration, to the detriment of the complex, multiple human.

Middlemarch (1872) is the novel that deals most ostensibly with scientific issues. One of the main characters, Lydgate, is a doctor with a deep passion for scientific discovery. *Daniel Deronda* (1876) explores, among other things, the imaginative underpinnings of science and the realms that lie beyond the scientific known.

References

Beer, Gillian. *Darwin's Plots: Evolutionary Narrative in Darwin, George Eliot and Nineteenth-Century Fiction*. London/Boston: Routledge, 1983.
Shuttleworth, Sally. *George Eliot and Nineteenth-Century Science*. New York: Cambridge UP, 1984.

Heather V. Armstrong

Eliot, Thomas Stearns (1888–1965). Recipient of the 1948 Nobel Prize for Literature and author of many important works of poetry, criticism, and drama, including the epoch-defining poem *The Waste Land* (1922). Early studies of the role of science in his poetry, such as Hyatt Howe Waggoner's *The Heel of Elohim* (1950), tended to characterize Eliot as following Irving Babbitt, F.H. Bradley, and Henri Bergson in situating himself against the "scientism" of the age even as he relied on works of **anthropology**, such as Bessie Weston's *From Ritual to Romance* and Sir James Frazer's *The Golden Bough*, to structure his work. More recently, in *Myth, Rhetoric and the Voice of Authority* (1992), Marc Manganaro has examined the role of "anthropological authority" and Frazer's "comparativist discursive form" in Eliot's poetry. According to Daniel Albright, modern **physics** supplied Eliot with a model for "a wave-theory of poetry" along with a slew of metaphors and images, biological as well as physical; and in *Modernism, Technology and the Body* (1998), Tim Armstrong reads *The Waste Land* as a study in the regimentation of mental and physical hygienes, with "waste" figured antithetically as both central to the poem's production and requiring elimination.

Reference

Albright, Daniel. "Eliot's Waves." *Quantum Poetics: Yeats, Pound, Eliot and the Science of Modernism*. Cambridge: Cambridge UP, 1997. 218–87.

Steven Meyer

Ellison, Ralph Waldo (1914–1994). Author of *Invisible Man* (1952), which chronicles the unnamed protagonist's search for self and community. **Electricity** is a source of illumination and alienation as he struggles to control its power in his life. Science, according to the "Brotherhood," is another reminder of estrangement from a society where the machinations of reason and order dominate.

Shelly Jarrett Bromberg

Emerson, Ralph Waldo (1803–1882). Essayist and poet, the dominant intellectual force in nineteenth-century American speculative thought, both in his early Transcendentalist and subsequent radical empiricist phases. Most studies of Emerson's poetic understanding of science, from Harry Hayden's seminal essay on "Emerson and Science" of 1931 to Lee Rust Brown in *The Emerson Museum* (1997), concentrate on his early work—roughly, *Nature* (1836) through "The Poet" (1844)—which subordinate science to **poetry**. However, in his later writing Emerson shifted his emphasis, viewing the scientist as the true poet and speculating on the "natural history of intellect," as he titled a series of lectures delivered at Harvard University in 1870–1871.

Reference

Robinson, David M. "Fields of Investigation: Emerson and Natural History." *American Literature and Science*. Ed. Robert J. Scholnick. Lexington: UP of Kentucky, 1992. 94–109.

Steven Meyer

Empiricism. The view that all legitimate knowledge is based upon sensory experience of physical phenomena. In positivist accounts of science, empiricism is the bedrock of **scientific method**: The only valid way to test theories and hypotheses is through experiential (observational) data. Empiricism further claims that data speak for themselves—that science proceeds inductively, naturally, and without distortion from observation to explanation. While many scholars maintain that empiricism inaccurately describes how science works, others have called for a revised empiricism that preserves methodological rigor while acknowledging how background assumptions and tacit beliefs shape the observation and analysis of sensory data. Contemporary literary theory ostensibly opposes empiricism: Texts do not speak for themselves but require interpretations; moreover, specific textual meanings depend on the reader/critic. However, literary critic Jules Law sees potential value in certain aspects of empiricism for literary studies.

References

Law, Jules David. *The Rhetoric of Empiricism: Language and Perception from Locke to I.E. Richards*. Ithaca, NY: Cornell UP, 1993.
Longino, Helen. *Science as Social Knowledge: Values and Objectivity in Scientific Inquiry*. Princeton, NJ: Princeton UP, 1992.

Michael A. Bryson

Encyclopédie, ou Dictionnaire raisonné des sciences, des arts, et des métiers. (Encyclopedia, or Descriptive Dictionary of the Sciences, Arts, and Trades), (1751–1772).

Multivolume reference work, coedited by **Denis Diderot** and the mathematician Jean d'Alembert, which epitomized the intellectual ambition, critical spirit, and disciplinary fluidity of the French **Enlightenment**. Designed to change the common way of thinking through its innovative presentation of a vast range of subjects, the *Encyclopédie* was a collaborative project involving experts in the fine **arts**, literature, mathematics, **medicine**, economics, **natural history**, and the physical sciences. It included eleven volumes of plates illustrating everything from anatomy to shipbuilding. These plates, along with the ingenious system of cross-references that Diderot devised to interconnect the *Encyclopédie*'s articles in occasionally subversive ways, played a fundamental role in engaging the work's readers in a particular way of viewing and interpreting the world and of understanding the relationship between knowledge and nature. Despite official disapproval of its calls for religious and sociopolitical reform, the *Encyclopédie* became a bestseller throughout eighteenth-century Europe and served as a major vehicle for disseminating such notions as toleration and **progress** through reason.

References

Anderson, Wilda. "Encyclopedic Topologies." *MLN* 101 4 (1986): 912–29.
Brewer, Daniel. "The Work of the Image: The Plates of the *Encyclopédie*." *Stanford French Review* 8.2–3(1984): 229–44.
Lough, John. *The Encyclopédie*. London: Longman, 1971.

Anne C. Vila

Energy. Defined by **physics** as the ability to do work, and divided into energy being dissipated (kinetic energy) and energy stored (potential energy). The term and concept take their rise in several works of **Aristotle**, especially those with significance for literature and science, respectively, as well as for the study of literature and science. In the *Rhetoric*, Aristotle uses the term *energeia* to characterize metaphor's ability to create "actuality" (*Rhetoric* 1411 b 2) by means of transference, thus making more vivid that which it represents. Henry Fielding writes of energy in his *Covent-Garden Journal* entry for April 11, 1752, citing (and translating) the *Nicomachean Ethics* (1098 b 33) in the process. "Let us leave the Merit of good Actions to others, let us enjoy the Pleasure of them. *In the Energy itself of Virtue* (says Aristotle) *there is great Pleasure.*" (I: 308). In the *Physics*, Aristotle raises the concept in his discussion of "matter" and "form." The latter term refers to the underlying and essential constitutive principle of matter. As his successors have done, Aristotle divides energy into actual (kinetic) and potential. "And finally in every case it may be either (a) a potentiality or (b) an actual energizing" (*Physics* 195 b 16–17).

In its modern, physical acceptation, the term appears first in Thomas Young's *A Course of Lectures on Natural Philosophy and the Mechanical Arts* (1807; 1845), where Young formulates energy as $e = mv^2$, or "the product of the mass or weight of a body, into the square of its velocity" (I: 59). Within the context of the Second Law of **Thermodynamics**, which sets forth the principle of the conservation of energy, the term and concept are taken up by Hermann Helmholtz in an essay of 1847 originally entitled "On the Conservation of Force" ("Über die Erhaltung der Kraft") but retitled "On the Constancy of Energy" ("Über die Constanz der Energie").

Energy is a term and concept so central to the nineteenth and twentieth centuries that it is difficult to conceive of it as being disreputable, or even marginal. Nevertheless, during the Newtonian Revolution (*see* Newtonianism), the term was notable by its absence. As Yehuda Elkana (26) notes, for example, the word *energy* appears nowhere in the original Latin version of Newton's *Principia* (1687), and only once in Andrew Motte's English translation (1729), which renders "tanquam efficaciam quandam" as "a certain power or energy." The reasons for Newton's disavowal of the word and concept are not far to seek: His mechanical model privileges transcendent causation over the immanent alternative, and Newton expresses special suspicion of, and disdain for, such models of immanentism as Aristotle's occult qualities and Spinoza's substance. Newton also privileged the exact, physical sciences over the natural. In turning to such works as **John Ray's** *The Wisdom of God Manifested in the Works of Creation* (1691), one finds no such reticence. Ray argues for the necessity of an immanently acting life-force. "Let Matter be divided into the subtilest Parts imaginable, and these be moved as swiftly as you will, it is but a senseless and stupid Being still, and makes no nearer Approach to Sense, Perception or vital Energy" (49), Ray argues.

Elsewhere, the term and concept became associated with religious enthusiasm.

John Wesley, for example, in a 1775 sermon tellingly titled "Working out Our Own Salvation," defines the principle of energy ("*to energein*") as the vehicle of grace, as "all that power from on high, all that energy which works in us every right disposition" (VI: 508).

The date of Young's use of the term and concept—1807—is not coincidental. While the Newtonian synthesis held sway during much of the eighteenth century, there was little need to talk of inward-working phenomena, let alone to study them. Everything, up to and including the operations of the human mind itself, could be reduced to and discussed in mechanical terms, as David Hartley does in his *Observations on Man* (1749). But that synthesis began to seem at best incomplete, at worst questionable, as the eighteenth century waned. Just as Young called Newtonian **optics** into question in his first Bakerian Lecture (1803), so he called Newtonian mechanics into question some four years later.

In literature, the term and concept came, in the two decades marking the end of the eighteenth century and the beginning of the nineteenth, to denote the inward working powers of the **imagination** and, above all, of poetic genius. In **Blake's** words, from *The Marriage of Heaven and Hell* (1790–1793), "Energy is the only life and is from the Body. . . . Energy is Eternal Delight" (pl. 4).

References

Elkana, Yehuda. *The Discovery of the Conservation of Energy.* Cambridge: Harvard UP, 1974.

Harman, P.M. *Energy, Force, and Matter: The Conceptual Development of Nineteenth-Century Physics.* New York: Cambridge UP, 1982.

Stuart Peterfreund

Engineer(s)/Engineering. Designers and constructors of engines and machines and the study or application of scientific understanding to **technology**. Paradoxically crucial to the advance of civilization, sometimes strikingly indifferent to the civilizing influence of **culture**, but particularly vital in American cultural thought and writing, engineering has played a decisive role in shaping everyday American life. From the harsh criticisms of **Henry David Thoreau** (see "Sounds" in *Walden* [1854]) and **Nathaniel Hawthorne** (most famously in "The Celestial Railroad") to the celebratory **Walt Whitman** ("To a Locomotive in Winter"), American writing encompasses a broad range of responses to this theme.

Contemporary authors have, in keeping with the times, been generally concerned with the issues attending the rise of biogenetic and computer engineering. Fay Weldon's *The Cloning of Joanna May* (1989) wittily confronts certain problems arising from the advent of bioengineering (*see* Biotechnology), while Richard Powers's *Galatea 2.2* (1995) plausibly depicts an encounter with the sort of artificial intelligence (*see* Virtual Reality and Artificial Intelligence) whose realization has long been the goal of **computer science**.

Michael B. McDonald

Enlightenment. Intellectual and reformist movement, widespread in eighteenth-century Europe and America, and characterized by the belief that advances in science, **philosophy**, and the understanding of man and nature would lead to a new morality and sociopolitical order. Although geographically diverse, the Enlightenment was primarily associated with French *philosophes* like **Voltaire** and **Denis Diderot**, whose writings illustrate the productive convergence of literary and scientific discourse that typified the movement.

The term "enlightenment," as defined in 1784 by the German metaphysician Immanuel Kant, had both a private and a public dimension: It denoted, first, an ongoing process of learning to use one's own reason critically, without prejudice or direction from others; and second, an effort by sagacious scholars and statesmen to further the improvement of human nature and society. The Enlightenment had its roots in three conceptual and cultural developments: the Scientific Revolution, which was held to have infused not only science but also ethics, political theory, and literary criticism with a new "geometric" spirit; the empiricist approach to nature and to the mind championed by seventeenth-century English philosophers like **Francis Bacon** and **John Locke**; and finally, the sense of public mission with which contemporary intellectuals had become imbued as a result of such diverse factors as the expanding book trade, the growth of salons, scholarly academies and related institutions, the **popularization** of science, and the emerging ideal of a cosmopolitan Republic of Letters.

As the universally recognized model of reason, science—or rather, **natural philosophy**, the heading under which fields like **physics**, **astronomy**, **chemistry**, and physiology were placed at the time—held enormous symbolic and methodological prestige. Figures like Isaac Newton (*see* Newtonianism) took on heroic proportions in the narratives of scientific achievement that abounded in both scholarly and popular literature, and the notion of uncovering nature's secrets pervaded the Enlightenment's aesthetics and sociomoral **theory** along with its scientific endeavors. The title of "philosopher" was thus claimed by novelists and poets as well as mathematicians, chemists, and naturalists, whereas everything from probability theory to sentimentalism was included among the so-called sciences of man, and debates over the operations of matter and the body had implications extending into the political and religious realms.

Despite its optimistic view of the **progress** humankind could make through reason and toleration, the Enlightenment movement was rife with tensions and contradictions. Although many theologians strove to reconcile the new science with **religion**, the Enlightenment's secularist tendencies often veered toward anticlericalism and materialism, particularly in France. Writers like **Jean-Jacques Rousseau** attacked the very notion that civilization and learning were progressive. Finally, central Enlightenment principles like the existence of a universal form of virtue and **rationality** were challenged by the fascination with "exotic" peoples and with **gender**, areas of difference that deeply preoccupied eighteenth-century **physicians**, moralists, and literary authors.

References

Hankins, Thomas L. *Science and the Enlightenment*. Cambridge: Cambridge UP, 1985.
Outram, Dorinda. *The Enlightenment*. Cambridge: Cambridge UP, 1995.
Porter, Roy, and Mikuláš Teich. *The Enlightenment in National Context*. Cambridge: Cambridge UP, 1981.

Anne C. Vila

Entropy. A term originally introduced by Rudolf Clausius to quantify **energy** that cannot be put to useful work. It was subsequently shown by Ludwig Boltzmann to be a measure of a system's disorder and later related (though not rigorously) by Claude Shannon to **information theory**. According to the Second Law of **Thermodynamics**, the entropy of a closed system tends toward a maximum. Hence entropy has become a ubiquitous metaphor for degeneration, **chaos**, and noise in the (post)modern world. **Thomas Pynchon's** short story "Entropy" (1959) and novels *The Crying of Lot 49* (1965) and *Gravity's Rainbow* (1973) are notable illustrations.

Jay A. Labinger

Environment. One's surroundings, natural and otherwise, including one's perception of those surroundings. While ecology studies the interaction between organisms and their environment, Literature and the Environment studies the literature that treats the interaction between organisms and their environment. Though the term *ecology* dates only to the late nineteenth century, the study of nature is as old as human history. Attempts to understand and explain nature and humanity's role within it have taken many forms, including scientific investigation, legal analysis, and artistic expression. Out of these investigations have sprung myths that have permeated the **culture**, creating multiple ways of seeing the world and humanity (throughout this entry, I adopt Barthes's definition of the term myth, using it to mean not a superstitious or erroneous belief but rather an accepted story explaining the workings of the world). Often these views clash, generating social upheaval and deep-seated conflicts in humanity's relationship with the natural world. Those myths, conflicts, and repercussions form the focus of environmental literature as well as of Literature and the Environment.

This entry attempts to cover some of the most important components of Literature and the Environment. It will first examine the concept of myth and its importance to the larger field of Cultural Studies, of which Literature and the Environment forms a part. Next, we will look at **ecocriticism**, the critical apparatus used in "green cultural studies." The third section discusses **nature writing** as a genre and attempts to situate it within the field of Literature and the Environment.

There are, Roland Barthes argues, three ways of reading myth (129). If I see a picture of the space shuttle and decide it is a symbol of American ingenuity and technological supremacy, then I am acting as a producer. If I believe the shuttle does not just represent American technological supremacy but *is* that supremacy, then I am a reader, accepting without question the union of symbol and signifier. Lastly, if I decipher the work of the producer by divining that a human agent decided what the shuttle symbolized in order to further a specific agenda, then I am a mythologist. Throughout history and literature, examples of the first two ways of reading myth abound. The study of Literature and the Environment provides a scholarly apparatus through which to attempt the third.

Of course, Literature and the Environment does not own the franchise for the study of myth nor of culture. All intellectual pursuits share the task. Societies rely on common myths; we must assume that we share a similar world in order for language and its embedded metaphors to function. Without an agreement as to shared experience, human interaction could not occur. Following Kant, Ludwig von Bertalanffy suggests that such "moral concepts as Freedom, God, Immortality, and Human Dignity are fictions but nonetheless of immense importance: for we have to behave 'as if' they were reality. . . . [T]he myths of tradition are fictions based on the mythical experiences of man and later invested in historical narratives" (67). Accepting this premise can prove terrifying. Without the assurance of a common **reality**, societal **entropy** hovers disturbingly nearby. Attaching **objectivity** and incontrovertibility to a given web of myths removes the burden of subjectivity from the need to obey social norms. In Neil Evernden's view, this ruse of objectivity is all but inevitable: "[T]he tendency to practice the subterfuge of mythmaking is very understandable. In practical terms, it may very well afford us some measure of comfort by legitimating a belief in the certainty of at least a few features of existence and a few behavioral norms" (29–30).

Shared myths inevitably mutate as societies change. The concepts of God and immortality have undergone radical revisions in the last 150 years. In the United States many of our common myths revolve around the frontier and the absence of history. They form crucial components of the mixed bag of fictions that together form the American Dream. Circumstances have changed since the Dream's inception, however, partially due to the repercussions of these myths and partially because societies, like ecosystems, must evolve or die.

The focus on ecosystems and humanity's role within them distinguishes Literature and the Environment from other genres of literary criticism. It provides a critical apparatus, ecocriticism, with which to interpret culture and literature and to situate the human condition within the natural world. Perhaps because their field of study is so mutable and the discipline so new, ecocritics often differ on how to define what they do. Some jokingly refer to themselves as "compoststructuralists" in an attempt to differentiate ecocriticism from the other critical schools that emerged from the 1980s and 1990s. Broadly defined, ecocriticism adds place to the categories of **race**, class, and **gender** commonly used in literary analysis. For some, that means looking at how texts represent the physical world; for others, at how literature raises moral questions about human interactions with nature.

Ecocriticism's indefinability stems from its focus on three of the most flexible terms in language: literature, environment, and nature. *Literature* has been a contested term for some time, as scholars have drawn and redrawn the boundaries of the canon and argued over what makes a piece of writing "literature." *Environment*, briefly defined as one's surroundings, is inherently subjective, constantly shifting and calling into question the boundaries of self. *Nature*, meanwhile, may have more definitions than any other word in the language, ranging from "a creative and controlling force in the universe" to "the inherent character or basic constitution of a person or thing" (*Merriam Webster's Collegiate Dictionary*, 10th ed.).

Nature's multifarious meanings raise serious epistemological questions. **C.S. Lewis** argues that there exists a fundamental paradox at the root of the human relationship with nature, one that is most clearly displayed in the competing visions of the law of nature. On the one hand, natural law decrees what is good and enjoins what is bad. Hence, a law of nature is "conceived as an absolute moral standard against which the laws of all nations must be judged and to which they ought to conform." On the other hand, a law of nature could decide that which is "least specifically human." By this reasoning, natural law dictates "the way in which non-human agents behave until they are trained not to" (61–62). In other words, humans should obey the laws of nature until they make better ones. The precivilized state during which natural law governs would then form the Hobbesian "state of nature." The act of forming a civilization would overthrow natural law, turning nature into a force to be conquered and tamed.

The schism created by the opposing visions of natural law points to a fracture at the base of our relationship with nature. That division infuses every facet of human culture. Depending on which view one subscribes to, the primary values or beliefs underlying the state's authority can seem fundamentally inconsistent. That realization leads to a loss of faith in the central authority causing what Habermas has called a "legitimation crisis." Legitimation crises are particularly problematic for modern societies because of their reliance on reason rather than **religion** and tradition. Because the dispute over the role of natural law and humanity's relationship with its surroundings dates from the dawn of human civilization, it follows that a large segment of the population resides in perpetual legitimation crisis. Ecocritics focus on this uncertain relationship with our surroundings and with the central authority that is a product of that relationship, using it as a guiding principle in the study of culture. In this sense, Literature and the Environment is much less about literature and the environment than it is about the forces that create them.

Every work of literature both reflects and helps create the forces that affect our relationship with our surroundings. Every word is environmental and, for that reason, contestable. For example, we take the term "pollution" to refer to an environmental impurity or contamination. Yet attempts to categorize and quantify the contaminants in our surroundings only distract from moral issues underlying the data. Acceptable standards as to parts per billion of a given material constantly change. That is because exposure levels are merely a symptom of the larger disagreement between environmentalists and industrialists over what constitutes an adequate standard of living. Environmentalists may advocate a small-scale, cooperative society that stresses sustainability over growth. Industrialists might reply that lost jobs, food shortages, and a much less comfortable lifestyle are incompatible with the human need to improve ourselves. As Evernden notes, "To the environmentalists, what is at risk is the very possibility of leading a good life. To the industrialists, what is at risk is the very possibility of leading a good life. The debate, it appears, is actually about what *constitutes a good life*" (5).

The pollution issue is morally rooted because the factions' competing visions on the right way to live derive from their position on obedience to the laws of nature. The environmentalists believe that the laws of nature should and do dictate the highest good, whereas the industrialists maintain that humanity has transcended the state of nature and can and should make its own laws. Fealty to one or the other view concerning natural law determines the "morality" of one's actions.

While the debate over natural law is ontological, its effects are ecological. In the American West, for example, the idea that humans can and should conquer nature inspired a century and a half of "reclamation," as Americans sought to remake the desert into an Eden. Wishful thinking, coupled with a desire to remake the **landscape** in the image of human needs and wants, led, during the settling of the West, to what Henry Nash Smith labeled the "Myth of the Garden." "Rain," nineteenth-century proponents insisted, would "follow the plow." Allegedly, one needed but to till the soil for rain to fall commensurate with the tiller's needs. This notion eventually fell into disfavor, but not before many settlers homesteaded the arid region, lured by the vision of hydrological abundance. That which was not already Edenic would soon become so through human ingenuity and American perspicacity.

Imagining the land as virgin and Edenic ignored the geographical realities of a large indigenous population and a varied terrain and climate. Westward expansion, rather than puncturing these myths, fueled an extraordinary campaign to remake the land in the image of that mythic landscape. **Emerson** counseled "action proportioned to nature"; when nature did not yield freely, human industry should refashion it to better suit human needs. This transformative relationship with nature harmonized, in Emerson's view, with nature's status as the ultimate commodity. Humans fulfill their destiny through working the land and forcing ever-greater harvests. In an essay in *Nature* aptly entitled "Commodity," Emerson holds that nature has no greater purpose than to serve "Man." And Man has no greater purpose than to work the land and take his place in the productive cycle: "A man is fed not that he may be fed but that he may work"

(26). The policies born of them led, unsurprisingly, to ecosystemic catastrophe, the full implications of which are yet to be felt.

Emerson's views were both a product of the American relationship with the land as well as a shaping force upon it. So it is with all literary endeavors in all parts of the world. The creative act simultaneously reflects the culture at work on the artist and the artist at work on the culture. The ecocritic begins with the fundamental assumption that there is an "extratextual" reality that affects human beings and their artifacts and that human beings and their artifacts in turn impact that reality.

But Literature and the Environment is not just a synonym for **ecocriticism**. It also includes the rich body of literature that is often called "nature writing." Nature writing as a genre also defies easy categorization. It has generally been conceived as variations of the nonfiction **essay** popularized by **Thoreau**—a blend of scientific observation and self-analysis. Recently, though, its boundaries have begun to expand. To the class of literature that includes **Charles Darwin's** journals of discovery, **John Muir's** paeans to the Sierra, and **John McPhee's** accounts of the interworkings of people, places, and things, we might add **John Updike's** tales of the city and John Cheever's stories of suburban life. Even with the trend toward inclusiveness in nature writing, though, the popular notion of it remains the proto-Thoreauvian investigation of place.

Annie Dillard sent ripples through the nature writing and scholarly community when she admitted that she had made up a number of the incidents and descriptions in her classic work *Pilgrim at Tinker Creek*. This revelation left many feeling betrayed. Yet all Dillard had done was what any good writer does—construct a literary environment through language. Nevertheless, some of her public felt deceived and wondered what, if any, literature they could "trust."

The issue is not an easy one. Does a nonfiction, descriptive writer have a higher duty to **truth** and accurate reporting than other writers? Should this perceived duty limit an author's literary license? If so, what standard of accuracy should they aspire to meet? Nature writing must now struggle with the unreliable narrator, an issue that has dogged **fiction** since the Modernist era. Yet the issue is not new within nature writing either. Even Thoreau, the godfather of nature writing, compressed two years of living at Walden into one and conveniently left out of his solipsistic ramblings that he dined at his mother's house every Saturday. His selective omissions have not disturbed *Walden*'s place in the literary pantheon.

All descriptive writing attempts to recreate an experience already passed. **Time**, a crucial component of all experience, has marched on; the writer can only try to invoke through words that which can never come again. According to Lyotard, "In description, writing tries to meet the challenge of being equal to its momentary absence" (188). Furthermore, since language exists only through metaphor (words merely evoke; they are not themselves the thing described), their "truth" must always be once removed from experience.

Given these limitations, it seems unwise to set a standard of accuracy for any type of **art,** particularly art that seeks to convey personal experience. Yet if not truth, what should we expect of nature writing, or indeed of any writing that aspires to convey an accurate sense of the world? Seamus Heaney explored this question in his speech accepting the 1995 Nobel Prize for Literature. He first cites Archibald MacLeish's maxim that "A poem should be equal to:/not true." But then he acknowledges that

There are times when a deeper need enters, when we want the poem to be not only pleasurably right but compellingly wise, not only a surprising variation played upon the world but a retuning of the world itself. We want the surprise to be transitive, like the impatient thump which unexpectedly restores the picture to the television set. . . . We want what the woman wanted in the prison queues in Leningrad, as she stood there blue with cold and whispering for fear, enduring terror of Stalin's regime and asking the poet Anna Akhmatova if she could describe it all, if her art could be equal to it.

The misery of the woman in Leningrad demands a truth the writer cannot reach. Even as she asks the question, she knows that no words can ever convey her bone-wrenching cold. Like Lyotard, she understands that poems can only act as the staging ground for the power of language. Language cannot capture the human experience; it can only try to do it justice.

That attempt to capture the human experience is quintessentially the task of literature. Because the human experience takes place in nature, all literature is, in a sense, nature writing. The controversy over truth in nature writing is thus a question for Literature and the Environment. It deals with the human experience and the levels of veracity in relating humans interacting with their surroundings.

The field of Literature and the Environment looks to distill cultural truths from the artifacts of human interaction with other humans and with their surroundings. Those truths, if they exist, lie less on the surface of the written word than in the aggregate of the literary experience—the writing, reading, and dissemination of the work. Literature and the Environment offers a set of tools with which to investigate all three.

References

Barthes, Roland. *Mythologies.* Trans. Jonathan Cape. New York: Hill and Wang, 1982.

Bertalanffy, Ludwig von. *Perspectives on General System Theory.* Ed. Edgar Taschdjian. New York: George Braziller, 1975.

Emerson, Ralph Waldo. *Selections from Ralph Waldo Emerson.* Ed. Stephen E. Whicher. Boston: Houghton Mifflin, 1957.

Evernden, Neil. *The Social Creation of Nature.* Baltimore: Johns Hopkins UP, 1992.

Lewis, C.S. *Studies in Words.* 2nd ed. Cambridge: Cambridge UP, 1967.

Lyotard, Jean-François. *The Inhuman: Reflections on Time.* Trans. Geoffrey Bennington and Rachel Bowlby. Stanford: Stanford UP, 1991.

Smith, Henry Nash. *Virgin Land: The American West as Symbol and Myth.* Cambridge, MA: Harvard UP, 1978.

<http://www.nobel.se/literature/laureates/1995/heaney-lecture.html>.

David N. Cassuto

Epistemology. The term given in **philosophy** to the field of discourses about knowledge. The key concerns are: What constitutes knowledge? How is it derived? Why is it relevant? Where are its limits? In sciences, epistemological concerns focus on how knowledge is distilled from nature. Raw knowledge is derived through experimentation and is shaped by theories, which in turn are checked by further experiments (*see* Experimental Science). Laws are given the highest density of epistemic content. In literature, the most commonly identified epistemic content is knowledge about human nature and aspects of the world. Yet these classical views of the epistemologies of science and literature have been shown to rest on highly problematic foundations. It is increasingly recognized that truths do not stand objectively on their own but are intimately linked to theories, ideologies, **cultures**, and interpretations, all of which blur any possible objective view.

In science, the central debate is to what extent laws are about nature itself. **Albert Einstein** exemplifies the belief in an absolute epistemology attainable through science. Ilya Prigogine describes a more subjective and fluid epistemology at ease with uncertainty even about its own nature. Jacques Derrida has stressed that epistemology itself, as a discourse, is of a literary nature and as such is subject to the play of creation. **Annie Dillard** points out that when it comes to understanding, all is **fiction**, and **art** can model possible relationships among ideas and materials. If literature seems more epistemologically chaotic, it is perhaps because it does not exclude any point of view.

Luis O. Arata

Essay. A literary text for purposes of communication between writer and reader, today broadly defined as nonfictional, expository prose generally of a length readable in one sitting. The essayist "essays" or attempts to instruct, entertain, and persuade the reader through his or her observations, perceptions, opinions, and feelings.

As a literary form, the essay has long been a product of the doubt and questions surrounding the structuring or encoding of literary conventions and expectations into a code for **classification**. The interpretation of any text involves a hermeneutic decoding process that brings the text into a context of comprehensibility, a literary common ground or forum of relationships and affinities. When such conventions and expectations undergo deviation and dislocation through sociohistorical forces, the traditional genre system—for example, the classical trio of epic, **drama**, and lyric—expands to include new literary texts. The essay with its versatility and chameleon existence at the borders of the more traditional literary forms was a product of such an expansion, an expansion that arose out of the social and historical reappraisal of **culture** and literature.

The essayistic content typically derives (1) from the author's personal experiences, (2) from the author's cultural experiences, or (3) from other writers or artists, resulting in one of the most popular types of essay, the literary biography. Significantly, the essay seldom speaks of new topics but rather of old topics in a new manner. What is more, as a particular thing, event, or experience, the content of the essay serves mainly to carry the idea, theme, or meaning within the social, historical, and cultural context.

So varied and versatile is the essay's subject matter and its thematic communication and so great is its degree of polycentricity that it often has been lost among or confused with closely related forms—memoir, letter, oration, dialogue, meditation, manifesto, preface, review, and so on. Since all the above doubtless demonstrate essayistic qualities, the reader may confuse all or part of them with an essay, making the task of delineation all the more difficult. As a hybrid form, the essay has conventionally appropriated sundry methodologies and structures from other literary forms that have traditionally served as stylistic or thematic sources, examples, or models for the essay. What is more, the essay does not belong to the belles lettres, a mode that organizes language into a mimetic mirror held up to **reality**, but rather to expository prose, a rhetorical, didactic, and transparent lens that directly examines, "exposes," and comments upon reality.

Paradoxically, the methodology and structure of the essay are often said to be characterized by a lack of methodology and structure, that is, by free association, digression, multiperspectivity, subjectivity, and open-endedness. The essay is difficult to systematize, due to its own antisystematism. Yet these "artistic" qualities are balanced by objective experiment and empirical observation, as well as by deductive, analytical methodology. Like an empirical treatise, the essay may proceed from an appraisal of a question, problem, or dilemma to suggestions and hypotheses and subsequently move on to criteria in order to determine the truth of such hypotheses. But the essay organizes this inductive strategy within a personal and cultural context, not in the controlled, objective, and verifiable context of the laboratory. **Art** and the artistic—intuitive, associative, autonomous subjective, fragmented, open-ended—and science and the scientific—abstract, verifiable objective, systematic, complete, conclusive—constitute the binary opposition that continues to function as the foremost paradigm by which the essay is oriented theoretically.

As mediator between art and science, the essay may well be understood as an epistemological bridge between nature or myth and culture or history, that is, between the two main cognitive modes that began to split apart during the Renaissance and had completed their division by the time of the **Enlightenment**. Apart from periodic "romantic" revivals or attempts at returning to a monistic paradigm, modern thought and society demonstrate a chasm larger than ever between "hard" science and "soft, playful" art.

Like science, the essay does not deploy **fiction** or fable to mediate between the author's perception and articulation of reality. Like science, it describes, reports, and analyzes reality. Unlike science, however, and like art, the essay is limited neither to accuracy of observation nor rigor of analysis. Whereas science adamantly separates the experience of reality from the analyzing and knowing of that reality, the essay's subjective and imaginative consciousness relates reality, experience, and knowledge. By mediating among subjective experience, objective reality, and theoretical knowledge, the author's and the reader's **imagination**, which remains both critical and fantastic, frees the discourse to the realization of "what might have been" and "what might yet be." The essay's ambivalent questioning of reality, knowledge, and experience may serve to lend meaningful truth to scientific fact.

The confusion of methodology and structure, and of content, theme, and function, lies at the base of the essay's very identity and ontology. But amid this confusion, one overlying phenomenological as well as historical typology adheres. All essays may be readily divided into two major subclasses, the formal, or critical, essay and the informal, or occasional, essay.

The formal essay shares a border with the philosophical, scientific, or historical treatise. Once the major medium of Scholasticism, the treatise allows, indeed requires, the author to retreat behind the principles of rationalism and **objectivity**. Starting from steadfast premises and proceeding logically through experiment and analysis, the "truths" of the treatise are presented as unquestioned conclusions of the system. Significantly, matters of art, aesthetics, and style, such as authorial subjectivity, elegance, caprice, and wit, are unwelcome here as factors that may undermine the treatise's objectivity and scientific qualities.

Although also impersonal and didactic, the formal essay distinguishes itself from the treatise to the extent that it is neither exhaustive in content nor rigorously critical or scientific in method. Its beginnings may be found in the writings of **Francis Bacon**, whose *Essays. Counsels, Civil and Moral* (1597) reveal a high degree of affinity to the treatise. As instructions for the political life, they typically articulate a theme or thesis representing Bacon's prescription for political action.

In contrast to the formal essay the informal essay shares common ground with imaginative or fictional literature. Entertaining, conversational, even whimsical, it nevertheless remains an essay, because in its attempt to speak the truth, it utilizes the lens of direct communication between author and reader and not the mimetic mirror of a fictional world.

Because the informal essay lays no claims to being all-inclusive, exhaustive, definitive, or inventive, it is privileged to begin and end its discourse on what it will, when it will. Reminiscent of an intellectual walk, the informal essay emphasizes the question over the answer, the skeptical attitude over the conclusion, the conversation over the sermon. Entertainment and persuasion play as large a role in the essay's intention as instruction.

The French nobleman **Michel de Montaigne**, with his *Essais* (1580, 1588), remains the undisputed father of the informal essay. The classical, contemporary, and historical culture from which Montaigne chose his subjects was organized under the sole principle of Montaigne's skeptical and individual understanding of the human condition, which, for him, began and ended with himself. Montaigne's essays are thus an endless conversation with Montaigne about the world in order to search out the truths of that world. Neither cynic nor polemicist but moralist, Montaigne is more content to observe and witness than judge and prescribe.

As the first true essayist, Montaigne received all earlier literary forms from classical and medieval sources that demonstrated essayistic qualities and may be understood as essays *avant la lettre*—dialogue, epistle, oration, confession, treatise, sermon memoir, meditation, and so on—and channeled their essayistic influence into the new genre of the essay. Central to Montaigne's new literary form is its conversational quality, its intimacy, and sincerity. The writer Montaigne and the reader of his essays are both operative principles around whom Montaigne structured his observations, quotations, anecdote, and metaphors. The novelty of Montaigne's awareness of his readership and its relevance for what and how he wrote continued and grew during the **Enlightenment**, the rise of the bourgeois class and the concurrent flourishing of the journals, the literary monthlies, and the moral weeklies, particularly in England, France, and Germany. The eighteenth-century journal essay or article essay that resulted from the bourgeois apotheosis of enlightenment and education offered a pleasing and inviting conversation that involved the moral, practical, and cultural instruction and refinement of the reading public, the private and domestic bourgeoisie.

Nineteenth-century **Romanticism** and realism and twentieth-century **modernism** and postmodernism all have employed the general form of the essay in a specific fashion and for their respective purposes. But whatever the changes the essay has undergone from Montaigne to the present, it remains an essay on the basis of its essayistic methodology, its infinite themes of the human condition, its function of enlightenment, diversion, and persuasion, and the writer's consciousness of the reader, as well as the reader's awareness of the writer.

References

Butryn, Alex J., ed. *Essays on the Essay*. Athens: U of Georgia P, 1985.
Lopate, Phillip, ed. *Art of the Personal Essay*. New York: Andover, 1994.

Ralph W. Buechler

Essay, Popular Scientific. A specialized form of nonfiction prose. The phrase implies that "scientific essay" is normative, its content meant for professional communication and not for popular, even trivial, education and amusement. Nonetheless, the range of sites in which **popularizations** of scientific knowledge appear—from mass market paperbacks to the publications of university presses and learned societies—urges caution in accepting these connotations. "Popular" does not differentiate a professional few who produce scientific knowledge from a largely unsophisticated audience who consume that knowledge in debased form. Such a distinction trivializes the reader of science popularizations as much as it demeans their authors. Viewed from rhetorical, historical, and social perspectives, the popular scientific essay is anything but intellectually jejune. Popular scientific writing is rhetorically complex, enjoys a rich history, and provides a multitude of insights into the relationship between science and society.

Popular scientific essays appear in a variety of media addressed to different audiences. There are science popularizers such as **Stephen Jay Gould**, **Carl Sagan**, and **Stephen W. Hawking**, whose book-length treatments of scientific topics are perennial best-sellers. News reports in scientific journals such as *Science, Natural History, Scientific American*, and *Nature* often serve to bring new scientific topics to a wider *scientific* as well as popular audience. The publications of scientific organizations, such as *Physics Today* (from the American Institute of Physics) or *Chemical and Engineering News* (from the American Chemical Society), also disseminate scientific knowledge from one scientific field to wider audiences of nonspecialist scientists and engineers. Even mass market scientific media such as *Science News* or *Discover* are not solely intended for a supposedly trivial, popular audience. It is perhaps only in daily newspapers, radio broadcasts, or **television** programming that scientific topics are subjected to extensive trivialization, but even here, television programs such as *Nova* and cable channels such as *The Discovery Channel* often tackle scientific topics with great care.

That a scientific topic is treated in some venue other than a scientific journal, monograph, or academic conference does not make it intellectually suspect. Because many popularizations of scientific knowledge have as much interest for the practicing scientist as for the nonspecialist reader, it is better to think of popular scientific writing as a rhetorically flexible category, within which there are degrees of concern about formalization, technical precision, and controvertibility of arguments. Publications such as *Discover* and *Science News* may treat scientific truths as incontrovertible, though the same publications do not often render their descriptions of scientific knowledge in highly formalized or precise language. By contrast, a review article intended for nonspecialists, such as might appear in *Physics Today*, often displays a high degree of controvertibility of arguments because the specialists reviewing a field often elaborate upon and justify their conclusions, yet such review articles also exhibit highly formalized and precise language. In terms of **Bruno Latour** and Steve Woolgar's useful five-part classification of statement types, in other words, popularized treatments of scientific knowledge are no more likely to make their claims in highly unmodalized ways (type four or five statements) than in relatively more qualified or even speculative language (type one, two, or three statements).

Indeed, given the variety of ways in which specialized scientific knowledge is conveyed to diverse audiences, it makes far more sense to think of popular scientific writing as something other than an act of translation, with popularizations displaying inadequate technical precision and conceptual difficulty. Like other kinds of writing, popular scientific writing establishes a social relationship between the writer and the audience. In fact, popular scientific writing may very well be the site where **C.P. Snow's two cultures** of literature and science meet most effectively. Regardless of its connotations, in other words, "popular" does not categorically identify a "professional" science that is, or ought to be, divorced from the larger **culture**. Such a view of scientific knowledge is neither consistent with the history of scientific discourse, nor does it adequately account for the prominence of scientific popularizations in recent years.

In fact, it is possible to regard the rhetorical tradition begun by **Robert Boyle**, in which writers of professional scientific discourse self-consciously separate themselves from the social world, as historically aberrant. Consider **Lucretius's** efforts to displace Stoic fatalism with Epicurean atomism, or **Galileo's** defense of **Copernicus's empiricism** against scholastic pronouncements about celestial motion, or **Thomas Henry Huxley's** spirited advocacy of **Charles Darwin's theory** of natural selection against nineteenth-century biblical **creationism**, or even Stephen Jay Gould's debunking of the ways mistaken views of evolution continue to foster racism, sexism, and a foolish regard for progress as the pattern of history. All of these writers preeminently illustrate the historically rich tradition of the scientist whose discourse intentionally links scientific with social knowledge. What is sometimes dismissed as merely "popular" scientific writing extends this Lucretian tradition. An intelligent appreciation of popular scientific writing thus calls for relating it to the ideologies, values, habits of thought, and linguistic and rhetorical practices that define a culture. Popular scientific writing is yet one further expression of the rhizomatic networks that link scientific and social knowledge within the culture in which they circulate. Popular scientific writing is precisely the site, in other words, where the social construction of scientific knowledge is most transparent, where knowledge expressed in one site reexpresses knowledge in another.

The resurgence of a dogmatic Baconianism in recent years finds little value in paying attention to the networks that connect popular and professional scientific discourse with the larger social world. Even so, gifted researchers from a variety of scientific fields persist in their desire to open the borders that presumably separate their disciplines from each other and from society and culture. Understood in this way, popular scientific writing not only contributes to reducing the levels of scientific illiteracy that unfortunately continue to affect modern society, but it also functions to bridge gaps between science and culture that might never have opened had the historically recent tradition of professional scientific discourse remained as deeply committed to the social world as it has to describing the natural one.

References

Latour, Bruno, and Steve Woolgar. *Laboratory Life: The Construction of Scientific Facts*. 2nd ed. Princeton, NJ: Princeton UP, 1986.

McRae, Murdo William, ed. *The Literature of Science: Perspectives on Popular Scientific Writing*. Athens: U of Georgia P, 1993.

Shinn, Terry, and Richard Whitley, eds. *Expository Science: Forms and Functions of Popularisation*. Dordrecht: Reidel, 1985.

Murdo William McRae

Evolutionary Theory. Any **theory** designed to explain transformations over **time** but now predominantly identified with the Darwinian theory of biological adaptation by means of natural selection. In *The Origin of Species,* **Charles Darwin** rejected the commonly accepted idea that all species were created in their current form. Before Darwin, the main **hypothesis** put forth to explain the transformation of species over time was Lamarck's theory that organisms have an inherent tendency to progress and that they can inherit characteristics their ancestors acquired by learning. Darwin himself regarded the inheritance of acquired characteristics as a possible contributory force in evolution, but he argued that the primary **mechanism** was natural selection: the differential survival and reproductive success of heritable variations within organisms.

Darwin supported his theory with evidence from **paleontology**, embryology, comparative anatomy, and the geographical distribution of species. **Mendel's** work on **genetics** was not available to Darwin, and the one largest gap in Darwin's theory was the absence of any specific mechanism of inheritance. Because of this gap, the theory of natural selection remained controversial until it was integrated with genetics in the 1930s and 1940s. Since this "modern synthesis," Darwin's theory of evolution has been the central coordinating principle in **biology**. The idea of descent with modification provides a historical rationale for the relations among species, and the idea of adaptive change provides a causal explanation for the development of all complex functional structures within organisms. The discovery of DNA in 1953 extended the total explanatory network of **Darwinism** to molecular biology, hence to **chemistry**, and through chemistry to **physics**. At present, then, Darwin's theory of evolution is a central link in the chain of causal relations that connects the physical and biological sciences and that gives evidence for the unity both of the natural order and of scientific knowledge.

In *The Descent of Man, and Selection in Relation to Sex* (1871), Darwin argued that human behavior is necessarily rooted in biological predispositions, and he thus extended the explanatory scope of his theory to include psychology (*see* Anthropology/Psychology/Sociology) and the sciences of social organization. In the last two decades of the nineteenth century and the first decade of the twentieth, many social thinkers and literary artists assimilated the Darwinian vision, particularly the social Darwinists (*see* Social Darwinism) and the naturalists. In the second decade of the twentieth century, an anti-Darwinian counterrevolution took place in the social sciences. Social theorists such as Émile Durkheim, Franz Boas, Alfred Kroeber, and Robert Lowie propounded the doctrine that **culture** is an autonomous agency that produces all significant mental and emotional content in human experience. In this view, innate, evolved characteristics exercise no constraining influence on culture. The idea of cultural autonomy became the cornerstone of standard social science, and until the 1970s, Darwinism essentially disappeared from professional social theory.

In the 1960s, ethologists writing for a popular audience analyzed human behavior in terms of animal instincts, but the first major professional challenge to the idea of cultural autonomy appeared in 1975, with the publication of **Edward O. Wilson's** *Sociobiology: The New Synthesis*. Wilson offered a comprehensive analysis of the social behavior of animals within the explanatory framework of natural selection. His final chapter, extending this analysis to the human animal, provoked a series of violent rebuttals, but it also inaugurated a line of research that has since grown at ever-accelerating rates. Evolutionary thinking in the social sciences and the humanities is still vehemently contested, but over the past two decades, Darwinism has made major advances in **philosophy, psychology, anthropology**, political science, linguistics, aesthetics and literary theory.

Four main types of evidence are used to illuminate the biological foundations of human behavior: theoretical biology; the continuity between human behavior and that of other animals, especially primates; the study of human universals or the comparative analysis of similar behavioral patterns in diverse cultures; and the analysis of specific biological mechanisms—genetic, neurological, endocrinological, and physiological. Disciplines that have contributed to these interlocking forms of evidence include **sociobiology**, ethology, anthropology, evolutionary psychology, physiology, the **neurosciences**, and behavioral genetics. Sociobiology concerns itself with the way in which fitness maximization or differential reproductive success regulates all processes of evolutionary adaptation, and it thus provides the largest theoretical framework for these disciplines. Ethologists offer a zoological perspective on human behavior. Evolutionary psychologists and anthropologists identify human universals and seek to correlate them with evolved cognitive structures—sensory, emotional, and intellective. Evolutionary psychology in the broadest sense encompasses cognitive psychology, linguistics, and the study of personality and emotion. Physiology and neuroscience provide information on the specific mechanisms that regulate behavior, and behavioral genetics seeks to identify the genetic basis of such mechanisms.

Antagonism to Darwinism in the social sciences and the humanities has three main sources: political, disciplinary, and spiritual. The belief in cultural autonomy is closely associated with the impulse toward liberal political reform. The idea that social order is constrained by innate biological characteristics seems to limit the range of possible reform and to justify distributions of power widely regarded as unjust. In the social sciences and the humanities, a commitment to liberal social reform has joined hands with the desire to establish fields of study as distinct disciplines, each with its own autonomous regulative principles. Disciplinary motives of this sort animated much of the formalist theory associated with the New Critics and with the totalizing system of literary organization put forth by Northrop Frye in *The Anatomy of Criticism*. Since the poststructuralist (*see* Poststructuralism) revolution of the 1970s, the claims that language and culture have primary causative power have become the commonly accepted creed of academic literary scholars. The spiritual antagonism to biological **determinism**, in philosophy and in literary study, has close affinities with all idealist philosophy in the Western cultural tradition—with **Plato**, Christianity,

Romantic transcendentalism, and Kantian and Husserlian idealism. Both New Criticism and Frye's archetypal myth criticism have spiritualist and antinaturalist associations. Acolytes of deconstruction invert the rhetoric of idealist philosophy but remain within its frame of philosophical reference.

The imaginative impact of Darwinian biology on the literary mind extends from the broadest metaphysical concerns through all the problems of human nature and human social identity. Many Victorian theorists of culture formulated teleological conceptions of cultural progress that derive from pre-Darwinian historicist traditions. (**Matthew Arnold** is representative in this respect.) But even before *The Origin of Species,* **Tennyson** had already assimilated enough information from geology and paleontology to realize that a naturalistic universe undermined any providential conception of nature. Literary writers who have most fully registered the metaphysical implications of the Darwinian vision include **Joseph Conrad, H.G. Wells, Jack London,** Richard Jeffries, **Thomas Hardy,** and **Aldous Huxley.** On the level of human motivation and human social interaction, Darwinism directs attention both to the elemental, animal basis of human behavior and to the intimate relation between organism and environment. Naturalistic **fiction** includes clinically detached "experiments" in behavioral analysis, like those of **Émile Zola, Frank Norris,** and Henrik Ibsen, richly evocative depictions of animal sensation, like those in Hardy, Jeffries, Guy de Maupassant, and D.H. Lawrence, and fantastic evocations of the beast within, like those in **Stevenson's** *Dr. Jekyll and Mr. Hyde* and Wells's *The Island of Dr. Moreau.* As a distinct movement, **naturalism** reached its apex in the later nineteenth century, but as a broad set of ideas, attitudes, and literary techniques, it has diffused itself throughout the literature of the twentieth century.

The philosophers, speculative psychologists, and literary critics and theorists who have been most heavily influenced by the Darwinian vision include **Herbert Spencer, T.H. Huxley,** Hippolyte Taine, Leslie Stephen, Friedrich Nietzsche, **William James, Sigmund Freud, Carl Jung, Karl Popper,** and Konrad Lorenz.

References

Barkow, Jerome H., Leda Cosmides, and John Tooby, eds. *The Adapted Mind: Evolutionary Psychology and the Generation of Culture.* New York: Oxford UP, 1992.

Carroll, Joseph. *Evolution and Literary Theory.* Columbia: U of Missouri P, 1995.

Degler, Carl N. *In Search of Human Nature: The Decline and Revival of Darwinism in American Social Thought.* New York: Oxford UP, 1991.

Mithen, Steven. *The Prehistory of the Mind: The Cognitive Origins of Art, Religion, and Science.* London: Thames and Hudson, 1996.

Wilson, Edward O. *On Human Nature.* Cambridge: Harvard UP, 1978.

Joseph Carroll

Experimental Novel. An extended prose narrative characterized by formal or thematic experimentation. Novels create a fictional yet coherent context, with the effect of an open and possibly infinite world. The name "novel," with its connotations of "news" or "unprecedented occurrences," already defines itself as experimental. The possibilities for representing everyday life in detail lead to comparisons between fictional worlds and the objectivity demanded by science, while the flexibility of the form allows the novel to be an agent of inquiry and even scientific change, as in the case of **William Gibson's** invention of **cyberspace** in *Neuromancer* (1983). Novel-length prose works include Roman satires and medieval chivalric romances, but the novel form is typically dated from **Miguel de Cervantes's** *Don Quixote* (1604). **Daniel Defoe** (1660?–1731), Samuel Richardson (1689–1761), Henry Fielding (1707–1754), and **Laurence Sterne** (1713–1768) made England the center of the novel's rise and development. The range of their works—including mock biography, epistolary, and epic—indicates that the form of the novel was experimental from the first. Experimental novelists frequently attempt to stylistically recreate scientific or technical processes, such as the use of **cybernetics** and **film** in **Thomas Pynchon's** *Gravity's Rainbow* (1973). The theory set out in **Émile Zola's** *The Experimental Novel* (1880) draws an analogy between writing and the experimental methods of physiognomic observation and testing in **medicine**. More recently, nonlinear electronic **hypertext** realizes and expands the fragmented and playful postmodern novel. It remains debatable whether novelistic experimentation must necessarily thematize science, but the imaginative expansion or alteration of narrative possibility inevitably challenges the limits of science.

Charles A. Baldwin

Experimental Science. A set of analytical methods and/or procedures by which scientists test ideas and suppositions about natural phenomena. For the purposes of this entry, the phrase encompasses experimental investigations and investigators and experimental scientific ideas and metaphors in Western imaginative literature, as well as the relationship between experimental and literary activity. From the dawn of the experimental sciences in the sixteenth, seventeenth, and eighteenth centuries to their maturation, enculturation, and professionalization in the nineteenth and twentieth centuries, science and scientists have been well-represented in **poetry**, **drama**, **fiction**, and other imaginative literature such as literary **essays** and personal narratives. Ideas from **astronomy** and **physics** are evident in literature across the centuries, from **Ben Jonson's** moon voyage drama and the **telescope** in **John Milton's** *Paradise Lost* (1667) to magnification in **Jonathan Swift's** *Gulliver's Travels* (1726) and electromagnetism in **Mary Shelley's** *Frankenstein* (1818); uses of physical concepts of **time, space**, power, and **entropy** pervade twentieth-century literature, especially fiction. *Frankenstein* is a pivotal work historically, at once looking back to alchemical magic and facing forward in anticipation of the moral dilemmas inherent in the powerful creations of experimental science as it advanced beyond her century to bring an unsuspecting world new potential monsters like nuclear power and genetic engineering (*see* Biotechnology), major motifs in twentieth-century fiction.

Shelley's Frankenstein, **Nathaniel Hawthorne's** Rappaccini and Aylmer, **Robert Louis Stevenson's** Jekyll, and **H.G. Wells's** Moreau represent a beginning of an eventually widespread presence in fiction of the life sciences and **genetics**, particularly after **Charles Darwin** and **evolutionary theory** and, in the twentieth century, the birth of molecular biology, the advent of genetic engineering, and revolutionary advances in biomedicine. Ideas and metaphors from these sciences are pervasive in twentieth-century fiction, from **Aldous Huxley's** cloners in *Brave New World* (1932) and various biological themes in **science fiction** from the 1930s onward to the prevalent themes in the 1980s and 1990s of genetic and pharmacological control.

A few examples of novels in which biological research and ideas figure crucially are John Brunner's *Stand on Zanzibar* (1968), **Ursula K. Le Guin's** *The Left Hand of Darkness* (1969), William Kotzwinkle's *Doctor Rat* (1971), Kate Wilhelm's *The Clewiston Test* (1976), **Frank Herbert's** *The White Plague* (1982), Harry Adam Night's *Death Spore* (1985), Greg Bear's *Blood Music* (1985), Harold King's *The Hahnemann Sequela* (1984), **Nancy Kress's** *Brainrose* (1990), and Robert Charles Wilson's *The Divide* (1990). Examples of novels in which physicists and ideas from physics are of central significance are **Stanislaw Lem's** *The Invincible* (1967), Ursula K. Le Guin's *The Dispossessed* (1974), James Hogan's *Inherit the Stars* (1977), **Arthur C. Clarke's** *Space Odyssey* novels, Martin Cruz Smith's *Stallion Gate* (1986), and Stephen Leigh's *Alien Tongue* (1991).

Fiction dealing with the scientific life and manners and with revolutionary advances in the experimental sciences, such as in physics and genetics, has been written by scientists and physicians. Much of this fiction is preoccupied thematically with the scientific ethos and with morally responsible research and development. Examples of novels that provide a close look at the working life of experimental scientists are **C.P. Snow's** *The Search* (1934) and *In Their Wisdom* (1974) and **Carl Djerassi's** *Cantor's Dilemma* (1989) and *The Bourbaki Gambit* (1994). Examples of such fiction by physicians are Steve Pieczenic's *Blood Heat* (1988), Michael Palmer's *Flashback* (1988), **Michael Crichton's** *Terminal Man* (1972) and *Jurassic Park* (1990), Primo Levi's *The Periodic Table* (1984), and **Robin Cook's** *Coma* (1977) and *Mutation* (1989). With *Mutation*, fiction about experimental science comes full circle for in geneticist Victor Frank and his secretively engineered monster Cook presents a high-tech version of the dilemmas faced by Shelley's Frankenstein.

Physicists (and close students of physics) have written fiction that explores ideas about space, time, being, nuclear power, extraterrestrial contact, and interplanetary travel; some examples are Thomas McMahon's *Principles of American Nuclear Chemistry: A Novel* (1970), **Russell McCormmach's** *Night Thoughts of a Classical Physicist* (1982), **Carl Sagan's** *Contact* (1985), **Gregory Benford's** *Artifact* (1985), **David Brin's** *The River of Time* (1986), and

Alan Lightman's *Einstein's Dreams* (1993). The fiction by Asimov, Brin, and Benford, with that of such writers as Aldous Huxley, Le Guin, **Octavia Butler**, and Kress, project future histories: societies and worlds shaped in fundamental ways by ideas and advances from the physical sciences, robotics, **computer science**, and the life sciences.

Images of the experimental scientist, as well as a diversity of scientific ideas and metaphors, are also evident in poetry and drama, though not as markedly as in fiction. Poetry containing scientific ideas, metaphors, and images spans several centuries. Scientific poetry (an oxymoron of sorts) explores and critiques scientific modes of thought, revolutionary advances, and the place and responsibility of science in society. Examples of collections of poetry about science are Ralph B. Crum's *Scientific Thought in Poetry* (1931), John Heath-Stubbs and Phillips Salman's *Poems of Science* (1984), Bonnie Bilyeu Gordon's *Songs from Unsung Worlds: Science in Poetry* (1985), and Joan Digby and Bob Brier's *Permutations: Readings in Literature and Science* (1985). Examples of plays dealing with experimental science are **G.B. Shaw's** *Back to Methuselah* (1921), **Karel Capek's** *Rossum's Universal Robots* (1923), **Friedrich Dürrenmatt's** *The Physicists* (1964), **Bertolt Brecht's** *Galileo* (1966), and Heinar Kipphardt's *In the Matter of J. Robert Oppenheimer* (1968).

Literary works also reflect and comment on scientific positivism, especially since the late nineteenth century, when the **Industrial Revolution** and the Scientific Revolution were in full stride. Scientific thought and advances are explored and critiqued in a broad range of works: empirical objectivism in **Charles Dickens's** *Hard Times* (1854); rationalism in Jane Austen's *Pride and Prejudice* (1813); **Darwinism** in Eugene O'Neill's *The Hairy Ape* (1921); mechanism in Elmer L. Rice's *The Adding Machine* (1923); scientific construction of characters and plots in the fiction of Aldous Huxley, D.H. Lawrence, and **John Steinbeck**; **entropy** in **Thomas Pynchon's** *Gravity's Rainbow* (1973); scientific attitude and technological overkill in *Nineteen Eighty-Four* (1949), Martin Caidin's *The God Machine* (1968), and Don DeLillo's *Ratner's Star* (1976) and *White Noise* (1984).

The presence of the experimental sciences in fiction also means the presence of scientists. Roslynn D. Haynes identifies six recurrent stereotypes of scientists in Western fiction: the alchemist, obsessed with ethically questionable research; the stupid **virtuoso**, absent-minded and socially neglectful; the unfeeling scientist, unemotional and hermitic; the heroic adventurer, optimistic, superpowerful, and controlling; the helpless scientist, who has lost control over his creation; and the idealist, readily accepted as working in the interest of human progress. Most of these character "types" often overlap in fictional scientists, as is the case with Victor Frankenstein.

Other forms of imaginative literature beside fiction, poetry, and drama are concerned with the experimental sciences and their relationship with literary art. Much of these writings explore in various ways, directly or indirectly, the nature of "doing science" versus that of literary art. Scientists and literary artists collectively have produced a substantial body of works—personal essays and reflective narratives, often using poetic prose and fictional license—that grapple with issues of differences, as well as complementarities and reciprocities, between experimental science and literature.

A major example is the famous debate between C.P. Snow and F.R. Leavis, to which contributions were made by such works as Aldous Huxley's *Literature and Science* (1963), Jacob Bronowski's *Science and Human Values* (1965) and *The Visionary Eye* (1978), and Peter B. Medawar's *The Hope of Progress* (1974). The scholarly and public essays of these and other writers—including **Loren Eiseley**, **Richard Selzer**, **Lewis Thomas**, and Robert Coles—constitute an ongoing exploration and dialogue focused on the intellectual and practical relations between science and literature. Some writers, like Bronowski and Eiseley, have attempted to articulate the idea of an organic wholeness of the intellect that transcends the perceived boundaries between the scientific and literary.

References

Haynes, Roslynn D. *From Faust to Strangelove: Representations of the Scientist in Western Literature*. Baltimore: Johns Hopkins UP, 1994.
Isaacs, Leonard. *Darwin to Double Helix: The Biological Theme in Science Fiction*. London: Butterworths, 1977.
Shapin, Steven, and Simon Schaffer. *Leviathan and the Air-Pump: Hobbes, Boyle, and the Experimental Life*. Princeton, NJ: Princeton UP, 1985.

Robert C. Goldbort

Expositions/World's Fairs. International exhibitions, principally European and American, organized periodically as testaments to Western "progress." The first international exposition to capture wide attention was the British Crystal Palace of 1851, which displayed the produce of empire within a huge, specially constructed glass pavilion. Subsequent world's fairs included those at Philadelphia (1876), Paris (1889, 1900), Munich (1890), Chicago (1893), St. Louis (1904), and San Francisco (1910). Typically these included buildings designed to represent individual nations, buildings designed to display particular fields of technical or economic progress, as well as large amusement parks called—after the Chicago fair—"midways." As testaments to progress, the fairs often sought to represent contemporary knowledge as a unified accomplishment that included literary, pedagogic, and other social advances, as well as scientific discoveries and technological innovations. The **typewriter** was introduced to a large public at the Philadelphia exposition, for example, while Frederick Jackson Turner's frontier thesis was first expounded in conjunction with the World's Columbian Exposition in Chicago, and Esperanto was promoted in Paris (1900). Noteworthy midway attractions included the first Ferris wheel, early motion picture displays, a "village" of Philippine islanders, and a southern "plantation," complete with "slaves." Many millions attended each exposition, and each comprised a powerfully magnetic spectacle of cultural self-definition and consumption, frequently punctuated by exoticist, imperialist attractions. The American naturalist writer Hamlin Garland wrote his parents from Chicago, "Sell the cook stove if necessary and come. You *must* see this fair." **Henry Adams** found the twentieth century bearing down on him in Paris (1900), where he fell with his "historical neck" so famously broken before the dynamos in the Hall of Machines. President William McKinley was shot by anarchist Leon Czolgosz at the Buffalo, New York, Pan-American Exposition of 1901.

References

Brain, Robert. *Going to the Fair: Readings in the Culture of Nineteenth-Century Exhibitions.* Cambridge: Whipple Museum of the History of Science, 1993.
Rydel, Robert W. *All the World's a Fair: Visions of Empire at American International Expositions, 1876–1916.* Chicago: U of Chicago P, 1984.

Lisa Gitelman

Extraterrestrials. Supposed material and intelligent inhabitants of regions beyond the Earth. The question of the existence of extraterrestrial beings or, as it was long known, of a **plurality of worlds** has fascinated humans throughout nearly all Western history. In antiquity, Epicurus and **Lucretius** championed this idea, whereas **Aristotle** and **Plato** resisted it. In the Middle Ages, Thomas Aquinas opposed it, but Nicholas of Cusa advocated inhabitants of the sun and moon. In the sixteenth century, **Nicholas Copernicus's** heliocentric theory added to the plausibility of extraterrestrial beings, as **Giordano Bruno** was quick to stress.

The support given to belief in extraterrestrial life by such seventeenth- and eighteenth-century scientists as **Johannes Kepler**, Isaac Newton (*see* Newtonianism), Christian Huygens, and **William Herschel** inspired literary, religious, and philosophical authors to embrace and to embellish this belief. Among the more prominent **Enlightenment** humanists who incorporated this belief into their writings were **Alexander Pope**, Edward Young, Friedrich Klopstock, Immanuel Kant, **Bernard de Fontenelle**, and **Voltaire**.

Enthusiasm for extraterrestrials has not diminished in the nineteenth and twentieth centuries, even as scientists have gradually recognized the complexities involved in resolving the question of life elsewhere. Moreover, the modern passion for **science fiction** writings has stimulated the debate on whether our planet contains the only intelligent beings in the universe.

Reference

Crowe, M.J. *The Extraterrestrial Life Debate 1750–1900: The Idea of a Plurality of Worlds from Kant to Lowell.* Cambridge: Cambridge UP, 1986.

Michael J. Crowe

F

Faraday, Michael (1791–1867). British scientist whose most important work was in **electricity** and magnetism. Faraday built the first electric motor and dynamo and laid the foundations for James Clerk Maxwell's electromagnetic **field theory**. Faraday's work led to the "electric revolution," which altered life dramatically during the second half of the nineteenth century as generators began to supply electric power to major cities in Europe and the United States. Electricity became an important literary trope in the writing of such authors as **Charles Dickens**, **Honoré de Balzac**, **Mark Twain**, and **Theodore Dreiser**, where it was associated with a newly mechanized modern world.

Kristine Swenson

Faulkner, William (1897–1962). American fiction writer known for innovations in the modern novel form, experiments in narrative technique, and range of psychological types in characters. Faulkner's work reflects a layperson's knowledge of influential intellectual theories of his time, especially **Freud's psychology** (*see* Anthropology/Psychology/Sociology), Bergson's **philosophy**, and **Einstein's relativity** theory. The presence of the latter can be sensed in particular in *The Sound and the Fury*, where the relations between light, velocity, and **time** are subjected by characters to **thought experiments** that use the terminology of relativity **physics**.

Paul A. Harris

Feuilleton. From the French for "leaf or sheet of paper," refers to a journalistic category, a short and light section intended for the entertainment of the general reader. In 1800 Abbé Julien Louis Geoffroy first featured the feuilleton in his *Journal des Débats* by supplementing the various announcements with short and lively observations and commentary on the arts, travel, and everyday life. Since then, the feuilleton has developed into the feature, lifestyle, or arts and entertainment section of the daily and weekly press, offering a rich resource for social scientists, cultural critics, and others through which to trace trends in popular **culture**.

Ralph W. Buechler

Feynman, Richard Phillips (1918–1988). American physicist, instrumental in bringing quantum theory to its modern form. Feynman was known for his insight into quantum mechanics and for his unique methods of mathematical analysis. During World War II he worked on the atomic bomb project at Los Alamos, New Mexico. In 1948 he refined quantum electrodynamics, or QED—the **theory** of electrons and photons that had been stymied since the 1920s—into meaningful form, for which he shared the 1965 Nobel Prize in **Physics**. He sat on the panel investigating the *Challenger* space-shuttle disaster of 1986, playing a leading role in identifying and publicizing the cause of the explosion. A professor at the California Institute of Technology, he was an excellent teacher, and his *Lectures on Physics* (1966) is a classic text. Feynman's career was punctuated by irreverent episodes, such as pranks he played on security forces at Los Alamos. He was also known for playing the bongo drums and for his paintings. He was the author of a number of important works of popular science, including two best-selling memoirs about his life and ideas in science, *"Surely You're Joking, Mr. Feynman"* (1984) and *What Do YOU Care What Other People Think?* (1988).

References

Feynman, Richard Phillips. *QED: The Strange Theory of Light and Matter*. Princeton, NJ: Princeton UP, 1985.
———. *Six Easy Pieces*. Reading, MA: Helix Books, 1995.
Gleick, James. *Genius: The Life and Science of Richard Feynman*. New York: Pantheon Books, 1992.

Sidney Perkowitz

Fiction. From the Latin *fingo*, to feign or imagine, is, together with **poetry**, the literature with which science has historically been least comfortable, and vice versa. It was Newton's (*see* Newtonianism) view (*Queries to Opticks*, 1704–1706) that every "**hypothesis**" was "feigned" and that good science differed from bootless metaphysics in having as few as possible. Science, of course, has a literature, professional and otherwise, including forms like the treatise, the **essay**, the letter, or the presentation to the learned society, standard in Western science from the sixteenth and seventeenth centuries. Some scientists in that period, however, wrote fiction (**Kepler**, *Somnium*, c. 1610; **Bacon**, *New Atlantis*, c. 1627), **Galileo** concocted a dialogue for his censored masterpiece (*On the Two Chief World Systems*, 1632), and in the eighteenth century **Alexander Pope** and **Erasmus Darwin** put science into verse. In the nineteenth and twentieth centuries, **science fiction** (earlier called scientific romance and scientifiction) has rivaled scientific journalism as the most compelling way to report and argue science; and if "**thought experiments**" like Maxwell's Demon (1867) or **Einstein's** light-traversed gravitational **elevator** (1907) be labeled fictions, then this period has been prodigal with them. Arguments made by, among others, Ernst Mach at the end of the nineteenth century (**positivism**) and **Donna Haraway** and **Bruno Latour** at the end of the twentieth (constructivism) suggest that all science, in effect, is thought experiment and hypothesis, so fundamentally shaped by **cultures** and subcultures that it cannot be said to have any separate or special reliability as a source of knowledge, despite any apparent "**objectivity**" (or commonality in perceptions) of the external world. In the same period an accurate awareness of the consequences of science and the effects of **technology** has been increasingly important to the success of any kind of literature, and perhaps especially of fiction all the way from **Émile Zola** (*Les Rougon-Macquart*, 1871–1893) to **Kurt Vonnegut** (*Cat's Cradle*, 1963) and **Thomas Pynchon** (*Gravity's Rainbow*, 1973).

The dialogue between science and fiction has therefore taken place on several levels. Each must suspect the other while including it. Fiction must feign science. Science, to progress, must feign hypotheses. Fiction may make a fiction of the fact that it is fiction (like **Defoe's** *Robinson Crusoe* and other early English novels). Science remains uncomfortable with the fact that it invents fictions and tries to make facts of them (despite Einstein's 1933 statement in "On the Method of Theoretical Physics," that physical theories are "fictitious . . . freely formed concepts . . . produced by a creative act"). The central hypothesis of fiction must remain, however, that worlds that never were can be imagined, while the central hypothesis of science has remained that any hypothesis imagined about the existing world must be both verifiable and falsifiable: able to be confirmed by properly recorded events and able to be abandoned if events do not confirm it. A scientist and a novelist (**Charles Darwin** and **Herman Melville**, for example) may approach exactly the same subject (nature in the Galapagos Islands) at the same time (1835, 1842) and produce equally compelling prose (*The Voyage of the Beagle*, "The Encantadas"), but the scientist can be distinguished by his or her appeal to verifiability, objectivity, and generality, or at least to the possibility of these things.

The tension admits of no permanent resolution. There is of course a long tradition of science fiction in which invented characters deal with the consequences of an invented science or an extrapolated technology. The hellenistic satirist **Lucian** wrote the first voyage to the moon in the second century and Thomas More, François Rabelais, and the real Cyrano de Bergerac all made use of his work. However, the use of fiction by Western scientists probably begins with **Johannes Kepler's** *Somnium*, and the use of science by fiction writers might be said to begin if not with satires like **Jonathan Swift's** Laputa (1726) and **Voltaire's** *Micromegas* (1758), then certainly with **Mary Shelley's** *Frankenstein* (1818). **Jules Verne** defined the genre in the 1870s, and **H.G. Wells**, who had taught science, may be said to have perfected it, with the double aim of instruction and prophecy. His *Time Machine* (1895) together with Edwin A. Abbott's *Flatland* (1884), both critical visions of late-nineteenth-century society and class, are still used as introductions to the multidimensional geometry they popularized, and the **popularization** is thought to have affected developments as disparate as Einstein's **physics** and the abstract **art** of Marcel Duchamp and Kasimir Malevich. Science fiction in the twentieth century has included a range of writers from every national literature, and a large range of attitudes toward science and **technology**, from the unambiguous celebration of material progress (Hugo Gernsback, **Isaac Asimov**) to dark visions of decay (E.M. Forster, John W. Campbell, **Philip K. Dick**) and attempts to imagine all forms of economic, social, and sexual alternatives (**Ursula K. Le Guin, Charlotte Perkins Gilman**). Science fiction can be political, whether on the Right (**Robert Heinlein**) or on the Left (Frederick Pohl and C.M. Kornbluth). There is science fiction set in postnuclear times describing the failure of science and technology (Russell Hoban, Walter M. Miller), science fiction designed to challenge the received ideas of science (**Italo Calvino, J.G. Ballard**, "James Tiptree"), and science fiction narrowed again to the exposition of what science knows or can predict (Larry Niven, Hal Clement). Of course, there are also novels about science and scientists, from Sinclair Lewis's *Arrowsmith* (1925) to Russell McCormmach's *Night Thoughts of a Classical Physicist* (1982). Indeed, suggests science fiction writer Samuel Delany, science fiction is as much a protocol of reading as a mode of writing, and it is possible to read any text as science fiction, even a Jane Austen novel. By the same token, it has become possible, through the efforts of social constructionists or constructivists, to read any scientific publication as fiction. For many thinkers, this is the core of something they call postmodernism, but it must be said that the problematic was there from the beginning.

William R. Everdell

Field Theory. Not a physical **theory** (despite its scientific-sounding name) but a phrase denoting a way of understanding the fabric of the world. The "field theory" outlook emphasizes the interconnected nature of **reality**; the world is a whole irreducible to its component parts, and "observers" are inextricably bound participants in the field. Any "language" used to describe the field (verbal, mathematical) is part of the field it describes. There is thus a self-referential aspect of both language and any "subject" or "observer" located in the field.

In physics, a field is a region in which bodies act on one another through forces; a field represents how bodies not in direct contact influence one another. Types of fields include gravitational, electric, and magnetic. **Michael Faraday** and James Clerk Maxwell may be regarded as pioneers of field theory; in the later nineteenth century, they defined electric and magnetic fields in relation to one another. Maxwell then united the two into the electromagnetic field, providing the foundation for **Albert Einstein's** special theory of **relativity**. Relativity and quantum theory are the physical theories from which field theory has drawn its primary philosophical and literary inspirations.

Field theory manifests itself in literature through an underlying sense that not only are characters and events enmeshed in a single field, but language itself, in depicting the fictional world, changes its nature as well. A preliminary list of twentieth-century writers who have explicitly deployed field theory includes **John Barth, Samuel Beckett, Jorge Luis Borges**, John Fowles, **James Joyce, Vladimir Nabokov, Thomas Pynchon**, and **Kurt Vonnegut**. Perhaps the most sustained meditation on field theory in literature is **Lawrence Durrell's** *The Alexandria Quartet*.

Paul A. Harris

Film. A medium that merges **technology** and **art** and is thus crucial for understanding how various aspects of science and literature have often been opposed, played out, and where possible, synthesized. Taken as a whole, the course, and indeed evolution, of cinematic developments marks one of the great triumphs of twentieth-century science and technology. The thematization of science and technology in film suggests, however, a rather more curious, oddly spotty story. The first, charming paeans to technology as art were committed to celluloid in the late nineteenth century by the likes of **Edison** and the brothers Lumière. Soon thereafter, however, we are more likely to encounter the theme of technology as, at best, a relentless annoyance, as in the technologically assisted buffooneries of the Keystone Kops, or as a manifestation of something downright insidious, as in Chaplin's great masterwork *Modern Times* (1936).

As one might expect, given the coincidence of World War II with the development of a more sophisticated, technologically polished cinema, this era is marked by more sympathetic portrayals of science and technology. Both the Allied and Axis Powers encouraged the making of films that celebrated not only the courage of their fighting men and women but, more spectacularly, the technological sophistication and power of their weaponry. Mervyn LeRoy's biopic of *Madame Curie* (1943) signaled the eventual celebration of the scientific and technological investigations that resulted in the atom bomb and subsequently the long period of nuclear anxiety we now remember as the Cold War. Between LeRoy's film and the merely nominal ruefulness of *Fat Man and Little Boy* (1989), Stanley Kubrick's *Dr. Strangelove* (1963) heralded a long period wherein the nuclear age was parodied, satirically criticized, and even polemically insulted on film. Of the many films of this era that deal with such issues, Alain Resnais's *Hiroshima mon Amour* (1960—with its screenplay by the eminent French novelist Marguerite Duras—arguably offers the most subtle consideration of the impact of the nuclear age on human emotions and overall attitudes toward life.

With Stanley Kubrick's *2001: A Space Odyssey* (1968), the criticism of the nuclear age so prevalent in the cinema of the 1950s was simultaneously projected out, into the **cosmos**, and effectively countered by the depiction of an ultimately benign, if relentlessly interfering and manipulative, alien science and technological culture. Curiously, even as the film's premise follows from the notion that scientific advancement is crucial to the evolution of humankind, human science and technology are shown to be useful only in positioning humanity to encounter—and be saved by—a far superior, more intelligently conceived and accomplished, alien science. Underlying the film's superficial message of hope and self-transcendence, therefore, rests a surprisingly bleak sense that humanity would remain no more evolved than chimps but for the happy interference of a wiser scientific culture. This underlying pessimism is every bit as evident in the film's sequel, *2010* (1986), but finds its most exemplary expression in **Clarke's** *Childhood's End* (1953), a novel wherein human evolution is baldly equated with human extinction.

The tendency to depict science and technology in negative, even apocalyptic terms is reflected in the relative dearth of films that address science as a heroic or even basically praiseworthy activity. *Infinity* (1996), a film nominally about the life of **Richard Feynman**, an American Nobel laureate in **physics**, is quite instructive in this regard. The film glosses over Feynman's life as a scientist, using the few scenes that have any scientific content primarily for color. Such scenes are used merely to portray Feynman's famously eccentric and colorful personality rather than to help the viewer understand the nature of his life as a scientist. Indeed, with its overall focus on the pathos of Feynman's troubled relations with his first wife, this film is essentially a love story, with a little science thrown in for flavor.

Science and technology are obviously cornerstones of modern life and culture, yet one could scarcely tell that this is so from viewing contemporary cinema. In the 1990s, Hollywood has proven itself capable only of portraying the scientist as corrupt and easily corruptible, like Richard Attenborough's character in *Jurassic Park* (1993), as downright demonic (Anthony Hopkins's Hannibal Lector in *The Silence of the Lambs*, 1991, exemplifies the tendency to portray extraordinary analytical lucidity as tantamount to a kind of madness), or as a kind of delightfully eccentric maverick, working on the fringes of the scientific establishment until special circumstances enable him (hardly ever her) to use his expertise to save the day. Jeff Goldblum's charmingly wacky computer scientist in *Independence Day* (1995) nicely exemplifies this trend.

Rather than look to the level where science and scientists are explicitly thematized and portrayed, it is rather at the level of myth—and in the mythic aspect of science fiction—that contemporary filmmakers wrestle with the impact of science and technology on twentieth-century life. Lee Drummond has decisively shown, for instance, how George Lucas's portrayal of intelligent **cyborgs** in the *Star Wars* trilogy of the 1970s enables a contemporary audience to contemplate the burgeoning—and increasingly problematic—role of intelligent machines in modern life and to engage this issue at a mythic rather than simply celebratory or critical level.

References

Drummond, Lee. *American Dreamtime: A Cultural Analysis of Popular Movies, and Their Implications for a Science of Humanity.* Lanham, MD: Littlefield Adams, 1996.

Nowell-Smith, Geoffrey, ed. *The Oxford History of World Cinema.* Oxford: Oxford UP, 1996.

Michael B. McDonald

Finch, Anne (1661–1720). Countess of Winchilsea. While her Pindaric ode "The Spleen" (1701) was widely invoked in the eighteenth century as providing an accurate compendium of the symptoms associated with "the spleen," recent criticism reads the poems as a critique of the gendered ideology of late-seventeenth-century nervous disorders. Finch's poem suggests that, as applied to male sufferers, the "spleen" serves as a mark of genius, while for women it denotes feminine debility and **irrationality** (*see* Rationality). Finch's complex critique represents her own experience of "the spleen" as a response to the public ridicule visited upon women writers in a **culture** that views women's literary ambitions as transgressive and hence pathological. Ruth Salvaggio has observed that in verses such as "Petition for an Absolute Retreat" and "Adam Pos'd," Finch identifies herself with a feminized natural world that was "increasingly subjected to the invasive scrutiny and technological discipline of the experimental natural philosopher" and represents both woman and nature as eluding systematization within **Enlightenment** science.

References

Hellegers, Desiree. *Handmaid to Divinity: Science, Politics and the Gendered Poetics of Resistance in Seventeenth-Century England.* Norman: U of Oklahoma P, 1999.

McGovern, Barbara. " 'The Spleen': Melancholy, Gender and Poetic Identity." *Anne Finch and Her Poetry, a Critical Biography.* Athens: U of Georgia P, 1992. 159–78.

Salvaggio, Ruth. "Histories, Theories, Configurations" and "Anne Finch Placed and Displaced." *Enlightened Absence, Neoclassical Configurations of the Feminine.* Chicago: U of Illinois P, 1988. 3–28; 105–32.

Desiree Hellegers

Finke, Gary (19?–). American poet. His poems "Calculating Pi" and "The Butterfly Effect" use the paradoxes of calculation and **chaos theory** to develop the theme of the human relationship to the natural world. Finke's work in general is shot through with a critical fascination for scientific subjects and the troubled relations between reductionism and **imagination**.

References

Finke, Gary. "Calculating Pi." *New England Review and Bread Loaf Quarterly* 12.4 (1989): 350.

———. *Handing the Self Back.* Maryville, MO: Green Tower, 1990.

Joseph Duemer

Finlay, Ian Hamilton (1925–). Scottish poet, **landscape** gardener, and small press publisher. His major work is his garden at Little Sparta in southern Scotland. Has created numerous permanent installations throughout Europe, including the garden of the Max Planck Institute, Stuttgart, and in North America. Finlay views nature in terms of cultural history, incorporating into his designs a wide range of references, from the **pre-Socratic philosophers** to the **technology** of modern warfare.

References

Abrioux, Yves. "Géométrie du paysage et dynamique culturelle: Bernard Lassus et Ian Hamilton Finlay." *T.L.E.* 12 (1994): 229–54.
———. *Ian Hamilton Finlay : A Visual Primer*. 2nd ed. Boston: MIT, 1992.

Yves Abrioux

Fitzgerald, Penelope (1917–2000). British author of several award-winning novels. *The Gate of Angels* (1990) takes up such questions as scientific thought, religious faith, and the new **physics** as they affect a young physicist, Fred Fairley, when he falls in love with a nurse, Daisy Saunders, in Cambridge in 1912. In *The Blue Flower* (1997), she recreates the world of eighteenth-century German life, centering her narrative upon the personal life and love of the philosopher–poet **Friedrich von Hardenberg (Novalis)**.

Kristine Swenson

Flaubert, Gustave (1821–1880). French author, most notably of *Madame Bovary* (1857), in which he criticizes the bourgeois use of science, typified by Charles Bovary and the chemist Homais. In *The Temptation of Saint Antony* (1874) he shows the powerful allure of science, making the cell the final temptation that overcomes his protagonist. *Bouvard and Pecuchet* (unfinished, 1880) dwells at length on the wonders and hideous inconsistencies of scientific inquiry, from **agriculture** to anatomy. Flaubert's works demonstrate an ambivalent attitude toward science—fascinated, yet critical. His writing resembles scientific discourse: distinctness and specificity of observation, **objectivity**, authorial effacement, the striving for precise and perfect form.

Reference

Troyat, Henri. *Flaubert*. Trans. Joan Pinkham. New York: Viking Penguin, 1992.

Heather V. Armstrong

Fludd, Robert (1574–1637). English physician, occultist, inventor of the thermometer. His writings involved Rosicrucian, hermetic, alchemical **symbolism**, utilized by later writers. Flood was the major British Paracelsian discussed and criticized by European scholars. He combined alchemical themes and biblical doctrines of creation and defended number mysticism against **Johannes Kepler**.

Val Dusek

Fontenelle, Bernard le Bovier de (1657–1757). French author of numerous works including the *Entretiens sur la pluralité des mondes* (*Conversations on the Plurality of Worlds*, 1686), a landmark in the **popularization** of science. Designed to interest Paris's social elite in Copernican **astronomy**, these witty dialogues between a philosopher and a marquise illustrated the ambiguous role of class and **gender** in the transmission of scientific knowledge. Fontenelle was criticized by later *philosophes* like **Voltaire** for his ornate prose and persistent allegiance to Cartesianism, yet his writings and long service as perpetual secretary to the Académie des Sciences nonetheless made him a major spokesman for science in **Enlightenment** culture.

Reference

Harth, Erica. "Fontenelle and the Ladies." *Cartesian Women: Versions and Subversions of Rational Discourse in the Old Regime*. Ithaca, NY: Cornell UP, 1992. 123–67.

Anne C. Vila

Ford, Henry (1863–1947). American industrialist and automobile manufacturer. With the introduction of his Model T in 1908, Henry Ford captured the American imagination. The car was a relatively affordable machine, available to many, and its manufacture would lead Ford to his assembly-line production method. The assembly line, with its roots in "scientific" management, interchangeable parts, and continuous process production, required the standardization of labor, repetitive, mechanical, unthinking actions. **Modernism** developed in part as a reaction against the ideals of mass production and bourgeois commonality that Ford came to represent. A few literary modernists tackled Ford, including **John Dos Passos** in his *U.S.A.* trilogy (1936) and Harte Crane in *The Bridge* (1930). For some the "fordism" of modern industrial production became associated with the quirks of Henry Ford's personality, his nativist antiintellectualism, and his rabid anti-Semitism, as well as with the intractable antagonisms between labor and management. Further fictional representations include **Upton Sinclair's** scathing *The Flivver King* (1937) and E.L. Doctorow's *Ragtime* (1975).

References

Hounshell, David A. *From the American System to Mass Production, 1800–1932*. Baltimore: Johns Hopkins UP, 1984.
Sinclair, Upton. *The Flivver King: A Story of Ford-America*. 1937. Chicago: Charles H. Kerr, 1987.

Lisa Gitelman

Fossil Record. Evidence of past life forms, petrified in layers of rock. The concept scarcely in human minds prior to the beginning of the nineteenth century, when Cuvier and Brongniart in France and William Smith in England together founded the science of stratigraphy. Two realizations were fundamental: First, that in normally ordered strata, age increases with depth; and second, that each stratum has a complement of life forms peculiar to itself. From these re-alizations, two generalities emerged: First, that strata are of the same age if they contain the same complement of life; and second, that the complement of life changes throughout time. Because the transition from one stratum to another was often abrupt, it was possible to hold (as the earliest stratigraphers did) that the changes from one fauna to another had been catastrophic and sudden rather than gradual and slow. This seeming verification of repeated destructions and creations was a major difficulty for **Charles Darwin**, who could respond only by emphasizing the incompleteness of the record. Early examples of stratigraphy in English literature include **Shelley's** *Prometheus Unbound*, IV; and **Byron's** *Don Juan, Cain*, and *Heaven and Earth*. **Tennyson** agonized over the impli-cations of the fossil record in *In Memoriam*; another famous example appears in **Thomas Hardy's** novel *A Pair of Blue Eyes*. The longer version of Langdon Smith's poem "Evolution" ("When you were a tadpole and I was a fish") in-cludes several individuals named after strata.

Reference

Darwin, Charles. "On the Imperfection of the Geological Record." *The Origin of Species.* London: J. Murray, 1859. ch. 10.

Dennis R. Dean

Fourth Dimension. With the development of non-Euclidean geometry by J. Bolyai, N.I. Lobachevsky, and G.F.B. Riemann in the mid-nineteenth century, writers began to popularize the concept of a fourth dimension for **fiction**, oc-cultism, and **philosophy**. Geometrical fantasies such as Edwin A. Abbott's *Flat-land* (1884) preceded **H.G. Wells's** stories about time machines and spatial inversions. Multidimensional worlds became a favorite topic in later **science fiction** and led to the subgenre of alternative histories.

Reference

Henderson, L.D. *The Fourth Dimension. Non-Euclidean Geometry in Modern Art.* Prince-ton, NJ: Princeton UP, 1983.

Elmar Schenkel

Fractals/Fractal Geometry. Essentially, an attempt to complement tradi-tional geometry, with its emphasis on straight lines and smooth curves, with a geometry that is appropriate to many of the shapes we encounter in nature: jagged edges, indentations, and discontinuities. Constructed by Benoit Mandel-brot, a computer scientist at IBM, fractal geometry seeks to account for nature's tendency to produce irregularities.

Whereas regular shapes have regular dimensions, Mandelbrot argues that highly irregular shapes have fractional dimensions. For example, a Koch snowflake—generated by taking an equilateral triangle and adding a new equilateral triangle to each of its sides and then iterating the process repeatedly—has so much detail that its dimension is higher than that of a simple line, yet lower than that of a plane. Specifically, a Koch curve has a dimension of 1.2818 . . .

A famous example of a fractal is a coastline. How long is the Gulf coast from Galveston to Corpus Christi? In fact, this seemingly simple question cannot be answered because the answer depends on the length of the ruler used to make the measurements. The smaller the ruler, the longer the coast, and if the ruler were small enough, it is conceivable that the coastline has infinite length. In other words, it is impossible to measure the length of the Gulf coast without a prior specification of the scale used to make the measurement. Furthermore, the more closely we look at the coastline, the more detail we will see. Although the new detail brought into focus by higher and higher magnification will not be identical to the general shape of the coast at larger scales, it will tend to be self-similar to it; that is, like all fractals, a coastline will reproduce its general pattern in finer and finer scales.

Alex Argyros

Frankenstein. (Character and work). **Mary Shelley's** novel *Frankenstein; or, The Modern Prometheus* (1818; rev. 1831) and its protagonist, Victor. It is simplistic to view *Frankenstein* only as a pioneering work of **science fiction** and to neglect the novel's psychological dynamics in the context of both Shelley's life and the Gothic (*see* Gothicism) tradition. Victor Frankenstein's actions and motives, as well as the central imagery of electromagnetism, nonetheless symbolize at once the passing of alchemical **magic** and the coming of modern science. As a "future myth," Victor and his creation of the monster anticipate the inescapable dilemmas faced by twentieth-century scientists in exercising their moral responsibility *vis-à-vis* the societal effects of their creations (*see* Leonard Isaacs). Shelley's use in the novel of electromagnetic and biologic theory was influenced by her exposure to the ideas of, among others, **Erasmus Darwin**, Luigi Galvani, and **Humphry Davy**.

Reference

Ketterer, David. *Frankenstein's Creation: The Book, the Monster, and Human Reality.* Victoria, British Columbia: U of Victoria P, 1979.

Robert C. Goldbort

Franklin, Benjamin (1706–1790). Diplomat, scientist, inventor, writer, and one of the major American statesmen in the years leading up to 1776. Franklin represented with his personality, thought, and work the **Enlightenment** in North America as few others did. Franklin's optimism, humor, candor, and industriousness and his common, pedagogical, and practical sense are perhaps best evident in his *Poor Richard's Almanac* (1733–1758) and his *Autobiography*, begun in 1771.

Franklin's writing proved to be both an organizing principle and a witness to his thought on theoretical science, **politics**, and ethics. Many of his ideas subsequently found concrete transformation into such projects as would secure his future fame: the demonstration of the identity of lightning and **electricity**, the inventions of bifocal lenses and the Franklin stove, and the founding of the University of Pennsylvania and of the first subscription library.

Reference

Franklin, Benjamin. *Autobiography*. New York: Heritage, 1951.

Ralph W. Buechler

Freud, Sigmund (1856–1939). Founder of psychoanalysis. His influence on modern thought cannot be overestimated. His conception of subjectivity, sexuality (*see* Gender and Sexuality), and the unconscious formed a critique of the Cartesian rational subject that influenced philosophers, novelists, historians, filmmakers, intellectuals, and others throughout the twentieth century. Psychoanalytic talk therapy, with its emphasis on free association, childhood experience, and the meaning of psychical symptoms, created a profession in the United States that barely existed prior to Freud's arrival. His writings continue to provide rich, engaging texts for scholars and theorists of psychology (*see* Anthropology/Psychology/Sociology), **culture**, and society.

Freud's belief in the value of insight into the repressed unconscious impulses that motivate human behavior provides the basis for his **theory**. After studying medicine in Vienna and working briefly under neurologist Jean Martin Charcot in Paris, Freud pursued his interest in hysteria, and in his practice with Joseph Breuer he developed (with ample support from certain patients) elements of what would become psychoanalysis, particularly free association and "the talking cure." Freud's own self-analysis and the subsequent publication of *Die Traumdeutung* (The Interpretation of Dreams) led him to articulate the rest of the early theoretical touchstones of psychoanalysis, including his theory of dream interpretation, the unconscious, the Oedipus complex, and infantile sexuality. Later, Freud revised these concepts and developed others, including transference, the triad of ego, id, and superego, and the death drive.

While Freud conceived of psychoanalysis as a science, the importance of his work to literature and science is its theoretical and philosophical legacy. The profound impact of psychoanalysis on clinical psychology and psychiatry in the United States has meant not only that most psychotherapy remains indebted to Freud but also that our basic vocabulary about human behavior—repression, being defensive, having a big ego—is rooted in Freud's thought. This particularly American version of psychoanalysis, which critics decried as "ego psychology," also had an impact on cultural production, particularly novels and **film**, and on scholarly production, particularly in literary criticism, **anthropology**, and history.

Too often, the reductive critiques that sometimes resulted from such scholarship are taken as typical examples of the impact Freud's theories had on intellectual life in the United States. Such a perspective ignores the last thirty years of astonishingly productive engagements with Freud's writing in literary theory, linguistics, anthropology, and history, many of which start with the "return to Freud" engendered by the French psychoanalyst Jacques Lacan. Lacan's emphasis on language, meaning, and subjectivity produced new readings of Freud's texts that became influential in **poststructuralism**, feminist theory, film theory, and **semiotics**. Just as important have been less complimentary but no less rigorous rereadings of Freud and psychoanalysis, such as Michel Foucault's rejection of the repressive hypothesis in his *History of Sexuality*, French feminist critique of Freud's phallocentrism, and so on. What remains crucial to LS is Freud's ongoing analysis of the relationship between the rational thought of science and the realm of fantasy, **irrationality** (*see* Rationality), and the unconscious.

Chris Amirault

Frontier. "The meeting point between savagery and civilization," according to Frederick Jackson Turner. Turner's **theory** held that the receding western frontier and the accompanying need to civilize an unconquered wilderness were more important than the European legacy in shaping American society. This **hypothesis**, though vastly influential and widely accepted for many years, has fallen into disfavor due to internal contradictions. According to Turner's scheme, the yeoman farmer is simultaneously the apotheosis of American **culture** and a mere midpoint in the stages of social evolution. Though those who live in primitive conditions and conquer the wilderness form the soul of the nation and embody the highest social values, by Turner's logic, they were the advance guard for urban industrial society, whose values and mechanized way of life would eventually displace them. Turner's ideas remain powerful because they continue to embody this contradiction at the heart of the American ethos.

References

Slotkin, Richard. *The Fatal Environment: The Myth of the Frontier in the Age of Industrialization 1800–1890*. New York: Atheneum, 1985.
————. *Regeneration through Violence: The Mythology of the American Frontier, 1600–1860*. Middletown, CT: Wesleyan UP, 1973.
Smith, Henry Nash. *Virgin Land. The American West as Symbol and Myth*. Cambridge: Harvard UP, 1978.
Turner, Frederick Jackson. *The Frontier in American History*. Foreword by Ray Billington. New York: Holt, Rinehart and Winston, 1962.

David N. Cassuto

Frost, Robert Lee (1874–1963). American pastoral poet, four-time winner of the Pulitzer Prize for Poetry. At Harvard, Frost studied the works of **William James** and subsequently taught James's *Principles of Psychology* and *Talks to*

Teachers on Psychology to high school students. **Darwin** and Bergson also influenced his understanding of **poetry**, and in a 1987 article Guy Rotella provides evidence for his acquaintance with work by Eddington, **Heisenberg**, and **Bohr**.

Reference

Faggen, Robert. *Robert Frost and the Challenge of Darwin*. Ann Arbor: U of Michigan P, 1997.

Steven Meyer

Fulton, Alice (1952–   ). American poet who puts scientific language to metaphorical purpose and demands of science that it offer its language to **art**. In her third book, *Powers of Congress* (1990), she describes a **computer's** memory expansion board's "soldered subdivisions/exposed yet unembarrassed as a city seen from the air."

Joseph Duemer

G

Galen (c. 129–c. 210+) Greek physician; follower and interpreter of **Hippocrates**; author of over 300 works treating **medicine**, language, and logic. Galenic medicine synthesized deductive reasoning and clinical observation and shaped medical practice and education in medieval Europe as well as in the medieval Arab world. The sixteenth- and seventeenth-century anatomical studies of Vesalius and **William Harvey** challenged Galenic authority. Renaissance literature—**Donne, Shakespeare, Jonson**, and others—used the traditional Hippocratic/Galenic theory of the four bodily humors to explain and depict human **psychology** (*see* Anthropology/Psychology/Sociology).

Anne Bratach Matthews

Galileo (Galileo Galilei) (1564–1642). Italian astronomer, mathematician, and natural philosopher. Exploiting the observational potential of the **telescope**, Galileo made astronomical observations that he believed offered strong support for Copernican heliocentrism. In *A Dialogue on the Two Chief World Systems* (1632), he overtly obeyed the Catholic edict forbidding Copernicanism by presenting his science as hypothetical. However, covertly he subverted the Church by putting its doctrines into the mouth of "Simplicius," who argues ineffectually for the priority of **Aristotle** and book-bound scholasticism, whereas "Salviati" presents Galileo's ideas and the virtues of direct observation. Church leaders saw through the ironies, convicted Galileo for disobedience, and confined him to house arrest.

The figure of Galileo is laden with various cultural **representations** of science: the hero of **truth** against superstition; the brilliant pioneer doomed in his day; the betrayer of science and reason. All these are present in **Bertolt Brecht's** play *The Life of Galileo* (1940, 1952). Brecht's Galileo is a people's revolutionary who sells out to power, compromising science's high social ideals and prefiguring the atomic bomb. Galileo is central to discussions of the nature of the Scientific Revolution; the construction of science as a uniquely powerful zone independent of social constraints; and the denigration of literary humanism against a science whose truths are universal and real.

References

Albanese, Denise. *New Science, New World.* Durham, NC: Duke UP, 1996.
Biagioli, Mario. *Galileo, Courtier: The Practice of Science in the Culture of Absolutism.* Chicago: U of Chicago P, 1993.

Laura Dassow Walls

Gamow, George (1904–1968). Russian-born American physicist whose work on the origin of the universe established a foundation for Big Bang **cosmology**. Gamow's diverse scientific interests are reflected in several popular books including those depicting the whimsical adventures of "Mr. Tompkins." In 1956 Gamow received UNESCO's (the United Nations Educational, Scientific, and Cultural Organization) Kalinga Prize for the **popularization** of science.

JoAnn Palmeri

García Márquez, Gabriel (1928–   ). Prolific Colombian novelist, winner of the 1982 Nobel Prize for Literature. While references to science do not abound in his work, his novel *One Hundred Years of Solitude* (1967) presents science and **technology** as alien objects in a setting marked by García Márquez's well-known **magic realism**. Associated with the gypsy character Melquiades, science comes to symbolize the advanced outside world in contrast to the provincial, magical Macondo that serves as the setting for the novel.

J. Andrew Brown

Garden. The natural **environment** under human or divine creative influence and a pervasive metaphor of transformation, both actual and potential. Western European literature is replete with garden imagery evoking prelapsarian perfection, postlapsarian decay, and the human ability to act in (and upon) the world (**Edmund Spenser**, **John Milton**, **Alexander Pope**, **William Wordsworth**). Fifteenth-century Spanish explorers who traversed the American Southwest deemed it an inhospitable wasteland, unfit for human habitation. Yet by the nineteenth century, the West had been rehabilitated by the American **imagination** into a new Eden capable of supporting hundreds of millions in bucolic splendor. This wishful thinking, coupled with a desire to remake the **landscape** in the image of American needs and wants, led to what Henry Nash Smith labeled the "Myth of the Garden." The policies borne of the Garden Myth (including the Homestead Acts, the Newlands Act creating the Bureau of Reclamation, and many others) have played seminal roles shaping the social and terrestrial **geography** of the United States. In many cases, the Garden Myth's legacy is also one of ecosystemic catastrophe, the full implications of which are yet to be felt.

References

Cassuto, David N. "Turning Water into Wine: Water as Privileged Signifier in *The Grapes of Wrath.*" *Steinbeck and the Environment.* Birmingham: U of Alabama P, 1996.

Charlesworth, Michael, ed. *The English Garden: Literary Sources and Documents.* Robertsbridge: Helm Information, 1993.

Marx, Leo. *The Machine in the Garden.* New York: Oxford UP, 1964.

Simpson, Lewis P. *The Dispossessed Garden: Pastoral and History in Southern Literature.* Athens: U of Georgia P, 1975.

Smith, Henry Nash. *Virgin Land: The American West as Symbol and Myth.* Cambridge: Harvard UP, 1978.

David N. Cassuto

Gender and Sexuality. Varied and numerous studies in LS that participate in several fields within gender inquiry and science studies generally. Sandra Harding, Evelyn Fox Keller, and **Donna Haraway** have been the most central thinkers in this area, establishing or articulating most forcefully what have become the major veins of thought concerning gender and sexuality in relation to science and literature. For those just beginning to study this field, a useful source is Gill Kirkup and Laurie Smith Keller's anthology *Inventing Women: Science, Technology, and Gender.*

Following the early work of such writers as Ruth Bleier and Anne Fausto-Sterling, themselves among the first scholars and scientists in the United States to argue the profound role of gender in science, Sandra Harding has examined the ways in which science is gendered (and raced) and has been central in the critique of scientific objectivity generally, the belief in the purity of which has become associated with the elitist and corporatist institutional structure of masculinist science. After the fashion of contemporary sociology of science and along with many who have followed her, from epistemologists to ecofeminists (*see* Ecofeminism), Harding has called for a reformulation of science along the lines of standpoint **epistemology**, a type of knowledge that acknowledges its own material and historical biases.

Evelyn Fox Keller has called similarly for the reconception of **objectivity**, which she argues has been constructed since the seventeenth century in two problematic ways: as uncontaminated reflection of **reality** as it is; as a mode of knowledge impervious to the location of the knower in the material world. Keller, with historians like Carolyn Merchant, has been among the first to examine the roles of women and gender in the **history of science**. Keller has also led the way, most crucially for LS, in the examination of **rhetoric** in scientific constructions of self and other.

This application of gender analysis to the history of science now constitutes a large subfield of gender and science. Some of the representatives of the field, like Nancy Tuana, provide epic examinations of Western history generally. More often, studies of gender and the history of science are more specifically focused.

Londa Schiebinger, for example, examines gender **politics** in seventeenth- and eighteenth-century European developments in taxonomy and physical **anthropology**. Ludmilla Jordanova draws from medical texts as well as scientific in her examinations of images of gender between the eighteenth and twentieth centuries. Because of the breadth of this particular subfield, one might turn most usefully to anthologies and essay collections, like those edited by Marina Benjamin, which draw together the work of many respected historians of science and gender.

The study of scientific rhetoric, which provides a bridge to the larger field of composition and rhetoric studies, is a slightly smaller subfield of gender and science studies. Following Keller, who highlights the role of language in the social construction of science, writers like Bonnie Spanier have gone on to examine particular uses of gendered metaphor and narrative in their general critique of the scientific discourses.

The third most central figure in the study of gender, science, and **philosophy** has been Donna Haraway, generally credited with representing—if not inventing—the postmodern branch of the field. Her work critiques systems of traditional ideological control—military, economic, social—in favor of a relatively utopian vision of a new science, a new language, and a new conception of gender. She is best known for her celebrations of the **cyborg**, the half-human, half-machine entity that puts into question the basic distinction between nature and culture, female and male.

Haraway's cyborg, the embodiment of disruption, has come to be the central metaphor for **technology** studies, one of the largest and fastest-growing subfields of gender, science, and literature. Mark Dery's special 1993 issue of *South Atlantic Quarterly* (92.4), "Flame Wars," articulated most forcefully the nexus of technology, gender studies, and literary criticism that has powered the new field. In that issue and in independent work since then, Anne Balsamo has led this particular field in uniting feminism, postmodernism, and Foucauldian **theory** over the issues of the body (*see* Corporeality/Body), embodiment, gender, and the cultural uses of technology. Along more purely Marxist lines, Carol Stabile has examined the extent to which technological representation obscures the material economic conditions of women's lives in the late twentieth century.

A closely related field, often crossing over into issues of technology, is **science fiction** studies. The case is commonly made that science fiction has been unfairly excluded from the postmodern canon, and feminist writers and critics in particular have called for the revaluation of the genre. As a part of this general project, Marleen Barr has studied contemporary science fiction for evidence of a reconception of gender, and Robin Roberts has examined gender issues within the history of the genre, turning finally to recent, feminist science fiction. Lucie Armitt has brought together a collection of essays on a variety of feminist issues in regards to the writing and criticism of science fiction throughout the history of the genre.

Studies of **medicine**, science, and literature represent a field equally close to technology studies. The central project of the field is the examination of the extent to which "disease" and "illness" are conceptually gendered categories. Histories of medicine and literature might examine the changing **representations** of hysteria, for example, as in the work of Elaine Showalter, or of feminine illness generally, as in the work of Diane Price Herndl, as well as representations of **pregnancy**, maternity, and **reproduction**. Contemporary representation of disease is also of interest, and here again Donna Haraway has been influential. Of central concern to this particular area of study is the subject of HIV and **AIDS**. Steven Kruger, for example, among many others, has argued that the language of scientific and literary texts alike has made AIDS an exclusively gendered, gay disease.

Weaving its way through all of these fields and subfields is the individually crafted work of LS itself. Research is extremely varied and depends upon particular triangulations of individual critics, so that the "field" as a whole encompasses subjects as different as eighteenth-century literary representations of hysteria, **Mary Shelley's** *Frankenstein*, feminized late-twentieth-century representations of **chaos**—the diversity is witnessed in contributions to *Configurations: A Journal of Literature, Science, and Technology*. Scholars interested in exploring the field generally might most usefully begin with an edited volume such as Marina Benjamin's *A Question of Identity: Women, Science, and Literature*, which brings together a number of essays that explore how women have been traditionally categorized in scientific and literary texts and how women writers have struggled with that legacy, or with individual articles published in journals like *Configurations* or *Mosaic*. At the time of this study, the field is young enough that very few book-length studies have been published in the field of literature, science, and gender or sexuality outside the categories listed above, although the number of dissertations in this area has blossomed, promising substantial future work.

References

Armitt, Lucy, ed. *Where No Man Has Gone Before: Essays on Women and Science Fiction*. New York: Routledge, 1991.

Balsamo, Anne. *Technologies of the Gendered Body: Reading Cyborg Women*. Durham, NC: Duke UP, 1996.

Barr, Marlene. *Alien to Femininity: Speculative Fiction and Feminist Theory*. Westport, CT: Greenwood, 1987.

Benjamin, Marina, ed. *A Question of Identity: Women, Science, and Literature*. New Brunswick, NJ: Rutgers UP, 1993.

————, ed. *Science and Sensibility: Gender and Scientific Inquiry*. Cambridge, MA: Basil Blackwell, 1991.

Bleier, Ruth, ed. *Feminist Approaches to Science*. Elmsford, NY: Pergamon, 1986.

Fausto-Sterling, Anne. *Myths of Gender: Biological Theories about Women and Men*. New York: Basic Books, 1986.

Haraway, Donna. *Modest_Witness@Second_Millennium.FemaleMan©_Meets_Onco Mouse,™ Feminism and Technoscience*. New York: Routledge, 1997.

————. *Simians. Cyborgs and Women: The Reinvention of Nature.* New York: Routledge, 1997.

Harding, Sandra. *Is Science Multicultural? Postcolonialisms, Feminisms, and Epistemologies.* Bloomington: Indiana UP, 1998.

————. *The Science Question in Feminism.* Ithaca, NY: Cornell UP, 1986.

————. *Whose Science? Whose Knowledge? Thinking from Women's Lives.* Ithaca, NY: Cornell UP, 1991.

Harding, Sandra, and Jean F. O'Barr, eds. *Sex and Scientific Inquiry.* Chicago: U of Chicago P, 1987.

Herndl, Diane Price. *Invalid Women: Figuring Feminine Illness in American Fiction and Culture, 1840–1940.* Chapel Hill: U of North Carolina P, 1993.

Jordanova, Ludmilla. *Sexual Visions: Images of Gender in Science and Medicine between the Eighteenth and Twentieth Centuries.* Madison: U of Wisconsin P, 1989.

Keller, Evelyn Fox. *A Feeling for the Organism: The Life and Work of Barbara McClintock.* San Francisco: W.H. Freeman, 1983.

————. *Reflections on Gender and Science.* New Haven, CT: Yale UP, 1985.

————. *Secrets of Life, Secrets of Death.* New York: Routledge, 1992.

Kirkup, Gill, and Laurie Smith Keller, eds. *Inventing Women: Science, Technology, and Gender.* Cambridge, United Kingdom: Polity Press; Cambridge, MA: Basil Blackwell, 1992.

Kruger, Steven F. *AIDS Narratives: Gender and Sexuality, Fiction, and Science.* (Gender and Genre in Literature). New York: Garland, 1996.

Merchant, Carolyn. *The Death of Nature: Women, Ecology, and the Scientific Revolution.* New York: Harper and Row, 1980.

Roberts, Robin. *A New Species: Gender and Science in Science Fiction.* Urbana: U of Illinois P, 1993.

Schiebinger, Londa. *Nature's Body: Gender in the Making of Modern Science.* Boston: Beacon, 1993.

Showalter, Elaine. *The Female Malady.* New York: Pantheon, 1985.

Spanier, Bonnie. *Im/partial Science: Gender Ideology in Molecular Biology.* Bloomington: Indiana UP, 1995.

Stabile, Carol. *Feminism and the Technological Fix.* Manchester: Manchester UP, 1994.

Tuana, Nancy. *Feminism and Science.* Bloomington: Indiana UP, 1989.

Sharon Stockton

Genethics. Term referring to a hybrid discourse emerging during the 1930s and 1990s (crucial periods in the history of molecular **genetics**) in which scientists have responded to the challenge of integrating exposition of the complexities of the new genetics with critique of its political, cultural, and ecological consequences. Uniquely positioned at the intersection of scientific and popular **culture**, their texts provide rich material for a literary-historical case study of the ideological implications of science.

Geneticist **David Suzuki** and science writer Peter Knudtson have applied the label "genethics" to this popular discourse, which they distinguish from technical scientific writing and scholarly ethical debate. Critiques of racism, eugenics, **determinism**, and reductionism are common threads linking the 1990s discourse—including Suzuki and Knudtson's *Genethics* (1989), R.C. Lewontin's *The Doctrine of DNA* (1993), and Ruth Hubbard's *Exploding the Gene Myth* (1993—with the popular works of their 1930s counterparts—among them **J.B.S. Haldane's** *Heredity and Politics* (1938), H.S. Jennings's *The Biological Basis of Human Nature* (1930), Mark Graubard's *Genetics and the Social Order* (1935), and H.J. Muller's *Out of the Night* (1935). In these texts, the ideological work of genetics in providing biological bases for new cultural and political distinctions and groupings is inseparably intertwined—indeed, analogous—with the work of metaphor; that is, changes in genetic knowledge and its attendant popular metaphors are central to historical modulations of the fundamental concepts equality and inequality—especially in popular **representations** of **race**, normality, and disease.

Dialogic interplay between different expository metaphors—each bearing its particular social implications—informs this rhetorically and ideologically complex popular discourse. For example, Jennings's metaphor of "diverse recipes" of genetic individuality is a contradictory mix of determinism and a passion for difference. In contrast, Hubbard's antideterminist use of a cookery metaphor for the complex interaction of DNA, cells, organism, and **environment** emphasizes chance and adaptive compensation and prefigures her critique of the uncertainties and fallacies of geneticists' claims and predictions.

Suzuki and Knudtson's choreographed "dance of the chromosomes" mixes concepts of machinelike control and intricate cooperative interaction; it thus lends an ambiguous determinist coloring to their insights into the limits of our knowledge of "stunning" biological complexity and their commentary on social and ecological misuses of genetics. Though Hubbard finds fault with the mechanistic "balls on a string" model of genes, Jennings and Muller employ elaborate metaphors of chromosomal strings to represent the exceedingly complex biochemical and historical networks of heredity. Haldane's ingenious explication of Mendelian principles using an analogy between chromosome pairs and hyphenated surnames serves his purpose of uniting theoretical genetics with its social context.

References

Hubbard, Ruth, and Elijah Wald. *Exploding the Gene Myth*. Boston: Beacon, 1993.
Kevles, Daniel J. *In the Name of Eugenics: Genetics and the Uses of Human Heredity*. 1985. Harmondsworth: Penguin, 1986.
Suzuki, David, and Peter Knudtson. *Genethics: The Ethics of Engineering Life*. 1988. Cambridge, MA: Harvard UP; London: Unwin, 1989.

Doug Russell

Genetics. The study of the patterns and mechanisms of inheritance. Classical genetics derives from the work of Gregor Mendel, who quantitatively characterized the inheritance of distinct traits in pea plants in the 1860s, and from early twentieth-century cell biologists, who determined that chromosomes carried the physical units of heredity. Modern genetics employs biochemical analysis to determine gene location, structure, and function; analyzes the relationship between genes and disease; and explores methods of gene manipulation. Scientist and feminist critic Evelyn Fox Keller has made significant contributions to the historical, literary, and philosophical analysis of twentieth-century genetics and molecular biology. Literary theorist Richard Doyle analyzes the **rhetoric** and dominant metaphors (such as "life's code" and the "language of life") of genetics and molecular **biology**.

References

Doyle, Richard. *On Beyond Living: Rhetorical Transformations of the Life Sciences.* Stanford, CA: Stanford UP, 1997.
Keller, Evelyn Fox. *Secrets of Life, Secrets of Death: Essays on Language, Gender, and Science.* New York: Routledge, 1992.

Michael A. Bryson

Geography. A broadly defined science dealing with the surface of the earth, has been fundamental to literature since its beginnings, influencing well-known works by, among others, **Homer**, **Vergil**, **Chaucer**, **Marlowe**, and **Shakespeare** (his seacoast of Bohemia being the most famous mistake). Michael Drayton's "Poly Olbion" is a versified gazetteer of England. Narratives of exploration, collected by Hakluyt and others, greatly expanded literary **imaginations**. The sixteenth-century *Lusiads* of Luis de Camoes, researched by an actual trip to India, was followed in the nineteenth century by **Whitman's** "Passage to India" and then Forster's in the twentieth. The discovery of America was reflected in Marlowe's plays, Shakespeare's *The Tempest*, Drayton's ode "To the Virginian Voyage," Marvell's "Bermudas," and innumerable later celebrations of Columbus. The plants, animals, and peoples of newfound lands have been immensely influential in all areas of human knowledge and their literary impact almost incalculable in magnitude, modern interest in other worlds and **space travel** (seventeenth century to the present) being only an updated version of it.

Reference

Kish, George, ed. *A Source Book in Geography.* Cambridge: Harvard UP, 1978.

Dennis R. Dean

Germanicus Caesar (15 B.C.E.–A.D. 19). Roman general, grandson of Augustus, adopted son of Tiberius, poisoned at thirty-four. Known for his humanitarianism and learning, he wrote two Greek comedies and a translation of **Aratus's** astronomical-astrological poem *Phaenomena*, which influenced **Cicero**, **Vergil**, and **Milton**.

Pamela Gossin

Giants. Beings of immense stature. Because giants are mentioned in the King James Bible (Gen. 6:4), in classical literature, and in the accounts of early European explorers to the New World, they have proved resilient inhabitants of the shifting frontier between fact and **fiction**. From the voyage of Magellan to that of **Darwin**, giants were thought to inhabit Patagonia, South America.

Lisa Gitelman

Gibson, William (1948–   ). In the prototypical **cyberpunk** novel *Neuromancer* (1984), Gibson introduced the term **cyberspace** to **science fiction** and popular culture. The "terminal identity fictions" (Bukatman 9) of cyberpunk science fiction mark both the end of the modernist subject and the construction of new posthuman subjectivities within global information networks.

Reference

Bukatman, Scott. *Terminal Identity: The Virtual Subject in Postmodern Science Fiction.* Durham, NC: Duke UP, 1993.

Noel Gough

Gilman, Charlotte Perkins (1860–1935). American feminist, social critic, and author, whose widely read utopian novel *Herland* (1915) depicts an isolated but scientifically advanced and ecologically self-sustaining society of women who are discovered by three male explorers. The novel exposes and critiques the biases and limitations of androcentric **culture**, science and exploration. *The Yellow Wallpaper* (wr. 1890; pub. 1899) is a semiautobiographical account of a woman writer's psychological breakdown and her physician-husband's ill-fated attempts to cure her.

Michael A. Bryson

Glanvill, Joseph (1636–1680). Divine, Fellow of the **Royal Society**, and an important Latitudinarian Anglican apologist for the Royal Society. In such works as *Scepsis Scientifica* (1665), *Plus Ultra* (1668), and *Philosophia Pia* (1671), Glanvill argued that the new science promoted piety (through **natural theology**), social unity, and utilitarian learning. He also argued for a belief in witchcraft grounded on observed evidence (**Joseph Addison** based his 1715 comedy *The Drummer* on a spirit-rapping incident described in *Saducismus Triumphatus*). Glanvill's advocacy of a "plain style" in prose (see Jones) has recently been reconsidered as contributing to a "propagandist" "self-validating" "myth of plainness" constructed by the established church (Vickers 45).

References

Jones, Richard Foster. *The Seventeenth Century: Studies in the History of English Thought and Literature from Bacon to Pope.* Stanford: Stanford UP, 1951.
Vickers, Brian. "The Royal Society and English Prose Style: A Reassessment." *Rhetoric*

and the Pursuit of Truth: Language Change in the Seventeenth and Eighteenth Centuries. Los Angeles: William Andrews Clark Memorial Library, 1985. 1–76.

Lisa Zeitz

Gleick, James (1954–   ). American popular science writer. In *Chaos: Making a New Science* (1987), he traces the revolutionary development of nonlinear systems study in **biology**, **physics**, and other fields and discusses how scientists uncover ordered patterns in complex, randomly determined phenomena. His *Genius: The Life and Science of Richard Feynman* (1992) offers a tour de force scientific biography as instructive for its creative use of the genre as for its historical detail.

Michael A. Bryson

Gnosticism. Religious heresy, denounced by the early Church from the time of Irenaeus's *Adversus haereses* (c. 180–192) onward and by the established churches of the Middle Ages and Modern Period. Gnosticism is the belief in indwelling *gnosis*, or knowledge, propagated by the efficacious workings of an immanent principle (*pneuma*) in the material world. The belief takes its rise from the understanding that the hexameral account of the Creation (Gen. 1–2: 7a) is the misunderstanding of a misbegotten and misshapen being known as *Yaldabaoth* ("begetter of the heavenly powers") and that the material world maintains its connections with its heavenly origins in a being known as *Pistis Sophia* (Faith Wisdom) only because of the operation of *pneuma* in the world, which is chronicled imperfectly in the second account of the Creation (Gen. 2: 7b–25).

Since the discovery, in 1945, of the Nag Hammadi codices, the most diverse and richest compendium of gnostic literature and liturgy currently known, scholarly interest in gnostic beliefs and practices has increased. Most particularly, interest has picked up since the publication, in 1977, of the *Nag Hammadi Library*, an English translation, by several hands, of the codices, followed some two years later by Elaine Pagels's *The Gnostic Gospels*.

The importance of gnosticism for literature and science has to do with its insistence on the primacy and fundamentality of the immaterial as the basis of material phenomena and cognition and on the instrumentality of personal revelation as the basis for social, political, and religious order. As a system of positions and beliefs, gnosticism resists such tactics as reification, **argument from design**, and public demonstration. Adopted as a credo by such millenarian radicals as John Everard, who translated *The Divine Pymander of Hermes Trismegistus* in 1650, and **William Blake**, who professed his gnostic commitment to Henry Crabb Robinson, gnosticism also influenced those who attempted to respond to the materialist science of the Newtonian Revolution (*see* Newtonianism), such as **Joseph Priestley** and **Goethe**. In recent times, gnosticism has figured prominently in the fiction of **Thomas Pynchon**—most particularly in *Gravity's Rainbow* (1973).

References

Jonas, Hans. *The Gnostic Religion: The Message of the Alien God and the Beginnings of Christianity.* 2nd rev. ed. London: Routledge, 1992.

Pagels, Elaine. *The Gnostic Gospels.* New York: Random House, 1979.

Robinson, James M., ed. *The Nag Hammadi Library in English.* New York: Harper and Row, 1977.

Rudolph, Kurt. *Gnosis: The Nature and History of an Ancient Religion.* Trans. Robert McLachlan Wilson. Edinburgh: T. and T. Clark, 1983.

Stuart Peterfreund

Goethe, Johann Wolfgang von (1749–1832). German poet, playwright, novelist, amateur biologist, color theorist, geologist. Goethe's work is perhaps the prime example of the unity of literary and scientific activity, and he is revered in Germany for his literary achievement and universal talents. His literary works refer to themes of **alchemy** and **chemistry**. His scientific works embody an aesthetic (*see* Art and Aesthetics) approach to nature and knowledge.

Goethe was interested in alchemy. In *Faust*, he portrayed the life of a Renaissance alchemist resembling **Paracelsus**. The Faustian bargain with the devil became symbolic of the dilemmas of modern science and its power for good and evil. In *The Parable*, Goethe utilized alchemical **symbolism**. In *Elective Affinities*, he used that contemporary chemical doctrine, a forerunner of valence bonding, to structure a series of romantic relationships of his protagonists.

Goethe brought an aesthetic perception to **botany**, anatomy, geology, and **optics**. He believed that there were primordial phenomena that yield insight into the nature of things. He developed his botany in terms of the primordial plant. He searched for continuities and discovered the intermaxillary bone in the human skull, similar to other mammals. His geological interests involving the debate between theories of sedimentation and vulcanism (*see* Volcanoes) appear early in Part Two of *Faust*. His *Theory of Colors* challenged Newton's (*see* Newtonianism) analysis of white light into colors and claimed that white and black are colors. The latter **theory** was a defense of direct perceptual intuition against analytic abstraction. It resembles some psychological theories of vision based on warm and cool colors.

Goethe's attempt to keep science united to direct, aesthetic perception of primordial forms failed, but his particular achievements in science have gained recognition. Scientists Hermann von Helmholtz, **Werner Heisenberg**, and Charles Sherrington have been both attracted to and highly critical of his aesthetic approach to color theory. Some reverberations of Goethe's theory appear in **Thomas Pynchon's** *Gravity's Rainbow*.

Val Dusek

Goldbarth, Albert (1948–   ). American poet, essayist, and professor who combines **Whitman's** inclusiveness with the ironies and juxtapositions of postmodernism. An eccentric scientist, he is interested in everything, from Leeuwenhoek and Percival Lowell to comic books and **religion**. More than any American poet of his generation, Goldbarth has embraced the language of science and **science fiction** to shape the metaphors and images of his **poetry**. His language is an amalgam of technical jargon, popular **culture**, and the logos of **Romanticism**. This vocabulary is sometimes deployed to treat scientific subjects but more often is used to defamiliarize the reader's response by filtering familiar situations through strange language, as in "We're Just About to Observe the Edge of the Universe," as well as most of the poems from *Marriage and Other Science Fiction* (1994). Beginning as a poet, Goldbarth has in recent years produced two collections of pyrotechnic essays saturated with the language of science and the popular culture of science. Goldbarth's work is so original it has repelled disciples but could we time-travel (as we can in some of his poems) we would discover in the future his central place in our literature.

References

Goldbarth, Albert. *Arts & Sciences*. Princeton, NJ: Ontario Review, 1986.
————. *A Sympathy of Souls*. Minneapolis: Coffee House, 1990.

Joseph Duemer

Goncourt, Edmond de and Jules de (1822–1896; 1830–1870). Brothers and lifelong collaborators who honed their powers of observation in watercolor sketches and journals detailing social life and offered unflinching documentation of lower-class living conditions, prostitution, prisons, and hospitals. Emphasizing the influence of **environment** upon the character and potential of the individual, they produced some of the first French novels of **naturalism**, *Germinie Lacerteux* (1864) and *Madame Gervaisais* (1869).

Pamela Gossin

Gosse, Edmund (1849–1928). Biographer, translator, and essayist. Gosse's autobiography, *Fathers and Sons* (1907), recounts his relationship with his father, the zoologist Philip Henry Gosse, who rejected Darwinian (*see* Darwin) natural selection in favor of his religious fundamentalism. Gosse's interest in new scientific ideas caused a break with his father.

Kristine Swenson

Gothicism. Literary genre first appearing in the mid-eighteenth century with Horace Walpole's novel *The Castle of Otranto* (1764) but reaching its prime in the 1790s in the work of Ann Radcliffe, Matthew Lewis, and numerous others. Through its conventional motifs (sublimely imposing and confusing architecture, chiaroscuro description, enclosure and bondage, violence, psychological doubling, **supernatural** occurrences, and more), the genre suggests a dissatisfaction with rationalist certainty, particularly as it is expressed through **theories** of ocular perception. The seeds of modern-depth psychology (*see* Anthropology/Psychology/Sociology) are present in the Gothic novel as well, symbolically expressed through scenes of subterranean imprisonment and pursuit. With **Mary Shelley's** *Frankenstein* (1818) the genre's possibilities are extended into an analysis of scientific ethical risks, and Gothicism's connection with **science fiction** is established. Endemic in novels of the nineteenth and twentieth centuries, Gothicism and its conventions continue to provide writers with a powerful, multifaceted mode of cultural analysis.

Reference

Punter, David. *The Literature of Terror: A History of Gothic Fictions from 1765 to the Present Day.* London: Longmans, 1980.

Stephen D. Bernstein

Gould, Stephen Jay (1941–2002). Evolutionist, historian, popularizer, coauthor of the **theory** of punctuated equilibrium, claiming that species are mostly in a static state, punctuated by rapid changes. Gould was probably the best regarded popular science writer of the late twentieth century. He said he attempted to recapture the quality of Victorian **natural history essays**. His elegant essays on evolution were laced with literary allusions and humor. They placed theories in social context and emphasized contingency and nonadapted structures. Gould criticized notions of progress, **determinism**, and hierarchy in evolution, as well as **sociobiology** and beliefs in innate group differences in human intelligence.

Val Dusek

Gravity/Antigravity. Terms used to refer to attractive and repulsive effects or forces perceived to operate in the universe. **Aristotle's** notion of gravity as roughly equivalent to weight differs tremendously from Newton's (*see* Newtonianism) description of the relations of mass and distance and **Einstein's** conceptualizations of the curvature of space. Recently cosmologists have postulated that dark energy may act as an antigravitational force, perpetuating the expansive effects of the Big Bang. Writers have capitalized on the fact that the nature of gravity is unknown despite Isaac Newton's formulation of the laws governing it. Gravity and antigravity have thus been important elements in speculative **fiction** ranging from **Johannes Kepler's** *Somnium* to **Jules Verne, H.G. Wells**, and modern fantasies. Antigravity devices abound in early **science fiction** (*apergy, cavorite*, fluids, rays, etc.). Weightlessness has been linked to psychological states as well, as in the works of George MacDonald, Franz Kafka, or Paul Auster.

Reference

Schenkel, Elmar. "Antigravity: Matter and the Imagination in George MacDonald and Early Science Fiction." *Northwind* 14 (1995): 46–56.

Elmar Schenkel and Pamela Gossin

Gray, Alasdair (1934–   ). Scottish writer and artist whose works frequently address the social costs of scientific and technological development. In *Lanark* (1981) individual use of **technology** is paid for through accelerated aging. *Poor Things* (1992) questions Victorian scientific procedure, medical education, and epistemological certainty. The short story "Near the Driver" (1993) features discussions concerning the history of rail innovation, British imperial decline, and blind adherence to official dogma. In *A History Maker* (1994) Gray asks what societies would do should a technological **utopia** be achieved, suggesting a dissonance between human character and a peaceful existence where most work is done by "power plants."

References

Bernstein, Stephen. *Alasdair Gray*. Lewisburg, PA: Bucknell UP, 1999.
Crawford, Robert, and Thom Nairn, eds. *The Arts of Alasdair Gray*. Edinburgh: Edinburgh UP, 1991.

Stephen D. Bernstein

Gribbin, John (1946–   ). English science writer and novelist. A prolific popularizer of science who has written books and articles on **astronomy**, climate change, potential natural disasters, geology, evolution, and modern **physics**. Gribbin has also written biographies of scientists: *Einstein: A Life in Science* (1994) and, with Michael White, *Stephen Hawking: A Life in Science* (1992). His **popularizations** of modern physics include an account of quantum theory entitled *In Search of Schrödinger's Cat* (1984), followed by *Schrödinger's Kittens and the Search for Reality* (1995), and a speculative piece about **relativity theory** entitled *In Search of the Edge of Time* (1992).

June Deery

Grunwald, Lisa (1959–   ). American journalist and writer whose first novel, *Summer* (1986), provides a poignantly accurate psychological account of a family's response to the mother's diagnosis of cancer. In *The Theory of Everything* (1991), the protagonist is a physicist at the crux of thirty whose work with grand unifying **theories** must expand to include the alchemical and astrological beliefs of his mother and the emotional and personal strings of his girlfriend. Her other works include another novel, *New Year's Eve* (1996), a children's book on **time**, and an epistolary social history, *Letters of the Century: America 1900–1999* (1999).

Pamela Gossin

Gynecology. The medical term referring to the study of female physiology is, in radical feminist literature and **theory**, wrested from phallotechnic space by the wordplay "gyn/ecology." This term refers to the need for women to preserve a female, nonpatriarchal, nontechnological space and was coined in *Gyn/ecology: The Metaethics of Radical Feminism* (1978), an important feminist text by Mary Daly. Daly reflected a growing awareness of the **politics** of language and the social construction of identity found in subsequent theorists, including Alice Jardine (*Gynesis: Configurations of Women and Modernity*, 1985), Julia Kristeva (*Desire in Language*, 1980), and many novelists, including Joanna Russ (*The Female Man*, 1977) and Monique Wittig (*The Lesbian Body*, 1975), and influenced the concept of "writing the body," or écriture femininé. (*See* Corporeality/Body.)

Mary Libertin

H

Haldane, J.B.S. (1892–1964). Leading British theoretical biologist and popular science writer. He popularized his important neo-Darwinian **genetics** in *The Causes of Evolution* (1932). His command of a range of genres—including scientific prophesy (*Daedalus*, 1924) and the newspaper column (*Science and Everyday Life*, 1939)—and his reflection on the intellectual and linguistic rigors of **popularization** ("How to Write a Popular Scientific Article," 1946) exemplify the role of literary form in science's social interrelations. Haldane employs striking analogies (*see* Analogy) linking science with **philosophy**, **politics**, and everyday experience; conversely, in *Heredity and Politics* (1938) and "Human Genetics and Human Ideals" he strongly critiques analogies inherent in racial and eugenic thought.

Reference

Haldane, J.B.S. "Human Genetics and Human Ideals." *Scientific Progress*. James Jeans et al. London: Allen, 1936. 143–73.

Doug Russell

Haraway, Donna J. (1944–). American historian of science, trained in **biology** (Ph.D. Yale). Haraway critiques the natural sciences from a socialist-feminist perspective. Much of her writing focuses on the androcentric and constructed nature of Western science, on scientists' rhetorical strategies, and on the feedback loop between ideology, socioeconomics, and scientific discovery.

In her first major work, *Primate Visions: Gender, Race, and Nature in the World of Modern Science* (1989), Haraway draws on scientific accounts and popular **culture** to examine how nature is constructed by Western science, and she identifies androcentric, imperialist, and patriarchal roots in the science of primatology. As a historian, she traces specific networks of power within academia that have influenced the production of knowledge. The essays collected in *Simians, Cyborgs, and Women: The Reinvention of Nature* (1991) identify each of these as boundary creatures, as historically contingent constructions of others that can destablize official Western narratives. A particularly influential essay, "A Cyborg Manifesto" (1985), suggests that the idea of a **cyborg** (a creature part organic, part machine) could be an important imaginative resource for expressing new hybrid, multiple, postgender identities and overcoming such dualisms as natural/artificial, mind/body, human/animal, self/other, male/female, nature/culture, whole/part, active/passive, maker/made. Here and elsewhere, Haraway urges feminists to engage with science and reinvent it in their own images.

Reference

Haraway, Donna J. *Crystals, Fabrics, and Fields: Metaphors of Organicism in Twentieth-Century Developmental Biology.* New Haven, CT: Yale UP, 1976.

June Deery

Hardy, Thomas (1840–1928). English novelist, short story writer, and poet, son of a stonemason, trained as an architect; produced some of the nineteenth century's most sophisticated syntheses of literature and science, especially treating the personal and social consequences of the **Industrial Revolution**, contemporary **astronomy** and **cosmology**, geology, and Darwinian (*see* Darwin) **evolutionary theory**. In a cosmos where "God is not in his heaven and all is wrong with the world" (*Tess of the d'Urbervilles*, 1891), Hardy's fictional characters attempt to fit themselves for survival against biological, psychological, and social forces, often finding themselves caught up in a complex web of expectations and potentials, hopes and desires, mistakes and losses, blind chance, and circumstance. Hardy seems to have believed that natural selection had blundered in allowing living beings to evolve consciousness of their own mortality; but given the "facts" of such a universe, individuals ought to do all they can to enable each other's ability to adapt and thrive during their transient existence. Such themes figure strongly in the emplotment of his novels, characterizations, and settings—for example, the cliff-hanging scene in *A Pair of Blue Eyes* (1873), where the intellectual, Henry Knight, comes face to face with his own mortality, his coequality with the lowest forms in the **fossil record**, and the most primitive fears within his own highly developed, but apparently expendable, psyche; the meticulous analysis of sexual selection and evolutionary fittedness in the characters of Gabriel Oak and Bathsheba, the rural **environment**, and farms of *Far From the Madding Crowd* (1874); the haunting introductory description of the natural and archaeological environs and later lunar eclipse episode between Clym and Eustacia in *The Return of the Native* (1878); the high drama of the astronomical observing scenes in *Two on a Tower* (1882) and the comparative treatment throughout of scientific and religious views of the heavens; the complex—and simple—incommensurability of the individual and the universal for Tess and Jude and the ways their fictional lives play out the tensions among the ideal, the natural, and the real within Gothic, melodramatic, and tragic narrative elements. Hardy's poetry explores similar thematic concerns and highlights (as do the rural characters of his fiction) his ear for local, natural speech patterns as well as his anthropological interest in the folklore and rituals of his native region of Dorset. His intense engagement with contemporary science was lifelong, and in the final year of his life he corresponded with **Einstein** about **time** and **relativity**.

References

Beer, Gillian. *Darwin's Plots: Evolutionary Narrative in Darwin, George Eliot and Nineteenth-Century Fiction.* Boston/London: Routledge, 1983.

Dale, Peter Allan. *In Pursuit of a Scientific Culture: Science, Art, and Society in the Victorian Age.* Madison: U of Wisconsin P, 1989.

Gossin, Pamela. *Thomas Hardy's Novel Universe: Astronomy and the Cosmic Heroines of His Major and Minor Fiction.* Aldershot, United Kingdom: Ashgate Publishing, expected 2003.

Pamela Gossin

Harvey, William (1578–1657). English physician; discoverer of the circulation of the blood. His seminal work *Du Motu Cordis* (1628) is as much an argument for the empirical method as it is a demonstration of the motion and function of the heart. His dissections having led him to question received knowledge derived from **Galen** and his medieval commentators, he asserts that he will learn anatomy from nature rather than books. Harvey's investigations are governed by the microcosmic/macrocosmic relationship between the body and the world—a central metaphor in Renaissance **art** and **poetry**. His metaphor-laden *Du Motu Cordis* insists on plain speaking as well as on the simplest explanation of a phenomenon. Later in the century, the **Royal Society** will elaborate Harvey's observations concerning language and skeptical inquiry.

Anne Bratach Matthews

Hawking, Stephen William (1942–   ). British theoretical physicist who popularized his seminal contributions to **cosmology** in the best-seller *A Brief History of Time: From the Big Bang to Black Holes* (1988). Often ranked with the greatest scientists of history, Hawking portrayed himself in a Star Trek episode, alongside fellow Lucasian professor of mathematics, Isaac Newton (*see* Newtonianism).

JoAnn Palmeri

Hawthorne, Nathaniel (1804–1864). American novelist whose work reflected the Romantic prejudice against science, distrusting **rationality** in favor of emotions as a guide to moral and mental health. In his fiction, intellectual curiosity (epitomized in science) without compassion is regarded as the "unpardonable sin," destroying all in its path (Martin 99).

Hawthorne's interest lay in psychology (*see* Anthropology/Psychology/Sociology) and contemporary fringe sciences, from phrenology to **mesmerism**, and his characters are symbolic alchemists rather than realistic scientists. Aylmer, the chemist protagonist of "The Birthmark" (1845), is obsessed with the scientific challenge presented by his beautiful wife's minor blemish. Her subsequent death, when he removes the flaw, is both the literal and symbolic result of his desire. In "Rappaccini's Daughter" (1844) another heartless scientist cultivates a garden of exquisite but poisonous flowers to study their fatal effect on other life forms. His daughter Beatrice becomes an extension of his experiment as her suitors inhale her poison.

In Hawthorne's most famous novel *The Scarlet Letter* (1837), the aptly named Chillingworth, elderly physician-cum-alchemist, is obsessed with identifying his young wife's lover, but his great sin lies in his invasion of a human heart in order to destroy it. *Septimus Felton or the Elixir of Life* (1871) features another Faustian scientist, a mere spectator of life. These scientists, originally idealists, are all variants of Faustian hubris, desiring to transcend the limitations of human knowledge, but Hawthorne includes a warning that when science progresses more rapidly than society's moral development, it creates its own ethical standards.

References

Bell, Millicent, ed. *New Essays on Hawthorne's Major Tales*. Cambridge: Cambridge UP, 1993.
Heilman, R.B. "The Birthmark: Science as Religion." *South Atlantic Quarterly* 48 (1949): 573–83.
Martin, Terence. *Nathaniel Hawthorne*. Boston: Twayne, 1983.
Stoehr, Taylor. *Hawthorne's Mad Scientists: Pseudoscience and Social Science in Nineteenth-Century Life and Letters*. Hamden, CT: Archon, 1978.

Roslynn D. Haynes

Heinlein, Robert A(nson) (1907–1988). A graduate in naval engineering, much of whose **science fiction** focuses on the military-industrial uses of space. Some of his most inventive and engaging stories, including *Have Space-Suit— Will Travel* (1958), are "juveniles"—novels written for explicitly teenage (and implicitly male) readers.

Noel Gough

Heisenberg, Werner Karl (1901–1976). German physicist, a major figure in the early history of **quantum physics**. In 1925, Heisenberg developed matrix mechanics, a form of quantum mechanics later shown to be equivalent to the alternate formulation in terms of waves due to Erwin Schrödinger. Heisenberg is most famous for his **Uncertainty Principle** of 1927. It states that for certain pairs of physical quantities, such as momentum and position, or **energy** and **time**, the more one knows about one member of the pair, the less one knows about the other. This fundamental indeterminacy is a consequence of the wave-particle duality of quantum physics and has deep implications for our ability to predict and understand the physical world. Heisenberg's *Physical Principles of Quantum Theory* (1930) is a classic, and in other works he explored the philosophical meaning of the quantum. He won the Nobel Prize for Physics in 1932, along with his fellow quantum pioneers, Schrödinger and Paul Dirac.

References

Frayn, Michael. *Copenhagen.* London: Methuen Drama, 1998.
Heisenberg, Werner. *Philosophic Problems of Nuclear Science.* Translated by F.C. Hayes. New York: Pantheon, 1952.
———. *Physics & Philosophy; The Revolution in Modern Science.* New York: Harper and Row, 1958.

Sidney Perkowitz

Herbert, Frank (1920–1986). **Science fiction** writer best known for his ecological novel *Dune* (1965) and its five sequels. Exploring political, economic, and technological ramifications of desertification on a planetary scale, *Dune* reproduces the "discourse of apocalyptic ecologism" (Ellis 104) that flourished in many Western countries during the 1960s.

Reference

Ellis, R.J. "Frank Herbert's *Dune* and the Discourse of Apocalyptic Ecologism in the United States." *Science Fiction Roots and Branches: Contemporary Critical Approaches.* Ed. Rhys Garnet and R.J. Ellis. London: Macmillan, 1990. 104–24.

Noel Gough

Hernández, Francisco (c. 1515–1587). Noted Spanish **physician** and medical humanist, court physician to Philip II. From 1570 to 1577, he headed a scientific expedition to study the **natural history**, medicinal plants, animals, and minerals of New Spain (Mexico). Portions of his writings are included in *Rerum medicarum Novae Hispaniae thesaurus* (Rome, 1651) and Franciso Ximénez's *Quatro Libros de la Naturaleza* (Mexico, 1615).

Rafael Chabrán

Herschel, Caroline (1750–1848). Sister of the astronomer William Herschel who assisted her brother in his research and also made important independent contributions to the field. Born in Germany, she came to England with her brother in 1757, and after a period in which the two earned their livings by **music**, she joined him when his interests turned to **astronomy**. At first, she polished the lenses of the **telescopes** William built and accompanied him in his nighttime observations, recording the results and making the necessary calculations in the daytime. But then, at his suggestion, she undertook observations of her own and made several discoveries, including three new nebulae and eight comets. She compiled extensive catalogs of stars and nebulae and corrected errors and omissions in earlier catalogs. After William died in 1822, she went back to Germany and devoted herself to organizing her brother's papers, work that earned her the gold medal of the **Royal Society** in 1828.

References

Cedering, Siv. "Letter from Caroline Herschel (1750–1848)." *Letters from the Floating World: Selected and New Poems*. Pittsburgh: U of Pittsburgh P, 1984.

Lubbock, Constance A. *The Herschel Chronicle: The Life-Story of William Herschel and His Sister Caroline*. New York: Macmillan; Cambridge: Cambridge UP, 1933.

Herschel, Mrs. John. *Memoir and Correspondence of Caroline Herschel*. New York: D. Appleton, 1876.

Jacob Korg

Herschel, John (1792–1871). The son of William Herschel, who carried on and extended his father's work in **astronomy** and made brilliant contributions to a number of different sciences, including mathematics, **chemistry**, and photography. He became the model scientific figure of his time and was elected to the **Royal Academy** at the age of twenty-one in recognition of his work in mathematics. John at first worked with his father and collaborated with another author in publishing astronomy catalogs that won him prizes from the Royal Academy and the Paris Academy of Sciences and a knighthood. He lived in South Africa from 1833 to 1838 in order to observe the skies of the Southern Hemisphere. After completing this work, he was rewarded with a baronetcy and was later appointed Master of the Mint. Herschel was the author of many scientific publications and works of popular science. His *Outline of Astronomy* had strong influence on the creative writers and poets of his day, including **Thomas Hardy**.

References

Buttman, Gunther. *The Shadow of the Telescope: A Biography of John Herschel*. New York: Scribner, 1970.

Crowe, Michael J. *Modern Theories of the Universe: From Herschel to Hubble*. New York: Dover, 1994.

Evans, David S., et al., eds. *Herschel at the Cape. Diaries and Correspondence of Sir John Herschel*. Austin: U of Texas P, 1969.

Jacob Korg

Herschel, William (1738–1822). British astronomer and founder of the science of observational **cosmology**. His discovery of the planet Uranus in 1781, the first new planet to be seen since ancient times, made him famous and inspired a simile in a sonnet by **John Keats**. Keats, describing his feelings on first reading a translation of **Homer**, referred to Herschel in writing: "Then felt

I like some watcher of the skies/When a new planet swims into his ken." Herschel was born in Germany and moved to England in 1757, where he earned his living as a musician before becoming interested in making **telescopes** and observing the heavens. He did not turn to **astronomy** full-time until the age of forty-three. His major accomplishments as a pioneer in the field were the construction of improved telescopes, the exploration of the universe beyond the solar system, the resolution of nebulae into individual stars, and the **theory** that they underwent evolutionary changes. His work was recognized by the award of a Copley Medal, election to the **Royal Society**, appointment as court astronomer, and from George III, an annual pension of 200 pounds and a generous grant for the construction of a very large telescope.

References

Armitage, A. *William Herschel*. Garden City, NY: Doubleday, 1963.
Hoskin, Michael A. *William Herschel and the Construction of the Heavens*. New York: Norton, 1963.
Sidgwick, J.B. *William Herschel, Explorer of the Heavens*. London: Faber and Faber, 1953.

Jacob Korg

Hesiod (c. eighth century B.C.E.). After **Homer**, second greatest writer of Greek literature. Three principal works are attributed to Hesiod: the *Theogony, Works and Days*, and the *Catalogue of Women*. While these epic poems continue the spirit of Homeric tradition, Hesiod's approach toward his subject matter is suggestive of scientific analysis. He examines the behaviors of the gods, explores their and the world's origins, and creates a genealogical catalog of their unions with mortal women.

Shelly Jarrett Bromberg

Hildegard of Bingen (1098–1179). Abbess at the Disibodenberg convent near Bingen, Germany, her mystical visions inspired innovative perspectives in **cosmology**, **music**, theater, **poetry**, and theology. Among her many writings, *Liber Divinorum Operum* (Book of Divine Works) best embodies her holistic views of the interconnectedness of nature, the soul, and God.

Reference

Flanagan, S. *Hildegard of Bingen, 1098–1179: A Visionary Life*. London: Routledge, 1989.

Philip K. Wilson

Hippocrates (c. 460–c. 377 B.C.E.)/**Hippocratic Writings.** Greek physician and founder of Western **medicine**, whose **theory** of the four bodily fluids or humors formed part of the underpinning of medicine until the seventeenth century. According to this theory, the human body consists of blood, phlegm, yellow bile, and black bile; the healthy body maintains a balance among these fluids. The anonymous Hippocratic writings, written from about 430 to about 260 B.C.E., treat medical subjects ranging from ethics to methodology; they comprise a remarkable dialogue about the nature of man, the causes of disease, and the relationship between reason and sensation. **Galen**, the second-century Greek physician, adopted Hippocrates's humoral theory as the basis for his own medical practice.

Anne Bratach Matthews

Hispanic World (LS in). Can be traced to the twelfth century, when King Alfonso X, the Wise, wrote the *Cantigas*, where, for instance, in "cantiga" 321 he writes about illness as a rationalist would and fuses numerology with **religion** (Castro 371–72). Besides writing literature he was an astronomer as well. A century before Alfonso X became king, Greek and Roman classics began to be translated in Spain, but it was in the famous school of translators of Toledo that the greatest quantity of translations took place, in the twelfth and thirteenth centuries (García-Yebra 90). According to Jacob Bronowski, the conception of the Renaissance took root in Spain because the ancient texts were turned from Greek through Arabic and Hebrew into Latin in Toledo (Bronowski 177). This served as the spark plug that ignited the Renaissance in **Italy**. Also in the fifteenth century in pre-Columbian America, the Aztec king of Tezcoco—in what is now Mexico—Nezahualcóyotl (1402–1472)—was a poet and engineer. He wrote **poetry** infused with the **philosophy** and science of his times.

The European invasion of the American continent in 1492 was made possible by the new technological applications of mathematics, which solved the problem of overcast skies and brought into being the compass, **astronomy**, and new techniques in shipbuilding. Abraham Zacut (1452–1515), working with the Mathematical Council of Lisbon in the application of Greco-Arabic doctrines of Alfonso X, the Wise, was instrumental in some of these scientific developments.

Along with the atrocities committed by the Europeans came a knowledge of the different scientific fields, which were used by the "criollos" (Europeans born in the Americas) to develop their own worldview. In Mexico a poet–mathematician, Carlos de Sigüenza y Góngora (1645–1700), wrote *Libra astronómica y filosófica*, a modern view of comets, and Sister Juana Inés de la Cruz (1651–1695) wrote "Primero sueño" (First Dream), a 975-verse poem where she addressed the categories of scientific discourse. Sor Juana was also the first feminist of the Western Hemisphere. She defended the rights of women to be educated and attend college (Catalá, *Ciencíapoesia*).

In Spain, novelists like **Miguel de Cervantes** (1547–1616) and playwrights such as Félix Lope de Vega (1562–1635), Tirso de Molina (1584?–1648), and Pedro Calderón de la Barca (1600–1681) were expressing in their work the scientific and philosophic ideas of their time. Their sources included, for example, the work of the natural philosophers Domingo de Soto (1494–1560) and Francisco Suárez (1548–1617). De Soto worked on the latitude of forms and investigated laws of motion as mathematical possibilities (Bynum et al. 229). Suárez, influenced by **Aristotle** and Thomas Aquinas, wrote the *Disputationes metaphysicae* (1597), the first systematic and comprehensive work on metaphysics written in the West that went beyond mere commentary on Aristotle's *Metaphysics*. Suárez's work became a very important and lasting influence on **Descartes**, Leibniz, Wolff, and Schopenhauer. Its influence was felt not only in Europe but in Latin America as well. The Suarezian system dominated thought at Catholic and Protestant German and Dutch universities of the seventeenth and eighteenth centuries. A contemporary of Suárez, Juan Huarte de San Juan (1529–1588), wrote a book on the nature of human intelligence, *Examen de ingenios para las ciencias* (1575). This book also strongly influenced Descartes, as Noam Chomsky pointed out in *Cartesian Linguistics* (n. 78–79) and *Language and Mind* (9–11). Juan Luis Vives (1492–1540) wrote *De disciplinis* (1531), a book on **epistemology**, and *De Anima et Vita* (1538), a pioneer work in the field of psychology (*see* Anthropology/Psychology/Sociology). Vives's and Huarte's books were translated into many European languages and saw many editions and reprints over the next two centuries. The scientific ideas of these writers, as well as other Spanish scientists like the mathematician Juan Caramuel Lobkowitz (1606–1682), Juan de Cabriada (1665–1714), professor of medicine at the University of Valencia, the physician José Lucas Casalete (1630–1701), and the astronomer Vicente Mut (1614–1687), plus other European scientists, were major influences in the work of the poets and writers of Golden Age Spain (López-Piñero et al).

During the nineteenth and early twentieth centuries the works of the botanist Gregor J. Mendel, the biologist **Charles Darwin**, and the psychoanalysts **Sigmund Freud** and Carl Jung sparked new images in the literary minds of the world. They renewed the relationship between science and literature as we can witness in the work of **Benito Pérez Galdós** (1843–1920), **Emilia Pardo Bazán** (1851–1921), **Pío Baroja** (1872–1956), **Miguel de Unamuno** (1864–1936), Ramón del Valle Inclán (1866–1936), Antonio Machado (1875–1939), Gabriel Miró (Spain, 1879–1930), Antonio Buero Vallejo (1916–2000) and many others. Critics such as Rafael Chabrán have studied the scientific subtext in Unamuno; Kevin Larsen has worked on the medical sciences in Galdós (1996) and **thermodynamics** in Gabriel Miró (*La ciencia*; "Miró"); and Jerry Hoeg has studied communication and **information theory** in Valle Inclán ("Communication"). In Hispanic America, novels like *Cecilia Valdés* by Cirilo Villaverde (Cuba, 1812–1894), *Sin rumbo* by Eugenio Cambaceres (Argentina, 1843–1888), *La vorágine* by Eustasio Rivera (Colombia, 1889–1928), *Doña Bárbara* by Rómulo Gallegos (Venezuela, 1884–1959), *Cuentos de amor de locura y de muerte* by Horacio Quiroga (Uruguay, 1878–1937), and the work of two major figures in the sociohistorical discourse, Eugenio María de Hostos (Puerto Rico, 1839–1903) and **Domingo Faustino Sarmiento** (Argentina, 1811–1888) are a few examples of how **genetics**, the theory of evolution, and psychoanalysis found their way into the literature of Spain and Hispanic America.

From the 1920s and 1930s the impact of the theory of **relativity** and quantum mechanics began to resonate in poetry and **fiction**. This momentum continues today with **chaos theory** and Benoit Mandelbrot's fractal geometry, **Gregory Bateson's** view of communication and ecology, and David Bohm's *Wholeness and the Implicate Order*. The momentum is magnified with the new **biology**, which the Santiago Theory exemplifies. This is the product of two Chilean biologists, Humberto Maturana and **Francisco Varela**, who developed the study of **autopoiesis**, a term they coined to describe the self-organization and maintenance of living systems. Their books *Autopoiesis and Cognition* (Spanish 1972, English 1980) and *The Tree of Knowledge* (Spanish 1984, English 1987) have brought a new dimension to the way we think of life as process and cognition.

This constant succession of epistemological evolution can be studied in the works of Macedonio Fernández (Argentina, 1874–1952), **Jorge Luis Borges** (Argentina, 1899–1986), Alejo Carpentier (Cuba, 1904–1980), Clemente Soto Vélez (Puerto Rico, 1905–1994), **Julio Cortázar** (Argentina, 1914–1984), Octavio Paz (Mexico, 1914–1998), Nicanor Parra (Chile, 1914–   ), Camilo José Cela (Spain, 1916–   ), Miguel Delibes (Spain, 1920–   ), Lucila Velázquez (Venezuela, 1927–   ), **Gabriel García Márquez** (Colombia, 1928–   ), Juan Goytisolo (Spain, 1931–   ), Severo Sarduy (Cuba, 1937–1992), **Rafael Catalá** (Cuba, 1942–   ), Leopoldo Castilla (Argentina, 1947–   ), Vilma Bayron-Brunet (Puerto Rico, 1946–   ), David Jou (Spain, 1953–   ), Lourdes Sifontes-Greco (Venezuela, 1961–   ), and many others. Of all the writers just mentioned, Borges is perhaps the best-known writer in Spanish language whose fiction has dealt most deeply with the relationship between science and literature. Borges's works deal with many problems of science that have captivated the mind for centuries.

The explicit discourse on the relationship between literature (and the humanities) and science began with **José Martí** (Cuba, 1853–1895) (Catalá, "La cultura," 1983; "Para une teoría," 1990; "What is Sciencepoetry?" 1988). Martí wrote several essays on the importance of bringing together the sciences and literature. Later on he brought this vision to practice in the poem "Yugo y estrella" (The Yoke and the Star), where he fuses the theory of evolution and ethics in an aesthetic expression.

José Vasconcelos (México, 1881–1959), a philosopher and fiction writer, was also a major figure in this discourse. In his books *Ética* (1932) and *Estética* (1936), Vasconcelos writes about the need to integrate **quantum physics** and the theory of **relativity** with the humanities and religion. He stated that in discovering these relationships a new cultural synthesis would ensue (Catalá, Lectures, 1992).

The work begun by these writers continued in the writing of Octavio Paz, Severo Sarduy, and Rafael Catalá. Paz explored science-humanities relations in *Alternating Current* (Spanish 1967, English 1973) and *El signo y el garabato* (1973). Luis Jiménez has written of Paz that he "insists upon the need of communication through language since 'the cosmos is the language of languages.'"

His main concern is to tie the expression of human thoughts to physics" ("Paz" 113). Sarduy's *Big Bang* (1974) is a collection of poems emanating from the different cosmological theories; *Barroco* (1974) is a theoretical study that deals with science, literature, and art from the times before the baroque to our day; and *Steady State* (1980) is a series of six poems on cosmology using a mixed-media technique. Ulloa points out that Sarduy "writes for readers in the future about the present moment by laughably integrating in fragments the epistemology of the XX century" (Ulloa 73–74). He along with Alejo Carpentier and José Lezama Lima are representatives of the Latin American neo-Baroque. In 1986 Catalá wrote *Cienciapoesía* (Sciencepoetry), a book with a theoretical introduction and a collection of sciencepoems (one word). He describes **sciencepoetry** as the holistic vision of reality in which science and the humanities are actively engaged in an aesthetic work (Jiménez, "Octavio Paz," 110). Jerry Hoeg calls sciencepoetry a "strategic innovation that consists in making a basic change in the way in which we conceive our relationship with others and the universe" ("Cienciapoesía"). The work of these three writers is engaged in the theoretical exploration and creative expression of the relationship between literature and science.

The Argentinian novelist Ernesto Sábato (1911–   ) expressed this relationship by rejecting science. After earning his Ph.D. in physics in 1937 and working for a year at the Curie Laboratory in Paris, he began to leave science for literature. His conflict seems to have emerged from his disenchantment with communism, on the one hand, and with modern science and the misuse of **technology**, on the other. In *Uno y el universo* (One and the Universe) (1945), he writes that "[t]he power of science is acquired by a sort of pact with the devil: a progressive evanescence of our daily life. Science becomes the monarch, but when it attains this, its realm is but a kingdom of ghosts" (45). Sábato rejected the hard sciences because of their supposed cold objectivity and lack of moral values. He writes that "scientific analysis is depressive: like men who upon entering a prison become numbers," but a few years before writing this statement, between 1938 and 1942, he developed a theory on the concept of temperature in phenomenological **thermodynamics**. In 1943 he left science forever. According to a biography by Carlos Catania, Sábato "felt nauseated by the path the spirit of science had taken, its brutal abstraction" (41). On the other hand, Sábato writes in this book about the morality of scientists who are willing to accept that a theory is wrong when so proven. It seems to me that what we are seeing here is a profound ideological conflict between scientific discourse and practice. Even though he had chosen to be a novelist, he could not exclude himself from his scientific background. The discourse of science in Sábato's novels is an interesting aspect that has not been studied yet (Catalá, "Literatura y clencia," 1998).

Another poet–physicist is the Chilean Nicanor Parra. He did not reject science, but he did not incorporate science into his poetic discourse until much later in his career as a poet. This may very well be due to the pedagogical split in primary and secondary schools and colleges throughout the world that teaches that the humanities and the sciences are opposites—what **C.P. Snow** has called the **two cultures**, thus creating a psychological schism impossible to reconcile in some writers such as Parra and Sábato.

In the 1980s and 1990s there was an explosion of creative works where the relationship between science and literature is very apparent. **Ernesto Cardenal's** (Nicaragua, 1925–   ) *Cántico cósmico* (Cosmic Canticle) (1989) was called by Enrique Lamadrid an "astrophysical epic" (147). In it we find a synthesis of cosmology, ethics, and ecology. In Argentina, Arturo Alvarez Sosa's (1935–   ) *La singularidad desnuda* (Naked Singularity) weaves together eroticism and quantum physics; in Venezuela, Lucila Velazquez's *El arbol de Chernobyl/The Tree of Chernobyl* (1989) deals with the misuse of technology; in Puerto Rico, Eduardo Forastieri-Braschi's *Sobre el tiempo de los signos* (On the Time of Signs) (1992) is a dialogue between physics, cosmology, philosophy, and other humanities through writers and scientists like Charles Sanders Peirce and Juan de Valdés.

In 1989 the **Ometeca** Institute (New Brunswick, New Jersey) was founded. It is devoted to the study of the relationship between science and the humanities in general, with an emphasis on Hispanic and Luso-Brazilian literatures and cultures. It publishes the journal *Ometeca* and sponsors working sessions/conferences throughout the Americas.

References

Bohm, David. *Wholeness and the Implicate Order*. London: Routledge and Kegan Paul, 1980.

Bronowski, J. *The Ascent of Man*. Boston: Little, Brown, 1973.

Bynum, W.F., et al. *Dictionary of the History of Science*. Princeton, NJ: Princeton UP, 1981.

Castro, Américo. *La realidad histórica de España*. 3rd ed. México: Porrúa, 1966.

Catalá, Rafael. *Cienciapoesía*. Minneapolis: Prisma Institute, 1986.

———. "La Cultura en la practica de la liberta." Ideologies and Literature 4.16 (1983): 197–212.

———. Lectures. "What is Sciencepoetry?" Given at University of Connecticut-Storrs, November 23, 1992; and "A Possible Integration of the Humanities and Science." Given at Hostos Community College of the City University of New York, December 23, 1992.

———. "Literatura y ciencia en las culturas de habla española." *La Torre* 3.9 (1998): 529–550.

———. *Para una lectura americana del barroco mexicano: Sor Juana Inés de la Cruz y Sigüenza y Góngora*. Minneapolis: Prisma Institute, 1987.

———. "Para una teoría latinoamericana de las relaciones de la ciencias con las humanidades: La cienciapoesía." *Revista de Filosofía* (U of Costa Rica) 28.67–68 (1990): 215–23.

———. "What Is Sciencepoetry?" *Publication of the Society of Literature and Science* 3.4 (Aug. 1988): 1, 14–15.

Catania, Carlos. *Genio y figura de Ernesto Sábato*. Buenos Aires: Editorial Universitaria de Buenos Aires, 1987.

Chabrán, Rafael. "Miguel de Unamuno: Traductor de Herbert Spencer." *Anuario del Departamento de Filsofía*. Universidad Autónoma de Madrid, Cursos 1986–1987 y 1987–1988: 33–43.

————. "Unamuno's Early Salamanca Years." *Revista Canadiense de Estudios Hispán- icos* XI.2 (1987): 244–56.

Chomsky, Noam. *Cartesian Linguistics.* New York: Harper and Row, 1966.

————. *Language and Mind.* Enlarged ed. New York: Harcourt Brace Jovanovich, 1972.

García-Yebra, Valentín. *Traducción: Historia y teoría.* Madrid: Gredos, 1994.

Hoeg, Jerry. "Cienciapoesía: Una innovación estratégica." *Rafael Catalá: Del 'Círculo cuadrado' a la 'Cienciapoesía.'* Ed. Luis A. Jiménez. New Brunswick, NJ: Ome- teca Institute, 1994.

————. "Communication, Information, and Literature: Los cuernos de Don Friolera." *Ometeca* 3.2–4.1 (1996): 128–41.

Jiménez, Luis A. "Octavio Paz and Sciencepoetry: Theoretical Convergences." *Ometeca* 1.2–2.1 (1989–1990): 110–18.

————, ed. *Rafael Catalá: Del 'Círculo cuadrado' a la 'Cienciapoesía.'* New Bruns- wick, NJ: Ometeca Institute, 1994.

Lamadrid, Enrique. "The Quantum Poetics of Ernesto Cardenal." *Ometeca* 2.2 (1991): 147–151.

Larsen, Kevin. *La ciencia aplicada.* Madrid: Editorial Alpuerto, 1997.

————. "Gabriel Miró, Lucretius, and Thermodynamics." *Ometeca* 1:1 (1989): 77–92.

López-Piñero, José, et al. *Diccionario histórico de la ciencia moderna en España.* 2 vols. Barcelona: Península, 1983.

Maturana, Humberto, and Francisco Varela. *Autopoiesis and Cognition.* Dordrecht: D. Reidel, 1980.

————. *The Tree of Knowledge: The Biological Roots of Human Understanding.* Boston: Shambala, 1987.

Sarduy, Severo. "Steady State." *Severo Sarduy.* Catalog. Madrid: Museo Nacional Centro de Arte Reina Sofía, 1998. 57–64.

Ulloa, Leonor A. "Signos en rotación en el neobarroco pictórico de Severo Sarduy." *Ometeca* 1.1 (1989): 62–76.

Rafael Catalá

History of Science. Can be conceived as a distinct literary genre that con- stitutes an important but often overlooked intersection of literature and science. To a great extent, our view of science as the engine and index of **progress** and as a hallmark of Western civilization was established by histories of science, which emerged as a distinctive literary form in the early nineteenth century, approximately 100 years before history of science was established as a discipline and during a period when science had not yet attained the prestige it enjoyed by the end of the nineteenth century.

Although histories of individual sciences and biographies of great scientists have been written since ancient times, the comprehensive narrative history of science, which treats all the sciences as opposed to a single science or scientist, is a product of the same early-nineteenth-century forces that led to the coining of the term "scientist," the formation of the British Association for the Advance- ment of Science, and the proliferation of publications aimed at broad dissemi- nation of scientific knowledge. These forces sought to establish a clearly defined intellectual and cultural identity for science.

As a literary form, the history of science holds interest for students of LS for several reasons. To begin with, the comprehensive history of science, which unifies the sciences and puts science at the center of history, constitutes an elegant and highly successful rhetorical strategy. Moreover, as historians of science have sought to create valid, useful, and appealing historical accounts, they have drawn on a wide range of literary sources and themes, and they have experimented with an even wider range of genres. This entry provides a historical overview of the themes and genres used by historians of science from the early nineteenth century up to the present. The designation "historian of science," as it is used here, refers not only to professional historians of science but also to the many scientists, general historians, teachers of science, and journalists who have produced historical writing about science.

Aims and Audiences

The literary strategies used by historians of science are best understood in light of the enduring aims and typical audiences for the history of science. Histories of science have been designed to achieve one or more of three interrelated aims: (1) conveying the substance of science and the view of the natural world that emerges from scientific study (the pedagogical aim); (2) associating science with positive cultural values, establishing the centrality of science to progress and to **culture**, and creating a heroic image for scientists (the persuasive aim); and (3) distinguishing science from other forms of knowledge and discerning the principles by which science advances so that its advancement can be accelerated (the philosophical aim). Although scientists have been important both as writers and readers of the history of science, historians of science have often addressed a broad audience consisting of educated readers who were neither scientists nor academic historians.

For all of these audiences and aims, writing the history of science has meant interpreting science by defining it and explaining its significance. Achieving excellence as a historian of science has almost always required a strong interdisciplinary background that combines knowledge of science with the standards of scholarship associated with humanistic learning.

Strategies and Themes

The rhetorical strategy embodied in the comprehensive history of science has become so entrenched that it is hard to recognize *as* a strategy, largely because it has become one of the master narratives of Western culture. The heart of the strategy is a monolithic conception of science as a unified activity with a very broad scope, as opposed to a number of separate lines of inquiry with much narrower scope. The comprehensive history places unified science at the center of a historical narrative in which the history of science becomes coextensive with the history of civilization "from the earliest to the present times." Once this frame of reference is established, a single event, science, or figure can be viewed as an instance or part of the larger entity.

Historians of science use a number of literary techniques to support this rhetorical strategy. They have used dramatization, thick description, strong characterization, and evocative language to engage the reader's **imagination**; to make it possible for readers to visualize remote, invisible, or microscopic processes; and to make individual scientists seem heroic and appealing. Historians of science have also made extensive use of metaphor and **analogy**, along with images, themes, and quotations from literature.

The metaphors and images drawn from literary sources are used to give a recognizable shape to the pattern by which science developed or to scientific knowledge as a whole. One of the most common metaphors used by historians of science is the metaphor of the tree or river of knowledge in which branches or rivulets form increasingly large trunks. This metaphor provides a model of science as able to capture both general and particular truths, to unite disparate pieces of knowledge into a unified whole, and to recognize distinct branches of inquiry while still maintaining the unity of the larger entity.

Historians have also used literature to interpret science. In interpreting and attaching positive value to science, historians of the nineteenth century devoted surprisingly little attention to its practical value but instead linked science to traditional religious and moral values. Historians of science drew and continue to draw on themes established by poets inspired by science in the seventeenth and eighteenth centuries, such as Isaac Watts. Perhaps the most important of these themes is the idea that the wisdom of God is revealed in the order, harmony, immensity, plenitude, and beauty of the natural world. In this view, science becomes a pathway to God, and nature becomes a source of moral truth. Many historians of science set up chapters by quoting literary responses to science or to nature. They draw on a wide range of sources ranging from Greek and Roman writers, **Milton**, and **Shakespeare**, to eighteenth-century and Romantic poets. As a way of validating and diffusing criticisms of science, historians of science often quote poets such as **Pope** who emphasize the limitations of science but still embrace science as a pathway to God. All of these aims, tendencies, and strategies are exemplified in **Whewell's** *History of the Inductive Sciences from the Earliest to the Present Times* (3 vols., 1837). Although several interesting comprehensive histories of science were written in the nineteenth century, Whewell's *History* provides one of the earliest and most influential examples of comprehensive history of science.

Significant Historical Changes

Comprehensive history achieved the persuasive and pedagogical aims of history of science but was less adequate for achieving philosophical aims or the scholarly aims of professional historians of science, who began to emerge in the late nineteenth and early twentieth centuries. Encyclopedic histories of science emerged after science had established a secure cultural identity but before history of science became a recognized academic specialty. These monumental works responded to a need to assemble an exhaustive set of resources for professional scholarship. Lynn Thorndike's *A History of Magic and Experimental Science* (8 vols., 1923–1958) and George Sarton's *Introduction to the History of Science* (3 vols. in 5 parts, 1927–1948) are well-known examples of encyclopedic history.

The years following World War II saw increasing levels of activity in the history of science and changed the kind of history that was written. Although courses in the history of science had been taught in universities since the 1890s and the History of Science Society was founded in 1924, history of science did not become an established university discipline with a recognizable career path for academic historians until after World War II. Increasingly uneasy about celebration and legitimization of science as the primary aims of the historical enterprise, the emerging group of academic historians frequently rejected the progress narrative form of history. They embraced **objectivity** and depth of detail.

These changes had two main consequences: (1) a narrowed scope with a corresponding emphasis on representative history and (2) the relegation of dramatic techniques, evocative language, and celebratory themes to a new genre, the dramatic history. Dramatic history was more clearly aimed at popular audiences and designed to provide entertainment along with information and the celebration of science. It was significantly influenced by the emergence of **television**. Jacob Bronowski's *The Ascent of Man* (1973) and Daniel Boorstin's *The Discoverers* (1983) are examples of successful dramatic histories.

The representative or case study history became the genre of choice for professional historians. Representative history allows for testing theories about history and makes it easier to achieve professional norms of depth and detail. Two of its most common forms are intellectual history and biography. Thomas Kuhn's (*see* Revolutions) *The Copernican Revolution: Planetary Astronomy in the Development of Western Thought* (1957) provides an interesting example of intellectual history of science.

Contemporary Issues and Future Prospects

The contemporary scene in the history of science is characterized by a great deal of literary experimentation, most of which is aimed at transcending the limitations of traditional genres and capturing the complex interactions of science with other aspects of culture and human experience. In the last quarter of the twentieth century especially, histories of science have both shaped and been shaped by a growing awareness of science as an actor in and product of culture, as a significant component in cultural change, and as an important element of problem creation and solution.

New genres, mostly versions of representative history, have emerged as a result. Sociocultural history has emerged from the effort to understand the history of cultural practices in which science plays a part. Although sociocultural history does not assume an adversarial relationship with science, it also does not take the legitimation and celebration of science to be its primary goal. Deconstructionist history goes beyond sociocultural history to reveal the ways that science has exercised influence and been connected to exclusionary practices in culture. Shapin and Schaffer's *Leviathan and the Air-Pump: Hobbes, Boyle, and the Experimental Life* (1985) and Cynthia Eagle Russett's *Sexual Science: The Victorian Construction of Womanhood* (1989) are, respectively, examples of sociocultural and deconstructionist history.

Attention has also turned to the history of metascience, which is broadly defined as the history of thought and talk about science and includes the literary history of the history of science. Sociocultural history, deconstructionist history, and history of metascience reflect growing awareness of the ways that history of science has functioned in a powerful but unremarked way to interpret science. The development of interdisciplinary LS studies is in large part a response to the same forces that stimulated these new forms of history.

As scholars have recognized the many levels on which science operates, they have sought to create texts that operate on many levels as well, making creative use of the tension between the panoramic view offered by comprehensive history and the detailed, vignette-style portrayals of context that have been achieved in recent versions of intellectual history, biography, sociocultural history, deconstructionist history, and other forms of representative or case study history. In the effort to recreate the experience of science and to connect science to positive values, authors continue to employ the techniques and themes of dramatic history.

The enduring concern of historians of science with the literary quality of writing on science reflects how important techniques, standards, and themes drawn from literature and the humanities have been in creating valid, useful, and appealing historical accounts of science. From a literary point of view, writing the history of science is very demanding; it requires telling a detailed, absorbing, well-documented story while keeping larger issues in sight.

So far, little systematic attention has been given to the literary aspects of historical writing about science. As the foregoing discussion has demonstrated, however, histories of science have an interesting literary history of their own, and the late twentieth century is one of the most interesting periods in that history. For students of LS, the literary history of science constitutes a rich and promising area for future work.

References

Jones, William Powell. *The Rhetoric of Science: A Study of Scientific Ideas and Imagery in Eighteenth-Century English Poetry.* Berkeley: U of California P, 1966.

Laudan, Rachel. "Histories of Science and Their Uses: A Review to 1913." *History of Science* 21 (1993): 1–34.

Sarton, George. *A Guide to the History of Science.* Waltham, MA: Chronica Botanica, 1952.

Servos, John W. "Research Schools and Their Histories." *Osiris* 7 (1993): 3–15.

Thackray, Arnold, "The Pre-History of an Academic Discipline: The Study of the History of Science in the United States, 1891–1941." *Minerva* 18 (1988): 448–73.

Thackray, Arnold, and Robert K. Merton. "On Discipline Building: The Paradoxes of George Sarton." *ISIS* 63 (1972): 473–95.

Yeo, Richard. *Defining Science.* Cambridge: Cambridge UP, 1993.

Kathryn A. Neeley

Hobbes, Thomas (1588–1679). Materialist political philosopher and apologist for monarchy during the English Civil War. Hobbes associated with leading scientific figures such as **Francis Bacon**, Pierre Gassendi, **Galileo**, **Descartes**, and Marin Mersenne. His primary work, *Leviathan* (1851), applies mechanical forces to human behavior, reenvisioning the state of nature as a vacuum for the independent testing of social variables.

Reference

Boonin-Vail, David. *Thomas Hobbes and the Science of Moral Virtue*. New York: Cambridge UP, 1994.

Alison E. Bright

Hoffmann, Ernst Theodor Amadeus (1776–1822). German musician and Romantic writer of fantastic novels, trained as a lawyer. His *Fantastic Tales* (*Fantasiestücke*) (1814) and *Weird Tales* (*Nachtstücke*) (1817) are reminiscent of **Edgar Allan Poe's** stories in their blend of fantasy, horror, and scientific **realism**. Two of the *Weird Tales*, "Ignaz Denner" and "The Sandman," reflecting Hoffmann's own ambivalent fascination and horror at **technology**, were inspired by an exhibition of automata in Dresden in 1813. Both stories examine the destruction of innocent victims by evil scientists. Ignaz Denner is a demonic physics professor whose father has entered into a Faustian pact with the Devil to obtain illicit knowledge, while the title character of "The Sandman," Dr Coppelius, overtly a lawyer, is also a closet alchemist, intent on producing an automaton. Discovering a child, Nathanael, observing his experiments, Coppelius threatens to drag out his eyes, for Hoffmann associates the desire for artificial vision, symbolic of the attempt to improve on nature, with the pretensions of science. Coppelius subsequently returns as Coppola, an Italian hawker of scientific glasses that distort the vision, and gazing through one of his telescopes, Nathanael becomes infatuated with a seemingly flawless woman, Olimpia. Eventually her automaton nature is revealed and the devastated Nathanael, deluded about distance by Coppola's telescope, flings himself to his death from a tower, another Romantic victim of science.

References

Ellis, J.M. "Clara, Nathanael and the Narrator: Interpreting Hoffmann's *Der Sandmann*." *German Quarterly* 54 (1981): 1–19.
Prawer, S.S. "Hoffmann's Uncanny Guest: A Reading of *Der Sandmann*." *German Life and Letters* 18 (1965): 297–308.
Warrick, Patricia S. *The Cybernetic Imagination in Science Fiction*. Cambridge: MIT, 1980.

Roslynn D. Haynes

Hoffmann, Roald (1937–   ). Theoretical chemist, Nobel laureate, poet, and author/coauthor. His most well-known works of popular science include *Chem-

istry Imagined (1993), illustrating connections between science and **art;** *The Same and Not the Same* (1995), an explication of chemical themes for both professional and layman, focusing on the key role of the tension between polar opposites; and *Old Wine, New Flasks* (1997), which explores relationships between science and **religion**.

Jay A. Labinger

Holub, Miroslav (1923–1998). Czech poet and scientist. At the time his highly influential book of poems and prose poems *Sagittal Section* was published (1980), Holub was chief research immunologist at the Institute for Clinical and Experimental **Medicine** in Prague. Holub's poems are colloquial and expressive of an intelligent tenderness toward the world; neither materialist nor idealist, he celebrates the realms of matter and spirit with equal affection. Like **Czeslaw Milosz**, his attitude toward the world is best described as religious and moral.

Joseph Duemer

Homer (fl. eighth–seventh century B.C.E.). Greek poet first to record Greek **mythology**. His epic poems the *Iliad* and the *Odyssey* are the earliest written accounts of the **geography** and topography of Ancient Greece. In these poems the whims of the gods are now tempered by natural law, and heroes are free to act. With the rise of the Allegorists in the second century B.C.E., Homer's descriptions of the gods and their exploits were reinterpreted in terms of scientific phenomena.

Shelly Jarrett Bromberg

Hooke, Robert (1635–1703). Author of *Micrographia* (1665), a record of observations using the compound **microscope**. Employing techniques similar to those utilized to arrive at **representations** of life in literature, Hooke deployed his artistic training to summarize information gleaned via multiple viewings of specimens through the imperfect lenses available into highly detailed, accurate representations.

Maria F. Ippolito

Hopkins, Gerard Manley (1844–1889). Jesuit priest whose formally experimental poems of "inscape" and "instress" remained unpublished until after World War I. In recent discussions of the impact on his protomodern **poetry** of **Darwinism** and Victorian wave theory, critics have drawn attention to several letters Hopkins published on atmospheric phenomena as well as remarks he made on John Tyndall's **energy physics**.

Reference

Zaniello, Tom. *Hopkins in the Age of Darwin*. Iowa City: U of Iowa P, 1988.

Steven Meyer

Horace [Quintus Horatius Flaccus] (65–8 B.C.E.). Latin writer, under the patronage of Augustus and Maecenas. He wrote elegant odes, epodes, and verse epistles, some with a political and social satiric edge. His *Ars Poetica* influenced literary criticism and **aesthetics** into and beyond the seventeenth and eighteenth centuries, emphasizing the vital function of poets in society as important commentators on political and moral life.

Pamela Gossin

Hoyle, Fred (1915–   ). Unorthodox and distinguished British astronomer who developed the steady state **cosmology** later modified as quasi-steady state, an alternative to Big Bang cosmology. Hoyle wrote **science fiction** works such as *Black Cloud* to give his ideas more breadth. He often wrote in collaboration with his son Geoffrey.

Luís O. Arata

Hugo, Victor (1802–1885). The most prolific and celebrated of French Romantic authors. His novel *Notre-Dame de Paris* (The Hunchback of Notre Dame, 1831) contributed to a renewed interest in and appreciation of the Middle Ages. Hugo uses this historical background for a fictional story that revolves around a nameless and ill-defined character, the hunchbacked bell-ringer. He and the cathedral are monstrous beings evolving over the narrated time into **strange attractors** within a discourse that resembles a nonlinear dynamical system. Describing a society at the edge of **chaos** and order, Hugo projects creative conditions for a postrevolutionary nation in search of stable societal norms.

Maria L. Assad

Humanism. A system of education and mode of inquiry (fourteenth to sixteenth centuries). The *studia humanitatis*, consisting of grammar, **poetry**, **rhetoric**, history, and moral **philosophy**, was held to be the equivalent of the Greek *paideia*. The humanist Francesco Petrarch combined **Cicero** and St. Augustine to develop a Christian-rhetorical position, claiming language and rhetoric as the ultimate arbiter of truth. By 1600, humanism was primarily a literary pursuit, with philosophy left to develop on its own.

Diana B. Altegoer

Humboldt, Alexander von (1769–1859). German geographer, naturalist, explorer, and writer. Humboldt's encyclopedic works, including *Ansichten der Natur* (Aspects of Nature, 1808) and *Kosmos* (1845–1862), profoundly shaped nineteenth-century **geography**, **biology**, and ethnography and influenced the nascent science of ecology (*see* Deep Ecology; Environment) in the mid-1800s. Humboldt's writings synthesized German **romanticism**, geographical exploration, and nineteenth-century **empiricism**. Humboldtian science proceeded by collecting and analyzing all conceivable kinds of data—mineral, biological, geographic, linguistic—while striving for a holistic **representation** of nature.

Michael A. Bryson

Hutton, James (1726–1797). A philosopher of nature in Edinburgh, best known for his geological "theory of the earth" (1788, 1795), which is often regarded as the first modern one. Ignoring Genesis and all those who sought to explain the surface of the earth by evoking catastrophic forces not now at work, Hutton emphasized the age of the earth and its central heat. While fully aware of the efficacy of erosion, he theorized that the earth's heat was creating new continents from the ruins of the old, divine contrivance intended to maintain the fertility of soils. For both scientific and religious reasons, Hutton was controversial in his own time. An exhumation of his geological theory by **John Playfair** (1802) provoked a lasting dispute within the scientific community of Edinburgh. Hutton's arguments were then greatly strengthened by **Charles Lyell** in his *Principles of Geology* (1830–1875) and eventually predominated in a modified form. Hutton directly influenced **Erasmus Darwin**, **Coleridge**, Scott, **Shelley**, **Carlyle**, **Tennyson**, and—more profoundly—**Emerson** ("Compensation," 1841).

References

Dean, Dennis R. *James Hutton and the History of Geology*. Ithaca, NY: Cornell UP, 1992.
———. *Tennyson and Geology* (monograph). Lincoln, England: Tennyson Society, 1985.

Dennis R. Dean

Huxley, Aldous (1894–1963). English novelist and essayist, grandson of Darwinist **Thomas Henry Huxley** and brother of biologist **Julian Huxley**. A major concern of his was to establish closer relations between literature and science and to formally compare their products and methods; see, for example, his book-length essay *Literature and Science* (1963). Huxley was interested in how literary artists can and should incorporate scientific ideas into their work, and there are numerous references to contemporary developments in **biology**, **chemistry**, and **physics** in his own **fiction** and nonfiction. Huxley is best known for the technocratic **dystopia** *Brave New World* (1932), which anticipated developments in genetic engineering (*see* Biotechnology/Genetic Engineering) and warned against the application of scientific principles to social organization. While Huxley admired much about scientists and the **scientific method**, he also pointed to their limitations. He argued for more recognition for what lies outside the scientific grasp, such as **art** and **religion**, and he counseled scientists to examine the metaphysical foundations and assumptions of their worldview. One of Huxley's most profound ambitions was to reconcile science and religion in order to resuscitate religious faith in a scientific era. He believed he found such an opportunity in the apparent consonance between modern physics and the mystical tradition.

References

Baker, Robert S. *Brave New World: History, Science, and Dystopia*. Boston: Twayne, 1990.
Deery, June. *Aldous Huxley and the Mysticism of Science*. London: Macmillan, 1996.
June Deery

Huxley, Julian (1887–1975). English biologist, educator, and administrator. Grandson of **Thomas Henry Huxley**, the Darwinist, and elder brother of **Aldous Huxley**, the novelist. Sir Julian was a prolific writer who published scientific research (*The Elements of Experimental Embryology*, 1934, and *Evolution: The Modern Synthesis*, 1942), **popularizations** of science (*The Science of Life*, 1929), religious speculations (*Religion without Revelation*, 1927), autobiographical material (*Memories*, 1970), and **poetry** (*The Captive Shrew*, 1932). Huxley regarded himself as a scientific humanist who wanted to establish a religious belief for a scientific era. He was a well-known broadcaster and public intellectual whose diverse scientific interests included evolution, embryology, **ornithology**, and ecology. Admired as an explicator of science in various media, he was at different times a college professor, the secretary of the London Zoo (1935–1942), and the first director-general of UNESCO (the United Nations Educational, Scientific, and Cultural Organization) (1946–1948).

Reference

Squier, Susan Merrill. *Babies in Bottles: Twentieth-Century Visions of Reproductive Technology*. New Brunswick, NJ: Rutgers UP, 1994.
June Deery

Huxley, Thomas Henry (1825–1895). Biologist, essayist, and educator. Huxley is perhaps best known now for his aggressive defense of Darwin's theory of evolution (*see* Darwin, Charles; Darwinism; Evolutionary Theory), but he has a more general significance as a spokesman for science. In essays of high literary merit, Huxley argued that science has radically altered traditional conceptions of nature and of man's place in nature. He believed that science is progressive and that it gives access to the rationally intelligible order of nature. He maintained that scientific knowledge should take precedence over religious faith and humanistic traditions and should assume a much more prominent place in modern education.

References

Huxley, Thomas Henry. *Method and Results*. New York: D. Appleton, 1899.
———. *Science and Education*. New York: A.L. Fowk, 1880.
Joseph Carroll

Hypertext. A mode of writing in which verbal text is broken into units that may be read in a variety of orders. These units, sometimes called *lexia* and usually consisting of a sentence or a paragraph, are connected by electronic links. A hypertext system running on a **computer** presents one of the lexia to the reader and then allows the reader to choose which link to follow. The reader's choice then determines or at least influences the order of presentation of the subsequent lexia. Hypertexts can consist of multiple media, including static graphics, animation, sound, and video as well as verbal text. Such multimedia hypertexts are called hypermedia.

History

Vannevar Bush, science adviser to President Franklin Delano Roosevelt, is often credited as the originator of the concept of hypertext. In 1945, Bush envisioned a device for textual storage and retrieval that he called the "memex." Bush's memex, which was never built, was to be a desk-size hypertext system in which information would have been recorded photographically and stored on microfilm: links would presumably have been recorded electromechanically. Using the memex each scientist would be able to manage the coming information explosion by fashioning his or her own hypertextual library. In the 1960s, Theodor Nelson coined the term "hypertext" and was the first to envision a fully electronic and globally networked system, which he called Xanadu. Nelson's Xanadu was also never built. In the 1980s, the workstation and the personal computer made hypertext practical for the first time. Authoring environments as Notecards and Hypercard were used to create literary and pedagogical hypertexts. In 1990, Tim Berners-Lee, a physicist working at CERN in Geneva, proposed and constructed a system for networked hypertextual communication, the **World Wide Web**. Berners-Lee's World Wide Web had some technical similarities to Xanadu and had a goal similar to that of the memex. Berners-Lee wanted a system that would allow scientists around the world to exchange ideas and drafts of their papers at the speed of electronic communication on the **Internet**. Since 1993, with the introduction of the first graphical browser, the World Wide Web has become a medium for recreation, entertainment, and business and commerce as well as scientific and academic discourse.

Writing Technologies

Enthusiasts have sometimes claimed that hypertext provides a model for human cognition: that hyperlinks mirror the associative character of human thought itself. Some educational technologists have suggested that the associative links of hypertext present information more "naturally" than do the hierarchies favored by print. A less extreme form of this claim is that hypertext is especially appropriate for domains of knowledge that are inherently nonhierarchical: In such ill-structured domains ordinary printed textbooks do a poor job.

Contemporary literary and social theorists, however, would reject any claim for a special affinity between hypertext and the human mind, on the grounds that such universalist claims ignore the socially constructed character of the concept of mind. Such theorists would prefer to regard electronic hypertext as another **technology** of writing, one that takes its place alongside of such earlier technologies as the ancient papyrus roll, the medieval handwritten codex, and the printed book. Contemporary **culture** invested each of the technologies with certain defining characteristics. In particular, the printed book has been valued for its precision, stability, and authority. Our culture now appreciates a different set of characteristics in electronic hypertext. A hypertext is dynamic: It is called forth in the act of reading, and it may be different with every new reading. The author of a hypertext does not define the text as precisely as did the author in print. Instead the hypertextual author defines the overall shape and limits of the text and then allows the reader to realize a particular linear text from among these possibilities. The author of a hypertext shares with the reader some of the responsibility for creating the text. For the past thirty years poststructuralist critics, such as Jacques Derrida, Stanley Fish, and Roland Barthes, have made similar claims about the indeterminacy and instability of all written or printed text. Ironically, the qualities that these critics identified as belonging metaphorically to printed text seem now to belong literally to hypertext. Electronic hypertext seems to be the embodiment of poststructuralist literary **theory**.

It is particularly fiction that has revealed the poststructuralist qualities of hypertext. Stand-alone hypertext as well as Web fiction by such authors as Michael Joyce (*afternoon*, 1987; rev. 1993), Stuart Moulthrop (*Victory Garden*, 1995), and Judy Malloy (*its name was Penelope*, 1990) demonstrate the instability of the text and foreground the importance of the reader's role in constituting the text. Although these fictions command small audiences in comparison to popular printed fiction, on the one hand, and commercial Web sites and multimedia, on the other, they have nevertheless influenced the cultural meaning of hypertext.

The Future of Verbal and Visual Communication

Electronic hypertext refashions the technology and cultural practices of print. What is new about hypertext is the opportunity it provides writers and readers to reinterpret the roles familiar to them from the age of print. Likewise, hypermedia refashions not only the printed book but earlier visual technologies, as the increasingly hypermediated World Wide Web illustrates. Web sites borrow from and refashion almost every earlier form of verbal and audiovisual communication, including printed encyclopedias, novels, newspapers, and magazines as well as painting, photography, **film**, radio, and **television**. This process of refashioning allows Web sites as well as other forms of hypertext both to establish their continuity with and to define their differences from their predecessors.

One of the most important differences between the new electronic media and print technology is redefined relations between word and image. In forms of print, especially in books but also in newspapers and magazines, the verbal text tended to be dominant: Images and illustrations were explained and constrained by the text. Multimedia and hypermedia applications of the World Wide Web and in **CD-ROM** and DVD suggest a new relationship, in which static and moving images free themselves from the constraint of verbal text. Because hyperlinks can be attached to images as well as words, images can be integrated into the operational structure of a hyperdocument. Meanwhile, streaming audio and video are displacing verbal text in the World Wide Web and on the Internet in general. This renegotiation of the relationship of word and image may prove to be a far more significant cultural event than the survival (or loss) of the printed book as a material artifact.

References

Bolter, Jay David, and Richard Grusin. *Remediation: Understanding New Media.* Cambridge: MIT, 1998.

Bush, Vannevar. "As We May Think." *Atlantic Monthly* 176.1 (July 1945): 101–8.

Joyce, Michael. *Of Two Minds: Hypertext Pedagogy and Poetics.* Ann Arbor: U of Michigan P, 1995.

Landow, George. *Hypertext 2.0: The Convergence of Contemporary Critical Theory and Technology.* Baltimore: Johns Hopkins UP, 1997.

Lanham, Richard. *The Electronic Word: Democracy, Technology, and the Arts.* Chicago: U of Chicago P, 1993.

Rouet, Jean-Francois, Jarmo J. Levonen, Andrew Dillon, and Rand J. Spiro. *Hypertext and Cognition.* Mahweh, NJ: Erlbaum, 1996.

Jay David Bolter

Hypothesis. A predictive statement explaining the connection between two variables, the relationship among empirical observations, and so on. Although hypothesis formation and data collection typically are considered independent processes, in fact the two are concurrent and codependent. Thus hypotheses guide data collection by determining which data are worth considering, while observed data test hypotheses and/or suggest alternatives. Hypotheses frequently are generated through intuitive or accidental insight, rather than by formal analysis of observations.

Reference

Davenport, Edward. "Scientific Method as Literary Criticism." *Et Cetera* 42.4 (Winter 1985): 331–50.

Michael A. Bryson

I

Illness Narratives. Related to **pathography**, descriptive accounts of the experience of illness ("the innately human experience of symptoms and suffering") as opposed to clinical accounts of disease processes (Kleinman 3).

Reference

Kleinman, Arthur. *The Illness Narratives: Suffering, Healing and the Human Condition.* New York: Basic Books, 1988.

Anne Hunsaker Hawkins

Imagination and Creativity. Important cognitive processes in both literature and science. In his manual of advice to prospective scientists, *The Incomplete Guide to the Art of Discovery*, Jack E. Oliver distinguishes discovering in science from creating in **art**: If a particular composer had not lived, his **music** "would probably never have been written"; if a particular scientist had not lived, "his discoveries would have been made . . . by someone else" (185). For Robert Scott Root-Bernstein, this distinction between the scientist as instrument, detecting what would be there, whether found or not, and the artist as **inventor**, creating all but ex nihilo, is less easily maintained. Through his series of Galilean dialogues, *Discovering*, Root-Bernstein insists that the divide between discovering and inventing reflects strategies of exploration *within* science, too. Claude Louis Berthollet, pointed toward the principle of mass action by observing the seemingly anomalous **chemistry** of the Natron Lakes, discovers. **Albert Einstein**, imagining how changes in reference frames change perception, invents.

Einstein epitomizes, for Root-Bernstein, the scientist acting intuitively rather than empirically: by imaginative power, transforming our idea of nature. Ariana, artist as well as endocrinologist, and a participant in the fictive colloquium informing *Discovering*, asks the physical chemist Hunter whether he will assent to "ways of knowing—understanding—that transcend verbal and mathematical understanding" (98). Yes, Hunter replies, if she changes "transcend" to "augment"; and he invokes Einstein, explaining to Jacques Hadamard how he thinks, to make his case. "The words or the language," Einstein writes, ". . . do not seem to play any [initial] role in my mechanism of thought." Instead, he visualizes, quarrying his conceptual building-blocks from "signs and . . . images . . . 'voluntarily' reproduced and combined" (Hadamard 142).

This dynamic of **visualization** and combination places him inside events that he has himself devised: aboard an **elevator** falling at light speed or a lightbeam chasing another lightbeam. He becomes protagonist in his own stories (**thought experiments**). So doing, he acts out what **John Keats** labeled "negative capability."

Keats appropriated the notion of negative capability (though not the term) from William Hazlitt, whose *Essay on the Principles of Human Action* develops it as a cognitive strategy: "[T]he imagination . . . must carry me out of myself into the feelings of others by one and the same process by which I am thrown forwards . . . into my future being, and interested in it" (1–2). "Carrying me out of myself" sums up the momentary transport of the persona in "Ode to a Nightingale," who, yearning to fly to the bird "on the viewless wings of Poesy," finds himself "Already with thee!" It also suggests the transaction, between ourselves and the Keatsian speaker, that constitutes, for Kenneth Burke, our experience of "Ode on a Grecian Urn." By reading the "Ode," we reenact it. Participating in the scenes circumscribing the urn, we collaborate in shaping the poem (458).

Burke offers his response to "Ode on a Grecian Urn" as an example (almost a thought-experimental demonstration) of what he calls "Dramatism" at work. Dramatism, he explains, involves seeking a "representative anecdote" (59)—of the sort, say, that Einstein finds, imagining himself pursuing a lightbeam. The maker of the urn finds his representative anecdote in the scenes etched on its frieze. Keats finds his not only in these scenes but in his encounter with the urn itself, silent testimony to the craftsman(woman?)ship of its maker, even against the force of slow time. We find ours by sharing with Keats the unfolding process of the encounter, dramatized in the act of experiencing (reading) the poem.

To read literarily, then, entails projecting oneself into the scene. As Keats reads the urn, we read his "Ode." We too exercise a form of negative capability. Or, to use a term Root-Bernstein uses to characterize how Joshua Lederberg thinks, we "playact." As Lederberg puts it, a scientist "needs . . . the ability to think. . . . What would it be like if I were one of the chemical pieces of a bacterial chromosome? And to try to understand what my environment was, try to know *where* I was, try to know when I was supposed to function in a certain way" (Root-Bernstein 97). What Lederberg recommends as procedure Barbara McClintock reports as practice: "I found that the more I worked with them, the bigger . . . [the chromosomes] got, and when I was really working with them, I was right down there with them, and everything got big. . . . I actually felt as if

I was right down there and these were my friends. . . . As you look at these things, they become part of you. And you forget yourself" (Kroeber 34).

McClintock's absorption in studies that eventually gained her a Nobel Prize resembles, almost uncannily, Fergus's quest for knowledge in **W.B. Yeats's** dialogic poem "Fergus and the Druid." Having metamorphosed into the visual phenomena around him, Fergus finds that he has "grown nothing, knowing all." He foregoes himself.

In contemplating an object, to become what one beholds is either, as Yeats would have insisted, to perform a magical act or, as a rationalist would presumably argue, to indulge a childlike fantasy. Even as rigorous an empiricist as Oliver acknowledges the relation between discovery and childlike thinking: " 'What is it made of?' and 'How did it get that way?' are the basic questions of geology. To answer these childlike but fundamental queries has always been the prime goal of basic earth science" (13–14).

That discovering starts with childlike curiosity is what Isaac Newton (*see* Newtonianism) is suggesting when he portrays his discovering self as "a boy playing on the sea shore," diverted by "now and then finding a smoother pebble or a prettier shell than ordinary"; and what Einstein affirms when, in his foreword to the *Opticks*, he pronounces Newton a "happy child of science," ranging his experiments "in order like playthings." Einstein reads Newton, moreover, as Burke would have us read Keats: "He who has time and tranquility can by reading this book live again the wonderful events which the great Newton experienced in his young days." He too exercises negative capability, joining Newton in the darkened room where he conducted his optical experiments. And as we envision Keats recognizing in the urn the manifestation of its maker, Einstein envisions Newton recognizing in the various effects he induced from light one expression of its author: "Nature was to him an open book, whose letters he could read without effort" (*Opticks* lix).

Einstein's Newton grasps knowledge in a way analogous to the way of the "little Actor" in **William Wordsworth's** "Ode: Intimations of Immortality from Recollections of Early Childhood," who "cons" parts one after another. He reads the Book of Nature. And to read the Book of Nature—as, indeed, a literary critic might read a poem—comprises, for Rom Harré, the aim toward which a scientist's training points: "[L]earning to make reports, to use sentences to convey information, is learning to read the world, in much the same sense as one learns to read words, signs and symbols" (192).

In an age when scientific and humanistic study are, thanks to **C.P. Snow** (and more recently **Francis Crick**), considered mutually exclusive, if not adversarial, the idea that scientists and literary critics operate analogously may appear dubious, even outlandish. It requires supposing that (at least great) scientists think like poets. Yet this supposition precisely underlies the claim of David Bohm and F. David Peat that "Metaphoric thinking is . . . fundamental to all science and involves bringing together previously incompatible ideas in radically new ways" (35). Einstein, in his letter to Hadamard, describes this conjunction of previously incompatible ideas as "combinatory play" and declares it "the essential feature in productive thought" (Hadamard 142). He is asserting the importance of analogical reasoning, or what (as Phillips Salman has observed) a poet might redefine as building conceits.

A conceit is a figure yoking apparently incommensurate objects or concepts, revealing them in the end to be tellingly commensurate. (" 'Tis with our judgments as our watches, none /Go just alike, yet each believes his own"—**Alexander Pope**.) It was this sort of combinatory—and conceptual—imagining that enabled, say, **Niels Bohr** to visualize atoms as microscopic solar systems, or enables all of us to grasp **electricity** as dynamic flow, "current." It renders the intangible tangible and implies a world comprehending what **Roald Hoffmann** images, in a poem built on the metaphor of string theory, as a "Grand Unification."

Hoffmann—who, both a Nobel laureate in chemistry and the author of two finely crafted books of verse, might be said to embody a conceit himself—nicely illustrates this rhetorical device not only in his poems but in the conclusion to his recent gathering of essays on science and society, *The Same and Not the Same*: "Centaurs are the incarnation of the same and not the same. Man and beast, not whole human, not wild beast. Stationary and fleet, a tenser, complex, yet integrated being. Capable of harm, seeking for the good. Like chemistry" (259). Who, before reading Hoffmann, would have associated a mythic creature, extant alone through the fantasies of ancient poets, with perhaps the hardest of hard sciences? But then, having followed the combinatory play by which Hoffmann brings them together, who will fail to see their association? Hoffmann is acting out, in his prose meditation, a crucial aspect of creative thought in science and poetry alike: discovering the same in what appears not the same.

References

Bohm, David, and F. David Peat. *Science, Order, and Creativity*. New York: Bantam, 1987.

Burke, Kenneth. *A Grammar of Motives*. 1945 Berkeley: U of California P, 1969.

Hadamard, Jacques. *The Psychology of Invention in the Mathematical Field*. 1945. New York: Dover, 1954.

Harré, Rom. *The Principles of Scientific Thinking*. Chicago: U of Chicago P, 1970.

Hazlitt, William. "Essay on the Principles of Human Action." *The Complete Works of William Hazlitt*. Ed. P.P. Howe. Vol. 1. New York: AMS, 1967.

Hoffmann, Roald. *The Same and Not the Same*. New York: Columbia UP, 1995.

Kroeber, Karl. *Ecological Literary Criticism: Romantic Imagining and the Biology of Mind*. New York: Columbia UP, 1994.

Newton, Sir Isaac. *Opticks*. 1730. 4th ed. New York: Dover, 1952.

Oliver, Jack E. *The Incomplete Guide to the Art of Discovery*. New York: Columbia UP, 1991.

Root-Bernstein, Robert Scott. *Discovering*. Cambridge: Harvard UP, 1989.

Barton Friedman

Industrial Revolution. A complex set of significant economic, social, and cultural changes wrought by the rapid development and application of steam-powered machinery and factories to the means of production. Dating from roughly 1725 to 1900, these changes appeared first in Great Britain, later expanded to the United States and throughout Europe, and are still affecting the development of countries throughout the world. Many of the earliest literary responses to the Industrial Revolution in England were critical. John Clare's **poetry** mourns the loss of a rural way of life to urban growth, which was caused by enclosure and the depopulation of the land. While not sharing Clare's agrarianism, **William Blake** castigated the new factories as "dark, Satanic mills" in *Milton* (1804–1808) and identified industrialization with the kinds of social and economic misery evoked in *Songs of Experience* (1794). Unemployment and other social consequences of industrialization led to urban and agricultural "machine-breaking." These subversive acts were important catalysts for the development of industrial fiction in England. **Harriet Martineau's** "The Rioters" (1827), Benjamin Disraeli's *Sybil* (1845), and Charlotte Brontë's *Shirley* (1849) all reprimanded machine-breaking and defended the virtues of laissez-faire capitalism. **Charles Dickens's** *Hard Times* (1854) (one of the first novels to use railways as a significant plot device) and the novels of Elizabeth Gaskell treated industrial workers more sympathetically, while continuing to frown upon strikes and other militant union activities. Later in the nineteenth century, **John Ruskin** and **William Morris** advocated a pastoral antiindustrialism, and while **H.G. Wells** explored the utopian potential of industrial **technology**, the antiindustrialism typical of Fabian Socialism characterized the writings of **Hardy**, **Woolf**, Lawrence, **Orwell**, and many others. As late as 1959, **C.P. Snow's** *The Two Cultures and the Scientific Revolution* chided literary intellectuals' inability to embrace the benefits and significance of the Industrial Revolution.

In the United States both nature and industry were frequently regarded as powerful symbols of the age, as evidenced by the writings of **Ralph Waldo Emerson** and **Henry Adams** on the figurative nature of steam and electrical technology. In *Moby-Dick* (1851) and "The Tartarus of Maids" (1855), **Herman Melville** investigates industrial society, and Rebecca Harding Davis's "Life in the Iron-Mills" (1861) and Elizabeth Stuart Phelps's *The Silent Partner* (1871) denounce the socially destructive effects of industrialism. Edward Bellamy's *Looking Backward* (1888) and **Mark Twain's** *A Connecticut Yankee in King Arthur's Court* (1889) advocate free technological advancement as the solution to the inequities of industrialization. The rapid industrialization of the South in the twentieth century was condemned on conservative grounds by the other authors of *I'll Take My Stand* (1930). Writers' continued engagement with the Industrial Revolution is apparent in the "steampunk" writing of James Blaylock, Tim Powers, and most notably, **William Gibson** and **Bruce Sterling's** *The Difference Engine* (1991).

References

Gallagher, Catherine. *The Industrial Reformation of English Fiction: Social Discourse and Narrative Form 1832–1867.* Chicago: U of Chicago P, 1985.
Kovacevic, Ivanka, ed. *Fact into Fiction: English Literature and the Industrial Scene, 1750–1850.* Leicester, United Kingdom: Leicester UP, 1975.

Nicholas Spencer

Industry. The practice of trade and manufacture, especially with reference to technological developments in manufacturing and the rise of industrial capitalism. Frederick Taylor's book *The Principles of Scientific Management* (1911) introduced the concept of rationalization (the science of efficiency and its application to the human worker) to industrial manufacturing. Introduced into practice by **Henry Ford** under the term "Fordism," this concept of the workplace and human worker as a scientifically designed apparatus continues to exert powerful influences over factory design and industrial relations. In the 1980s, these ideas were challenged in an era of downsizing and recession; the result has been the institution of decentralized work practices, flex-time, and the informating (automating and computer-streamlining) of the workforce.

Helen J. Burgess

Information Superhighway. Catchall term for the proliferation of computer-mediated forms of electronic communication. The information superhighway gained widespread attention in the 1980s as government-based electronic networks were extended and adapted for widespread educational, commercial, and personal use. By the early 1990s, the term was widely used to denote the increasing speed and flexibility of such forms of communication as email and the **World Wide Web**. The metaphor of information exchange as a superhighway invokes an idealized vision of the Interstate Highway System, built in the United States in the 1950s and 1960s; this image emphasizes the speed of "super" communication rather than the ecological costs, the wear and tear, of systems of transportation. This transformation of the superhighway from the material transportation of people and cargoes to the dematerialized exchange of information becomes a barometer for changing perceptions of the basis of economic profit: On the information superhighway, information itself becomes a commodity.

References

Coyne, Richard. *Designing Information Technology in the Postmodern Age: From Method to Metaphor.* Cambridge: MIT, 1995.
Haraway, Donna. *Simians, Cyborgs, and Women: The Reinvention of Nature.* New York: Routledge, 1991.
Hayles, N. Katherine. "The Materiality of Informatics." *Configurations* 1 (1993): 147–70.

Rheingold, Howard. *The Virtual Community: Homesteading on the Electronic Frontier.*
Reading, MA: Addison Wesley, 1993.

Robert Markley

Information Theory. Analysis and thinking applied to the problem of efficiently communicating information over noisy communication channels. In *A Mathematical Theory of Communication* (1948), Bell Laboratories' Claude Shannon introduced a new way of thinking about the problem of information transmission in terms of probabilistic theory. Shannon's seminal work seeks to apply statistical methods to data communications and thence to the problem of decoding information. Shannon's key insight was to posit the relationship in any channel between wanted information (or signal) and extraneous information (or noise). The key problem, then, in information theory becomes finding the best way in which to separate signal from noise so that the message remains intact; a problem with clear applications in data compression. In another application, researchers in machine learning use Shannon's insight to design automatic methods for exploring data. Ross Quinlan's C4.5 machine learning algorithm, for example, treats massive amounts of loosely organized incoming data as a "message" and then attempts to extract meaningful information from it.

In the humanities, **Michel Serres** has appropriated and mutated information theory as a way of attempting to talk about the philosophical notion of the "excluded third." Noise, Serres argues, cannot ultimately be separated from signal since it is constitutive of information; in other words, noise becomes an excluded third in communication without which no meaning is possible. Noise, in other words, is inherent in, and even constitutive of, meaning.

References

Hayles, N. Katherine. *How We Became Posthuman: Virtual Bodies in Cybernetics, Literature, and Informatics.* Chicago: U of Chicago P, 1999.
Serres, Michel. *The Parasite.* Trans. Lawrence R. Schehr. Baltimore: Johns Hopkins UP, 1982.
Shannon, Claude. "A Mathematical Theory of Communication." *Bell System Technical Journal* (1948).

Helen J. Burgess

Internet. The overarching network of **computer networks** that connects millions of machines, principally in North America, Europe, and other developed areas. It serves as the channel through which a variety of communication services can flow; the most important of these are email and the **World Wide Web**.

Jay David Bolter

Inventor(s). Creative agents, particularly those engaged in the conception of new **technology**. Literature and inventing involve each other on several levels.

The inventor has proved a resilient fictional character, particularly in America, where a national myth developed around the figure of a male yeoman inventor who has an idea that he parlays into fame and fortune. Starting with **Benjamin Franklin** and **Thomas Jefferson**, ingenuity and invention were seen to be part of the American character, and inventors appear, for instance, in **Herman Melville's** short stories, in **Mark Twain's** Colonel Sellers series (starting with *The Gilded Age*, 1873), and in works by **Nathaniel Hawthorne** and William Dean Howells. Later this figure of the inventor was transmuted by a more civil, technocratic ethos, and the fictional engineer appeared as a literary protagonist with similar regularity.

Complementing these instances of inventing in literature are present considerations of literature in inventing. Like the processes of formulating new scientific knowledge, the processes of inventing new technological knowledge involves much discursive (if not specifically literary) action. The pen and pencil are never far from the inventor's hand. An inventor's standing within a research program, the nomination, description, and promotion of invented goods, the application for and defense of patent rights are all differently rhetorical activities that routinely form part of the invention process. Beyond nuts and bolts, the inventor's literature includes experimental notebooks, patent applications, legal and other correspondence, product labels, litigious **representations**, and an ongoing narrative of invention into which the inventor seeks to enroll financial backers, civil and jural authorities, and consumers.

Lisa Gitelman

Ireland, Scotland, Wales (LS in). Specific geographical areas within Great Britain that display unique language and cultural backgrounds. All three regions are noted for their picturesque **landscapes**, which invariably incorporate superb river systems, beautiful lakes, impressive mountain ranges, and a vast variety of flora and fauna. Indeed, the unique geographical, social, and national contexts of these regions are strongly reflected in the writings of many eminent individuals.

From an Irish perspective, the **poetry** of **William Butler Yeats** (1865–1939) is very much concerned with natural knowledge and the beauty of the Irish landscape, as evidenced in such works as "The Wind among the Reeds" (1899) and "The Wild Swans at Coole" (1917). His relationships with his contemporaries are frequently compared with natural and physical phenomena. **James Joyce** (1882–1941) reflected upon and explored the mundane events of human life and social living, as depicted in *Ulysses* (1922) and *Finnegans Wake* (1939). In *Dubliners* (1914), Joyce portrays the social malaise of Irish life. Joyce was also extremely interested in human psychology (*see* Anthropology/Psychology/Sociology) and the creative process, particularly its gestation and development, as is evidenced in *A Portrait of the Artist as a Young Man* (1916). For Joyce, the physical phenomena of the world were important elements in explaining the mind's engagement with **reality**.

The range of Irish writing in LS is aptly represented by the works of Patrick Kavannagh (1905–1967) and Dame Kathleen Lonsdale (1903–1971). Kavannagh's **poetry** stems from his experience as a farmer. His poem "The Great Hunger" (1942) explores the cultural anomalies of the Irish archetype and stereotype. Lonsdale, a renowned Irish scientist, was deeply concerned with the moral responsibilities of scientists and with world peace. The latter she explores in her book *Is Peace Possible?* (1957).

Irish poets' deep association with the natural world can be seen in Michael Longley's (1939–) poetry, which expresses an intimate understanding of the Irish landscape. Indeed, he makes frequent references to the flora and fauna of Ireland and also employs scientific ideas and imagery to explore a range of issues associated with personal, social, and cultural concerns. Similarly, the poetry of Seamus Heaney (1939–) is essentially rooted in the natural world, as portrayed in *Death of a Naturalist* (1966) and *Door into the Dark* (1969). However, Heaney moves beyond this in terms of his analysis and exposition of the creative process, as evidenced in *Seeing Things* (1991).

In historical **fiction**, **John Banville** (1945–) demonstrates a keen interest in exploring the duality of artistic expression and scientific discovery. In a number of his works he employs eminent scientists of the past to investigate the nature of the scientific **imagination**, for example: *Doctor Copernicus* (1976), *Kepler* (1981), *The Newton Letter* (1982), and *Mefisto* (1986).

Arguably, Robert Burns (1759–1796) reflects, more than any other writer, the cultural and national identity of Scotland. Indeed, much of his poetry is concerned with poverty, injustice, and the concept of equality. He was uniquely responsible for producing many songs, satires (*see* Satire), and animal poems. However, there are many other Scottish writers and scientists who have made significant contributions. **James Thomson** (1700–1748) is particularly renowned for his topographical poetry, which essentially relates to his engagement with the landscape of his local area. Andrew J. Young (1885–1971) was also interested in the varied and picturesque landscape of Scotland. Indeed, many of his works convey his concern for the natural world and portray his reflections on God and humankind. His prose work *A Prospect of Flowers* (1945) demonstrates his keen interest in **botany** and offers a detailed account of his many journeys in pursuit of his interest. Norman Alexander MacCraig was also very much inspired in his poetry by the landscapes of the West Highlands and of life in Edinburgh.

There are a number of Scottish scientists who distinguished themselves with their writing. Andrew Lang (1844–1912) was one of the most versatile writers of his day, being recognized as a poet, essayist, reviewer, historian, translator, biographer, editor, and anthropologist. His works include *Myth, Ritual and Religion* (1887), *A History of Scotland from the Roman Occupation* (1900), and *A History of English Literature from Beowulf to Swinburne* (1912). Another is **Arthur Conan Doyle** (1859–1930). He trained as a medical doctor but wrote many stories about the amateur eagle-eyed detective, Sherlock Holmes, and many of his works reflect his considerable medical and scientific background. Frank Fraser Darling (1903–1979), a naturalist and an ecologist, has written numerous books on humankind's relationship with, and responsibility for, the environment. Indeed, *Wilderness and Plenty* is the published version of his 1969 Reith Lectures.

The works of Welsh writers also offer compelling perspectives on literature and science. Edward Lhuyd (1660–1709), a talented writer, was also a botanist, palaeontologist and a philologist (one engaged in the scientific study of languages and their development). In 1895, Lhuyd wrote an elaborate two-volume **natural history** of Wales. In this work, he not only included the abundant flora and fauna of Wales but also made reference to its geology, history, and language. Arthur Llewellyn Macken (1863–1947) was also very much influenced by the Welsh landscape and the folklore of his local region. Dylan Thomas (1914–1953) wrote both poetry and prose, much of which keenly reflects his experiences of life in Wales. Perhaps *Under Milk Wood* (1953), a **drama** of poetic prose, intermingled with songs and ballads, best mirrors his perceptions of the social and cultural life of Wales.

Ronald Stuart Thomas (1913–2000) is a Welsh poet whose works are uniquely colored by his experiences of working in remote local communities as a clergyman. The earth, the trees, and the wild creatures of his locale feature throughout his works, and there are occasions when Thomas effectively unites religious and rural imagery. In many instances, the bleak and barren landscape of remote rural communities are used to convey a certain resentment, on the poet's part, of the Welsh and of Wales. Dannie Abse (1923–   ) is a doctor and a poet. His poetry is very much based on his domestic and professional experiences, as portrayed in *Tenants of the House: Poems 1951–1956* and in *Collected Poems: 1948–76*. His volume of autobiography *A Poet in the Family* (1974) offers stimulating perspectives on his role as both physician and creative writer.

Significant and potent interrelations of literature and science inform the creative life of Ireland, Scotland, and Wales. Furthermore, many writers and scientists within these regions have contributed and continue to contribute to the diverse and expanding area of research and scholarship in LS.

References

Banville, John, "Physics and Fiction: Order from Chaos." *New York Times Book Review*, April 21, 1985, pp. 41–42.
Ellmann, Richard. *James Joyce.* Oxford: Oxford UP, 1959.
Kearney, Richard, ed. *The Irish Mind: Exploring Intellectual Traditions.* Dublin: Wolfhound Press, 1985.

Liam F. Heaney

Isaacs, Leonard N. (1939–1988). U.S. scientist, professor of Science and Technology Studies at Michigan State University, and five-time director of the

Clarion Speculative Fiction Writers' Workshop. Isaacs's career as a teacher–scholar exemplifies the creative intellectual opportunities called for by **C.P. Snow**. He was immersed in interdisciplinary approaches in science studies, and in *Darwin to Double Helix: The Biological Theme in Science Fiction* (1977) he advocated the study of **science fiction** as a reflective, projective, and dramatic expression of the relations between science and society. In the 1980s, Isaacs embarked on a bold reassessment of the Baconian (*see* Bacon) vision, articulated in two 1987 essays, "Molecular Biology and Bacon's Vision" and "Creation and Responsibility in Science," the latter showing how the ethical dilemmas in twentieth-century scientific creation, notably in **physics** and **genetics**, are anticipated in **Mary Shelley's** *Frankenstein*. Near the end of his life, Isaacs began to explore the ontological basis of molecular biology.

Robert C. Goldbort with special acknowledgment to Professor Katherine O. See, Michigan State University

Italy (LS in). Early birthplace of scientific literature and literary science. It was her own **Galileo** who said that the book of the universe was written in mathematical signs. **Lucretius's** poem on nature and Boethius's (480–526) works on arithmetic and **philosophy** are heralds of this vision. Poets of the medieval Sicilian school and the *dolce stil nuovo* wove **natural philosophy** into their love songs. Contemporary to these authors is Marco Polo (1254–1324), who kept close observational notes in his *Milione*, recording the life he encountered. Such integration of objective observation and subjective interpretation will return in the travel diaries of Christopher Columbus (1451–1506), Antonio Pigafetta (1480–1536), and Lazzaro Spallanzani (1729–1799).

In the Renaissance, the philosophical treatise emerged as a hybrid genre of literary expression, protoscience, **rhetoric**, and logic. We can see this early on in Francesco Petrarch's *De remediis utriusque fortunae*, which speaks about the healing power of words. This notion is later echoed in Lorenzo Valla's (1405–1457) discussions on how truth is inextricable from language. Marsilio Ficino's (1433–1499) *Three Books on Life* and Pico's (1463–1494) *On the Dignity of Man* are but two other treatises that integrate the literary and scientific. In essays on education, we find Coluccio Salutati's (1331–1406) *Epistolario* and Pier Paolo Vergerio's (1370–1444) *De ingenuis moribus et liberalibus studiis*, both defending the study of mathematics as part of the liberal arts, especially in training orators. Interestingly, it was the mathematician Giorgio Valla (1447–1500) who was the first to translate **Aristotle's** *Poetics* into Latin. Some other Renaissance treatises that fused the scientific and the literary are Leone Ebreo's (1463–1523) *Dialogues on Love*; Girolamo Fracastoro's (1478–1553) poem on syphilis; Pietro Pompanazzi's (1462–1525) theories of the soul; Girolamo Cardano's (1501–1576) autobiography; Giambattista Della Porta's (1535–1615) *Natural Magic;* **Giordano Bruno's** dialogues on infinity and infinite worlds; and Tommaso Campanella's (1568–1623) utopian *City of the Sun*. One could argue that Leon Battista Alberti's treatise *On Painting*, which theorizes on the science of perspective, has much that is literary about it. Similarly, Francesco Colonna's (1433–1527) architectural dream narrative, the *Hypernotomachia Poliphili*, and the observational and theoretic notebooks of **Leonardo da Vinci** utilize the literary in their efforts to present the empirical and theoretical. Epic poetry, too, is a genre in which contemporary scientific notions were presented, though often for the purpose of exaltation and critique. We can see this, for example, in **Dante's** *Divine Comedy*; Ludovico Ariosto's (1474–1533) *Orlando Furioso*, and Giambattista Marino's (1569–1625) *Adone*.

In the seventeenth and eighteenth centuries, while scientific writing continues to augment, Italian literary production decreases. What literature there is, however, often nods to science. There are the "science poems" of Francesco Redi (1626–1698), Lorenzo Mascheroni (1750–1800), and Vincenzo Monti (1754–1828); Niccolò Tommaseo's (1802–1874) **naturalism**; Antonio Fogazzaro's (1842–1911) spiritualistic **Darwinism**; and Giacomo Leopardi's (1798–1837) poetic musings on nature and the **cosmos**. As in earlier centuries, many "scientific" works utilized the literary and philosophical format of the dialogue. Galileo's *Discourse on the Two World Systems*, Francesco Algarotti's (1712–1764) *Newton's Optics for the Use of the Ladies,* **Giambattista Vico's** *New Science*, and Ludovico Muratori's (1672–1750) reflections on "good taste" in the sciences and the arts are but four examples.

In late-nineteenth- and early-twentieth-century Italy, we find Giovanni Pascoli's (1855–1912) notion that the poet must transform scientific **truth** into a world vision man can understand. Shortly after this, there emerge anti-technology novels, such as Luigi Pirandello's (1867–1922) *Shoot!*, alongside the Futurists' explosion of protechnology propaganda. **Magic realism/science fiction** surfaces in the works of Massimo Bontempelli (1878–1936), Alberto Savinio (1891–1952), Dino Buzzati (1906–1972), and Tommaso Landolfi (1908–1979), articulating further into the poetic prose of **Italo Calvino**. With Calvino, Elio Vittorini (1908–1966) founds the journal *Menabò* (1959) where experimentalism in literature—and oft the scientific—is presented.

When we think of twentieth-century scientists writing literature in Italy, the first person who comes to mind is likely Primo Levi. In his *Periodic Table*, chemist and writer self-consciously unite to record the author's memories of World War II. The physicist Daniele Del Giudice (1949–   ) employs a similar, though less systemic, integration of his scientific expertise in his novels and short stories, as do the engineers Carlo Emilio Gadda (1893–1973) and Leonardo Sinisgalli (1908–1981). And finally, there is **Umberto Eco**, who displays in his essays and narrative a fascination with science's history, especially as it pertains to signs, codes, human language, and information technology. Italian authors continue to be active contributors to the growing discussion of "Literature and Science," and their work will certainly help spin the direction in which the future of this interdisciplinary dialogue will go.

References

Branca, Vittore, et al., eds. *Letteratura e scienza nella storia della cultura italiana.* Palermo: Manfredi Editore, 1978.
Raimondi, Ezio. *Scienza e letteratura.* Torino: Einaudi, 1978.

Arielle Saiber

J–K

James, Henry (1843–1916). Writer often described by critics as disliking science. His fascination with human psychology (*see* Anthropology/Psychology/Sociology), particularly the emphasis on that unknown that lies beyond the conscious, however, gestures to his interest. The close relationship to his brother William informs his investigations of human development. His short novel, *The Turn of the Screw*, a precursor to contemporary feminist **science fiction**, explores the tensions inherent to the unconscious and the terrors associated with the **supernatural**. The *Princess Casamassima* emphasizes the powers of observation in a manner informed by scientific practices and narratives. His prefaces, written after completing many of his novels, recall a scientist's analysis.

References

Clark, Harry H. "Henry James and Science: The Wings of the Dove." *Transactions of the Wisconsin Academy of Sciences, Arts, and Letters* 52 (1963): 1–15.

Purdy, Strother B. *The Hole in the Fabric: Science, Contemporary Literature, and Henry James*. Pittsburgh: U of Pittsburgh P, 1977.

Sandra J. Chrystal

James, William (1842–1910). Leading turn-of-the-century pragmatist philosopher and radical empiricist psychologist. Although the influence of James's brand of **pragmatism** on twentieth-century American **poetry** has received greater attention, his physiological psychology (*see* Anthropology/Psychology/Sociology)—articulated in works ranging from the 1884 essay "What Is an Emotion?," the two-volume *Principles of Psychology* of 1890, the 1896 *Lowell Lectures* on extraordinary mental states, the 1899 *Talks to Teachers on Psychology*, and the 1902 *Varieties of Religious Experience*—played a key role in the development of writers as disparate as **Robert Frost, Gertrude Stein, Marianne Moore**, Ludwig Wittgenstein and Alfred North Whitehead.

Steven Meyer

Jeffers, Robinson (1887–1962). One of the most influential American poets of the twentieth century. Jeffers was a writer who saw tremendous danger in the technological advances of modern science. In post–World War I poems such as "Science" (1925), Jeffers warned that humanity had fallen victim to its own scientific excesses, stating that "Man . . . Like a maniac with self-love and inward conflicts cannot manage his hybrids" (*Selected Poems* 39).

The era's military and political turmoil, coupled with what Jeffers saw as dangerous and unchecked technological advances, gradually moved the poet toward a position of contempt for much of what human society had to offer. "I'd sooner, except the penalties, kill a man than a hawk," Jeffers wrote in the 1928 poem "Hurt Hawks" (*Selected Poems* 45). Often chastised as an "anti-humanist" for such strident refusals to accept an anthropocentric view of nature, Jeffers instead found solace in the vision of organic wholeness presented by the burgeoning scientific discipline of ecology (see his poem "The Answer," 1938). As one of the first modern literary proponents of an ecological worldview, Jeffers has had an impact far beyond the scope of his own immense talents. The biocentric, ecological themes of his poetry made him an important literary influence on future generations of ecologically conscious writers, such as **Gary Snyder** and **Edward Abbey**.

References

Jeffers, Robinson. *The Double Axe and Other Poems*. New York: Random House, 1948.
———. *Selected Poems*. New York: Vintage 1963.

Philip K. Wilson

Jefferson, Thomas (1743–1826). Author of *Notes on the State of Virginia* (1781), containing observations on **natural history** that refuted **Buffon's theory** that nature in the New World had degenerated for want of cultivation and was inferior to Europe's. His skepticism about theoretical reasoning was based on the empiricist **philosophy** of science.

Raymond F. Dolle

Johnson, Samuel (1709–1784). Lexicographer, master essayist, and moral poet. Johnson probably contributed to Robert James's early *Medical Dictionary* (1743), and he manifested a more than ordinary interest in **medicine**, though his study never advanced beyond the level of well-educated amateur. He maintained a similar amateur interest in arithmetic, which he described as "a species of knowledge perpetually useful and indubitably certain" (*Letters* 4: 138). Johnson was much impressed with the empirical **philosophy** of **Francis Bacon**, and he and **John Locke** are the two most cited prose writers in the *Dictionary*.

References

Letters of Samuel Johnson. Ed. Bruce Redford. 5 vols. Princeton, NJ: Princeton UP, 1992–1994.

Schwarz, Richard B. *Samuel Johnson and the New* Science. Madison: U of Wisconsin P, 1971.

Richard Nash

Jones, William Powell (1901–1989). Author of *The Rhetoric of Science: A Study of Scientific Ideas and Imagery in Eighteenth-Century English Poetry* (1966), a comprehensive history of the influence of science on **poetry**. Jones traces the **history of science** as a stimulus to poetic imagination, beginning with the **telescope** and **microscope**, which were most influential in the first half of the century, and continuing with **natural history**, which took over as the dominant subject after 1760. As the scientific subjects shifted, Jones argues that the poetry itself became less sublime, but the theme of science as a way to perceive God as revealed in nature persisted, even among poets who rejected science as cold and mechanistic.

Kathryn A. Neeley

Jonson, Ben (1572?–1637). Jacobean playwright and poet who produced satirical comedies based on the four humors (e.g., *Every Man in His Humour*, 1598). His play *The Alchemist* (1610) represents the most extensive satirical treatment of **alchemy** in English literature. Jonson evinces not only familiarity with alchemy but also with **Paracelsus**, **astrology**, and **magic**. He is perceptive as to the satirical potential of scientific discoveries as his numerous allusions to the new astronomy or magnetism show (*News from the New World Discovered in the Moon*, 1621; *The Magnetic Lady*, 1632). In *The Staple of News* (1625), Jonson caricatures the emerging systems of communication.

Reference

Partridge, Edward B. *The Broken Compass. A Study of the Major Comedies of Ben Jonson.* New York: Columbia UP, 1958.

Elmar Schenkel

Josselyn, John (fl. c.1608–c.1700). Author of *New-Englands Rarities Discovered* (1672) and *Two Voyages to New-England* (1674), which offer a **natural history** of the region, interspersed with folklore, **poetry**, wit, and tales. Intended for the **Royal Society**, Josselyn's catalogs of animals, plants (especially *materia medica*), minerals, and native culture promote the image of an earthly paradise to colonize.

Raymond F. Dolle

Joyce, James [Augustine Aloysius] (1882–1941). Author of the modern epics *Ulysses* (1922) and *Finnegans Wake* (1939), works designed to function, in Franco Moretti's phrasing, as "world texts" due to "the supranational dimension of the represented space." According to Moretti, "the protagonists of *Ulysses*" are not the central characters, "Stephen Dedalus and the Bloom couple, but two techniques—the [Jamesian] stream of consciousness," dominating the first half of the novel, and an assortment of "polyphonic devices" that "end up . . . master of the Joycean universe." Philip Kuberski draws numerous parallels in his 1994 study, *Chaosmos: Literature, Science and Theory*, between the polyphony found in *Finnegans Wake*—"dissipative structures, neither stable nor unstable, neither ordered nor unordered, neither cosmic nor chaotic," which, "in Joyce's coinage, . . . present us with a 'chaosmos' "—and similar structures in **quantum physics, chaos** and complexity **theories**, fractal geometries (*see* Fractals/Fractal Geometry), and the science of ecology. Critics have also discussed Murray Gell-Mann's appropriation of the term "quark" from *Finnegans Wake* as well as parallels (including false parallels) in Joyce's work to **Einstein, Heisenberg**, and Newton (*see* Newtonianism) and his use, and deliberate misuse, of mathematics and geometry. Finally, Christine Froula, in *Modernism's Body: Sex, Culture and Joyce* (1996), has explored the ramifications of the "trope of vivisection" in "Joyce's autobiographical art."

References

Kuberski, Philip. *Chaosmos: Literature, Science and Theory*. Albany: SUNY P, 1994.
Moretti, Franco. "Ulysses and the Twentieth Century." *Modern Epic: The World System from Goethe to García Márquez*. London: Verso, 1996. 123–229.

Steven Meyer

Keats, John (1795–1821). Major Romantic poet and a licensed surgeon. His physiological understanding of the brain informs *Ode to Psyche* (1819), and chemical knowledge is often taken as the source of the synaesthetic blending that characterizes all of his work. Keats's *Isabella* (1818) evidences close awareness of **technology** in the early **Industrial Revolution**. Long seen as a critic of Newton's **optics** (*see* Newtonianism) in *Lamia* (1819), Keats also increasingly appears as a prophet of post-Newtonian mechanics in presenting space.

Reference

De Almeida, Hermoine. *Romantic Medicine and John Keats*. Oxford: Oxford UP, 1990.

William Crisman

Kees, Weldon (1914–1955). Born in Beatrice, Nebraska, a poet, abstract painter and collagist, jazz pianist and composer, experimental photographer and filmmaker, art critic, screenwriter, and novelist. As his extensive correspondence indicates, Kees knew everyone who was someone in **art** and literary circles on both coasts during the 1940s and 1950s. Kees collaborated with **Gregory Bateson** and Jurgen Ruesch on a psychological study of nonverbal communication. Having written the script for the film shorts of the Bikini Island Atoll **atomic** tests, his art and **poetry** express the existential futility of the postatomic era (*The Last Man*, 1943; *The Fall of the Magicians*, 1947; *Poems 1947–1954*), while his **music** and experimental **films** combine ironic curiosity with the detached charm of a Hoagy Carmichael–style cool. He is presumed to have committed suicide at forty-one by stepping into a heavy fog off the Golden Gate Bridge.

References

The Collected Poems of Weldon Kees. Ed. Donald Justice. Rev. ed. Lincoln: U of Nebraska P, 1975.
Weldon Kees and the Midcentury Generation: Letters, 1935–1955. Ed. Robert E. Knoll. Lincoln: U of Nebraska P, 1986.

Pamela Gossin

Kepler, Johannes (1571–1630). Founder of modern **astronomy**. Kepler's planetary laws formed a theoretical bridge from **Tycho Brahe** to Isaac Newton (*see* Newtonianism). Through mathematical formulations he was able to show, for the first time, that the planets had elliptical rather than circular orbits. By contemporary standards, Kepler's prose is a somewhat impassioned blending of scientific fact with **poetry, analogy**, and metaphor. Kepler's most creative endeavor is a prototypical **science fiction** work *Somnium* (The Dream, 1634), published posthumously by his son. While the cosmic voyage itself and several other details are clearly fantastic, Kepler relies primarily on Copernican (*see* Copernicus) science to describe what happens on the moon's surface.

Reference

Bozzetto, Roger. "Kepler's *Somnium*; or, Science Fiction's Missing Link." *Science-Fiction Studies* 17.3 (1990): 370–82.

Shelly Jarrett Bromberg

Kingsley, Charles (1819–1875). English author, Christian Socialist, and amateur naturalist who advocated study of nature both as **natural theology** and as part of his nationalist stance (*Glaucus*, 1855; *Scientific Lectures and Essays*, published 1880). An apologist of **Charles Darwin**, Kingsley linked scientific advancement to social reform in novels such as *Two Years Ago* (1857).

Reference

Uffelman, Larry K. *Charles Kingsley*. Twayne's English Authors Series. Boston: G.K. Hall, 1979.

Alison E. Bright

Koestler, Arthur (1905–1983). English writer of Austro-Hungarian origin. Koestler became famous for his dystopian novel *Darkness at Noon* (1940), which reflects his disappointment with communism. In his collection of essays *The Yogi and the Commissar* (1945), Koestler argues for the union of saint and revolutionary. After 1955, Koestler publishes essays and books on science, **religion**, and psychology (*see* Anthropology/Psychology/Sociology). *The Sleep-*

walkers (1959) is a history of **astronomy** embedded in **culture** and biography. In *The Act of Creation* (1964) and in *The Ghost in the Machine* (1967), he outlines a psychology of "bisociation" that constitutes the creative act in science as well as in **art** and literature. *The Roots of Coincidence* (1971) is a cautious evaluation of parapsychology.

Elmar Schenkel

Kress, Nancy (1948–   ). American writer who turned to publishing hard **science fiction** in 1988. Kress's fiction speculates on genetic engineering (*see* Biotechnology/Genetic Engineering), bioethics, and future history, employing ideas from cultural **anthropology**. Her novel *Brain Rose* (1989) explores the response of medical science to an **AIDS**-like memory-eating disease, dubious treatment for which causes disastrous and unanticipated side effects.

Robert C. Goldbort

Krutch, Joseph Wood (1893–1970). A popular nature essayist in the 1950s and 1960s, also wrote a scholarly study (*Henry David Thoreau*, 1948) and an influential anthology, *Great American Nature Writing* (1950). His scientific outlook was formed by two scientists known for their popular essays: the Harvard entomologist William Morton Wheeler and the influential conservationist **Aldo Leopold**. A believer in evolution, Krutch argued in his nature essays based upon close observation of mysterious animal behavior that intelligence and love, among other qualities, could be the mechanism for evolution rather than natural selection. Author of a dozen books on nature-related topics, his best-known essays are collected in *The Best Nature Writing of Joseph Wood Krutch* (1969).

Reference

McClintock, James I. "Joseph Wood Krutch: Metabiologist." *Nature's Kindred Spirits: Aldo Leopold, Joseph Wood Krutch, Edward Abbey, Annie Dillard, and Gary Snyder*. Madison: U of Wisconsin P, 1994.

James I. McClintock

Kuhn, Thomas S. *See* **Revolutions/Crises/Paradigms/Kuhn**.

L

Laboratory. A place for modern scientific experimentation. An early example can be found in the description of Salomon's House in **Francis Bacon's** *The New Atlantis* (1624). While Bacon's dream vision anticipates laboratory research in such areas as **meteorology** and crop science, the shroud of secrecy that envelops Salomon's House also makes its way to the laboratories in the **fiction** of the nineteenth and twentieth centuries. The secret laboratory of **Mary Shelley's** Victor **Frankenstein** is pivotal historically: It looks at once backward to alchemical magic and forward to anticipate the moral dilemmas inherent in the revolutionary creations of modern laboratory science. Other famous laboratories in nineteenth-century fiction are those of **Nathaniel Hawthorne's** Rappaccini, **Robert Louis Stevenson's** Jekyll, and **H.G. Wells's** Moreau.

The twentieth century spawned a plethora of fictional laboratories, from **Karel Capek's** robotics lab in *Rossum's Universal Robots* (1923) and **Aldous Huxley's** human cloning labs in *Brave New World* (1932) to the dinosaur cloning labs in **Michael Crichton's** *Jurassic Park* (1990), and from the labs that pervade mainstream **science fiction** to the politicized corporate and academic labs in the novels of **Robin Cook** and chemist **Carl Djerassi**. Laboratory fiction both reflects and evaluates the Baconian program; it sets forth variations on the timeless motif that the power of **experimental science** can be used to shape humanity's biocultural progress for either good or ill.

References

Goldbort, R.C. " 'How Dare You Sport Thus with Life?': Frankensteinian Fictions as Case Studies in Scientific Ethics." *Journal of Medical Humanities* 16 (1995): 79–91.

Latour, Bruno, and Steve Woolgar. *Laboratory Life: The Construction of Scientific Facts.* Princeton, NJ: Princeton UP, 1986.

Robert C. Goldbort

Landscape(s). Historical, aesthetic, and literary entities that involve science and the **history of science** in several ways. Through **theories** of geological and climatic evolution, or the history of agricultural and industrial **technologies**, science shapes the landscapes of **art** and literature. Just as important is the impact of exploration and expansionism. Visions of colonial landscapes bear the imprint of imperialism's "scientific" exploitation of its dominions; indeed, the proliferation of people of European descent throughout the world's temperate zones was largely the biological triumph of their weeds, domestic animals, vermin, and bacteria. Students of travel literature have become sensitive to the scientific dimension of landscape descriptions, while **geography** as a discipline has begun to recognize the rhetorical status of its **representations** (e.g., maps). Finally, landscaping as an aesthetic practice is dependent on technological innovation and may also form an imaginative response to the impact of scientific discovery. Thus the classical French **garden** was made possible by advances in surveying techniques (and ballistics), while landscaping projects in eighteenth-century England could simultaneously register the discoveries of the explorer James Cook and contribute to the rationalization of **agriculture**. Environmentalist dreams to the contrary, historical landscapes are poised far from equilibrium.

Reference

Barnes, Trevor, and James S. Duncan, eds. *Writing Words: Discourse, Text & Metaphor in the Representation of Landscape.* London and New York: Routledge, 1992.

Yves Abrioux

Lapidary Lore. A common component of literature prior to the advent of modern **mineralogy** in the late seventeenth century. Theophrastus, **Aristotle's** successor in the Lyceum, wrote the first known treatise on stones, *Peri Lithon*. In *Lithica*, a thousand-line poem in classical Greek of unknown authorship and uncertain date, Theodamus, a son of Priam, recounts the virtues of precious stones to the author as they go to assist at a sacrifice to the sun. **Dante's** many references to the mineral kingdom have been traced not only to **Pliny the Elder** but also to such medieval intermediaries as Albertus Magnus, Isidore of Seville, and Uguiccione de Pisa. A medieval tradition of Anglo-Norman lapidaries influenced many English poets, especially **Chaucer** and Gower. Renaissance continuations of the same tradition influenced **Shakespeare** and **Milton**.

References

Austin, Herbert D. "Dante and the Mineral Kingdom." *Philology* 4(1950): 79–153.
Duncan, Edgar H. "The Natural History of Metals and Minerals in the Universe of Milton's *Paradise Lost.*" *Osiris* 11(1954): 386–421.
Heather, P.J. "Precious Stones in Middle English Verse of the Fourteenth Century." *Folk-Lore* 42(1931): 217–64, 345–404.
Kunz, George F. *Shakespeare and Precious Stones.* Philadelphia: Lippincott, 1915.

Dennis R. Dean

Lassus, Bernard (1929–   ). **Landscape** architect and theoretician, studied under Fernand Léger. Lassus has developed a concept of the "de-mesurable" as a means of reintroducing infinity into a world rendered finite by the mastery of space achieved by science and **technology**. He has incorporated into his land- scape designs and theoretical writings the imaginative impact of changes in the world picture produced by the great explorers of the past (*Garden of the Returns*, Rochefort, France) and the contemporary exploration of space (plan for a *Gar- den of the Planets*, Paris), as well as seeking solutions to the problem of post- industrial sites (Duisberg-North, Germany).

Reference

Abrioux, Yves. "Géométrie du paysage et dynamique culturelle : Bernard Lassus et Ian Hamilton Finlay." *T.L.E.* 12 (1994): 229–54.

Yves Abrioux

Latour, Bruno (1947–   ). Influential, prolific, and controversial French so- ciologist of scientific knowledge. Latour rejects the split between "nature" and "society," "text" and "context," arguing that splitting human and nonhuman, then using either to explain the other, violates the principle of symmetry by which nothing can be "reduced to" or used to explain anything else. He thus opens up science as a broadly based cultural practice. *Laboratory Life* (with Steve Woolgar, 1979), employs **anthropology** and literary criticism to study the working lives of scientists. *Science in Action* (1987) examines science as the production and stabilization of facts via networks composed through the align- ment of heterogeneous entities, or "actors," both human and nonhuman; *The Pasteurization of France* (1988) offers a historical case study. Latour disartic- ulates the concept of "modernity" altogether (and with it, postmodernity) in *We Have Never Been Modern* (1993), and in the innovative *Aramis* (1996), he lov- ingly tells the story of a failed Paris rapid transit system.

Laura Dassow Walls

Le Guin, Ursula K(roeber) (1929–   ). One of the most influential and intensively studied authors of contemporary **science fiction**, many of her best- known works explore the complex interrelations of nature and **culture** in the context of alternative worlds. *The Left Hand of Darkness* (1969) is a vividly personalized account of a solitary human's interactions with the androgynous inhabitants of a world in the grip of an Ice Age that problematizes the **politics** of **gender**. In *The Dispossessed* (1974), the social functions of science and language are compared in a story of twin worlds, one very like earth and one an arid planet that is home to a convincingly realized anarchistic **utopia**. Many of Le Guin's short stories, such as can be found in collections like *The Compass Rose* (1984), *Buffalo Gals and Other Animal Presences* (1987), and *A Fisher- man of the Inland Sea* (1994), weave complex threads of science, ethics, lan- guage, and criticism into deceptively simple narratives. For example, "Sur: A

Summary Report of the *Yelcho* Expedition to the Antarctic, 1909–1910" (1984), a seemingly straightforward tale of nine South American women who journey to the South Pole several years before Amundsen's and Scott's all-male expeditions, explores new articulations of the contradictory positions to be found within and between liberal (modernist) and postmodernist discourses of identity, gender, science, nature, and narrative. Le Guin's nonfictional writings also provide many perceptive critical insights on the discursive relations of literature, science, and **technology**.

Reference

Le Guin, Ursula K. *Dancing at the Edge of the World: Thoughts on Words, Women, Places*. New York: Grove, 1989.

Noel Gough

Lem, Stanislaw (1921–   ). Polish writer whose ingenious and witty uses of **science fiction** include *Memoirs Found in a Bathtub* (1971, trans. 1973), a satire upon militarism, and *The Cyberiad* (1967, trans. 1974), a collection of whimsical fables about robotic engineering (*see* Engineers/Engineering). Lem's metaphysical novel *Solaris* (1961, trans. 1970; filmed in 1972 by Andrei Tarkovsky), in which the limits of human knowledge are explored through encounters with the sentient ocean on an alien planet, is especially noteworthy.

Noel Gough

Leonardo da Vinci (1452–1519). Known primarily as an artist, **engineer, inventor**, naturalist, anatomist—and to himself as "uomo sanza lettere"—he was also the developer of what some consider the first scientific prose. He adds to this prose, however, flashes of pathos, the apocalyptic, and love for the marvelous, though reminding us that the poetic is inferior to the artistic and scientific. In Leonardo's notebooks there are a series of short fables and prophecies, which have been titled posthumously the *Pensieri, Favole, Il Bestiario, Profezie,* and *Facezie*. He reveals, through empirical evidence, **thought experiments**, and debts to earlier natural philosophers, how man—his virtues and vices—is a microcosm of nature. Consequently, Leonardo's literary production is a prosopopoeic exploration and attempt to forecast patterns in both the natural and human worlds.

References

Marinoni, Augusto, ed. *Leonardo da Vinci: Scritti Letterari*. Milan: Rizzoli, 1987.
Richter, Jean Paul, ed. *The Literary Works of Leonardo da Vinci*. Berkeley: U of California P, 1977.

Arielle Saiber

Leopold, Aldo (1886–1948). Author of the often-quoted environmental classic *A Sand County Almanac* (1947) and proponent of a "land ethic," Leopold was also a pioneering conservationist. A distinguished field biologist, Leopold became the first professor of wildlife ecology at the University of Wisconsin and was elected president of the Ecological Society of America. The scientific basis for Leopold's environmental ethic is 1920s and 1930s ecology, particularly Frederic Clements's concepts about plant ecology and succession and Charles Elton's theoretical foundations for modern ecology.

In the most influential essay from *Almanac*, "The Land Ethic," Leopold blends scientific and philosophical outlooks to argue that we should enlarge the boundaries of "community to include soils, waters, plants, and animals, or collectively: the land" (239). If we do include biotic "citizens" in the community, then an "ecological conscience" says "a thing is right when it tends to preserve the integrity, stability and beauty of the biotic community; is wrong when it tends otherwise" (262). Leopold's conversion to this biocentric, rather than human-centered, morality is dramatically presented in another essay from *Almanac*, "Thinking Like a Mountain."

Leopold's influence on contemporary nature writers and environmental advocates has been pervasive, and Leopold's writings are frequently alluded to in popular outdoor magazines as well as scholarly works on the environment. Leopold joins **Henry David Thoreau** and **John Muir** as an environmental prophet.

References

Callicott, J. Baird, ed. *Companion to* A Sand County Almanac: *Interpretive and Critical Essays.* Madison: U of Wisconsin P, 1987.
Leopold, Aldo. A Sand County Almanac: *With Essays on Conservation from Round River.* New York: Oxford UP, 1966.
Meine, Curt. *Aldo Leopold: His Life and Work.* Madison: U of Wisconsin P, 1988.

James I. McClintock

Lewis, C(live) S(taples) (1898–1963). Classical scholar, novelist, literary critic, and Christian apologist, vehemently opposed to scientific materialism. His **science fiction** trilogy *Out of the Silent Planet* (1938), *Perelandra* (1943), and *That Hideous Strength* (1945) reflects both his friendship with J.R.R. Tolkien and Charles Williams and his public controversy with the Marxist geneticist **J.B.S. Haldane** over the degree of influence that science should exert in society. Lewis regarded reductionist materialism and the Darwinian (*see* Darwin) emphasis on chance as equally incompatible with religious values. His character Weston (Western man), a physicist, who is both ruthless and simplistic in his understanding of the universe, embodies the various facets of scientism that Lewis vigorously denounces through his spokesperson Ransom, a philologist and Christian humanist. Unlike most science fiction writers, Lewis had no interest in the technical side of his story, which he regarded as merely a vehicle for the philosophical debate that was his overriding purpose, and despite his two realistic disputants, the trilogy is closer to fantasy than science fiction.

In *Out of the Silent Planet*, as Weston and Ransom travel to Mars (Malacandra), Weston affirms his Darwinian and racist beliefs in the rights of the human species over the individual and, summoned before the all-wise Oyarsa of Malacandra, foolishly asserts humanity's right to conquer and colonize other worlds, a premise of much pulp science fiction of the 1930s. *Perelandra* attacks what Lewis regarded as two other scientific "heresies"—the pantheistic view of a purposeful Life-Force directing evolution, and scientific utilitarianism. In *That Hideous Strength* (1945) Lewis specifically denounces behavioral psychology (*see* Anthropology/Psychology/Sociology), represented as N.I.C.E. (National Institute of Co-ordinated Experiments), a sinister foundation planning to introduce eugenics, prenatal education, vivisection, brainwashing, and environmental control. Underlying this program is the same rationale enunciated by Weston in the first two books—materialism, utilitarianism, the belief that the ends justify the means, the sacrifice of the individual for the species, etc.—in fact, all the values that Lewis ascribed to science and scientists and associated with intellectual arrogance and ruthlessness. As well as attacking Haldane, the trilogy takes issue with **H.G. Wells** for his glorification of science, Olaf Stapledon for his evolutionary beliefs, and what Lewis called the "scientification" of science fiction magazines.

References

Haldane, J.B.S. "Auld Hornie, F.R.S." *Shadows of Imagination*. Ed. M.R. Hillegas. Carbondale: Southern Illinois UP, 1969. 15–25.
Lowenberg, Susan. *C.S. Lewis: A Reference Guide, 1972–1988*. New York and Toronto: G.K. Hall, Maxwell, Macmillan, 1993.
Wilson, A.N. *C.S. Lewis: A Biography*. London: Collins, 1990.

Roslynn D. Haynes

Lichtenberg, Georg Christoph (1742–1799). Physicist, editor, and lifelong professor at the University of Göttingen, best known today for his literary achievements: his private journals or sketch books, the posthumously published *Sudelbücher*, which formed the source of his many aphorisms; his essays popularizing science and criticizing contemporary German **culture**; and his famous essays on the English artist William Hogarth. Lichtenberg's writing reveals a paradox of thought and awareness of language that not only expressed the contradictions of the late-eighteenth-century German **Enlightenment** but also anticipated and deconstructed many of its structures of psychology (*see* Anthropology/Psychology/Sociology) and language. Both his enlightened and dialectical critique of the Enlightenment from the perspective of personal experience instead of rational analysis and his superior consciousness of language and image as media that play a key role in what is thought have guaranteed an ever-growing interest in Lichtenberg, his personality, and his work.

Reference

Stern, Guy. *Lichtenberg. A Doctrine of Scattered Occasions.* Bloomington: U of Indiana P, 1959.

Ralph W. Buechler

Lightman, Alan P. (1948–   ). Physicist and writing teacher (MIT), author of many essays about science and humanities, and a novelist. He is best known for *Einstein's Dreams* (1993), an exploration of the nature and experience of **time** framed by an account of **Albert Einstein** completing his work on special **relativity.** *The Diagnosis* (2000) is a Kafkaesque narrative in which Lightman juxtaposes the surrealism generated by the speed and tempo of contemporary life, **information** overload, and the medicalization of the mind and body with a narrative account of the ancient trial of Socrates and the intergenerational and philosophical differences of his persecutor, Anytus, and his son.

Jay A. Labinger and Pamela Gossin

Lindbergh, Anne Morrow (1906–2001). Spouse of aviator Charles Lindbergh (1900–1975), author of books of travel, poetry, fiction, and diaries and letters. Before World War II, she traveled extensively with her husband in a two-person floatplane across Canada to the Orient and Europe. She is best known for her first two works, *North to the Orient* (1935) and *Listen! The Wind* (1938), based on her 1931 and 1933 flights with her husband. Lindbergh's greatest success lies in her ability to transform the experience of flight to the understanding of the nontechnical reader. *Orient* is externally focused, examining the physical nature of the world through which she traveled with her husband from New York to China before their plane was capsized. *Wind* is internally focused, as she reviews personal responses as plane's copilot and wife during flight, especially in the area of the Canary Islands and the **Africa**–South America flight. Later works remain in this mode, especially responding to women's adjustments to pressures of family and life (particularly in *Gift from the Sea*, 1955). Lindbergh's most lasting contribution to the literature/science interface is her early recognition of the impact of science through **technology** on human living.

David Kirk Vaughan

Literary Representations of the Scientist. Fictional depictions of the scientist, or his predecessors the alchemist and the natural philosopher, dating back at least to the sixteenth century. Such depictions are characterized by (1) the frequency with which six basic images have recurred, with minor differences; and (2) by the preponderance of unattractive and ill-intentioned figures. These primary stereotypes can be classified as: the evil alchemist, the noble scientist, the stupid scientist, the inhuman researcher, the scientist as adventurer hero, and the scientist out of control.

The Evil Alchemist

Originally practiced in ancient Egypt, **alchemy** was introduced to medieval Europe via translations of Arabic writings and hence was popularly associated with heresy and the black arts. Alchemists often lived in fear of their lives, working in secret and disguising their knowledge in arcane symbols and language that were perceived by the uninitiated as a further threat. Despite its evil reputation, alchemy also fascinated by its promises of fabulous wealth (by turning base metals into gold), power (through a perpetual motion machine), longevity (through an elixir of youth that would banish death), and the creation of a homunculus. Because science continues to offer variants of these allurements (medical cures for once-fatal diseases, nuclear power, in-vitro fertilization, and genetic engineering [*see* Biotechnology/Genetic Engineering]), the alchemist stereotype has been anachronistically retained, and writers have perpetuated the image of scientists as intellectually arrogant, power-crazed, secretive, and even insane in their pretensions to transcend human limitations.

The prototypical alchemist in literature was Doctor Faustus, based on a real person but mythologized as a figure whose intellectual pride led to a pact with the devil and hence eternal damnation. Although the first written account of Faust, the anonymous *Historia von D. Johann Fausten* (1587), was highly moralistic, later versions have varied in their interpretation from condemnation (for humanistic rather than religious reasons) to regret for the tragic waste of a gifted individual. **Christopher Marlowe's** play *Doctor Faustus* (1604), an early example of the latter view, influenced the heroic Faust characters of German **Romanticism**, the most famous being **Goethe's** *Faust* (Pt. 1, 1805; Pt. 2, 1832).

More recent alchemists in **fiction** and **film** have been inspired by **Mary Shelley's** *Frankenstein* (1818). Shelley's protagonist has provided a universal byword to condemn scientists who fail to warn society of the consequences of their research, particularly in **physics**, **biology**, and medical science. Examples of the Frankenstein complex that focus on the destruction wreaked by power-crazed weapons producers are found in Georg Kaiser's plays *Gas I* (1918) and *Gas II* (1920), **J.B. Priestley's** novel *The Doomsday Men* (1938), **Philip K. Dick's** *Dr Bloodmoney* (1965), and Stanley Kubrick's film *Dr Strangelove* (1964), while **Robert Louis Stevenson's** *The Strange Case of Dr Jekyll and Mr Hyde* (1886), **H.G. Wells's** *The Island of Doctor Moreau* (1896) and *The Invisible Man* (1897), Maurice Renard's *New Bodies for Old* (1908), Somerset Maugham's *The Magician* (1908), and numerous short stories in pulp fiction explore the psychology (*see* Anthropology/Psychology/Sociology) of the Faust and Frankenstein prototypes in the field of biology, usually in strongly moralistic terms suggesting that such experimentation is not only dangerous but sinful.

The Noble Scientist

The first literary work depicting scientists positively was **Francis Bacon's** *New Atlantis* (1626), describing a **utopia** governed by a scientific elite, the

House of Salomon. Bacon's scientists pursue long-term research, emphasizing experimental method and promoting internationalism, the open sharing of knowledge, team effort, and individual altruism for the common good. Potentially harmful research is immediately discontinued. Bacon's ideals were the motive force for the founding in 1662 of the **Royal Society** of London, whose most prestigious member, Isaac Newton (*see* Newtonianism), became the archetype of the wise and noble scientist. Humble where Faust had been proud, he appeared to his contemporaries to explain rather than mystify, to bring harmony and order to the hitherto confusing **cosmos**, and in the process, deliver considerable economic spin-offs from his laws of mechanics and **optics**. So successful was the scientific hagiography attached to Newton that his obsession with closet alchemy, revealed by John Maynard Keynes in 1946, seemed at first unbelievable, then a betrayal.

The belief that scientists alone might be selfless and wise enough to be entrusted with government was reaffirmed in the nineteenth century by Kurd Lasswitz in *Two Planets* (1897) and in the twentieth century by H.G. Wells in a series of scientific utopias including *The Food of the Gods* (1904), *A Modern Utopia* (1905), *The World Set Free* (1914), and *Men Like Gods* (1923) and by the psychologist Burrhus F. Skinner in *Walden Two* (1948). The interwar period saw the reemergence of the scientist–ruler in numerous American and European utopias where peace is achieved only by entrusting world government to a noble scientist, invariably of the same nationality as the author. Since World War II, the image of the scientist as world ruler has ceased to appeal, and such stereotypes are rarely invoked, except as a yardstick against which to measure the deficiencies of contemporary scientists.

More commonly in twentieth-century literature the noble scientist is presented as a victim of society, a lone protester against what he perceives as immoral activities. This was a common theme during and immediately after World War II in Nigel Balchin's novels *The Small Back Room* (1943) and *A Sort of Traitors* (1949), where British scientists are unwillingly coerced into working on weapons production, and in Charles Morgan's plays *The Flashing Stream* (1942) and *The Burning Glass* (1953), where the protagonists refuse to work for military intelligence. This theme of the scientist repudiating what was popularly believed to be his patriotic duty became even more controversial during the Cold War when the trials of the so-called atom spies elicited numerous literary explorations of the moral questions involved. Among these are James Hilton's *Nothing so Strange* (1947), James Aldridge's *The Diplomat* (1949), Ruth Chatterton's *The Betrayers* (1953), Mitchell Wilson's *Meeting at a Far Meridian* (1961), and Carl Zuckmayer's play *Cold Light* (1955). Recent **science fiction**, especially that by women writers, has attempted to break away from the former simplistic heroes of the genre. **Ursula K. Le Guin's** *The Dispossessed* (1974) and **Marge Piercy's** *Body of Glass* (1991), for example, examine what morality in science might entail in the twenty-first century.

The Stupid Scientist

The early members of the Royal Society and their contemporaries, the **virtuosi** (usually untrained dilettantes in **natural philosophy**) were ridiculed on the Restoration stage. The virtuosi, in particular, with their vast and expensive *cabinets* of miscellaneous objects, which they believed would contribute to the Baconian project of collating universal knowledge, were satirized as obsessively collecting useless, foul-smelling trivia while ignoring important events. Sir Nicholas Gimcrack, in **Thomas Shadwell's** play *The Virtuoso* (1676), pursuing fake "wonders" while ignoring social responsibilities, provided a stereotype that has reappeared in more or less sinister forms. In the Projectors of Book III of *Gulliver's Travels* (1726) **Jonathan Swift** arraigned stupid, shortsighted specialists who produce widespread disasters, but in the early twentieth century when science was revered, absentminded professors in numerous comic strips, pulp fiction, and films were treated as merely humorous. Since 1945, however, eccentric scientists have been placed under scrutiny and found guilty of crimes against humanity, as in **Kurt Vonnegut's** satire of Dr. Felix Hoenikker in *Cat's Cradle* (1963).

The Inhuman Researcher

The Romantic movement of the late eighteenth and early nineteenth centuries generated the most enduring scientist stereotype, that of the researcher who sacrifices the emotional to the rational, abandoning human relationships in an obsessive pursuit of science. English Romantic writers in particular realized that the reductionist procedures of scientific materialism epitomized in Newtonian science denigrated, if they did not altogether banish, questions of value, and they responded by depicting scientists as emotionally retarded and deficient in creative **imagination**. **William Blake** regarded Newton as a dangerous advocate of materialism and in *Jerusalem* linked him with Francis Bacon and **John Locke** as constituting an infernal trinity.

Emotionally deficient scientists range from the pitiful to the sinister, depending on the degree of power they achieve. The protagonists of **Charles Dickens's** story *The Haunted Man* (1848) and **Robert Browning's** poem *Paracelsus* (1835) repent, but most are beyond help. **Honoré de Balzac's** *The Search for the Absolute* (1834) and Mary Shelley's *Frankenstein* (1818) epitomize the Romantic fallen angel who rejects love and family for research. Shelley's novel also explores the psychological consequences of a life of research. In the twentieth century accounts of the unconcern of atomic weapons scientists during World War II and the Cold War about the human cost of their research revived this stereotype, causing the impersonal scientist to become the amoral scientist. Physics, mathematics, and **computer science** have provided the best-known examples of the emotionless, amoral scientist, prepared to wreak worldwide disaster. The third version of **Bertolt Brecht's** *Life of Galileo* (1947), **Pearl Buck's** novel *Command the Morning* (1959), **Friedrich Dürrenmatt's** play *The Phys-*

icists (1962), and Heiner Kipphardt's *In the Matter of J. Robert Oppenheimer* (1967) exemplify this concern.

The Scientist As Adventurer Hero

This stereotype, which emerged with the late-nineteenth-century belief in **progress** and the benefits of technology, found its first, perhaps supreme, expression in the novels of **Jules Verne**. His debonair scientist heroes, equipped with fast and novel means of transport, conquer all dangers and limitations of nature, affirming bravery, optimism, and reverence for scientific knowledge and technology. *A Journey to the Centre of the Earth* (1864) and *20,000 Leagues under the Sea* (1870) are the best known of Verne's *Les Voyages extraordinaires.* **Arthur Conan Doyle's** Professor Challenger stories with their mix of science, adventure (both physical and intellectual), courage, and moral superiority are in the same mold. Their descendants are the **inventors** and space travelers of science fiction, such as Garrett P. Serviss's *Edison's Conquest of Mars* (1898), and of the pulp magazines that sprang up in the 1930s and 1940s, such as *Amazing Stories, Astounding Stories*, and *Marvel*. **Isaac Asimov**, **Arthur C. Clarke**, and other well-known science fiction writers retained the same simplistic optimism about science and its moral status expressed in the early Verne stories and the scientific utopias of H.G. Wells, and their unquestioning valorization of the scientist continued in the popular *Star Trek* and *Dr. Who* series. Feminist critics have located in such science fiction a major source of sexism and racism, since female characters are either absent or passive sex objects to be attacked by evil aliens and rescued by macho space travelers who purvey an uncomplicated message of rightful imperial domination over the cosmos and its dissenting inhabitants.

The Scientist Out of Control

The theme of the scientist whose experiment has misfired or become uncontrollable expresses one of the major fears of twentieth-century civilization, in response to the real and imagined disasters inherent in atomic power, nuclear weapons, genetic engineering, cloning, artificial intelligence (*see* Virtual Reality and Artificial Intelligence), organ transplants, and ecological disasters. Not surprisingly, it is one of the most common modern stereotypes, and here again *Frankenstein* has provided an archetype. **Karel Capek's** play *R.U.R.* (1923), Philip Wylie's novel *The Gladiator* (1930), and **Fred Hoyle** and John Elliot's *A for Andromeda* (1964) depict robots or computers overpowering their creators; **C.P. Snow's** *New Lives for Old* (1933) deals with the problems of experiments in rejuvenation redounding on naive biologists; **Stanislaw Lem's** *His Master's Voice* (1968) focuses on the consequences of scientists' inability to communicate; Howard Brenton's play *The Genius* (1983) considers the irreversible transition from pure math formulae to atomic weapons; aspects of environmental pollution are discussed by Heinrich Böll's *The Safety Net* (1979), Günter Grass's *The Rat* (1986); and Christa Wolf's *Störfall* (1987) examines the implications of the Chernobyl disaster and the unwitting guilt of the scientists involved. In most recent literature of this kind, actual events have preceded their fictional representation.

These archetypes are the continuing folklore of our time. Like all myths they may appear simple but in fact represent complex ideas and suppressed fears that transcend time, place, and race.

References

Cohen, John. *Human Robots in Myth and Science*. London: Allen and Unwin, 1966.

De Camp, L. Sprague, and Thomas D. Clareson. "The Scientist." *Science Fiction: Contemporary Mythology*. Ed. Patricia Warrick, Martin H. Greenberg, and J. Olander. New York: Harper, 1978. 196–206.

Haynes, Roslynn D. *From Faust to Strangelove: Representations of the Scientist in Western Literature*. Baltimore: Johns Hopkins UP, 1994.

———. *H.G. Wells: Discoverer of the Future*. London: Macmillan, 1980.

Levine, George, and U.C. Knoepflmacher, eds. *The Endurance of Frankenstein*. Berkeley and Los Angeles: U of California P, 1979.

Philmus, Robert M. *Into the Unknown: The Evolution of Science Fiction from Francis Godwin to H.G. Wells*. Berkeley and Los Angeles: U of California P, 1970.

Smeed, J. William. *Faust in Literature*. London: Oxford UP, 1975.

Warwick, Patricia S. *The Cybernetic Imagination in Science Fiction*. Cambridge: MIT P, 1980.

Roslynn D. Haynes

Literature and Science (Chronological Periods)

Antiquity (500 B.C.E.–A.D. 476)

A historical period associated with the rise of Greek civilization beginning with Pericles and ending with the fall of the Roman Empire. The earliest examples of the meeting of science and literature in Greece are found in the epic works of two poets in the ninth century B.C.E. **Homer's** (c. 800 B.C.E.) *Iliad* and *Odyssey* are important instances of a mythological world imbued with natural law. **Hesiod's** (c. 800 B.C.E.) *Theogony* and *Works and Days* continue Homer's exploration of myth while also evidencing a further move toward scientific rationalism characteristic of Grecian science. Against the backdrop of centuries of war, migration, and colonization, Grecian culture came into its own between the eighth and seventh centuries B.C.E. Fifth century B.C.E., however, is designated as the start of Antiquity with the incorporation of Ionia in 479 B.C.E. when Greece at last expelled Persia. The reign of Pericles (c. 490–429 B.C.E.) beginning in 460 B.C.E. signals the most important period known as the *Periclean Age*, during which the arts and sciences flourished as never before and never since.

Ancient philosophy, the progenitor of both science and literature, antedates the Periclean Age with the advent of the **pre-Socratic philosophers** in seventh century B.C.E. Many of these early explorations into the physical world would become known as natural philosophies. Myth was still strong, and nature was animate, but scientific inquiry became the primary means of understanding both. Thales of Miletus (c. 624–546 B.C.E.), founder of the Ionian school, was the first to speculate on primary material elements, of which, for Thales, water was the most important. Thales was considered one of the founders of Greek geometry and **astronomy** and wrote epic rhymes about the cosmos inspired by Greek **mythology**. Thales would be followed by many pre-Socratics including Pythagoras of Samos (c. 580–520 B.C.E.), Parmenides, (c. 515 B.C.E.), and Zeno (c. 490–430 B.C.E.), all of whom, in varying degrees, sought to understand nature and myth through systematic analyses. Democritus (c. 460–370 B.C.E.), considered the father of modern science, was the last of the pre-Socratics and is best known for creating mechanical explanations for all of nature that surrounded him. As with his fellow pre-Socratics, Democritus's attempts to rationally explain the earthy and mythological realms signaled steady progress toward scientific rationalism (*see* Rationality).

During the Periclean Age, first philosophy and then science began to replace myth and **religion**. Here was a new kind of faith based upon reason rather than superstition. The accomplishments of the period are numerous, influencing all areas of science from **astronomy** to zoology (*see* Biology/Zoology). Protagoras of Abdera (c. 480–411 B.C.E.), founder of the Sophists, would be the first to make a definitive break with religion, replacing myth with natural law. **Hippocrates** (c. 460–390 B.C.E.), the father of modern **medicine**, would go further, establishing the study of medicine as a scientific rather than religious practice. The literature of this period, however, remained tied to religion and myth, and even well-known poets such as Pindar (c. 522–443 B.C.E.), originator of the Pindaric ode, had little to say of science.

The move toward science and away from religion was gradual. Socrates (c. 470–399 B.C.E.), for instance, while clearly skeptical in outlook, made few contributions to science and is considered by some critics to have frustrated its advance. Ironically, Socrates played an interesting and perhaps unwitting role in the history of science and literature during the Periclean Age as a character in the comedy *Clouds* (423 B.C.E.) by **Aristophanes** (c. 445–385 B.C.E.). Aristophanes was highly critical of science, and in the play he parodies the Sophist Anaxagoras (c. 500–428 B.C.E.) and his concepts of World Mind and the rotary vortex by relegating the explanations of both to the voice of Socrates. Among the poets and dramatists of the day, however, there were those, like Euripides (c. 480–406 B.C.E.), one of the originators of Greek tragedy, who were familiar with the works of the Sophists and understood the dramatic possibilities scientific rationalism afforded. Of his many tragedies, *Medea* (431 B.C.E.) is a fitting example of Euripides's turn away from superstition and toward rational, perhaps even psychological, explanations, for in the drama the magical powers of Medea now are insufficient to control her destiny or that of her husband Jason. Moreover, it is her character and its flaws that lead to the ultimate tragedy.

Socrates's most famous follower, **Plato** (427–347 B.C.E.), continued the work of his teacher and revealed only a kind of mystical interest in mathematics similar to that of the Pythagoreans. Plato also is credited with denouncing the study of mechanics, opting instead to focus on the soul and the state. What Plato lacked in scientific inquiry, however, was greatly offset by his literary prowess found in the thirty-six remaining dialogues of his work.

Science and literature in the Periclean Age were best represented in the works of **Aristotle** (384–322 B.C.E.), whose death also signals the end of this remarkable period. Of the many areas of science Aristotle explored from **physics** to astronomy, his most famous and accurate work would be in **biology**, where he developed his Ten Categories that would lead to the first **classification system** of nature. His work in **rhetoric** and **poetry** were equally influential. He extended his scientific analyses into literary treatises discussing a range of ideas from the unities of form for drama to an explanation of imitation and mimesis in poetic expression.

By the end of the third century B.C.E., science had reached its apogee in Greece. The conquests of Alexander the Great, stretching from Hellas to Alexandria the Farthest, created a steady stream of new knowledge often for the first time seen by the philosophers of the era. This would be the age of Euclid (c. 300 B.C.E.) and his *Elements*, one of the earliest and most enduring textbooks on geometry. Another important figure of the time would be Archimedes (c. 287–212 B.C.E.), whose principles of weights and floating bodies are still of scientific importance. Zeno of Citium (350–260 B.C.E.) was a central figure of science and literature. Zeno, who founded the Stoic school, would continue the cynicism of Socrates with the addition of a fundamental interest in scientific research. The stoics reappropriated mythological tradition as allegories of natural science. Drawing upon Homer, they reformulated the mythical world, subjecting the various gods and their actions to scientific analysis. Zeus, for example, was now allegorically tied to the ether they believed permeated the outer limits of the **cosmos**.

While science clearly dominated this era, particularly through the Alexandria school, literature gradually moved toward more pastoral or religious themes such as those found in the poetry of Theocritus. This turn toward well-wrought but philosophically vacuous poetry was a reflection of the larger attitudes of the day wherein the analytical and critical ways of thinking were softened as religion regained prominence.

By the time of the Roman conquest (214 B.C.E.) Hellenistic culture was waning, and little of the scientific spirit of exploration and discovery remained. Literature had become institutionalized, with form valued over content. Greece, however, would conquer Roman culture. Grecian **physicians** and philosophers began arriving in Rome shortly after the incorporation of Greece into the Roman state. So, too, the famous museums and schools of Alexandria and Athens continued to flourish under Roman rule for several centuries.

From the first century B.C.E. to the fall of Rome at the hands of Odovaker in A.D. 476, advances in science and literature slowed as more of the empire's resources were bound up in the long and protracted battles to protect and expand its power. In the last century B.C.E., three of the Greco-Roman world's most famous poets appeared, **Vergil** (70–19 B.C.E.), **Horace** (65–8 B.C.E.), and **Ovid** (43 B.C.E.–A.D. 18). Ovid's *Metamorphoses* spans the creation of the world to Julius Caesar, based upon the notion that matter can assume any shape.

In the years directly before and after the birth of Christ, Seneca (4 B.C.E.–A.D. 65) was one of the last philosopher–poets of Antiquity. His *Questiones Naturales* was a study of natural science based on Democritus's mechanical explanations of nature. More interestingly, however, was his interpretation of the drama *Medea* in which reference is made to another continent beyond the Atlantic centuries before the discovery of the New World.

Up to the fall of the Roman Empire, science was confined to the universities where advances were made, most notably in medicine and **chemistry**. Science, like literature, however, gradually became overshadowed by religion. The *Confessions* of Saint Augustine (A.D. 354–430) exemplifies this symbolic turn away from scientific rationalism toward religious mysticism, for within its pages, he claims that it was his knowledge of science that led him to Christianity.

Advances in science and literature became the pillars of Antiquity and helped to define it as an age of exploration and creation unparalleled in the history of Western civilization. As philosophers, scientists, and poets sought to demythologize the world around them, science and literature, often as interdependent modes of expression, heralded new ways of describing nature that would forever change the course of Western thought.

References

Durant, Will. *The Story of Civilization: Part II, The Life of Greece.* New York: Simon and Schuster, 1939.

Kirk, G.S., et al. *The Presocratic Philosophers: A Critical History with a Selection of Texts.* Cambridge: Cambridge UP, 1995.

Titchener, Frances B., ed. *The Eye Expanded: Life and the Arts in Greco-Roman Antiquity.* Berkeley: U of California P, 1999.

Wright, M.R. *Cosmology in Antiquity (Science in Antiquity).* New York: Routledge, 1995.

Shelly Jarrett Bromberg

Middle Ages

The time period from roughly A.D. 500 to 1400. Medieval science and **philosophy** viewed nature as the universe created by God. Human beings had an assigned place and duties in the natural order of the universe; failure to assume the place and duties was unnatural and, therefore, immoral. Since, however, morality is not actually perceptible in the physical world, a new mode of interpreting and of writing had to be developed in order to express the moral order of the universe. This was the "poetic mode." The poetic mode for the Middle Ages was allegory. In its simplest terms, allegory is metaphorical language; that is, words mean literally one thing (the letter) and, at the same time, figuratively something else. Indeed, the figurative meaning may be multiple, thus conveying one or more allegorical meanings in addition to the required literal sense.

Medieval literature, like any literature, reflects the science of its time. For example, the medieval optical principle of extramission may explain the play of eyebeam and vision in works ranging from mysticism to love's "first sight." Similarly, in Joseph of Exeter's *Ylias* (c. 1183), an epic poem on the Trojan War, Helen's passion for Paris is explained by the domination of her liver, the seat of lust, over her heart and brain. However, the characterization of a strong sexual attraction as lust reveals the important moral dimension of much medieval science. The liver is a literal explanation based on medieval science, but with a significant moral component not evident in the scientific facts alone. The explanation for Helen's conduct approaches the multiple levels of meaning in allegory.

As poetic mode, we can see how the moral level of meaning interprets heterogeneous natural phenomena. For example, Alan de Lille's *Complaint of Nature* (*De planctu Naturae*, c. 1160–1175) faults human perversity in two areas: language and sexuality (*see* Gender and Sexuality). Language is incorrect when modifiers fail to agree in gender with their nouns—for example, when a masculine adjective is joined to a feminine noun (such as *bonus femina* instead of the grammatically correct *bona femina*). Unnatural sexuality occurs when nature's laws are violated. This occurs in unreproductive sexual intercourse, including homosexuality. God wanted the two sexes to reproduce (Gen. 1:28). Since this is impossible between persons of the same sex, homosexuality was deemed unnatural even though it could, like heterosexual relations, give pleasure. The two moral faults in language and sexuality do not refer to one another but to their underlying meaning: natural human activity. Language is natural to human beings and requires agreement in grammatical gender for effective communication; sexuality is just as natural, but it requires both sexes for reproduction. In these two cases, the letter has another meaning besides speech and sexual intercourse, a meaning relating to natural law and medieval morality. Alan de Lille offers a clearer illustration of allegory in the poetic mode in his *Anticlaudianus* (1182–1183). This work describes the construction of a cart, likening it to the acquisition of knowledge of the seven liberal arts by having personifications of the trivium and the quadrivium construct the cart's different parts— grammar makes the guide pole, logic the actual cart, and rhetoric its ornaments, while arithmetic, geometry, **music**, and **astronomy** make one wheel each; the cart is drawn by four horses, which signify the five senses, whereas personifications of reason and prudence direct the team through the universe. The cart and its team of horses become the vehicle for exploration of the scientific and philosophical world, exploration possible through acquisition of the seven arts of the trivium and the quadrivium as well as by direct experience.

Not all allegories are as simple as these examples. In fact, the poetic mode was especially useful in treating more difficult or abstruse subjects. For example, to speak of God, writers could not escape using temporal and spatial language, as when God is said, metaphorically, to "stand" outside of **time** and space. In his *Consolation of Philosophy* (c. 523–526), for example, Boethius uses words like *eternal* and *infinite* as metaphors for God. Boethius makes time and space, terms drawn from the language of science that refer to ways we perceive the natural world, into vehicles referring to the divinity, which is timeless and unbounded. To adapt human language to speak of the Creator of the universe makes language metaphorical; as such, the language uses allegory, the poetic mode.

In the poetic mode, literature, philosophy, and science are not treated separately but in a special kind of medieval writing called "fabulous narrative." Macrobius defines this kind of narrative as a fable that covers a **truth**, as with a veil (*Commentary on Cicero's "Dream of Scipio,"* c. 430–440). Common terms for such writing are *narratio fabulosa, integumentum*, and *involucrum*, all of which suggest the veiling or covering typical of allegorical writing in which the fictional letter is said to cover its allegorical or figurative truth. In this way, medieval writers could salvage ancient **mythology** by treating myths as fables and then giving them a different, allegorical meaning. For instance, Ovid's *Metamorphoses* was glossed and rewritten in historical, scientific, and moral terms. For example, Jupiter's actions could represent a historical ruler's achievements, the planet in the geocentric world, lust in his pursuit of a nymph, or Jesus Christ as king of the world. As Abelard (c. 1079–1142) noted, to understand universal topics in science and philosophy, one must construct a fictional vehicle (*res ficta*) (*see* Fiction) through which the mind projects its thought. He thereby links the invention of such fictional images to the imaginative faculty (*see* Imagination and Creativity). The value of the poetic mode depends on its being modeled on an accepted truth. Allegory assumes an important role in such writing, even when the truth relied on what we would term scientific evidence.

Other authors besides Macrobius authorized the use of images and fables in the poetic mode to express scientific, philosophical, and religious truths. Calcidius (first half of the fourth century) translated and commented on part of Plato's *Timaeus*. The *Timaeus* provided a model of the universe that, alongside the Bible, accounted for Creation. The poetic mode permitted the reader to see both the biblical account and the *Timaeus* account of Creation as two readings of the same event. The biblical account related the story, whereas the Timaean account elaborated upon the forces at work that made that story possible. The two accounts of creation, although different, are complementary in the same way that language and sexuality are in Alan of Lille's comparison. Martianus Capella's *Marriage of Mercury and Philology* provides the model of the seven liberal arts in a fictional marriage ceremony; the marriage is the image or vehicle through which we are made to understand what the seven arts teach.

A number of medieval works illustrate the poetic mode in ways analogous to these predecessors. That is, they were rewritten by medieval authors in order to explore and illustrate both philosophical and scientific knowledge and inquiry. For example, Bernardus Silvestris's *Cosmographia* (c. 1143–1148) represents the creation of the universe, or macrocosm, and of the human being, or microcosm, by drawing on models like the *Timaeus*. Alan of Lille uses a similar technique in his *Anticlaudianus* to show how a perfect man may be recreated, using the motif of the journey through the geocentric universe and beyond that Calcidius describes as well as the triumph of virtue over the vices.

Starting in the thirteenth century, the poetic mode was also adapted to works written in a number of vernacular languages, as in, for example, *The Romance of the Rose* by Guillaume de Lorris (c. 1235–1240) and Jean de Meun (c. 1275–1280), **Dante's** the *Divine Comedy* (c. 1308–1320), **Geoffrey Chaucer's** *House of Fame* (c. 1379–1380), and Christine de Pizan's *Path of Learning* (*Chemin de long estude*, c. 1402–1403) and her *Vision* (*La Vision Christine*, c. 1405–1406). All these works use the model of the geocentric universe to show forth, allegorically, the moral hierarchy deriving from God and visualized and put into language through the image of the geocentric universe. In this way, the language of literature, science, and harmony harmonize in the poetic mode of allegory.

References

Dronke, Peter. *Fabula: Explorations into the Uses of Myth in Medieval Platonism*. Mittellateinische Studien und Texte, 9. Leiden and Cologne: Brill, 1974.

Lewis, C.S. *The Discarded Image: An Introduction to Medieval and Renaissance Literature*. Cambridge: Cambridge UP, 1964.

Lindberg, David C. *The Beginnings of Western Science: The European Scientific Tradition in Philosophical, Religious, and Institutional Context, 600* B.C. *to* A.D. *1450*. Chicago: U of Chicago P, 1993.

Stock, Brian. *Myth and Science in the Twelfth Century: A Study of Bernard Silvester*. Princeton, NJ: Princeton UP, 1972.

Douglas Kelly

Sixteenth and Seventeenth Centuries

Appear in many forms of Early Modern discourse, especially in Great Britain. "And God said let Newton be, and all was light" wrote **Alexander Pope** in a 1727 epitaph intended for the mathematician's tomb in Westminster Abbey. Pope was eulogizing as well the greater regularity and **rationality** that seemed to govern much of intellectual life after 1660 and the achievements of the "new science" in creating a more modern and simpler style of thinking and writing. The dominance of the scientific attitude began with the astronomers **Nicholaus Copernicus** (1473–1543), **Galileo Galilei** (1564–1642) and **Johannes Kepler** (1571–1630) and ended with the mechanistic and materialist ideas of **Thomas Hobbes** (1588–1679) and **Robert Boyle** (1627–1691). In between, **Francis Bacon** (1561–1626) promulgated new disciplinary boundaries regulating the protocols of learning, thereby separating traditional humanistic studies from the work of natural philosophers, while **René Descartes** (1596–1650) applied scientific method to metaphysics in order to prove the existence of God and the soul. With the advent of Isaac Newton (*see* Newtonianism) (1642–1727), intellectuals became accustomed to probing the physical world by sensory observation, experiment, inductive reasoning, and mathematical measurements. Both scientists and literary writers contributed to the period's attempt to reenvision the human position in a vastly more dynamic and plural universe.

In the beginning of the period, the Tudors had inherited a medieval and Ptolemaic worldview whereby a coherent system of beliefs about human physiology and psychology (*see* Anthropology/Psychology/Sociology) had been tied to a theological **cosmology** governed by divine will. From the four physical elements of air, fire, water, and earth up to the pure intelligence of angels, Tudor theorists claimed that the "body politic" (i.e., families, corporations, and state institutions) was regulated by natural laws characterized by unity and subordination under a single head, the monarch. Richard Hooker's (1553?–1600) *Laws of Ecclesiastical Polity* (1593–1597) ensured that divine, natural, and man-made laws were grouped under the same definition as a general "Law" of nature. In **drama**, the importance of degree and hierarchy in the name of social order could be seen in Ulysses's notable speech on degree and place in **William Shakespeare's** (1564–1616) *Troilus and Cressida*.

Ironically, alongside this concern for hierarchy and order came a desire to master and understand Nature, not only to obey her using the texts of **Aristotle** and scholastic theologians. The Schoolmen had been attacked by humanists since the fourteenth-century writings of Francesco Petrarch (1304–1374). The Italians had formalized Neoplatonism into a coherent philosophical system with the work of Pico della Mirandola (1463–1494) and had propagated that system throughout Europe through such books as Baldassare Castiglione's (1478–1529) *Courtier* (1528; Hoby's translation, 1561) and Roger Ascham's (1515–1568) *Schoolmaster* (published 1570). The Neoplatonists looked for harmony of mind and body in the universe, worshiping beauty and cultivating the soul through courtly love, interpreted as geometrical proportion. This Neoplatonism rejected the Ptolemaic earth-centered universe and inspired the heliocentrism of Copernicus and Kepler.

In England, humanists **Edmund Spenser** (c. 1552–1599) and **Philip Sidney** (1554–1586) promoted a Neoplatonic and courtly view of society and nature while still validating a monarchical worldview. In the *Faerie Queene* (1590, 1596) Spenser used a Platonic vision of the universe and the individual's harmonic integration with the natural in his Garden of Adonis episode linking form and matter. He combined Neoplatonism with medieval scholastic theology when he represented the House of Alma (or Temperance) using conventional medieval faculty psychology to describe bodily and mental processes. Shakespeare's *Hamlet* (1599?) and John Webster's (1580?–1625?) *The Duchess of Malfi* (printed 1623) had similarly attempted to study **melancholy** and violent passion within the frame of a conventional revenge **tragedy**. Traditional modes of **representation** were combined with a new awareness of individual personality and psychology in the 1621 work of **Robert Burton** (1577–1640), *Anatomy of Melancholy*. Here, the human organism was pictured as a little state wherein the "humors" or bodily fluids (blood, phlegm, melancholy, choler) could become diseased, unruly, and passionate if not governed by the faculties of the soul whose agents were the vital spirits.

Within sixteenth-century culture, however, there was considerable resistance to the Tudor's Neoplatonic reshaping of the medieval and Ptolemaic system. Religious controversies between Protestants began to criticize the divine right of kings, while the influx of emigrants from Spain (Arabs, Jews, and Moors) led to a questioning of social and racial groupings. In the drama of Shakespeare and **Christopher Marlowe** (1564–1593), the transgression of social boundaries by members of differing **races** and classes (and by women) proved that human ambition was not easily confined within the notion of static degrees paralleling a closed and predictable universe. In addition to the Neoplatonic and mathematical theorists, the "new science" attracted a group of "empirics," that is, medical men and women, navigators, mining engineers, land surveyors, and a host of other so-called quacks and charlatans who combined a belief in witchcraft and **magic** with **alchemy** and **astrology**. These pseudoscientific "empirics" were part of a movement fostered by **Philippus Aureolus Paracelsus** (1493–1541) on the Continent and the sixteenth-century followers of Roger Bacon (1214–1294) in England, and which stressed sensory observation and experience. In Shakespeare's *All's Well That Ends Well*, the diseased king of France charged the healer Helena with the name "empiric" and claimed that her interference with natural processes contradicted the Royal College of Physicians, a corporate body consisting primarily of established medical men following **Galen** and Aristotle. The empirics were commonly linked in this period to a movement challenging the established notion of a fixed natural and social hierarchy.

Sir Walter Raleigh (1552–1618), Marlowe, and the Cambridge humanist Gabriel Harvey (1545–1631) were likewise advocating the alliance of **natural philosophy** with experiment and observation, often for politically subversive purposes. Harvey counseled young men in 1593 to abandon **poetry** for more utilitarian pursuits, to study engineering and the "commodious devices for war and peace." He advised reading Hakluyt's *Principle Navigations*, as well as the works on alchemy and **geography** by John Dee and Thomas Hariot. These empirics made direct contributions to early-seventeenth-century experimental science in England, which can be seen in William Gilbert's (1540–1603) work on magnetism in 1600 and **William Harvey's** (1578–1657) theories on the circulation of the blood in 1628. Ironically, while both Gilbert and Harvey claimed that knowledge resided in things themselves rather than in books, both were members of the conservative Royal College of Physicians, which relied heavily on Galen. In fact, while Harvey was influenced by the empirics, he would continue in his scientific work to use metaphors validating a traditional monarchical and authoritarian form of government.

Generally, the early seventeenth century could find no real consensus in the speculations of the "new science." Raleigh, while ambitiously promoting the natural magic of the alchemists and Neoplatonists, was generally skeptical that the essence of Nature could ever fully be determined through experiment and observation. Not until Francis Bacon's elaborate system of educational reform in the *Advancement of Learning* (1605) did the Neoplatonic cult of the human intellect give way to a need for a systematic method of discovery, that is, induction, given Bacon's argument that the Idols of Mind continually distorted the perception of natural processes. He claimed that the simplicity of natural laws should be reflected in, or represented by, a plainer and simpler linguistic and verbal style, shorn of the abundant metaphors favored by the Neoplatonists. Not only did Bacon's reform of learning change the way natural philosophers conceptualized the universe, but it also led to a skepticism regarding the poetic **imagination's** ability to construct and describe the world.

Following Bacon, the most important achievement of the seventeenth century proved to be the formulation of a regular scientific society and the institutionalization of an official scientific mode of writing. Gresham's College was established in London in 1598, and the "Invisible College" at Oxford in 1645. The **Royal Society**, incorporated in 1662 under a charter by the newly restored Charles II, was officially titled the Royal Society of London for the Promotion of Natural Knowledge. Its motto was *Nullius in verba,* "We don't take anybody's word for it." Thomas Sprat (1635–1713) wrote the first *History of the Royal Society* (1667). In addition to opening the Society to working-class men and artisans, he advocated a scientific style of writing that would be plain, simple, and clear, thereby reducing the number of words to the number of things. **John Wilkins** (1614–1672) in *An Essay towards a Real Character and a Philosophical Language* (1668) conceptualized a universal language scheme that would guarantee epistemic consistency in the representation of philosophical ideas and that would therein resemble the language of mathematics and **physics**.

The Society was independent of Church and crown and tended to promote free inquiry and expression in the investigation of scientific ideas. The Society admitted volunteer members who were known as the **virtuosi**, dilettantish intellectuals more interested in collecting exotic phenomena and constructing cabinets of curiosities than in promoting a scientific agenda of detached observation. While the organizing members of the Society succeeded in limiting the function of the virtuosi, the latter made significant contributions not to scientific progress but to the growing literary use of **realism** in visual arts and in poetic description and representation.

The intellectual climate had become, by the end of the seventeenth century, unfavorable to poetry and literary prose, causing a depression of the baroque poetic imagination that had seen a high point in the verse of **John Donne** (1572–1631). **Thomas Browne** (1605–1682) saw himself as "a great amphibian . . . living in a divided and distinguished world," both medieval (theological) and modern (scientific). With the advances achieved by the new science, the later period was marked by a dissociation of thought and feeling, as **T.S. Eliot** would claim in his 1921 essay "The Metaphysical Poets." According to Eliot, this gap was most evident in the later work of **John Milton** (1608–1674) and the last books of *Paradise Lost* (1667). The newly postulated systems of the universe replaced the more comfortable and limited Ptolemaic cosmogony and with it the older idea of a microcosm mirroring the macrocosm that regulated the physical and psychological realm of human reality. The period culminated in England with Newton's demonstration of the laws of gravitation and motion by which the planets move in their orderly and regular courses, a descriptive system that would find its complement in the tightly regulated verse of the Augustan poets.

References

Tillyard, E.M.W. *The Elizabethan World Picture*. London: Chatto and Windus, 1943.
Webster, Charles. *The Great Instauration: Science, Medicine and Reform 1626–1660*. New York: Homes and Meier, 1975.

Diana B. Altegoer

Post-Restoration Eighteenth Century

A period rich in interaction between the fields of literature, science, and **philosophy**, spanning the years from Isaac Newton's (*see* Newtonianism) profoundly influential *Principia* (Mathematical Principles of Natural Philosophy, 1687) to Jean-Antoine-Nicolas de Caritat de Condorcet's *Esquisse d'un tableau historique des progrès de l'esprit humain* (Sketch for a Historical Picture of the Progress of the Human Mind, 1795), a classic statement of **Enlightenment** optimism and faith in science. Although often called "the Age of Reason," the eighteenth century was also an age of emotionalism—evident in the vogues of sensibility and sentimentalism that shaped the period's aesthetics (*see* Art and Aesthetics), moral philosophy, and social practices—and of antirationalism (*see* Rationality/Irrationality), a pronounced element in the mesmerist and Gothic fads of the 1780s and 1790s. Literature and science were mutually implicated in all of the eighteenth century's diverse tendencies; moreover, in their desire to "enlighten," their concern with language and method, and their shared preoccupation with the underlying **mechanisms** of matter and mind, they were often remarkably close in spirit and aim.

Despite the delight that authors like **Jonathan Swift** took in satirizing scientific theorists and experimentalists, science enjoyed unprecedented prestige in learned and popular **culture** throughout eighteenth-century Europe and America. It was at once a privileged form of cognition, a methodological model, and a major source of recreation and entertainment. As described by apologists like **Bernard le Bovier de Fontenelle**, influential secretary to the French Academy of Sciences, the pursuit of science was a courageous, virtuous activity that served all of humanity by advancing the understanding of nature and fostering the principle of orderly, critical thinking. Science—or, rather, **natural philosophy**, as it was more commonly called—was thus an essential part of the politically reformist, ideologically emancipatory strain of Enlightenment culture. Along with the salons of France and coffeehouses of England, scientific societies and academies like Fontenelle's were considered to be central sites within the "Republic of Letters," a self-consciously new social order whose members valued freedom of thought, skepticism toward authority, and the convivial exchange of ideas.

In literary and scientific writing alike, the critical, analytical spirit of the day was frequently embodied by the figure of the discoverer: that is, a candid onlooker whose unprejudiced observations provided a fresh, often unsettling perspective on what had previously seemed familiar. Whether applied to nature or to European society, the technique of defamiliarization—used with particular skill by Charles-Louis Secondat de Montesquieu in both *Les Lettres persanes* (Persian Letters, 1721) and *L'Esprit des lois* (The Spirit of the Laws, 1748), his famous contribution to political science—broke down common beliefs and assumptions, forcing readers to reevaluate existing categories of knowledge, political structure, or sociomoral convention. The theme of quest and discovery took on heroic overtones in the period's narratives of scientific accomplishment, which depicted men of science as daring, noble visionaries who carried the torch that would light the way for the rest of humanity. Although literary authors (including the libertine novelist Donatien-Alphonse-François de Sade) occasionally parodied the self-aggrandizing rhetoric that filled eighteenth-century expedition accounts and histories of science, they also drew from it, producing similarly elitist, gendered descriptions of the "serious" novelist or playwright as a natural philosopher in his own right.

Among the major vehicles for such rhetoric were **popularizations**, a genre that included everything from John Newberry's *Tom Telescope's Philosophy of Tops and Balls* (1761) to the *Encyclopédie* (1751–1772), which was both the chief *machine de guerre* of the Enlightenment and a massive effort at scientific popularization. Popularizers included renowned naturalists, **physicians,** and men of letters; **Voltaire,** for example, undertook to explain **John Locke's** empiricist philosophy and Newton's **optics** to French readers. Popular science books, compendiums, and periodicals played a significant role in the diffusion of scientific views of nature to the lay public. Although often directed at audiences deemed to be outside the ranks of the intelligentsia, like women or children, such texts also provided an important mode of communication among eighteenth-century natural philosophers, as did epistolary correspondence.

A veritable cult surrounded Newton: English poets embraced his theories of color and light and eulogized him for decades after his death in 1727; French, Italian, and German thinkers wrestled with his vision of the universe; and his ideas were broadly disseminated in popular accounts like Francesco Algarotti's *Il Newtonianismo per le Dame* (1737), translated in 1739 as *Sir Isaac Newton's Philosophy Explained for the Use of Ladies.* Newtonianism did not, however, dominate eighteenth-century science as much as this popular enthusiasm might suggest. Rather, specialists in **physics, astronomy, chemistry, natural history,** and the life sciences had fierce debates over Newtonianism versus Cartesianism, idealism versus materialism, monism versus dualism, **mechanism** versus vitalism, and the role of observation versus experimentation in **scientific method**.

Such debates were rooted in questions like the existence of the soul, the freedom of human reason and volition, the activity and passivity of matter, and the role of a divine or extramaterial force in the workings of nature. Those disputes shaped laboratory investigations into subjects ranging from mechanics to neurology, while also spilling over into the period's philosophical and imaginative literature. For example, although sensationalist philosophers like Etienne Bonnot de Condillac emulated Locke in avoiding inquiry into the physical causes of ideas, they commonly used physiological analogies like mental "fibers" to construct their models of the mind and sense organs. Natural philosophy also inspired writers like Julien Offroy de La Mettrie, whose blatantly materialistic, atheistic *L'Homme machine* (Man a Machine, 1748) provoked a scandal throughout Europe, and **Denis Diderot**, who used **fiction** and philosophical dialogues to explore the epistemological, moral, political, and aesthetic implications of the latest theories on life and matter.

Language was another area of intense concern to scientists and nonscientists. Theories on the origin and evolution of language abounded, often intertwined with theories on the origin and evolution of society. Botanists like Carolus Linnaeus and chemists like Antoine-Laurent Lavoisier strove to develop systems of nomenclature (*see* Classification Systems) that would mirror the structure of the material world as well as the natural, logical procedures one should follow in observing it. In his *Méthode de nomenclature chimique* (Method of Chemical Nomenclature, 1787), Lavoisier frequently cited the theories of Condillac, who sought both to devise a universal method of analytic thinking and to remodel modern languages according to the principles of algebra, which he viewed as the only field to have attained the status of a truly "well-made" language. Condillac's analytic method, described in treatises like *La Logique* (1780), was based on his conviction that philosophical and scientific language had to be purged of poetic figures like metaphor. His self-authorizing rhetoric and neutral, denotative language served as a model of a new style of scientific writing, one that was exuberantly applied in the positivistic natural sciences of the following century.

The fundamental secularism of Enlightenment natural philosophy—expressed in the principle established by **René Descartes** that God might well exist but was not a necessary component to scientific thinking—was bound to clash with the religious worldview that continued to govern the average European's habits of thought and behavior. One answer to that conflict was **natural theology**, whose eighteenth-century proponents argued that recent scientific discoveries and instruments like the **telescope** and **microscope** showed that God's design for the universe was observable in every creature, every star, and every blade of grass. This brand of nature piety, expressed in works like *Physico-Theology, or a Demonstration of the Being and Attributes of God from His Works of Creation* (1713) by the clergyman and amateur scientist **William Derham**, was particularly prevalent in England and Germany during the first half of the century. The effort to mediate between science and theology was central to Gottfried Wilhelm Leibniz's system of preestablished harmony, which became one of the eighteenth-century solutions to the mind/body problem. It also contributed to a widespread substitution of "Nature" for "God" in **poetry**, aesthetics (*see* Art and Aesthetics), and natural-philosophical discourse and coincided with the sentimental back-to-nature movement that is typically associated with **Jean-Jacques Rousseau** but actually predated him.

Natural theology can be seen as a mystical extension of the deep Enlightenment impulse to find unity within all fields of human knowledge. **Georges-Louis Leclerc de Buffon's** *Histoire naturelle* (1748–1804) was one of the period's most celebrated attempts to create a universal explicatory system that classified the whole of nature. The same impulse underlay the idea of founding a unitary "science of man," a project championed by the Scottish philosopher David Hume along with *philosophes* from the Encyclopedists to Condorcet. This endeavor encompassed the fields of cognitive psychology, ethics, aesthetics, sociopolitical theory, **anthropology**, and **medicine**; it brought to the fore such questions as the nature of the self, of sociability, and of the relation between mind and body.

The holistic conception of human nature implicit to the science of man also clearly informed the period's literature, especially as biomedical notions of sensibility, sympathy, and nervous disorder permeated contemporary **culture**. In England, physiological notions of madness, **melancholy**, and the "diseased" **imagination** appeared in novels like **Laurence Sterne's** *Tristam Shandy* (1759–1767), a work whose strategic digressions and disruptions can be seen as a literary attempt to combat the "spleen" that so preoccupied popular physicians such as George Cheyne. On the Continent, Rousseau employed his best-selling sentimental fiction *La Nouvelle Héloïse* (1761) to promote a system for controlling moral and physical sensibility that mirrored the comprehensive hygienic programs found in treatises like the *Essai sur les maladies des gens du monde* (An Essay on the Disorders of People of Fashion, 1770), by the renowned Swiss doctor Samuel-Auguste-André-David Tissot.

Tissot and other proponents of the "philosophical" medicine that emerged at the mid-century went to great lengths to broaden the scope of their field by extending it into all areas of knowledge, including **pedagogy**, ethics, law, and social theory. To that end, they exploited the experimental studies of nerves and muscles that physiologists like Albrecht von Haller and Robert Whytt had conducted in the 1740s and 1750s and argued that the newly discovered property of vital sensibility would explain the myriad phenomena of human experience: organic function, disease, the interconnections of the physical and the moral, intellectual capacity, and the diversity of human types. This medical theory was part of the complex constellation of ideas that developed around sensibility throughout eighteenth-century Europe, producing not only the cult of sentiment evident in the period's plays and novels but also the epidemic of "vapors" that physicians believed was raging in large cities like Paris—most particularly among rich female urbanites who indulged in insalubrious pursuits like gambling, theatergoing, and novel-reading.

Vapors and related nervous illnesses were a complex cultural problem involving questions of **gender**, moral-physical hygiene, and the ambiguous privileges of sensibility. They were linked to the increasingly dimorphic notions of sex, class, and race that arose in medicine, anthropology, and sociopolitical theory during the century's final decades. The introduction of these sharply drawn categories of difference into the discursive framework of the "science of man" illustrates that the monistic, universalist conception of human nature that had dominated eighteenth-century thought was beginning to fracture. As a result of that fracturing—a process whose causes also included Romantic spiritualism and antiscientism, the growing specialization of the sciences, and the social upheavals triggered by the French Revolution—literature and science would no longer have the degree of mutual permeability they had enjoyed during the heady, ever "philosophical" days of the Enlightenment.

References

Anderson, Wilda. *Between the Library and the Laboratory: The Language of Chemistry in Eighteenth-Century France.* Baltimore: Johns Hopkins UP, 1984.

Christie, John, and Sally Shuttleworth, eds. *Nature Transfigured: Science and Literature, 1700–1900.* Manchester: Manchester UP, 1989.

Ferrone, Vincenzo. *The Intellectual Roots of the Italian Enlightenment: Newtonian Science, Religion, and Politics in the Early Eighteenth Century.* Trans. Sue Brotherton. Atlantic Highlands, NJ: Humanities, 1995.

Flynn, Carol Houlihan. "Running Out of Matter: The Body Exercised in Eighteenth-Century Fiction." *The Languages of Psyche: Mind and Body in Enlightenment Thought.* Ed. G.S. Rousseau. Berkeley and Los Angeles: U of California P, 1990. 147–85.

Mullan, John. "Hypochondria and Hysteria: Sensibility and the Physicians." *Sentiment and Sociability: The Language of Feeling in the Eighteenth Century.* Oxford: Clarendon, 1988.

Nicolson, Marjorie Hope. *Newton Demands the Muse: Newton's "Opticks" and the Eighteenth Century Poets.* Princeton, NJ: Princeton UP, 1946.

Saine, Thomas P. *The Problem of Being Modern, or, The German Pursuit of Enlightenment from Leibniz to the French Revolution.* Detroit: Wayne State UP, 1997.

Schatzberg, Walter. *Scientific Themes in the Popular Literature and Poetry of the German Enlightenment, 1720–1760.* Berne: Herbert Lang, 1973.

Terrall, Mary. "Heroic Narratives of Quest and Discovery." *Configurations* 6.2 (1998): 223–42.

Vila, Anne C. *Enlightenment and Pathology: Sensibility in the Literature and Medicine of Eighteenth-Century France.* Baltimore: Johns Hopkins UP, 1998.

Anne C. Vila

Nineteenth Century

A period that saw the beginnings and ends of sweeping alliances between science and literature. At one extreme, **Alexander von Humboldt** was widely respected as the last thinker to have a science of everything, and **Louis Agassiz** enjoyed a reputation as simply "the scientist." At the other extreme, the positivist character Bazerov in Turgenev's *Fathers and Sons* (1861) proclaims that science does not exist, merely a plurality of sciences. Deductive science seemed to meet its end with Hegel's **natural history** lectures of 1817 (the eventual *Encyclopedia* of 1830), only to be reborn for the literary **imagination**, though in different form, in the **field theory** of **Faraday**.

Revisions of theoretical models and their technical applications across the fields of **physics** influenced literature considerably. Some poets used a scheme of near physical formulas in their **poetry**, as **Blake** did in his prophecies and **Emily Dickinson** did in her riddles. Non-Euclidean geometry, which was pioneered by Riemann, and which would gain further theoretical underpinnings in the Michelson-Morley disproof of ponderable ether and its replacement by a space with its own tropic characteristics, saw literary prefiguration in **Keats**. Popular elaborations by Helmholtz and Clifford eventuated in late-century fantasies like Edwin Abbott's *Flatland* (1884). Conventional kinetics and dynamics became matters of personal experience in the development of rapid transit, inspiring popular amusements like the panorama and influencing the perceptions of **landscape** and people from **De Quincey** to Eichendorff, **Baudelaire**, and Stephen Crane.

Electrical phenomena in the aftermath of Galvani and their mystical elaboration in Mesmer appear in the poetry and **fiction** of both **Shelleys, E.T.A. Hoffmann**, **Poe**, and **Novalis**. Lord Kelvin's investigation into work as a function of heat provided an analogue to the role of work as labor in the developing Victorian novel and in the nonfiction of **Mill** and Engels. Faraday's conception of the magnetic field has been drafted in support of various discussions of imagination, including **Emerson's** and Keats's. Maxwell, himself a poet, sparked considerable interest in **entropy**, which joined devolutionary thinking about lost human energy in **George Eliot's** novels and among the naturalists. Maxwell's own **thought experiment** about the "Demon" that can trace individual atoms instead of recording a statistical sampling has received a nearly unique status as a scientific literary fiction.

Specific research into acoustics produced literary interest in Ørsted among Danish Romantics. A rethinking of Newtonian **optics**, especially in **Goethe**, produced an antimechanistic model of seeing in **Wordsworth**, **Coleridge**, and others that would depart from Hartley's Associationism and eventually lead to Gestalt psychology (*see* Anthropology/Psychology/Sociology). Technical interest in lens grinding, microscopy, and telescopy appears in Poe, Hoffmann, and **Hawthorne**. An extended occupation with technical optics in its advanced guise of **photography** and **X-rays** appears in **Zola** and the Scandinavian naturalists.

Apart from rapid transit and acoustical/optical inventions, technological uses of physics dominated the nineteenth century. Although the pace of industrialism differed from country to country, the **Industrial Revolution** obsessed western Europe through the relocation of families as a workforce. Elizabeth Gaskell's novels provide documentation. Keats presents insights into problems of relocation and personal distance in *Isabella* (1818). Difficulties of employee abuse and adjustments to clocked time, which occupy modern popular notions of industrialism, were products of the middle and late factory **culture** portrayed in **Dickens's** *Hard Times* (1854) and by a variety of realist and naturalist novelists (the **Goncourts**, Zola, Eliot, **Hardy**).

In responding to **chemistry**, nineteenth-century literature was inspired by theories of combination and dissolution. Goethe's *Elective Affinities* (1809) established a valence theory of human interaction related to Tornberg Bergmann's work. Both Keats and Friedrich Schlegel relied on combinatory properties of chemicals in their writings. **Davy's** and Beddoes's work with gases influenced models of **imagination** in Wordsworth and Coleridge. Historical models were influential as well, as can be seen in the Lucretian atomism of **Byron** and Hawthorne and the alchemical arcana of *Frankenstein* (1818), Hoffmann, and **Rimbaud**.

Laplace's **nebular hypothesis** in **astronomy** received public notice in O.M. Mitchel and John Nichol's American lectures of the 1840s, and this model of an expansion and contraction theory of the universe found its way into Poe's *Eureka* (1848) and **Whitman's** *Song of Myself* (1855). The debunking of a nebular "liquid," already in place with **William Herschel**, continued with De Quincey's fascination with the nebular shape revealed by Rosse's advanced telescopes. Herschel's own discovery of Uranus produced a rhapsodizing about astronomical discovery and poetic invention from John Bonnycastle to Keats's "On First Looking into Chapman's Homer" (1816). Herschel, long a proponent of extraterrestrial life (*see* Extraterrestrials), was joined by Percival Lowell's fancied observations of Martian "canals" to produce considerable popular literature as well as **H.G. Wells's** *War of the Worlds* (1898).

Nineteenth-century geology derived in large part from a dispute over whether to prefer gradualism or catastrophism as a model for Earth's formation. Thomas Burnet, a seventeenth-century proponent of catastrophe on biblical grounds, colored Coleridge and Wordsworth's visions of the Alps. His catastrophist view gained support from **Abraham Gottlob Werner**, the charismatic teacher of many German Romantics, whose doctrine of Neptunism at the Freiberg **mining** college essentially held that geological change occurs only at catastrophic boundaries between sedimentary rocks. This model, which accounted for rocks as deluvial accretions, was enormously influential in forming literary notions of the unconscious as stratigraphic layers in G.E. Schubert, and in Tieck and Hoffmann, both of whom wrote prominent mining fictions. **Lyell's** work with sedimentation had a similar effect in the English-speaking world. **Hutton's** Vulcanism, or Uniformitarianism, which posited subterranean fire as a source of never-ending, gradual change, did not have the same effect on the literary mind that Neptunism had, partly because of a lack of style (until **John Playfair's** 1802 paraphrase) and partly because Uniformitarianism posed problems for the biblical calendar. Still, such works as Shelley's *Queen Mab* (1813) showcase Neptunist-Vulcanist disputes, as does Byron's use of the catastrophist Cuvier.

In addition to terraformative speculations, Werner also inspired his literary students with his revolutionary taxonomy of minerals, which was to find direct analogues in biological sciences. In the light of increased exploration in non-European areas, animal and plant taxonomies were becoming more and more problematic. The literary result was to attempt more precision, along several lines. Harking back to Goethe's ideas of morphology in his essays and poems on mountains and plants, Wilhelm von Humboldt's thoughts on epigenesis encouraged the Bildungsroman, one of whose main representatives, Stifter's *Indian Summer* (1857), climaxes with the blooming of the exactly named and perfectly performing *Cereus peruvianus*. In mainstream **Realism, Balzac** famously styled himself the biologist of literature and categorized the denizens of Paris according to Linnaean types, with a method reminiscent of **Harriet Martineau** and Adolphe Quetelet.

The intersection of **biology** and human physiology appears in Keats's detailed awareness of brain structure in the *Ode to Psyche* (1819) and was pronounced through the persistence of physiognomy and phrenology in Goethe, George Sand, Balzac, and Turgenev, overlapping even into a physiognomy of the landscape in **Alexander von Humboldt**. Finally, the line between biological and robotic existence came to obsess such prominent literary artists as Hoffmann, Hawthorne, and Villiers de l'Isle-Adam.

The most striking shift in nineteenth-century biology is that toward evolutionary speciation (*see* Evolutionary Theory). Associated with **Charles Darwin** with (sometimes unacknowledged) addenda by **Herbert Spencer**, theories of evolution have a long pedigree, including nineteenth-century work preceding Darwin's, such as the ethnological speculation popular in America at **Thoreau's** time. Darwin's notion was that species in relative isolation mutate to produce phenotypes of greater or lesser adaptability and thus produce new lineages. His thoughts, though suggestive of human nature in *On the Origin of Species* (1859), aimed squarely at humankind in *The Descent of Man* (1871), which includes reflections on women's genetic passivity and men's genetic aggressiveness. Biology and literary response to it here pass into the social arena. A great stylist in his own right, Darwin unfortunately and inadvertently lent his name, through association with Spencer, to "**Social Darwinism**," a variety of cynical beliefs that do not appear often in Darwin's own writings on natural selection but that have become his literary legacy. An emerging beast in humanity appears in **Swinburne**, Baudelaire, and the Pre-Raphaelites; tied to the "heat death" of the Second Law of **Thermodynamics**, a decline in human mental and moral potential appears fatalistically in Hardy and **Norris**; and a connection with depopulation in *fin de siècle* France led French naturalist novelists to conclude that a bestial devolution had occurred. In England, Mr. Hyde represents the latent beast in Stevenson's Dr. Jekyll, just as **Wells's** half-transformed beasts in *The Island of Dr. Moreau* (1896) suggest partly humanized forms that are doomed to revert.

The gloom that attended the frequent misapprehension of evolutionary thought abated a bit in consideration of **medicine**. Although unavoidable physiological or psychological doom remains in the reaction to cholera (Poe's *The Masque of the Red Death* [1842]) and the newly contrived "moral insanity" (his *The Tell-Tale Heart* [1843]), much of developing epidemiology stressed bad sanitation, instead of a moral condition, as a disease cause, as can be seen in **Melville's** *Redburn* (1847). Indeed, Zola considered himself as "innoculating" his readers. The effect on Dickens of William Farr's studies of urban mortality is pronounced. Literary treatment of syphilis becomes increasingly accurate in writers like Balzac and Ibsen. Medical procedures like birthing receive emphasis in **Blake's** *Book of Urizen* (1795–1815) and Mary Shelley's *Frankenstein*. Orthopedics comes into discussion through the grisly clubfoot operation in **Flaubert's** *Madame Bovary* (1857). Among diseases, tuberculosis receives treatment in numerous works including Keats's poetry and Tolstoy's *Anna Karenina* (1876); smallpox lies in the background of Dickens's *Bleak House* (1852); eye maladies become a prominent theme in Balzac's *Père Goriot* (1834–1835); and addiction and **alcoholism** assume their modern status as diseases in De Quincey and Stephen Crane. In addition to physical afflictions, mental illnesses were either discovered or invented, like the neuraesthenia that plagues more than one **Henry James** heroine. As both judge and professional literary figure, Hoffmann was among the first to advocate and critically to scrutinize the insanity plea in his jurisprudence and fiction.

References

Cunningham, Andrew, and Nicholas Jardine, eds. *Romanticism and the Sciences*. New York: Cambridge UP, 1990.
Degler, Carl. *In Search of Human Nature: The Decline and Revival of Darwinism in American Social Thought*. New York: Oxford UP, 1991.
Lenoir, Timothy. *Instituting Science: The Cultural Production of Scientific Disciplines*. Stanford: Stanford UP, 1997.

William Crisman

Twentieth Century

The period from which much of the scholarship in the cross-disciplinary, Euro-American field of LS dates, with most studies examining developments in Renaissance and post-Renaissance Western thought. Historical accounts generally agree that the bifurcation of literature and science into specialist professional institutions began in the eighteenth and nineteenth centuries. Disciplinary edges subsequently hardened in the late nineteenth and early twentieth centuries, when both natural science and literature became established as university subjects and professional careers.

For most of the early twentieth century, relations between artists and scientists were strained, resulting in little communication across institutional boundaries. Like their Romantic predecessors, Modernist writers and critics expressed fear, disgust, or indifference regarding scientific reductionism and mechanization, envy of science's cultural prestige, and in some instances, a genuine interest in incorporating scientific ideas into their work. One or several positions were frequently adopted simultaneously, even to the point of contradiction. The literary author's imitation of science often amounted to producing "experimental" works that were as difficult, as inaccessible, and as "technical" as scientific works. Rarely did literary texts or commentaries on these texts demonstrate a profound insight into their epoch's increasingly impenetrable science, though few could avoid recognizing the general populace's admiration both for scientific ideas and for their technological applications. Actually, the distinction between science and **technology** was commonly lost in intellectual circles and in the public mind, though clearly there are significant differences: Indeed, in some regards, theoretical science is more akin to literary **art** and **theory** than any of them are to technology. Meanwhile, an international, cosmopolitan **Modernism** garnered considerable prestige for literature and the arts, but only some of its members acknowledged that technological developments in transportation and communication enabled this to occur.

In the mid- to late twentieth century, artists and theorists have been somewhat less inclined to demonize science or to deny their own intimate relationship with a technological environment. Current and futuristic technology and science have appeared in prestigious postmodern works, and there has been a concomitant mainstreaming of **science fiction** (e.g., so-called **cyberpunk**). However, a sustained or deliberate use of scientific ideas is still comparatively rare in postmodern literature.

Another form of literary engagement with science has been in the field of literary criticism, where critics have consciously or unconsciously recognized the heuristic value of scientific concepts or techniques. There have been several waves of scientific influence in the twentieth century, especially on the work of I.A. Richards, on Russian formalism, New Criticism, psychoanalytic approaches, and **structuralism**. These and other theorists in search of a method looked to scientific models once science became regarded as the normative mode of knowledge. Many continued to emulate positivist models of scientific method even after these became outdated. Hence various attempts have been made to establish literary criticism as progressive, verifiable, and objective as scientific method has been perceived to be. In actual fact, altogether different approaches can and have laid claim to being "scientific," from highly abstract theory (structuralism) to focus on the empirical example (New Criticism). The aim in most cases has not so much been to recapture a central place for literature in the general **culture** as to establish a niche for professional critics and secure literature as a rigorous academic discipline.

The sociopolitical repercussions of the perceived division between literature and science came to a head in the so-called **two cultures** debate that was provoked by **C.P. Snow's** Rede lecture of 1959 (*The Two Cultures and the Scientific Revolution*). In what was to some extent a revisiting of the Victorian **T.H. Huxley–Matthew Arnold** debate, scientist-novelist C.P. Snow expressed concern over the estrangement and hostility between the scientific and literary intelligentsia and, in a Cold War context, urged the West to undertake educational reform in order to maintain technological prowess. The effect was to firmly establish that the relation between literature and science was a "problem" of considerable sociopolitical significance. Snow's proposals were enthusiastically debated for a time in popular and journalistic venues as well as more scholarly works. The main concerns were educational, moral, and political reform, though T.H. Huxley's grandson, **Aldous Huxley,** was one who tried to refocus attention on to methodological comparisons, language use, and the incorporation of scientific ideas into literary texts.

Sustained scholarship along these lines developed later in the century. What emerged as LS studies were fostered by developments in the history of ideas, in the philosophy and sociology of science, in literary theory and linguistics. The field has been especially active since the 1980s, when there was a marked increase in scholarly interest and the formation of professional bodies to encourage and organize this activity. While Literature and Science became a division of the Modern Language Association (MLA) as early as 1939, it was at the 1985 meeting of the International Congress of the History of Science (ICHS) that the Society for Literature and Science (SLS) was established. This organization now attracts several hundred members, sponsors an annual conference, and supports an award-winning journal (*Configurations*).

Approaches and Major Issues

Literature and Science (LS) is a field predominantly inhabited by literary critics, though the Society for Literature and Science has tried and has had some limited success in encouraging participation by scientists. The motives for undertaking a study of LS are diverse. Typical claims are that the comparative method clarifies and deepens one's understanding of each field and method, that an interdisciplinary perspective helps elucidate particular texts or writers, or that studying the relations between and across disciplines uncovers the ideologies, values, and nature of the wider culture. In recent decades, the categories of "literature" and "science" have themselves been problematized so that commentators are less willing to accept either point of comparison as a stable or easily definable term, as either temporally or culturally fixed. Nor are all theorists content to accept that each field is, at any point in history, a monolithic or exclusive formation. While earlier studies did make such assumptions, the overall thrust of LS studies since their inception has been toward viewing literature and science as more alike than their institutional segregation would suggest, a conclusion that is often made into an argument for granting literature and other arts a higher status in relation to science and for devaluing the construction of knowledge offered by science as an academic institution or method.

Various models for conceptualizing the precise relations between literature and science have been offered. Initial studies generally assumed a linear causal relation in which science (prior) was seen to influence literary texts (subsequent), and critics were content to catalog references to scientific ideas without delving into larger epistemological, ontological, or cultural issues. In the last two decades, models have emerged that argue for a more reciprocal relation between literature and science. Some scholars argue that literature and science come from a common cultural source, which may result in a parallel development or in mutual influence (e.g., N. Katherine Hayles). Other scholars make an even stronger case for literary influence by arguing that in certain instances literature anticipates or even engenders scientific ideas (e.g., David Porush). Most attempts to establish any type of influence are difficult to verify, and commentators face the speculative nature of their discussion with varying degrees of comfort. But whichever model is selected, there has been an emphasis in recent years on fundamental epistemological and sociopolitical relations and a view of both literature and science as culturally embedded. As such, science is regarded by LS scholars as permeable to broader cultural forces. Like literature, it is seen as a creative, linguistically determined and historically positioned activity.

The majority of writings in LS are specific studies centered on a literary text or texts, generally critically acclaimed works. The more popularist works of science fiction, despite their obvious engagement with science, feature less prominently; although this attitude is changing. Broader studies also look at the historical and institutional relations and what these reveal about cultural history. When studies center on specific literary works, they typically look at the influence or presence of science in ideas, themes, characters, form, or language. The focus may be on isolated references to scientific ideas or technology, or how these have affected the author's general worldview. In addition to recording scientific citations, scholars may investigate their ontological status and the transformations concepts undergo when they are refracted, misunderstood, or reutilized in a different context.

As in other fields, scholars in LS have recently become preoccupied with language, and several have advanced the idea that how one views literature and science in part depends upon how one understands language. The earlier, positivist view of scientific language as nonfigurative, unambiguous, rhetorically neutral, impersonal, and inherently different from literary language has been largely overturned. Since the 1960s there have been studies of the use of metaphor and models in scientific accounts that have suggested that these are not extraneous, decorative features but crucial and innate components of scientific knowledge formation (e.g., Mary Hesse, Gillian Beer). The very ambiguity and polysemy of metaphors, features that were devalued in a positivistic scheme, are now more often regarded as an advantage for scientific development as well as for literary exploration. In the last few decades, a growing number of studies have identified "literary" or rhetorical features in scientific texts in a manner previously reserved for the study of literary writings (e.g., Charles Bazerman, Alan Gross, Lawrence Prelli)—the premise being that facts do not stand alone as positivists had imagined and that therefore scientists need to persuade their audience through an effective use of language as well as other means. A further, related development is the view of science as a narrative, inspired by arguments that history is a narrative (e.g., Hayden White) and structuralist and poststructuralist assertions that all cultural formations can be viewed as narratives.

Some LS studies have examined the possible connection between scientific findings and literary form, the connection, for example, between twentieth-century **physics** and the literary preoccupation with subjective viewpoints, unreliable narrators, nonlinear narratives, and self-referentiality. As well as drawing on linguistics, on rhetoric, and on some strains of poststructuralist literary theory, LS scholars have benefited from developments in the **philosophy** and sociology of science. Of particular interest to such scholars, and to those in the humanities in general, has been the mid-century shift away from strict **positivism** to constructivism or relativism. Particularly influential were philosophical and historical studies conducted in the 1960s and 1970s by Thomas S. Kuhn (*see* Revolutions), Paul Feyerabend, **Karl Popper**, Richard Rorty, and Michel Foucault, sociological studies by **Bruno Latour**, Barry Barnes, David Bloor, and others, as well as recent feminist, deconstructivist, Marxist, and ethnographic perspectives. Many of these studies contend that there is bias, error, subjectivity, and even **irrationality** (*see* Rationality) in scientific method or methods. An early and seminal account was Thomas Kuhn's study of the various pressures that eventually persuade scientists to switch from one theoretical framework, or paradigm (*see* Revolutions), to another. Kuhn's notion of a paradigm shift and his distinction between normal science and revolutionary science (during which the paradigm shift occurs) were widely adopted as a model in LS studies and in other fields. Other authors have begun to demonstrate how scientific projects affect and are affected by specific sociopolitical and economic forces; for example, in the context of Western capitalism and its spawning of specializations and utilitarian rationales. Sociologists of science and feminist historians have worked to uncover the sociopolitical networks and hierarchies that determine what kind of science is done, by whom, and why (e.g., **Donna Haraway**). The picture of **scientific method** that such studies produce more closely resembles the movements and disciplineships associated with artistic development.

In recent years, new forms of **realism** and more limited constructivist accounts have gained ground. Opponents of extreme constructivism object that denying science's predictive powers and material accomplishments not only is unfair and unrealistic but is a weak defense of literature that reduces the credibility of its defenders. Nevertheless, the use of constructivist models did usefully complicate the status of science and uncover its ideological and philosophical foundations. Though it can be used in a facile manner to simply debunk science, this perspective has also made science more rich and amenable to humanistic inquiry and encouraged questions of interest to students of both literature and science: For example, Is there a scientific method, or method? Is literature a field determined by its method or object of study?

Yet there has not been much of a two-way dialogue. Most natural scientists continue to regard their method as more objective than do those who observe them—Kuhn, for example, has been more influential among nonscientists than scientists—while artists relate scientific ideas to metaphysical or ethical issues in ways scientists would never countenance.

Although literary writers and critics have touched on numerous developments in science and technology, some areas have proven to be of particular interest. Among scientific concepts prior to the twentieth century, **evolutionary theory** has attracted most attention, and there have been pioneering studies of the rhetorical and sociopolitical foundations and impact of **Darwin's** ideas (e.g., Gillian Beer, George Levine). As for twentieth-century science, writers have been intrigued by **relativity** theory and quantum mechanics, especially issues of indeterminacy, complementarity, the field concept, and the role of the observer in subatomic observations. In addition, literary authors most often refer to the discovery of DNA, genetic engineering (*see* Biotechnology/Genetic Engineering), medical science, reproductive technologies, **cybernetics**, and artificial intelligence (*see* Virtual Reality and Artificial Intelligence), and in the last couple of decades, **chaos theory**, **virtual reality**, and **cyberspace**. There has also been considerable discussion in both fictional writing and theory about technology's impact on the literary process, whether it be the publication and distribution of texts or the composition on or by **computers**. New communication technologies have rapidly begun to alter how information is disseminated in science and in literature and from one field to another. The growing use of electronic forums like the **Internet** and the **World Wide Web** has led to a rethinking of copyright and intellectual property issues, as well as an exploration of the hypertextual possibilities of these new media—all of which may present interesting possibilities for future research in LS.

However, one issue of theoretical and practical significance for the future of LS studies is the organization of academic institutes. For all the recent theoretical gestures toward interdisciplinarity, nineteenth-century taxonomies and resulting disciplinary territories remain largely intact. This presents intellectual and professional difficulties for those already in academic positions and is of obvious pragmatic concern for those in search of an academic post that will allow them to research and teach LS. It may be that in the next century this and other interdisciplinary approaches will find a home under the broader banner of Cultural Studies.

References

Jordanova, Ludmilla, ed. *Languages of Nature: Critical Essays on Science and Literature*. London, NJ: Free Association Books, 1986.

Levine, George, ed. *One Culture: Essays in Science and Literature*. Madison: U of Wisconsin P, 1987.

Livingston, Paisley. *Literary Knowledge: Humanistic Inquiry and the Philosophy of Science*. Ithaca, NY: Cornell UP, 1988.

Peterfreund, Stuart, ed. *Literature and Science: Theory and Practice*. Boston: Northeastern UP, 1990.

Schatzberg, W., R. Waite, and J. Johnson, eds. *The Relations of Literature and Science: An Annotated Bibliography of Scholarship, 1880–1980.* New York: MLA, 1987.

June Deery

Twenty-First Century

The century beginning in the year 2001, a period in which LS studies will take on new formulations and configurations. Discoveries in physical sciences, especially the new **physics** and sciences of nonlinear dynamics, had a profound impact on traditional assumptions about the nature of **reality** and the representational role of language and literature in the twentieth century. The postmodernist movement accordingly showed a preoccupation with the problematics of language that shaped the literary discourse of the latter half of this century and produced self-reflexive **fiction** that was fiction about writing fiction. It embodied the destabilization and deconstruction of traditional concepts of **truth**, meaning, and knowledge as it turned inward to a linguistic labyrinth with no center or foundation, no origin or end. The literary fiction of the last decade shows a shift that has been termed by some as "radical **realism**." It combines realistic details with a skillful incorporation of postmodern narrative strategies to depict an experience that is profoundly affected by scientific and technological reorganization of the sociopolitical, cultural, and economic conditions of production as well as consumption.

To understand the current shift, it is useful to invoke the discourse of **cognitive science** with its interdisciplinary relationships with computer science (*see* Computers), psychology (*see* Anthropology/Psychology/Sociology), **philosophy**, linguistics, and neurophysiology. Recent developments in brain science have led to a better understanding of cognitive processes that have produced intellectual discourses on the contemporary human condition that are mutually constituting and reciprocally illustrating. The two reigning paradigms in cognitive science in the last few decades have been a cognitivist paradigm that is based on the description of mental processes in terms of symbolic **representation** and a connectionist model that gives up representation all together and describes the operations of the mind from the bottom up as being constituted of simple units working together to produce global behavior. **Gerald Edelman's** work shows that human cognition involves decentralized operations in the brain. In the absence of any central processor, the processes of memory and perception involve creation and recreation of representations without recourse to stored memory. Whereas the cognitivist paradigm is based on the model of the mind as a computer, the connectionist paradigm, which has become increasingly popular since the 1970s, models the mind after the brain. The philosophical implications of the connectionist or emergent model in artificial intelligence (*see* Virtual Reality and Artificial Intelligence) research have led to mechanistic theories that reduce consciousness to brain processes and depict the mind as an information processor. For example, Daniel Dennett, a cognitive philosopher, describes the mind as a virtual machine that sits on top of the biologically hardwired brain. Since there is no central self, the mind, according to Dennett, operates as a stream of consciousness wherein narratives get written and rewritten with no one in charge.

The information-processing metaphor has affected recent literary production as well as criticism and has led to constructions of the body or bodies of fiction in terms of coded information patterns or information systems. **Donna Haraway** argues that communications and **biotechnology** are tools that are recrafting our bodies and changing social relations, both technologies reducing the world and the bodies into a problem of coding. The organism, she notes, is no longer the object of knowledge but an information-processing device that can be disassembled, reassembled, and appropriated. N. Katherine Hayles specifically addresses the trend in information narratives where the interiority of the humanist subject is displaced by the flatness of the posthuman subject. In information narratives that include the **cyberpunk** genre, **technology** creates an invasive space that becomes the unexplored frontier where both the human subject as well as the body (*see* Corporeality) are reconfigured and redesigned, leading to transcendental visions of other modes of being or earthly visions of human surrender to technological innovations or to alien species. Even as these narratives problematize the neat distinctions that have traditionally been made between the outer and the inner, human and machine, natural and artificial, physical space and **cyberspace**, they construct posthuman subjectivity exclusively in terms of dispersal, fragmentation, and alienation.

Both cognitivist and connectionist paradigms ultimately postulate the mind as an information processor and are unable to explain the sense of self that all of us have in spite of the decentralized operations of the mind or the world. Both promote concepts of cognition and experience that are reifications of actual experience. While the former approach leads to the return to conservative realist epistemologies, the latter promotes descriptions of the world and human experience in terms of fragmentation and alienation that seem to have become the predominant theme in contemporary **culture. Francisco J. Varela** et al. argue that human experience ought to be an important part of any description of mind. They postulate an enactive model of mind as the middle way between cognitive realism and connectionist paradigm. The approach moves away from the description of mind as an information processor to that of mind as the creator of information. Since human experience emerges from the interaction of the mind and the world, it turns the background knowledge and cultural matrix as well as the physical, psychological, and culturally gendered and racially marked body of the agent into an integral part of both being as well as becoming in the world.

Writers of literary fiction, too, are beginning to explore this middle space between the cognitivist and connectionist paradigm, by locating the experiencing self or selves in a cultural matrix that in a pluralistic global society appears decentered, groundless, nonlinear, and complex, in the meshes of which metaphysics and politics of bodies unfold. Already we see narratives that reflect on serious philosophical, psychological, or ethical issues as science and technology increasingly define contemporary society. Fictions produced by **Richard Powers**, William T. Vollman, and David Foster Wallace show a sophisticated understanding of information technology, either in the form of the role of computers or other entertainment media in society. Powers's *Galatea 2.2* is not only a novelistic rendering of the current issues in artificial intelligence research, but it also reflects on artistic **creativity** and human experience. In Vollman's *You Bright and Risen Angels*, the narrative focuses on the conflict between the reactionaries and revolutionaries; the former are portrayed as allies of technological imperialism. One of the main narrators is Big George, a pure electrical consciousness, which flows in and out of stories and machines, thereby not only controlling the author's computer at times but also the direction of the narrative. **Marge Piercy's** recent fiction has dealt with the ethical dilemmas society faces as technology advances. If the current narratives are an indication, the narratives of the twenty-first century should celebrate the transformative power of language that connects the body and the world together. It would envision fictional spaces where the boundaries between human-machine, self-other, inner-outer, past-present become permeable and the subjectivity that is formulated is based on fluid connections. These narratives will continue to explore the displacement of the human subject with the posthuman subject that is subject to a different epistemological and ontological status. However, the construction of the posthuman subject will not be exclusively in terms of dispersion and dissolution. The disunity of self that has been revealed by cognitive scientists as well as humanist theorists could thus become a source of creativity as it opens space for the construction and reconstruction of identity. Instead of dispersing into cyberspace, TV space, outer space, or the material space of the cities of this planet, these narratives would turn inward, exploring the human condition from multiple perspectives while at the same time revealing the intricate relationship of science and technology to social, psychological, and political constructions in contemporary society.

References

Dennett, Daniel C. *Consciousness Explained*. Boston: Little, Brown, 1991.
Edelman, Gerald. *Bright Air, Brilliant Fire*. New York: Basic Books, 1992.
Varela, Francisco J., Evan Thompson, and Eleanor Rosch. *The Embodied Mind*. Cambridge: MIT, 1996.

Jaishree K. Odin

Literature and Science Programs

Drew University

Modern History and Literature (MHL) and Medical Humanities (MH). The Graduate School at Drew University in Madison, New Jersey, offers two programs with an interdisciplinary approach to science and literature: the M.A. and Ph.D. in MHL and either a certificate or master's in MH. MHL offers a subspecialty in the **history of science**, candidates for the Ph.D. in history being required to take one course in this area. Medical Humanities takes a humanistic approach to **medicine**, bringing medical science into dialogue with literature, history, and **philosophy**. Further information is available through the Office of Graduate Admissions. Phone: (973) 408–3110; email: qradm@drew.edu; or <http://www.drew.edu/>.

Alison E. Bright

Lafayette College

Values and Science/Technology (VAST) Program. Begun in 1994–1995 as a required sophomore-level writing course taught by professors from all divisions of the college, "VAST" aims to bridge disciplinary divisions between the natural and social sciences, humanities, arts, and engineering. Instructors design their own courses around an area of inquiry too large for any single discipline to address adequately; each course includes both scientific and humanistic perspectives and considers ways in which the values of science and of society interact. See: <http://www.lafayette.edu/~vast/vasthp.html>.

Laura Dassow Walls

University of Missouri, Rolla

Literature and Science Minor. An undergraduate program offered at the University of Missouri system's technological campus. UMR primarily attracts students interested in engineering and the sciences. The English Department's literature and science minor invites them, along with UMR's humanities students, to examine theoretical and methodological issues as well as cultural connections between literature and science. The minor includes an introductory core course and three electives. See: <http://www.umr.edu/~english/programs/minors.html>.

Anne Bratach Matthews

University of Texas, Dallas

Medical and Scientific Humanities Minor (MaSH). An eighteen-hour undergraduate minor offering students majoring in Pre-Health, the sciences, engineering, and interested others courses in interdisciplinary humanities that explore the interrelations of **medicine**, science, **technology**, and **culture**. MaSH features course work in medical and scientific ethics, the **history of science** and medicine, literature and science, literature and medicine, and advanced composition taught in an interdisciplinary preprofessional format. For more information, contact the adviser for MaSH, Pamela Gossin, psgossin@utdallas.edu or see course listings and links available at: <http://www.utdallas.edu/dept/ah.html>.

Pamela Gossin

Locke, John (1632–1704). English philosopher and political theorist whose works included *An Essay Concerning Human Understanding* (1690), a pioneering empiricist examination of the conditions and limits of knowledge. Locke stressed reason over faith and rejected the doctrine of innatism, arguing instead that experience, observation, and reflection are the source of ideas. Although condemned by theologians, Locke's **philosophy** profoundly influenced eighteenth-century views of the self, the mind and senses, and **scientific method**. In Britain, David Hume extended Lockean philosophy to psychology (*see* Anthropology/Psychology/Sociology) and social science, while writers like **Laurence Sterne** playfully satirized it in **fiction**. In France, Locke was widely praised by the *philosophes* and broadly linked to sensationalism, materialism, and the **Enlightenment**.

Reference

Yolton, John, ed. *John Locke: Problems and Perspectives. A Collection of New Essays.* Cambridge: Cambridge UP, 1969.

Anne C. Vila

Lomonosov, Mikhail Vasilievich (1711–1765). Scientist, poet, and philosopher who dominates eighteenth-century Russian science and letters. Lomonosov's 1739 *Letter on the Rules for Russian Versification* established the syllabotonic system still used in Russian **poetry** today. His analysis and codification of the stylistic norms inherent in the Russian language made possible the development of Russian literary and scientific discourse, which had previously been limited to nonvernacular Church Slavonic and Latin, respectively. His contributions to theoretical **physics**, **chemistry**, and **optics** are essentially extensions of the corpuscular or mechanical **philosophy** of his day; as such the significance of his scientific findings have been exaggerated by some Soviet historians but not yet embedded in the linguistic, philosophical, and social contexts that Lomonosov did much to reshape.

Lomonosov's humble origins in a peasant family near the White Sea port town of Kolmogory located him in the potentially stimulating atmosphere of a foreign trade nexus and a remote northern haven for political and religious dissenters. By concealing his origins he managed to enroll in Moscow's Slavo-Greco-Latin Academy. In 1735 he was sent to Europe to study **mining** and chemistry; he was placed at Marburg University under the supervision of Christian Wolff. Most scholars agree that Lomonosov, like Wolff, never fully separated physics from metaphysics. In a number of brilliant experiments (conducted at Moscow University, which he helped found in 1755 and now bears his name) Lomonosov sought evidence to buttress his qualitative interpretation of the physical properties of matter but rejected the mathematical approach championed by Newton (*see* Newtonianism).

Lomonosov's scientific work produced no disciples, although his literary achievements and polymath genius are the basis of a potent Russian cultural myth that denies the essential separation of scientific and literary inquiry.

References

Brown, W.E. *A History of Eighteenth-Century Russian Literature*. Ann Arbor: Ardis, 1980. 74–110.

Leicester, M., ed. *Mikhail Vasilévich Lomonosov and the Corpuscular Theory*. Cambridge: Harvard UP, 1970.

Pavlova, Galina, and Aleksandr Fedorov. *Mikhail Vasilievich Lomonosov: His Life and Work*. Trans. Arthur Aksenov. Moscow: Mir Publishers, 1984.

Yvonne Howell

London, Jack (1876–1916). American author renowned for stories of elemental struggle—of man against nature, man against man, and class against class. In his tales of the Klondike (most famously, *The Call of the Wild*, 1903), he gave authentic descriptions of the harsh realities of the natural **environment** and survival instincts of both human and animal. Largely self-taught in sociology and **politics**, London was both a **Social Darwinist** and a socialist. His social views are reflected in such works as *The Iron Heel* (1908) and *The Valley of the Moon* (1912). His semiautobiographical novel *Martin Eden* (1913) registers the predominating influence of **Herbert Spencer**. Also autobiographical is his memoir *John Barleycorn* (of the same year), in which he recounts his struggles with **alcoholism**.

References

London, Jack. *Novels and Social Writings*. Ed. Donald Pizer. New York: Library of America, 1982.

———. *Novels and Stories*. Ed. Donald Pizer. New York: Library of America, 1982.

Joseph Carroll and Pamela Gossin

Lopez, Barry (1945–   ). Best known for his National Book Award–winning *Arctic Dreams: Imagination and Desire in a Northern Landscape* (1986). He has also written a number of other widely admired books concerning the natural **environment**. Individually and collectively they move from alienation to affirmation through integrating a range of information and ideas from science, **anthropology**, and personal experience. The sources for *Arctic Dreams* are not only Lopez's scientific reading, which informs the text and appears in both appendices and the bibliography, but also his travels with marine ecologists, Eskimo hunters, Canadian landscape painters, and oil crew roughnecks. His objective is to harmonize the outer **landscape** of weather, plants, animals, and geology and the inner landscape that is "a kind of projection within a person of a part of the exterior landscape" (*Crossing* 64–65). To be in a proper relationship with particular natural landscapes, Lopez believes, one must pay attention to ideas and information from scientists, mystics, and local inhabitants. Even then, mystery remains. The order that is perceived in nature through this kind of attention is, for Lopez, "the face of God" (Anton 17). In his mission to know the land through science and experience and to grow spiritually so that we heal the land and ourselves, he refers to such like-minded writers as **Loren Eiseley**, **Rachel Carson**, Richard Nelson, and Gary Nabhan, all of whom join scientific outlooks with spiritual questing expressed in **essays** about the natural environment.

References

Anton, Jim. "An Interview with Barry Lopez." *Western American Literature* 21.1 (May 1986): 17.
Lopez, Barry. *Crossing Open Ground.* New York: Vintage Books, 1988.

James I. McClintock

Lowell, Amy (1874–1925). Poet and leader, after **Pound's** departure, of the Imagist movement. In *Legends* (1921), Lowell distinguishes between scientific (proven) **truth** and literary (imaginative or speculative) truth. Although Lowell was critical of the indiscriminate use of scientific "phraseology" in **art**, she often uses Latinate botanical terms in her poems. Her brother Percival (1855–1916), an astronomer, founded the Lowell Observatory, wrote about life on Mars, and paved the way for the discovery of Pluto.

Elizabeth J. Donaldson

Lucian (second century A.D.). Syrian-Greek satirist and prolific author of works parodying Greek and Roman philosophical, religious, and literary traditions. Dialogues comprise the bulk of Lucian's extant corpus, but the corpus also includes a diverse collection of critical **essays**, biographies, and satiric narratives (*see* Satire). Because of their fantastical nature (in depicting journeys to the moon and interplanetary adventures) the dialogue *Icaro-Menippus* and the prose work *True History* are classified by some as prototypical examples of the **science fiction** genre.

Reference

Fredericks, S.C. "Lucian's True History as SF." *Science Fiction Studies* 3.1 (Mar. 1976): 49–60.

JoAnn Palmeri

Lucretius (first century B.C.E.). Roman poet and author of *De Rerum Natura* (On the Nature of Things), the major epic poem on nature surviving from antiquity. His didactic, materialistic explanation of **cosmology**, meteorology, life, disease, and death relied upon the rational conceptualization of atoms acting beneath the sensate realm of nature. This popular dissemination of Democritus's pre-Socratic atomism within the context of Epicurus's **philosophy** of the senses influenced countless literati through the Romantic period.

Reference

Winspear, A.D. *Lucretius and Scientific Thought*. Montreal: Harvest House, 1963.

Philip K. Wilson

Luria, Aleksandr Romanovich (1902–1977). A twentieth-century Russian neuropsychologist who is best known among literary scholars in the West for his clinical biographies. Luria's intent in these biographical case histories, which he calls "unimagined portraits" (178 in *The Making of Mind*, 1979), is to understand a clinical feature in relation to the whole configuration of the individual's personality. The neurologist and writer **Oliver Sacks** appears to have used Luria's histories as a model for *Awakenings* and subsequent "clinical tales."

References

Luria, Aleksandr Romanovich. *The Man with a Shattered World*. Trans. Lynn Solotaroff. New York: Basic Books, 1972.
———. *The Mind of the Mnemonist*. Trans. Lynn Solotaroff. New York: Basic Books, 1968.

Anne Hunsaker Hawkins

Lyell, Charles (1797–1875). Victorian geologist and author, wrote the classic *Principles of Geology* (twelve editions between 1830–1833 and 1875), which made **Darwin's** *Origin of Species* (1859) possible and was of major literary influence on such writers as **Tennyson, Emerson**, and **Hardy**. By discrediting the supposed seven-day Creation and universal Flood of Noah, it effectively excluded Genesis from serious consideration as a valid history of nature and did much to free scientists from attempted control by the clergy. Lyell also defended the earlier ideas of **James Hutton** and **John Playfair** regarding an extended age of the earth and the virtual identity of geological forces in the past with those now observable. He overestimated the vertical mobility of continents; underestimated the efficacy of subaerial erosion; and was slow to accept the Ice Age. Lyell also withheld his acceptance of Darwin's theory of evolution (*see* Evolutionary Theory) for a time. Once convinced, however, Lyell reversed himself to endorse natural selection publicly in the tenth edition (1867) of the *Principles*. Even before then, his second major work, *The Antiquity of Man* (1863, 1874), had forcefully established the reality of human prehistory. Lyell traveled widely within Europe and wrote two well-received books about his experiences in the United States. In them and elsewhere, he was an outspoken critic of Victorian higher education and an effective voice in its reform. He was one of the first geologists to be knighted.

References

Bailey, Edward. *Charles Lyell*. London: Nelson, 1962.
Dean, Dennis R. " 'Through Science to Despair': Geology and the Victorians." *Victorian*

Science and Victorian Values: Literary Perspectives. Ed. James Paradis and Thomas Postelwait. 1981. New Brunswick, NJ: Rutgers UP, 1985. 111–36.

Wilson, Leonard G. *Charles Lyell. The Years to 1841: The Revolution in Geology.* New Haven: Yale UP, 1972.

Dennis R. Dean

Lytton, Edward George Bulwer- (1803–1873). First Baron Lytton, was one of the most versatile and prolific writers of his age, producing plays, poetry, essays, and twenty-four novels, including three works of science fiction, *Zanoni* (1842), *A Strange Story* (1862), and *The Coming Race* (1871). These last reflect his interest in vitalism and form part of his assault on scientific materialism, yet ironically in terms that mimic those of the very science he is condemning. In particular, Bulwer-Lytton was fascinated by the then-unexplained phenomenon of **electricity**, which he saw as one manifestation of a supernatural, all-pervading power or vital principle. His early novel, *Zanoni*, is an allegorical onslaught on the mechanistic interpretation of life, in which Mejnour, the representative of true wisdom, described as "Contemplation of the actual—SCIENCE," attacks contemporary experimental science and defends the occult practices of the Rosicrucians. Yet the universal power to which Mejnour is privy, the true basis of **medicine**, is described in terms of electricity, and even the passages attacking science are bolstered with copious references to contemporary scientists. The net effect is a curious pastiche of occult theories, physical science (*see* Physics), and a cult of the Will combining animal magnetism and Schopenhauer's impersonal, cosmic Will. In *The Coming Race*, which appeared in the same year as **Darwin's** *The Descent of Man*, Bulwer-Lytton broached the controversial evolutionary implication of the possible extinction of humanity when forced into competition with a more "fit" species. His subterranean **race**, the Vril-ya, have superior powers by virtue of their control over a form of fluid kinetic energy, Vril. Although *The Coming Race* satirizes Darwinian theory (*see* Darwinism; Evolutionary Theory) along with the emancipation of women, it inspired numerous successive evolutionary romances.

Reference

Christensen, Allan Conrad. *Edward Bulwer-Lytton: The Fiction of New Regions.* Athens: U of Georgia P, 1976.

Roslyn D. Haynes

M

Magic Realism. A term first used by Franz Roh in 1925 and applied to German painters of the time, it is now more frequently applied by literary critics and publishers to a practice in Latin American literature in which authors describe reality as a mixture of the mundane and the magical. One of the salient features of the novels of the Latin American Boom, many have found elements of magic realism in the works of such authors as **Jorge Luis Borges, Gabriel García Márquez, Julio Cortázar**, and Alejo Carpentier among others. Alejo Carpentier's concept of the Marvelous Real, the idea that the uniqueness of Latin American **reality** requires the marvelous as a mode of description, strengthened the connection between Latin American **fiction** and the use of magic realism. Science, when it does appear, tends to occupy the role of outsider, contrasting with the magical reality depicted in novels such as García Márquez's *One Hundred Years of Solitude* (1967). Even so, writers such as Cortázar and Borges use elements of the new **physics** in their depiction of a fantastic reality. The term has lost much of its explanatory power in Latin American criticism due to overuse and to a discrediting of Carpentier's position.

J. Andrew Brown

Mallarmé, Stéphane (1842–1898). French symbolist poet ("L'après-midi d'un faune," 1865) and author of many essays on poetic **theory**. In "La Musique et les Lettres" (1891) and in the language of late-nineteenth-century literary practices, Mallarmé posits poetic activity as a nonlinear process and thereby reveals a close affinity between metaphoric expression and complex dynamical systems.

Maria L. Assad

Malthus, Thomas (1766–1834). Author of the influential treatise *An Essay on the Principle of Population* (1798). Malthus argued that population tends to increase exponentially, while food resources go up only arithmetically, creating pressure on population growth—which will inevitably be checked. Malthus's work had an immediate impact in his own time and later inspired writers ranging from **Darwin** (who credits Malthus with a central tenet of natural selection) to **Aldous Huxley** and other writers of **science fiction**. Malthus's ideas continue to engage economists, birth control activists, and population theorists today.

Reference

Goran Ohlin, "The New Breed of Malthusians." *Family Planning Perspectives* 6.3 (1974): 158.

Leonard Cassuto

Manga. An extremely popular—indeed the best-selling—form of literature in Japan, comprised of pulp "comic" books or graphic novels, often published as weekly serials. Written in virtually every conceivable genre to appeal to virtually every market demographic, some of the most important stories concern serious issues of science, **technology**, and the human relationship to the natural **environment**, as well as explorations of social conformity, **gender and sexuality**, the potentials and discontents of **cybernetics** and cyberculture. Offering fascinating experiments in narrative **representation** through their combination of drawings and text, the most sophisticated manga have inspired full-length feature **anime** (animated films), often with apocalyptic themes.

Reference

Schodt, Frederik L. *Manga! Manga! The World of Japanese Comics*. Toyko: Kodansha, 1986.

Pamela Gossin

Mann, Thomas (1875–1955). German writer who won the Nobel Prize for Literature in 1929. Mann's increasingly complex style reflected his complex mind and study of the history of ideas. His works analyze the physical and mental state of modernity and depict the forces of ideology within social change. *Buddenbrooks* (1900) examined bourgeois society, while *Doktor Faustus* (1947) examined the German character during the Nazi regime. The status of the artist in society is equated in his early works with the decadence in society (*Death in Venice*, 1912, for example), but his later works (*The Confessions of Felix Krull, Confidence Man*, 1922, rev. 1955, and *The Magic Mountain*, 1924) emphasize the constructive role of the artist in society. The last title, for its depiction of **pathography** and illness, has become a classic text in medical humanities and ethics courses.

Mary Libertin

Mantell, Gideon Algernon (1790–1852). Professionally a surgeon, the first person to devote himself to collecting **dinosaur** relics and reconstructing the animals' original appearance. He discovered Iguanodon, Hylaeosaurus, Regnosaurus, and Peolorosaurus outright while augmenting the understanding of other saurian genera. Through his popular books, Mantell impressed the Age of Reptiles on Victorian minds. The frontispieces of his *Geology of South-East England* (1833) and *Wonders of Geology* (1838) contributed the "scarpe'd cliff" of **Tennyson's** *In Memoriam*, poem 56. Mantell's paleontological influence extended to **Bulwer-Lytton**, **Hardy**, and other writers, including such scientific ones as Cuvier, **Robert Chambers**, and **Darwin**. Mantell also helped popularize the study of microscopics.

Reference

Dean, Dennis R. *Gideon Mantell, Discoverer of Dinosaurs.* New York and London: Cambridge UP, 1997.

Dennis R. Dean

Marlowe, Christopher (1564–1593). Dramatist and poet, writing for the Elizabethan theater c. 1586 and murdered in a tavern brawl in 1593. Marlowe is the author of *Doctor Faustus, Tamburlaine the Great, The Jew of Malta, Edward II, Dido, Queen of Carthage, The Massacre at Paris*, and the unfinished epyllion *Hero and Leander*, all c. 1586. Marlowe created characters who voiced an often insatiable desire for scientific knowledge and the power concomitant with that learning. Ultimately, Marlowe expressed doubt about the accessibility of the Real and was certain only about the ideological power plays of his protagonists.

Diana B. Altegoer

Martí, José (1853–1895). Cuban poet and writer. He wrote on the necessity of bringing together science and the humanities in education. He practiced what he preached in several essays and poems. In the poem "Yugo y estrella" (Yoke and Star), he fuses the theory of evolution (*see* Evolutionary Theory) with ethics in bringing forth a new man. Martí wrote for many newspapers throughout Latin America and in New York. He spent most of his life in the struggle for the independence of Cuba from Spain.

References

Catalá, Rafael. "Para una teoría latinoamericana de las relaciones de la ciencia con la literatura: La cienciapoesía." *Revista de Filosofía* 28 (1990): 28.67/68: 215–223.
Jiménez, Luis A. "José Martí, Darwin and the Behavior of Animals." *La edad de oro? Ometeca* 3.2–4.1 (1996): 265–69.

Rafael Catalá

Martineau, Harriet (1802–1876). English writer best known for her *Illustrations of Political Economy* (1832–1834), which fictionalized the theories of **Malthus**, David Ricardo, and Adam Smith. An important precursor to Victorian industrial novelists, Martineau advocated free trade and utilitarianism, opposed strikes, and welcomed factories and industrial machinery as being beneficial to workers.

Nicholas Spencer

Martín-Santos, Luis (1924–1964). Spanish psychiatrist and novelist. Martín-Santos's only complete novel, *Tiempo de silencio* (Time of Silence, 1962), concerns a medical researcher working in 1940s Madrid. The novel, often compared to **Joyce's** *Ulysses*, marks a move away from the silent (and therefore conservative) narrator of social **realism** toward multitiered discourses drawn from competing ideologies. The promises and frustrations of scientific research constitute the fundamental signs of the text and allegorize the political tensions inherent in the authoritarian regime of Francisco Franco. The later Ortega and his postwar lectures on perspectivism suffer blistering **satires** in the novel.

Reference

Rey, Alfonso. *Construcción y sentido en "Tiempo de silencio."* 3rd ed. Madrid: José Porrúa Turanzas, 1988.

Dale J. Pratt

Mather, Cotton (1663–1728). Theologian and author of *The Christian Philosopher* (1721), a collection of **essays** on the natural sciences, **chemistry**, and Newtonian (*see* Newtonianism) **physics**. His **natural philosophy** forged a link between New England Puritan orthodoxy and enlightened rationality. For him, the experimental New Science revealed the minute and infinite wonders of God's mysterious universe.

Raymond F. Dolle

Mather, Increase (1639–1723). Theologian and author of *Essay for the Recording of Remarkable Providences* (1684), a study of New England's strange natural phenomena, such as thunderstorms and earthquakes, and supernatural phenomena, such as witchcraft. Employing **rationality** and empirical science to defend Puritan orthodoxy, Mather collected eyewitness accounts to support his **hypothesis** that God's hand is behind such events.

Raymond F. Dolle

Maxim, Hudson (1853–1927). American **inventor**, industrialist, and writer. Brother of Sir Hiram Maxim, the inventor of the machine gun, Hudson Maxim invented a high explosive he called "maximite." After this success, inventing and literature formed his twin avocations. He served as president of the early Aeronautical Society and in 1910 published *The Science of Poetry and the Philosophy of Language*, a work in which he intended to systematize literary criticism. The influence of Maxim's mechanist views about language, his appeals to the efficiency and practicality of **poetry**, and even his devotion to lethal

technology can all be variously glimpsed in the work of **Ezra Pound** and Wyndam Lewis.

Reference

Tichi, Cecelia. *Shifting Gears; Technology, Literature, Culture in Modern America.* Chapel Hill: U of North Carolina P, 1987.

Lisa Gitelman

McClure, Michael (1930–   ). Beat Generation poet, essayist, and environmental advocate. Since his first public reading at San Francisco's Six Gallery in 1955, Michael McClure has worked to integrate the disciplines of **biology**, biophysics, and ecology into his art. The author of over thirty collections of poems, essays, and plays, McClure's writing has taken him from the Beat era of the 1950s, through the counterculture of the 1960s and 1970s, and has made him one of the preeminent American literary voices for the environmental cause. Throughout his career, he writes, "My interest in biology has remained a constant thread through my searching" (11 in *Scratching the Beat Surface*, 1982). McClure's early work, such as *Hymns to St. Geryon* (1959) and *Poisoned Wheat* (1965), presents a worldview that is based in the realities of biology rather than what he sees as the abstract illusions of **politics**. Heavily influenced by biophysicists H.T. Odum and Harold Morowitz, as well as ecologist Ramon Margalef, McClure's later poetry, such as *Fragments of Perseus* (1983) and *Rebel Lions* (1991), endeavors to reconnect his readers to what he calls their "mammalian" roots.

Reference

McClure, Michael. *Lighting the Corners: On Art, Nature, and the Visionary.* Albuquerque: U of New Mexico P, 1993.

Rod Phillips

McCormmach, Russell (19?–   ). American writer and historian of science. His novel *Night Thoughts of a Classical Physicist* (1982) presents the reader with a character who works in the shadow of several early-twentieth-century scientists, especially **Max Planck** and Hermann von Helmholtz. Narrated by a practitioner of what Kuhn (*see* Revolutions) names "ordinary science," the book effectively reconstructs the world of European, especially German, **physics** at the beginning of the century. The central theme of the novel is the transition between the predictable world of classical physics and the new world of **quantum physics** that emerged at the beginning of the twentieth century. Extensive notes provide a rich source of historical detail. His more recent work in the **history of science** and scientific biography draws upon the strong narrative style of *Night Thoughts.*

References

McCormmach, Russell, and Christa Jungnickel. *Cavendish: The Experimental Life.* Cranbury, NJ: Bucknell UP, 1999.
————. *Intellectual Mastery of Nature: Theoretical Physics from Ohm to Einstein: The Now Mighty Theoretical Physics 1870–1925.* Chicago: U of Chicago P, 1990.

Joseph Duemer

McPhee, John (1931–   ). "A lover of small details, . . . a passionate list maker, a reverent collector of facts," according to Michael Pearson. Small details, lists, and facts are not usually accorded such emotionally charged modifiers, but they provide a key insight into McPhee's work: The most specialized concepts and phenomena, when explored with creative understanding, when placed in the context of human endeavor, become accessible and interesting to lay audiences and acquire literary significance as well. Whatever topic he chooses for his books (he has averaged a book a year for the past quarter century)—be it orange growing (*Oranges*, 1967), environmentalism (*Encounters with the Archdruid*, 1971), nuclear science (*The Curve of Binding Energy*, 1974) (*see* Nuclear Energy/Nuclear Science), or geology (*Annals of the Former World* tetralogy, 1981–1993), McPhee saturates himself in the subject matter by interacting on a very human level with the experts involved. When working on his geology books he embarked on cross-country excursions with geologists who became his mentors as well as figured prominently in the narratives. For example, in the series' fourth book, *Assembling California* (1993), he describes one geologist's talent "for seeing through the topography" and another geologist's delightful ability to describe the dynamics of seismic fault rupture by using clever hand gestures.

Through his metaphor- and story-rich inquiries into science, **technology**, and industry, McPhee calls dramatic attention to the inseparability of ideas from those who work with and produce those ideas.

References

Pearson, Michael. "Profile: Twenty Questions: A Conversation with John McPhee." *Creative Nonfiction* 1.1 (1993): 76–87.
Roundy, Jack. "Formal Devices in the Prose of John McPhee." *Literary Nonfiction: Theory, Criticism, Pedagogy.* Ed. Chris Anderson. Carbondale: U of Southern Illinois P, 1989. 70–92.

Fred D. White

McPherson, Sandra (1943–   ). American poet. McPherson is more openly passionate than her reserved teacher Elizabeth Bishop. From her first book, *Elegies for the Hot Season* (1982), to her most recent, *Edge Effect* (1996), McPherson has regarded the world with a naturalist's fierce and loving gaze. Not a "nature poet," she draws metaphors from nature's objects, especially plants and flowers, making them stand for the varied states of human consciousness.

References

McPherson, Sandra. *The God of Indeterminacy.* Urbana: U of Illinois P, 1993.
———. *Radiation.* New York: Ecco, 1973.

Joseph Duemer

Mechanism. The philosophical system explaining natural processes using metaphors drawn from machines. Mechanism eliminates the spiritual properties associated with organicism or vitalism, leaving a lawful, structured universe, where causal series of connecting parts are subject to local forces and interactions. Mechanistic explanation methodically reduces any object to the machine. More complex processes, events, or organisms can be explained in terms of more complex, more encompassing machines. Mechanism presumes that the totality of the machine itself always remains beyond human comprehension, if only in its smallest part, such as the initial act setting the universal machine in motion.

In theory, mechanism exactly follows known physical laws; however, its development is determined by the type of machine used in the metaphor. The Archimedean lever presupposes physical contact and provides a basic but limited possibility for pushing and pulling. By contrast, a watch presupposes a more complex mechanism of regular ongoing operations but still requires a maker or ordering force. Philosophical mechanism is associated with the clockwork world found in seventeenth-century thinkers such as **Thomas Hobbes** and **René Descartes**. In the nineteenth century the dominant metaphor was the steam engine, where control involved the **thermodynamics** of consumption and expenditure. More recent forms of mechanism, such as **cybernetics** or quantum theory, deal less with specific machines than with a field of mechanistic forces. Each version of mechanism involves tension between the machine as metaphor for universal structure and historically specific mechanisms. There are always gaps in the machine, redistributions of functions and directions of momentum, subject to historical reception, translation, and transformation.

Literature historicizes the machine, making visible its gaps. Literary thematization of machines allegorizes and names what was otherwise a physical absolute, bringing out the latent consequences of mechanism. These themes come in many forms, from **utopias** of progress, to dystopic satires of the sterility of utopias, to gloomy prophecies of science gone out of control. At the same time, any formalist or structuralist description of literature is inevitably mechanistic. Mechanistic explanation presumes the combinatory production of new but ordered outcomes. Literary form is predicated on the mechanistic coherence and interaction of the text as machinelike. Literature as a machine provides a metaphor for what occurs in reading. The literary machine does not involve the forces and interactions of a physical system, but literary form provides the metaphorical definition of mechanism. Literature clarifies and extends the possibilities of the machine. In this sense, the text is a machine without gaps or breakdowns, working without expenditure.

Reference

Pepper, Stephen C. *World Hypotheses: A Study in Evidence.* Berkeley: U of California P, 1942.

Charles A. Baldwin

Medical Case History. An oral or written account by medical staff of a particular patient's illness and course of treatment. "Case history" can refer to the patient's chart or progress notes, to the extended history or clinical biography such as is written today by **A.R. Luria** and **Oliver Sacks**, or to the patient narrative by premodern **physicians** ranging from **Galen** to Henry Head. In its typical form, the case history begins with the patient's presenting problem, called the chief complaint, then the history of the present illness, the past medical history, review of systems, family history, and social history, concluding with notations as to physical examination and laboratory tests. The medical case history has only recently come under analysis by literary scholars.

Reference

Banks, Joanne Trautmann, and Anne Hunsaker Hawkins, eds. "The Art of the Case History." *Literature and Medicine* 11.1 (Spring 1992): 1–179.

Anne Hunsaker Hawkins

Medicine. A genuinely interdisciplinary field that challenges many common assumptions about the allegedly opposed **cultures** of science and the humanities. Literature is generally thought of as "soft"—as concerned with ideas and interpretations and not with facts; as primarily affective rather than cognitive and logical; as aesthetic rather than utilitarian. Medicine, in contrast, is generally considered a practical application of scientific knowledge. But medicine is a human science, a science that is also an **art**. It demands interpretive skill as well as factual knowledge, and the capacity to empathize and intuit can be as important in diagnosis and treatment as scientific data and logical deduction. The responsible **physician** must be grounded in knowledge both of the sciences and the humanities in order to render effective patient care. And because of the need in actual medical practice for such humanistic qualities as imaginative and emotional empathy, the ability to listen and the ability to communicate, ethical sensitivity, and the awareness of and respect for cultural difference, literature has come to play a significant role in medical training. Indeed, literature and medicine is one of the few areas of study in which such learning can take place.

Literature and medicine is an academic field with its own body of **theory**, heuristic strategies, and research agendas, and likewise its own scholarly journals and professional societies. It is also a pedagogic discipline with characteristic course topics, canonical texts, and appropriate teaching methods. Common to both the field and its pedagogic application are theoretical bases and conceptual frameworks that give the study of literature and medicine systematic coherence and intellectual rigor. But these are constantly evolving in response to developments in literary theory and medical reality. Like the **two cultures** it seeks to synthesize, literature and medicine is less a static body of knowledge than an ongoing and dynamic project, a creation that is always in the act of recreating itself.

Literature and medicine can be conceptualized in three different ways: there is literature itself in all its genres, both literary and scientific; there is its functional or educational dimension; and there is scholarship and its theoretical and conceptual framework.

Literature

"Medical literature" ranges from the literal to the figurative and from actual case histories to cultural diagnoses and analogies. Literary texts that are taught in the classroom and analyzed in the pages of scholarly journals include the old canon of Western literature as well as contemporary works by such authors as Alice Walker, Keri Hulme, Joanna Russ, **Marge Piercy**, Cao Xuequin, Marie Cardinal, and D.M. Thomas.

Medicine, as compared with more abstract sciences, is peculiarly culture-bound. The ongoing problems with U.S. health care policies and provision reminds us how deeply and pervasively the actual practice of medicine is conditioned by economic, social, and political forces and less obviously but just as important by ideologies and systems of value. To some degree, medicine reflects the culture from which it emerges, and it is not surprising that literature often resorts to medical **analogy** in analyzing the pathology of a given era or society. **Swift** brilliantly sums up the madness of late-seventeenth-century society in *A Tale of a Tub;* **Mann** makes a tuberculosis sanitorium a symbol of prewar European history in *The Magic Mountain*; Camus portrays France under German occupation in *The Plague* (1947–1948); Solzhenitsyn's *Cancer Ward* (1968) is a figure of Stalinist Russia.

This kind of metaphor or analogy by which medicine becomes a symbol for other realities can be reversed: It is possible to read stories or plays or poems that do not literally deal with disease and healing as texts that illumine these things by analogy. Most familiar are the "case histories" of Dr. Watson in which **Conan Doyle**—himself a physician—shows a detective employing methods of close observation and skilled deductive reasoning that resemble a medical diagnosis, methods modeled on those of the Edinburgh physician Joseph Bell. Less obviously, the stories in **Joyce's** *Dubliners* are also case histories in which the former medical student traces the symptoms of spiritual paralysis that afflict modern Ireland. Kafka's "Metamorphosis" (1915) can be read as providing vivid and surrealistic images of the transforming effects of sickness as experienced by a patient and his family. And **Dante's** *Inferno* can be seen as the descent into illness, combining images of physical and mental agony with a precise clinical classification of spiritual disease: This Hell is a kind of hospital in which no one is cured.

Such analogies can extend the field of medicine and literature—if only for pedagogic ends—to literature that is not "about" medicine. But of course there is no lack of works that deal directly with sickness, disability, and death—from Sophocles' *Philoctetes* to Tillie Olson's *Tell Me a Riddle* (1961) or Helena Maria Viramontes's *The Moths* (1985). *The Plague* is a recent example of the literature of pestilence—a literature that ranges back to the Athenian plague in Thucydides, reflections of the Black Death in **Chaucer** and Boccaccio, and **Defoe's** realistic chronicle of the Great Plague of London in *Journal of the Plague Year* (1722); proceeds through **Poe's** eerie evocation in "Masque of the Red Death" (1842), Manzoni's *The Betrothed* (1825–1827), and Katherine Anne Porter's novel of the great flu pandemic of 1916, *Pale Horse, Pale Rider* (1939); and appears now in the outburst of plays, stories, poems, and pathographies about **AIDS** in our own day. Images of the doctor or the healer—not necessarily the same—range from the religious, as in biblical stories of healing, to the satiric, as in **Molière's** *The Doctor in Spite of Himself* (1666) or Samuel Shem's *House of God* (1978); the realistic, as in Sinclair Lewis's *Arrowsmith* (1925); the surrealist, as in Kafka's "Country Doctor" (1917); or the symbolic, as in Ibsen's *Enemy of the People* (1882) or Vonda McIntyre's *Dreamsnake* (1978). Doctors themselves sometimes turn writer: Rabelais's graphic physical imagery and **Chekhov's** blend of sympathy and detachment would seem to derive from their medical experience as well as their individual temperaments.

Recently, individuals of all kinds have been writing autobiographical accounts of their experience of illness or disability. These pathographies constitute a distinctively modern genre, though **John Donne's** *Devotions upon Emergent Occasions* (1623–1624) offers a brilliant earlier example. In **pathography** the merger of medicine and literature is as obvious as is the relevance of such narratives for medical teaching and practice: They affirm the centrality of the patient to the medical transaction and give voice to experiential dimensions of sickness that are all too often ignored.

Felice Aull at New York University has established a literature and medicine online database that is accessible and an email discussion group: these are accessible through the address <http://mchipOO.med.nyu.edu/lit-med/medhum. html>.

Teaching

As an academic discipline, literature and medicine is still relatively new. The first full-time appointment in the field was that of Joanne Trautmann Banks, in 1972, at the Pennsylvania State University College of Medicine. Formal courses in literature and medicine are available in medical school as well as undergraduate curricula. Moreover, in the medical setting, literature has proved helpful in hospital chaplaincy and clinical ethics programs, in teaching rounds, and in residency training. The most extensive programs in continuing education are offered by The Center for Literature and the Health Care Professions, which is jointly sponsored by Hiram College and Northeastern Ohio Universities College of Medicine. Courses or workshops are regularly offered by such professional societies as the Association of American Medical Colleges (AAMC), the Society of Teachers of Family Medicine, the American College of Physicians, and the Society for General Internal Medicine.

Courses in literature and medicine are themselves models of interdisciplinarity, taught sometimes by literary scholars, sometimes by physicians, and sometimes by both together. Early on, teaching tended to focus on contemporary literature explicitly dealing with medical subjects, on realistic portrayals of doctors and disease, and on poems and stories written by physicians. These emphases continue, building up a repertoire of texts like Tolstoy's *The Death of Ivan Ilych* (1886), Chekhov's *Ward Six* (1892), and **Charlotte Perkins Gilman's** "The Yellow Wallpaper" (1892) and of the works of physician-authors such as **William Carlos Williams** and **Richard Selzer**. In more recent years, adventurous teachers have explored other kinds of texts and ways of teaching. Creative writing workshops have attracted students, doctors, and patients. Courses are now offered in which the techniques and insights of literary theory are brought to bear on the analysis of both literary and medical texts. Works such as Dante's *Inferno* and **Henry James's** *The Wings of the Dove* (1902) find their way into syllabi. Role-playing exercises in the classroom have developed into ambitious medical theater programs offering readings or performances of often original plays for the medical community or the general public.

The study of literature aims to instill and strengthen humane qualities and humanistic skills. It is not designed to correct the imbalance of the mainly scientific training students receive before and in medical school or to provide cultural enrichment after they become physicians. It does not seek to make doctors into better human beings, except in the ways that better human beings make better doctors. Literature develops and hones the empathetic **imagination**, helping medical caregivers identify with individuals who may be very different from themselves. **Freud** has said that we cannot imagine our own death: Though this may be true, we can imaginatively understand what it is like to die through the deaths of Tolstoy's Prince Andrey and Ivan Ilytch or through poems by **Emily Dickinson**, Dylan Thomas, and Denise Levertov. There is a powerful tendency in medicine to regard the patient as an embodied disease and to reduce the human experience of illness to the data of medical charts and records: This tendency is countered by the rich particularity and emotional force of the "case histories" provided in stories, poems, plays, and pathographies. And there is also a tendency in medical ethical thinking to rely on the abstractions and generalities of principle-based ethics: These are countered by literature's way of exploring moral conflict and choice in all their particularity, complexity, and ambiguity.

Scholarship and Theory

In the 1990s, scholarship in literature and medicine attests to an explosion of interest in popular culture, cultural studies, textuality, and theory. In the journal *Literature and Medicine* one finds, side by side with studies of **Melville**, **George Eliot**, and **Henry James**, essays on such diverse topics as the tradition of satirical skits in medical schools; on family conferences in hospice work and on the comparison of the discourse of midwifery and obstetrics; on pathographies of all kinds; on poster art about breast cancer and on the obeah woman in Derek Walcott's *Omeros* (1990); on the temporal dimension of narrative in psychoanalytic discourse and on the ways in which narrative theory illumines clinical medicine.

Scholarship in literature and medicine tends to fall into two categories. The first focuses on works of literature that concern medical or medically related topics (death, suffering), medical issues (abortion, euthanasia), or medical figures (physician, patient). The second kind of scholarship in literature and medicine applies literary methodologies to the medical enterprise itself. Medical texts have come under scrutiny in recent years: The medical case history, the hospital chart, students' case presentation, and physicians' own narratives have been discussed as interpretive narratives embodying and reflecting the point of view of the author.

Scholarship in literature and medicine has taken a "narrativist turn" in recent years, as the insights of narrative theory are employed by literary critics to deconstruct the medical enterprise itself. Kathryn Montgomery Hunter (in *Doctors' Stories*) persuasively shows how the daily practice of medicine is filled with stories—especially the experience-based stories that patients tell their physicians and the diagnostic stories that physicians return to the patient and record in the medical record. Narrative ways of knowing help explain both the patient's representation of experience and the physician's reformulation of the patient's narrative. Rita Charon demonstrates that there are interpretive parallels between acts of reading and acts of diagnosis. She argues that physicians need "narrative competence"—a competence that can be developed and honed by literary study. Evaluating patients requires the skills that are exercised by the careful reader: Careful attention to language, the ability to adopt alien points of view, skill in integrating isolated phenomena so that they suggest meaning, and the capacity to sustain multiple (and sometimes discordant) interpretations.

A narrative approach has also been found helpful in medical ethics. Narrative theory provides the entering wedge for literary scholars who seek to contribute to a field that has been dominated by philosophers over the past thirty years. The approach that is often called "**narrative ethics**" positions the examination of ethical dilemmas within the framework of a patient's biography and culture. Most recently, narrative techniques have been extended to the analysis of case histories reported (or created) by medical ethicists.

Of course, not all scholarship in the field concerns narrative and narrative theory. An entire issue of *Literature and Medicine* is devoted to **drama** and another to **film**, and in each issue there is an essay on some aspect of the visual arts. Though poetry tends to be underrepresented in literature and medicine scholarship, essays can be found on **Tennyson's** "The Princess" and **Homer's** *Iliad,* on poetry about AIDS and poetry about mental illness, and on the contribution that lyric poetry in its epiphanic dimensions can make to understanding issues in medical ethics. Short essays on particular poems are often the subject of the regular column "Medicine and the Arts" in *Academic Medicine,* the journal of the Association of American Medical Colleges.

The primary source for theoretical as well as pedagogical publications is the journal *Literature and Medicine,* which began as an annual in 1982 with the State University of New York Press at Albany and is now published biannually by Johns Hopkins University Press. Other venues for scholarship include literary journals, general medical journals, general humanities journals, publications of the medical specialities and the medical subspecialties, and journals on ethics, philosophy, or religious studies. Presentations on topics relevant to literature and medicine occur at the conventions of such groups as the Modern Language Association, the Society for Literature and Science, the Association of American Medical Colleges, and The Society for Bioethics and Humanities.

The double title of the field—"literature and medicine"—suggests its dual allegiance. The medical establishment expects literature to be enlightening, useful, and relevant to the practice and **epistemology** of medicine; the literary establishment requires theoretical sophistication, analytic complexity, and ideological ferment. How can scholars and teachers in literature and medicine satisfy both imperatives? By its very interdisciplinarity, the evolving field of literature and medicine is committed to the tension between these two sets of expectations—a tension that is at the same time its challenge and its promise.

References

Brody, Howard. *Stories of Sickness.* New Haven, CT: Yale UP, 1987.

Charon, Rita. "Medical Interpretation: Implications of Literary Theory of Narrative for Clinical Work." *Journal of Narrative and Life History* 3.1 (1993): 79–97.

Charon, Rita, et al. "Literature and Medicine: Contributions to Clinical Practice." *Annals of Internal Medicine* 122 (1995): 599–606.

Coles, Robert. *The Call of Stories: Teaching and the Moral Imagination.* Boston: Houghton Mifflin, 1989.

Hawkins, Anne Hunsaker. *Reconstructing Illness: Studies in Pathography.* West Lafayette, IN: Purdue UP, 1993.

Hawkins, Anne Hunsaker, and Marilyn Chandler McEntyre, eds. *Approaches to Teaching Literature and Medicine.* Options for Teaching. New York: MLA Publications, 2000.

Hunter, Kathryn Montgomery. *Doctors' Stories: The Narrative Structure of Medical Knowledge.* Princeton, NJ: Princeton UP, 1991.

———. "Literature and Medicine: Standards for Applied Literature." *Applying the Humanities.* Ed. D. Callahan, A.L. Kaplan, and B. Jennings. New York: Plenum, 1985.

Hunter, Kathryn Montgomery, Rita Charon, and John L. Coulehan. "The Study of Literature in Medical Education." *Academic Medicine* 7.9 (1995): 787–94.

Literature and Medicine. no.1+ continuing. Especially Tenth Anniversary Retrospective issue. Ed. Anne Hudson Jones. 10 (1991): xi–197.

Morris, David B. *The Culture of Pain.* Berkeley: U of California P, 1991.

Sontag, Susan. *Illness as Metaphor.* New York: Random House, 1977.

Anne Hunsaker Hawkins

Melancholy. State of despondency, misanthropy, and mournful longing, also called "vapors" or spleen, associated since **Aristotle** with both artistic talent and bodily dysfunction. According to ancient humoral theory, melancholy arose from an overabundance of black bile, which could lead to madness yet was also deemed a temperamental precondition for poetic inspiration. Melancholy's double-edged quality has long preoccupied **physicians**, artists, and literary writers, including **Robert Burton**, **William Shakespeare**, **Charles Baudelaire**, and **Sigmund Freud**.

Reference

Klibansky, Raymond, Erwin Panofsky, and Fritz Saxl. *Saturn and Melancholy: Studies in the History of Natural Philosophy, Religion, and Art.* New York: Basic Books, 1964.

Anne C. Vila

Melville, Herman (1819–1891). American novelist and poet whose youthful experience on a whaling expedition informed *Moby-Dick* (1851) and other stories of seafaring. Though often studied as an epic tragedy of human obsession, much of the text of *Moby-Dick* can also be read as a handbook of cetology, marine engineering, navigation, and oceanography. Crawford has described it as "decidedly Latourian" (18)—a narrative that exemplifies **Bruno Latour's** actor network theory.

Reference

Crawford, Hugh. "Networking the (Non) Human: *Moby-Dick*, Matthew Fontaine Maury and Bruno Latour." *Configurations* 5.1 (1997): 1–21.

Noel Gough

Meredith, George (1828–1909). English novelist and poet who satirized false system-builders in the characters of Sir Willoughby Patterne in *The Egoist* (1879) and Sir Austin Feverel, whom he calls ironically, a "scientific humanist" in *The Ordeal of Richard Feverel* (1859). However, he was not opposed to science, and his long novels sometimes reflect a Darwinian (*see* Darwinism) vocabulary. Meredith's **poetry** employs conventional star imagery, but he goes beyond this in "Meditation under Stars" (1888) where he recognizes the "links" between the organic and inorganic in the **cosmos**: "The fire is in them [the stars] whereof we were born." Meredith's most notable use of celestial imagery occurs in his sonnet "Lucifer in Starlight" (1883) where we are told that the rebellious angel is defeated by "The army of unalterable law," that is, the order of the heavens and the morality it reflects.

Jacob Korg

Mérimée, Prosper (1803–1870). Romantic and Realist French author, master of the short story. Mixing **realism** with mystifying or eerie events, Mérimée's tales are spun around concrete settings but evolve into illogical states that are analogous to chaotic tendencies of nonlinear dynamical systems. *La Vénus d'Ille* (1837) and *Lokis* (1869) are good examples of stories based on nonlinearity.

Maria L. Assad

Merrill, James (1926–1995). Author of the visionary, mock mock-epic *The Changing Light at Sandover* (1982), a "poem of science" and product of twenty-five years of sessions at the Ouija board. Mixing domestic experience, magpie mythology, echoes of **Dante**, **Blake**, **Shelley**, and **Yeats**, and reading in **popularizations** of twentieth-century science, Merrill allegorizes powers who "speak from within the atom." He thereby makes the imaginative nature of scientific tropes inescapable even as he finds "revelations," as Kuberski observes, in "the interplay of rule and chance, the **cosmos** and **chaos** within the alphabet and the periodic table of elements."

Reference

Kuberski, Philip. "Merrill's Other World." *Chaosmos: Literature, Science and Theory.* Albany: State U of New York P, 1994. 170–85.

Steven Meyer

Mesmerism. Therapeutic technique popularized by the Viennese physician Franz Anton Mesmer (1734–1815), who claimed to cure nervous disorders by acting as a conductor of an invisible cosmic fluid he called animal magnetism. Mesmerism, which exploited medical vitalism and the **Enlightenment** vogue of science, captivated fashionable Parisians during the 1780s. It was widely influential in nineteenth-century **culture**, attracting literary followers like **Honoré de Balzac**, and is now considered a precursor to the modern practice of hypnotism.

References

Darnton, Robert. *Mesmerism and the End of Enlightenment in France.* Cambridge: Harvard UP, 1968.
Tartar, Maria. *Spellbound: Studies on Mesmerism and Literature.* Princeton, NJ: Princeton UP, 1978.

Anne C. Vila

Metaphysical Poets. A group of poets writing in seventeenth-century England whose verse tended toward intense personal and intellectual complexity and concentration. The chief practitioner was **John Donne**, and his disciples included the minor amorous lyrists Edward Herbert, Henry King, and John Suckling. These poets are most often linked in terms of style with the great religious lyrists of the mid-seventeenth century, such as George Herbert, Richard Crashaw, Henry Vaughan, and Thomas Traherne. Andrew Marvell fused the metaphysical practices of Donne with the urbane sophistication of the Cavalier poets **Ben Jonson** and Robert Herrick, the school most in opposition to the metaphysicals, in order to transform both poetical attitudes and create a neo-classical style that would anticipate the Augustan poets in the next century. Europeans writing in this tradition include Jean de Sponde (France), Francisco Quevedo y Villas (Spain), Paul Fleming (Germany), and Constantijn Huygens (Holland).

The style was to blend emotional intensity with intellectual ingenuity through the verse's primary metaphorical device, the conceit. This figure of speech, a major source of the poem's wit, forms a fanciful parallel between apparently dissimilar or incongruous objects and situations. The metaphysical conceit is the most intricate and intellectual device in **poetry**, establishing an **analogy** between one body's spiritual properties or qualities and an object in the physical world, a paralleling that ultimately controls the whole structure of the poem. One of the most famous conceits is from "A Valediction: Forbidding Mourning" where Donne compares two lovers' souls to a draftsman's compass. Because of the violent yoking together of unconnected ideas and natural objects, the reader is forced to think through the argument of the poem, thereby analyzing both feeling and thought.

In the seventeenth century, the phrase "metaphysical poetry" was used disparagingly. The Scottish poet William Drummond criticized those contemporaries who tried to "abstract poetry to metaphysical ideas and scholastic quiddities" (1630). **John Dryden** condemned Donne for affecting metaphysics and perplexing "the minds of the fair sex with nice speculations of philosophy" rather than engaging their hearts with the softness of love. In 1779 **Samuel Johnson** called this verse "a kind of discordia concors . . . a discovery of occult resemblances in things apparently unlike," through which "the most heterogeneous ideas are yoked by violence together." Not until **T.S. Eliot's** influential essay "The Metaphysical Poets" (1921) was the association of sensibility, the fusion of thought and feeling, finally rehabilitated.

References

Eliot, T.S. "The Metaphysical Poets." *Selected Essays*. New York: Harcourt, 1950.
Gardner, Helen, ed. *The Metaphysical Poets*. London: Penguin Books, 1957.

Diana B. Altegoer

Meteorology. The science of weather and the atmosphere that came into being at the end of the eighteenth century and was immediately reflected in literature. Well-known examples include **Erasmus Darwin**, "The Economy of

Vegetation"; **Coleridge**, "The Aeolian Harp," the *Ancient Mariner*, and "Frost at Midnight"; **Shelley**, "Mount Blanc," "Ode to the West Wind," and "The Cloud"; and **Goethe's** poems on Luke Howard, the originator (in 1822) of modern cloud type **classification**. Howard's influence is also apparent in Goethe's *Faust II*. The unusual weather of 1816, caused by the previous year's eruption of Tamboro volcano (Dutch East Indies), was noticed by many commentators in Europe and the United States. Earlier references to atmospheric phenomena, common in Renaissance literature, derived most usually from **Aristotle**, but classical writers like **Homer** (Aeolus in the *Odyssey*) had their influence, as did Genesis, with its flood-preceding rainbows. The French Renaissance poets Jean-Antoinede Baif (1567) and Isaac Habert (1585) both published long poems versifying the weather lore of their times; and **Shakespeare** refers to numerous meteorological phenomena (in *King Lear* and *The Tempest* especially). Sea stories, like **Conrad's** *Typhoon* (1903) often depend on weather, as does naturalistic **fiction** of other kinds (**Jack London**, "To Build a Fire"). Nor may one forget a Kansas tornado and a little girl named Dorothy (Frank Baum's *The Wonderful Wizard of Oz*, 1900).

References

Heninger, S.K. Jr. *A Handbook of Renaissance Meteorology, with Particular Reference to Elizabethan and Jacobean Literature.* Durham, NC: Duke UP, 1960.
Hennig, John. "Goethe's Interest in British Meteorology." *MLQ* 10 (1949): 321–37.

Dennis R. Dean

Microscope. An optical device that provides magnified images of the invisibly small. Its invention (probably around 1590 by Zacharias Janssen) triggered both serious interest in the microcosmic dimension and fantasies about new worlds. **Francis Bacon** predicted the importance of the microscope for future science in *New Atlantis* (1626). **Robert Hooke's** illustrations in *Micrographia* and van Leeuwenhoek's studies on the microcosmic worlds provided abundant material for literature. Obsession with the microscope was satirized by seventeenth-century writers and by **Swift** in his *Gulliver's Travels*. **Romanticism** and nineteenth-century literature stress the horrific qualities of the microcosmic worlds, as can be seen in **E.T.A. Hoffmann, Edgar Allan Poe**, or Fitzjames O'Brien, while Louis Pasteur's and Robert Koch's discoveries led to the widespread fear of microbes at the turn of the century.

Reference

Wilson, Catherine. *The Invisible World. Early Modern Philosophy and the Invention of the Microscope.* Princeton, NJ: Princeton UP, 1995.

Elmar Schenkel

Mill, John Stuart (1806–1873). At first an adherent of Benthamism, and of the quasi-scientific rationalism it advocated, he eventually achieved a balance in his thinking between the claims of logic and emotion. He came to realize the inadequacy of the purely rational life of the mind through literature as the *Mémoires* of Jean-François Marmontel, and more especially **William Wordsworth's** lyric **poetry**, enabled him to recover from a severe depression and convinced him of the value of feelings and the **art** that expressed them. Mill's extensive writings on **politics** and society emphasize the importance of literary and artistic **culture**, and some of his most durable works are **essays** in literary criticism. In his "Inaugural Address" at St. Andrew's University he declared that education should include both literature and science. His *System of Logic* (1843) envisions ethics as a collaboration of "Art" and "Science" in which Science proposes actions whose moral value is decided by Art.

Reference

Mill, John Stuart. *Autobiography*. New York: Columbia UP, 1960.

Jacob Korg

Miller, Andrew (1961–   ). English-born writer, now living in Ireland. He won the International Dublin Literary Award of 1999 for *Ingenious Pain* (1997), a historically exacting novel of eighteenth-century **medicine** that recounts the life and work of a fictional surgeon born without the ability to feel pain. His second novel, *Casanova in Love* (1998), offers a graphic tour of the dark side of **Enlightenment** London as experienced by his over-the-hill title character. Both works offer recreations of Newtonian (*see* Newtonianism) **culture**, including occasional appearances by historic figures such as **Samuel Johnson**.

Pamela Gossin

Miller, Hugh (1802–1856). Scottish stonemason and man of letters who pioneered the **popularization** of geology. As editor of *The Witness*, Miller wrote a series of popular journal articles on Devonian fish, which he collected into the immensely popular book *The Old Red Sandstone* (1841), a precursor of **Robert Chambers's** *Vestiges of the Natural History of Creation*. Miller's other widely read works included *Footprints of the Creator* (1849) and *My Schools and Schoolmasters* (1854).

Reference

Shortland, Michael, ed. *Hugh Miller and the Controversies of Victorian Science*. New York: Oxford UP, 1996.

James G. Paradis

Milosz, Czeslaw (1911–   ). Lithuanian-born Polish and American poet, essayist, and novelist; Nobel Laureate for Literature in 1980; among the most important poets of the twentieth century. Considerably affected by the horrors of modern history, he distrusts the philosophical materialism and reductionism of modern science, preferring instead a fully humanized universe. He is critical in *The Year of the Hunter* (1994), for instance, of ethological filmmaking because it suggests that man is merely an animal among animals, sanctioning human viciousness.

Milosz's greatest concern is the horror of twentieth-century history, which he associates with science and **technology**; his answer is an old and inviting one: a sensualized and celebratory religious attitude toward the objects of **reality**. In *Unattainable Earth* (1986), Milosz includes whole poems by **Whitman** and D.H. Lawrence. Milosz would probably agree with **Wallace Stevens** that modern **poetry** and **philosophy** are largely concerned with perception, but unlike Stevens, Milosz is a profoundly religious poet, though also a sensualist, a poet of praise.

References

Milosz, Czeslaw. *Collected Poems: 1931–1987*. New York: Ecco, 1988.
————. *Provinces: Poems 1987–1991*. New York: Ecco, 1991.

Joseph Duemer

Milton, John (1608–1674). Poet and Puritan educator and administrator. Author of "L'Allegro" and "Il Penseroso" (c. 1631), *Comus* (1634), *Lycidas* (1638), *The Doctrine and Discipline of Divorce, Areopagitica* (1644), *Paradise Lost* (1667; rev. 1674), and *Paradise Regained* and *Samson Agonistes* (both 1671). Milton was appointed Latin Secretary to Oliver Cromwell in 1649. In 1638, while on a tour of Italy, Milton visited **Galileo Galilei** during the time when he was under house arrest due to his astronomical views and observations on the universe conflicting with the doctrine of the Roman Catholic Church—an event later recorded in the *Areopagitica*. While at Christ's College, Cambridge, Milton criticized the Scholastic logic that dominated university curriculum at the time. In his last prolusion (1631–1632?) he claimed an affiliation with a Renaissance **humanism** that combined Christian ideas with Neoplatonism. In his later writings, he demonstrated an affinity with Baconian **empiricism**, though no recorded evidence exists that he read **Francis Bacon**. In his pamphlets *Of Education* and *Areopagitica*, Milton placed a notable emphasis on science. In the latter, he expressed his belief in the power of **truth** to win the day and to be sought through free inquiry and discussion, showing himself to be a scholar, philosopher, poet, and lover of books. As a supporter of the Arminian doctrine of salvation for all believers, Milton insisted upon humans' rational freedom and responsible power of choice. Following this doctrine, he espoused a materialistic and animist **natural philosophy** that linked him with the "vitalist" scientific movement of his day.

References

Fallon, Stephen M. *Milton among the Philosophers: Poetry and Materialism in Seventeenth-Century England*. Ithaca, NY: Cornell UP, 1991.

Rogers, John. *The Matter of Revolution: Science, Poetry, and Politics in the Age of Milton*. Ithaca, NY: Cornell UP, 1996.

Diana B. Altegoer

Mineralogy and Petrology. The sciences of minerals and rocks. As scientific disciplines, they developed slowly and did not clearly separate themselves from traditional predecessors before the middle of the seventeenth century. By the end of the eighteenth century, modern **chemistry** and the geological theories of **A.G. Werner** gave increasing prominence to both mineralogy and petrology as components of the earth sciences. The nineteenth century's emphasis on fossils and strata then diminished that prominence, which was partially reclaimed in the 1860s when a way was found to put thin sections of rock under the **microscope**. Too technical since then for general literary use, mineralogy and petrology are only occasionally reflected in later belletristic works. **Wordsworth** satirized Wernerian mineralogists in *The Excursion* (1814), but **Tennyson**, Auden, **Snyder**, and numerous moderns have all carefully distinguished one type of rock (and less often, mineral) from others. Gemstones had been so distinguished since the time of the Old Testament.

References

Adams, Frank Dawson. *The Birth and Development of the Geological Sciences*. 1938. New York: Dover, 1954.
Laudan, Rachel. *From Mineralogy to Geology: The Foundations of a Science, 1650–1830*. Chicago: U of Chicago P, 1987.

Dennis R. Dean

Mining and Metallurgy. The process of taking minerals from the earth and the science and **technology** of minerals. Both are relatively uncommon topics for early literature, except for the familiar use of gold, silver, bronze, and iron ages in classical and later verse. Prior to the eighteenth century, metals were usually discussed in alchemical terms, **Milton's** *Paradise Lost* being particularly rich in references. **Chaucer**, **Shakespeare**, **Spenser**, and Du Bartas all disparaged the mining of metals. During the conquest of the New World, however, the search for gold gave rise to a plethora of fantastic tales. El Dorado—the mythical City of Gold—was sought after by both Spanish and Portuguese conquistadores. Owing to the influential teaching of **Abraham Gottlob Werner** in the mining academy at Freiberg, the negative attitude toward mining changed notably among German writers around 1800—preeminently **Goethe** but also **Novalis**, Jean Paul, Tieck, **Hoffmann**, and others. The various gold rushes of the nineteenth century produced an abundant literature, with authors such as **Mark Twain** (*Roughing It*, 1872), Bret Harte, and **Robert Louis Stevenson** (*The Silverado Squatters*, 1883) producing the best-known examples. In **García Márquez's** *One Hundred Years of Solitude*, gold-making is linked to the circularity of **time**.

References

Duncan, Edgar H. "The Natural History of Metals and Minerals in the Universe of *Paradise Lost.*" *Osiris* 11 (1954): 386–421.

Durler, Josef. *Die Bedeutung des Berghaus bei Goethe und in der deutschen Romantik.* Frauenfeld: Huber, 1936.

Taylor, Georg C. "Milton on Mining." *MLN* 45 (1930): 24–27.

Dennis R. Dean and Shelly Jarrett Bromberg

Möbius Bodies. One-sided surfaces, developed by Augustus Möbius in the early nineteenth century. Visually striking in M.C. Escher's lithographs, these surfaces describe the narratives of some twentieth-century **fiction**, including the Korean Yu Miri's *Kazoku shinema*, Argentine **Jorge Luis Borges's** *Labyrinths*, and various works of the Irishman **James Joyce**, including *Ulysses*. The technique refers to problematics in the **time**-space continuum; the semiosis of the subject/object/interpretant within the narrative sign-system; and the inversion and impossible synthesis of third- and first-person perspectives—giving a telling twist to the character/narrator/author paradox.

Mary Libertin

Modernism. A style in all Western arts and sciences, arising just before the twentieth century and still characteristic of it, *pace* "Postmodernism." The word "Modernismus" first appeared in the Germanic languages c. 1880 to describe Naturalist theater, and "Modernismo" in Spanish referred to the loose prosody of American poets; but it was thereafter applied to (among others) the art styles of **Cubism**, Futurism, and Expressionism, the **physics** of **relativity** and quanta, the architecture of Otto Wagner and Louis Sullivan, the demolition of monistic idealism in **philosophy**, and the stream-of-consciousness **fiction** of Arthur Schnitzler and **James Joyce**. The Modernist common trait may be a bias in favor of **discontinuity**, linking neuron, gene, quantum, particle, and "bit" with the habit of analysis and a preference for juxtaposition over transition.

Reference

Everdell, William R. *The First Moderns: Profiles in the Origins of Twentieth-Century Thought, 1872–1913*. Chicago: U of Chicago P, 1997.

William R. Everdell

Molière (Jean-Baptiste Poquelin) (1622–1673). Great dramatist of seventeenth-century France. Although he wrote no treatises on science or **epistemology**, his comedies express many valuable intuitions on these topics. Drawing upon and surpassing the techniques of the traditional Italian farce, he relentlessly mocked pedantic verbalism, academic skepticism, fashionable intellectual posturing, and dogmatic pseudoscience. Molière sided with the moderns in the ongoing debate over the authority of the ancients, contending that contemporary findings could justifiably supplant received doctrine. The opposite thesis is defended in his plays by a gallery of venal and ridiculous doctors.

An oft-cited example comes at the end of *Le Malade imaginaire* (1673), where a medical student is applauded by his teachers when he purports to explain opium's soporific effect by saying that it has a *virtus dormativa* (Molière, II: 906). Béralde, the *raisonneur* or voice of reason in the same play, argues that since the workings of the human "machine" are still largely a mystery, the doctors' verbalisms, ceremonies, and crude techniques are both deceptive and dangerous. In a fine example of literary self-reference and circular argumentation, Béralde advises Argan to go and see one of Molière's comedies to see how ridiculous the doctors are.

Although Molière consistently contrasts reasonable and unreasonable characters, the words of reason—Béralde's speech being a perfect example—fail to bring about the resolutions of his comic plots. Often it is not the *raisonneur* but a crafty and deceptive maid (the *fantesca* of the *commedia dell'arte*) whose theatrics cure the ills of the household. While Béralde's reasonings simply anger Argan and cause him to become more entrenched in his error, Toinette's deceptive exaggeration of the doctors' abuses finally achieves the needed change of attitudes. Again and again in both the early farces and the mature **dramas**, it is clowning and not argument that corrects passionate errors and resolves the central conflict. And in some cases, only the physical blows of the *argumentum ad baculum* (the argument by the club) do the job, forcing the Pyrrhonist philosopher to admit that at least some sense impressions—such as his own sensations of pain—are perfectly reliable. An interesting counterexample, perhaps, is Elmire's defeat of Tartuffe. Elmire, it is true, fails to use words of reason to persuade her husband that Tartuffe is a dangerous imposter and must resort to deceptive trickery to make her point. But as Mette Hjort has argued, her method amounts to the staging of a "crucial strategic experiment" in which Orgon is presented with self-validating evidence of Tartuffe's vile intentions. As Béralde claims, "truth and experience" can at times prevail over dogma and passion.

References

Gossman, Lionel. *Men and Masks: A Study of Molière*. Baltimore: Johns Hopkins UP, 1969.
Hjort, Mette. *The Strategy of Letters*. Cambridge: Harvard UP, 1993. Ch. 4.
Millepierres, François. *La vie quotidienne des médecins au temps de Molière*. Paris: Hachette, 1964.
Molière. *Oeuvres complètes*. 2 vols. Ed. Maurice Rat. Paris: Gallimard, Bibliothèque de la Pléiade, 1956.

Paisley Livingston

Montaigne, Michel de (1533–1592). French nobleman, moralist, and skeptic. He is known as the first true essayist on the basis of his *Essais* (1580, 1595), in which his singular intellectual personality, his classical learning, his observations on history, country life, and travel, and his radical self-analysis all converge into a new literary form. Independently wealthy from the family vineyards outside of Bordeaux (whose citizenship elected him twice to mayor), Montaigne retreated from active life in his thirties to embrace the contemplative life.

Montaigne's writing emerges from his perceived dilemma of incongruence between individual experience of life and any intellectual construct, concept, idea, or **theory** of knowledge. As anthropological empiricist, Montaigne felt nevertheless ever ill at ease with the scientific bridge connecting experience with theory and system, so that he begins and ends with the individual phenomenon. Since knowledge lies at the border between the self and the world, the former was for Montaigne as vital a component in the process of cognition as the latter. Ultimately, the unifying theme of Montaigne's essays was always Montaigne himself ("c'est moi que je peins").

It is with Montaigne that for the first time the experience of the human condition becomes a dilemma in the modern sense. Montaigne talks of himself through the literature of the **essay**, and his essays are realized through his self-observation and self-analysis. As moralist and skeptic, but never cynic or polemicist, Montaigne is content to observe, describe, and comment. He wrote for various audiences: "thoughts addressed to myself" were clearly essays written for private contemplation; but he also wrote for a closed, intimate circle of learned acquaintances and for the nobility of leisure and for the developing, educated bourgeoisie.

Montaigne combined conversation and letter into an intimate tone far removed from the contemporary, humanistic **rhetoric**. Employing description, quotation, anecdote, and metaphor for a discourse of divergence, he eschewed the logic of syllogism and hierarchy. His sentences led away from conclusions and answers and toward conjecture, speculation, and questions.

Ralph W. Buechler

Moore, Marianne [Craig] (1887–1972). Twentieth-century American author of hybridized poems, composed of phrases cited from works ranging from zoology to advertisements—the "words cluster[ing]," as she put it, "like chromosomes." Having nearly majored in **biology** at Bryn Mawr, Moore regularly transcribed passages of **natural history** and biology into her journals. Lisa M. Steinman examines Moore's redefinition of twentieth-century science and **technology** in *Made in America* (1987), and Kadlec argues that her "adaptation of genetics to poetry" enabled her to "confront the essentialist logic of modern eugenics."

Reference

Kadlec, David. "Marianne Moore, Immigration and Eugenics." *Modernism/Modernity* 1.2 (Apr. 1994): 21–49.

Steven Meyer

Morris, William (1834–1896). English artist, poet, and novelist. Influenced by **John Ruskin**, Morris attacked machine-based industrial **culture** as impersonal, both in terms of its products and its treatment of labor. This found practical application in the Victorian Arts and Crafts movement, emphasizing handicraft particularly in the production of textiles. Morris's social vision is best expressed in *News from Nowhere* (1891), which depicts a socialist artisanal society peculiarly devoid of scientific pursuit despite reliance upon electrical power.

Reference

Thompson, E.P. *William Morris: Romantic to Revolutionary.* New York: Pantheon Books, 1955.

Alison E. Bright

Morrison, Toni (1931–   ). Novelist and literary critic. In *Beloved* (1987), the character Schoolteacher illustrates Morrison's critique of racially biased scientific practice. As an expression of a language structured by white privilege, Schoolteacher's science exercises the subjugation of African Americans, a defining concern of all of Morrison's work. Morrison's emphasis on freeing language from its "racially informed and determined chains" suggests that all science may be examined in light of the formative influence of racist concepts.

Reference

Morrison, Toni. *Playing in the Dark: Whiteness and the Literary Imagination.* New York: Vintage, 1993.

Elizabeth J. Donaldson

Muir, John (1838–1914). American naturalist who transformed a stifling religious upbringing into an almost saintly veneration for the beauty of nature. Muir is closely associated with Yosemite Valley in California, where he lived for a time, and with the High Sierras more generally. In direct contradiction to the state geologist J.D. Whitney, Muir advocated a glacial rather than a tectonic origin for Yosemite and other Sierran valleys resembling it. He was later able to visit still-living glaciers in Alaska, one of which is named for him. Muir's writings and advocacy of wilderness conservation deeply influenced such contemporaries as **Emerson** and Theodore Roosevelt (both of whom visited Yosemite with him), furthered a continuing tradition of **nature writing** in America, and were of major significance in winning popular support for the establishment of national parks.

References

Dean, Dennis R. "John Muir and the Origin of Yosemite Valley." *Annals of Science* 48(1991): 453–85.

Miller, Sally M., ed. *John Muir: Life and Work*. Albuquerque: U of New Mexico P, 1993.

Dennis R. Dean

Museums. In their earliest form, extensive collections and cabinets of curiosities owned by private collectors and early proponents of the New Science. These eventually became the centerpiece of early National Museums. The British Library and British Museum began with the collections of Sir Hans Sloane, president of the **Royal Society**, and from those origins to the present day, the museum operates as a liminal space where knowledge is institutionalized in the service of cultural formation.

References

Anderson, Benedict. *Imagined Communities*. London: Verso, 1991.
Findlen, Paula. *Possessing Nature: Museums, Collecting and Scientific Culture in Early Modern Italy*. Studies on the History of Society and Culture, No. 20. Berkeley: U California P, 1996.
Haraway, Donna. *Primate Visions: Gender, Race, and Nature in the World of Modern Science*. New York: Routledge, 1989.

Richard Nash

Music. The science and **art** of composing sounds and tones. Considered by the ancient Greeks to be the first science, due to the importance of its practitioners' skill in the observation and recognition of pattern. It is a convention of modernity to separate the arts of pattern from the sciences of pattern. Since the **Enlightenment**, science has depended upon reductionist strategies of analysis that, while very powerful, are antithetical to musical practice and to artistic practice in general. Whether recursive or iterative, music is concerned with its own extension and elaboration, and so not only resists reductionism but stands in opposition to it. This is as true of John Adams's minimalism as it is of Bach's recursive structures. It is possible, of course, to imagine conditions in which these oppositions do not prevail; in Western societies since the Scientific and **Industrial Revolutions**, however, music has tended to take an oppositional stance toward science, even while employing its techniques.

In the twentieth century, musical practice has been extended and modified by technological developments in **physics** and **computer science**. Futurist composer F.T. Marinetti (1876–1944) declared in 1909 that "a roaring motorcar . . . is more beautiful than the Victory of Samothrace" and composed music employing industrial sirens and other noisemakers. Karlheinz Stockhausen's (1928–) *Gesang der Junglinge* (1955) pioneered the use of programmed musical computers and tape recording to create sounds never heard in nature or produced by traditional instruments, including the human voice. The Moog synthesizer, invented by Robert Moog and first marketed in 1964, allowed musicians to dispense with elaborate programming techniques; the prototype for most contemporary electronic instruments, the Moog moved electronic music from the realm of premeditation to improvisation.

Joseph Duemer

Mythology (Greco-Roman). Stories and legends of the gods and heroes of Greek and Roman cultures. The earliest examples are often dated from the works of **Homer** and **Hesiod**, who set forth the lives and deeds of the gods in epic **poetry**. Here was a mythic realm inhabited by gods human in appearance who traversed the **landscapes** of Greece and other known areas of the ancient world. Attitudes toward nature and natural phenomena in mythology also were important. Because everything on the mythical plane was animate, from the land to the stars, myths were a means of exploring and explaining the natural world. From the thunderbolts of Zeus to the Promethean gift of fire, mythic tales were an early source of scientific inquiry and explanation. With the rise of the **pre-Socratic philosophers** (seventh century B.C.E.) the belief that the gods and their deeds were the primary cause of natural phenomena was called into question, prompting such thinkers as Heraclitus to doubt the veracity of myths found in works like the *Iliad*. With the rise of the Sophists (fifth century B.C.E.), mythology was divested of its authority as a source of natural law and became useful only as a didactic tool for teaching morals and values. The purpose of myth changed once more with the allegorists (second century B.C.E.) as these philosophers rationalized myth and used the gods and their deeds to explain the physical universe. Many of their early correlations between myth and science continued well into the modern age. Further allegorical use would be made of mythology in scientific writings in the twentieth century such as **Freud's** adoption of the Oedipal myth to explain the complex relationship between a mother and son.

Shelly Jarrett Bromberg

N

Nabokov, Vladimir (1899–1977). Novelist, poet, and translator who studied zoology (*see* Biology/Zoology) his first year at Cambridge in the late 1910s, published eighteen scientific papers on entomology, and used the money from his first literary publications for butterfly-hunting expeditions. *Pnin* (1957), a novel about an émigré professor of entomology, is based in part on his experiences while teaching Russian and European literature at Cornell University, Ithaca, New York. His novels, from *Pale Fire* (1962) to *Transparent Things* (1972), are self-reflexive metanarratives, full of irony, wit, and paradoxes about the seeming isomorphism between inner and outer events.

Mary Libertin

Narrative Ethics. A methodological approach to ethics based on understanding personal identity as a narrative construct. Narrative ethics grounds moral evaluation and decision not so much in principles and rules as in an understanding of the "narrative coherence" of a particular patient's life as that life has been shaped over time, privileging the particular over the universal and recognizing the importance of personal, historical, and cultural context. Using this approach, the ethicist takes on skills of the good reader: He or she recognizes metaphorical systems, is able to adopt different points of view and thus allow for contradictory meanings of a story, and—perhaps most important—understands the limitations of interpretation, recognizing the extent to which any interpretation is affected by the reader's own values and assumptions.

References

Chambers, Tod S. "The Bioethicist as Author: The Medical Ethics Case as Rhetorical Device." *Literature and Medicine* 13.1 (1994): 60–78.
Charon, Rita. "Narrative Contributions to Medical Ethics." *A Matter of Principles? Fer-*

ment in U.S. Bioethics. Ed. E.R. Dubose et al. Valley Forge, PA: Trinity Press
International, 1994. 260–83.
Nelson, Hilde Lindemann, ed. *Stories and Their Limits: Narrative Approaches to Bio-
ethics.* New York: Routledge, 1997.

Anne Hunsaker Hawkins

Narrative Knowledge. The mode through which particular events are con-
figured into a meaningful story. Jerome Bruner compares narrative knowledge
to logicoscientific knowledge, which, in contrast, achieves understanding
through general categories or abstract conceptualizations. In **medicine**, **physicians** rely on both kinds of knowing in order to make sense of clinical information. Logicoscientific knowledge encodes events and facts as examples of
some general paradigm; narrative knowledge, on the other hand, involves the
selection and temporal ordering of facts and events, the imposition of causal
connections between them, and the construction of some overall unifying meaning. The physician's understanding of the story a patient tells is itself an interpretative retelling of that story. The narrative contract between writer and reader
can serve as a metaphor for what goes on between patient and doctor in the
production of meaning: Central to both are the act of writing (or telling) with
its implied author, the narrative frame, temporality and sequence, and the
reader's (or listener's) response, with its implied reader.

References

Bruner, Jerome. *Actual Minds, Possible Worlds.* Cambridge: Harvard UP, 1986. 11–43.
Charon, Rita. "Medical Interpretation: Implications of Literary Theory of Narrative for
    Clinical Work." *Journal of Narrative and Life History* 3.1 (1993): 79–97.
Hunter, Kathryn Montgomery. *Doctors' Stories: The Narrative Structure of Medical
    Knowledge.* Princeton, NJ: Princeton UP, 1991.

Anne Hunsaker Hawkins

Natural Classicism. An aesthetic **theory**, based on the evolution of the
physical universe, intended to supplant late modernist and poststructuralist aesthetics. It contains two main lines of argument. The first attributes aesthetic
behavior among animals and among humans in all cultures to the practice of
ritual and to the reproductive success of individuals adept at ritual practice and
thus the spread of genes suited to the intricate behaviors and sensitivities required by ritual. Ritualization drove genetic change, and genetic change drove
further elaborations of ritual, in a nonlinear feedback process. Gene-ritual coevolution generated new values, such as the loyalty of goose pair-bonding, and
new aesthetic forms, such as the mating songs of humpback whales and the
elaborate constructions of bowerbirds. Humans in this view are the most highly
ritualized of all animals and unique in that ritual is at least as much a learned
behavior as an inherited one. Nevertheless, certain genres, forms, and techniques
(dubbed "neurocharms" by Frederick Turner) underlie the artistic practices and

aesthetics of all human cultures, including storytelling, melodic structure, poetic meter, dramatic pretense, and visual **representation**. **Art** and literature depart from these inherited abilities at their own risk; poetic meter, for instance, is not an arbitrary European invention but a culturally universal psychic **technology** based on the three-second periodic cycle of the poetic line, whose measurable effects include the activation of the brain's neurochemical reward system, the integration of left and right brain modes, and the attunement of neural with somatic arousal.

The second proposition of natural classicism is that since the experience of beauty and the possession of neural mechanisms for recognizing it are so universal, found not only in all human cultures but also among animals, it is likely that the experience must have a real object. In a world where many species possessed eyes, it would be implausible to doubt the objective existence of light and of visual phenomena. Thus beauty is an objective characteristic of the universe. Aesthetic pleasure seems to be associated with the following properties: (1) unity in multiplicity; (2) complexity within simplicity; (3) generativeness and creativity; (4) rhythmicity; (5) hierarchical organization; (6) self-similarity. These properties would be immediately recognized by scientists in many fields as belonging to feedback processes and the structures that are generated by them. What we recognize as beautiful, both in nature and in art, seems to be reflexivity or feedback and the structures that are its result. As with any turbulent dynamic nonlinear open feedback process, the universe continually generates new frames and dimensions, new rules and constraints, and its future states are too complicated to be calculated by any conceivable **computer** made out of the universe as it is. The process of emergence is what we see as beautiful. Evolution itself is a prime example of a generative feedback process. Variation, selection, and heredity constitute a cycle, which when iterated over and over again produces out of this very simple algorithm the most extraordinarily complex and beautiful life forms. Variation is the novelty generator; selection is a set of alterable survival rules to choose out certain products of the novelty generator; and heredity, the conservative ratchet, preserves what is gained. All such processes produce patterns with the characteristics of branchiness, hierarchy, self-similarity, generativeness, unpredictability, and self-inclusiveness. Art, in this view, is a continuation at a higher level of reflexiveness of the generative process of nature.

References

Dissanayake, Ellen. *Homo Aestheticus: Where Art Comes From and Why.* New York: Free Press, 1992.

Rentschler, Ingo, David Epstein, and Barbara Herzberger, eds. *Beauty and the Brain: Biological Aspects of Aesthetics.* Basel: Birkhauser, 1988.

Turner, Frederick. *Natural Classicism.* Charlottesville: UP of Virginia, 1991.

Frederick Turner

Natural History. Accounts and artifacts that record or depict human understanding of the development of nature over time. Natural history has been
closely associated with literature from earliest times. Indeed, even before the
invention of written language, Paleolithic artists were depicting animals in paintings and sculptures; Neanderthals decorated their burials with flowers; and seasonal variations governing the appearances of both animals and plants were
surely known. Certain artifacts have been interpreted as attempts to record the
lateral movement of the sun throughout the year. An oral culture rich in natural
history must therefore have existed.

Both Egyptians and Mesopotamians, in their early civilizations, made frequent
use of natural history. In each case we have extensive artistic legacies, often
devoted (as in the Paleolithic) to the theme of hunting. The zoomorphic deities
of Egypt also come easily to mind. But the most frequently depicted animals
were domesticated ones, particularly cattle. In the written documents and literatures of both river civilizations, animals figure primarily as commodities,
though Egypt has also given us an informal legacy of anthropomorphic caricature. Numerous hieroglyphics and symbols derived from insects (the scarab
beetle), fish, beasts, and plants. Several animals, late in the tradition, were regarded as sacred and therefore mummified, including cats, falcons, bulls, ba-
boons, and the ibis. Unwrapped in the early nineteenth century, they would
convince Cuvier and other naturalists that species did not change.

With the spread of **agriculture** and the consequent destruction of habitats,
lions, giraffes, rhinos, hippos, and elephants tended to drop out of both literature
and **art** as animals actually observed. Only one lion, for example, appears in
the Old Testament, and Samson killed it easily in a vineyard. Soon afterward,
he tied torches to the tails of foxes and drove them into a wheat field, setting
it ablaze. The lion, bees, and foxes of the Samson story (in Judges) are clearly
interlopers, their former wilderness having disappeared.

Complementing this literary emphasis on agriculture, the New Testament in
particular is rich in the imagery of pastoralism, the shepherd and his flock.
Together with such classical examples as Theocritus, Bion, Moschus, and **Vergil**, the pastoral tradition and its imagery survived well into modern times, particularly as an elegiac convention (**Spenser**, **Milton**, **Shelley**, and **Arnold**).
Pastoralism was also a fundamental component in the rise of **landscape** art and
therefore of landscape **poetry**.

Despite its pervasive influence, pastoralism was not fundamentally analytical
and so had limited value as a model for the inclusion of natural history in
literature. The Book of Genesis, contrarily, was unequaled as a stimulus. It
began, after all, with a majestic narrative (two separate ones, as we have since
discovered) of the Creation of nature, including light, earth, water, air, and all
creatures that inhabit them. Paradise, as depicted in Genesis, is one of the fundamental metaphors of Western thought, the asserted proprietorship of man over
animals being another. In both literature and art, we find Adam surrounded by
tame yet toothsome carnivores (at a time when death did not exist) that it was

his prerogative to name—yet a third fundamental metaphor. Finally, there was the Fall, by which the supposed hostility of nature to man was rationalized. These short passages in Genesis strongly influenced European thinking about nature for upward of 1,500 years. They influence us still.

The Bible is of such fundamental importance to the use of natural history in literature that much more could be written about it. Among further stories of great influence are those of the Flood of Noah (geological theories), the dispersal of Noah's sons (origin of **races**), the Tower of Babel (origin of languages), and the destruction of Jericho (**astronomy**, geology). The Ten Lost Tribes of Israel were sometimes cited to explain the peopling of the New World; Leviathan, to explain fossil bones.

Whether science and literature are compatible or antagonistic is partly a matter of definition and partly of theoretical commitment, but poets throughout the history of Western civilization have seldom hesitated to versify the natural history of their times. Some philosophers have even considered poetry ideally suited to scientific discourse. In classical Greece, for example, such early rationalists as **Hesiod**, Xenophane, Empedocles, and Parmenides all expounded their theories of nature in verse—most of which, unfortunately, have been lost. **Aristotle**, of course, was the first great naturalist (marine **biology**, many theories) followed by his nephew Theophrastus (**botany**, petrology). Any poems written by them have been lost. In prose, Posidonius, Strabo, and Ptolemy were all important geographers, with Ptolemy outstandingly influential for his long-accepted geocentric astronomy.

Among the poets of ancient Rome, **Vergil** (in the *Georgics*) begged the muse to show him nature's secrets; his sixth *Eclogue* celebrates the creation of the world; his *Aeneid* calls attention to the volcanic landscapes of southern Italy. **Ovid** versified a remarkable geological treatise in the fifteenth book of his *Metamorphoses*. An unfinished poem of his on fishing describes various species and their food chains. Grattius (on hunting, dogs, and horses), Manilius (on astronomy), **Aratus** (on weather and astronomy), Nicander (on bees, influencing Vergil), and under Caracalla, two poets named Oppian (on fishing and hunting) devoted whole or significant parts of their poetic works to natural history, as Xenophon, **Pliny the Elder**, Seneca, and Plutarch (*On the Intelligence of Animals*) did in prose.

The greatest and most influential scientific poet of classical times, combining Greek and Roman sources, was **Lucretius** (first century B.C.E.), the author of *De rerum natura* (On the Nature of Things), an incomplete long poem in six books that attempted to free mankind from the fears and superstition of **religion** by proving that worldly vicissitudes are wholly material in origin. Books I and II assert an atomistic theory of matter; III and IV deal with the nature of mind and soul (both wholly material); IV with sensation and emotion. The most important natural history, in books V and VI, describes the world, its creation and astronomical situation, and the beginnings of vegetable, animal, and human life, including primitive man and the evolution of human **culture**. Other topics include storms, waterspouts, earthquakes, and volcanoes. Lucretius strongly influenced Vergil and survived the hostility of the Middle Ages to achieve his greatest success as a model of scientific poetry in the eighteenth and nineteenth centuries, when he was both translated and imitated. There is a fine verse tribute to him by **Tennyson**.

After the fall of Rome, in northern Europe especially, much of this classical legacy was lost. The earliest nature poems in English literature, therefore, present a world totally different from that of Lucretius. But the remarkably vigorous natural descriptions of *Beowulf* and "The Seafarer" did not become standard. For more obviously Christian writers of the Middle Ages, the material world was important not primarily for itself but for the spiritual truths that it embodied as a manifestation of God. Some of their earliest poems, such as the Angle-Saxon "Wyrta" (perhaps c. 1000), are half medical and half magical, listing in this case plants believed efficacious against poison, infirmities, and demons. The bestiary tradition, derived from allegorical reinterpretation of the Roman author Pliny's fanciful assertions about animals, often influenced literature. In the twelfth century, when Anglo-Norman had become the literary language of England, Philippe de Thaon versified the signs of the zodiac, the allegorical significance of each zodiacal animal, and the astronomical origin of the calendar. Another poem of his explained the lion, crocodile, elephant, sea-serpent, and siren, among other creatures, all of which existed for him as reminders of spiritual truths and had not been seen in life.

Also of literary importance during the Middle Ages (and beyond) was the Hexameral tradition of Basil, Ambrose, and others, in which all the phenomena of nature were classified according to their day of creation in Genesis. Massive prose encyclopedias (like that of Bartholomaeus Anglicus, c. 1240) facilitated such compilers. In England, the northern dialect poem *Cursor Mundi* (World Survey c. 1300, 24,000 lines) divided the history of God's work into seven ages, beginning with the Creation and ending with the Last Judgment. The Hexameral tradition continued to be viable as late as the seventeenth century, when Du Bartas and Milton, together with prose writers like John Swan, adapted its conventions to the learning of their time.

Two outstanding medieval poets utilized natural history in very different ways. **Dante Alighieri's** *Divine Comedy* (c. 1320) includes a sustained vision of the geocentric **cosmos** and its nested spheres. Like other authors of his time, however, Dante was seldom concerned with the literal **truth** of his science; the interpretation of nature-in-actuality formed no part of his intentions. **Geoffrey Chaucer**, on the other hand, wrote a treatise on the astrolabe. His *Canterbury Tales* (1387–1400) begins with a passage of natural description and alludes frequently to current learning regarding earthly and celestial phenomena. Neither poet was particularly observant regarding plants, or animals other than birds, though Chaucer's Chauntecleer affirms traditional clichés about the rooster.

From the fourteenth century to the beginning of the seventeenth, European writers generally endorsed a fairly predictable body of assumptions about nature, including belief in the historicity of Genesis, a round earth central to concentric planetary spheres, a further sphere of equidistant stars, astrological influences (which inclined but did not compel), alchemical transformations, four elements, and four humors in man, who was a microcosm of the cosmos as a whole. Throughout these same years, however, all of these assumptions were challenged in various ways and would eventually collapse. Meanwhile, attention to real plants, animals, and natural phenomena of all kinds was growing.

Because of the fame and bulk of his life's work, the plays and poems of **Shakespeare** have long ago been searched for all the birds, beasts, bugs, and whatever other allusions to nature they were held to contain. Except for *King Lear* (1605–1606), landscape description is noticeably sparse; Plinean natural history and astrology are generally rejected; but his universe is complacently geocentric, not Copernican. **Marlowe's** *Dr. Faustus* had earlier dramatized the religious problems created by the new knowledge, in astronomy especially; **Ben Jonson's** *The Alchemist* (1610) is more about greed than science. John Webster's *Duchess of Malfi* (1613–1614) borrows from both Pliny and Ovid but also alludes specifically (in II: iv) to "Galileo, the Florentine" and his **telescope**, which was destined to explode the bounded medieval cosmos.

Thoughtful contemplations of nature and its mutability were common at the end of the sixteenth century, which had seen the worst of the Reformation. Among poetic ones are the "Mutability" cantos of **Spenser's** *Faerie Queene* (1590–1596); the sonnets of Shakespeare and others; two long poems by Sir John Davies, *Orchestra* (1596, alluding to **Copernicus**), and *Nosce Teipsum* (1599); and John Norden, *Vicissitudo Rerum* (On the Changes of Things, 1600), "an Elegiacall Poem, of the interchangeable courses and varieties of things in this world." Much of this literary mutability was inspired by the *Metamorphoses* of Ovid, whose works were translated frequently throughout the later sixteenth century, most notably by Arthur Golding (1565, 1567). The political situation accounted for some of the literary popularity of mutability, as did the bothersome earthquake of 1580.

By the final years of the sixteenth century, natural changes of every kind were apparent to Elizabethan writers, even in the supposedly immutable realm of the fixed stars. In 1572, a new star (supernova) appeared in Cassiopeia and continued to shine brightly for two years. An exceptionally bright comet in 1577 and—incredibly enough—a further supernova in 1604 convinced many Europeans that a fundamental reassessment of their traditional cosmology was required. Astrologers were full of dire predictions, but three great astronomers (**Tycho Brahe**, **Johannes Kepler**, and **Galileo Galilei**) instead helped to create a new, and ultimately less theological, cosmos. Poets, too, heeded the astronomers and their theories.

The new cosmos affected almost every major English poet (and an American one) throughout the seventeenth century, including George Chapman, George Herbert, Edward Taylor, Henry Vaughan, Thomas Traherne, Andrew Marvell, and **John Milton**, but none other expressed their intellectual dilemma so memorably as did **John Donne** ("First Anniversary," 1610), who also cited Copernicus, Kepler, Galileo, and William Gilbert in a satire against the Jesuits (*Ignatius His Conclave*, 1611). Besides the decay of the world, as emphasized by Donne, other astronomical themes appearing in seventeenth-century poetry include the motion of the earth, the immensity of the universe, the telescope and its revelations, the habitability of other worlds, and the possibility of **space travel**. Skepticism regarding traditional knowledge was widespread, but literary works affirming the old world view continued to appear throughout the century, with Du Bartas and Milton creating great poems on its behalf. In Book VIII of Milton's *Paradise Lost* (1667; 1674), Adam discusses the competing geocentric and heliocentric astronomical systems with archangel Raphael and is told to regard the matter with indifference. Within a few years, however, Newton's (*see* Newtonianism) *Principia* (1687) would establish the truth of heliocentricity, thereby discrediting the authority of Aristotle and Ptolemy, who had maintained the contrary for 2,000 years.

Though Newton would dominate public apprehension of science well into the eighteenth century, the more humble study and appreciation of nature advanced steadily throughout the seventeenth. God's Creation seemed a much less controversial revelation of Himself than the thorny problems associated with biblical exegesis, with which Jesuit controversialists and outright skeptics were having a field day. "Thus are there two books from whence I collect my divinity," wrote **Sir Thomas Browne** in 1635; "besides that written one of God, another of his servant nature, that universal and public manuscript that lies expansed unto the eyes of all." And a little later on: "nature is the art of God." In a further work, familiarly called *Vulgar Errors*, Browne endeavored to expose the inadequacy of that too-often-fanciful natural history solemnly asserted by credulous classical writers. Both the telescope and the **microscope**, moreover, were revealing worlds of which the ancients had known nothing.

By 1700 or so, skepticism and **empiricism** replaced faith as the basis of natural history. A most important stimulus to this fundamental transition was the immense expansion of the known world brought about by the explorers. As intrepid (if greedy) mariners like Vasco Da Gama and Columbus found previously unsuspected lands, the geographical adequacy of received authorities like the Bible and classical writers naturally became suspect. Knowledge, it now seemed, lay not with the past but with the future. The improvement of maps and charts was only the most obvious of many examples.

Though the explorers were motivated by other reasons as well, theirs was primarily an economic enterprise. They reported at length the existence of previously unknown plants, animals, and peoples, often bringing examples of each back to Europe. As a result, traditional maps had to be redrawn, so as to account for new continents, new climates, new flora and fauna, new peoples, new languages, new cultures, and new products. All of this new information needed to be assimilated, not only in natural history but also in theology. European assumptions regarding the Creation, regarding the ordinary and logical, were shattered. As with astronomy for a time, no one knew what to believe, but there was a sustained effort (lasting into the nineteenth century) on the part of some of the best minds, like **John Ray**, to interpret facts of nature as evidence of divine wisdom and goodness.

Throughout the seventeenth century and onwards, accounts of voyages and travels were regarded as uniquely valuable sources of knowledge. They appeared in great numbers, relaying information of varying quality about such far-flung places as China, India, Egypt, black **Africa**, and the Americas. Rather than indulging themselves with philosophical reflections or displays of classical learning, travelers were urged to ascertain and record factual information of all kinds, much of it natural history. A foremost stimulus to this enterprise was the **Royal Society** of London (1662), which specifically instructed would-be authors as to what was needed. It was the Society's intention, according to its "Directions for Seamen, bound for far voyages," to "study nature rather than books, and from the observations made of the phenomena and effects she presents to compose such a history of her as may hereafter serve to build a solid and useful philosophy upon." The Society's *Philosophical Transactions* (begun 1665, two years before Milton's *Paradise Lost*) readily published communications from within Britain and abroad relative to natural history.

The advocacy of the Royal Society on behalf of **truth** to nature (as expressed by **Thomas Sprat** in his 1667 *History of the Royal Society*, for instance) had an immense literary impact extending well into the nineteenth century as Shakespeare, Milton, and other prescientific writers were criticized by later ones for their ignorance of natural history. Throughout the eighteenth century, major poets such as **James Thomson** and others, all writing in imitation of Lucretius (whose *De Rerum Natura* was now accorded high prestige), attempted to versify the science of their time, which was frequently Newtonian but encompassed the whole of nature. Anxious to prove that their occasionally abstruse information was responsible and up-to-date, poets sometimes resorted to footnotes.

This neoclassical revival of Lucretius, a major literary phenomenon in both Germany and England, culminated in the verses of **Erasmus Darwin** (1731–1802). Utilizing the Linnaean system of botanical **classification** (which did much to sort out a Magee's closet of finds and greatly popularized the collection of plants), Darwin ingeniously created a two-part poem called *The Botanic Garden* (1789–1791). Scientific in and of itself, Darwin's poem included not only prodigious scientific footnotes but essay-length scientific backnotes as well; it was embellished with attractive hand-colored plates, some of them (not scientific) by **William Blake**. Having by no means restricted himself to botany, Darwin created what was virtually an encyclopedia of contemporary science. His information (and often his verse) influenced all of the major Romantic poets, including Blake, **Wordsworth**, **Coleridge**, Robert Southey, **Byron**, **Shelley**, and **Yeats**. Only John Clare continued to write of nature in the old way.

Much of the information about nature that we find in the Romantic poets derived from the kind of close personal observation advocated by the Royal

Society. Much of the rest came from travel books, which all of them read assiduously; as a group, they traveled more widely than had any previous generation of writers. More so than Wordsworth and his contemporaries, for whom nature generally meant birds and flowers, Byron and Shelley were strongly influenced by the rising popularity of geology, which had begun to dominate conceptions of nature by about 1815.

By 1816, a year famous for its unusual weather, and certainly by 1820, the previously benign view of nature advocated so memorably by Wordsworth and Coleridge was being repudiated by more naturalistic thinkers. "Nature," wrote the geologist **Charles Lyell** in 1827, "is not repose, but war. It is not rest, but change. It is not preservation, but successive production and annihilation." **Keats** had had a similar vision earlier, prompting his poem to Reynolds, and **Tennyson** would have another later on, with his "Nature, red in tooth and claw." No longer a fit guide for human conduct, Nature and man, **Arnold** would eventually declare, "can never be fast friends." This more realistic view of animals, prompted in part by the futility of the Napoleonic wars, enhanced public acceptance of the extinction of species throughout time, an idea seldom endorsed before about 1800, and multiplied the repugnance of any suggestion that man may be an animal himself. Naturalists now were professional investigators—no longer genially puttering clergymen like **Gilbert White** but genuine scientists (the word having originated c. 1840). The growth of knowledge and the importance of scientific controversies about nature tended to make amateurish observations less acceptable, particularly when clerical bias was suspected. The Bible had lost the whole of its once-great authority as a textbook of natural history. Travel books therefore became more specialized and their authors more professional, often concentrating on a single natural science, like geology. Reviewers of them, sometimes specialists themselves, called attention to assertions having theoretical import and thereby instructed the public regarding controversies of note. They responded savagely to incompetence, however well intentioned.

Though some Romantics declared themselves hostile to the **Enlightenment** and its rationalism, few writers of their time escaped the influence of science. Among those who shared its interests, and sometimes participated in its controversies, was Coleridge, whose liberal reading of the Bible found ample room for modern natural history. In France, the prolific and more secular **Stendhal** fought a running battle with the lingering influence of **Buffon**. Among the sciences appearing in his novels are astronomy, **meteorology**, **chemistry**, **mineralogy**, geology, botany, and zoology. Even better known as an imaginative writer utilizing science was **Goethe**, a contributor to several sciences himself. **Optics**, chemistry, meteorology, anatomy, morphology, botany, geology, and mineralogy were among his subjects. Inspired by Lucretius, Goethe (like Coleridge) once planned to write a comprehensive epic poem that would synthesize his view of nature but never did.

Of all the nineteenth-century poets and novelists whose views of nature are scientific in part, none was eventually so reputable for the modernity of his knowledge as Tennyson. Apart from the quality of his poems, Tennyson was remarkable for his lifelong devotion to natural history, which for him included astronomy, botany, and geology primarily. He made lesser use of many other sciences in passing and was particularly concerned with theories of evolution—the origin and fate of the cosmos, but especially man. For Tennyson, as for many other Victorians, the prognosis from science was grim. Accordingly, he once referred to astronomy and geology, normally his favorite sciences, as "Terrible Muses!"

That nature is governed by **time** was an idea of fundamental importance to the nineteenth century, which had received a legacy of **evolutionary theories** from the eighteenth. Buffon, Laplace, Monboddo, and Erasmus Darwin soon found their echoes in the later theories of Lamarck, Lyell, **Chambers**, Wallace, and **Darwin**, to name only the most prominent. All of them had literary influence, but Darwin (despite a revival of Lamarck that attracted several writers) had more of it than all the others put together. Relatively soon after the appearance of Darwin's *Origin of Species* in November 1859, the struggle for existence that had been apparent to the thoughtful a generation earlier became the received conception of the natural world. As such, it could be found endorsed, regretted, illustrated, or denied in vast bodies of late-nineteenth- and twentieth-century literature. **Tennyson, Browning, Swinburne, Meredith, Hardy, Wells**, Crane, Bierce, and **London** are especially known for their reactions to Darwin, but almost everyone else who has written on nature since 1859 has also taken his prominence for granted.

Despite such later, more humanistic studies such as ecology, and value-based advocacy of one sort or another (e.g., eugenics), there is still pervasive agreement that Darwin's description of the way nature works is basically correct. Much of the popularity of science fiction since 1859 has derived from its implicit (and perhaps naive) reassurance that human **technology** can save us from the consequences of evolutionary mortality.

References

Alcorn, John. *The Nature Novel from Hardy to Lawrence.* New York: Columbia UP, 1977.

Allen, Don Cameron. *The Legend of Noah: Renaissance Rationalism in Art, Science, and Letters.* 1949. Urbana: U of Illinois P, 1963.

Arthos, John. *The Language of Natural Description in Eighteenth-Century Poetry.* 1949. New York: Octagon, 1966.

Dean, Dennis E. "The Influence of Geology on American Literature and Thought." *Two Hundred Years of Geology in America.* Ed. Cecil J. Schneer. Hanover, NH: UP of New England, 1979. 289–303.

Economou, George D. *The Goddess Natura in Medieval Literature.* Cambridge: Harvard UP, 1972.

Fleischmann, Wolfgang B. *Lucretius and English Literature 1680–1740.* Paris: Nizet, 1964.

Henkin, Leo J. *Darwinism in the English Novel, 1860–1910: The Impact of Evolution on Victorian Fiction.* 1940. New York: Russell, 1963.

Jordanova, Ludmilla, ed. *Languages of Nature: Critical Essays on Science and Literature.* London: Free Association Books, 1986.

Paradis, James, and Thomas Postlewait, eds. *Victorian Science and Victorian Values: Literary Perspectives.* 1981. New Brunswick, NJ: Rutgers UP, 1985.

Piper, Herbert W. *The Active Universe: Pantheism and the Concept of Imagination in the English Romantic Poets.* London: Athlone, 1962.

                                                                Dennis R. Dean

Naturalism. A late-nineteenth-century outgrowth of **realism** in **art** and literature that features a harsh, fatalistic worldview. Notable for a rigorous **determinism**, naturalism has lent itself easily to the expression of social causes because the typical narrative depicts outmatched individuals fighting against an oppressive order—hereditary, social, economic—of some kind. The naturalistic enterprise is traceable to nineteenth-century evolutionary thinking—principally the science of **Darwin** and the **philosophy** of **Spencer**. French novelist **Émile Zola** used the term to describe his **fiction** where, in Spencer's words, "events are the proper products of the characters living under given conditions." Zola influenced many fin-de-siècle American writers, including **Dreiser**, **Norris**, **London**, and **Wharton**.

References

Howard, June. *Form and History in American Literary Naturalism.* Chapel Hill: U of North Carolina P, 1985.

Michaels, Walter Benn. *Naturalism and the Gold Standard.* Berkeley: U of California P, 1987.

Pizer, Donald. *Realism and Naturalism in Late Nineteenth-Century American Literature.* Rev. ed. Carbondale: U of Southern Illinois P, 1984.

                                                                Leonard Cassuto

Natural Philosophy. The variety of mathematical and experimental practices in medieval and early modern Europe that since the nineteenth century has been termed "science." Before 1800, "science" generally denotes a specific skill, craft, or body of knowledge; "natural philosophy" is the general term used to describe humankind's knowledge of the natural world. Encompassing what we would now call **biology**, zoology, **astronomy**, **medicine**, geology, **physics**, and **chemistry**, natural philosophy predates the advent of disciplinary knowledge— the post-Kantian belief that science and the humanities are opposed ways of investigating, representing, and understanding the world. These strategies of scientific investigation, almost without exception, are described as divinely inspired and in England are identified with the institutional authority of the **Royal Society** (founded 1662) and the work of Isaac Newton (*see* Newtonianism), **Robert Boyle**, and **John Ray**, among others.

Natural philosophy is premised on the metaphor of the two books, the perceived correspondence between the book of Nature and the Bible. The coherence of natural philosophy as a process of inquiry and a body of knowledge is guaranteed not by an internal logic or a distinct method but by an overriding **analogy** to the Bible: The world is ordered because it manifests divine wisdom. Precisely because humankind's knowledge of the universe is theocentric, the options for investigating how it works become different paths to contemplating and comprehending, as far as human nature allows, the beauties of God's creation. Paradoxically, the efforts of Newtonians in the eighteenth century to abstract mathematics as a self-sufficient system that reflects the harmony of a theocentric creation begins to dissociate the study of the natural world from theology. The principles of order that natural philosophy attributes to divine wisdom do not disappear but are displaced into the internal logic of increasingly sophisticated scientific practices. By the early nineteenth century, natural philosophy gives way to modern usages—and conceptions—of science.

References

Bono, James. *The Word of God and the Languages of Man: Interpreting Nature in Early Modern Science and Medicine.* Madison: U of Wisconsin P, 1995.

Hunter, Michael. *Science and Society in Restoration England.* Cambridge: Cambridge UP, 1981.

Jacob, Margaret. *The Cultural Meaning of the Scientific Revolution.* New York: Knopf, 1988.

Markley, Robert. *Fallen Languages: Crises of Representation in Newtonian England, 1660–1740.* Ithaca, NY: Cornell UP, 1993.

Shapin, Steven. *A Social History of Truth: Civility and Science in Seventeenth-Century England.* Chicago: U of Chicago P, 1994.

Shapin, Steven, and Simon Schaffer. *Leviathan and the Air-Pump: Hobbes, Boyle, and the Experimental Life.* Princeton, NJ: Princeton UP, 1985.

Robert Markley

Natural Theology. Religious studies in which knowledge of God is arrived at through the use of reason. In its broadest sense, natural theology includes: (1) the ancient **argument from design**, with its teleological and empirical proof for the existence of God founded upon the order and purposiveness legible in nature; (2) the derivation of religious knowledge from common notions (that is, from beliefs held "universally"); and (3) the cosmological argument (God is the First Cause of all effects). Of these the first (also known as **physicotheology**) is most important. In its heyday in the seventeenth and eighteenth centuries (when its most influential proponents were **John Ray** and **William Derham**) this rational *a posteriori* theology, with its vision of a stable law-governed universe (and a **rhetoric** and method discourse it shared with contemporary science), played an important social role in promoting and legitimizing scientific inquiry (through its sanctioning of the pursuit of **natural philosophy** as a religious duty); defending Christianity; and "confirming" divine design in both social and political structures.

Natural theology was widely popularized in lengthy scientific poems (such as **James Thomson's** *Seasons*, 1730–1746), sermons, and periodical **essays**; this central cultural discourse—"the lay model for understanding the natural and human world before Darwinism" (Levine 16)—shared the conventions of eighteenth-century narrative including "its teleological unfolding; its providential use of coincidence; its implicit faith in the ultimate coherence, rationality, and intelligibility of the world being described; its movement to closure" (Levine 25). Despite the critiques of David Hume and Immanuel Kant, this resilient and adaptable theology retained its popularity well into the nineteenth century—in William Paley's hugely popular *Natural Theology* (1802) and the Bridgewater treatises of the 1830s—until it was undermined by Darwin's theory of evolution (*see* Evolutionary Theory). Recently natural theology has reemerged in reformulated teleological and cosmological arguments.

References

Barbour, Ian G. *Issues in Science and Religion*. Englewood Cliffs, NJ: Prentice-Hall, 1966.
Brooke, John Hedley. *Science and Religion: Some Historical Perspectives*. Cambridge: Cambridge UP, 1991.
Jaki, Stanley L. *The Road of Science and the Ways to God*. Chicago: U of Chicago P, 1978.
Levine, George. *Darwin and the Novelists: Patterns of Science in Victorian Fiction*. Cambridge: Harvard UP, 1988.
Paley, William. *Natural Theology; or, Evidences of the Existence and Attributes of the Deity, Collected from the Appearances of Nature*. London: R. Faulder, 1802.

Lisa Zeitz

Nature Writing. Embraces a range of subgenres that includes travel narratives as well as literary almanacs and **poetry** as well as prose, but readers generally identify the phrase with the "nature essay." The most celebrated example is **Henry David Thoreau's** *Walden* (1854). Literary historian and nature essayist **Joseph Wood Krutch** writes that nature **essays** combine "scientific knowledge with both philosophical interest and an emotionally charged attitudes toward nature" based in a "sense of oneness" with our "fellow creatures" (6). They bring into alliance close observation of external nature with intense subjective experience, often leading to epistemological and metaphysical speculation. They link the ordinary with the sacred and the natural with the social. The earliest examples predate Thoreau, notably **Gilbert White's** *The Natural History and Antiquities of Selbourne* (1789). The best-known American practitioners include **John Muir**, John Burroughs, **Aldo Leopold**, **Loren Eiseley**, and **Rachel Carson** as well as contemporaries **Edward Abbey**, **Annie Dillard**, John Hay, **Barry Lopez**, Gary Nabhan, and Ann Zwinger. Adding the authority of modern ecological science to nineteenth-century Romantic ideas, nature essayists collectively offer a vision that runs counter to the alienation of most contemporary literature.

References

Buell, Lawrence. *The Environmental Imagination: Thoreau, Nature Writing, and the Formation of American Culture.* Cambridge: Harvard UP, 1995.

Finch, Robert, and John Elder, eds. *The Norton Book of Nature Writing.* New York: W.W. Norton, 1990.

Fritzell, Peter A. *Nature Writing and America: Essays upon a Cultural Type.* Ames: Iowa State UP, 1990.

Krutch, Joseph Wood. *Great American Nature Writing.* New York: Sloane, 1958.

McClintock, James I. *Nature's Kindred Spirits: Aldo Leopold, Joseph Wood Krutch, Edward Abbey, Annie Dillard, and Gary Snyder.* Madison: U of Wisconsin P, 1994.

James I. McClintock

Naylor, Gloria (1950–   ). Writer of powerful African American novels. Her works show womanist healing—physical, emotional, and spiritual—through women's words, herbal remedies, holistic methods, conjuring, and voodoo as well as through small communities of love. Mattie Michael in *Women of Brewster Place* (1982), Willa Nedeed in *Linden Hills* (1985), the eponymous magician of Mama Day, and Eve in *Bailey's Café* (1992) show Naylor's evolution from depicting healers magically to revealing them symbolically.

Mary Libertin

Nebular Hypothesis. Theory concerning the origin of the planetary system presented by French mathematician Pierre-Simon Laplace in his *System of the World* (1796). Laplace's naturalistic creation account of planets coalescing out of an extended solar atmosphere informed nineteenth-century evolutionary debates and influenced American writers **Ralph Waldo Emerson** and **Edgar Allan Poe**.

Reference

Numbers, Ronald. *Creation by Natural Law: Laplace's Nebular Hypothesis in American Thought.* Seattle: U of Washington P, 1977.

JoAnn Palmeri

Neuroscience(s). The study of brain function and brain organization, ranging from the molecular level to distributed sensory, central, and motor systems; often used synonymously with "neurobiology." Three areas of inquiry dominate discussions of neuroscience and literature. The first involves considerations of how the specifically literary mind or brain actually works, as in Norman N. Holland's *The Brain of Robert Frost* (1988) and Mark Turner's *The Literary Mind* (1996). Second, critics of **poetry** such as Karl Kroeber and Michael G. Miller argue for continuities between Romantic theories of mind and recent theories of brain functioning. Finally, critics of **science fiction**—among them

David Porush and N. Katherine Hayles—analyze literary **representations** of brain organization.

Steven Meyer

Newton, Isaac. *See* Newtonianism.

Newtonianism. The direct and indirect influence of Isaac Newton (1642–1727) on eighteenth-century science and **culture**, often used to describe the philosophical and ideological implications of the belief that the universe is mathematically ordered and therefore comprehensible. Because Newtonianism encompasses a wide range of beliefs and practices, it has become a subject of intense debate. Through the mid-twentieth century, Newtonianism frequently, and inaccurately, was reduced to a strict mathematical **determinism**.

Since the 1970s, with attention focused on Newton's unpublished manuscripts, the term has been broadened to include Newton's influence in antitrinitarian theology, **alchemy**, ancient history, and even **politics**. In this view, Newtonianism implies a voluntaristic, nondeterministic science (the belief that God intervenes miraculously in creation instead of operating by ironclad laws), an antitrinitarian theology (the denial of Christ's divinity), and a Whiggish politics (the belief in a limited, constitutional monarchy). These aspects of Newtonianism emerge most clearly in the attacks of Newton and his followers on the system-builders of European science, notably **René Descartes** and Gottfried Wilhelm Leibniz. Ironically, then, Newtonianism, understood in its historical context, means almost exactly the opposite of what most people take it to mean: Rather than a label for a deterministic, mathematical order, it implies the rejection of all forms of systematizing in science, theology, and politics.

Newtonianism is characterized as well by the competing efforts of Newton's followers to gain scientific legitimacy by seeking his approval or, after his death in 1727, laying claim to his legacy. Chief proponents of Newton's **natural philosophy** between 1700 and 1750 include William Whiston, Colin Maclaurin, Henry Pemberton, Samuel Clarke, and John Keill, most of whom published book-length introductions to Newtonian science. These works tend to downplay Newton's work in theology, ignore his alchemy (about which Newton was obsessively secretive), and emphasize those aspects of his mathematics that demonstrate an aesthetic order to the universe and thus allow his popularizers to attribute the regularities of celestial motion to the designs of a benevolent deity.

References

Dobbs, Betty Jo Teeter, and Margaret C. Jacob. *Newton and the Culture of Newtonianism.* Atlantic Highlands, NJ: Humanities, 1995.
Force, James. *William Whiston: Honest Newtonian.* Cambridge: Cambridge UP, 1985.
Jacob, Margaret C. *The Newtonians and the English Revolution, 1689–1720.* Ithaca, NY: Cornell UP, 1976.

Markley, Robert. *Fallen Languages: Crises of Representation in Newtonian England, 1660–1740.* Ithaca, NY: Cornell UP, 1993.

Stewart, Larry. *The Rise of Public Science: Rhetoric, Technology, and Natural Philosophy in Newtonian Britain, 1660–1750.* Cambridge: Cambridge UP, 1993.

Robert Markley

Nicolson, Marjorie Hope (1894–1981). Professor of English at Columbia University, dean of Smith College, and pioneering scholar in the field of literature and science. Nicolson studied under A.O. Lovejoy and served as editor of the *Journal of the History of Ideas*; her work illustrates the overlap of literature and science with the history of ideas.

Though the central theme of Nicolson's work was science and **imagination** in the seventeenth and eighteenth centuries, her work holds broad interest for students of literature and science. Of Nicolson's eleven books, *Newton Demands the Muse: Newton's "Opticks" and the Eighteenth-Century Poets* (1946), which received the Rose Mary Crawshay Prize of the British Academy in 1947, is perhaps the best known. In *Newton Demands the Muse*, Nicolson traces the influence of Newton's (*see* Newtonianism) *Opticks* on **poetry** from his poetic deification following his death in 1727 to his poetic damnation roughly thirty years later. Viewing science-inspired poetry within the tradition of science for the layman, she argues that Newton's *Opticks* was more influential than the *Principia*, largely because it was written in English and dealt with phenomena more easily grasped by nonexperts.

Insight into the range and influence of Nicolson's work can be gleaned from *Science and Imagination* (1956), a collection of her essays dealing with **Milton**, **Donne**, and **Swift**, among others, and *Reason and the Imagination: Studies in the History of Ideas 1600–1800*, a collection of essays by her former students and some of her most distinguished contemporaries, which was published in her honor in 1962.

Kathryn A. Neeley

Nöosphere. The next evolutionary stage of the biosphere, in which human reason acts as the dominant geological force shaping planetary phenomena. The Russian geochemist **V.I. Vernadsky** uses the term (literally, "sphere of reason") to designate his empirically formulated concept of the importance of living organisms—most potently, human beings—in determining the composition of the earth's crust and atmosphere (the biosphere). Vernadsky's emphasis on the role of human cognitive and spiritual advances, as well as technological ones, in shaping the earth's evolutionary ecology establishes an optimistic basis for regarding the nöosphere as the goal of human creative endeavor.

Reference

Borisov, V.M., F.F. Perchonok, and A.B. Roginsky, "Community as the Source of Vernadsky's Concept of Nöosphere." *Configurations* 1.3 (Fall 1993): 415–38.

Yvonne Howell

Norris, Frank (1870–1902). American naturalist author whose **fiction** was deeply engaged with evolutionary debates of his time. Influenced most prominently by the philosopher **Herbert Spencer**, Norris's brief literary career (cut short by fatal illness) showed a preoccupation with physical evolution in the atavistic *Vandover and the Brute* (1914) and the savagely violent *McTeague* (1899). He explored social change as the product of interacting forces in *The Octopus* (1901) and *The Pit* (1903), the two completed parts of an unfinished economic trilogy on wheat.

Reference

McElrath, Joseph, Jr. *Frank Norris Revisited*. New York: Twayne, 1992.

Leonard Cassuto

Novalis, Friedrich Leopold Freiherr von Hardenberg (1772–1801). German Romantic lyric poet and political philosopher. His *Hymns to the Night* (1800) and *Christianity or Europe* (1826) exemplify his **poetry** and thought. Novalis studied mathematics, **philosophy**, and geology. He developed a unitary theory of mathematical and poetical signs and wrote on medical and biological topics. His visionary conceptualization of a universal spirituality that would transcend the scientific and political influenced Herman Hesse and **Thomas Mann**, among others.

Val Dusek

Novatores. A group of innovative Spanish scientists in the areas of **medicine** and **chemistry** in the latter part of the seventeenth century. At the center of the movement was the **physician** and chemist Juan de Cabrida (c. 1665–post-1714), author of the "The Medico-Chemical and Philosophical Letter" (1687), which was a manifesto that demanded the renovation of medicine in terms of the latest research of iatrochemistry.

Rafael Chabrán

Nuclear Energy/Nuclear Science. Fields based on the understanding that nearly all the mass of matter is contained in atomic nuclei and that nuclear transformations are responsible for the already-known phenomenon of **radioactivity**. These ideas originated around 1910 with **Ernest Rutherford** and were followed by developments of liberation of **energy** by nuclear fission or fusion. The dominant role of this topic in literature is, of course, the ubiquitous theme of nuclear warfare, especially in the post–World War II period, although a few literary writers presciently anticipate such superweapons even before the underlying science was worked out (notably **H.G. Wells** in *The World Set Free*, 1914).

Jay A. Labinger

Number Theory. Branch of mathematics dealing with the properties of integers, positive and negative whole numbers. It began with Greek algorithms for determining prime numbers; and in 1997 Andrew Wiles proved its best-known proposition, Fermat's Last Theorem. Late-nineteenth-century number theory was revolutionized by Richard Dedekind's definition (1872) of irrational numbers. Subsequent efforts to define number by Charles S. Peirce (c. 1880), Gottlob Frege (1884), and Edmund Husserl (1887–1891) launched the "analytic" and "phenomenological" schools of twentieth-century **philosophy**. The literature on number theory, or involving it, has primarily been limited to mathematicians, with novelist and theorist **Don DeLillo** a notable exception (*Ratner's Star*, 1976).

Reference

Dantzig, Tobias. *Number, The Language of Science*. 1930. 4th ed. New York: Free Press, 1953.

William R. Everdell

O

Objectivity. The state, condition, or quality of being uninfluenced by prejudice, emotion, or outside values, usually identified with the belief in a **reality** that is independent of human observation or intention. Traditionally, objectivity has been seen as the default condition of science; in this sense, it denotes the actual existence of phenomena that can be experimentally verified in different circumstances and by different scientists. Debates about objectivity have been a staple in the **philosophy** of science since the nineteenth century: Realists affirm a belief in a mind-independent reality; constructivists argue that there can be no unmediated access to the natural world and that therefore scientists invariably promote values and agendas of which they may be only partially aware.

Recently, feminist scientists have challenged the terms of this debate, focusing on what N. Katherine Hayles calls "constrained constructivism," the dependence of perception on the embodiment of the observer as well as on her cultural, political, social, and religious investments. In historical terms, James Bono and Robert Markley suggest that objectivity did not arise from within science as it developed in the early modern period but was imported from theology, a projection onto the scientist of God's all-knowing perception—and command—of the universe (*The Word of God and the Languages of Man*, 1995; *Fallen Languages: Crises of Representation in Newtonian England, 1660–1740*, 1993). **Donna Haraway** offers an alternative to traditional concepts of objectivity and their dependence on this "God-trick" by emphasizing "situated knowledges" as a means to break through the oppositions of subject and object, realism and constructivism. Situated knowledges are always value-laden; making explicit the investments of particular observers and parties can lead, Haraway maintains, beyond the binary logic that sustains traditional ideals of objectivity to a dynamic mosaic of partial knowledges and perspectives that are dialogically rather than hierarchically related (*Simians, Cyborgs, and Women*, 1991).

References

Bordo, Susan. *The Flight to Objectivity: Essays on Cartesianism and Culture*. Albany: State U of New York P, 1987.
Gillespie, Charles C. *The Edge of Objectivity*. Princeton, NJ: Princeton UP, 1960.
Hayles, Katherine. "Constrained Constructivism: Locating Scientific Inquiry in the Theater of Representation." *New Orleans Review* 18 (1991): 77–85.
Rorty, Richard. *Objectivity, Relativism, and Truth*. Cambridge: Cambridge UP, 1991.

Robert Markley

Ometeca. The title of a poetry and scholarly journal devoted to the study of the relationship between science and the humanities, and the name of an institute located in New Brunswick, New Jersey, devoted to the same purpose. The word "ometeca" comes from the Nahuatl language of the Aztecs, meaning "two in one": science and the humanities. The journal was founded in 1989 by the Cuban American poet **Rafael Catalá** and Professors Rafael Chabrán of Whittier College and Kevin Larsen of the University of Wyoming. It publishes **sciencepoetry** and articles in the three major language groups of the Americas: English, Portuguese, and Spanish. Theoretical articles are published in English and a romance language (Spanish or Portuguese). The Ometeca Institute was founded in 1991. It sponsors a Working Conference every other year, symposia, lectures, readings of sciencepoetry, and publishes books. Mailing address: P.O. Box 38, New Brunswick, NJ 08903–0038, USA.

In 1996 the Ometeca Foundation was formed in San Ramón, Costa Rica. It is developing programs to bring an awareness of the importance of the relationship between science and the humanities to the intellectual community and the general public in that country and Latin America.

Rafael Catalá

Optics. That branch of **physics** that theorizes, measures, and describes the physical characteristics and properties of light and color. Because of the prominence of light in the Book of Genesis—the Creation begins with it (1:3) and God uses the rainbow as the sign of his covenant with Noah and his descendants (9:13)—the study of optics, up to the beginning of the nineteenth century, was underwritten by a heavily theological agenda. From no later than the time of John Pecham (1240–1292) to at least that of Isaac Newton (*see* Newtonianism) (1642–1727), discussions of optics tended to harmonize **theories**, descriptions, and measurements with the Genesis **cosmology**.

As a consequence of this harmonization, it became, in the eighteenth century, a common practice to look to the work of Newton—at least in part his work in optics—as testifying, in a manner rivaling that of **poetry** itself, to the divinely artificed design of the known universe, as well as to humanity's place in that design. No less than the Bible (the Book of Books), the Book of Nature from Newton's time onward could be seen as the validation of God's plan for humanity. What one sees and how one sees, no less than the meaning of what may be seen, was taken as evidence of the workings of a transcendent Deity, who created the material world, absconded, and now contains all that has been created, as well as all that there is to be seen. In Richard Glover's words from his "A Poem on Newton" (1728), "Newton demands the Muse." The Newtonian model, based on what is known as the emission theory, predicated and explained the phenomena of reflection, refraction, and diffraction on the movement of discrete particles through the subtle medium known as ether. The diffraction of white light into the colors of the rainbow, for example, was held to result from the differing size—hence, the differential refrangibility—of the particles as they passed through a prism (or water vapor). In much the same manner, the light transformed from inchoate matter to white light by the hexameral Creator made its presence known to Noah and his family through the mists of the receding flood waters as a rainbow.

But while it validated the hexameral account of the Creation, Newtonian optics ultimately did not save all of the optical phenomena it undertook to explain, especially not phenomena such as polarization and interference. This perceived explanatory inadequacy left the way clear to revisit the alternative wave (undular) theory originally developed by Newton's near-contemporary Christian Huygens. The negative response to the Newtonian theory came from quarters as diverse as those of Thomas Young, **Johann W. v. Goethe**, and **John Keats**. Young's First Bakerian Lecture, "On the Theory of Light and Colours" (1801), proposed the wave theory. Goethe, while no adherent of the wave theory or the particle theory—Young in 1814 called Goethe's *Zur Farbenlehre* (1810) "a striking example of the perversion of the human faculties"—explored the subjective dimension of seeing to an extent that problematized the likelihood of any demonstration attaining the status of a theoretically crucial or defining experiment (*experimentum crucis*). Keats, writing in *Lamia* (1819), asks, derisively, with Newton in mind,

> Do not all charms fly
> At the mere touch of cold philosophy?
> There was an awful rainbow once in heaven:
> We know her woof, her texture, she is given
> In the dull catalogue of common things. (II: 229–32)

The wave-particle debate, which raged through the nineteenth century and involved such major scientific thinkers as Young, **William Whewell**, and **John Herschel**, was largely laid to rest by the rise of quantum theory, which accounted for the full range of optical phenomena by noting that under certain conditions light appears to behave like a particle phenomenon, while under other conditions, it appears to behave like a wave phenomenon. During the twentieth century, quantum mechanics has played an integral role in the development of **field theory**, with its elaborations of the **uncertainty principle** and the problematic relation between observing subject and observed object. The implications of field theory for the narrative strategies of modern and contemporary **fiction** has been discussed admirably and at length by N. Katherine Hayles. Less work has been done on the implications of field theory for **poetry**, but two recent admirable treatments are those of Steven Carter and Guy Rotella.

References

Cantor, G.N. *Optics after Newton: Theories of Light in Britain and Ireland, 1704–1840.* Manchester: Manchester UP, 1983.

Carter, Stephen. "Fields of Spacetime and the 'I' in Charles Olson's *The Maximus Poems.*" *American Literature and Science.* Ed. Robert J. Scholnick. Lexington: UP of Kentucky, 1992.

Hayles, N. Katherine. *The Cosmic Web: Scientific Field Models and Literary Strategies in the Twentieth Century.* Ithaca, NY: Cornell UP, 1984.

Nicolson, Marjorie Hope. *Newton Demands the Muse: Newton's "Opticks" and the Eighteenth Century Poets.* Princeton, NJ: Princeton UP, 1946.

Rotella, Guy. "Comparing Conceptions: Frost and Eddington, Heisenberg, and Bohr." 1987. *On Frost: The Best from American Literature.* Ed. Edwin H. Cady and Louis J. Budd. Durham, NC: Duke UP, 1991.

Stuart Peterfreund

Ornithology. The scientific study of birds. Ornithology is historically a descriptive science, but contemporary ornithological research emphasizes behavior and evolutionary development, as well as how birds function within specific ecosystems. Notable nature writers, such as Susan Fenimore Cooper, Florence Merriam and John Burroughs, were active birders. Similarly, scientist–illustrators John James Audubon and Roger Tory Peterson were prolific and gifted writers. Ornithological literature thus ranges from field guides to literary **essays** to **poetry** to children's books.

Reference

Brooks, Paul. *Speaking for Nature: How Literary Naturalists from Henry Thoreau to Rachel Carson Have Shaped America.* Boston: Houghton Mifflin, 1980.

Michael A. Bryson

Ortega y Gasset, José (1883–1955). Philosopher and essayist who stands as one of the premier Spanish intellectuals of the twentieth century. Educated under Hermann Cohen, Paul Natorp, and Ernst Cassirer, Ortega held the chair of Metaphysics at Madrid from 1910 to 1936. In Ortega's **philosophy**, individual life is the fundamental **reality**. Throughout his writings Ortega consistently turns to science, especially Einsteinian **physics**, as an intellectual template for the revitalization of Spanish culture. In his well-known book-length essay *The Rebellion of the Masses* (1930), Ortega uses **Einstein** as an example of the type of scientist he feels should be countering what he terms the "mass-man"—a highly specialized, yet culturally ignorant scientist. His emphasis on the individual also shows the influence of his understanding of Einstein's **theory** of special **relativity**. Following the Spanish Civil War much of Ortega's originally liberal **rhetoric** was coopted to promote Francoist doctrines, including platitudes about the importance of science to the autocratic regime.

References

Dust, Patrick H., ed. *Ortega y Gasset and the Question of Modernity*. Minneapolis: Prisma Institute, 1989.
Gray, Rockwell. *The Imperative of Modernity: An Intellectual Biography of José Ortega y Gasset*. Berkeley: U of California P, 1989.
Ortega y Gasset, José. *Meditaciones del Quijote*. Ed. Julián Marías. Madrid: Cátedra, 1984.

Dale J. Pratt and Shelly Jarrett Bromberg

Orwell, George (1903–1950). Novelist, essayist, and author of two satirical attacks on totalitarianism. Born Eric Arthur Blair in Motihari, India, Orwell fought and was wounded in the Spanish Civil War, where he fought with the Loyalists. Deeply suspicious of totalitarian and nationalist impulses, whether on the Left or Right, Orwell wrote *Animal Farm* (1945), an attack on Stalinism, and *Nineteen Eighty-Four* (1949), a novel set in a dystopian future of bureaucratic totalitarianism. The novel includes some chilling descriptions of the scientific reshaping of the English language into politically sound bureaucratic "newspeak," under the premise that what cannot be expressed cannot be thought.

Helen J. Burgess

Osiander, Andreas (1498–1552). German Lutheran professor of theology with serious avocational interests in mathematics and **natural philosophy**, especially **astronomy**. He was the infamous author of an anonymous prefatory letter to *De revolutionibus* that (against the wishes of **Copernicus** and his advocate Rheticus) asserted that the heliocentric system proposed by the text was intended as a provisional and hypothetical model only and not as a description of the physical **reality** of the heavens. The case provides a powerful early modern example of the importance of **rhetoric** in the **history of science**.

References

Westman, Robert S. "Proof, Poetics, and Patronage: Copernicus's Preface to *De revolutionibus*." *Reappraisals of the Scientific Revolution*. Ed. David C. Lindberg and Robert S. Westman. Cambridge: U of Cambridge P, 1990. 167–205.
Wrightsman, A. Bruce. "Andreas Osiander's Contribution to the Copernican Achievement." *Copernican Achievement*. Ed. Robert Westman. Berkeley: U of California P, 1975. 213–43.

Pamela Gossin

OuLiPo. The "Ouvroir de Litterature Potentielle," or "Workshop for Potential Literature," cofounded in Paris in the early 1960s by mathematician and writer Raymond Queneau and François Le Lionnais. Oulipian writers impose constraints that must be satisfied to complete a text, constraints ranging across all levels of composition, from elements of plot or structure down to rules regarding letters. OuLiPo thus pushes a structuralist conception of language to a level of mathematical precision; technique becomes technical when language itself becomes a field of investigation, a complex system made up of a finite number of components. The informing idea behind this work is that constraints engender creativity: Textual constraints challenge and thereby free the **imagination** of the writer and force a linguistic system and/or literary genre out of its habitual mode of functioning. The results of these experiments can be acrobatic. Famous Oulipian texts include Queneau's *Cent Mille Millard de Poemes* (1961), a sonnet where there are 10 possible choices for each of the fourteen lines, thus comprising 10^{14} potential poems, and **Georges Perec's** *La Disparition/A Void*, a novel without the letter "e," which constantly refers to the vowel's disappearance.

Paul A. Harris

Ovid (Publius Ovidius Naso) (43 B.C.E.–A.D. 18). Roman poet and author of numerous works including the fragmentary *Medicamina faciei feminae* (Facial Preparations for Women), a mock-didactic poem on the care of women's complexions. In addition to his famous mythohistorical *Metamorphoses*, Ovid also wrote the *Fasti*, a compilation of myth and custom structured according to the Roman calendar.

Jacqui Sadashige

P

Palacio Valdés, Armando (1853–1938). Popular Spanish realist who flirted with **Zola's naturalism**. In *La fe* (Faith) (1892), Father Gil spends chapters pondering the conflicts between religious dogma and his readings in science and **philosophy** under the direction of the sympathetic town atheist. In a leap of faith ironically inspired by a passage in Kant's *The Critique of Pure Reason*, Gil rejects modern science in favor of a mystical quietism. At the novel's end he is jailed for a rape he did not commit and is symbolically crucified by pseudoscientists who claim his cranial and body measurements testify of his depravity.

References

Dendel, Brian J. *Spain's Forgotten Novelist: Armando Palacio Valdés (1853–1938)*. Lewisburg, PA: Bucknell UP, 1995.
O'Connor, D.J. "Filiation, the Eucharist and the Grotesque in Palacio Valdés' *La Fe* (1892)." *Letras Peninsulares* 1 (1988): 51–69.
Palacio Valdés, Armando. La fe. *Obras escogidas*. 3rd ed. Madrid: Aguilar, 1942. 933–1059.

Dale J. Pratt

Paleontology. The study of fossils, not so named until the 1830s. In earlier forms, it was called oryctology or fossil comparative anatomy. That fossils (*see* Fossil Record) represented the remains of once-living creatures was not established until the beginning of the eighteenth century. That once-living forms had become extinct was not recognized until the beginning of the nineteenth. The first fossil animal to attract widespread literary attention was the mammoth. **Dinosaurs** (as opposed to other fossil reptiles) were not discovered until the 1820s; the name "dinosaur" dates from 1842. From the 1860s onward, extinct forms of humans have generated the most literary interest. **Byron's** play *Cain*

(1821), **Tennyson's** *In Memoriam,* **Jack London's** *Before Adam* (1907), and **Conan Doyle's** *Lost World* were influenced fundamentally by paleontology.

References

Buffetaut, Eric. *A Short History of Vertebrate Palaeontology.* London: Croom Helm, 1987.
Rudwick, Martin J.S. *The Meaning of Fossils: Episodes in the History of Palaeontology.* New York: Science History Publications, 1976.

Dennis R. Dean

Paracelsus, Philippus Aureolus Theophrastus Bombastus von Hohenheim (c. 1493–1541). Physician, chemist, philosopher. Paracelsus rejected ancient **medicine** and founded chemical medicine. He traveled across Europe, challenging the establishment with a mixture of **alchemy, astrology,** and **philosophy**. A number of novels and plays portray his life. His alchemical **symbolism** was revived by **Johann W. von Goethe** and by German Romantics.

Val Dusek

Pardo Bazán, Emilia (1852–1921). Spanish novelist and essayist. Pardo Bazán is probably the most important nineteenth-century Spanish short story writer, with over 500 stories to her credit. As the writer of her generation most engaged with science, Pardo Bazán published numerous essays that popularize or critique the scientific ideas of the day, including organic evolution, caloric **theory, electricity,** ether, and criminology. She frequently mentions **Charles Darwin**, Ernst Haeckel, Cesare Lombroso, and Max Nordau. Though her style resembles **Zola's naturalism** more closely than does that of any other Spanish realist, she maintains a Catholic sense of free will throughout her works.

References

Otis, Laura. "Science and Signification in the Early Writings of Emilia Pardo Bazán." *Revista de Estudios Hispánicos* 29 (1995): 73–105.
Pardo Bazán, Emilia. *Obras completas.* Ed. Federico Carlos Sainz de Robles and Harry L. Kirby, Jr. 3 vols. Madrid: Aguilar, 1947–1957.
Pattison, Walter. *Emilia Pardo Bazán.* New York: Twayne, 1971.

Dale J. Pratt

Patents. Units of intellectual property granted by civil authorities to protect an invented device, material, or process. The word "patent" derives from the Latin meaning "disclosed, lying open"; in its early English use, "letters patent" meant an open, public document granting territorial rights or similar privileges to an individual or corporate body for an explicit period of time. In its more narrow modern form, the patent grants an inventor's rights at the price of publishing her or his invention. The patent document, a genre legislated and prescribed, seems, then, to be inherently deconstructive in form, with a double burden of revealing and concealing technological knowledge. **Inventors** make their works public, but try to do so in such a way that they are protected against as many unforeseen adaptations and alternatives as possible. The different components of the genre work together: The "specification" needs to be as specific and as vague as possible. The "claims" then offer readings of the specification that assert the novelty, invention, and utility of specified components. Patent rights have retained an important analogical relation to territorial rights. Like undiscovered **mining** properties, inventions await claims, and **technology** is assumed to consist of adjacent and divisible parcels of describable knowledge.

Lisa Gitelman

Pathography. An autobiographical or biographical narrative describing a personal experience of illness or disability, treatment, and sometimes dying. Book-length pathographies seem to belong almost exclusively to the second part of the twentieth century. In contrast to the **medical case history**, which is a narrative written by medical staff about a patient's illness and treatment, pathography is concerned with the experiential dimensions of illness and treatment. Recent examples include books by Paul Monette (about **AIDS**) and William Styron (about clinical depression). **Freud** used the term "pathography" in a somewhat different sense to refer to a biographical study that focuses on how pathological elements affect an individual's life. Some scholars prefer the term "autopathography." Others, like Arthur Frank, prefer the term "**illness narrative**," which can refer to oral as well as written narratives about the experience of illness.

References

Frank, Arthur Frank. *The Wounded Storyteller: Body, Illness, and Ethics.* Chicago: U of Chicago P, 1995.
Hawkins, Anne Hunsaker. *Reconstructing Illness: Studies in Pathography.* West Lafayette, IN: Purdue UP, 1993.
Monette, Paul. *Borrowed Time: An AIDS Memoir.* San Diego: Harcourt Brace Jovanovich, 1988.
Styron, William. *Darkness Visible: A Memoir of Madness.* New York: Random House, 1990.

Anne Hunsaker Hawkins

Peacock, Doug (1941–   ). Self-styled grizzly bear researcher, wilderness activist, and writer. Following a tour of duty as a medic during the Vietnam War, Peacock sought refuge in the American West and there developed a fascination for grizzlies and the wilderness they inhabit. The result of his years of research among the big bears is the 1990 volume *Grizzly Years: In Search of the American Wilderness*. Although written ostensibly as Peacock's own personal narrative, the book sets forth what may be the most complex **natural**

history of an endangered species ever written, examining the grizzly's ecological, cultural, and political niche on the North American continent.

Rod Phillips

Peary, Josephine Diebitsch (1863–1955). Author of the expedition narrative *My Arctic Journal: A Year among Ice-Fields and Eskimos* (1893). She also wrote *The Snow Baby: A True Story with True Pictures* (1901) and *Children of the Arctic* (1903), based on her experiences accompanying her husband, **Robert E. Peary**, on his Arctic expeditions.

Reference

Bergmann, Linda S. "Woman against a Background of White: The Representation of Self and Nature in Women's Arctic Narratives." *American Studies* 34 (1993): 53–68.

Linda S. Bergmann

Peary, Robert E. (1856–1920). Polar explorer. Inspired by Elisha Kent Kane's Arctic narratives and driven by the desire for fame, Peary adopted native expertise for his five major Arctic expeditions. He produced the expedition narratives *Northward Over the "Great Ice"* (1898), *Nearest the Pole* (1907), and finally *The North Pole* (1910), in which he claims to have reached the Pole.

Reference

Herbert, Wally. *The Noose of Laurels: Robert E. Peary and the Race to the North Pole.* New York: Atheneum, 1989.

Linda S. Bergmann

Pedagogy. Issues relating to teaching methods as well as to the goals and design of LS courses. It is useful to approach the pedagogy of LS from two perspectives: (1) Course **Philosophy** and Design: Why are LS courses important in the academy? What are the central curricular issues, and how might courses be designed around those issues? What specific topics and readings might such courses include? (2) Teaching Methods: What are some of the ways that one may effectively organize an LS course? Present the material? What activities should be included to supplement class lectures and discussions? What are the advantages and disadvantages of interdepartmental team teaching?

Course Philosophy and Design

LS courses are important to interdisciplinary and core-curriculum programs because they call attention to the commonalities and relationships among traditionally separate knowledge domains. Students who come to realize, for example, that aesthetics are important to both **art** and science (e.g., that **physics**, like **poetry**, engages in metaphoric discourse, as Roger S. Jones demonstrates in *Physics as Metaphor*, 1983), that certain scientific texts may themselves be regarded as "literary" (such as **Darwin's** *Origin of Species*, 1859; **Lyell's** *Principles of Geology*, 1833; **Carson's** *Silent Spring*, 1962), or that **relativity** and **thermodynamics** can be used to describe literary texts as well as the natural world, tend to develop a deep sense of the interconnectedness of all knowledge: a crucial goal in undergraduate education.

Teachers of LS often design their courses to answer this central question: "In view of the fact that institutions of higher learning separate literary study from scientific study, what are the fundamental properties of each mode of inquiry that warrant the separation?" This inquiry usually takes one of three possible approaches: (1) the **two cultures debate** approach; (2) the scientific themes in literature approach; and (3) the topical approach.

The Two Cultures Debate Approach

Such a course typically begins with the classic lecture-debates of **T.H. Huxley** ("Science and Culture," 1881) and **Matthew Arnold** ("Literature and Science," 1882), followed by their twentieth-century counterparts: **C.P. Snow** ("The Two Cultures," 1959) and F.R. Leavis (*Two Cultures? The Significance of C.P. Snow*, 1960). Responses to these debates, particularly the Snow-Leavis debates—because of the notoriety they created—are numerous; the most noteworthy include Lionel Trilling's "The Leavis-Snow Controversy" (1962), **Aldous Huxley's** *Literature and Science* (1963), and **Loren Eiseley's** "The Illusion of the Two Cultures" (1964). Admirable anthologies were assembled during the 1960s to meet the flowering of LS courses that followed this track. One fine example is George Levine and Owen Thomas's *The Scientist vs. the Humanist* (1963), which included, along with excerpts from "The Two Cultures" lectures, the Trilling essay mentioned above, an essay by H.J. Muller defining science, and essays by **Asimov**, Rabi, Oppenheimer, Bridgman, and others who address possible relationships between science and humanities, reason and **imagination**, or the nature of knowledge. In addition, Levine and Thomas include excerpts from "imaginative" literary texts such as **Swift's** *Gulliver's Travels* and **Dickens's** *Hard Times*. These are important works to consider for such a course because they call attention to the "ancients versus moderns" controversy that accompanied the rise of modern science from the seventeenth through nineteenth centuries (see Richard Foster Jones's invaluable study *Ancients and Moderns*, 1961).

A more recent and versatile LS anthology is Joan Digby and Bob Brier's *Permutations: Readings in Science and Literature* (1985). Digby and Brier include poems, stories, and excerpts from novels and treatises in philosophy and in four branches of science (**astronomy**, physics, **chemistry**, **biology**). In their introduction they point out how poets and essayists of science, although always "willing to give their opinions on the value and proper position of science," rarely discuss "the more central and more difficult question of what science is" (19). A good question to raise in an introductory LS course, certainly, is the extent to which belletristic writing, regardless of genre, can approach such a concern. Moreover, one cannot assume that rigorously analytic discourse, such as Sir **Karl Popper's** *The Logic of Scientific Discovery* (1959), F.S.C. Northrop's *The Logic of the Sciences and the Humanities* (1959), or Hans Reichenbach's *The Rise of Scientific Philosophy* (1951), can establish unambiguous distinctions between scientific and nonscientific discourse.

Not only do the two cultures debates compel undergraduates to reassess their ideas regarding the kinds of knowledge that are most worth having; they also compel them to examine key terms involved—terms they had always assumed to be simple and unambiguous: "knowledge," "**culture**," "humanities," "art," "literature," "science"—and their relationship to human conduct.

To complement the debate commentary, fictive texts that draw from traditionally scientific culture as well as from traditionally literary culture are particularly useful. Three important authors whose works accomplish this are **Thomas Pynchon**, whose *The Crying of Lot 49* (1966) gives literary richness to **information theory** and the Second Law of Thermodynamics; **Richard Powers**, whose *The Gold Bug Variations* (1992) invokes encryption theory and molecular biology; and **Alan Lightman**, whose exquisite *Einstein's Dreams* (1993) includes terse and lyrical parables about the human experience of time.

An important corollary concern to the two cultures scenario is that of scientific and literary *activity*. In other words, before students can fully appreciate the subtle interconnectedness of the two cultures, they need to understand how practitioners in either domain do what they do, and where the similarities and differences essentially lie. How do biotechnologists get through a typical day? How do artists and writers? **James D. Watson** in *The Double Helix* (1968) shares his insights into the way scientists, not unlike painters, poets, or architects, engage in creative, metaphoric thinking in order to solve problems. Watson also sheds light on the interactive, collaborative (although at least for the 1950s, often sexist) nature of scientific work. The well-known scientific romances that depict the scientist as a kind of Faustian, isolated demigod (think of Victor **Frankenstein** or Aylmer of **Hawthorne's** "The Birthmark," or the narrator of **Poe's** "Facts in the Case of M. Valdemar") do not characterize typical scientists, of course; and it is startling to discover how many nonscience majors continue to harbor this stereotype of scientific activity. Uncommon is the literary work that depicts real-world scientists in action. C.P. Snow's *The Search* (1934) is a good example. A more recent novel that depicts the interactions of biologists is **Carl Djerassi's** *Cantor's Dilemma* (1989). Like Watson in his memoir, Djerassi, a Stanford University chemistry professor who synthesized the first oral contraceptive, focuses on the intense competition driving scientists—sometimes to the point of unethical behavior.

The "Scientific Themes in Literature" Approach

Instead of focusing on the debate between the cultures of scientific work and literary work, this approach concentrates instead on the way literary texts—including classics of world literature—integrate scientific concepts or may be regarded as reactions to scientific concepts. One might teach *Gulliver's Travels*, for example, as a satire on **modernism;** *Hard Times* as a satire on industrialism. *Moby-Dick* could be approached as a dramatization of the human struggle—and ultimate failure—to understand nature. The creative tension **Melville** generates between modes of thought and discourse—meditation versus methodical analysis, for example—is astonishing. In *The Periodic Table* (1984), Primo Levi uses chemical elements to represent persons, attitudes, and episodes of his life as a chemist in Fascist Italy—and subsequently as a prisoner in Auschwitz. "Chemistry, for me . . . led to the heart of Matter, and Matter was our ally precisely because the Spirit, dear to Fascism, was our enemy" (52). For poetry, one might choose *Songs from Unsung Worlds: Science in Poetry* (1985), edited by Bonnie Bilyeu Gordon, containing poems by **Holub**, Cedering, **Ackerman**, Clampitt, **Ammons**, Swenson, and many others on such topics as the space shuttle (Ackerman), cancer research (Parlatore), and subatomic particles (Benedikt). The last section in the anthology contains poems that criticize and satirize science.

Topical Approaches to Literature and Science

Instead of trying to take on literature and science as monolithic wholes, many LS courses limit the scope to a single genre or to one scientific discipline, such as: literature and physics (or even poetry and physics), literature and the **environment**, or literature and **medicine**; or even to one concept common to both literature and science, such as relativity in literature and science. Literature and medicine is an especially popular option because of its obvious links to traditional humanistic concerns. Teachers are able to draw from a wealth of themes:

Theme	Possible Text(s)
Death and dying	Leo Tolstoy, *Death of Ivan Ilyich*
Healing and spirituality	Echo Heron, *Intensive Care: The Story of a Nurse*
Illness, disease, and daily life	**William Carlos Williams**, *The Doctor Stories*
Medicine and language	**Lewis Thomas**, *The Lives of a Cell* Susan Sontag, *Illness as Metaphor*
Mental illness	**Anton Chekhov**, "Ward Six" Ken Kesey, *One Flew over the Cuckoo's Nest*
Neurological illness/injury	**Oliver Sacks**, *The Man Who Mistook His Wife for a Hat*

Another popular topic is literary responses to environmental issues. One might begin with *Walden* (1854), or **Muir's** *The Mountains of California* (1894), or with Native American narratives, such as Lame Deer's "Talking to the Owls and Butterflies," from *Lame Deer, Seeker of Visions* (1972)—a good text to use in a literature and medicine course as well because Lame Deer was a Sioux medicine man. One of Henrik Ibsen's greatest plays, *An Enemy of the People* (1882) is an amazingly prophetic work dramatizing the clash between private enterprise and public welfare. A scientist discovers that the water feeding a new health spa—his small community's pride and joy—designed to attract thousands, thereby boosting the impoverished economy, has been dangerously contaminated by a mill upstream. The scientist must confront his brother, who just happens to be the town's mayor and represents the business investors of the spa.

Several fine anthologies focusing on the literary dimensions of environmentalism have recently been published, two of which particularly deserve mention: *Deep Ecology* (1985), edited by Bill Devall and Roger Sessions; and *Being in the World* (1994), edited by Scott H. Slovic and Terrell F. Dixon. For poetry, teachers may wish to use *Poetry for the Earth* (1991), edited by Sara Dunn and Alan Scholefield.

Ecological **science fiction** (SF) should also be considered. **David Brin's** *Earth* (1990) is a good example. Adopting a **Dos Passos**-like collage of parallel story lines, Brin depicts an environmentally ravaged world fifty years hence in which the ultimate environmental accident has occurred: A lab-manufactured microscopic black hole has escaped confinement and falls to the earth's core, where it begins devouring the planet. A good anthology of environmental SF is Kim Stanley Robinson's *Future Primitive: The New Ecotopias* (1994), which features stories by Carol Emshwiller, **Ursula K. Le Guin**, Robert Silverberg, and Ernest Callenbach (well known for his utopian novel *Ecotopia*, 1975). As with all science fiction, as Kim Stanley Robinson points out in his introduction, ecological SF presents "implicit histories connecting their futures back to our present. . . . It is a mode of thought that is utopian in its very operating principle, for it assumes that differences in our actions will lead to . . . predictable consequences later on" (9).

As is apparent from these different topical approaches to LS, the **essay** predominates over **fiction**, poetry, or **drama**. The old boundary lines separating "expository" from "creative" writing no longer hold up—a learning experience in itself for students, in view of the fact that students have been subtly conditioned to compartmentalize aims and modes of discourse from first-year composition onward. Boundaries are of course useful: One needs at least a general sense of what is included in or excluded from a discipline before one can investigate it in depth. At the same time, firm boundaries can interfere with creative thinking, which often transgresses disciplinary boundaries.

Teaching Methods

Even before LS teachers ask their students, "Why should we concern ourselves with relationships between literature and science?" they ought to call attention to the problem of defining the operative terms, "literature" and "science." Parity is assumed to exist between them, but does it? To begin with, would not "art" rather than "literature" be a more appropriate counterpart to "science"? Also, could not one argue for a literature *of* science or a science *of* literature just as well? And what is one to make of the blanket term "science": applied or theoretical? Doing science or thinking science? Or thinking *about* science? Such questions are bound to get the course off to a provocative if unsettling start. By deconstructing these operative terms, teachers automatically historicize the inquiry. They do so first via the etymologies of the terms (e.g., *litteria* is Latin for "letters"; *ars* most likely stems from an Indo-European word, *ar*, meaning "to join together," as in *arm* or *army*).

An LS course ought to inspire pedagogical strategies as innovative as the subject matter it embraces. Science courses tend to be visually oriented and often include **laboratory** practica. Literature courses (quite unlike other arts courses as well as science courses) typically lack visual media, unless the course focuses on literary works that have specific ties to the visual arts, such as dramatic works or literary movements that parallel artistic movements (pre-Raphaelitism, impressionism, surrealism, and so on). For the most part, multimedia approaches to literature direct attention away from critical analyses and toward interdisciplinary comparison (say, between a novel and its **film** adaptation). But in LS courses multimedia approaches are more integral to course objectives. For example, a course in which *The Origin of Species* is studied as both a literary and a scientific text can include, along with close textual analysis, a video or slide show depicting life on the Galapagos Islands, or a film tracing the history of evolution and profiling the scientists who contributed to it. Contemporary authors whose works can be studied as both literary and scientific texts, such as James Burke (*Connections*, 1978), **Carl Sagan** (*Cosmos*, 1980), **Diane Ackerman** (*A Natural History of the Senses*, 1991), have also written and coproduced video series based on them—and even appeared as the narrator/host. Courses in which these works and their video analogs are used would also want to include discussion of the ways in which visual and textual elements work interactively to produce a more holistic understanding of the material.

Guest speakers can certainly enrich the experience of an LS course. It is not necessary to bring in celebrity author–scientists either. Scientist–writers abound, very likely on one's own campus. The chemist who writes poems, no matter if they have not been published, the poet who loves astronomy, no matter if she has "credentials," can spark invaluable discussion about the role that one mode of intellectual activity is capable of stimulating in the other.

Guest speakers might also be brought into the LS class to "ionize" student-managed debates on the similarities versus differences between literary and scientific activity. A professor of chemistry and a professor of literature might launch a debate on the role of imagination in writing and in creating molecular models. A professor of mathematics and a professor of linguistics might launch a debate on the nature of ambiguity or uncertainty in syntactic/semantic structures and in mathematical equations. A professor of psychology (*see* Anthropology/Psychology/Sociology), or a professional psychologist or psychiatrist, along with a professor of literature might use their particular perspectives to launch a debate on psychoanalytic versus formalist or new historicist critical approaches to a given literary work or author (**Poe**, **Whitman**, **Dickinson**, Dostoevsky, **Woolf**, Plath, Berryman being ideal candidates). Few academic experiences can provide as much intellectual stimulus as that of experts debating the very issues students are studying and wrestling with. Knowledge, whether scientific or literary, is in its very essence unstable.

An LS course is an adventure in teaching and learning: Artistic and epistemological assumptions rarely brought into question are scrutinized. Agreeing to disagree, students and teachers alike engage in a learning experience rare in academe: exploring the possibilities of integrating modes of perception and experience hitherto assumed to be nonintegrable.

References

Eiseley, Loren. "The Illusion of the Two Cultures." *The Star Thrower*. New York: Harcourt, 1978. 267–79.
Jones, Richard Foster. *Ancients and Moderns*. New York: Dover, 1961.

Fred D. White

Pepys, Samuel (1633–1703). Famous diarist. He recorded detailed accounts of daily social life, **music**, theater, food, dress, churchgoing, domestic relations and extramarital affairs, street violence, disease and disasters, such as the plague and great fire of London, and demonstrations of experimental science, providing an early example of the use of a personal journal to document social history. He became president of the **Royal Society** in 1684, just in time to usher in the greatest achievements of Isaac Newton (*see* Newtonianism) and welcome their first female visitor, "mad Madge," **Margaret Cavendish.**

Reference

Nicolson, Marjorie H. *Pepys and the New Science*. Charlottesville: UP of Virginia, 1965.

Pamela Gossin

Percy, Walker (1916–1990). American **physician–writer** whose works notably reflect his existentialist **philosophy** and view of symbolic language as definitively human. These beliefs grew from his medical training and personal experiences. At age twenty-six, Percy himself developed tuberculosis; his subsequent confinement fueled examination of human existence as limited within a technological society, a theme common to his later works. Moreover, the birth of his hearing-impaired daughter accentuated a keen interest in symbolic language. Of his essays, the collection titled *The Message in the Bottle* (1975) typifies Percy's existentialist theme of the castaway human shipwrecked in an alienating society.

Robert J. Bonk

Perec, Georges (1936–1982). French-born writer of Polish Jewish emigré parents. A member of **OuLiPo**, he is renowned for acrobatic literary achievements governed by precise formal constraints: the longest known palindrome (over 5,000 letters); experiments in heterogrammatic **poetry** (a form in which all verses are anagrams of one another, whose letter combinations follow precise combinatoric rules); a novel without the letter *e*, *La Disparition/A Void* (1969); and *Les Revenentes* (1972), a novel where *e* is the only vowel.

Paul A. Harris

Pérez Galdós, Benito (1843–1920). One of the greatest Spanish novelists since Cervantes. A realist writer, Galdós wrote over seventy-five novels, whose plots and characters intermingle. Many include descriptions of characters suffering from disease, epilepsy, apoplexy, **alcoholism**, migraines, and other maladies and also details about drugs used in treatment. Galdós viewed science as a progressive cultural force, although he depicts the scientific climate in Spain with irony. Important characters linked to science include such figures as Teodoro Golfín in Marianela (1878), a surgeon who gives sight to the blind; the title character in *La Familia de Léon Roch* (The Family of Léon Roch, 1878), a geologist with the patience of Methusaleh; and Pepe Rey, an engineer murdered in a provincial town, and Augusto Miquis, a doctor.

References

Dendle, Brian J. "Marianela, el descubrimiento del nuevo mundo y las limitaciones de la ciencia." *Insula* 48.561 (Sept. 1993): 29–30.
Franz, Thomas R. "Galdós the Pharmacist: Drugs and the Samaniego Pharmacy in *Fortunata y Jacinta*." *Anales Galdosianos* 22 (1987): 35–46.
Pérez Galdós, Benito. *Obras completas*. Ed. Federico Carlos Sainz de Robles. 6 vols. Madrid: Aguilar, 1970–1986.

Dale J. Pratt

Philosophy. Encompasses, within LS, two central questions: (1) What makes an approach to literature, science, and their relations a *philosophical* one? And, (2) What results have such approaches yielded?

Consider an example. A scholar publishes a study of the works of **Émile Zola**, focusing on his programmatic statements about the "**experimental novel**," his naturalist conception of biological **determinism**, his varied stylistic techniques, as well as his work's relation to other aspects of the sciences of his time. Such a study is clearly about literature and science, but is it philosophical? Not if the commentator remains neutral with regard to the claims made by Zola and his contemporaries, failing to challenge or develop any of the ideas and arguments. Philosophical inquiry is one thing, and historical reportage is another. Such a study would, however, be philosophical if the reading of Zola were undertaken as a way of solving some more general intellectual problem. For example, the scholar could intend, in discussing Zola's works, to explore and develop arguments on free will and determinism, and this intention could be realized in an engagement with the relevant philosophical assumptions and arguments. So the goal of achieving general, theoretical insights by means of conceptual analysis and factual inquiry is *necessary* if an approach to literature and science is to be philosophical, which is not to say that such an approach is always successful or better than other approaches.

The search for generalities or regularities does not, however, *suffice* to make an approach philosophical. Some descriptive historical accounts are at once highly general and unphilosophical, an example being a large-scale socioeconomic study of professorial salaries in nineteenth-century Europe. What suffices to make many general, problem-solving investigations of science and literature philosophical is that they deal with topics belonging squarely within one of the established areas of philosophical inquiry, such as metaphysics, ethics, or **epistemology**. This claim would be viciously circular, however, if we did not go on to say what makes these long-standing approaches and topics philosophical. It has been proposed, in this regard, that a work is philosophical when it targets questions that are deeper or more fundamental than descriptive, historical topics, but one needs to hear more about how this spatial metaphor is cashed out.

Philosophers are interested not only in what is known in **art** and in science but in how it is known, which leads to the suggestion that philosophical inquiry is a second-order inquiry, a matter of thinking about thinking. Yet such higher-order thinking should also be concerned with what the first-order thinking was about. If conceptual analysis and empirical research are the two extremes of an unbroken continuum, philosophical inquiry is closer to the former but cannot be defined as purely logical analysis. Even so, while psychologists run experiments with relatively small numbers of subjects and do statistical analyses of the results, philosophers are more likely to use **thought experiments** to explore what is logically possible. Perhaps what suffices to make a study philosophical is the attempt to engage in systematic, explicitly critical, rational thinking about general features of the nature of **reality** and knowledge.

Not everyone agrees that what makes an approach philosophical is an admirable ambition of doing conceptual spadework and taking on fundamental issues. Ludwig Wittgenstein, for example, blamed a "craving for generality" as the source of philosophy's pseudoproblems. In this regard he carried forward the neo-Kantian tradition's idea that generalizing, "nomothetic" projects are inappropriate with regard to historical topics. According to this family of prevalent views, which is exemplified by Heinrich Rickert, the sciences are "nomethetic" and look for explanations and regularities, while the humanities are "idiographic" and describe particular, nonrecurrent cases. If the lives, works, and events involved in literature and science are viewed as historical topics calling for idiography, it follows that philosophical approaches to them are inappropriate, unless, that is, philosophy's proper role is radically reconceived. It has been proposed in this vein that the philosopher's proper task is the "therapeutic" one of criticizing such generalizing projects. In that case, philosophy becomes a self-critical enterprise, a kind of gadfly's gadfly. Another overly exploited strategy in this vein is to approach or even to replace philosophy's epistemic goals with various poetical and self-expressive impulses, so that the philosophers's stylistic experiments and personality come to the fore.

It is far from clear that we have good grounds for accepting such challenges to philosophy's traditional contemplative and theoretical ambitions. It is certainly true that some excessive versions of world-historical philosophizing deserve a gadfly's bite, but it is not obvious that this is honorable work for an entire discipline. One wonders, as well, to which branch of the tree of knowledge the neo-Kantian conception of that tree is supposed to belong. In this regard the neo-Kantian position faces a trichotomy: (1) it has an idiographic role alongside other particularist, descriptive inquiries; (2) it shares the generalizing, explanatory ambitions of science; or (3) neo-Kantian philosophy has a different status, above or outside the nomethesis/idiography distinction (which, then, is not exhaustive). Neither of the first two options are coherent with the neo-Kantian's more general claims about the tree of knowledge: If it is not appropriate to theorize about the history of the arts and sciences, it is also inappropriate to theorize about our knowledge of them, since such knowledge is the product of human activity. Yet in the absence of theorizing there can be no neo-Kantian picture of the tree of knowledge. The third option avoids this problem, but at the price of having to posit another mode of knowing, which is usually left undefined. Option three easily leads to the making of untestable and dogmatic claims about a privileged form of philosophical insight that somehow transcends the very dichotomies it posits. So it is best to abandon the neo-Kantian schema and accept some version of option two, according to which philosophy resembles the sciences in attempting to provide general explanations, while differing from them in *some* of its methods and topics.

What are some of the general conclusions yielded by philosophical approaches to literature, science, and their relations? Three families of views should be mentioned in this regard: (1) Science and literature are not fundamentally different; (2) science and literature are different, but in the effort to understand, explain, or assess them, their similarities and interactions are at least as important as the differences; and (3) science and literature are different, and in the effort to understand, explain, or assess them, these differences are more important than the similarities. The first view is exemplified by extreme versions of a rhetorical approach to science, which claim that science, like literature, is reducible to a series of rhetorical devices aiming at power and persuasion. View two is exemplified by moderate versions of the rhetorical approach and by macrosociological accounts that focus on the institutional dynamics involved in both science and literature. View three is exemplified by the idea that literary works have a primarily artistic or aesthetic function, while scientific works primarily target explanatory goals.

Theories of type one are popular among scholars in the humanities but unpromising. They purport to reduce both science and literature (and the arts more generally) to the functioning or effect of some other item, such as discourse, textuality, the will to power, class conflict, symbolic capital, or the history of Being. Such speculative "macro" accounts tend to obscure salient differences, stumbling, for example, over the rather conspicuous fact of the terrific instrumental efficacy that results from the application of modern science's results. If science is just one discursive formation or rhetorical system among others, why are its results often so *explosive*, even for those who do not understand and are not persuaded by its symbols? Literature, it is true, also has important consequences, but not of the same sort. The publication of a controversial novel cannot cause ecological disasters, eliminate species, or produce a cure for cystic fibrosis. If science and literature are both just social constructions, why does the one intervene in nature in causally effective ways that the other cannot? Philosophy of science is a complex field, and literary theorists have a regrettable tendency to neglect its best arguments in favor of self-serving, romanticist viewpoints designed to demote the epistemic successes of science (for the book-length version of this claim, see Livingston; for background, see Boyd, Gasper, and Trout).

Views two and three require careful development and comparison in order to approach a better understanding of reasons for favoring the one or the other.

The intuitive appeal of view two is strong. Writers as diverse as **Edgar Allan Poe**, **Molière**, **Stanislaw Lem**, Robert Musil, and **Virginia Woolf** are widely recognized as having produced works of literature, but it seems a mistake to contend that their ambitions—as well as the functions of their texts—should be sharply disjoined from the kinds of cognitive aims that one associates with (scientific) knowledge. Many are the literary authors who understood themselves to be attempting to make a contribution to one or more of the sciences of their time. And in the long, complex, and ongoing tradition of the Counter-Enlightenment, many are the literary authors whose intended contribution to *science* involves a perceived corrective to the excesses and limitations of the dominant, natural-scientific mode of inquiry. In this vein, literature is praised for its antirationalist, skeptical impulses, for its emphasis on complexity and lived experience, for its antimechanistic qualities, and for its manifestation of dimensions of subjectivity that are said to be ignored or repressed by science. Even if one holds that the actual successes of such antiscientific tendencies are often exaggerated in literary circles (did **William Blake** really give the lie to Newtonian **physics**?), it is appropriate to observe that literary and scientific cultures do not exist in separate "systems" or universes. Such an observation moves in two directions: Literary works, while possessing their specifically literary characteristics, nonetheless draw upon, react against, and sometimes contribute to scientific thinking. And science, while possessing its own procedures, social conditions, aims, and results, sometimes draws upon, reacts against, contributes to, and detracts from the art of literature. The description and explanation of such processes is a valuable research agenda.

Philosophers have on the whole favored view three, perhaps because they tend to focus on conceptual boundaries and definitions. It seems right to ask how scientific and literary works differ before one inquires into their similarities and interactions. Otherwise, why go on using these distinct terms at all? It makes sense to observe, along with such philosophers as Roman Ingarden, that symbols function differently in literary as opposed to scientific works, the basic idea being that in literature, language is foregrounded and employed to aesthetic ends. Scientific discourse, by contrast, is designed to reduce ambiguity so as to serve a literal, denotative function. Aestheticians, literary critics, and philosophers have made various, more detailed proposals about the defining or symptomatic features of a literary use of language, listing, for example, fictionality, figurative language, foregrounding, the use of multiple voices and perspectives, nonstandard narrative techniques, a heavy reliance on implicit meanings, and what Nelson Goodman calls nondenotative reference and syntactic and semantic density.

Are there any *general* grounds for preferring view two or three? The answer depends on how these views are developed. Oddly enough, professors of literature tend now to disfavor view two and spend most of their time exploring variants of view three, while those who do not specialize in literature think of it predominantly along aesthetic and artistic lines.

The basic contrast at the heart of view three can be developed and construed in strikingly different ways. For some thinkers, Siegfried J. Schmidt being an influential example, the distinctions in question are a matter of the use to which people put a text: "Literariness" is in the reader's attitude and is produced when readers adopt certain aesthetic and semantic conventions (i.e., suspending instrumental attitudes and actively developing multiple interpretations). A single text can be either literary or scientific, depending on how it is used, but not both at the same time. Agents are on the whole capable of adopting either attitude, but no general rule governs the appropriateness of so doing. It is sometimes contended, contrary to this view, that the literature/science distinction is inherent in either the textual artifact (e.g., in its semantic and other features), in the producers' aims and attitudes (e.g., in the authors' referential and other intentions), or as Robert Stecker argues, in some more complex combination of these (and other) factors.

The functionalist thesis on the ontology of art is that texts and other artifacts can be put to strikingly divergent uses and that our categorizations should be attuned exclusively to them. An objection to the functionalist line is that there is an aesthetically or artistically significant difference between something's being made with an aesthetic or imaginative goal and something's being put to such a use. Even if one manages to read one's bank statement as a poem, that does not make it one, for the document was designed with other aims in view. Although it may be psychologically possible, for some people in some contexts, to adopt a literary attitude to any and every text, it does not follow that our literary and other interests are typically or best served in this manner. The fact of this broad psychological possibility (if it is one) tells us nothing about the constraints that actually determine literary practices or promote their flourishing. It is also possible, perhaps even very likely, that readers' beliefs about a text's provenance routinely inform their decisions about what to do with that text. Believing that the document was mailed to me in order to inform me about the balance in my bank account, I am not inclined to attempt to discover or to invent this text's artistic or aesthetic value. Believing that a creative person has designed a **fiction** with the goal of stimulating my **imagination**, I have an additional reason (but not necessarily a decisive one) to read the text with the aim of enjoying an aesthetic experience and appreciating the writer's artistry.

As our beliefs about texts' provenances make a difference, one might think that reliable beliefs are to be preferred over misinformation and wishful thinking. Yet proponents of extreme versions of the functionalist approach deny this, claiming that an antiinstrumental and polysemic stance is more generally ethical, rewarding, or fun than science's tediously literal and dangerously instrumental attitudes. Why murder to dissect when you can let it be and enjoy? One wonders, however, how such an attitude can be an appropriate way to deal with crippling and fatal childhood diseases or discourses of hatred and persecution. Neither actual readers nor the "ideal readers" of aesthetic doctrine are systematically oblivious to the causal histories and contextual situations of texts. In sum, although the precise nature of the literary/nonliterary distinction remains as elusive as the art/nonart distinction to which it is closely related, historical and causal factors are likely to figure prominently in an adequate descriptive or normative account of this demarcation, and we should prefer a **classification** that is sensitive to events in the history of a text's or artifact's production. Such a classification does not, however, dictate specific uses of texts in any simple way.

As utterances can be put to many different uses, the assessment of a general approach to literature and science often comes down to the following question: Assuming that a given end or goal is justified, in what way must a particular means fit this goal for its adoption to be warranted? One tendency is the insistence on a unique fit between means and ends. A familiar philosophical move with regard to the question of knowledge and literature is to ask, not whether literary works can convey knowledge but whether what is specifically literary in them can do so. The question is a good one, but it sometimes leads to an excessive emphasis on literature's specificity. It is claimed, for example, that it is not enough to say that literature contributes to knowledge whenever writers use the expressive means of literary art to express the right sort of beliefs; instead, the literary employment of tropes, fiction, point of view, or other stylistic devices must make the contribution. When carried to the extreme, this line of thought leads to a situation where a nonparaphrasable literary *je ne sais quoi* is charged with making literature's truly specific and uniquely valued contribution to thought. This is an exaggeration of the sensible view that the philosophical content of a novel is not to be found uniquely in the ideas and arguments uttered by the characters. For example, in the first part of *Notes from the Underground* (1864) we hear the absurdist's reasoning, but in the second part we are told a story about how he lives. Fyodor Dostoevsky had some good reasons for juxtaposing these two sections, and we are likely to learn more about Dostoevsky's views if we read the work as a whole, engaging imaginatively in the experience it evokes. But the fact remains that it is also possible to find some interesting philosophical claims in a snippet from this and other literary works. Sometimes reading a text leads people to think of valuable arguments that the author never dreamt of and would not have accepted.

Another question is whether looking at literary works as a means to epistemic ends is always the most reasonable option. Literary fiction is sometimes treated like a window on the world, a window that either displays or fails to display the really important extraliterary matters. But if the latter are what really matters, how significant and important are the literary windows? Is fiction the sole, or even a viable, means to the desired end of learning about the actual world? If, for example, racism is one's topic, social history and **biology** (qua ideology and explanatory science) are the royal roads, and literature, though relevant, comes in much later. The injunction to read literature qua literature, that is, solely with an eye to the *art* of literature, can have the unfortunate consequence of obscuring literature's social and scientific relations; but the injunction to read literature with only epistemological (or political) issues in mind dispenses with artistic and aesthetic values on the assumption that this is the price that must be paid in order to promote other valued ends. But if such a promotion fails, and if other, more reliable means were overlooked, specifically literary values have been needlessly sacrificed. In response to this worry, one may hold that an emphasis on ways in which science and literature are similar and interact can nonetheless provide a useful supplement to a purely aesthetic approach to literature. Once we have noted that fictionalizing is a typical symptom of a writer's literary aims and that fiction has its specific uses and pleasures, we may also observe that those very artistic and aesthetic means can be adopted in order to serve a variety of ulterior intentions. Sometimes make-believe is a means to the promotion of sincerely held beliefs. A failure to see this leads to a badly truncated account of literary history. On the other hand, literature is not just a vehicle for science or knowledge, and treating it as such may lead to a failure to realize both literary values as well as the other sorts of values being promoted.

References

Boyd, Richard, Philip Gasper, and J.D. Trout, eds. *The Philosophy of Science*. Cambridge: MIT, 1991.

Goodman, Nelson. *Languages of Art*. New York: Bobbs-Merrill, 1968.

Ingarden, Roman. *The Cognition of the Literary Work of Art*. Trans. R.A. Crowley and K.R. Olson. Evanston, IL: Northwestern UP, 1973.

Livingston, Paisley. *Literary Knowledge: Humanistic Inquiry and the Philosophy of Science*. Ithaca, NY: Cornell UP, 1988.

O'Hear, Anthony. *What Philosophy Is*. Harmondsworth: Penguin, 1985.

Rickert, Heinrich. *Kulturwissenschaft und Naturwissenschaft*. Freiberg: J.C.B. Mohr, 1899.

Schmidt, Siegfried J. "Conventions and Literary Systems." *Rules and Conventions: Literature, Philosophy, Social Theory*. Ed. Mette Hjort. Baltimore: Johns Hopkins UP, 1992. 215–49.

Stecker, Robert. *Artworks: Definition, Meaning, Value*. University Park: Pennsylvania State UP, 1996.

Walsh, Dorothy. *Literature and Knowledge.* Middletown, CT: Wesleyan UP, 1969.
Wittgenstein, Ludwig. *Philosophical Investigations.* New York: Macmillan, 1953.

Paisley Livingston

Phonograph. Invention made by **Thomas Alva Edison** in 1877 to record and reproduce sounds mechanically. Edison early projected that his device would be used to record and replay literature, newspapers, and correspondence, though by the mid-1890s musical amusement became its primary function. Also called the "talking machine" (and the "gramophone"), the phonograph was acknowledged by the United States Copyright Act of 1909 to be a *reading* machine, able to read the grooves on a record, which were therefore deemed copies of constitutionally protected "writings." Early literary **representations** of the phonograph include Edward Bellamy's "With Eyes Shut" (1889) and **Mark Twain's** *American Claimant* (1892): Bellamy posits a future world in which the phonograph dominates all of the discursive functions of **culture**, whereas Twain's Colonel Sellers adapts the phonograph into a safety device, able to play curses to steady storm-tossed men at sea. Twentieth-century treatments include Walter Van Tilburg Clark's "The Portable Phonograph" (1941) and George Steiner's "Desert Island Disc" (1993).

Lisa Gitelman

Physician(s)/Physician–Writers. Authors in all societies, past and present, who practice the **art** of **medicine**, as defined within that society. Writings by or about physicians on patients, diseases, and treatments abound in Western **culture** since classical times but can also be found in African, Chinese, Native American, and other non-Western societies. As understanding of medicine continued to evolve, particularly during the **Enlightenment**, literary **representation** of physicians and patients, as well as the metaphor of disease, also changed. Nevertheless, writings by or about physicians retain a commonality of complex relationships between healer and patient—and the disease that temporarily unites them.

This breadth of literature captures progression of medical arts from **magic** or **religion** to technological science. In the Middle Ages, medical texts emphasized words to isolate medical knowledge within the educated classes, whereas early modern writings celebrated the human form through combining the skills of artisans and scientists. With the Enlightenment emerged a satirical view of physicians more concerned with **classification** and codification than with patients and healing.

The nineteenth century heralded the rise of **technology** as the physician's tool, a theme further developed in the twentieth century. Modern physician-writers—among them **Walker Percy**, **Richard Selzer**, **Lewis Thomas**, and **William Carlos Williams**—explore philosophical and psychological reverberations of the technological disassociation of physician from patient in modern society. Thematic material now comes full circle with the literary exploration of diseases, notably **AIDS** (acquired immunodeficiency syndrome), as physiological maladies rather than as **supernatural** retribution.

Reference

Carmichael, A.G., and R.M. Ratzan, eds. *Medicine: A Treasury of Art and Literature.* New York: Harkavy Publishing Service, 1991.

Robert J. Bonk

Physicotheology. "Divinity enforced or illustrated by natural philosophy," as **Samuel Johnson** defined it, concisely expressing its inseparability from science (Philipp 1257). Often used synonymously with **natural theology**, physicotheology may be distinguished from that more general term by its sole focus on the order and purposiveness discernible in the natural world and its exclusive reliance on ancient design arguments for the existence of God. By vigorously cultivating the relationship between contemporary science—from which it drew its copious illustrations of divine design—and **religion**, this rational empirical theology (most popular in England and Germany) facilitated the cultural acceptance of **natural philosophy**; it also helped to popularize knowledge of the natural world: The influential physicotheologies of **John Ray** and **William Derham** may be read as both encyclopedic natural histories and religious texts.

It is important to carefully distinguish this theology (with [1] its insistence on God's continuing providence and maintenance of the systems of nature and [2] its acceptance of Revelation) from the "natural religion" of deism and from nonempirical a priori arguments. Orthodox physicotheologians often express the agreement between their theology and revealed religion through the metaphor of the two "books" of God—the Bible and the Book of Nature. Physicotheology's techniques, imagery, and conventional motifs (which include the superiority of Nature to **Art**, and the ideas of order, plenitude, the chain of being, contrivance, purposiveness, and general and particular providence) are found in a large range of eighteenth-century literary texts—in popular periodical literature (best represented by **Joseph Addison**), in scores of lengthy physicotheological scientific poems (such as Richard Blackmore's *Creation* [1712], **James Thomson's** *The Seasons* [1730–1746], and **Alexander Pope's** *Essay on Man* [1733–1734]), and in countless references to the order and design of nature in providential fiction.

References

Glacken, Clarence J. *Traces on the Rhodian Shore: Nature and Culture in Western Thought from Ancient Times to the End of the Eighteenth Century.* Berkeley: U of California P, 1967.

Jones, William Powell. *The Rhetoric of Science: A Study of Scientific Ideas and Imagery in Eighteenth-Century English Poetry.* Berkeley: U of California P, 1966.

McKillop, Alan Dugald. *The Background of Thomson's "Seasons."* 1942. Hamden, CT: Archon, 1961.

Philipp, Wolfgang. "Physicotheology in the Age of Enlightenment: Appearance and History." *Studies on Voltaire and the Eighteenth Century* 57(1967): 1233–67.

Lisa Zeitz

Physics. From the Greek word *phusis*, meaning "nature"; originally connoting philosophical inquiries into the nature of all natural phenomena. **Aristotle's** "Physics" influenced the definition and development of this branch of science for over 2,000 years. Classical, that is to say, Newtonian (*see* Newtonianism), **physics** established fundamental laws of motion and basic concepts of mass, **energy**, force, acceleration, inertia, and momentum. Newton's mathematical description and analysis of the behavior of planetary orbits, comets, tides, and light made these natural phenomena intelligible in ways that transformed our understanding of the universe as a whole. Modern theories of **relativity** and **quantum physics** offer refinements of Newtonian concepts that are especially relevant to research into the nature of subatomic particles.

Historically, **astronomy** and **cosmology** have provided visual imagery, metaphors, and themes for **poetry** and **fiction** in far greater quantities than physics proper. In the early modern period, **John Donne** alluded to the Galilean concept of shared motion in the *Epithalamion*, written to celebrate the wedding of the Earl of Somerset (1613); **James Thomson** versified Newton's achievements in planetary dynamics and **optics** (among other things) in *An Ode to the Memory of Sir Isaac Newton* (1727); and **Laurence Sterne** employed the notions of rectilinear motion, centrifugal force, and vortices as structural metaphors for his experimental novel *Tristram Shandy* (1760+). **Jonathan Swift** satirized both Cartesian mechanism and Newtonian experimental science in *Tale of a Tub* and *Gulliver's Travels*, emphasizing the primacy of moral **philosophy** over **natural philosophy** (mathematical, or not). Poet, essayist, and dictionary editor **Samuel Johnson** was a serious reader of Newtonian science, including Newton's experimental work on electrical attraction and concepts of matter and ether. In his personal synthesis of faith and reason, Johnson saved the phenomena of religious belief and praised natural investigators who acted upon spiritual motivations to seek deeper understanding of God's creation and His role as caring creator (albeit occasional maintenance mechanic). The nineteenth-century Romantics alleged anti-Newtonian sentiments have been well publicized (**Blake, Keats, Wordsworth,** and others), although recent analyses offer revised views of how these poets incorporated knowledge of the natural sciences into their thought and work. At the fin de siècle and into the Modernist period, popular ideas of **entropy** and relativity, respectively, entered the creative **arts, music,** and literature, especially inspiring experiments with narrative form and **time (H.G. Wells, Conrad, Woolf, Eliot).**

Most late-twentieth- and early-twenty-first-century students of the interrelations of literature and physics know that physicist and Nobel Laureate Murray Gell-Mann bestowed the term "quark" on the smallest subatomic particle from the cry of a seagull heard in **James Joyce's** *Finnegans Wake*. Physicist N. David

Mermins also borrowed a term from literature when he named a phenomenon in liquid helium a "boojum" after the mysterious unseen creature in Lewis Carroll's nonsense epic *The Hunting of the Snark* (1876). Given the battle Mermin waged to get the term accepted, it is perhaps understandable why such borrowings do not occur more often.

Twentieth-century instances of literature borrowing ideas and concepts from physics are much more plentiful. Not surprisingly, physics and physical ideas appear most frequently in **science fiction**, although it seems that many science fiction writers find it creatively convenient to ignore or break the laws of physics in their narratives. *Star Trek, Star Wars*, and other space opera stories unapologetically present starships zipping between star systems in a matter of hours or days instead of the decades or centuries it would actually require. Some short stories and novels, however, do attempt to present realistic views of the physical universe according to physics. **Ursula K. Le Guin's** Hannish stories (among them, *The Left Hand of Darkness*) posit a universe where only sublight-speed travel is allowed between the few closest human-inhabited star systems. Scientifically accurate science fiction stories most often appear within "hard science fiction," best exemplified by the work of such writers as **Isaac Asimov** and **Arthur C. Clarke** (who helped found the subgenre) and by the fiction that has appeared for over sixty years in the magazines *Analog* (1961–present) and its predecessor *Astounding* (1938–1961). One of the most authentic presentations of the life of a working physicist in science fiction may be that of Gregory Benford in his novel *Timescape*. Benford (himself a physicist on the faculty of the University of California at Irvine) presents a physics professor protagonist who must deal with the travails of a "publish or perish" academic universe, replete with interdepartmental infighting and graduate students who fail their candidacy exams, all the while attempting to fit in some actual scientific research in his remaining free time.

Physics is less prevalent in so-called mainstream fiction, perhaps because some writers fear that the inclusion of such ideas or themes would unfavorably label their work as science fiction. Probably the best-known novels containing physics themes are **Thomas Pynchon's** *The Crying of Lot 49* and *Gravity's Rainbow*. The former follows the odyssey of Oedipa Maas through a surreal California **landscape** in the 1960s searching for the truth of a centuries-old underground postal system that may or may not be a hoax. Along the way she encounters the concepts of entropy, Maxwell's Demon, and their roles in **information theory**. In the latter, the central governing metaphor is the V2 rocket during the closing days of World War II and the early days of the occupation. Just about every technical aspect of the rocket is touched upon at some point in the narrative. Even the title "Gravity's Rainbow" is an allusion to the parabolical path the rocket takes as a ballistic object falls under the influence of **gravity**.

More recent (though less well known) literary works have tended to focus on the quantum mechanics part of modern physics. Carol Hill's *The Eleven Million*

Mile High Dancer (1985) is a comic romp as seen through the eyes of a NASA astronaut and physicist, Amanda Jaworski, and her pet cat (Schrödinger, of course) as they encounter an alien being. The title character (the alien) is taken directly from an example given by Heinz Pagels in his popular science book on quantum theory, *The Cosmic Code*. Eric Kraft's novel *Where Do You Stop?* (rpt. 1995) and Jane Hamilton's short story "When I Began to Understand Quantum Mechanics" (1989) both portray teen-aged protagonists who are encountering their own alien worlds—adulthood and quantum mechanics—with a variety of comparisons linking the two.

Other creative writers have taken the structure of the historical record of physics in the twentieth century and interwoven fictitious characters into it. In *Mrs. Einstein* (1998), novelist Anna McGrail takes the historical fact that **Einstein** and his first wife had a baby girl in 1902 who they subsequently placed for adoption. In McGrail's fictional account, the child grows up to become a physicist in her own right, and her life intersects, in 1938, with another historical figure from physics, Lise Meitner, just as Meitner discovers how to split the atom. In *Night Thoughts of a Classical Physicist,* **Russell McCormmach** offers a fictional recreation of the world of German physics in the early twentieth century as the twin revolutions of relativity and quantum mechanics upset the world of classical physics.

In some literary works, the world of physics and physicists serves primarily as a backdrop or setting. In *Properties of Light: A Novel of Love, Betrayal and Quantum Physics* (2000), Rebecca Goldstein tells a story of ambition and manipulation when a young physicist seeks to collaborate with an older physicist, only to fall in love with the elder man's daughter. In *First Light* (1995), Charles Baxter relates the life stories of a brother and sister. He is a car dealer, and she is an astrophysicist. The intriguing conceit of this book is that the story is told in reverse sequence, opening with the most recent events and working backward to the beginning, echoing the way astrophysicists study the universe: from the nearest objects first, then on out to the most distant (and earliest occurring) events. The title refers to astronomers' search for the light from the first (and thus most distant) objects in the universe.

In theater, physics and physicists have figured prominently in several well-known plays. **Bertolt Brecht's** play *Life of Galileo* is a historical **drama** about the great physicist and astronomer that (in keeping with Brecht's politics) casts him as a social revolutionary of his day. **Friedrich Dürrenmatt's** play *The Physicists* tells the story of a physicist hiding in an insane asylum to protect a dangerous formula he has discovered. The play debates the role of science and scientists in taking responsibility for the consequences of their discoveries. Playwright Tom Stoppard alludes to physics and scientific ideas in several of his plays but has done so most notably in *Hapgood*, where the dual slit experiment in quantum physics and the question "Which path did the photon take?" are played out on stage in the form of a hunt for spies who may be double agents. The hit play of the year 2000, *Copenhagen*, by Michael Frayn, dramatizes the early days of World War II. **Werner Heisenberg** (then head of the German atomic bomb project) and **Niels Bohr** (later to flee to Britain and then to the United States to help with the Manhattan Project) meet to discuss the possibility of creating nuclear weapons. In the play, Frayn brings the two men back from the dead to discuss physics and the historical record. In the process, they give conflicting accounts of what transpired during that meeting. Ultimately, Frayn uses the concept of complementarity from quantum mechanics as a dramatic metaphor to show the impossibility of determining which version of the historical phenomena is correct.

Physics appears in contemporary popular **culture** in a variety of media. A witty song by singer-songwriter Christine Lavin recounts the scientific debate over whether Pluto should be considered a planet or not ("Planet X"). The song is also notable for being the first to include a working URL for a scientific Web site as part of its lyrics (<http://www.christinelavin.com/022200planetx.html>). Physics toys and decorative items (Galilean thermometers, desktop pendula) are ubiquitous in gift catalogs and "educational" stores, marketed to adults and children alike. Einsteinian coffee mugs, posters, bumper stickers, and pop cultural references to his stereotypical absent-minded professor's "mug" occur worldwide in advertising and commercial films (*I.Q, Young Einstein*).

In a more serious vein, several extremely popular nonfiction works have attempted to connect modern physics with Eastern philosophies (most notably **Fritjof Capra's** *The Tao of Physics* and *The Dancing Wu Li Masters* by **Gary Zukav**). They have continued to attract a wide audience (including, in the case of Zukav, the millions of viewers of *Oprah)* and have sold well for over twenty years. Although it may be fair to say that the philosophical forays of Heisenberg and Bohr, among others, may have encouraged such cross-disciplinary and cross-cultural ventures to some extent, the opinions of physicists toward such works typically range from "interestingly flawed" to the decidedly uncomplimentary, "new age pseudoscience" (see: "Why Fred Allen Wolf, Tao of Physics, 'Quantum Healing,' et al. Are Interesting, But Aren't Science" at <http://myweb.onramp.net/~jet/writings/physics.html>).

In the classroom, however, physics teachers purposefully and perennially rely upon literary texts, art, and other sources materials from popular culture for pedagogical purposes. Astronomy professor and popular "interdisciplinary" astronomy textbook author Andrew Fraknoi distributes annotated bibliographies ("Science Fiction Stories with Good Science" and "Suggestions for Further Reading") from his "Physics for Poets" course on Modern Physics at Foothill College. His lists feature titles of highly readable physics textbooks, biographies, autobiographies and histories of science, fiction and science fiction by physicists, and a wide array of novels, short stories, poetry, **essays**, music, art, and other sciences that draw upon or depict concepts and discoveries from physics, astronomy and cosmology (<http://www.foothill.fhda.edu/ast/afraknoi.htm>).

Individual physicists, physics research communities, and their work have become the subjects/objects of linguistic, sociological, and cultural studies (Bazerman, Locke, Traweek). Physicists have also been active participants in the ongoing experiment to test the attractive/repulsive forces between science and culture (most notoriously, Alan Sokal). Given the long tradition of individual physicists' personal involvement in literature, art, and culture (**Snow, Feynman, Sagan, Lightman**) and the ever-pressing need for cogent and compassionate public science education and **popularizations** of science, it is the hope of this entry's coauthors that personally and professionally enriching collaborations between literature and physics (like the collegial relationship they enjoy) may gracefully calm the crossfire.

References

Bazerman, Charles. *Shaping Written Knowledge: The Genre and Activity of the Experimental Article in Science.* Madison: U of Wisconsin P, 1988.

Crease, Robert P., and Charles C. Mann. *The Second Creation: Makers of the Revolution in Twentieth-Century Physics.* New York: Macmillan, 1986.

Friedman, Alan J., and Carol C. Donley. *Einstein as Myth and Muse.* Cambridge: Cambridge UP, 1985.

Gossin, Pamela. "Literature and the Modern Physical Sciences." *Cambridge History of Science.* Ed. Mary Jo Nye. Vol. 5. Cambridge: Cambridge UP, 2002.

Locke, David. *Science as Writing.* New Haven, CT: Yale UP, 1992.

Lussier, Mark S. *Romantic Dynamics: The Poetics of Physicality.* New York: St. Martin's, 1999.

Mermin, N. David. "E Pluribus Boojum: The Physicist as Neologist." *Physics Today* (Apr. 1981): 46.

Nadeau, Robert L. *Readings from the New Book on Nature: Physics and Metaphysics in the Modern Novel.* Amherst: U of Massachusetts P, 1981.

Strehle, Susan. *Fiction in the Quantum Universe.* Chapel Hill: U of North Carolina P, 1992.

Traweek, Sharon. *Beamtimes and Lifetimes: The World of High Energy Physicists.* Cambridge: Harvard UP, 1988.

Marc Hairston and Pamela Gossin

Piercy, Marge (1936–   ). American poet and novelist whose two utopian novels explore futuristic **technologies** from a feminist perspective. *Woman on the Edge of Time* (1976), which depicts proto–**virtual reality** devices and artificial wombs, suggests some liberatory potential for men and women in **cyberspace** and reproductive technology (*see* Reproduction). *He, She and It* (1991) portrays a more full-blown cyberspace and other human-machine interfaces; for example, virtual reality entertainments, intelligent **computers**, cleaning robots, and humans with prosthetic devices. Most important is the **cyborg** protagonist who raises questions about human identity and the ethics of creating and owning artificial intelligences.

References

Shands, Kerstin W. *The Repair of the World: The Novels of Marge Piercy.* Westport, CT: Greenwood, 1994.

Walker, Sue, and Eugenie Hamner, eds. *Ways of Knowing: Critical Essays on Marge Piercy*. Mobile, AL: Negative Capability Press, 1984.

June Deery

Planck, Max Karl Ernst Ludwig (1858–1947). German physicist whose insight that **energy** comes in discrete packages rather than a continuous flow formed the basis of quantum mechanics. In 1900, Planck considered the puzzle called the ultraviolet catastrophe; according to classical **physics**, a hot object like the sun (called a blackbody for historical reasons) would radiate infinite power at the short wavelengths of the ultraviolet, a physically absurd result. Planck resolved the problem by assuming that atoms within the body vibrate only at specific discrete energies, as if water could be dipped from a pond only in exact multiples of a gallon, never in odd amounts such as one and a quarter gallons. Planck also determined the fundamental constant of nature named after him, which defines the minuscule quantum of energy and appears throughout quantum theory. For his discovery (which he himself never fully accepted, considering the quantum only a mathematical trick) he received the Nobel Prize for Physics in 1918. Literary perspectives on Planck's ideas are explored in **Russell McCormmach's** novel *Night Thoughts of a Classical Physicist* (1982).

Reference

Wheaton, Bruce R. *The Tiger and the Shark: Empirical Roots of Wave-Particle Dualism*. Cambridge: Cambridge UP, 1983.

Sidney Perkowitz

Planetarium. An optical device for projecting images of the sun, moon, planets, and stars onto a hemispherical surface. Initial donors wished planetarium experience could mitigate human differences and unify strained relations between **race**, class, and **gender**. Planetaria offered the stars to city dwellers who had lost their understanding and appreciation of that natural spectacle. Amateur (principally female) **poetry** extolled wonder and awe at the exactness and versatility of the "artificial heavens." Verses described the serenity of night, the medium's ability to "transport" viewers into a different **reality**, and the renewal of one's mental equilibrium with the approaching "dawn." Poetic themes addressed the mechanical display of God's "handiwork" or "plan" and recurrent expressions of twentieth-century **natural theology**.

Nathalie Sarraute's novel *Le Planétarium* (1959) became an important contribution to the movement known as *nouveau roman*, sometimes regarded as the literary counterpart of nonreferential (abstract) painting. Sarraute's discarding of literary conventions and the ordering of reality invoked psychological turbulence that mirrored the behaviors of planets and satellites around their parent bodies.

Jordan Marché

Plato (c. 427–347 B.C.E.). Student of Socrates, teacher of **Aristotle**, founded the Academy for the study of **philosophy**, mathematics, and science. His sophisticated and wide-ranging dialogs influenced literature, literary criticism and aesthetics (*see* Art and Aesthetics), political and analytical philosophy, **astronomy**, **cosmology**, and the other natural sciences (*Symposium, Gorgias, Phaedo, Republic, Timaeus*). Together with Aristotle, he was a primary founder of the Western intellectual tradition, contributing such concepts as the great chain of being, the mathematical description of physical nature, and the **argument from design**. His idealistic philosophy elevated the study of mathematics, astronomy and cosmology to the pinnacle of abstract thought, attracting **Copernicus, Kepler**, and Newton (*see* Newtonianism). The forms of his works were as influential as their content, with the *Republic* directly inspiring later utopian writing and his cosmological dialogs serving as models for **Galileo's**.

References

Brisson, Luc, and F. Walter Meyerstein. *Inventing the Universe: Plato's Timaeus, the Big Bang, and the Problem of Scientific Knowledge.* Albany: State U of New York P, 1995.
Hutchison, Keith. "Why Does Plato Urge Rulers to Study Astronomy?" *Perspectives on Science* 4 (1996): 24–58.

Pamela Gossin

Playfair, John (1748–1819). Writer of the most readable book on geology to appear in Britain during the first third of the nineteenth century. His friend **James Hutton** had managed only an incomplete *Theory of the Earth* in 1795, dying two years later. Realizing both the importance of Hutton's book and its verbal deficiencies, Playfair published *Illustrations of the Huttonian Theory of the Earth* (1802). Throughout the ensuing controversy, combatants on both sides recognized the excellence of Playfair's exposition, which included more recent ideas not in Hutton's original. Though not always agreed with, Playfair's book was widely read, influencing **Wordsworth, Coleridge**, Scott, **Shelley**, and poets lesser known. *Illustrations* also had major influence on **Charles Lyell**, whose *Principles of Geology* (1830–1833) was indebted to Playfair for its title and much else.

References

Dean, Dennis. *James Hutton and the History of Geology.* Ithaca, NY: Cornell UP, 1992.
      (Includes chapters on Playfair and Lyell)
———. "John Playfair and His Books." *Annals of Science* 40 (1983): 179–87.

Dennis R. Dean

Pliny the Elder (Gaius Plinius Secundus) (A.D. 23–79). Author of *Natural History*, a thirty-seven-book encyclopedia covering the natural sciences, the history of **art**, descriptions of "wonders," the uses of plants and minerals in **med-**

icine, and many other topics. Pliny died while investigating the eruption of Mount Vesuvius. His nephew, Pliny the Younger, records the story of his death in a letter to the historian Tacitus.

Jacqui Sadashige

Plurality of Worlds. The idea that the universe contains not only our own planet but also other celestial bodies inhabited by intelligent beings. Proposed in Greek antiquity, this idea provoked discussion especially after the introduction in the sixteenth century of the heliocentric theory, which by claiming that the Earth is a planet implied that planets are Earths and that stars are suns orbited by planets. The term **"extraterrestrial,"** introduced in the nineteenth century, has largely supplanted "plurality of worlds." However labeled, the notion of life elsewhere in the universe has for centuries deeply influenced various genres of literature, especially **poetry** and **science fiction**.

Reference

Crowe, M.J. *The Extraterrestrial Life Debate 1750–1900: The Idea of a Plurality of Worlds from Kant to Lowell.* Cambridge: Cambridge UP, 1986.

Michael J. Crowe

Poe, Edgar Allan (1809–1849). Author of *Eureka* (1848), a defense of La-place's **nebular hypothesis** and a deductive explication of the expansion and contraction of the universe. He read and plagiarized **John Herschel** on **astronomy** and showed intense research into physiology in *The Premature Burial* (1844). **Mesmerism** inspired several tales, including the effective scientific hoax *The Facts in the Case of M. Valdemar* (1844; 1850).

William Crisman

Poetry. A much older discourse than science. Poetry, almost certainly, emerged simultaneously with language, whereas science (in the modern sense) is a later historical development. **Aristotle's** science is really a form of literature, rather than a recognizable precursor to the set of practices now collected under the term "science." The foundations of modern scientific discourse were laid by **René Descartes** and **Francis Bacon** in the sixteenth century. Descartes, emphasizing rational over sensual experience, drove a wedge between inner and outer **reality**, as well as between mind and matter; Bacon, privileging general statements over particular description, emphasized induction and generalization based on empirical observation. By the seventeenth century the Copernican revolution, along with developments such as **Harvey's** discovery that blood circulates in the body and the invention of the **telescope** and **microscope**, had shaken and then replaced the older orders of knowledge inherited from antiquity, codified during the Middle Ages, and elaborated in the Renaissance.

Though the discourse now named science began to coalesce in the late sixteenth century, the word only took on its present meaning of specialized study of material phenomena in the mid-nineteenth century. As early as the seventeenth century, however, poets were becoming anxious about the compatibility of the new scientific knowledge and poetry. Notably, **John Donne's** "First Anniversarie" decries the fragmentation of thought resulting from the doubt that lies at the heart of scientific enterprise.

Poets have ever since been obliged to come to terms with the **epistemology** created by the new discourse. It is perhaps only coincidental that both Bacon and Descartes first distinguished themselves in the law, with its obvious need to discover general truths out of the welter of human behavior. Previously, it had been poetry itself that had been granted responsibility for making general claims regarding the human place in the **cosmos**. **William Wordsworth's** discussion of the "philosophical" qualities of poetic language in the preface to *Lyrical Ballads* recalls this heritage. The rise of scientific rationalism continues to force poets to defend **imagination** from reductionist claims about the nature of reality.

Romanticism, early in the nineteenth century, was the first aesthetic movement for which the rise of science precipitated a full-scale epistemological crisis. Poets such as **William Blake** and Wordsworth located authenticity and autonomy within the self, which science was beginning to see as an epiphenomenon of natural physical processes. Though Wordsworth admired the clarity of empirical observation, he was troubled by an increasing poverty of spirit that he attributed to Utilitarianism, industrialization, urbanization, **technology**, and other results of the scientific revolution. Blake denounced the unbridled application of reason unchecked by imagination.

Only since the early nineteenth century have the competing truth-claims of science and poetry developed into a dialectical opposition, with science increasingly extending its influence. It is difficult to underestimate the degree to which the methodologies of science, with their attendant truth-claims, have been extended into every realm of human experience. In the twentieth century, science has taken from poetry the privilege of expressing the truth about both the physical world and the human place within it. The Modernist movement in literature and its successors have had to deal with the increasingly hegemonic claims of scientific discourse to define reality. The primary objection poetry raises to science and its methods is the partial account it offers, forced upon science by its methodology of analysis, **objectivity**, and reductionism.

Literary **Modernism** places the site of authenticity within the text, objectifying the work of art insofar as that is possible in an abstract medium like language. This Modernist reaction to Romanticism attempts to avoid subjectivism in favor of a supposedly scientific "objectivity." **Ezra Pound**, in *The ABC of Reading*, writes that the image-making writer is akin to the biologist comparing microscope slides. In order to validate its claims to objectivity, Modernism makes far greater claims on science than does Romanticism. Nevertheless, the underlying crisis remains forcefully present.

There have been, of course, scientists who accepted the poetic domain as useful and important, but scientific discourse has itself usually treated poetry as the antipode of scientific rationalism, and the imagination as an untrustworthy side effect of rational thought. Recent attempts to understand language biologically such as Steven Pinker's *The Language Instinct* (1994), Derek Bickerton's more sophisticated *Language and Species* (1990), and John McCrone's superficial *The Ape That Spoke* (1991) fail as poetics because they locate language in the natural world instead of in the imagination. Only Pinker's book contains an index entry for poetry, and his concern is exclusively on the conventions of rhyme and the inversions of wordplay. This is akin to describing science as the system by which we keep score in games.

Science, beginning with skepticism, seeks certainty; poetry—all the arts—beginning with perception, seeks knowledge. The procedures of poetry since the nineteenth century employ ambiguity as a mythos, placing the paradoxical figure of metaphor at the center of poetics. The procedures of science, on the other hand, are specifically designed to collapse ambiguity. Quantum theory remains at the center of scientific investigation because it appears to deny science this power.

The contemporary scene for the most part reproduces the oppositional stance toward science that first developed with Romanticism. Contemporary poets have tended to either ignore science completely or to embrace its language for their own often subversive purposes. Some of those who have accepted a scientific vision of the world will hold that poetry and science are merely different aspects of the same creative endeavor. Such poets have recently found much intellectual comfort in quantum mechanics and **chaos theory**, which they believe offer a potential foundation for free will and human creativity. Others, more skeptical, tend to see reductionism as a dividing line between poetry and science. Among these writers one is likely to encounter resistance to the claims, for example, of the artificial intelligence community (*see* Virtual Reality and Artificial Intelligence) that human consciousness might be reproducible outside human bodies. Some forms of postmodernism have taken the conventional nature of language as a starting point, producing texts that take this quality as their subject and method.

Though scientists will continue to protest the "misuse" of their concepts, in a rearguard and subversive action over the last decade of the twentieth century poets such as Claire Bateman, Joseph Duemer, **Alice Fulton**, **Albert Goldbarth**, Richard Kenney, Paul Lake, Frederick Turner, and others have begun to adopt scientific language, reenergizing it with metaphor. The precedents for this practice, however, go back as far as **Whitman** and Wordsworth. Though both have their sources in human imagination, because their ends are different poetry and science are not likely to form a unity, and only naive idealists would wish for such a unity in any event. Current cultural values tend to privilege science as an arbiter of truth, and poetry will likely continue to resist the hegemonic claims of scientific absolutism while borrowing from its language.

References

Fulton, Alice. *Powers of Congress.* Boston: David R. Godine, 1990.

Goldbarth, Albert. *Arts & Sciences.* Princeton, NJ: Ontario Review, 1986.

———. *Marriage and Other Science Fiction.* Columbus: Ohio State UP, 1994.

Holub, Miroslav. *Sagittal Section.* Oberlin, OH: Field Translation Series, 1980.

Kenney, Richard. *The Evolution of the Flightless Bird.* New Haven, CT: Yale UP, 1984.

———. *The Invention of the Zero.* New York: Knopf, 1993.

The New Princeton Encyclopedia of Poetry and Poetics. Ed. Alex Preminger and T.V.F. Brogan. Princeton, NJ: Princeton UP, 1993.

Joseph Duemer

Pointillisme. Or Divisionism, a painting style pioneered by Georges Seurat in finishing *Sunday on La Grande Jatte* in Paris in 1886. Named by Felix Feneon, used by Paul Signac, and taken up by Van Gogh, Matisse, and Giacomo Balla on their way to more modern styles, pointillism systematized the Impressionist technique of applying unmixed oil colors in patches, ignoring the academic stipulation that color areas shade into each other. By **analogy**, in literature, it is the juxtaposition of discontinuous scenes or touches of description.

William R. Everdell

Politics and Ideology. Normative collections of ideal beliefs and values, often strongly contended. Scientific ideology, for example, would include the belief that science should serve all citizens equally and therefore is not to be judged by social standards of fairness. For example, if fetal tissue possibly holds the promise to cure Parkinson's disease, it is ethically permissible to use dead fetuses for research purposes because such a scientific discovery would fairly benefit all. Science, here, is neutral. But what about the concern of the society at large for the dead fetus? The political system is left to decide the ethics of this conundrum.

In history, scientific ideology has been a figment of utopians; it has been nothing more than a horizon that is never reached. Science has never attained the ideology stage. The reason is that science policy is set by rhetorical exigencies as perceived by politicians—which policy has been influenced by popular literature and subsequently bought or rejected by a citizenry. Scientific policy responds to the social condition that is described by the amalgamated literature of a civilization. Social and scientific trends are sifted through literature, and the cake of political action comprises this literary flour. But for this literary business to be trusted and nobly acted upon by the politicians it must be left alone.

The intrusion of politics into scientific ideology has not changed much since **Frances Bacon** dreamed of a utopian science policy of which he wrote in *New Atlantis.* Bacon supported an apolitical science policy. He began his political campaign for independent science policy when he wrote *The Advancement of Learning (1605)* addressed to his ruler, James I of England, attempting to sweep away the myopic seventeenth-century **philosophy** of learning and to open a clearer future for scientific discovery. He felt that Renaissance education consisted of "lateral learning," that is, kneading classical Roman and Greek works until all the substance was squeezed out. Bacon distrusted scholastically popular logical appeal and rhetorical eloquence in scientific discourse. He characterized this lateral learning as making lace of broadcloth. Bacon argued for the opposite approach to learning—for discovery by methodical experimentation, which he characterized as inductive reasoning (cf., deductive reasoning). Although he campaigned for the removal of artistic proofs from scientific discovery, he used those rhetorical tools to sell his learning innovations to the political power. His literary works are quite eloquent, and there is a sense of literary ceremony in his writing.

He wrote *New Atlantis* (published posthumously in 1627) in the same didactic vein as *Advancement*, enlightening his world to the advantages of a scientific island. In fairy-tale fashion Bacon described a scientific **utopia**, in which man is not shackled by corrupting political influences but goes about his scientific business, with noble and pure discovery. Alas, even in Bacon's New Atlantis the people of science must remain hidden behind an opaque sea vapor, protected from corrupting politics.

Some prime examples of the mésalliance of science ideology to politics are the government policies of France from the seventeenth century forward, of Russia after the Bolshevik Revolution and into the 1980s, of China after the Cultural Revolution, and for that matter, of the present policies of the United States. French policies integrated elite social position with science education. The Soviet Union emphasized science **technology** over life comforts, which caused their nation's dire social sacrifices. China redirected pure scientific research toward technological application to keep its population from starving. The United States bandies national science priorities such as the space program, nuclear power production, eugenics, electronic data transmission, and environmental issues with regional political wiles.

Even programs that begin scientifically pure can be adulterated to yield benefits to politicians. The spectacular American space program became tainted on January 28, 1986. On that date the National Aeronautics and Space Administration (NASA) launched the *Challenger*, a manned spacecraft. At seventy-three seconds into the flight the space shuttle's rockets exploded, killing all seven astronauts. A faulty seal in the rocket booster apparently caused the explosion. The inferior gasket problem was well known to NASA administrators, but the damage had been superficially addressed so that the spacecraft could be launched before the eminent broadcast of the Presidential State of the Union message. In a follow-up report on the cause of the accident one member of the presidential commission, the prominent scientist **Richard Feynman**, hypothesized that the fundamental cause of the catastrophe was NASA's overconfidence. He said that

NASA had painted too rosy a picture of the agency's technological competence while it was lobbying for funding. NASA's management had served funding of the project instead of prioritizing reasonable mission safety. Feynman concluded that NASA's selling efforts to Congress interfered with its honesty as a science and engineering agency, a natural consequence of government funding.

The political process for forming national science policy is a child of seminal politics. From **Plato's** *Republic* we learn that a free government is born when a populace gives up some degree of individual rights to a sovereign authority, understanding, in turn, that the authority is to somehow better protect any rights that are retained by the individuals. The usual cost of that contract is that once the state is in power, it abuses its ascendancy by giving more benefits to those with the political power, and those without political power become exploited. The state begins to serve the most influential because the most influential control the state. This results in rapacity as each individual contends to get an unfair portion of the state's assets, because, of course, not everyone can get a fair share.

By the very nature of selection, politicians are the elite of a society. They cannot help ruling from the perspective of the elite. This creates a problem for an ostensibly value-free science policy. Politicians who are charged to set scientific policy always have an ulterior motive, which is to remain in power. Politicians always act to favor their own political survival and therefore set science policy to their own political benefit. The tendency is to reward the incumbent politicians with staying in power. **Karl Popper** (1902–1994), the philosopher of science, summarizes the issue of replacing durable power whether it be elitism or something else, with the suggestion that we admit we never can be certain we have the right answers. Hence, we have motivation to keep in place that machinery that can change authority. If a set of political leaders no longer provides what is obviously the best solutions, then, without violence, they can be replaced. For Popper the question is not who should wield the power but how, when necessary, the power should be passed on. Science priorities change and so must the politicians who set the policy.

In the United States 75 percent of all scientific research is assisted by some government funding. Realistically, the most money available for scientific funding is government revenue that is appropriated by popular choice. For instance, research funding for an **AIDS** cure swelled when AIDS became the favorite disease of the artists in this country. Their **rhetoric** in one form or another sold the public on the exigency of the AIDS. Arguably, popular selection of social priorities like this choice is fair; however, as Popper warned, what must be protected is the fairness of the selection process and, above all, the means to change it when the process becomes skewed. Natural order sets the rules of ruling, and the avenues of changing the ruler must be left open. For instance, when aberrations in nature occur, there is always a natural accommodation. So it should be with scientific policies. But how is informed political selection ensured?

In the free world the most powerful influence in setting public priorities is literature. It is the writers of literature who sense social priorities and fairness, *and* inequities, and enlighten their readers. These writers sound the tower bell and they awaken the town. Presumably the politicians will hear the knell, too. To achieve truth in consensus the process must be utterly open. It matters little which political process predominates, but that system also must be informed and oriented to the long-term benefit of those affected and, if necessary, be changeable.

Literature plays a critical part in the political process as it serves as a social measurement by keeping the priorities of long-term policy in perspective. Literature will reveal the wave of public opinion—or level it out. It gives us an average sounding of universal morality, not hard-case exception. Literature is a broad-crested weir, over which the aggregated stream of humanity flows—its level above the weir is a measure of the specific **energy** of a civilization. The passing of its gist depends little on whether the stream is laminar or turbulent; the essence of the fluid still flows past the observer at the weir. That time-polished dam measures both the smooth and chaotic flow in human events. Scientific ideology, too, must pass over the literary weir, as it is part of the stream of humanity.

References

Eiseley, Loren. *The Man Who Saw Through Time*. New York: Scribner's, 1973.
Feynman, Richard P. "An Outsider's View of the Challenger Inquiry." *Physics Today* Feb. 26, 1988: 26–37.
Lederman, Leonard L. "Science and Technology Policies and Priorities: A Comparative Analysis." *Science* 237 (1987): 1125–33.
Maynard-Mood, Steven. "Managing Controversies over Science: The Case of Fetal Research." *Journal of Public Administration Research and Theory* 5.1 (Jan. 1995): 5–18.
"Science and Politics." (Special issue) Ed. Margaret C. Jacob. *Social Research* (Fall 1992): 487–614.
Stephens, James. *Francis Bacon and the Style of Science*. Chicago: U of Chicago P, 1975.

Joseph C. Groseclose

Pope, Alexander (1688–1744). Perhaps the most popular and important English poet of the early eighteenth century. A master of the rhymed couplet, Pope wrote satiric verse and narrative poems and published translations of the classics—notably **Homer**—that made him a small fortune. Pope's famous couplet on Isaac Newton—"Nature and Nature's Law lay hid in Night,/ God said, 'Let Newton Be!' and all was Light"—testifies to his wit, the significance of Newton's reputation in the eighteenth century, and Pope's limited understanding of Newton's work. As an Anglo-Catholic and a Tory, Pope remained outside the dominant **culture** of **Newtonianism**; his fascination with gardening and his detailed and often moving descriptions of his physical afflictions make his poems and published letters important sources for understanding eighteenth-century perceptions of deformity, disease, and the body (*see* Corporeality/Body). Pope's **poetry** characteristically envisions nature as mediated and improved by careful cultivation and suggests that such refinement of nature is the proper role of the gentleman.

His gardens (*see* Garden; Landscape[s]) at Kew demonstrate an aesthetic concern for order and symmetry that is evident in his verse; his descriptions of his pain (caused primarily by a twisted spine) in letters to friends such as **Jonathan Swift** and the **physician** and satirist John Arbuthnot provide eloquent testimony to the suffering endured by patients in an era before modern surgery, antibiotics, and painkillers.

References

Deutsch, Helen. *Resemblance and Disgrace: Alexander Pope and the Deformation of Culture.* Cambridge: Harvard UP, 1996.
Martin, Peter. *Pursuing Innocent Pleasures: The Gardening World of Alexander Pope.* North Haven, CT: Archon, 1984.
Pollak, Ellen. *The Poetics of Sexual Myth: Gender and Ideology in the Verse of Swift and Pope.* Chicago: U of Chicago P, 1985.

Robert Markley

Popper, Karl Raimund (1902–1994). Realist and rationalist philosopher of science, critic of totalitarian ideologies, and a founder of evolutionary **epistemology**. Popper argued that knowledge develops through the testing of competing **hypotheses** and the correction of error. In opposition to Thomas Kuhn (*see* Revolutions), he argued that no single paradigm determines the content of our ideas, and he thus offers theoretical support for literary critics who reject the central contention of reader-response **theory**: the idea that meaning in literary interpretation is wholly determined by the reader's interpretive framework.

Reference

Schilpp, Paul Arthur, ed. *The Philosophy of Karl Popper.* La Salle, IL: Open Court, 1974.

Joseph Carroll

Popularization. The process of diffusing expert knowledge through the larger **culture**. Popularization covers activities ranging from education to entertainment but excludes magic and other displays that aim to stimulate wonder but not promote understanding. In contrast to scientific training, which in the West has typically proceeded via formal apprenticeship in institutions or through self-education, popularization has relied mainly on mass dissemination. Public lectures chiefly delivered popular science in the era before cheap printed materials, and the mass media took over thereafter—first newspapers, books, and magazines, then radio and **television**, and now the **Internet** and **CD-ROMs**. Motives for popularization differ not only by **time** and place but also for scientists and the public, who may have exclusive, if not opposing, interests. The public seeks access to specialized knowledge of certified social import because Western culture privileges objective, empirical knowledge of the universe as instrumental to material, and thus social, **progress**. However, the willingness of professionals to initiate laypeople into their specialized mysteries, and of non-specialists to appreciate that knowledge, varies considerably, depending on whether it requires extensive technical background as well as whether it threatens existing cultural and political values. Thus scientists have reluctantly discussed the fetal-tissue cloning that precedes research in cell development, while laypeople have resisted discoveries in conflict with biblical teachings on creation and sexual practice, among other topics. **C.P. Snow** decried the divergence between scientific and popular knowledge as the **two cultures**, but Nathan Reingold has pointed out that the divergence does not mean that earlier periods had a single, unified culture because America, at least, has always had "at least two—the learned culture and the vernacular culture" (48). Popular science belongs to that vernacular culture, which began in oral culture, flowered in print media, and is now colonizing electronic genres. Popular science literature thus includes not only nontechnical accounts of scientific activity in lectures, books (including exploration narratives and biographies), and documentary **film** and video but also projections of existing research into **science fiction** and critiques of science in verbal and graphic humor.

Popularization has particular importance for the United States. Puritanism promoted self-improvement and the empirical study of natural phenomena as signifiers of divine communication. The colonial condition initiated a tradition of publicly funded scientific research beginning in the seventeenth century with exploration of resources for economic development and commercial exploitation. By the nineteenth century the documentation of indigenous species for **agriculture**, of geographical features and geological assets for settlement and **mining**, and of ethnographic details of native peoples to be subdued were firmly established activities of the federal government through agencies as diverse as the Congress (which authorized various expeditions to explore the continent), the Smithsonian Institution (established 1835; organized 1846), the Geological Survey (established 1878–1889), the navy (for research in oceanography and **meteorology**), and the army (especially its West Point–trained corps of **engineers**, who surveyed the West for the transcontinental railroad). Like many other components of participatory democracy, these activities depended on the goodwill and tax dollars of an educated citizenry, and institutionally minded American scientists took care to maintain popular knowledge at a level that sustained public interest. Lay involvement had a long history as well, beginning with the transit of Venus in 1769, when amateurs helped David Rittenhouse calculate the sun's parallax with exceptional precision, and continuing throughout the nineteenth century, when rock and bone hunters collected mineral specimens and fossils essential to research in geology and **paleontology**—two sciences in which America led Europe.

As means for understanding the practice of popularization, rhetorical strategies such as information transfer, hagiography, and wonderment offer more insight than disciplinary categories (e.g., **astronomy** and zoology [*see* Biology/ Zoology]), genres (e.g., taxonomy and biography), or media (e.g., lectures and documentary film). By definition, however, popular science literature in all media diverges from the professional literature of the field. To borrow the terminology developed by Thomas S. Kuhn (*see* Revolutions) in *The Structure of Scientific Revolutions*, popular science comes into being as a discipline's paradigms become sufficiently set that the activities of normal science are professionalized. Or, conversely, science writing remains at the level of popular science until practitioners agree on disciplinary paradigms that close off participation by laypeople.

Information transfer, which enables the lay audience to rejoin the scientific community—peripherally, at least—represents the dominant form of popular science. The American appetite for information transfer runs back to the lyceum, begun in 1826 as public institutions for self-improvement within a democratic context—hence Carl Bode's description, "town meetings of the mind." By 1842, such popular science became a commodity for mass production and consumption, as Horace Greeley published transcripts of science lectures from the New York Lyceum, New-York Historical Society, and the Mercantile Library for sale first in daily (local) and then in weekly (national) editions of his New York *Tribune* and subsequently in pamphlets sold nationwide. John Tyndall's 1872 **physics** lectures in New York City sold 50,000 copies of the New York *Tribune*. The Appleton publishing house developed a list, under the leadership of the indefatigable popularizer E.L. Youmans, of popular works by major European and American scientists; the series aimed to promote, as the title of Youmans's collection of lectures put it, *The Culture Demanded by Modern Life* (1867). In 1871, the *Galaxy* magazine initiated its "Scientific Miscellany," briefly edited by Youmans, the first regular science department in a general-interest magazine. Today, newspapers have their own science sections, joining popular books on **chaos theory**, television programs on developments in cancer treatment, and Web pages with reports of scientific research (or the data themselves, as when the National Aeronautics and Space Administration [NASA] posts images sent from satellites) as they sustain popular interest in acquiring scientific knowledge.

The dominance of information transfer explains why accounts of discovery represent the largest genre of popular science literature: They blend history and laboratory report, thereby initiating the reader into scientific activity and its results. This staple of popular science also connects the dominant genre with two lesser-known types, the hoax and the **satire**. The most notorious American hoax occurred on August 25, 1835, when Richard Adam Locke, in the first article of a *New York Sun* series, claimed that the newest **telescope** by Sir **John Frederick William Herschel** had revealed "continuous herds of brown quadrupeds" on the moon. This so-called moon hoax imitated rather than debunked scientific reports, and similar counterfeits followed contemporary developments.

The American **fossil record**—critical in providing proof of evolution of species—proved particularly inspiring. As an identifiable subgenre, paleontological hoaxes began appearing with some regularity after 1831, when the Woodville *Mississippi Democrat* described "An Ossified Man," and continued through sketches by **Mark Twain**, who maintained a keen interest in science throughout his life. Parodies of scientific writing, which reached a high point in **Jonathan Swift's** satire of the **Royal Society** in *Gulliver's Travels* (1726) generated their own publication, *The Journal of Irreproducible Results* (1962–present).

The importance of information transfer accounts for the hero worship in many accounts of scientific activity, including scientific biography and narratives of discovery in both the **laboratory** and the **landscape**. Scientific biography reached its pinnacle in the nineteenth century, along with other manifestations of the Great Man School of History, at a time when scientific activity was turning less individual and more collaborative and institutional. Accounts of exploration, such as Biddle and Allen's *History of the Expedition under the Command of Captains Lewis and Clark* (1814), continue not only in Ken Burns's film on the subject, *Lewis and Clark* (1997), but also in heroic accounts of scientific triumph over travails large and small, including tales of polar and space exploration, including Tom Wolfe's *The Right Stuff* (1979). When scientists author their own popular accounts, as in **James D. Watson's** *The Double Helix* (1968), hagiography becomes self-promotion, a subset of autobiography. When the author seeks public funding of billions of dollars over the course of decades, as in the case of the Human Genome Project, heroics serve political as well as literary goals.

The literature of scientific wonderment—occasionally derided as the "Gee-Whiz! School of Popular Science"—reinforces the distinction between popular and professional science even as it appears to bridge it. This category focuses on phenomena themselves over explanations of them, emphasizing the unusual or remarkable over the typical or predictable. In focusing on effect rather than cause, the literature of wonder either ignores technical processes, thus maintaining the separation between expert and amateur knowledge, or keeps to the periphery of scientific activity, where investigation lacks the strong agenda of "normal science," with its communal agreement over open and closed questions. Thus the literature of wonderment treats research into so-called 'parascientific' phenomena, such as ESP (extrasensory perception), and dominates the imaginative genres of science fiction in all media from print to video game.

The importance of technical innovation in contemporary life continues to feed public interest in science, while the growing costs of research keep investigators beholden to the public. Popular science thereby sustains media industries—the factories of the information age—by transforming the raw materials of scientific activity into the infotainment that links popular culture today and yesterday.

References

Bode, Carl. *The American Lyceum: The Town Meeting of the Mind.* New York: Oxford UP, 1956.

Bruce, Robert V. *The Launching of Modern American Science, 1846–1876.* Ithaca, NY: Cornell UP, 1987.

Dupree, A. Hunter. *Science in the Federal Government: A History of Policies and Activities.* Baltimore: Johns Hopkins UP, 1986.

Lee, Judith Yaross. "(Pseudo-) Scientific Humor." *American Literature and Science.* Ed. Robert J. Scholnick. Lexington: UP of Kentucky, 1992. 128–56.

Reingold, Nathan. "Definitions and Speculations: The Professionalization of Science in America in the Nineteenth Century." *The Pursuit of Knowledge in the Early American Republic: American Scientific and Learned Societies from Colonial Times to the Civil War.* Ed. Alexandra Oleson and Sanborn C. Brown. Baltimore: Johns Hopkins UP, 1976. 33–69.

Scholnick, Robert J. " 'What We Mean by Science': The Diffusion of Science in Antebellum America and Beyond." Unpublished paper delivered at the Convention of the Society for Literature and Science, Oct. 1987.

Judith Yaross Lee

Positivism. A description of the logical methodology of scientific inquiry based upon the philosophies of **John Stuart Mill**, Auguste Comte (who coined the term), and others. According to positivism, science is empirical, normative, unified, and teleological; privileges mechanistic explanations of nature that can be experimentally verified; advances through the steady accumulation of knowledge; and contributes to social **progress**. In this view, science is the ultimate— indeed, the only valid—form of knowledge. Positivism is largely discredited as a valid **epistemology**; within literature and science studies, the term is usually pejorative. Yet positivist myths about science retain considerable currency in the larger culture.

Michael A. Bryson

Poststructuralism. The theoretical system that has dominated literary and cultural studies since the 1970s. The central doctrines of poststructuralism are textualism and indeterminacy. Textualism is the idea that language and **culture** constitute or construct the world according to their own internal principles, and indeterminacy identifies all meaning as ultimately self-contradictory. Together, textualism and indeterminacy eliminate the two criteria of **truth**: the correspondence of propositions to their objects and the internal coherence of propositions. By affirming that texts do not refer to objects but rather constitute them, textualism eliminates correspondence, and by affirming that all meaning is ultimately contradictory, indeterminacy eliminates coherence. In place of truth, poststructuralism yields epistemological and ontological primacy to **rhetoric** or discourse. The two basic poststructuralist doctrines are often integrated with concepts from Freudian psychology (*see* Freud) (*see* Anthropology/Psychology/ Sociology) and from Marxist social theory. In its political aspect, poststructuralism typically treats normative intellectual, moral, and social structures within the Western cultural tradition as arbitrary constructs that are designed to perpetuate the exploitative interests of social elites, particularly the interests of white male heterosexuals of the ruling classes. The main source for poststructuralist linguistic **theory** is the "deconstructive" **philosophy** of Jacques Derrida, and the main sources for its political theory are the concepts of "power" and "discourse" in the work of Michel Foucault. Derridean deconstruction and Foucauldian political criticism form the main antecedents for the cultural study of science. By attributing primacy to discourse, poststructuralism authorizes literary scholars to seek for the determining forces of scientific knowledge in language and culture.

References

Derrida, Jacques. *Of Grammatology*. Trans. Gayatri Chakravorty Spivak. Baltimore: Johns Hopkins UP, 1976.
Foucault, Michel. *Language, Counter-Memory, Practice: Selected Essays and Interviews*. Trans. Donald F. Bouchard and Sherry Simon. Ed. Donald F. Bouchard. Ithaca, NY: Cornell UP, 1977.

Joseph Carroll

Pound, Ezra Weston Loomis (1885–1972). Twentieth-century American poet and critic, author of the *Cantos*, an epic work sixty years in the making (1915–1970). Setting himself against the modern scientist's reduction of "all '**energy**' to unbounded undistinguished abstraction," Pound nonetheless insisted that **poetry** conform, as Maria Luisa Ardizzone has remarked, to a biological logic; and studies by Ian F.A. Bell and, more recently, Daniel Albright investigate his repeated use of scientific **analogy** in developing a critical vocabulary in which to discuss his poetry.

Reference

Pound, Ezra. "Cavalcanti." *Literary Essays of Ezra Pound*. Ed. T.S. Eliot. New York: New Directions, 1968. 149–200.

Steven Meyer

Powers, Richard (1957–   ). MacArthur Fellow and masterful novelist whose work evinces great concern with the interrelations of science, **technology**, **philosophy**, language, and human compassion. His narratives typically turn on contemporary scientific research and explore specific themes in considerable depth (such as the use of game theory in *Prisoner's Dilemma*, 1988). Powers's style has often been described as "fugue-like" in its multilayered presentation of themes and characterization. In *The Gold Bug Variations* (1991), molecular **biology**, **music**, and information science (*see* Information Theory) all figure strongly. In the semiautobiographical *Galatea 2.2* (1996), Powers creates a postmodern "Pygmalion" story, relating the collaborative efforts of a literature professor and cognitive scientist to develop artificial intelligence (*see* Virtual Reality and Artificial Intelligence). The resultant collection of neural networks eventually seeks knowledge of her identity, raising questions of purpose, free will, and the limits of the human search for knowledge and expression.

Jay A. Labinger and Pamela Gossin

Pragmatism. A perspective that focuses on practice rather than **theory**. The pragmatic stance tends to be flexible, open, and task oriented. Ernst Mach stressed sense perception. Richard Rorty derived the practical negotiating strategy of unforced agreement and stressed the value of diversity. Stanley Fish arrived at reader-response criticism. Other key pragmatists are **Ralph Waldo Emerson**, **William James**, Charles Peirce, and John Dewey.

In science, pragmatism is mostly confined to practice-oriented **laboratories** where, conceptually, **theories** are used as fuzzy tools for tinkering rather than dominant guides. The clearest example of pragmatic literature may be the work of **Jorge Luis Borges**. It sets its own rules at every turn in order to surprise the unknown within narratives and self-deconstruct its own assumptions without irony. Scientific and literary pragmatism share an interest in multiple approaches to a task, even if the approaches are mutually contradictory, as long as they tend to serve their purposes.

Luis O. Arata

Pregnancy. As studied within LS, a physical state rooted in the **politics** of **reproduction** and abortion rights. Such studies generally assume historical and cultural influence and stress the mutually supportive **rhetorics** of domination, penetrability, and opticalization employed within the histories and texts of **medicine** and literature. General branches of study include the historical evolution of "pregnancy" and the influence of a technological **imagination** on contemporary constructions of childbirth. Central works include those by Alice Adams, Barbara Duden, and Carol Stabile, which are in turn connected to general studies in **technology** and literature, and medicine and literature.

References

Adams, Alice. *Reproducing the Womb: Images of Childbirth in Science, Feminist Thought and Literature*. Ithaca, NY: Cornell UP, 1994.
Duden, Barbara. *Disembodying Women: Perspectives on Pregnancy and the Unborn*. Trans. Lee Hoinacki. Cambridge: Harvard UP, 1993.
Stabile, Carol A. *Feminism and the Technological Fix*. Manchester and New York: Manchester UP, 1994.

Sharon Stockton

Prehistoric Man. Humans living before the advent of written records of the past; hypothesized to have existed even in classical times, when **Hesiod, Lucretius**, and **Ovid**, among poets, speculated on cultural states prior to the advent of civilization. Greek travelers, like Herodotus, and Roman generals, like Caesar, had firsthand experience with people less technologically advanced than their own. Tacitus wrote a famous description of the Germans. The discovery of American Indians, and later of South Seas Polynesians, established beyond doubt that geographically diverse humanity represented differing cultural states. It was then seen that all of mankind had undergone a sequence of such states. In 1836, the Danish archeologist Christian Jurgensen divided prehistory into a stone age, a bronze age, and an iron age. A student of his, Jens Worsaae, then accepted the system and elaborated upon it in a book on the prehistory of Denmark (1849), one of the first of its kind. In 1865, Sir John Lubbock divided the Stone Age into an earlier Paleolithic (Old Stone Age) period and a later Neolithic (New Stone Age) period. But all of these designations were cultural only and did not presuppose the physiological evolution of mankind. This more controversial topic, made inevitable by the discovery of Neanderthal Man in 1856, was illuminated in turn by **Lyell** (*The Antiquity of Man*, 1863, 1874), **Huxley** (*Man's Place in Nature*, 1863), and **Darwin**, (*The Descent of Man*, 1871). After 1870 or so the theme was then taken up with enthusiasm by numerous popularizers, especially in France, where Louis Figuier, Gabriel de Mortillet, and Henri du Cleuziou all published before 1890. Prehistoric men entered such works as **Jack London**, *Before Adam* (1907); H. Rosny-Aine, *La Guerre du Feu* (1911, later filmed as *The Quest for Fire*); and **Arthur Conan Doyle**, *The Lost World* (1912). **H.G. Wells's** influential *Outline of History* (1920) and short story "The Grisly Folk" (1921) disparaged Neanderthals, as did William Golding's *The Inheritors* (1955). *The Long Journey* (1923–1924), a series of three novels by Johannes V. Jensen, traces the development of human civilization from the Stone Age to modern times. *Earth Children* (1980–1990), a series of four novels by Jean M. Auel (of which *The Clan of the Cave Bear*, 1980, and *The Mammoth Hunters*, 1985, are best known), is wholly prehistoric.

References

Grayson, Donald K. *The Establishment of Human Antiquity*. New York: Academic, 1933.
Trigger, Bruce G. *A History of Archaeological Thought*. Cambridge: Cambridge UP, 1989.

Dennis R. Dean

Pre-Socratic Philosophers (seventh to fifth centuries B.C.E.). Ancient Greek natural philosophers, traditionally divided into four main schools: the Milesians (Thales, Anaximander, and Anaximenes), Heraclitus, the Eliatics (including Parmenides and Zeno), the pluralistic naturalists (Empedocles and Anaxgoras), and the atomists (Leucippus and Democritus). While there are philosophical differences among these thinkers and their respective schools, the pre-Socratics are generally considered to be the originators of scientific thought. Thales (sixth century B.C.E.) first proposed that there was a unified and underlying substance of nature. Anaximander (seventh century B.C.E.), meanwhile, created the concept of four basic elements. As debates continued these philosophers moved further away from mythological explanations toward objective analysis of natural phenomena. Their work in **astronomy**, mathematics, and **natural philosophy** had broad consequences for traditional **mythology**. Among the Pythagoreans, mathematics reduced myth to a symbolic level, while for the Sophists scientific skepticism, rather than a belief in the gods, became the primary source for explaining natural phenomena.

Shelly Jarrett Bromberg

Priestley, Joseph (1733–1804). Chemist, unitarian minister, biblical scholar, considered, along with Lavoisier, to be responsible for the discovery of oxygen. Priestley shared many of Newton's unitarian beliefs—above all, the belief that trinitarianism was a false doctrine foisted on Christianity by the editorial policies of those who created the canonical version of the Bible. However, Priestley became a leader of the reaction to the Newtonian (*see* Newtonianism) synthesis of matter, motion, and force resulting from the acts of an absconded God. Causation, for Priestley, was both immanent and inward working.

In his first scientific publication, *The History and Present State of Electricity* (1767), Priestley credits the Newtonian synthesis with the gains that resulted from it, observing, "Hitherto philosophy has been chiefly conversant about the more sensible properties of bodies; electricity, together with chymistry, and the doctrine of light and colours, seems to be giving us an inlet into their internal structure, on which their sensible properties depend." Priestley's hope, based on the discoveries to that time, is that "[n]ew worlds may open to our view, and the glory of the great Sir Isaac Newton himself, and all of his contemporaries be eclipsed [*sic*] by a new set of philosophers, in a quite new field of speculation" (xiii). A decade or so later, in his *Replies* (1778) to Richard Price's *Remarks . . . on Several Passages in Dr. Priestley's Disquisitions on Matter and Spirit* (also 1778), Priestley notes that Price's attempt at a refutation "only shows, though in a clear and masterly manner, that the present laws of nature require an *intelligence and energy*, of which what we usually call nature is not capable" (IV: 10).

Within the context of literature and science, Priestley exemplifies one variety of the radical, dissenting reaction to the social consequences of the Newtonian synthesis—above all, the **argument from design** and the attempt to justify the social cruelties of eighteenth-century English society by presenting that society as conformable to "nature," as understood by the adherents of that synthesis. As such, Priestley operates in the realm of science much as **Blake** does in the realm of literature.

References

Fruchtman, Jack. *The Apocalyptic Politics of Richard Price and Joseph Priestley*. Philadelphia: American Philosophical Society, 1983.

Graham, Jenny. *Revolutionary in Exile: The Emigration of Joseph Priestley to America*. Philadelphia: American Philosophical Society, 1995.

Priestley, Joseph. *Autobiography of Joseph Priestley*. Ed. Jack Lindsay. Teaneck, NJ: Fairleigh Dickinson UP, 1971.

Stuart Peterfreund

Primates. Coined by Carl Linnaeus to describe a single descriptive category including humans among other apes, in the tenth edition of his *Systema* (1758). Thirty years earlier, **Swift's** Yahoos had challenged the boundaries of what constituted "human" and "nonhuman" physical identities. Whether in the evolutionary science that explores the kinship among primate species, the **neuroscience** that investigates various primate relations to language and subjectivity, or in the literary investigations of self and other (*see* Alterity) on the border of species identity, the category "primate" serves to unite as well as separate alternative constructions of what counts as "human."

References

Haraway, Donna. *Primate Visions: Gender, Race, and Nature in the World of Modern Science*. New York: Routledge, 1989.
Schiebinger, Londa. *Nature's Body: Gender in the Making of Modern Science*. Boston: Beacon, 1993.
Self, Will. *Great Apes*. New York: Grove/Atlantic, 1997.

Richard Nash

Problem Solving. The search for an explanation, answer, or solution to a puzzle, facilitated and improved, in literature, science, and LS by expertise in a knowledge domain. Expertise generally arises out of a decade or more of dedicated practice within a domain. A number of psychological studies have found that the successful problem solving of experts across fields is characterized by superior memory performance, an enhanced capacity to perceive complex patterns, and a profound **representation** of the problem. The problem solving of experts also tends to include the allotment of substantial time to qualitative analysis of the problem at hand as well as persistent self-monitoring.

Reference

Ericsson, K. Anders, ed. *The Road to Excellence*. Mahway, NJ: Erlbaum, 1996.

Maria F. Ippolito

Proctor, Richard Anthony (1837–1888). Most widely read author on **astronomy** in the English-speaking world in the last third of the nineteenth century. After graduating from Cambridge, Proctor authored at least fifty-seven books, mainly on astronomy. These volumes not only shaped public opinion concerning the heavens but also influenced such literary works as **Thomas Hardy's** *Two on a Tower*.

Michael J. Crowe

Progress. Often connoted, in Western culture, by science itself, as civilization is considered to improve through scientific insight and technological development. Progress *within* science implies that such knowledge develops through a steady process of accumulation. Philosophers, literary critics, historians and others have critiqued both assumptions. Thomas Kuhn (*see* Revolutions), in *The Structure of Scientific Revolutions* (1962), suggested that science proceeds via **paradigm** shifts rather than developing in a linear, accumulative manner. Progress thus becomes a positivist myth promulgated in heroic versions of scientific history. Within **biology**, progress is often falsely associated (through **social Darwinism** and other ideological frameworks) with evolution (*see* Evolutionary Theory), which instead is a directionless, purposeless process: Species change over time but do not strive toward an idealized endpoint.

Michael A. Bryson

Proust, Marcel (1871–1922). Author of *A la recherche du temps perdu* (In Search of Lost Time, 1913–1922), a multivolume work of **fiction** centered upon a philosophical exploration of the relationships among **time**, space, experience, and the individual's existence. Proust's emphasis on the role of the senses in triggering memory suggests a positivistic approach toward experience. His presentation of time as manifold or contemporaneous, meanwhile, is reminiscent of Henri Bergson's notions of time and space.

Shelly Jarrett Bromberg

Psychology. *See* **Anthropology/Psychology/Sociology**.

Public Science Writing. Since the eighteenth century, a discourse that self-reflexively sets about representing and instituting science in public life. Historian Jan Golinski argues that science as public **culture** involves scientific techniques and instruments as much as **rhetoric** (Golinski 3). However, in the late nineteenth century (for example, **T.H. Huxley**), the 1930s (J.D. Bernal), and the 1990s (the advocates and critics of the Human Genome Project), important roles have been played by texts by scientists aiming to persuade governments, private institutions, interest groups, other intellectual elites, and larger publics that science can best serve society's goals and interests and should thus be generously funded and incorporated into policy-making bodies.

Encompassing genres ranging from environmental impact statements to lectures and broadcasts, public science writing falls within the broad category of popular science; use of the term "public" represents a historical and sociological focus on institutions, publications, and practices that create common contexts—or public spheres—for debate. Alongside history and sociology, a key role exists for literary analysis of the semantic fluidity, novel metaphoric associations, and rhetorical and conceptual contradictions that characterize scientists' moves from the languages of their special fields into literary-political public discourse.

Significantly, Frank M. Turner urges fellow historians to read public science writing more closely and critically; and sociologist Richard Whitley points to the diffuse linguistic structures that accompany scientists' appeals to wider audiences. Of particular interest is historian Robert M. Young's detailed cultural analysis of literary and disciplinary specialization and the breakdown of public debate of science in the late nineteenth century. Theorist Jürgen Habermas offers a useful sociohistorical analysis of the disintegration of the public sphere of debate and the therapeutic role of cultural practices that represent everyday concerns in order to limit and modify the influence of scientific and other experts.

References

Golinski, Jan. *Science as Public Culture: Chemistry and Enlightenment in Britain, 1760–1820*. Cambridge: Cambridge UP, 1992.

Habermas, Jürgen. *The Structural Transformation of the Public Sphere: An Inquiry into a Category of Bourgeois Society*. Trans. Thomas Burger. Cambridge: MIT, 1989.

Turner, Frank M. "Public Science in Britain: 1880–1919." *Contesting Cultural Authority: Essays in Victorian Intellectual Life*. Ed. Frank M. Turner. Cambridge: Cambridge UP, 1993. 201–28.

Whitley, Richard. "Knowledge Producers and Knowledge Acquirers: Popularisation as a Relation between Scientific Fields and Their Publics." *Expository Science: Forms and Functions of Popularisation*. Ed. Terry Shinn and Richard Whitley. Dordrecht: Reidel, 1985. 3–28.

Young, Robert M. "Natural Theology, Victorian Periodicals, and the Fragmentation of a Common Context." *Darwin's Metaphor: Nature's Place in Victorian Culture*. Cambridge: Cambridge UP, 1985. 126–63.

Doug Russell

Pynchon, Thomas Ruggles (1937–   ). Author of *V.* (1963), *The Crying of Lot 49* (1966), *Gravity's Rainbow* (1973), *Slow Learner* (1984), *Vineland* (1990), and *Mason & Dixon* (1997), **fiction** in which sciences function as literary ground, theme, and motif. Although science and **technology** originate in aesthetic (*see* Art and Aesthetics), moral, or spiritual impulse, Pynchon suggests, they succumb to the Protestant capitalist ethic of control identified by Max Weber. According to Weber, Western bureaucracies divorce humans from nature by obscuring her chaotic energies. Pynchon's characters quest through historical mazes and **spy novel** labyrinths in search of novelty and surprise, hallmarks of information that can reveal signs of a sacred nature. Like language, science exhibits the saving grace of paradox: As an instrument it can rationalize and secularize, but as a way of knowing, it can also mystify and resacralize a world that persists beyond domestication of the planet. Weber's cycle of rationalization and charisma is the cultural equivalent of the Second Law of **Thermodynamics**, the statement of balance between order and **chaos** that Pynchon believes is crucial to natural and human systems. Pynchon traces the Second Law through its reformulations by disciplines as diverse as **physics**, ballistics, **astronomy**, **chemistry**, **biology**, **thermodynamics**, economics, and (especially) **information theory** and amplifies the Copenhagen Interpretation of **Reality** to include issues of free will and **determinism**. These metaphors illuminate the plight of characters who vibrate between poles of paranoia and uncertainty, trapped in an epistemological field bounded by fear of conspiracies of near-total control, on the one hand, and the equally frightening freefall of solipsism, on the other. Armed with language, **music**, and mathematics, Pynchon's protagonists seek organic nature behind corporate **landscapes** and industrialized systems that relentlessly subvert human aspirations. Chance and hard work permit a few to overcome psychological conditioning, commerce, and powerlessness to experience friendship, love, and freedom.

Reference

Slade, Joseph W. *Thomas Pynchon*. New York: Peter Lang, 1990.

Joseph W. Slade

Q

Quantum Metaphysics. Philosophical speculations pioneered by **Niels Bohr** and **Werner Heisenberg** that emphasized the indeterminate nature of knowledge about the results of the quantum phenomena. Whereas classical mechanics characterizes **reality** in deterministic and realistic terms, quantum mechanics describes the quantum domain in probabilistic and uncertain terms. David Bohm, following Louis DeBroglie and Erwin Schrödinger, focused on quantum reality per se and proposed a holographic paradigm based on the principle of nonlocality to explain the unbroken wholeness at the quantum level. The ground of this holographic reality, according to Bohm, lies in the "holomovement" that involves moments of the enfolding and unfolding of the totality.

References

Bohm, David, and B.J. Hiley. *The Undivided Universe: An Ontological Interpretation of Quantum Theory*. London and New York: Routledge, 1993.
———. *Wholeness and the Implicate Order*. London: Ark, 1983.
Heisenberg, Werner. *Physics and Philosophy*. New York: Harper and Row, 1958.

Jaishree K. Odin

Quantum Physics. The modern **theory** of matter and light (that is, electromagnetic radiation) and of their interaction. Its central ideas—that **energy** and other physical quantities come in indivisible units or quanta, that light and matter are simultaneously wave and particle, or equivalently that the universe is statistical in nature—break completely from classical theories that dominated physics through the nineteenth century. Quantum physics began in 1900, when **Max Planck** found he could not explain how light shone from a hot body without assuming that atoms within the body vibrate at discrete or quantized energies. In 1905, **Albert Einstein** concluded that light itself came in packets later called photons. But light had long been taken as a wavelike disturbance, a view that culminated in the nineteenth-century electromagnetic theory of James Clerk Maxwell. This was the first appearance of the paradoxical wave-particle duality.

In 1913 **Niels Bohr** used quantum rules to explain another puzzling observation, the specific wavelengths of the light emitted by hot hydrogen. And in 1923, Louis de Broglie concluded that matter had wavelike characteristics. By the late 1920s, physicists realized that light and matter were both wave and particle at the same time and that this dual nature was intimately related to quantum **reality**. In 1926, Erwin Schrödinger derived a general equation for the de Broglie matter wave, and Max Born interpreted the strength of the wave as the probability that a measurement would yield a specific result, the statistical interpretation we still use. Another ambiguity was uncovered in 1927, when **Werner Heisenberg** derived his **Uncertainty Principle** as a consequence of the wave-particle duality. In its simplest form, this states that the exact location and momentum of a particle can never be simultaneously known.

The last step toward modern quantum theory was to incorporate the theory of **relativity** to explain the behavior of light. Although first efforts were made in the 1920s, the final version of the theory came only in 1948, when **Richard Feynman** and others derived quantum electrodynamics, or QED, the full relativistic quantum theory of electrons and photons, an achievement that earned them a Nobel Prize.

Quantum physics is eminently successful. It agrees with experiment to a high degree of accuracy and underlies the **technology** of **computer** chips, lasers, and more. In imposing an indeterminate interpretation of nature, however, it has troubled many insightful physicists. Einstein never accepted the statistical view; Feynman called it "the *only* mystery" (Feynman, Leighton, and Sands). For LS, the great draw is that the quantum seems to allow certain compelling ambiguities in our world. But quantum physics is a theory of the microscopic, not of the human-sized. The wavelengths of its matter waves, and the uncertainties of Heisenberg's principle, are too small to affect any ordinary activity such as catching a baseball. And while quantum effects in principle operate in living matter, they are negligible on the scale where biological processes occur. In short, quantum physics cannot be expected to give meaningful predictions or descriptions of human affairs. Its literary value lies in its metaphorical use and in the recognition that the essential ambiguity of the quantum has rich implications for the philosophical underpinnings of the physical world.

References

Feynman, Richard P. *QED: The Strange Theory of Light and Matter*. Princeton, NJ: Princeton UP, 1985.

Feynman, Richard P., Robert B. Leighton, and Matthew Sands. *The Feynman Lectures on Physics*. 3 vols. Reading, MA: Addison-Wesley, 1963–1965.

Perkowitz, Sidney. *Empire of Light*. New York: Henry Holt, 1996.

————. "Strange Devices." *The Sciences* Jan.–Feb. 1995: 21–27.

Wheaton, Bruce R. *The Tiger and the Shark: Empirical Roots of Wave-Particle Dualism.* Cambridge: Cambridge UP, 1983.

Sidney Perkowitz

R

Race. A contested concept once considered denotative of biological difference, with complex personal, social, historical, and cultural implications. The confluence of literature, science, and race sprang from the Anglo-Saxon ideology of the English and European **Enlightenment**, but the combination flowered on American literary soil. America's historic obsession with racial difference found an outlet in science that widened in the early nineteenth century—when emerging scientific discourse sought power and authority. The two efforts reinforced each other: Scientists gained credibility for their work on race, while advocates of racial difference supported themselves with scientific evidence gained from craniometry, behavioral study of the "inferior races," and other dubious enterprises. Ethnologists like Samuel George Morton measured skulls, for example, while early evolutionists like Josiah C. Nott propagated religiously based theories of "polygenesis" (which held that each race had its own Adam and Eve).

The American slavery debate gave this work a political urgency, as each side tried to claim the authority of the new discourse. The result was a varied and combustible literature that helped to start the Civil War. It ranged from abolitionist propaganda, including slave narratives (whose clinical style was an implicit rebuttal to scientific assertions of Negro inferiority); to ethnological treatises on Indians, Negroes, and other races; to a body of **fiction** that represented racialist assumptions from both sides of the slavery debate. The "romantic racialism" of Harriet Beecher Stowe's colossally successful abolitionist novel *Uncle Tom's Cabin* (1852) set writers of proslavery plantation fiction scrambling to respond, but Stowe herself had indulged in scientifically influenced racial stereotyping—which was rebutted by William Wells Brown and other early black novelists.

Scientifically oriented debates on race continued past abolition, with **social Darwinism** providing impetus for antiblack books with titles like *The Negro a Beast* (1900) and rejoinders by the likes of Booker T. Washington, W.E.B.

Du Bois, and Frances E.W. Harper. Though science no longer exerts the same creative force on the literature of race in America, its echoes continue to be heard in books like Richard Wright's *Native Son* (1940) or **Toni Morrison's** *The Bluest Eye* (1970).

References

Fredrickson, George. *The Black Image in the White Mind: The Debate on Afro-American Character and Destiny, 1817–1914.* 1971. Middletown, CT: Wesleyan UP, 1988.

Horsman, Reginald. *Race and Manifest Destiny: The Origins of American Racial Anglo-Saxonism.* Cambridge: Harvard UP, 1981.

Jordan, Winthrop. *White over Black: American Attitudes toward the Negro, 1550–1812.* Chapel Hill: U of North Carolina P, 1968.

Sundquist, Eric J. *To Wake the Nations: Race in the Making of American Literature.* Cambridge: Harvard UP, 1993.

Leonard Cassuto

Radioactivity. Generated when the unstable nuclei of some types of atoms disintegrate, emitting elementary particles. The most common forms are alpha particles, beta particles, and gamma rays. Fantasies about powerful rays existed even before the discovery of **X-rays** and radioactivity (1895–1896), as in **Edward Bulwer-Lytton's** novel *The Coming Race* (1871). Around 1900, radioactivity appears in **fictions** where its power potential, military possibilities, and dangers are stressed. **H.G. Wells** discusses the impact of radioactivity on the world economy in *Tono Bungay* (1908) and predicts the atom bomb in his novel *The World Set Free* (1914). Early reactions can be found in novels by **Karel Capek** and Alexei Tolstoi. The full range of destructive potential became apparent after the explosion of atomic bombs over Japan and the Chernobyl disaster. Radioactivity has been linked to the nuclear holocaust in apocalyptic fiction (Walter M. Miller's *A Canticle for Leibowitz*, 1959; Russell Hoban's *Riddley Walker*, 1980) and in movies (*The Day After*, 1984).

Reference

Dowling, D. *Fictions of Nuclear Disaster.* London: Macmillan 1987.

Elmar Schenkel

Ramón y Cajal, Santiago (1852–1934). Spanish researcher who despite the unfavorable scientific climate in nineteenth-century Spain made significant, formative contributions to the science of histology. He shared the 1906 Nobel Prize for Medicine with Camilo Golgi. Cajal wrote prolifically, producing twenty-two books and hundreds of scientific monographs, as well as giving countless speeches to scientific and popular audiences throughout Europe. Cajal did not confine himself to scientific writing; he also penned his autobiographical *Recuerdos de mi vida* (Recollections of My Life, 1901, 1917), books of personal and philosophical reflections on life and Spanish society, most importantly *Char-*

las de café (1921) and *El mundo visto a los ochenta años* (The World through the Eyes of an Eighty-Years Old, 1934), and a popular scientific work—*Los tónicos de la voluntad* (Stimulants of the Spirit, 1899)—which vividly summarizes the state of Iberian science and outlines how and by whom science should be conducted. His series of short stories, *Cuentos de vacaciones*, which he subtitled "pseudoscientific narrations," were written in the mid-1880s but not published until 1905.

Cajal's writings frequently display his penchant for anthropomorphizing. In the stories, the referential power of scientific language ultimately fails the scientist protagonists; their efforts to exploit such language often lead into circular meditations about anthropomorphic cells and cell-like humans. Although in *Los tónicos* Cajal decries superfluous **rhetoric** in science, in his scientific texts he occasionally employs metaphors to glide over conceptual *lacunae* in his **theories**. For instance, in his discussion of nerve regeneration Cajal compares retrograde fibers with the losers in a race through the dark (*Degeneration* 205). The athletic metaphor imposes a set of relationships and desires on a phenomenon for which Cajal had no suitable explanation, though the discovery of the nerve growth factor in the 1950s later proved his intuitions about neurotrophic agents substantially correct.

References

Lizalde, Carlos Lorenzo. *El pensamiento de Cajal*. Zaragoza: Institución Fernando el Católico, 1991.

Ramón y Cajal, Santiago. *Degeneration and Regeneration of the Nervous System*. Trans. Raoul M. May. 2 vols. Oxford: Oxford UP, 1928. Rpt. in *Cajal's Degeneration and Regeneration of the Nervous System*. Ed. Javier DeFelipe and Edward C. Jones. Oxford: Oxford UP, 1991.

Dale J. Pratt

Randomness. In mathematics, the condition of a sequence whose values cannot be predicted, unless by an algorithm as incompressibly large and indeterminate as the sequence itself. The concept arose with Epicurus and other ancient materialists, becoming an important part of probability **theory** circa 1600–1800; but it was banished from **physics** until revived by quantum indeterminacy in the 1920s. By definition it is not really definable, but algorithmic information theory and **complexity** theory continue to try. In literature, it involves nonsystematic, aleatory composition.

Reference

Chaitin, Gregory J. *Information, Randomness, and Incompleteness*. 2nd ed. Singapore: World Scientific, 1990

William R. Everdell

Rationality/Irrationality. Concepts referring to the use of reason or its absence. They are applicable to human beings, to their behavior, and to products thereof (such as beliefs and arguments), but only if we accept an intentionalist **psychology** (*see* Anthropology/Psychology/Sociology) according to which people are capable of engaging in intentional action or, more generally, purposeful behavior explicable in terms of meaningful attitudes. Whether such an intentionalist psychology necessarily relies on assumptions about rationality is another question. Some thinkers defend, and others deny, the viability of an arational theory of agency. If rationality is assumed to be constitutive of the intentionalist psychological framework, a separate question concerns the specific nature of assumptions about rationality. In this regard, one may distinguish between synchronic and diachronic (or dynamic) topics, the former involving individual, "time-slice" units of behavior, the latter focusing on larger temporal units of deliberation, planning, and activity. Some writers defend a logically separate distinction between an agent's rationality and the rationality of belief or action. One may also focus on the rationality of this or that attitude, developing, for example, a theory of the rationality of belief, desire, or emotion. Beliefs, it is claimed, can be assessed in terms of epistemic or practical rationality, the former involving a belief's relation to criteria of knowledge, the latter involving the belief's tendency to advance the believer's other kinds of goals. Sometimes having a false belief can be advantageous, but on other occasions wishful thinking is disastrous. In addition to these distinctions, there is the question of collective rationality, which concerns the applicability of notions of rationality and irrationality to interagential relations, interactions, and such collective objects as institutions, conventions, and customs. A distinction pertinent to all of the topics just surveyed involves the contrast between subjectivist and objectivist criteria of rationality. As Jon Elster contends in *Sour Grapes: Studies in the Subversion of Rationality* (1983), between the thin theory of subjective expected utility and substantive theories of the true and the good there is room for a broad theory of the rational.

Conceptions of irrationality emerge against the background of various stances on the issues just surveyed. *Akrasia*, which is sometimes translated as "weakness of the will," is a paradigmatic example of irrational action where the agent does something that contradicts that agent's own unqualified best judgment about what to do. Self-deception is a paradigmatic form of irrational belief, as is wishful thinking, in which desire vitiates the weighing or gathering of evidence. It is irrational to believe a proposition and its contrary or contradictory (in the same sense at the same time).

It is important to recognize that these complex questions of rationality and irrationality apply both to science and to the **arts**. Science is often praised and blamed for its rationality, but providing a serious assessment of such claims is no small matter, and it is wise—perhaps even rational—to avoid snap decisions. Agents involved in various activities related to literature, such as writing and reading, can be meaningfully described and assessed in terms of rationality and irrationality, but such accounts do not yield any simple results on the question of works' artistic or other value. It is also possible that literary works (of many kinds, including **fiction**, **magic realism**, fantasy) express important insights into rationality and irrationality, largely by means of depictions of breakdowns and subversions of rationality.

References

Livingston, Paisley. *Literature and Rationality: Ideas of Agency in Theory and Fiction.* Cambridge: Cambridge UP, 1992.
Mele, Alfred R. *Irrationality: An Essay on Akrasia, Self-Deception, and Self-Control.* New York: Oxford UP, 1987.

Paisley Livingston

Ray, John (1627–1705). Botanist, naturalist, divine, Fellow of the **Royal Society**. By the time he published *The Wisdom of God Manifested in the Works of the Creation* (1691), his "most popular and influential achievement" and the "basis" of both **William Derham's** *Physico-Theology* and William Paley's *Natural Theology* (Raven, *John Ray* 452), Ray had completed extensive work on **classification** and taxonomy in the nascent fields of **botany**, **ornithology**, and ichthyology. In addition to its paradigmatic expression of the design argument, Ray's *Wisdom* (greatly expanded in subsequent editions) provided a systematic survey of **natural history**; "determined the character of the interpretation of nature till Darwin's time" (Raven, *Natural* 110); and established a **rhetoric** of **natural theology** (emphasizing consensus and accommodation) that contributed to the social and cultural ideology of post-Revolutionary England. As a dialect lexicographer inspired by "the empirical impetus" of the natural sciences (Gladstone 117), Ray published collections of proverbs and native English words that are now important sources for language historians.

References

Gladstone, Jo. " 'New World of English Words': John Ray, FRS, the Dialect Protagonist, in the Context of His Times (1658–1691)." *Language, Self, and Society: A Social History of Language.* Ed. Peter Burke and Roy Porter. Cambridge: Polity, 1991. 115–53.
Raven, Charles E. *John Ray: Naturalist.* 1950. Cambridge Science Classics. Cambridge: Cambridge UP, 1986.
————. *Natural Religion and Christian Theology.* The Gifford Lectures 1951. First Series: Science and Religion. Cambridge: Cambridge UP, 1953.
Zeitz, Lisa M. "Natural Theology, Rhetoric, and Revolution: John Ray's *Wisdom of God, 1691–1704.*" *Eighteenth-Century Life* 18(1994): 120–33.

Lisa Zeitz

Realism. A philosophical and **aesthetic** movement, generally associated with the nineteenth century, which (in its literary and artistic applications) sought to represent the everyday life of everyday (most often, lower- and middle-class) people as "objectively" and "truthfully" as possible. Realists eschewed romance and sensationalism, relying instead upon the observation and **representation** of precise detail. This reliance signals Realism's debt to the dominance by the nineteenth century of scientific **empiricism**. The coalescence of empiricism and literature can be seen in the early novel (e.g., **Defoe's** *Robinson Crusoe*, 1719) but it reaches its peak in late-nineteenth-century works such as **Flaubert's** *Madame Bovary,* **Eliot's** *Middlemarch*, and Leo Tolstoy's *Anna Karenina* (1875–1877).

Kristine Swenson

Reality. Ostensibly, a material realm (often associated with nature) that exists independently of ideas or perceptions about it. Although there is widespread agreement that reality as a whole cannot be captured in 500 words, opinion varies as to whether some aspect of reality can be reliably depicted by means of words or other symbols. Realists contend that reality is the fact of the matter targeted by our beliefs and by the symbols we use to express them. A belief is true when it stands in the right sort of relation (e.g., of matching or adequation) to what actually exists or is the case. Antirealists think it is mistaken or incoherent to try to make a mind-independent, external reality serve as an ingredient in knowledge, be it scientific, literary, or other. To do so implies that one can adopt a "God's eye view" from which to judge the relations between minds and mind-independent states of affairs. Cognition is conditioned and constrained in so many ways that it is naive to think that it functions as a pristine window on an ultimate reality. Realists reply that by the same token an antirealist cannot consistently claim to know that our beliefs do *not* stand in a particular relation to the world, for such a claim also depends on having a reliable external perspective. Coherent antirealism must be agnostic. When antirealists deny that reality could be anything other than what we take it to be (as in the Sophist's slogan that human beings are the measure of all things), they again presume to have surveyed the actual relation between the totality of human experience and a mind-independent sphere of being. If reality is a human or social construct (or historical series thereof), reality must have the essential feature of being constructible, this being a mind-independent fact that antirealists somehow have managed to discover, unless, however, it is merely the invention of one such construction. Realists think it is more plausible and coherent to hold that our evidence and experience are transcended by external states of affairs. Beliefs about the latter can be wrong, but it also looks like at least some of our beliefs may be right. Although it may be logically possible that we are all brains in a vat, victims of demonic manipulation, or fragments of textuality, the evidence does not on the whole look that way. The best available explanation may be that at least some of the time—but not always—our evidence serves as a reliable guide to the way things really are. If that is so, then the word "reality" is a convenient label for the sum total of actual states of affairs. The various sciences have a lot to say about the nature of reality, but little that is informative can be said about reality as a whole, so the term does little explanatory work in metaphysics.

It is important to observe that a realist conception of knowledge is compatible with but does not entail aesthetic doctrines associated with literary **realism** or **naturalism**. Some authors create literary works with the goal (among others) of sincerely expressing beliefs held to be true, and some of those beliefs may even be true of real states of affairs. But a writer's success in realizing these epistemic goals does not always contribute significantly to the work's artistic or **aesthetic** value, and works of **fiction** can be valuable for many other reasons. Questions of reality remain of continuing concern within **quantum physics** and **theories** of discourse, deconstruction, and postmodernism.

References

Haack, Susan. *Evidence and Inquiry: Towards Reconstruction in Epistemology*. Oxford: Blackwell, 1994.
Moser, Paul K. *Knowledge and Evidence*. Cambridge: Cambridge UP, 1989.
Munitz, M.K. *The Question of Reality*. Princeton NJ: Princeton UP, 1990.

Paisley Livingston

Relativity. A term used with differing connotations in **physics, theory** of knowledge, ethics, social **philosophy**, and social science. Epistemological relativity claims that knowledge is relative to the knower. Ethical or social relativity claims that morality is relative to the individual or society. **Albert Einstein** called his theories Special Relativity and General Relativity (theory of gravitation). Special Relativity asserts that simultaneity of distant events is observer-relative and that observed clock times and lengths of moving objects depend on velocity relative to the observer. General Relativity considers the effects of acceleration and is no more, and in some respects less, relative than Special Relativity. Young Einstein associated with relativistic anarchists and modernists, and his use of "relativity" for his theories was affected by this milieu. As his fame grew, references to Einstein's relativity were used to justify the claim that "everything is relative." Philosophers and physicists reacted against this simplistic definition, arguing that such claims were a misuse of the concept, which in Einstein's usage had nothing to do with moral or social relativism or with subjective relativism of knowledge.

The perspectivism involved in Einstein's theory did have parallels with doctrines of knowledge being developed by philosophers and novelists. Bertrand Russell claimed that objects were logical constructions, systems of perspectives. Perspectivalism stemmed from Renaissance perspective, but Einstein added **time** perspectives to the **space** perspectives. Process philosophers such as Alfred North Whitehead developed an "objective relativism" in which the structure of reality itself is perspectival but, like Einstein's theory, objective. **James Joyce** and **Virginia Woolf** experimented with temporal sequences and simultaneity around the time of Einstein's work. Critics drew parallels from this to Einstein's revolution. **T.S. Eliot** and **Ezra Pound**, meanwhile, opposed the moral relativism that popularly, but mistakenly, appealed to Einstein's authority. Most contemporary commentators have dismissed the tie between ethical or social relativism and Einstein's theory. **Bruno Latour**, however, has attempted to relink Einsteinian and social relativity in such works as *We Have Never Been Modern* (1991).

Reference

Friedman, Alan J., and Carol C. Donley. *Einstein as Myth and Muse*. Cambridge: Cambridge UP, 1985.

Val Dusek

Religion. Sets of beliefs regarding **supernatural** agency(cies) and their attendant ritual practices and moral values. In thinking about the relationship between religion and LS, we are doing nothing less than considering nature and the **supernatural** (God, the divine) in literary, religious, and scientific contexts. A survey of some of the interrelations of religion and science, and the literary dimensions and expressions of those interrelations, reveals an obvious but essential point: Religion is an integral part of the cultural context shared by both literature and science.

What people think about God shapes what and how they think about nature; what people think about nature shapes how and what they think about God. The late-nineteenth-century conflict model of the relationship between religion and science—exemplified in two works whose titles bear the marks of their authors' post-Darwinian battle scars, J.W. Draper's *History of the Conflict between Religion and Science* (1875) and A.D. White's *History of the Warfare of Science with Theology in Christendom* (1895)—is now recognized as inadequate. In its place are a number of more complex approaches that while acknowledging conflict as one possibility also see contiguous functions shared by these interpenetrating modes of discourse.

Religious language and content have been a significant part of the cultural context of scientific theories. Nowhere is this more apparent than in the **physicotheologies** of the late seventeenth and eighteenth centuries. By vigorously cultivating the relationship between contemporary science—from which it drew its copious illustrations of divine design—and religion, this rational empirical theology facilitated the social acceptance of **natural philosophy**; it also helped to popularize knowledge of the natural world, since physicotheologies were read as both encyclopedic **natural histories** and religious discourses. Newton's (*see* Newtonianism) *Principia* (1687) inspired that particularly Augustan form of natural theology: **astrotheology**; in the words of a famous hymn by **Joseph Addison**, "The spacious firmament on high,/With all the blue ethereal sky/And spangled heavens a shining frame,/Their great Original proclaim" (Barbour 37). The significance of arguments from design for both religion and science continues: Reformulated teleological arguments have emerged in the twentieth century, and it has been brilliantly demonstrated that modern ecological theory "owes its origin to the design argument: the wisdom of the Creator is self-evident, everything in the creation is interrelated, no living thing is useless, and all are related one to the other" (Glacken 423).

Science and religion have often shared metaphors—those "devices for the transfer of meaning between different disciplines" (Golinski 115). For centuries the agreement between science and revealed religion was expressed through the metaphor of the two "books" of God—the Bible and the Book of Nature. Metaphors also provide evidence of the way in which religious beliefs may influence the development of scientific **theory**. The concept of the "laws of nature," for instance, is intimately linked to voluntarist notions of the divine will: God works through the laws he imposed at Creation (though he is not bound by them). Both religious and scientific understanding has been reached through the use of the artisan **analogy** to express God's relationship to nature; while the "Clockmaker God" image accurately conveyed the notion of nature as perfect **mechanism**, its mechanical vehicle eventually overwhelmed its spiritual tenor. The "vast chain of being" celebrated in **Alexander Pope's** *Essay on Man* (1733–1734) is simultaneously a religious and a scientific image.

Of course, both religious and scientific language have important social dimensions: While religion helped to define a social role for science in the seventeenth and eighteenth centuries, science was also used to support religion. Religion contributed to the success of science in the sense that natural philosophy was promoted as a religious activity; so often were the works of nature used to prove the existence of a deity that "it would be difficult to find a seventeenth-century scientist who did not express this idea at one time or another" (Shapiro 92). The extent to which the two *shared* a language and **rhetoric** may be seen in **Thomas Sprat's** description (in his *History of the Royal Society*, 1667) of the miracles performed by Christ as "Divine *Experiments* of his Godhead."

It is important to recognize that a creationist position was held by most scientists up until the nineteenth century as a fundamental presupposition of their investigations into nature. As Roy Porter concisely describes this important aspect of the relationship between "science and religion" in the *Dictionary of the History of Science* (1981), Christian theology provided "a favourable framework for science's vision of an orderly and regular cosmos, Mediaeval scholasticism stressing the rationality of God's operations, early modern Protestantism underlining God as the giver of law, and eighteenth- and nineteenth-century liberal theology arguing the adaptation, integration, and design of Nature" (377). It has been persuasively argued (by scholars such as R. Hooykaas) that in the seventeenth century creationist views operating within science not only contributed the ideas of nature's intelligibility and predictability so central to the development of science but also influenced the process of theory selection. A growing number of historians of science now treat religious beliefs as a "constitutive factor" in the formulation and acceptance of generalized worldviews, specific scientific theories, and even "alleged observational 'facts' " (Rudwick 245). In other words, religious assumptions and ideologies must be taken into account in understanding not only the context but the content of scientific work.

The interrelations of religion and science, wherever they may be on the conflict-cooperation spectrum, are played out in the content, style, and formal structures of literary texts. **John Donne** found that the "new philosophy calls all in doubt"; Alexander Pope, a century later, affirmed that "the general order, since the whole began,/Is kept in nature, and is kept in man." The themes and imagery of religion and science are the very stuff of didactic **poetry** from the medieval *Cosmographia* through the Renaissance's *Les Semaines-Divine Weeks and Works*—and **Milton's** *Paradise Lost* to the "physico-theological epics" and lengthy scientific poems of the eighteenth century that celebrated Nature and Nature's God.

The assumption that the world is designed by a Creator and evinces both a natural and a spiritual order has formal implications. The divinely ordered universe of eighteenth-century "providential" narrative is to be found only fleetingly in nineteenth-century **fiction**, replaced by a new kind of "evolutionary" narrative. The **clock**, once the paradigmatic image of an ordered, beautifully maintained universe, comes to represent a diabolical mechanistic **determinism**. Newton's God became associated (unfairly to Newton) with a removed mechanic—**William Blake's** "Nobodaddy" and "Urizen" ("your reason"). It was against this mechanistic law-bound worldview that the Romantics reacted, recuperating the traditional idea of divine immanence and a nature permeated by spirit and replacing the clock metaphor with the language of organicism. **Thomas Carlyle's** 1834 phrase "natural supernaturalism" conveys the sense of a nature that embodies the miraculous and can inspire spiritual change. But this unity of mind and nature derived from German *naturphilosophie* was shortlived.

The implications for religion and literature of the geology of **Charles Lyell** and the natural history of **Robert Chambers** and Charles Darwin were immense: Value now seemed to inhere "not in permanence, but in change, not in mechanical design but in flexibility and **randomness**. Natural selection introduced the possibility of incorporating the random into scientific explanation" (Levine 94). The difference between an imagined world underwritten by natural theology and one underwritten by concepts of natural selection and survival of the fittest is memorably observed in **Thomas Hardy's** comment about **William Wordsworth**: "Some people would like to know whence the poet . . . gets his authority for speaking of 'Nature's holy plan' " (Beer 239). Nowhere is the human anguish and intellectual struggle of the Victorian "crisis of faith" better captured than in the poetry of **Alfred Lord Tennyson** and of **Matthew Arnold**. Indeed, Tennyson's "Nature, red in tooth and claw" and Arnold's retreating "Sea of Faith" have become paradigmatic expressions of the massive shift in ideas about Nature and God that occurred in the nineteenth century.

Of course, evolutionary narratives are not de facto deterministic structures: **Charles Kingsley**, author of *The Water-Babies* (1863), found religious meaning in the idea of transformation and made "natural selection itself an agent of divine power" (Morton 68). He retained a creationist view, but rather than being superintended by an interventionist male deity, his water-babies are observed by Mother Carey, a female sustaining principle of creativity and fecundity (Beer 137). Now the scientists have got rid of "an interfering God—a master-magician," Kingsley wrote in a letter in 1863; they have to choose between an "empire of accidents, and a living, immanent, everworking God" (Beer 136). Certainly, "everworking." In 1968 physicist Anthony Zee entitled his **aesthetic** and religious consideration of **quantum physics** *Fearful Symmetry* (after **William Blake's** "Tyger"). John Hedley Brooke's admonition that "there is no such thing as *the* relationship between science and religion" (Brooke 321) provides a salutary reminder to those interested in exploring this essential subject: While there are certain patterns, there are as many expressions of relationship as there are individuals and communities.

References

Barbour, Ian G. *Issues in Science and Religion*. Englewood Cliffs, NJ: Prentice-Hall, 1966.

Beer, Gillian. *Darwin's Plots: Evolutionary Narrative in Darwin, George Eliot and Nineteenth-Century Fiction*. 1983. London: Ark, 1985.

Brooke, John Hedley. *Science and Religion: Some Historical Perspectives*. Cambridge: Cambridge UP, 1991.

Glacken, Clarence J. *Traces on the Rhodian Shore: Nature and Culture in Western Thought from Ancient Times to the End of the Eighteenth Century*. Berkeley: U of California P, 1967.

Golinski, J.V. "Language, Discourse and Science." *Companion to the History of Modern Science*. Ed. R.C. Olby, G.N. Cantor, J.R.R. Christie, and M.J.S. Hodge. London: Routledge, 1990. 110–23.

Levine, George. *Darwin and the Novelists: Patterns of Science in Victorian Fiction*. Cambridge: Harvard UP, 1988.

Morton, Peter. *The Vital Science: Biology and the Literary Imagination, 1860–1900*. London: George Allen Unwin, 1984.

Porter, Roy, W.F. Bynum, and E.J. Brown, eds. *Dictionary of the History of Science*. Princeton: Princeton UP, 1981.

Rudwick, Martin. "Senses of the Natural World and Senses of God: Another Look at the Historical Relation of Science and Religion." *The Sciences and Theology in the Twentieth Century*. Ed. A.R. Peacocke. Notre Dame: U of Notre Dame P, 1981. 241–61.

Shapiro, Barbara J. *Probability and Certainty in Seventeenth-Century England: A Study of the Relationships between Natural Science, Religion, History, Law, and Literature*. Princeton, NJ: Princeton UP, 1983.

Lisa Zeitz

Representation. A philosophical **theory** of knowledge (associated with **realism**) that asserts that the mind perceives only mental images (representations) of material objects outside the mind, rather than the objects themselves. The doctrine can be traced to seventeenth-century Cartesianism, to the eighteenth-century **empiricism** of **John Locke** and David Hume, and in the idealism of Immanuel Kant. This **theory** demands that these mental images accurately correspond to external objects and thus calls into question, or considers with skepticism, the validity of much human knowledge.

Realism, considered alongside representation, is a set of representational practices, assumptions, and theories, whether aesthetic or philosophical, that is fixed to the idea that there exist tight links between something "real" and other versions (representations) of it constructed artificially by human skill and ingenuity. The artistic or technical representation refers the reader, viewer, or audience to something supposedly more authentic, genuine, or real. With the visual or musical arts, and with literature, the representation, while never losing its status as **art**, gives a sense of the world that is firm, secure, credible, and inviolable. Scientists and natural philosophers also deal with representational techniques, though they rarely acknowledge the artfulness of their reproductions. Their theories and discoveries are themselves representations of the real.

In aesthetics, representation has been used to address questions of how art symbolizes the world, the real, that is, ideas, feelings, objects, or states of affairs. In recent years, these questions have been answered with theories drawn from **philosophy** and linguistics, which argue that forms of art are similar to language and should be understood as language or **rhetoric** is understood, that is, in terms of conventions and semantic rules. These contemporary theories include Ernst Cassirer's philosophy of language and symbolic forms (inspired by the ordinary language **epistemology** of the later Ludwig Wittgenstein), Susanne K. Langer's theory of presentational symbols, and the works on semiology and **semiotics**, largely influenced by the writings of Roland Barthes. These theories suggest that representation in art (and science, philosophy, or **medicine**) is not so much a picture of sensory experience but is itself an instrument for acquiring knowledge about the structure of the world through the analysis of the structure of language and symbolic form.

The idea that philosophical and aesthetic problems are in some important sense linguistic can be called the "linguistic turn" in twentieth-century continental and Anglo-American analytical philosophy and is part of the attack on the entire philosophical tradition from **Descartes** to the twentieth century (primarily by continental philosophers) for its implicit or explicit dualism, that is, mind/body, thing/word, real/representational. The American pragmatist John Dewey (1859–1952) challenged the Cartesian idea that knowledge is primarily representations of mental intuitions. Dewey, along with Heidegger, Wittgenstein, and Richard Rorty, argues that experience is an interaction between a living being and the **environment**, with knowledge defined as a process of acting and being acted upon, and is not an issue of the *cogito* recreating mental or artistic representations.

References

Levine, George, ed. *Realism and Representation: Essays on the Problem of Realism in Relation to Science, Literature, and Culture*. Madison: U of Wisconsin P, 1993.
Rorty, Richard. *Philosophy and the Mirror of Nature*. Princeton, NJ: Princeton UP, 1979.

Diana B. Altegoer

Reproduction. The process, literal or figural, of conceiving and giving birth to offspring. In LS, studies center generally on the extent to which women have become associated with their potential for **pregnancy** and maternity and with their reproductive cycles generally (Oudshoorn), which have in turn been constructed as natural territory for social management (Rom; Spallone and Steinberg) and/or a basic process amenable to technological enhancement (Squier; Stanworth; Strathern) through the **technology** of **medicine**.

References

Oudshoorn, Nelly. *Beyond the Natural Body: An Archeology of Sex Hormones*. London: Routledge, 1994.
Rom, David. *Social Bodies: Science, Revolution, and Italian Modernity*. Princeton, NJ: Princeton UP, 1995.
Spallone, Patricia, and Deborah Lynne Steinberg, eds. *Made to Order: The Myth of Reproductive and Genetic Progress*. London: Pergamon, 1987.
Squier, Susan Merrill. *Babies in Bottles: Twentieth-Century Visions of Reproductive Technology*. New Brunswick, NJ: Rutgers UP, 1995.
Stanworth, Michelle, ed. *Reproductive Technologies: Gender, Motherhood and Medicine*. Cambridge, United Kingdom: Polity, 1987.
Strathern, Marilyn. *Reproducing the Future: Anthropology, Kinship and the New Reproductive Technologies*. New York: Routledge, 1992.

Sharon Stockton

Revolutions/Crises/Paradigms/Kuhn. The three major concepts of Thomas S. Kuhn's history and **philosophy** of science. Science is not a monolithic discourse. The many disciplines and subdisciplines of science have different **theories**, methodologies, and **rhetoric** for approaching the various phenomena of the universe. The discourse of microbiology, for example, radically differs from that of plasma **physics**. The discourse of each discipline develops over time as in the everyday practice of scientists new data are discovered, and theories explaining them are proposed, tested, and then accepted or discarded in favor of other theories. Scholars studying literature and science find historical changes within a scientific discourse, and the frontiers between the discourses of different fields, particularly fruitful areas of investigation because of the multifarious rhetorical strategies and motives involved in creating and negotiating these boundaries.

Kuhn, in his influential book *The Structure of Scientific Revolutions* (1962;

2nd ed. 1970), presents an interesting model of how these scientific discourses evolve as new ways of looking at the world arise. Kuhn sees the **history of science** in terms of normal science, theoretical crises, and scientific revolutions or paradigm shifts. Every science, according to Kuhn, provides an epistemological paradigm within which normal science is practiced. Vocabulary, rules governing the gathering of scientific data, instrumentation, and theory choice are contingent on the reigning scientific paradigm. The paradigm also defines what are considered worthwhile areas for scientific inquiry, what types of questions and answers are permissible, and often who is permitted or qualified to ask such questions and speak with authority.

Kuhn calls "normal science" those activities undertaken to explore the problems seen as particularly interesting or important under a given paradigm. The paradigm serves as a space for discussion wherein the statements of normal science are intelligible. When data are gathered, for which current theory offers no adequate interpretation, scientists hypothesize new explanations for the data based on tradition and the metaphysical framework of the paradigm. They then devise tests for the new **hypothesis** under cases in which they think it might fail, relying on research tradition to suggest factors that might plausibly influence the outcome of the experiment. In the main, scientists conduct experiments, hypothesize, and adopt or discard theories according to the paradigm under which they were educated, and most scientists spend their entire careers doing "normal science."

Times of scientific crisis occur when normal science uncovers data that are unaccountable under the prevailing theoretical conception of the world. In such periods, scientists will often suspend judgment and continue to practice normal science under the prevailing paradigm, always recalling and pondering possible explanations for the anomalous data. If the growing accumulation of data seems to controvert the current paradigm by forcing questions from outside the bounds of normal science, scientists will look for new ways of organizing their knowledge of the world through an alternative paradigm. These periods of scientific crisis end in one of two ways. Either a reevaluation of the current paradigm reveals ways of reconfiguring traditional theories to fit the new data, or else a scientific revolution takes place in which the old theoretical apparatus and methodologies are discarded in favor of a new paradigm suitable for explaining the previously inexplicable.

The crucial point of Kuhn's argument is that in moments of scientific crisis scientists will make their theory choices based on nonscientific grounds: "[T]his issue of paradigm choice can never be unequivocally settled by logic and experiment alone" (Kuhn, *Structure* 94). A person's status in the scientific community, personality, age, nationality, **race**, **gender**, social class, biases, and political and religious affiliations can influence his or her choice of paradigm. Any appeal to experiment must necessarily invoke a theoretical framework and methodology and is therefore useless in evaluating a competing paradigm that does not recognize that framework. Because of the lack of suitable evidentiary grounds to resolve scientific crises, decisions to adhere to a new scientific paradigm are subsequently much like religious conversions.

Scientific crises delineate methodological and semantic incommensurabilities between competing paradigms. Kuhn argues that during scientific revolutions two or more opposing camps of adherents to substantially different theories will organize themselves. Scientists working under one paradigm fail to communicate meaningfully with their counterparts under the opposing paradigm because of incompatibilities between the theories, methods, and rhetoric of the two groups. More important, the subject matter itself of the two paradigms differs. For Kuhn, the very worlds in which the two groups of scientists conduct their research are different. Scientific theories are underdetermined by data; a theory that makes accurate predictions can be replicated ad infinitum by empirically equivalent theories (however implausible or mutually contradictory they might seem under a given paradigm). The reigning paradigm indicates likely candidates among these myriad empirically equivalent theories purporting to be suitable conduits to information about the world and devises suitable means for testing their efficacy. Thus, scientific knowledge derives from a mixture of experimental data and the standard governing theory choice set forth by the paradigm. When a scientific revolution alters these standards with a shift in paradigms, scientific knowledge about the world undergoes radical changes. In normal scientific practice, scientists look for answers to questions posited by their paradigm as having a solution. A paradigm shift, however, is a change in the realm of possible answers scientists explore and hence a change in the world. Many of the words and concepts used to refer to the old way of viewing the world have neither epistemological nor ontological import in the new. Kuhn affirms that "paradigm changes do cause scientists to see the world of their research-engagement differently. In so far as their only recourse to that world is through what they see and do, we may want to say that after a revolution scientists are responding to a different world" (Kuhn, *Structure* 111). The new world is semantically incommensurate with the old and for this reason requires a new methodology and discourse for the puzzle solving of normal science to have any meaning.

The shift between the Ptolemaic and Copernican paradigms in **astronomy** presents a classic example of a scientific revolution. Ptolemaic astronomy offered fairly reliable predictions of planetary positions, but it required numerous ethereal spheres and equants to account for apparent retrograde motions in the planets' orbits. The perfectly circular orbits of **Copernicus's** heliocentric model provided predictions as adequate as the Ptolemaic system but no better. However, the model's parsimony held an aesthetic appeal, and its perceived incompatibility with Church doctrine made it alluring to the iconoclast or repugnant (or in **Galileo's** case, dangerous) for the orthodox. The competition between the opposing worldviews could not be adjudicated on evidential grounds; the personalities, biases, and religious and social commitments of the thinkers profoundly influenced their theorizing and ultimately decided the issue for each individually. Once the scientific paradigm used by astronomers in the sixteenth century had undergone this shift (for reasons not wholly rational), the normal science practiced under the Ptolemaic paradigm for the most part became meaningless under the Copernican. Normal science under the Copernican model then proceeded to investigate questions and solve problems rationally according to the theoretical constructs and methodology outlined by the new paradigm.

Scientists work and reason in theory-dependent worlds. All observational reports are cast in theory-laden vocabulary; theoretical and social conventions inform research, funding, publication, and teaching. While these conventions might appear to be obvious components of only modern scientific practice, even the earliest attempts to describe the workings of the natural world exhibit similar reliance on convention. Given that no reliable theory-independent methodology exists, rational scientific inquiry on the most basic level required significant amounts of theory making at the dawn of history to set up the world of inquiry.

According to Kuhn, scientific revolutions occur throughout the history of a discipline. Many of Kuhn's critics recognize a period of paradigm construction in the originary moments of a discipline, when the fledgling science first becomes normative and acquires a vocabulary and methodology, yet deny that any later adjustments in the discipline constitute radical shifts in perspective. Since the days of Newton (*see* Newtonianism) and Galileo, for instance, physics has maintained the same basic theoretical umbrella with no new paradigm creation. Although **Einstein's** theories are radically new, the critics argue, they arise from a 300-year tradition and represent but one step in the incremental progression of physics. Einstein's work connects to Newton's paradigm so fundamentally as to permit the deduction of Newton's equations as special cases of Einstein's more general rules. Kuhn, however, argues that Einstein's vocabulary differs so radically from Newton's as to make identical words (i.e., "mass" or "**energy**") have entirely different meanings in pre- and post-Einsteinian theorizing. Newton's and Einstein's equations may be syntactically similar, but Newtonian "mass" does not mean the same as Einsteinian "mass," so we cannot derive Newton's laws from Einstein's (see *Structure* 98–102). Kuhn views these semantic differences as critical: "[B]ecause it did not involve the introduction of additional objects or concepts, the transition from Newtonian to Einsteinian mechanics illustrates with particular clarity the scientific revolution as a displacement of the conceptual network through which scientists view the world" (Kuhn, *Structure* 102). Thus, Newton's world is incommensurable with Einstein's, and scientific revolutions have continued into the twentieth century in even ostensibly stolid disciplines like physics.

Since the year of its publication, *The Structure of Scientific Revolutions* has been one of the most oft-cited books in the *Social Sciences Citation Index*. Numerous misreadings have taken the book as asserting that social constructivism ineluctably entails absolute relativism and wholly arbitrary paradigm making. In the postscript to *Structure*, Kuhn denies these radical interpretations of his writings: "[T]hough scientific development may resemble that in other fields more closely than has often been proposed, it is also strikingly different. To say, for example, that the sciences, at least after a certain point in their development, progress in a way that other fields do not, cannot have been all wrong, whatever progress itself may be" (Kuhn, *Structure* 209). Kuhn focuses his arguments on the socially constructed methodologies and semantics of scientific discourses, and while the worlds of scientific practice may be paradigm-specific, Kuhn's model nevertheless neither admits the wholesale construction of reality nor denies the existence of a mind-independent world. The worlds of scientific practice are discursive worlds that relate to the natural world with varying degrees of success. Planes cannot fly merely because our paradigm says they will; they fly because the socially constructed paradigm we use to study nature relates to it in fundamental ways. Kuhn makes clear, however, that these discursive worlds, and not the natural world itself, constitute the objects of scientific investigation.

The strongest criticism of Kuhn's thesis touts a metaphysical **realism** shorn of naive objectivism. Hilary Putnam's notion of "internal realism" recognizes the social interactions Kuhn discusses in theory choice and avoids an external perspective on **reality** while simultaneously critiquing the notion of theory creation as purely ideological (Putnam 48–74, 103–26). Donald Davidson denies the possibility of Kuhnian "paradigm shifts" by arguing that any disagreements between speaker and listener are about specific propositions highlighted on an immense backdrop of shared, true beliefs. Since to communicate on even the most basic level a listener and a speaker must hold in common a multitude of beliefs about the world, the highly sophisticated scientific discourse among scientists educated under similar traditions precludes significant semantic incommensurabilities during scientific revolutions.

These criticisms and revised versions of metaphysical realism fail to diminish the evocative power of Kuhn's ideas. Kuhn's model of scientific revolutions has licensed the exploration of the social practices involved in scientific theorizing and rhetoric. Analysis of the construction and deployment of the tropes used in the creation and acceptance of new scientific paradigms forms an investigational bulwark for the fields of the history, philosophy, and sociology of science, LS, and cultural studies. The motivations for theory choice in historical and contemporary episodes of theoretical crisis in the sciences also merit attention. In a sense, Kuhn's model of paradigm shifts during scientific revolutions has itself brought about a paradigm shift in the ways philosophers, historians, and literary and cultural critics view science and their own disciplines.

References

Boyd, Richard, Philip Gasper, and J.D. Trout, eds. *The Philosophy of Science.* Cambridge: MIT, 1991.

Davidson, Donald. "On the Very Idea of a Conceptual Scheme." *Inquiries into Truth and Interpretation.* Oxford: Clarendon, 1984. 183–98.

Gutting, Gary. *Paradigms and Revolutions: Appraisals and Applications of Thomas Kuhn's Philosophy of Science.* Notre Dame: U of Notre Dame P, 1980.

Horwich, Paul, ed. *World Changes: Thomas Kuhn and the Nature of Science.* Cambridge: MIT, 1993.

Kuhn, Thomas S. *The Copernican Revolution: Planetary Cosmology in the Development of Western Thought*. 2nd ed. New York: Vintage, 1959.
———. *The Essential Tension: Selected Studies in Scientific Tradition and Change*. Chicago: U of Chicago P, 1977.
———. *The Structure of Scientific Revolutions*. 2nd ed., rev. Chicago: U of Chicago P, 1970.
Putnam, Hilary. *Reason, Truth and History*. Cambridge: Cambridge UP, 1981.

Dale J. Pratt

Rhetoric. The systematic study of means of persuasion. Rhetoric introduces itself into every use of language. Traditional rhetoric remains the oldest artifact dealing with discourse, but its contemporary status is uncertain. The sheer survival of techniques for finding "in each case the existing means of persuasion," as **Aristotle** put it, is too significant to ignore, yet modern rhetoric defines itself from after the decline of the rhetorical tradition and the rise of a logically based, scientifically oriented **theory** of discourse. Modern rhetoric is concerned with the systematic study of communication in all its forms: It generalizes the rhetorical tradition to approach discourse as inherently rhetorical. The rigorous differentiation of discourses is scientific, relating to the disciplinary matter of the discourses, to their referential status and claims to truth. Traditional rhetoric appears in such a hierarchy as a preliminary matter of learning or as a supplemental technique of ornamentation and style, while the modern concept of rhetoric appears as the production of a secondary discourse commenting on the conditions and success of communication. If science is the model of a discourse, the form of thought, it has little need of rhetoric.

Rhetorical approaches to science occupy a contested ground. Science must first of all be seen as made up of modes of observations and translation rather than objectively existing facts. At the same time, rhetoric must be granted its own **objectivity**, its scientificity. To speak of the rhetoric of a given discourse invokes strategies used to organize the presentation and to communicate with an audience. Science can be understood as primarily involved with the production of networks of texts that legitimate and transmit the presumptive real science occurring in the **laboratories**. Science is rhetorical because it deals with texts. The threat this position poses to the institution of science repeats the struggle between rhetoric as a set of practical techniques and the institutional place of rhetoric as a supplement to truth, a struggle that characterizes the history of rhetoric.

In the fifth century B.C.E., wandering teachers known as the Sophists brought rhetoric from Sicily to Greece. The best known is Gorgias, who arrives in Athens as ambassador in 427 B.C.E. Gorgias is credited with adding ceremonial (epideictic) rhetoric to the existing forms of judicial (forensic) and political (deliberative) rhetoric and with the use of rhymed prose as a rhetorical technique. Gorgias adapts poetics for rhetorical effect. By focusing on means of delivery, Gorgias turns rhetoric to matters of eloquence. **Plato** will criticize exactly this turn in his dialogues, where Gorgias comes under attack by Socrates. For Plato, the Sophistic rhetoric is based on effect or illusion and not **truth**, a teaching of mere technique rather than a development of logical thought (episteme). Plato admits the practical efficacy of Sophism but argues that rhetoric must persuade the listener only in the service of the truth. There must be a true rhetoric, modeled on dialectic and subordinated to the good of the republic. Throughout its subsequent history, the formalization of rhetoric as a stylistics will consistently be opposed to the philosophical rejection of rhetorical effects as epistemologically suspect.

Aristotle preserves the teachings of the Sophists while observing Plato's concern with the civic role of the rhetorician. The focus is on probability and belief rather than truth but emphasizes judicial and political settings, minimizing issues of eloquence. Aristotelian rhetoric is directed to the orator as a skilled craftsman, able to shape arguments based on a practical knowledge of psychology (*see* Anthropology/Psychology/Sociology), to prudently balance consideration of the character of the speaker (ethos) and the emotions of audience (pathos). The result is persuasion rather than dissimulation.

By the first century B.C.E., the center of rhetorical culture shifted to Rome. Rhetoric was integrated into the education system: The Roman citizen was educated as a rhetorician. Students first learned memorized topics and narratives. Literature was the material of rhetorical occasions. This was followed by practice in inventing and delivering oratory. The Roman rhetoricians were often political figures—Quintillian, for example, was the state-appointed rhetorician—and their works present the orator as the ideal citizen. All fields of knowledge were the subject of rhetoric. Eloquence became the medium of wisdom.

The basic techniques of the rhetorical tradition are already present in Aristotle. Three types of rhetorical scene are given: deliberative, forensic, epideictic. These genres determine the stage of any possible rhetorical transaction. Within such a setting, the orator must handle five parts of rhetoric: (1) invention (*inventio*); (2) arrangement (*dispositio*); (3) style (*elecutio*); (4) memory (*memoria*); (5) delivery (*actio*). This network structures the rhetorical act.

Invention (*inventio*) was the most important part, determining the facts and orientation of the rhetorical setting. It is better described as discovery. The orator worked with an existing body of knowledge, choosing from commonplaces or topics for their persuasive power. Rhetoric differs from poetics: It does not involve creation but presentation. Invention is the discovery of something to think with. The topics were a storehouse of arguments from the shared **culture** circumstances of the speaker and audience.

Arrangement (*dispositio*) was a kind of code determining the appearance of invented rhetorical material. It comes close to the modern idea of composition and involves knowledge of the formal parts of a speech. The general divisions set out by the rhetorical tradition continue to structure how texts are composed. Style (*elecutio*) is the commonsense notion of rhetoric: Here rhetoric is put into words. Emphasis on style minimizes issues of persuasion and audience while emphasizing discourse as a linguistic system. Style involves choosing from varying substitution sets, from single words to sentences and larger constructions. All elements produce effects. In terms of style, rhetoric is a collection of tricks, codes that form linguistic units. These units are "tropes" or turns, although this term is typically applied to individual words, and "figure" used for larger units. The handbooks that chart the history of rhetoric are a vast taxonomy of tropes. The best known are metaphor and metonymy, although attempts to reduce all style to variations on these two tropes proved unsuccessful. Rhetoric remains a flexible practice, an open system.

Memory (*memoria*) and delivery (*actio*) receive less attention in Aristotle. **Cicero** and Quintillian comment on them without the sustained attention and classification given the other parts. As a result, they are consistently undervalued in subsequent texts, yet these missing parts were metatopics, known to the orator and audience, learned from childhood; indeed, they were the basis of childhood learning. For the rhetorical tradition, they were implied in the techniques themselves. By the time of the Renaissance, however, literal reading of rhetorical treatises led to exclusion of memory and delivery. The objectivity of rhetoric is a historical constant. The suppression of a part of the rhetorical network makes this part implicitly structure the rest. In the history of rhetoric, memory and delivery return as symptoms of the history embedded in rhetoric. Memory and delivery reflect on "energia," rhetoric's ability to make something present, to speak directly to the listener and appeal to the heart or mind. Rhetoric uses ritualized action, performance, to bring something to mind, mnemotechnically.

The history of the classical rhetoric is understood as a decline. The Romans gave no priority to particular disciplines, but the Middle Ages divided the *artes liberales*, the seven arts of traditional learning, into two groups: the quadrivium (**music**, arithmetic, geometry, and **astronomy**) and the trivium (rhetoric, dialectic, grammar). On the one hand, arts dealing with nature and phenomena; on the other hand, arts dealing with discourse and language. The distinction of arts and sciences is found here, without yet including the epistemological and referential evaluations implied in the more modern terminology. What is the relationship of the parts of the trivium? While grammar was frequently assimilated to logic, bringing the assumption of logical rigor to grammatical analysis, rhetoric remained anomalous, lacking apparent method or logic. While a cultural interplay between the parts of the trivium lasted throughout the Middle Ages, logic was the dominant by the fourteenth century. Its rigorous organization made logic a medium between the trivium and quadrivium; as a result, all seven arts were seen as organized disciplines. The logical distinction between logic, grammar, and rhetoric was assured as long as it remained clear which of the three was at work. Rhetoric and grammar were subject to the rational ordering of logic on the assumption that they behaved logically. This assumption is implicit in the subsequent opposition of science to rhetoric, but it is the negative force of rhetoric, its encryption in apparently logical systems, that makes the rhetoric of science possible.

The Scientific Revolution was fought against rhetoric. **John Locke** argued that rhetoric could mislead, recasting Plato's critique from the position of empirical science. It is too simple to notice that such an argument is itself a piece of exhortative rhetoric. **Empiricism** was not a call for a higher or truer rhetoric but an attempt to exclude rhetoric entirely from scientific endeavor. When **Galileo** proposed that scientists read the Book of Nature, which lies always open before us but is written in mathematical symbols, he excluded rhetorical considerations, which are limited to the requirement that we must learn to read the language of mathematics. This learning is clearly preliminary, secondary to the business of observation and understanding. Learning is done so that it may be forgotten in a world positivized mathematically, made self-evident and readable.

If the Scientific Revolution attacked the epistemological status of rhetoric, theories of poetics attacked its aesthetic status. Following the retranslation of Aristotle's *Poetics* in the sixteenth century, the study of literature was no longer the exemplary part of rhetoric but was oriented toward problems of verisimilitude and authorship. The separation of rhetoric and literary study is completed with Romantic theories of artistic genius. The instrumental techniques of rhetoric find no place in a conception of **poetry** as a spontaneous creation.

Galileo made a clear distinction between the still-rhetorical bases of learning and experimental method. The new pedagogical methods of Peter Ramus made rhetoric a stylistic supplement to a dialectically principled logic, dividing the curriculum in terms of the uses of each art. Rhetoric was one subject among others. Finally, the material basis of culture was transformed with the rise of literacy and print culture. The institutional narrowing of rhetoric to written composition made invisible its role in other regions, while the proliferation and circulation of printed texts outgrew the capacities of the rhetorical education. Elements of the classical rhetorical education remained widespread until the nineteenth century, but rhetoric was increasingly limited to the study of written composition. It became stylistic and ornamental, marked by the pejorative "mere rhetoric." With certain significant exceptions, rhetoric is an anachronism, found in the "style manual" or book on how to be an "effective writer."

Science appears to understand and control rhetoric with little effort, presuming an ontology of stable, clearly manifested facts, subject to observation, induction, and formal abstraction. Corresponding to this epistemological basis is a method based on repetition and experimentation. Science is not a collection of experiments and texts but certain basic structures binding a range of practices. This is the self-evidence that gives science its rigor. Rhetoric is a supplement added to otherwise straightforward discourse whose aim is not persuasion but clear communication based on observation of **reality**. There is no need for persuasion if history is the filling in of discoveries and language simply the documentation of this progress.

By contrast, the rhetoric of science assumes that scientists are involved in the practice of persuasion and dissuasion. Scientific practice is a self-effacing discursive construct so rhetorical as to appear unrhetorical. The aim of the rhetoric of science is to make visible the circulation of knowledge among communities of agents. Scientific practice is seen as systematized persuasion supported by institutions and texts. The scientific text is broadened beyond published work to include journals, images, apparatuses, and so on. **Laboratories** are nodes in a network of circulating inscriptions making results transportable and historical. Texts are analyzed for a range of persuasive functions at work in the presentation of experimental methods and results, drawing on considerations of audience (ethos/pathos), arrangement, and style. Research models are topics or common-places in which science is performed. Rhetoric produces literal meaning through figuration. The literal is not equivalent to the true but rather to the institutionally readable, determining who will read the event, who the event addresses. Reading is the practice of both literature and science, and rhetoric the name for the shared medium. The horizon of the rhetoric of science is proof or truth as the aim and product of science. Facts are performed rhetorically.

Scientists are faced with forces that must be named. The rhetoric of science attempts to retell this encounter. By making visible science as a practice, rhetoric destabilizes self-evident scientific truths and certainties. The crisis that initiates the history of rhetoric is again repeated: The rhetoric of science would turn science into language, mere discourse, yet to find this crisis constitutive of the history of rhetoric suggests not a resolution but the source of rhetoric's power. Rhetoric reflects on constitutive events, apophantic conditions of possibility for science itself. The tropes of rhetoric are the positing and aggregation of discourse. What we take as scientifically true maintains our faith in the facts of the world; what we take as discursively constructed maintains our hope that the facts may yet come along. Rhetoric is precisely what guarantees the transparency of this effect. Rhetoric is not "mere rhetoric"—rhetoric is science.

References

Barthes, Roland. "The Old Rhetoric: An Aide-Mémoire." *The Semiotic Challenge*. Trans. Richard Howard. New York: Hill and Wang, 1982.
Gross, Alan G. *The Rhetoric of Science*. Cambridge: Harvard UP, 1990.

Charles A. Baldwin

Richardson, Robert Shirley (1902–1981). Astronomer and author of pop-ular science articles and books, plus **science fiction**/fantasy literature, including two novels and numerous short stories. Many were written under the pseudonym Philip Latham and evoked astronomical themes. Richardson's style employed first-person accounts by his alter ego, Latham, and drew upon extensive expe-rience as a professional scientist (spectroscopy) at Mt. Wilson Observatory. One of his stories ("N Day," 1946) has been adapted to the **planetarium**.

Reference

Reginald, R. *Science Fiction and Fantasy Literature*. Vol. 2. Detroit: Gale Research, 1979.

Jordan Marché

Rimbaud, Arthur (1854–1891). French Symbolist poet, author of *Une Saison en Enfer* (A Season in Hell, 1873) and *Illuminations* (1875; 1886), collections of poems that made him the exemplar poet rebel. His most celebrated poem is "Le Bateau ivre" ("The Intoxicated Ship," 1871). Rebelling against societal and cultural conformism, Rimbaud produces much of his sparse work at the dawn of the **Industrial Revolution**. His disdain for the growing phenomenon of urban sprawl and its ensuing "impurities" makes him a precursor of modern ecological concerns. After his breakup with fellow Symbolist Paul Verlaine, he spent sixteen years in outposts of various European empires, returning home from Ethiopia to die of cancer.

Reference

Perloff, Marjorie. *The Poetics of Indeterminacy: Rimbaud to Cage*. 1981. Evanston, IL: Northwestern UP, 1983.

Maria L. Assad and William R. Everdell

Roddenberry, "Gene" [Eugene Wesley] (1921–1991). Writer, film, and television producer best known for the creation of *Star Trek*. In his optimistic vision of humanity's future exploration of the final frontier, Roddenberry advocated "infinite diversity in infinite combination." While the original television voyages of the starship *Enterprise* coincided with Apollo (1967–1969), the 1970s revival of Roddenberry's vision coincided with early shuttle flights. The National Aeronautics and Space Administration's (NASA) naming of a test shuttle *Enterprise* is symbolic of *Star Trek*'s significance as cultural phenomenon. Themes addressed in scholarly studies include literary fandom, popular **culture** status, mythic elements, and analysis of the original and next-generation characters from the films, series, and paperback spinoffs.

Reference

Harrison, Taylor, Sarah Projansky, Kent A. Ono, and Elyce Rae Helford, eds. Enterprise *Zones: Critical Positions on* Star Trek. Boulder, CO: Westview, 1996

JoAnn Palmeri

Romanticism. A term applied to a period of literary and artist creativity, dating roughly from the last years of the eighteenth century into the early nineteenth, typified by lyrical, imaginative, and emotional expression and natural description. What we belatedly name Romanticism arose as a reaction against the rationalism of the previous era and the technological upheaval of the **Industrial Revolution**. Romanticism has usually been conceived as standing in opposition to the rising explanatory power of scientific reductionism and materialism, though even within Romanticism there was a countermovement that accepted the discoveries of science as appropriate poetic material.

Romanticism was the first artistic movement for which the confrontation with science reached the point of crisis, and romantic responses are both extreme and complex. In *The Mirror and the Lamp* (1953) M.H. Abrams notes an incident from the history of British Romanticism that may stand as an emblem of the complex Romantic response to the development of science: In December 1817 the painter Benjamin Haydon hosted a dinner at his studio. Among those present were Charles Lamb, **John Keats**, and **William Wordsworth**. Lamb, examining Haydon's painting *Jerusalem*, abused the painter for putting Newton's (*see* Newtonianism) head into his composition. Lamb and Keats agreed that Newton's *Optics* had "destroyed the rainbow" by providing rational explanation of the spectrum. Keats then proposed a toast "to the confusion of mathematics," to which many of the assembly drank, with the notable exception of Wordsworth. And **Whitman**, in his preface to *Leaves of Grass* (1855), was capable of saying that scientists are among "the lawgivers of poets and their construction underlies the structure of every perfect poem."

The Romantic Movement conventionally dates from 1798, the year in which William Wordsworth's *Lyrical Ballads* was published. In the famous *Preface* to that book Wordsworth establishes the terms under which **poetry** will be discussed for the next 200 years. Wordsworth located poetry's power in the poet's powerful, authentic feelings; the poet's language should also be authentic, free of artifice—"a man speaking to men." He also emphasizes that "the earliest poets . . . wrote from passion excited by real events." Indeed, although the motivations and the modes of expression between the poet and the "man of science" will ever differ, in Wordsworth's view, poetry may indeed be inspired by "real" scientific ideas and discoveries when such things have become "familiar" to the general reader as well as "manifestly and palpably material" to their lives.

To the extent that poetry and science both seek an **epistemology** that explains the relation of mind to nature, their concerns are similar. Romantic **theory** and practice has usually cast the opposition between physical science and the arts in terms of the position of the human subject, posited as an autonomous self conversant with nature. Rejected at the beginning of the twentieth century by the founders of **Modernism** who wished to establish a language for poetry free of romantic subjectivity, Romanticism remains a literary force at century's end. Romanticism shares with Modernism the desire to establish a natural and authentic language for poetry. Wordsworth believed that poetry is "naturally figurative language." Both Romanticism and Modernism seek to establish a transparent and natural language capable of inscribing the poet's understanding both of the self and of the exterior world.

References

Abrams, M.H. *The Mirror and the Lamp*. 1953. New York: Norton, 1958.
————. *Natural Supernaturalism*. New York: Norton, 1971.
Eaves, Morris, and Michael Fischer, eds. *Romanticism and Contemporary Criticism*. Ithaca, NY: Cornell UP, 1986.

The New Princeton Encyclopedia of Poetry and Poetics. Ed. Alex Preminger and T.V.F. Brogan. Princeton, NJ: Princeton UP, 1993.

Ruoff, Gene W., ed. *The Romantics and Us.* New Brunswick, NJ: Rutgers UP, 1990.

Joseph Duemer

Rousseau, Jean-Jacques (1712–1778). Swiss philosopher, writer, and composer whose works included the groundbreaking sociopolitical treatise *Du Contrat social* (1762), the best-selling sentimental novel *La Nouvelle Héloïse* (1761), and *Émile* (1762), a pedagogical fable whose account of **gender** difference greatly contributed to the biological **determinism** that pervaded European science, socioanthropological theory, and **culture** between the late eighteenth and twentieth centuries. In his celebrated *Discours sur les sciences et les arts* (Discourse on The Sciences and the Arts, 1750), Rousseau denounced the arts and sciences as decadent pursuits incompatible with virtue, patriotism, and true human nature. He developed this critique in his second *Discourse* (*Discours sur l'origine de l'inégalité* 1755), using a **noble savage** figure to decry the inauthenticity of civilized life. Despite his opposition to mainstream culture, his personal antipathy for *philosophes* like **Voltaire**, and the spiritualist leanings that made him a precursor to **Romanticism**, Rousseau embraced the **Enlightenment's** reformist tendencies and its holistic conception of mind and body (*see* Corporeality/Body), taking a sensationalist approach to education and promoting the idea of comprehensive moral-physical hygiene. Rousseau's *Confessions* (1782–1788), which did much to popularize autobiography as a distinct genre, continue to interest literary critics and psychoanalysts alike.

Reference

Starobinski, Jean. *Jean-Jacques Rousseau: Transparency and Obstruction.* Trans. Arthur Goldhammer. Chicago: U of Chicago P, 1988.

Anne C. Vila

Royal Society. Using the name "Royal Society of London for Improving Natural Knowlege" [*sic*], a group of scientists began to meet at Gresham College, London (1598) and Oxford (1645) to discuss new scientific ideas. This "Invisible College" became incorporated in 1662 under a grant chartered by the newly restored Charles II as the Royal Society of London for the Promotion of Natural Knowledge. Founders and early members included the chemist **Robert Boyle**, the scientist Bishop **John Wilkins**, the philosopher **Joseph Glanvill**, the mathematician John Wallis, the **inventor** and experimenter of the **microscope Robert Hooke**, and the architect Christopher Wren. It was Wren who wrote the preamble to the Society's charter and **Thomas Sprat** who wrote the first introduction to the *History of the Royal Society.* These philosophers were primarily supporters of the mid-seventeenth-century Puritan cause and were followers of and adherents to **Francis Bacon's** reform of learning and scientific education.

While independent of crown and Church financial support, the Royal Society still claimed moral and ideological identification with both restored monarchy and the Church of England. Perhaps because of its economic independence, the Royal Society succeeded in stimulating free expression in the development of scientific thought in England. Its publication *Philosophical Transactions* was begun in 1665 and became one of the earliest periodicals in Western Europe. Isaac Newton (*see* Newtonianism) was elected a member in 1671, and Edmond Halley, the astronomer, in 1678. **Abraham Cowley**, in an "Ode to the Royal Society," remarked upon the revolution in literary language introduced by that body, no doubt inspired by Sprat's preface to the *History*, which promised a style neat and plain, shorn of rhetorical flourishes. Augustan neoclassicism of the eighteenth century was influenced by this trend, enforced by the success of the modern scientific enterprise in its first 100 years of existence.

Reference

Hunter, Michael. *Establishing the New Science.* Woodbridge, United Kingdom: Boydell, 1989.

Diana B. Altegoer

Royer, Clemence (1830–1902). Author of influential French translations of **Charles Darwin's** *Origin of Species*. Her significance as popularizer extends beyond the role of mere transmitter, as demonstrated by reaction to her controversial preface in the 1862 translation. Self-educated in **philosophy** and the sciences, Royer wrote and lectured on **evolutionary theory** and its social implications.

Reference

Harvey, Joy. *"Almost a Man of Genius": Clemence Royer, Feminism and Nineteenth-Century Science.* New Brunswick, NJ: Rutgers UP, 1997.

JoAnn Palmeri

Ruskin, John (1819–1900). English author and art critic. An influential exponent of Victorian medievalism, Ruskin attacks machine **technology** and scientific **truth** in *The Stones of Venice* (1851–1853) and *Modern Painters* (1843–1860). Ruskin was nevertheless an avid naturalist, viewing scientific study as a tool by which the artist may achieve an enhanced wonder of nature.

Reference

Kemp, Wolfgang. *The Desire of My Eyes: The Life and Work of John Ruskin.* Trans. Jan van Heurk. London: HarperCollins, 1991.

Alison E. Bright

Russia and the Former Soviet Union. Contested **geographies** and **cultures** in which (according to Iurii Lotman's and Boris Uspenskii's seminal study

"Binary Models in the Dynamics of Russian Culture") there is a lack of relatively neutral political, social, economic, and legal institutions capable of mediating between the polarities of church and state, private and public, sacred and secular. As a consequence, for the last two centuries Russian literature and literary debate have assumed extraordinary significance as almost the sole realm of negotiating a collective as well as individual identity. The binary structure of Russian culture in large part characterizes the relationship between literature and science as well. Throughout modern Russian history, one finds either extreme tension between the two or radically synthetic attempts to erase the gap between different modes of knowledge altogether.

Few other cultures have been so defined, and self-defining, on the basis of their literary output as Russian culture. And no literary tradition has insisted more strongly on placing literature in the service of moral ideals, while simultaneously challenging hegemonic thinking. On the other hand, the self-proclaimed new Soviet culture that was meant to subsume Russian culture was defined by its thoroughgoing **scientism**. Soviet ideology (*see* Politics and Ideology) insisted that a single "scientific" **philosophy**—dialectical materialism—would inform not only scientific explications of the natural world but all fields of inquiry into human social and cognitive behavior, morals, and metaphysics. As is well known, the crude and dogmatic enforcement of this ideology resulted in tragic loss of life and perversion of scientific principles. Moreover, by restricting the purview of the humanities to a "Marxist-Leninist" philosophical framework, Soviet ideology deepened the divide between humanistic inquiry and science, since in the latter it was possible to avoid or even fruitfully apply the strictures of dialectical materialism, whereas work in the humanities that did not properly conform was silenced, "purged," or driven underground. Yet writers and scientists themselves were reluctant to concede that science and genuine humanistic inquiry were incompatible. Evgenii Zamiatin's antiutopian novel *We* (1920; published in USSR 1989) and his essay "On Literature, Revolution, and Entropy" (1923) are masterpieces of literary **imagination** deeply informed by scientific thought. The **poetry** and prose of such disparate writers as Mayakovsky, Bely, Mandelstam, Zabolotsky, and Bulgakov (all "silenced" in the 1930s by death, arrest, or censorship), as well as the work of Russian linguists and literary scholars (notably the school of Russian Formalism) in the first decades of this century, manifest an extraordinary interest in incorporating the perspectives of science into the realm of literature.

Today, when it is possible to retrieve more fully the legacy of the Soviet Union's suppressed writers and thinkers, the interdisciplinary vantage point of LS studies should be particularly instructive in illuminating a unique intellectual milieu, formed out of a peculiar tension between genuinely scientific, pseudo-scientific, and literary cultures in a twentieth-century setting. Furthermore, it is now possible to engage the innovative and fruitful contributions of recovered and new Russian scholarship in the area of science and culture. The chronological sketch provided below indicates some territory pertinent to the first issue and introduces the second.

At the beginning of the eighteenth century, European *Wissenschaft* was grafted onto Russian culture from above. Peter the Great (1672–1725), unlike his predecessors, was determined to modernize Russia by "opening a window to the West," and he understood that developing the conditions for scientific research to flourish on Russian soil was essential to ensuring the political and military clout of his empire. He mandated the establishment of the **Russian Academy of Sciences** (1725) and imported scientists in all fields to work in it and train Russian cadres. Science and the gloss of European **Enlightenment** were absorbed rapidly by a thin layer at the top of Russian society; the pattern of rapid but imitative and inconsistent development of scientific and technical knowledge according to the needs of the State has characterized Russian scientific culture ever since. The rise of a Russian literary language (a prerequisite alternative to ecclesiastic Church Slavonic and oral vernaculars) and a cultivated audience for literature also occurred relatively late and abruptly in comparison with the continuous development of Western European literary art. Early examples of Russian prose literature penned by Karamzin in the genre of the "sentimental sketch" can be shown to reflect the late-eighteenth-century scientific paradigm emphasizing the importance of the senses in human perception and cognition.

By the beginning of the nineteenth century, Russian literature had already produced its greatest artist, the versatile poet, dramatist, and prose fiction writer Alexander Pushkin. A late short story by Pushkin, "The Queen of Spades" (1830), contains topical allusions to scientific fads such as **mesmerism** and Montgolfier's balloon but retains its artistic freshness today precisely because innumerable critical attempts have fallen short of resolving its central narrative enigma, which is based on the interplay of chance and **complexity**. Thus, from the point of view of LS, the enduring work of narrative art seems to give temporal form to the paradoxical spatial incongruities implied by contemporary **physics**. In the second half of the nineteenth century, Western Europe's increasing confidence in the authority of science and the influence of positivist and materialist ideas reached Russia at a time of political reform and cultural reawakening. During the relatively liberal early reign of Tsar Alexander II (r. 1855–1881, assassinated by radical terrorists), the beginnings of real social and political reform, such as the abolition of serfdom, led to an intensification of the debate over the direction of Russia's future. In its broadest formulation, the debate pitted the Westernizers, who saw Russia's future in European modernization, against the Slavophiles, who saw salvation in resisting Western influence in favor of a "third path" expressing the unique destiny of Russia's Eurasian civilization. Nineteenth-century intellectuals hoping to push their nation westward or eastward enlisted literature and literary criticism, rather than the professional discourses of law and **politics**, to advocate (or undermine) Western theories in natural, physical, and social science.

Scholarship has taken account of the political and social factors shaping Russia's reception of new scientific ideas, but less attention has been paid to the lasting influence of literature and literary criticism on that reception. Indeed, the great polemical novels of Turgenev, Dostoevsky, and Tolstoy foreground the question of science's authority and incorporate this question into the larger argument over Russia's destiny. However, while Russia's intellectuals almost unanimously opposed the increasing conservatism that marked the second half of Alexander II's reign, that opposition seemed to be polarized into two camps: political radicals of varying hues who believed the efficacy of atheism, materialism, and rationalism as principles necessary for positive social change, and Idealist philosophers, writers, and many scientists, who shared a somewhat elitist distrust of the radicals and a common faith in humanistic and spiritual, if not religious, values. The radical social reformers (populists, anarchists, Marxists) endorsed **evolutionary theory**, for instance, as a potent ally in the battle against religious orthodoxy, Tsarist authority, and social backwardness. The most influential voices in this camp were literary critics, some of whom wrote their reviews from within Tsarist prisons. Broadly speaking, the radical literary critics judged literary worth on the basis of their own social and political ideals, which in turn were firmly linked to the scientific vindication of materialism and rationalism. The hero of Turgenev's novel *Fathers and Sons* (1862) can be interpreted either as a negative caricature or as a positive embodiment of the Russian tendency to harness science to extreme social and political radicalism. Dostoevsky, writing his major novels in the same pivotal decades of scientific advance, offers the Underground Man's famous diatribe against the limitations of rationalism's "two plus two equal four" and a gallery of "holy fools" (e.g., Sonia Marmeladova, Alesha Karamazov from *The Idiot*, 1868–1869) who defy modernity's diagnosis of "blessedness" as simply an organic pathology. In a different way, Tolstoy, no less than Turgenev and Dostoevsky, offers his literary masterpieces as proof of the narrowness and limitations of the scientific worldview, insofar as he could identify the latter with materialism, rationalism, and the European addiction to individualism.

At the turn of the century, writers and critics turned away from the scientific orientation of the nineteenth-century radical critics and the socially engaged, quasi-objective style of literary **realism**. Rather, **art** depicted a subjective realm and transcended material laws. Russian **modernism** defined itself in opposition to the nineteenth-century realistic novel, painting style, and classical **music** with the **Symbolist movement** (*see also* Symbolism) in poetry, abstractionism in the visual arts, and the twelve-tone scale in music. Recent scholars have fruitfully argued, however, that the Russian modernist dream of transcendence rests "on the solid positivistic substratum" (Paperno and Grossman 4) of nineteenth-century realism. The philosophers Nikolai Fedorov (1828?–1903) and Vladimir Soloviev (1853–1900) both developed highly influential moral and aesthetic doctrines proposing that the goal of human evolution is to achieve not only spiritual but also literal physical resurrection, or reconstruction of life forms here on earth. The disparate work of the two philosophers shares the premise that scientific **positivism** can be reconciled with Orthodox theology and (particularly in Soloviev) with the true function of artistic creation. Thus, one of the most striking facets of Russian modernism in the arts is its adherence to an aesthetic philosophy that goes beyond aesthetics and emerges as a synthetic worldview known as "life-creation." Life-creationism posits that the creative potential of human beings in both the arts and the sciences should be channeled toward conquering the ultimate cause of individual malaise and social injustice: death. The enduring influence of "the immortality project" in Russian literature and science is only beginning to be adequately investigated.

Recent scholarship has similarly taken a new look at the alleged **discontinuity** between modernism and the artistic style mandated by Stalinist ideology, socialist realism. Whereas socialist realism ostensibly represented a return to the civic engagement and "scientific" objectivity of nineteenth-century realism, it actually absorbed much of the modernist aesthetic that attempts to recreate life in "more evolved" biological and spiritual form. Life-creationism is transformed into a fundamental principle of Soviet cultural ideology, epitomized in Stalin's infamous dictum that Soviet writers and artists are the "**engineers** of human souls." Thus, nineteenth-century realism, modernism, and socialist realism take their place on a continuum, and all three rest on a consistent and enduring belief in science. One of the implications of this recent reconceptualization is that there is a greater link than has heretofore been explored between the modernist ethos of life-creation and the very real achievements of Russian cosmologists, geneticists, and psychologists in the Soviet period. Likewise, the crucial role science played and will continue to play in Russian notions of transforming individual and social life, whether biophysically or culturally, must be examined. In short, the polarized debate between science and humanism that invigorated prerevolutionary Russian literary life resolved itself first into an idealist aesthetic synthesizing the "**two cultures**," then into a dystopian social experiment in the name of "scientific materialism." In practice, though, the most significant writers and scientists of the Soviet period tended to valorize the (officially suppressed) connection between science and the entirety of Russian humanistic heritage. The almost cultlike status among the scientific intelligentsia of the Soviet science fiction writers **Arkady** and **Boris Strugatsky** can be attributed to the way the Strugatskys render this connection in popular literary form. On another level, the enormous moral prestige of the physicist Andrei Sakharov derived from the inextricable connection between his scientific and humanistic principles.

At the 1931 International Congress of the **History of Science** in London, it was a member of the Soviet delegation, the Russian physicist and historian Boris Hessen, who revolutionized the field with his "paradigm-setting analysis" of Isaac Newton's (*see* Newtonianism) contributions to science, which Hessen insisted could only be fully understood by taking into account external social and economic factors (Graham, *Science in Russia* 145). Hessen died in prison in 1938; his fate was shared by almost all early Soviet theorists exploring the possibilities of a sophisticated Marxist approach to both science and cultural studies. In fact, Stalinist ideological restrictions effectively channeled Soviet historians of science into a narrow "internalist" approach. As Daniel Alexandrov observes, this retreat ironically "left the sociology of science to philosophers who felt free to challenge both internalism and Marxism in their own way" (Alexandrov 331) and, it should be added, in their own "underground" or "kitchen seminar" space. With the collapse of the Soviet Union, these subterranean intellectual currents have surfaced to become the mainstream of a renaissance in Russian interdisciplinary studies of science and culture. Alexandrov highlights the Russian emphasis on viewing science as a type of "community of culture." Generally speaking, a Bakhtinian emphasis on the communicative nature of all intellectual activity inspires many areas of Russian science studies and points the way toward a fruitful common ground between literary studies and the microsocial history of science (Alexandrov 324). Recent Russian studies of the language of science have also been informed by dialogism, and in particular the theory of argumentation, in their efforts to reveal both the persuasive and logical structure of the scientific text and the dynamics of creative **problem solving** as it is manifested in the essentially dialogic verbal act, going beyond Bakhtin's own relegation of scientific discourse to "monologue."

References

Alexandrov, Daniel. "Introduction: Communities of Science and Culture in Russian Science Studies" and "Bakhtin's Legacy and the History of Science and Culture: An Interview with Anatolii Akhutin and Vladimir Bibler." By Daniel Alexandrov and Anton Struchkov. *Configurations* 1.3 (Fall 1993): 323–86.

Bailes, Kendall. *Science and Russian Culture in an Age of Revolutions: V.I. Vernadsky and His Scientific School, 1863–1945.* Bloomington: Indiana UP, 1990.

Graham, Loren. *Science in Russia and the Soviet Union: A Short History.* Cambridge UP, 1993.

———. *Science, Philosophy, and Human Behavior in the Soviet Union.* New York: Columbia UP, 1987.

Howell, Yvonne. *Apocalyptic Realism: The Science Fiction of Arkady and Boris Strugatsky.* New York: Peter Lang, 1994.

Lotman, Iurii, and Boris Uspenkii. "Binary Models in the Dynamics of Russian Culture (to the End of the Eighteenth Century)." *The Semiotics of Russian Cultural History.* Ed. Alexander D. and Alice Stone Nakhimovsky. Ithaca, NY: Cornell UP, 1985.

Lubrano, Linda, and Susan Gross Solomon, eds. *The Social Context of Soviet Science.* Boulder, CO: Westview, 1980.

Murav, Harriet. *Holy Foolishness: Dostoevsky's Novels and the Poetics of Cultural Critique.* Stanford, CA: Stanford UP, 1992.

Paperno, Irina, and Joan Delaney Grossman, eds. *Creating Life: The Aesthetic Utopia of Russian Modernism.* Stanford, CA: Stanford UP, 1994.

Todes, Daniel. *Darwin without Malthus: The "Struggle for Existence" and Russian Evolutionary Thought in the Nineteenth Century.* Oxford: Oxford UP, 1989.

Vucinich, Alexander. *Science in Russian Culture.* Stanford, CA: Stanford UP, 1963, 1970.
Zamiatin, Evgenii Ivanovich. *A Soviet Heretic: Essays.* Evanston, IL: Northwestern UP, 1992.

Yvonne Howell

Russian Academy of Sciences. Organization established in 1725 by Peter the Great; after the Bolshevik Revolution reorganized as the Academy of Sciences of the Soviet Union and in 1990 reassumed its original title. The Academy exists separately from the universities as the dominant and unifying body of scientific (including humanities) research. Its pyramidal structure institutionalized a complex answerability to state ideology (*see* Politics and Ideology) in both Tsarist and Soviet Russia, constituting an alternative to the social organization of scientific endeavor in other modern civilizations.

References

Lipski, Alexander. "The Foundation of the Russian Academy of Sciences." *Isis* 44 (1953): 349–54.
Vucinich, Alexander. *Empire of Knowledge: The Academy of Sciences of the USSR (1917–1970).* Berkeley: U of California P, 1984.

Yvonne Howell

Rutherford, Ernest (1871–1937). New Zealand–born physicist whose studies of **radioactivity**, and discovery of the alpha particle, underlie nuclear physics. His career began when he worked with **J.J. Thomson**, the discoverer of the electron, at the Cavendish Laboratory of Cambridge University. Rutherford became the leading experimentalist of his era, receiving the Nobel Prize in **Chemistry** in 1902. In 1911, he established that an atom consists of a nucleus of positive charge surrounded by negatively charged electrons. Rutherford bombarded thin gold foils with alpha particles, the nuclei of helium atoms. The particles were deflected in a manner that could be explained only if the gold atoms contained a small positive core.

Reference

Mitchell, Breon. "The Newer Alchemy: Lord Rutherford and *Finnegans Wake*." *A Wake Newslitter: Studies in James Joyce's Finnegans Wake*, n.s., 3 (1966): 96–102.

Sidney Perkowitz

S

Sacks, Oliver (1933–   ). Neurologist and author of extended case histories or clinical biographies about neurological conditions. These include *Awakenings* (1973), *The Man Who Mistook His Wife for a Hat* (1985), *Seeing Voices: A Journey into the World of the Deaf* (1989), *An Anthropologist on Mars* (1995), and a **pathography** about his own illness experience, *A Leg to Stand On* (1984). These "clinical tales," though they concern such relatively unusual problems as postencephalitic Parkinsonism, Tourette's syndrome, and total color-blindness, are seen by many as a model for a kind of history that centers the description of disease and its treatment within a picture of the patient and the patient's world. As Sacks himself observes, his aim is "to preserve what is important and essential—the real and full *presence* of the patients themselves, the 'feeling' of their lives, their characters, their illnesses, their responses—the essential qualities of their strange situation" (*Awakenings* xvii–xviii). Sacks's literary style draws through quotation and allusion on a wide range of disciplines, especially **philosophy** and literature, relating his **medical case histories** to a wider and deeper context of human knowledge. Sacks's very first book, *Migraine* (1970), though it is not clinical biography, nonetheless demonstrates the dual concern with physiology and personality that characterizes all his writings.

References

Hawkins, Anne Hunsaker. "Oliver Sacks's *Awakenings*: Reshaping Clinical Discourse." *Configurations* 1.2 (1993): 229–245.

Howarth, William. "Oliver Sacks: The Ecology of Writing Science." *Modern Language Studies* (1990): 103–20.

Sacks, Oliver. *Awakenings*. New York: HarperPerennial, 1990.

Anne Hunsaker Hawkins

Sagan, Carl Edward (1934–1996). American astronomer, exobiologist, and author who gained wide public recognition through his efforts to popularize science. Sagan devoted his scientific career to the study of planetary surfaces and atmospheres and to the problems of the origin of life on earth and the possible existence of **extraterrestrial** life. His literary efforts reflect a profound interest in these topics as well as with broader questions concerning humanity's place in a vast and wondrous universe. These efforts include *Intelligent Life in the Universe* (1966), *The Cosmic Connection: An Extraterrestrial Perspective* (1973), and the 1978 Pulitzer Prize–winning *The Dragons of Eden: Speculations on the Evolution of Human Intelligence* (1977). Sagan gained worldwide prominence in the 1980s with the public television series and best-seller *Cosmos* (1980). His interest in SETI (search for extraterrestrial intelligence) and questions of cosmic scope found fictional expression in the science fiction novel *Contact* (1985). Sagan's lifelong efforts to celebrate science, **rationality**, and the human spirit culminated in *The Demon-Haunted World: Science as a Candle in the Dark* (1996). The feature film *Contact* was released shortly after his death, as was his final book, *Billions and Billions: Thoughts on Life and Death on the Brink of the Millennium* (1997).

JoAnn Palmeri

Sarmiento, Domingo Faustino (1811–1888). Essayist, politician, and president of Argentina, 1868–1874. Sarmiento wrote extensively on the issues of **race** and the modernization of Argentina. In order to privilege his generally political objectives, Sarmiento often couched his discourse in popular scientific **theories** of the time. In his best-known *Facundo* (1845), he incorporated a taxonomy of gauchos, a pseudophrenological description of Juan Quiroga, and references to **Alexander von Humboldt** as he argued against the Argentine dictator Juan Manuel Rosas.

J. Andrew Brown

Sarton, George (1884–1956). Leader in establishing the **history of science** as a professional activity and independent academic discipline. Sarton received a doctorate in mathematics in 1911 and founded *Isis*, a journal of the history of science, in 1913. His monumental *Introduction to the History of Science* (3 vols. in 5 pts. 1927–1948) helped establish the bibliographic and methodological basis for the emerging discipline of history of science.

Sarton saw science as a form of human expression comparable to **art** or **religion** and hoped the history of science would link science and the humanities. His insistence on encyclopedic scope and his belief in the underlying unity of all knowledge distinguish him from most modern professional historians of science. Sarton's historical writing emphasizes important books related to science and often includes title pages, frontispieces, and illustrations, along with details regarding various editions and translations of the books he mentions. Because he conceived of the history of science so broadly, his work is a valuable source of bibliographic information for scholars working in LS. It also provides insight into the worldview that motivated the establishment of the discipline of the history of science.

References

Stimson, Dorothy, ed. *Sarton on the History of Science*. Cambridge: Harvard UP, 1962.
Thackray, Arnold, and Robert K. Merton. "On Discipline Building: The Paradoxes of George Sarton." *Isis* 63 (1972): 473–95.

Kathryn A. Neeley

Satire. The use of **poetry** or prose in mobilizing humor, irony, or wit for the purpose of social or moral critique. Two Roman poets, **Horace** and Juvenal, lend their names to the two most common forms of satire. Horatian satire, a social "comment with a smile," attempts to persuade its readers with gentle and sophisticated humor; while Juvenalian satire is cutting, angry, and no holds barred in its criticism.

The modern English resurgence of satire is popularly credited to the poets and essayists of the early-eighteenth-century **Enlightenment**, with acknowledgment to earlier accomplished Restoration satirists such as **John Dryden. Jonathan Swift, Alexander Pope, Joseph Addison**, and **Samuel Johnson** all made extensive use of Horatian and Juvenalian forms of satire, both in the service of a critique of social practices and the newly formed discipline of science. Swift's nonsensical depiction of the fictional Academy of Lagado in *Gulliver's Travels* (1726) suggests a relationship between science and the arts that was at its best ambiguous in the seventeenth century. Swift's indictments of scientific practice and his hilarious juxtaposition of pseudoscientific jargon point to a general wariness on the part of seventeenth-century intellectual and social **culture** over the burgeoning practice of "scientific" experimentation and the newly formed **Royal Society**.

In the nineteenth century, cultural anxieties over industrial practices and the technological innovations of the **Industrial Revolution** found their satirical expression in **Samuel Butler's** novel *Erewhon* (1871). In Butler's fictional country of Erewhon (nowhere), machines have been outlawed because the populace is afraid they will evolve into cruel artificial intelligences (*see* Virtual Reality and Artificial Intelligence). This nod to popular misreadings of **Darwin's** theories (and perhaps to the theories themselves, although this is denied by Butler in his preface to the second edition) is also an indicator of a more general anxiety at the growth of technological industries in which humans become slaves to mechanical production techniques. Also featured in *Erewhon* is Butler's satirical response to Victorian medical practices: In the novel, sick people are considered criminal and thrown in jail until they recover. This is a commentary on the passage of the Contagious Diseases Act, which allowed the sick to be forcibly detained, as well as the experimental and often cruel practices of Victorian authorities responsible for the treatment of mental illness.

In the twentieth century, sustained popular works of satire (as opposed to ephemeral newspaper columns, etc., which are in themselves often insightful commentaries) have mostly been aimed at topical political, rather than scientific, targets. One exception is the 1994 pseudoscientific hoax article appearing in *Social Text* and then exposed in *Lingua Franca* by its author, Alan Sokal, aimed at what Sokal believed to be the increasingly abstruse, jargon-filled, and possibly empty **rhetoric** of cultural studies of science. This act of one-upmanship in the so-called "Science Wars" (*see* Science/Culture Wars), however, served to reinforce, rather than expose, traditional disciplinary boundaries and ultimately suggested that cross-disciplinary understanding between science and the humanities was in this case poorly served by satire. A more gentle contemporary mode of satire, and one enthusiastically embraced by both the scientific community and the burgeoning Web community, is the *Journal of Irreproducible Results*, whose articles quietly poke fun both at scientific discourse and at the public's somewhat unrealistic expectations of science and social science.

The most powerful and enduring satires of science have been those that cross traditional disciplinary boundaries between science and the humanities, opening up closed discourses and suggesting ways in which they can be criticized, while recognizing that the populace at large is also complicit in the formation of disciplinary boundaries. This "human element" shows the value of satire at its best as a (sometimes shocking) tool for social change that forces its readers to recognize their own part in the farce. However, as Stephen Greenblatt has noted, any work of satire requires a rich knowledge of its cultural context, which limits its efficacy over time as a critical mode of writing (226).

References

Greenblatt, Stephen. "Culture." *Critical Terms for Literary Study*. Ed. Frank Lentriccia and Thomas McLaughlin. Chicago: U of Chicago P, 1990. 225–232.
Markley, Robert. "After the Science Wars: From Old Battles to New Directions in the Cultural Studies of Science." *After the Disciplines: The Emergence of Culture Studies*. Ed. Michael Peters. Westport, CT: Bergin & Garvey, 1999.

Helen J. Burgess

Savage (Noble). Primitivist figure of presocial, natural man, used throughout Western **culture** to embody an uncorrupted, wholesome life led in harmony with nature. From the Early Modern period to the **Enlightenment**, literary authors, philosophers, anthropologists, and **physicians** invoked the noble savage to attack European norms and support **theories** on health, the civilizing process, human diversity, and the origins of language and sociability.

Reference

Pagden, Anthony. *European Encounters with the New World: From Renaissance to Romanticism*. New Haven, CT: Yale UP, 1993.

Anne C. Vila

Schrödinger's Cat. A famous illustration of an ill-understood aspect of **quantum physics**, proposed in 1935 by one of its founders, Erwin Schrödinger.

The illustration compares the wave function, the mathematical entity that in quantum mechanics describes a physical system, to the condition of a cat in a sealed box where poison gas either has or has not been released by a random process. The wave function represents all possible states of a system such as an electron in an atom, only one of which is realized when a measurement is actually made. Similarly, the cat is definitively known to be alive or dead only when we open the box and look inside; until then, according to the rules of quantum physics, it is simultaneously alive and dead. In reality, quantum physics does not apply to complex living systems in so straightforward a way; the confused state of the cat is best taken as a scientific metaphor.

Reference

Gribbin, John R. *In Search of Schrödinger's Cat: Quantum Physics and Reality*. New York: Bantam Books, 1984.

Sidney Perkowitz

Science/Culture Wars. Ideological conflict in the 1990s between proponents of the cultural studies of science and adherents to the belief in the objective validity of scientific knowledge. The science wars succeeded the **culture** wars as a central arena of debate between radical and conservative intellectuals. Proponents of the cultural studies of science maintain that science does not progress toward an ever more exact and complete approximation of the natural order and that scientific knowledge is not regulated primarily by criteria of empirical evidence and rational coherence but rather by the ideological standpoint of scientists and by the social organization of science.

References

Gross, Paul R., and Norman Levitt. *Higher Superstition: The Academic Left and Its Quarrels with Science*. Baltimore: Johns Hopkins UP, 1994.
Ross, Andrew, ed. *Social Text*, nos. 46–47 (1996).

Joseph Carroll

Science Fiction. Initially applied as a generic label in the late 1920s to the types of stories that appeared in American "pulp" magazines such as *Amazing Stories* (first published in 1926) and *Astounding Stories of Super-Science* (from 1930). The term quickly gained currency as the popular designation for both previously published and contemporary literature from America and elsewhere dealing with similar themes, such as the technologically prophetic adventure stories of **Jules Verne**, the "scientific romances" of **H.G. Wells**, and the fantasies of other worlds (Mars, Venus, a world at the earth's core) by the creator of Tarzan, Edgar Rice Burroughs.

Some of the most common themes now associated with science fiction have long histories, including stories of natural cataclysm, interplanetary travel, and utopian (or dystopian) futures. For example, while visions of nature gone awry are now firmly associated with science fiction, the type of literary **imagination** they represent is also exemplified in premodern stories, including the deluges in the Babylonian epic of Gilgamesh and the biblical tale of Noah's ark. That natural catastrophe stories have become a species of science fiction reflects the cultural dominance of modern sciences in providing our basic understandings of nature. A contemporary story about the devastation wrought by a plague of locusts is more likely to offer a scientific (or plausibly pseudoscientific) explanation for its occurrence than to suggest that it is a manifestation of the wrath of Yahweh or some other **supernatural** force.

From its earliest archetypes, such as **Mary Shelley's** *Frankenstein*—which not only depicted the creation of monstrous life but also invented and simultaneously critiqued one of the first great myths of modern industrial society— science fiction has exhibited a deeply ambivalent attitude toward science as both a cultural practice and a body of knowledge. This ambivalence has become increasingly evident in postmodern **culture** and the fiction it produces, to the extent that the term "science fiction" has itself become problematic. Many writers now take advantage of the ambiguous acronym "SF" and use it to signify "an increasingly heterodox array of writing, reading, and marketing practices indicated by a proliferation of 'sf' phrases: speculative fiction, science fiction, science fantasy, speculative futures, speculative fabulation" (Haraway 5).

SF often appropriates scientific discourses, especially among writers who foreground the current truth claims of the natural sciences in their depictions of the earth and other worlds. Authors of what is sometimes called "hard" SF (**Arthur C. Clarke**, **Robert Heinlein**) tend to represent these claims faithfully and work within their limitations, whereas others (**J.G. Ballard**, **Ursula K. Le Guin**) question their narrative authority and adequacy. Nevertheless, few SF stories deliberately ignore, flout, or deny the evidence of science without at least gesturing toward plausible alternative **hypotheses**.

While much SF refers explicitly to science, a deeper continuity between SF and scientific texts is that which Damien Broderick describes as "attention to the object in preference to the subject" (155). This object-orientation is often manifested as a preoccupation with externalities and a corresponding deemphasis of nuanced characterization. Indeed, this attention to externalities marks SF as a form of environmental literature, since the narrative development of SF stories tends to privilege the effects of **environments** on the actions of characters, in contrast to the character-driven action of more conventional realist **fiction**. Most SF anticipates possible human responses to alternative conditions—an overpopulated earth, the environs of another planet, a new **technology**—and thus the alternative environment is emphasized rather than the characters who dramatize the effects of the hypothetical conditions on humanity writ large. This is especially evident in stories of alternative worlds—be they other (imagined or real) planets or this world as it might be (or might have been). Such alternative world stories subvert dominant assumptions about the relationships between nature and culture, including the tendency for modern industrial societies to define nature as Other (*see* Alterity) to culture.

The convergence of many SF themes with postmodernist concerns, such as the problematic boundaries between humans and machines explored in **cyberpunk** SF, has led some critics to argue that SF is the characteristic genre of postmodernist fiction. For example, Brian McHale argues that much modernist literature, exemplified by **detective fiction**, is epistemologically oriented (i.e., preoccupied with questions about knowledge of the world—Who knows what, and how reliably? How is knowledge transmitted, and to whom?), whereas postmodernist fiction, characterized by SF, is ontologically oriented (preoccupied with questions about what worlds are and how they are constituted—Are there alternative worlds? And if so, how do they differ and what happens when one passes from one world to another?).

Much SF draws attention to the ways in which social and cultural categories and binary divisions—natural/artificial, male/female, self/other, human/machine—are both constructed and destabilized by textual and technological practices. As the technologies of vitality, simulation, and bioengineering (*see* Biotechnology/Genetic Engineering) compel us to renegotiate the boundaries between such categories, SF dramatizes our new ontological insecurities and rehearses possible responses to them. In this respect, the thematic and linguistic convergence of feminism and SF since the 1970s has been at least as significant for SF as its convergence with postmodernism. Feminist SF has done much to bring the politics of difference to the fore in a genre that, for much of its history, has been dominated by authors, central characters and implied readers who are white, heterosexual, able-bodied males. Authors such as **Octavia Butler** have produced texts in which **gender**, **race**, and identity are central and which offer powerful critiques of existing social relations and power structures—especially of those relations and structures that are supported by Eurocentric and androcentric biological sciences (see also Haraway). As Jenny Wolmark demonstrates, SF that draws on feminist analyses of the construction of identity and difference, and simultaneously participates in the postmodern dissolution of boundaries between high and popular culture, has both unsettled the genre and expanded its possibilities, producing new and challenging perspectives on both scientific and literary discourses.

References

Broderick, Damien. *Reading by Starlight: Postmodern Science Fiction*. London and New York: Routledge, 1995.
Haraway, Donna J. *Primate Visions: Gender, Race, and Nature in the World of Science*. New York: Routledge, 1989.
McHale, Brian. *Constructing Postmodernism*. London and New York: Routledge, 1992.
Wolmark, Jenny. *Aliens and Others: Science Fiction, Feminism and Postmodernism*. Iowa City: U of Iowa P, 1994.

Noel Gough

Science Fiction Poetry. Verse using scientific speculation as the basis for an imaginary scenario or story. Much traditional mythological and epic **poetry**

could be classified as science fiction poetry under this definition, even if works based on pure fantasy are excepted—for instance, much of Vyasa's *Mahabharata,* **Homer's** *Odyssey,* **Dante's** *Divine Comedy,* and **Milton's** *Paradise Lost.* However, since the rise of empirical Western science the preferred mode for science fiction proper has been prose. Many poets, including major figures such as **Shelley, Whitman, Stevens, Eliot,** and Auden, have used scientific themes and ideas in their poetry, but the number of poetic fictions using plausible scientific speculations has been small. There are two possible reasons for the lack: the increasing predominance of lyric over narrative poetry during the modern period, due to the preference for the novel and short story forms in **fiction**; and the sharp ideological divisions between the avant-garde arts and the world of science and technology (*see* Art and Aesthetics).

In the last half-century there has been a modest increase in the production of short poems with science fiction themes (Fairfax; Tem). In addition, four larger and more ambitious fictions exist, which fully emulate prose science fiction in creating a fictional world, a cast of characters, a developed plot, and a carefully constructed machinery of plausible science. These are: Harry Martinson's *Aniara: A Review of Man in Time and Space* (1963; epic-length poem dealing with a space voyage); Dick Allen's *The Space Sonnets* (sonnet sequence about a futuristic ruined monastery in the aftermath of a catastrophe—not yet published in its entirety); Frederick Turner's *The New World* (1985; epic-length romance concerning a religious war in America 400 years in the future) and *Genesis: An Epic Poem* (1988; written in iambic pentameter about the terraforming of Mars).

The promise of science fiction poetry is that the traditional metaphorical and allegorical resources of poetry might be integrated with the subtle understanding of physical **reality** offered by science and the transformation of the physical world offered by **technology**. The metaphors of traditional poetry are usually based on superficial phenomenological resemblances; science should be providing poets with much deeper metaphorical material. Technological devices are in a sense concrete metaphors, expressing in form and function the idea and desire—and even the unconscious motivation—of their makers; the science fiction poet may be in a position not only to adopt but to help devise such metaphors. Prose science fiction must halt its storytelling, sometimes clumsily, to provide necessary scientific exposition; poetry, with its much greater economy and compression, should in theory be able to overcome this difficulty and at the same time bring out more smoothly the inherent lyricism in much scientific discovery. These advantages, however, require the development of new poetic techniques and a high degree of virtuosity to avoid bathos and obscurity.

References

Fairfax, John. *Frontier of Being: An Anthology of Space Poetry.* London: Panther, 1969.
Martinson, Harry. *Aniara. A Review of Man in Space and Time.* Adapted from the Swedish by Hugh McDairmid. New York: Knopf, 1963.

Tem, Steve Rasnic. *The Umbral Anthology of Science Fiction Poetry*. Denver, CO: Umbral, 1982.

Frederick Turner

Science in Literature. A traditional approach to LS, originating in the history of ideas, often associated with the groundbreaking work of Arthur Lovejoy and **Marjorie Hope Nicolson**. The resistance of literature to science dates from no later than **John Donne's** "An Anatomy of the World: The First Anniversary" (1611). There, Donne mourns not only the passing of "Mistress Elizabeth Drury" but "the frailty and decay of this whole world." Among those erstwhile certainties that no longer govern one's understanding of the physical world are the elemental **theory** of matter as something compounded of earth, air, fire, and water and the Aristotelian (*see* Aristotle) categories of substance, quantity, and relation. According to Donne, the rise of science—what he terms "the new philosophy"—is the precipitating cause of this phase of the world's long decline, which began with the Fall. In Donne's view, the

> . . . new philosophy calls all in doubt,
> The element of fire is quite put out;
> The sun is lost, and the earth, and no man's wit
> Can well direct him where to look for it.
> And freely men confess that this world's spent,
> When in the planets and the firmament
> They seek so many new; they see that this
> Is crumbled out again to his atomies.
> 'Tis all in pieces, all coherence gone
> All just supply, and all relation. (205–14)

Notwithstanding its tone of lament, Donne's poem does appropriate the very "new philosophy" that it questions, proclaiming the triumph of Copernican (*see* Copernicus) heliocentrism over Ptolemaic (and, ultimately, Aristotelian) geocentrism and noting the increasingly acute observations made by the science of **astronomy**, successor to judicial **astrology**. Donne, in other words, claims the Copernican Revolution for **poetry** as he proclaims it.

More copious in its erudition than Donne's poem, **John Milton's** *Paradise Lost* (1667) includes references to both the Ptolemaic and Copernican models of the universe, as well as to the full run of scientific knowledge of his day. But what may appear at first glance to be an uncritical retailing of scientific lore looks quite different in the sequel, *Paradise Regained* (1671). There, Christ resists a number of Satan's temptations in the wilderness, the last (and ostensibly the greatest trial) among which is numbered synoptic knowledge of the natural world. Satan cajoles Christ thusly:

> "Be famous then
> By wisdom; as thy empire must extend,
> So let thy mind o'er all the world,

> In knowledge, all things in it comprehend.
> . . . .
> The Gentiles . . . know, and write, and teach
> To admiration led by Nature's light." (IV.221–28)

But Christ is proof against this temptation, as he has been against all the others preceding it, arguing that the only knowledge worth having is direct, unmediated knowledge of God's grace working in the individual and that all other knowledge is insubstantial, pagan, or both of these. He replies to Satan thusly:

> "Think not but that I know these things, or think
> I know them not; not therefore am I short
> Of knowing what I ought. He who receives
> Light from above, from the Fountain of Light,
> No other doctrine needs, though granted true;
> But these are false, or little else but dreams,
> Conjectures, fancies, built on nothing firm." (286–92)

In several important respects, these two approaches underwrite much of the dynamic of resistance that follows. Writers either claim science by proclaiming it or resist it by belittling its potential for improving human knowledge or the human condition. In the eighteenth century, for example, **James Thomson** gained renown by appropriating Isaac Newton (*see* Newtonianism) to the cause of literature in his "To the Memory of Sir Isaac Newton" (1727), while **Alexander Pope**, in his *Essay on Man* (1733–1734), countered with this chilling **analogy**:

> Superior Beings, when of late they saw
> A mortal Man unfold all Nature's Law
> Admired such Wisdom in an earthly Shape,
> And show's a NEWTON as we show an *Ape*. (II.31–35)

What began as appropriation, then evolved into a dynamic of appropriation versus belittlement, evolved further at the turn of the nineteenth century. **William Wordsworth**, who subsequently expressed his awe-filled admiration for Newton, "Voyaging through strange seas of Thought, alone," in *The Prelude* (1850 [III.60–63]), was anything but admiring of science in general, if not Newton outright, in his earlier writing. In "The Tables Turned" (1798), for example, he characterizes scientific inquiry into the matter of animal anatomy and physiology this way:

> Sweet is the lore which Nature brings;
> Our meddling intellect
> Mis-shapes the beauteous forms of things:—
> We murder to dissect.
> Enough of Science and of Art. (ll.25–29)

It is the poet, according to Wordsworth, who humanizes science by recovering or discovering the affective dimension of that knowledge and, by so doing, making such knowledge apposite to the categories not only of human understanding but of emotion as well. In the "preface" to the second edition of *Lyrical Ballads* (1800), Wordsworth puts the case this way:

If the labours of Men of Science should ever create any material revolution, direct or indirect, in our condition . . . the Poet will sleep no more than at present; he will be ready to follow the steps of the Man of science, not only in those general, indirect effects, but he will be at his side, carrying sensation into the midst of the objects of science itself. The remotest discoveries of the Chemist, the Botanist, or Mineralogist, will be as proper objects of the Poet's art as any upon which it can be employed. . . . If the time should ever come when what is now called science, thus familiarised to men, shall be ready to put on, as it were, a form of flesh and blood, the Poet will be there to lend his divine spirit to aid in the transfiguration, and will welcome the Being thus produced, as a dear and genuine inmate of the household of man.

Writing in *A Defence of Poetry* (1821), **Percy Bysshe Shelley** makes very much the same point. The figural basis of science, according to him, is concealed by scientific method and the routines of what Thomas Kuhn (*see* Revolutions) calls "normal science." Along with such concealment comes the deemphasis on or disowning of the role that the poetic **imagination** has to play in scientific inquiry.

[W]e have more scientific and economical knowledge than can be accommodated to the just distribution of the produce which it multiplies. The poetry in these systems of thought, is concealed by the accumulation of facts and calculating processes. . . . We want [i.e., lack] the creative faculty to imagine that which we know; we want the generous impulse to act that which we imagine; we want the poetry of life; our calculations have outrun conception; we have eaten more than we can digest. The cultivation of those sciences which have enlarged the limits of the empire of man over the external world, has, for want of the poetical faculty, proportionally circumscribed those of the internal world; and man, having enslaved the elements, remains himself a slave.

In the America of the turn of the nineteenth century, the situation was somewhat different. America's foremost scientist of the Revolutionary War period, **Benjamin Franklin**, was a journalist and autobiographer as well. Charles Brockden Brown assayed the uses of Newtonian **empiricism** in his **fiction**, adapting the mathematical empiricism of Newton's *Principia* to the rationalistic narrative of *Arthur Mervyn* (1799) and the experimental empiricism of Newton's *Opticks* to the narrative of *Ormond* (1827).

It is hardly coincidental that Franklin and Brockden Brown were Philadelphians—the former by choice, the latter by birth—since Philadelphia was the home of the American Philosophical Society and the American Society for Promoting Useful Knowledge and was certainly one of the preeminent, if not *the* preeminent, centers for American science of the period. Later on, other writers of different regional affiliations did not share the accommodating position of Franklin and Brown.

Edgar Allan Poe, for example, derides science in his "Sonnet—To Science"

(1829), using the same sort of argument found in Wordsworth's "The Tables Turned," discussed above. Although science in Poe's view does not "murder to dissect," it does extinguish the Promethean spirit of poetry.

> SCIENCE! meet daughter of old Time thou art
> Who alterest all things with thy piercing eyes!
> Why preyest thou thus upon the Poet's heart,
> Vulture! whose wings are dull realities. (11.1–4)

In *Arthur Gordon Pym* (1838), Poe subjects the notion of scientific **progress** to critical scrutiny. Then Poe attacks **Bacon** and Baconianism in *Eureka* (1846), creating an anti-Baconian alternative science that bears some resemblance to the German *Naturphilosophie* of Lorenz Oken in its essentially immanentist and vitalist creed, although uncannily echoing the "General Scholium" of Newton's *Principia* ("in him are all things contained and moved") in its contention that the entire living universe exists "all within the *Spirit Divine*."

Poe's quarrel is not so much with science per se as with the Baconianism, with its creed of torturing nature to make her divulge her inmost secrets and toppling the idols on which much of Western culture is grounded. This Baconianism, as John Limon and George H. Daniels before him have noted, underwrote American science during the early part of the nineteenth century. *Eureka* is, in many ways a send-up of Baconianism and especially of *The New Atlantis* (1627).

Although he appears to champion science in *Nature* (1836), **Ralph Waldo Emerson**, like Poe, hews much closer to German *Naturphilosophie* than to English empiricism. Emerson prefaces his essay with this epigraph, drawn from Plotinus, by way of the English Neoplatonist Ralph Cudworth's *The True Intellectual System of the Universe* (1820): "Nature is but an image or imitation of wisdom, the last thing of the soul; nature being but a thing which doth only do, but not know."

Science, according to Emerson, "has one aim, namely, to find a theory of nature." *Find*, for Emerson, is not an idle metaphor. One must go out into nature to find that theory, and once out there, according to him, one finds that the informing wisdom in question is very much like the Spinozist (but *not* the Aristotelian) view of substance, that is, immanent, informing godhead, not merely that which persists through change. That substance, though occult, is made manifest throughout nature, thereby producing a unity that exists even between animate and inanimate nature. "The greatest delight which the fields and woods minister," says Emerson, once again using a verb-metaphor to maximum effect, "is the suggestion of an occult relation between man and vegetable. I am not alone and unacknowledged. They nod to me and I to them."

Ultimately, according to Emerson, what is occulted will be fully revealed. He looks forward, in the concluding paragraph of *The Divinity School Address* (1838; 1841), to a millennial time and "the new Teacher," who "shall see the world to be the mirror of the soul; shall see the identity of the law of gravitation with purity of heart; shall show that the Ought, that Duty, is one thing with Science, with Beauty, and with Joy."

Like Emerson, **Nathaniel Hawthorne** invokes Neoplatonism. As Alfred S. Reid has shown, the character of Aylmer in "The Birthmark" is modeled on the Neoplatonist Sir Kenelm Digby. Despite a good deal of debate as to whether this affiliation marks Aylmer's character as being in some way antiscientific, it seems clear that, as Limon notes, "we may specifically infer that he is a *Naturphilosoph*" (128), albeit a good deal closer to **Goethe** or Oersted in this respect than to Oken. For example, the statement, near the opening of the story, that Aylmer's attraction to, and love for, Georgiana is a "spiritual affinity . . . more attractive than the chemical one" both tropes and recalls the *leitmotif* of Johann Wolfgang von Goethe's *Elective Affinities* (*Wahlverwandtschaften*, 1809), which figures the shifting relationships between two men and two women in terms of chemical valences.

Ultimately, Hawthorne's quarrel is less with science than with the use of science and **technology** in the service of temporal power. Against "good" sciences, such as **alchemy** and magic, Hawthorne arrays "bad" sciences, such as mechanics and **medicine**, as well as technology. In "Rappaccini's Daughter" (1844), Doctor Rappaccini, the namesake of the title "distils . . . plants into medicines that are as potent as a charm."

The use of the adjectival form of *potentia*, the Latinate root of our word *power*, is hardly coincidental, for Rappaccini, a true Baconian in the sense of understanding that knowledge is power, uses his knowledge to ensure his control over his daughter Beatrice. Hawthorne, who opens up the possibilities for multilingual wordplay in a preface that attributes the story to M. de l'Aubepine, the French word for *hawthorn* (and Hawthorne), certainly intends that play with Beatrice's name, which in Italian means "blessed." Beatrice is blessed, both literally and ironically, by Rappaccini, who poisons her to guarantee his power over her by thwarting her growing attraction to Giovanni, the young student who has come to Padua to study. Aware that Rappaccini has poisoned her (and Giovanni through her), Beatrice

put Baglioni's antidote to her lips; and in the same moment the figure of Rappaccini emerged from the portal, and came slowly towards the marble fountain. As he drew near, the pale man of science seemed to gaze with a triumphant expression at the beautiful youth and maiden, as might an artist who should spend his life in achieving a picture or a group of statuary, and finally satisfied with his success. He paused—his bent form grew erect with conscious power, he spread out his hand over them, in the attitude of a father imploring a blessing on his children. But those were the same hands that had thrown poison into the stream of their lives!

The blessing of Beatrice is at the same time her mortal wounding. To recall the prefatory Anglo-French wordplay is also to recall that *blesser* in French means "to wound."

Rappaccini closely resembles Shelley's Count Cenci, father of another young woman named Beatrice and scion of the sanguinary and dysfunctional subject-family of Shelley's play *The Cenci* (1821). Indeed, Rappacini's name suggests the rapacity that is both his and Cenci's dominant characteristic. Moreover, like Cenci, Rappacini is a soulless creature, and his "scientific" view of it evokes Hawthorne's worst fears about the world as the site of nothing but soulless mechanisms and automata, a vision not all that different from that of **Carlyle**, whom he admired, and whose *Sartor Resartus* (1833; 1834) provides a conceptual template for the introductory remarks of M. L'Aubépine, whose work Hawthorne "edits," much as Carlyle "edits" the seven paper bags full of Herr Diogenes Teufelsdröckh's manuscript remains. Teufelsdröckh, his Blumine having run off with his best friend Towgood, glimpses the soullessness that will subsequently haunt Hawthorne.

"Doubt had darkened into Unbelief," says he [i.e., Teufelsdröckh]; "shade after shade goes grimly over your soul, till you have the fixed, starless, Tartarean black." To such readers as have reflected, what can be called reflecting, on man's life, and happily discovered, in contradiction to much Profit-and-Loss Philosophy, speculative and practical, that Soul is *not* synonymous with stomach; who understand, therefore, in our Friend's words, "that for man's well-being, Faith is properly the one thing needful; how with it, martyrs, otherwise weak, can cheerfully endure the shame and the cross; and without it, Worldlings puke-up their sick existence, by suicide, in the midst of luxury": to such it will be clear that, for a pure moral nature, the loss of his religious belief was the loss of everything.

Teufelsdröckh's goal, not unlike the goal of the *Naturphilosophen*, is the creation of an *Allgemeinewissenchaft* ("unified knowledge") that resolves the differences between literature and science by using the one discourse as a heuristic for the other. But that is clearly not **Matthew Arnold's** goal. Writing in "Literature and Science" (1882; 1885), originally drafted for delivery on his American lecture tour in 1883, Arnold concludes that

while we shall all have to acquaint ourselves with the great results reached by modern science, and to give ourselves as much training in its disciplines as we can conveniently carry, yet the majority of men will always require humane letters; and so much the more, as they have the more and the greater results of science to relate to the need in man for conduct, and the need in him for beauty.

Arnold's address came at a crucial juncture. The laws of **thermodynamics** and the theory of evolution (*see* Evolutionary Theory) had been discovered. The steam engine had been perfected, and electric power was beginning to be. The theory of **relativity** lay scarcely two decades in the future, and just beyond that the Great War, with quantum mechanics scarcely another decade beyond the war. Arnold's remarks offer some resistance to the professionalization of science, but they conceal, to some extent, another activity in full career at precisely the same time: the professionalization of higher education in general, and of the humanities and literary studies in particular. Arnold, himself a professional educator and education bureaucrat, stands as a witness to the birth and institutionalization of those antipodal twins, "the **two cultures**." If Western history is, as Alfred North Whitehead put it, "a footnote to Plato," then much of what follows from Arnold's remarks, which include the principled argument that "I must defend **Plato**, as to plead that his view of education and studies in general is in general, as it seems to me, sound enough and fitted to all conditions of men, whatever their pursuits may be," is a footnote to him—at least up to the time at which **C.P. Snow's** notion of "the two cultures" came in for some serious questioning.

One reason for the long duration of the idea of "the two cultures" is that those most apt to interrogate the idea were those most marginalized by it and the social formations that it prescribed. It is no coincidence, nor is it merely the result of the "gender-neutral" operation of English grammar, that the recurrent third-person pronoun in Arnold's discourse is *men*. Even though he realizes the imperative to improve the lot of the marginalized—witness his eloquent characterization of the unfortunate female infanticide Wragg in "The Function of Criticism at the Present Time" (1865)—Arnold does not let her speak in her own voice. Indeed, he claims she cannot, and he interposes his critically informed disinterestedness to supplant the politically motivated discourse of his two straw figures, the politicians Adderley and Roebuck.

Ironically, in part because of the very professionalization that seemed at first to marginalize them, women, who had been acquiring a presence in literature since the eighteenth century, began to acquire a presence in the university and in science in the nineteenth—in the latter instance at first as **laboratory** assistants, then as scientists in their own right. Following the abolition of the slave trade and slavery in England and America, Africans, especially African Americans, began to acquire a presence in science coeval with the one that they had earlier begun to acquire in literature.

Another result of the professionalization of science and the humanities was that literature, while it might resist the culture of science, could no longer resist its insights. Thermodynamics and **Darwin's** theory of evolution had a particularly strong impact on mid- and late-nineteenth-century British fiction, as Peter Allan Dale demonstrates in *In Pursuit of a Scientific Culture* (1989). And the effect of thermodynamics on late-nineteenth- and early-twentieth-century writers as diverse as **Henry Adams**, **Frank Norris**, **Jack London**, and **Theodore Dreiser** has been demonstrated by Ronald E. Martin in *American Literature and the Universe of Force* (1981). The naturalistic elements in Norris, London, and Dreiser, as well as later writers such as Eugene O'Neill and **Upton Sinclair**, owe a good deal to the biological discourse that arose out of Darwinian thought and theory.

It was not until after World War II, during which the pace of scientific discovery and technological innovation accelerated to meet the demands of the war effort, while at the same time unprecedented numbers of people were exposed to the workings and effects of science and technology, that science was subjected to the sort of social critique that once again allowed literature to resist it, to appropriate it—to do things with it—in the way that literature had done formerly. There were some early indications before and during the war of this nascent development, in the work of Marxist historians such as Boris Hessen, who published *The Social and Economic Roots of Newton's Principia* in 1937, and that of Marxist sociologists such as Edgar Zilsel, who published his *Origins of William Gilbert's Method* in 1941. But it was not until the postwar period that this social critique, with the resultant debunking of science's self-representation as a value-neutral, abstract, empirical, and quantitative enterprise, began in serious earnest, with the work of Jacob Bronowski, Herbert Feigl, Paul K. Feyerabend, Alexandre Koyré, Thomas S. Kuhn, Herbert Marcuse, Michael Polanyi, **Karl Popper**, and others.

This was, in the main, still a response mounted by white, middle-aged, European or American males. It took the rise of the civil rights movement in the 1950s, and that of the women's movement and the ecology movement a decade later, to broaden the social critique until it became broad-based and inclusive, accommodating such figures as the Hispanic scholar–poet **Rafael Catalá**, with his discourse of *cienciapoesía* (**sciencepoetry**), and such feminist critics as **Donna Haraway**, N. Katherine Hayles, Evelyn Fox Keller, Carolyn Merchant, and Londa Schiebinger. One recent outcome of the work of some of these last-mentioned feminist critics, and others such as Lorne Leslie Neil Evernden, has been the development of something like the unified discourse pursued by the *Naturphilosophen*, a discourse known as **ecocriticism**.

Some areas of inquiry have not developed as rapidly as those remarked above. There is not yet anything like an African American discourse of literature and science, although some sessions at recent meetings of the Society for Literature and Science suggest that this discourse is in the process of articulation. Neither is there a gay and lesbian discourse of literature and science, unless one wishes to propose Michel Foucault and Luce Irigaray as the avatars of such a discourse. Nor has postcolonial theory articulated such a discourse. However, notwithstanding the resistance to social, cultural, and above all, literary critiques of science manifest in such a book as Paul R. Gross and Norman Levitt's *Higher Superstition: The Academic Left and Its Quarrels with Science* (1994), scientific discourse is once again a discourse among discourses, there for literature to claim or to resist.

References

Catalá, Rafael. *Cienciapoesia*. Minneapolis: Prisma Institute, 1987.

Daniels, George H. *American Science in the Age of Jackson*. New York: Columbia UP, 1968.

Limon, John. *The Place of Fiction in the Time of Science: A Disciplinary History of American Writing*. New York: Cambridge UP, 1990.

Peterfreund, Stuart. "Literature and Science: The Current State of the Field." *University of Hartford Studies in Literature* 19.1 (1987): 25–36.

Reid, Alfred S. "Hawthorne's Humanism: 'The Birthmark' and Sir Kenelm Digby." *American Literature* 38 (1966): 349n.

Stuart Peterfreund

Sciencepoetry. Term coined by the Cuban American poet **Rafael Catalá** in his book *Cienciapoesía* (Sciencepoetry, 1986) to indicate that science and the humanities, as the expression of human consciousness, are one. In order to have a balanced worldview, both must be taken into account as a reasoning and as an intuitive process. Through this cognitive process we must learn to discern the commonality of principles that unify both subsystems of thought. In aesthetics (*see* Art and Aesthetics), for instance, the sciences and the humanities discover their oneness. Aesthetics is not the primary object of science or of history, yet beauty and elegance emanate from scientific and historical principles.

The deep ecologist (*see* Deep Ecology) William Homestead, in his essay "Practicing an Ecological Ethos: On Living Sciencepoetry" (*Ometeca* V 1996), points out that sciencepoetry is about refinding the potential that has always been ours. It is the process through which we integrate our scientific and humanistic selves in order to create a new ethos that has a deep sense of our relationship to other beings and the earth. It demands that we ask, How can ethics be separated from **biology**, **poetry** from **physics**, history from science or literature?

The forms of rational and nonrational behavior we have mastered for centuries are beginning to yield still another form of discerning our immediate **reality**. Poetry can communicate the emerging synthesis of science and the humanities in its creative practice through imagery and metaphors. This is sciencepoetry.

References

Cabral, Regis. Review. *Cienciapoesia. Publication of the Society for Literature and Science* 2.2 (Mar. 1987): 10–13.
Catalá, Rafael. "Para una teoría latinoamericana de las relaciones de la ciencias con las humanidades: La cienciapoesía." *Revista de Filosofía* 28. 67–68 (1990): 215–223.
———. "What Is Sciencepoetry?" *Publication of the Society of Literature and Science* 3.4 (Aug. 1988).
Jiménez, Luis A., ed. *Rafael Catalá: Del "Círculo cuadrado" a la "Cienciapoesía."* New Brunswick, NJ: Ometeca Institute, 1994.

Rafael Catalá

Science Reporting. The reportage and analysis of scientific news and information in mainstream media, such as newspapers and magazines. Science reporting vitally contributes to the public understanding of science: Science reporters educate the public about basic scientific issues and concepts, disseminate scientific information among specialists and nonspecialists, profile individual scientists or research groups, and report on controversies involving science and

technology. Science reporting is a subset of popular science writing characterized less by who does the work than by the subject matter itself—scientific news—and where the work is published (mainstream newspapers, general subject magazines, science-focused magazines, **Internet** publications, and non-text media such as radio and **television**). The scope and depth of coverage ranges from one-paragraph news releases to book-length studies of a working scientific **laboratory**. In LS studies, science reporting is considered a significant and constantly evolving discourse vital to the production and reception of popular scientific knowledge.

Publishing venues for science reporting have grown and diversified greatly over the past 150 years. Several important publications began in the nineteenth century, including *Scientific American* (1845), *Popular Science Monthly* (1872), and *Science News* (1878). Some magazines resisted the trend toward **popularization**, while others developed to fill a growing publishing niche during the late nineteenth and early twentieth century, as the profession of science rapidly expanded and underwent specialization. In 1922, Edwin Scripps founded the Science Service, a still-active syndicate for science news distribution. Today, many newspapers publish science news; others, notably the *New York Times*, regularly have sections devoted to science reporting. Mainstream magazines (*Time, Newsweek, U.S. News and World Report*, and *The New Yorker*) frequently feature items about science and technology. Science magazines are key outlets for science news; these include *Discover, Nature, Omni, Popular Science, Science News, The Sciences*, and *Scientific American*. Professional publications such as *Nature* and *Science* include editorials and news features, in addition to formal scientific reports on current research.

Who reports science has changed as dramatically as outlets for science news have grown and diversified. Before 1900, such work was done primarily by professional scientists who happened to be skilled writers. During this century, science reporting has evolved into a legitimate profession of over 5,000 diverse practitioners: trained journalists interested in science and technology; scientists who also write for the public, or who have become professional writers; and professional science writers who studied at one of several graduate programs in science writing that exist in the United States and elsewhere. Many organizations, both national and international, support the profession, including the National Association of Science Writers, begun in the United States in 1934. Notable contemporary science reporters include **Diane Ackerman**, Natalie Angier, Deborah Blum, John Crewdson, **James Gleick**, **John McPhee**, David Quammen, and Jonathan Weiner, all of whom are professional writers with varying backgrounds in science; some observers would include professional scientists such as **Edward O. Wilson** and **James Watson** in this group. Thus the distinctions among science reporter, popular science writer, and scientist–writer are blurred, signifying a rich heterogeneity within the field of science reporting.

Several key themes and contentious issues characterize the practice of science reporting. First, science journalism has at least three potentially conflicting goals:

the promotion of scientists, scientific institutions, and scientific discoveries; the education of the lay public about scientific matters; and the investigation and analysis of scientific issues and controversies. While sometimes goals may be achieved simultaneously, often one precludes another: For example, a newspaper dedicated to promoting new developments in science and/or individual scientists' careers consequently may neglect rigorous investigation and critique of scientific controversies. Analysts of science reporting also examine the multivalent tensions among key actors within scientific journalism—writers, editors, scientists (sources), and readers. Such tensions produce constraints, such as deadlines imposed by editors upon reporters, which may impact the technical accuracy of a given article, the type of information deemed newsworthy, the amount of research time devoted to a story, the style of writing, and the degree of analysis.

Contemporary analyses of science reporting, such as Dorothy Nelkin's *Selling Science: How the Press Cover Science and Technology* (1987), also address the **rhetoric** and **culture** of scientific journalism. Nelkin analyzes conflicts between journalists and scientists, prevalent metaphors and stylistic devices in science reporting, media effects upon public perceptions of science, and news coverage of risks and controversies associated with science and technology. Nelkin argues that metaphors are crucial to how readers perceive science; that science is generally portrayed as objective, progressive, and authoritative; and that journalistic constraints often preclude thorough analysis of risks and benefits associated with scientific controversies, particularly in the more conservative 1950s and 1980s. Other critics view this last issue differently: In *The New Science Journalists* (1995), Anton and McCourt characterize contemporary science reporting as a contentious, self-critical, and therefore vibrant field of journalism that has actively critiqued controversies and exposed scandals within science from the 1960s onward. This volume also reprints selections by eighteen science reporters and thus is an accessible introduction to the stylistic range of contemporary science writing.

Another resource for further study is *Scientists and Journalists: Reporting Science as News* (1986), edited by Friedman, Dunwoody, and Rogers, a collection of essays examining the relationship between scientists and journalists, as well as the role mass media plays in shaping public knowledge of science. Several case study analyses of how the press covers specific controversies, such as the Three-Mile Island disaster, are useful models for future critical studies of science reporting.

Michael A. Bryson

Scientific Article. A genre with unique historical roots and rhetorical conventions and direct relation to literary writing, usually written by scientists about their work and generally prepared for professional research journals published periodically. The first scientific journal in English is the *Philosophical Transactions of the Royal Society of London*, founded in 1662. Though there is no established formal typology of scientific articles, the major categories may be characterized as experimental, theoretical, review, and speculative. Scientists also write articles for the general public. Though hardly counted as holding professional significance in terms of career advancement, in an age of enormous public funding of scientific research such **popularizations** fulfill the major obligation of keeping the citizenry informed of major scientific developments that affect daily living.

The experimental article is the most important form of communication among **laboratory** scientists. As a genre, experimental articles proceed inductively by describing a series of laboratory or field events that lead to a general or broader statement about natural phenomena. Their typified arrangement may be seen as rooted in the inductive theory of **John Stuart Mill**, but the deeper influence is more likely found in the principles of Baconian (*see* Bacon) induction. Epistemologically, the pattern in scientific papers plays out and constantly reaffirms the scientific culture's belief in methodologies of inquiry and rhetorical strategies that permit the revelation and communication of the underlying characteristics and causes of natural phenomena. Thus, the artificial form of scientific papers, beyond serving to report information in a normalized fashion, is an idealization of scientific inquiry: a simplified progression from experimental design to collection and presentation of results to conclusions about the natural world. The structural paradigm of scientific papers also derives its sense of inevitability from the persuasive force of the Aristotelian (*see* Aristotle) syllogism (i.e., all A is B, all C is A, all C is B).

Experimental articles typically have in common certain structural components: an abstract just after the article's title; an acknowledgment of grant funding and/ or technical assistance; the report itself, arranged in what may be called an IMRAD pattern (introduction, methods, results, and discussion); visual elements, such as graphs, tables, diagrams, and photos; and citation of other scientists' research and ideas. In writing each of these parts, authors bring to bear rhetorical strategies that help persuade their readership of the authority, validity, and significance of their work: Contrary to the popular dictum, the data do not speak for themselves. Even the citations, beyond merely acknowledging prior work, have the rhetorical purpose of tactically situating the article's authors within the larger community of researchers (often anticipating peer review); and, for scholars of **rhetoric**, citations permit an understanding of the intertextuality of scientific texts.

While arrangement in scientific articles has an epistemological function, the role of style in papers is ontological. Inspired by Francis Bacon, adopted by the **Royal Society**, and announced by Bishop **Thomas Sprat**, the scientific plainness ethic rejected the Renaissance tradition of Ciceronian charm, with its tropes and figures and copiousness. As Bacon noted in his 1605 *Advancement of Learning*, the new science and its style of communication must seek "weight of matter, worth of subject, soundness of argument, life of invention, [and] depth of judgment." Words were to reflect physical reality, nature itself. Consequently, two fundamental stylistic hallmarks of scientific writing are the avoidance of the first person along with pervasive use of passive constructions. Ironically, however, studies of scientific language and writing have revealed that natural reality is individually and socially constructed utilizing a scientific rhetoric that is deeply dependent on, for instance, uses of **analogy** and metaphor (e.g., atomic structure, "lock-and-key" in enzyme **chemistry**).

The prose style of today's scientific articles and the organization of their parts, particularly in published experimental reports, are conventionalized and promulgated by various professional guidebooks. Examples are the American Psychological Association's *Publication Manual* (1994), the Council of Biology Editors' *Scientific Style and Format* (1994), the University of Chicago's *Chicago Manual of Style* (1993), Kate Turabian's *A Manual for Writers of Term Papers, Theses, and Dissertations* (1996), and Antoinette M. Wilkinson's *The Scientist's Handbook for Writing Papers and Dissertations* (1991).

Other types of scientific articles exist beside the experimental report. Theoretical articles, in contrast to the inductive process of experimental papers, proceed from a series of deductions that lead to or imply certain observations that confirm them. An example of how a theoretical article may be studied using literary theory is found in Jack Selzer's *Understanding Scientific Prose* (1993), in which a paper on **evolutionary theory** is critiqued using conceptual frameworks from such areas as cultural, **gender**, rhetorical, and reader-response **theory**. Also published by many scientific journals (such as *Nature*) are review articles, a form of secondary scholarship, which attempt critical syntheses from a survey of recent developments in a particular field of research. Such reviews compare and contrast experimental results from diverse studies and point to areas of consensus and areas where questions remain for further study. Finally, speculative articles, which bear some relation to theoretical papers, are likely to be published as popularizations of scientific information and ideas. They may, for instance, extrapolate from present developments to offer controlled opinions regarding the potential applications and influences of scientific knowledge in the future, such as in the areas of high-energy **physics** or recombinant DNA **biotechnology**.

The process of "writing up" scientific articles compares in important aspects to literary writing. Despite attempts to eliminate the writer in favor of facts and materiality, there is always a persona in the article's prose style. The author's perceived voice, whether terse, quasi-whimsical, baroque, aggressive, or reserved, may even influence its readers' reception of the argument set forth. In popularizations such as the **essays** of **Lewis Thomas** or **Richard Feynman**, the prose style is even closer to literary **art** and reflects the creativity and **imagination** of scientific discovery itself. Another literary quality of the language of scientific articles, mentioned earlier, is the reliance on analogy and metaphor for conceptualizing nature. An even more fundamental literary quality of scientific articles, especially in experimental reports, is their narrative structure: The write-up of laboratory methodology and the subsequent discussion of results in the context of natural processes poses a story, which ultimately might or might not turn out to be true, utilizing artifice and selectivity (e.g., in sequence of events or procedural quirks) for purposes of conventionalized style. As Karin Knorr-Cetina and others have shown, the laboratory drama is conveyed in words prudently selected to have the greatest persuasive impact on readers.

References

Bazerman, Charles. *Shaping Written Knowledge: The Genre and Activity of the Experimental Article in Science*. Madison: U of Wisconsin P, 1988.
Gross, Alan G. *The Rhetoric of Science*. Cambridge: Harvard UP, 1990.
Knorr-Cetina, Karin. *Epistemic Cultures: How the Sciences Make Knowledge*. Cambridge: Harvard UP, 1999.
Locke, David. *Science as Writing*. New Haven, CT: Yale UP, 1992.

Robert C. Goldbort

Scientific Explanation. The process of identifying, accounting for, and saving all the sub- or epiphenomena of a physical, chemical, biological, or other scientific event. The history of the concept of explanation and the Western scientific mind-set share common origins in the Renaissance. The word itself— from the Latin *ex-planare*, "to flatten out," and closely related to this acceptation—came into the English word-hoard in the middle of the sixteenth century. The infinitive *to explain* came to signify the activity of flattening the complexly tropaic folds—a near-synonym, *to explicate*, means "to flatten out the folds"—of a hitherto closed, mysterious, secretive, and occult nature, and to reduce that nature to a fully visualizable, if not actually visualized, understanding. The Baconian (*see* Bacon) program of putting a female-gendered nature, who possesses the sort of characteristics noted above, to the question, in order to wring her secrets out of her, to expose her inmost thoughts, owes a good deal to the metaphoric resonances of scientific discourse as a flattening out of, a revealing to a full visual inspection, of its object.

The problem with such a scientific program is, the pun duly noted, twofold. Such a program exercises a tyranny of the visual (and visualizable), even as it privileges visually recoverable evidence as the best sort of evidence for the scientific undertaking. And such a program deemphasizes or discountenances outright its own dependence on tropes (or tropaic folds—the Greek root, *trepein*, "to turn," describes one variant of the activity of creating folds), even though that dependence is clear in the inaugural premises of the discourse.

To cite two examples: Both **Giordano Bruno** (1548–1600) and **Galileo** (1564–1642) after him shared an atomistic view of light and colors, both holding that optical properties such as color were the result of differing aggregations of Democritan atoms. These atoms, in their turn, each described a geometric figure: "red" atoms might be circular; "yellow," triangular; "blue," square. Secondary and tertiary colors might, in their turns, be the result of differing aggregations of these "figures." To accept such a proposition is to move beyond the mystification bespoken by the Aristotelian (*see* Aristotle) concept of occult qualities, perhaps, but without the candid acknowledgment that "red" circles, "yellow" triangles, and "blue" squares are *figures* generally and, depending on whether one infers causation or does not, metonyms or metaphors in their own right. Thus this "explanation" of how colors originate is based on the understanding that circles are in a transferential relation with red, or are the cause of which red is the effect.

The second example is that of Isaac Newton (1642–1727) (*see* Newtonianism), who predicates the material on which forces act as being composed of corpuscles, the Latin word meaning "little bodies." Each of these corpuscles is endowed with five characteristics: extension, hardness, impenetrability, mobility, and inertia. The parallelism between endowing corpuscular "little bodies" with five characteristics and the understanding that human bodies possess five senses duly noted, it would seem that Newton's protest, *hypotheses non fingo* ("I do not frame [or feign] hypotheses"), is an overstatement and that his explanation of how things happen in a universe of matter, motion, and force is an extension of his sense of humanity's place in a material universe created by an absconded deity in whom all things—and all bodies—are contained and moved. By the terms of Newton's explanatory model, neither corpuscles nor the world itself possesses interiority, nor do causes act immanently, as Aristotelian occult qualities do, to produce any observable phenomena. But when Newton attempts to explain **gravity**, he is thwarted by the very tropaic categories of the explanatory model he has created. While he will not accept the notion that occult qualities are the cause of gravity, neither will he credit any explanation of an indwelling strong force as a function of mass and distance. Hence, Newton is left to proclaim that gravity results from action at a distance.

Over time, the practice of scientific explanation has shifted from an emphasis on flattening out the fold to not only acknowledging its durable presence but making that presence a part of explanation itself. Thus quantum mechanics notes that under certain circumstances photons behave more like particles of light, while under other circumstances, they behave more like light waves. Gravity is now part of grand unified theory, which deploys mathematical analysis as a way of viewing apparently contradictory or dissimilar forces, such as electromagnetic or weak forces, and gravitational or strong forces, as subject to the same laws, notwithstanding the very different ways in which such forces behave.

Stuart Peterfreund

Scientific Method. A formal prescriptive pattern of scientific investigation, traditionally comprised of these steps: pose a question about nature, develop a testable **hypothesis**, conduct controlled experiments, analyze observed data, and report results and conclusions. However, scholars from various fields have questioned whether the formal method accurately describes how science operates. Scientists may proceed by intuitive, unplanned leaps and starts; additionally, the implied separation between **theory** and fact, hypothesis and observation, and deduction and induction is misleading, for theories and assumptions direct data collection and interpretation. More radically, literary critics have suggested that scientific methodology is largely a narrative constructed through the rhetoric of science.

Reference

Gross, Alan G. *The Rhetoric of Science*. Cambridge: Harvard UP, 1990.

Michael A. Bryson

Scientific Models and Modeling. The use of figurative discourse, whether linguistic or mathematical, to analyze and/or describe the process by which a given phenomenon or set of phenomena takes place, starting with its simplest elements or constituents. Aristotelian (*see* Aristotle) science, which was rooted in principles of process such as substance, quantity, and relation, did not make widespread use of models. With the coming of Democritan science, however, early Western science underwent a shift from a belief in principle-based phenomena to a belief in matter-based phenomena. One of the outcomes of this shift was what was apparently the first of all scientific models in Western discourse: the atom. As its very name suggests, the atom is proposed as the least coherent unit of matter, the one that is "uncuttable." All of the phenomena and theories of Democritan science follow from this model. Sensation depends upon the size, velocity, and configuration of atoms. The principle of the conservation of matter, in conjunction with the model of the atom, precludes a belief in a cosmogony: There can be no creation *ex nihilo* if the quantity of matter in the universe is constant and always has been so.

The atom also satisfies the principle of Occam's razor, a scientific and/or philosophic principle that gives pride of place to the simplest theory that accounts for ("saves") the greatest possible range of phenomena and attempts to explain unknown causal **mechanisms** and/or mechanisms of process in terms of the known.

But in actual point of fact, the Democritan atom was every bit as much a principle as the Aristotelian categories noted above. No one isolated it in any sphere but the conceptual. So, too, with John Pecham's species as the model for **optics**, or with Isaac Newton's (*see* Newtonianism) corpuscle, or with Christian Huygens's wave, or with Newton's least interval, which we know as dy/dx, the basis of differential calculus; so, too, with John Dalton's atom, or Mendel's gene, or Kekule's benzine ring: It was not until scientific instrumentation caught up with scientific theory that models and the theories that those models underwrite could be validated by direct observation.

Such observation, in its turn, brings Occam's razor to bear anew. That is, as our powers of observation become ever more acute through improved instrumentation, we persist in the quest for ever smaller, more distant, more elusive first principles or building blocks. The atom is no longer the basic constituent of matter, nor are the subatomic particles—the electron, the proton, and the neutron. In their place we have the paired quarks, which comprise hadrons such as the electron and neutrino. The age of the universe keeps increasing, and its size keeps growing as we make use of the Hubble Telescope to take the measure of space-time. The gene is now composed of chromosomes, and these in their turn are made up of protein in the form of a double helix that we can study quantitatively and qualitatively by means of **chemistry** or visually by means of electron microscopy.

Scientific models tell us what we see and how we see. However, like any other figurative construct, such models have a finite lifespan, after which they recede to the status of cliché or common lived experience. Much in the same way that language renews itself through the coinages and other figurative workings of the literary **imagination**, science renews itself through the models and other figurative workings of the scientific imagination.

References

Black, Max. *Models and Metaphors: Studies in Language and Philosophy*. Ithaca, NY: Cornell UP, 1962.
Harré, Rom. *The Principles of Scientific Thinking*. Chicago: U of Chicago P, 1970.
Hesse, Mary. *Models and Analogies in Science*. Notre Dame, IN: U of Notre Dame P, 1966.

Stuart Peterfreund

Scientific Textbooks. A genre with its own formal and stylistic rules, shaped by disciplinary, national, and economic considerations. They represent a valuable resource for the study of scientific **rhetoric**. Scientific textbooks are likely to contain programmatic statements of the kind usually absent from research papers aimed at the already indoctrinated. Textbooks lay out methodological prescriptions, representational practices, and interpretive norms. They often contain mythologized bits of history that convey the discipline's self-image. Significant shifts in textbook format and content frequently reflect important changes in disciplinary methods, goals and alliances.

Stephen J. Weininger

Scientism. A general enthusiasm for science, and the belief that the empirical methods of natural science are the most authoritative, useful, and valuable means of acquiring knowledge, solving problems, and discerning truth. Like **positivism**, scientism claims that science is unified, objective, and conducive to social **progress**. Scientism further holds that nonscientific kinds of knowledge are of negligible value; consequently, the social sciences and humanities would benefit by becoming as scientific in their methods as possible. In most contexts, scientism is considered a discredited, uncritical view of science; the term "scientistic" is usually pejorative.

Reference

Sorell, Tom. *Scientism: Philosophy and the Infatuation with Science*. London: Routledge, 1991.

Michael A. Bryson

Scientist as Author. Consideration of every scientist as a professional author, since the results of scientific **theory** and experiment are mainly disseminated to the scientific community by publication in journals. In the highly specialized form of the research paper, scientists write for their peers within a narrowly defined mode, a form of expository writing that carries stringent constraints: limited length (because many scientific journals request a subsidy in the form of page charges to publish a paper, or because the volume of submission is so great that length must be limited); a defined order of presentation—introduction, methods, results, analysis and interpretation, and conclusions; a stylistic preference for clear and unadorned writing, exclusion of subjective elements, and inclusion of sufficient detail for other researchers to reproduce the result; the use of vocabulary, abbreviations, and idioms peculiar to the particular area; and dependence on tabular, graphical, or mathematical material in addition to text.

Contemporary scientists also write extensively in another specialized form, the grant or contract proposal, meant to justify to a scientific agency (usually a federal organization such as the National Institutes of Health, the National Science Foundation, or an arm of the Department of Defense) a request for funding by describing the research achievements expected to come as a result of the requested support. The style used in a proposal shares elements with the specialized research article but also requires a projection of future possibilities and a presentation of the author's scientific credentials and past achievements to demonstrate that the requested support is likely to be well used. The case must be made to a board of reviewers, often scientific peers but sometimes administrators. For this reason, the writing of proposals is best described as "writing to persuade."

The Scientist As General Author

Apart from these specialized forms of authorship, and more relevant to interactions between literature and science, there are scientists who convey scientific ideas or present their lives in science within standard literary modes such as biography and the personal **essay**, often for nonspecialist readers. Such writings can be seen as a return to older forms of science writing that prevailed into the early nineteenth century, when science began to develop into a profession with a specified style for the research article. Before that consolidation, scientific research was carried out by amateurs who wrote of their findings for a few peers and for the educated general reader. Such writing often attains a simplicity and a directness and displays a sense of enthusiasm and engagement with a problem, which are now absent in professional publications. The writing is often in the first person, as in Isaac Newton's (*see* Newtonianism) letters of the late seventeenth century to the **Royal Society** and to various correspondents describing his work on a new type of **telescope** and on the meaning of light. These present his experiments in full scientific detail, more than adequate for others to evaluate them; and yet also convey a sense of Newton working with his optical equipment, grappling with the meaning of what he observes, and deciding what line of investigation to pursue next.

Further, papers written at the dawn of new scientific ideas were often less abstract and less mathematical than later works when science had grown more sophisticated. The early forms of scientific concepts were easier to convey to nonspecialists. Modern scientists who write for a general readership frequently find that their greatest task lies in extracting the nub of the idea from the accretions of analysis, meaning, and jargon that surround it in the professional literature—in short, to give enough detail but not too much, a process that has been called "lying to tell the truth," a comment ascribed to the contemporary physicist Victor Weisskopf.

The accessible style of early science writing for a general audience can be seen in the famous nineteenth-century piece "The Chemical History of a Candle" by **Michael Faraday**, the greatest experimental scientist of his time, who discovered fundamental electromagnetic phenomena. He carried out his research at the Royal Institution in London, where he also presented Friday Evening Discourses, lectures for general audiences. "The Chemical History of a Candle" was originally presented to a group of children. Faraday's discussion of the composition and manufacture of candles, their applications, and the intricacies of their flames reads with straightforward lucidity. It carries a personal element as Faraday relates his own experiments with candles and tells of different forms of flame and candle he has seen in the streets of London.

The contrast between accessibility and specialization is not the only difference between general and professional writing by scientists. The Nobel Prize–winning physicist **Richard Feynman** commented that professional research papers leave an impression of a direct ascension to scientific truth, whereas the **reality** is that unfruitful turnings, intuitive jumps, and dead ends are an inherent part of research. (A similar criticism is often also leveled at science texts.) The open style of early science writing gives a clearer image of science as a human activity, an outcome still seen in contemporary general works by scientists. **James Watson's** memoir *The Double Helix* (1968) gives a broad picture of the successful search for the molecular structure of DNA. As Watson describes the science, he also points out the conflicting interpretations of the data, which had to be resolved. And in depicting the ploys used to get research funding, as well as the intense competition among scientists to find the answer, he goes even further to picture the scientific enterprise. In *The Hubble Wars* (1994), the astronomer Eric Chaisson clearly presents the scientific rationale for the Hubble space telescope, how it works, and what it tells us about the **cosmos**. To this he adds

extensive discussion about concerns over its $2 billion cost and about the tension
that arose when the telescope was found to be faulty once it was in orbit.

However, not every scientist who writes about a scientific idea presents it in
a style that sets it within a larger context or shows a personal element. Partly
that is determined by the particular scientific area. In some sciences, the researcher can interact directly with what is under study. In his essay "To See or
Not to See," the neurologist **Oliver Sacks** writes the true account of a man who
regained his sight in middle age, after forty-five years of blindness, and found
he could not understand what his restored vision showed. Sacks conveys the
details of the disease that caused the blindness and explains the role of interpretation in vision. He does this both as a medical scientist and as someone who
spends time with the man and observes the serious and depressing difficulties
that come from his restored sight. The result is a powerful weaving of the
personal and the scientific.

Other areas of science are more distant from what they observe. They examine
nature in the **laboratory** or through instruments, because that is the only way
to perceive the very small or the very distant. In such investigations, the scientist
is hard-pressed to present any direct interaction with the subject of study. In
The Double Helix, Watson does not deal directly with a DNA molecule, or even
see it; its scientific perception comes through intricate methods of **X-ray** analysis, and the heart of the discovery of its structure lies in gathering and interpreting data only remotely linked to direct sense experience. However, once the
structure is known, it can be described in words (and with drawings and models)
that appeal to ordinary perception.

At an even higher level of abstraction lies scientific thought that seems dis-
connected from the **reality** around us, or from our perceptions of reality. Mathematics and some reaches of theoretical **physics** fall into this category. Feynman,
a central figure in the modern understanding of the **quantum physics** of light
and matter, has related its meaning in his book *QED: The Strange Theory of
Light and Matter* (1985; the title abbreviates the name of the theory, quantum
electrodynamics). In explaining QED, he is presenting a theory whose premises
seem contradictory and whose effects appear on the submicroscopic level and
do not affect daily human experience. For all his penetrating understanding,
Feynman cannot viscerally engage the fundamental entities of light and matter
or the paradoxical quantum-mechanical duality of waves and particles. Although
he explains the theory simply and transparently for nonspecialists, he cannot
attain the immediacy of Oliver Sacks showing us a suffering individual while
explaining why he is suffering.

There are, of course, rhetorical methods and choices of style that help scientists write clearly about high abstraction or extremely complex ideas. One
approach is for the scientist–author to include the work of other scientists, illustrating different facets of the concept to help the reader. In *Taming the Atom:
The Emergence of the Visible Microworld* (1992), the theoretical physicist Hans
Christian von Baeyer discusses the modern quantum physics of matter. Along

with its philosophical and theoretical meanings, he presents the measurements of experimental physicists to show what the quantum means in the laboratory and in technical application. In *Eye, Brain, and Vision* (1988), the neurobiologist David Hubel places his own Nobel Prize–winning exploration of the visual cortex within the framework set by the research of many others, to illuminate the intricate system that senses and analyzes light. Historical development is another important tool. In *Wrinkles in Time* (1993), the astrophysicist George Smoot leads up to his work in measuring the light left over from the Big Bang by reviewing **cosmology** back to the time of the Greeks. And the powerful tools of **analogy**, metaphor, example, and comparison are invaluable to convey scale and meaning in science.

These aspects of writing by scientists for nonexperts point to one inescapable fact: The greatest scientists are not always the best authors for general audiences, for the remarkable ability to create breakthrough scientific ideas is not necessarily the same as the ability to convey their essence to nonspecialists. **Albert Einstein's** *Relativity: The Special and the General Theory* (1961) is nominally written for the general reader. The book is laudably straightforward and compact, and it presents the concepts of **relativity** in the sequence in which they originated. It does, however, include many mathematical equations—simple ones perhaps, but no matter how simple, each equation added may well lose half the remaining readership, the rule of thumb stated by the theoretical physicist **Stephen Hawking** (author of *A Brief History of Time*, 1988). And its compactness does not leave room for illuminating comparisons that help the reader interpret the strange phenomena of relativity in terms of the common world. The combination of deep scientific understanding and the ability to cast that understanding into a form that is true to the concept and yet easily grasped by others may be as rare as the insight that leads to new science.

References

Bowen, Elizabeth C., and Beverly E. Schneller, eds. *Writing About Science*. New York: Oxford UP, 1991.

Bowen, Mary Elizabeth, and Joseph A. Mazzeo, eds. *Writing About Science*. New York: Oxford UP, 1979.

Boynton, Holmes, ed. *The Beginnings of Modern Science: Scientific Writings of the 16th, 17th and 18th Centuries*. Roslyn, NY: Walter J. Black, 1948.

Sacks, Oliver. "To See or Not to See." *The New Yorker*, May 10, 1993: 59–73.

Sidney Perkowitz

Scientists in/and Society. A set of relationships and roles, under continual negotiation and critical scrutiny in LS. Scientists' popular literature on the social relations of science is crucial to the **representation** and interpretation of science as a political, cultural, and linguistic entity. The new synthesis of mechanico-organismic scientific concepts and metaphors, Marxist social critique, and Wittgensteinian language theory in the popular discourse of the 1930s signaled the transition to postmodernism in the ideological extension of science into popular **culture**.

Originating in the British scientific community in the early 1930s, then extending its effects into the United States and other countries during the decade, a "popular scientific revolution" took place that set in train the interpretation of science as a social and linguistic phenomenon. In an extensive and varied body of popular texts—among them many best-sellers—an influential minority of politicized scientists argued that science is part of society and has political and cultural implications. The 1930s was demonstrably the most important period in the development of scientists' popular social **rhetoric** and set the stage for the politically and ecologically informed popular scientific literature published today.

Scientists' popular cultural critique is a discourse that incorporates a wide range of genres, including travel writing, radio broadcasts, speeches, newspaper and magazine articles, and book-length studies. The works of eminent and innovative scientific specialists, the texts bridge the gap between the "expert culture" and the sphere of popular political and cultural debate. Associated with what historians label the science and society movement, the 1930s discourse popularized and drew together new ideas about nature, society, and language that are central to current description and interpretation of postmodern culture: from the natural sciences, the merging of mechanical and organismic models; from social theory, the transition from orthodox Marxism to an atomized post-Marxist cultural model; and from **philosophy**, Ludwig Wittgenstein's later language theory.

Literary study of this important popular discourse needs to work in dialogue with history, sociology, and philosophy of science in order to describe and interpret its institutionalization; its interaction with extrascientific discourses; the changes that popular writing wrought on the meaning of important terms and concepts; the uses and effects of metaphor in yoking social, linguistic, scientific, and other concepts; the extent to which scientists reflected on and theorized the linguistic and professional demands of writing popular science; the role of scientist-writers as publicists, critics, and editors; and the critical responses of literary figures. Further, there is considerable scope for literary-historical research of the periodic resurgence of this kind of literature.

Literature, Science, and Cultural Critique

In response to science's association in the popular press with the horrors of new technologies of warfare and with technology-related unemployment, scientists in the politically turbulent 1930s put forward a vigorous and prolific popular critique of the social apathy of the scientific community, on the one hand, and the political and educational mishandling of science, on the other. Not only had they turned science upside down to expose its social roots; they had also set out to show that society was grounded in science and **technology**.

The limited overlap between Gary Werskey's *The Visible College* (1978) and

Francis Mulhern's *The Moment of "Scrutiny"* (1979) symbolizes historians' adherence to the separation of science from other elements of culture that was the thesis of **C.P. Snow's** famous polemic *The Two Cultures and the Scientific Revolution* (1959). Therefore, neither Werskey's biographical history of the scientists' movement nor Mulhern's study of literary critic F.R. Leavis and others' "critical revolution" accounts for the intense interaction between the literary and scientific fields that occurred during the decade of the 1930s.

The "**two cultures**" controversy of the early 1960s between Snow and Leavis had its roots in the 1930s. Leavis's initial polemical forays into cultural critique in the early 1930s summarily dismissed cultural commentary by scientists. The argument and rhetoric of Snow's *Two Cultures* is redolent of the works of the 1930s by J.D. Bernal and colleagues, scientist–writers with whom Snow had been closely associated as a physicist and whom he greatly admired. However, Snow was more than a mere admirer; as editor of the Cambridge popular science magazine *Discovery* he was an important publicist and critical overseer of scientists' popular works.

In their influential journal *Scrutiny*, Leavis and others criticized the literary and analytical faults of the "scientific best-seller." Their reviews of popular works by leading scientist–writers Bernal, **J.B.S. Haldane**, Lancelot Hogben, and others—and of James Jeans's and Arthur Eddington's influential **cosmology**—strongly resisted scientists' entry into the field of cultural critique. At the same time they displayed an acute awareness of the importance of scientific knowledge and the need to develop an informed critique of the sciences' political, cultural, and educational influence.

There was no fundamental shaking of scientists' belief that social **progress** would be achieved by scientific knowledge—manifested in the technologies of air transport, hydroelectric power, electric communications, light metals, fertilizers, and applied **genetics**—harnessed to more scientifically managed political and educational systems. However, reaching beyond the scope of the social-historical accounts by William McGucken, Peter J. Kuznick, and others of the science and society movement's varied political structures and theoretical formulations, literary analysis of the scientists' popular texts demonstrates that negotiation of the tricky literary-political field of popular cultural critique opened scientists to ideas from other fields that profoundly reshaped their representation of science in society. Popular works by scientists set out to bridge the gap between specialist discourse and the everyday communication of the larger public. As soon as expert discourse enters the public domain it participates in a different discourse. In the popular scientific revolution of the 1930s, scientists brought together language theory, social theory, and science to self-reflexively create a new language, a way of knowing science as a sociolinguistic entity.

The Popular Scientific Revolution of the 1930s

The scientists' discourse of the 1930s revived the tradition of theoretically informed and socially and linguistically reflexive popular science initiated by

T.H. Huxley in the late nineteenth century. Far more widespread and generically heterogeneous, the 1930s discourse centered on the revision of Marxist social theory. At its most interesting and significant, that critique exploited the interplay between mechanical and organismic concepts and metaphors that was at the heart of the exciting new interdisciplinary science molecular biology. Origins of postmodern models of science in society can be observed in the metaphoric extension of the molecular analysis of biological structure to produce models for the microanalysis of social structure.

One of the more engaging genres was travel writing. A fine example is biologist **Julian Huxley's** *A Scientist among the Soviets* (1932), an at times eulogistic firsthand report on the Soviet experience of a science-based, planned society—viewed metaphorically by Huxley as a completely new kind of "social organism." Mathematical biologist Lancelot Hogben's *Author in Transit* (1940) is an account of a wartime around-the-world journey. In contrast to the Soviet Union, Hogben argues, the response to the social impact of science and technology in the United States is forward-looking; from the latter he draws a model of piecemeal planning based on a mechanico-organismic metaphor of society as a complex kaleidoscopic interplay of separate elements.

Anthologies of **essays** by scientists addressing social issues in which science was embroiled include Daniel Hall and others' *The Frustration of Science* (1937), a range of responses to criticism of the destructiveness of science and technology. The socialist physicist P.M.S. Blackett metaphorically depicts the scientist as part, rather than potential controller, of the highly complicated "machinery" of the modern state; and demographer and feminist Enid Charles mixes organismic and mechanical rhetoric in promoting social management of the "biological machinery" of population growth.

The 1930s witnessed the success of the "popular self-educator," a genre that mixes the new polemic about science's political and cultural implications with lucid exposition and historical overview of scientific knowledge. Hogben's two volumes *Mathematics for the Million* (1936) and *Science for the Citizen* (1938) were huge successes. Physicist and communist Hyman Levy produced an equivalent volume, *Modern Science* (1939). Though they may seem to exceed the limits of the popular, lengthy Marxist philosophical and sociological studies of the sciences in society—including Levy's *A Philosophy for a Modern Man* (1938) and communist physicist Bernal's influential *The Social Function of Science* (1939)—were intended for an educated general readership and might be best understood as stretching those bounds.

Scientists' speeches were published in collections such as John Boyd Orr and others' *What Science Stands For* (1937). In the lecture *The Retreat from Reason* (1937), Hogben argues that a true sociology must be cognizant of the development of electricity, biochemistry, and genetics and the enormous possibilities of an era of "biological inventions." Scientists were also quick to exploit the possibilities of radio. *Science in the Changing World* (1933), edited by Mary Adams, brings together BBC radio commentaries by scientists, writers, and philosophers. Wide-ranging radio discussions with fellow scientists comprise the text of Huxley's book *Scientific Research and Social Needs* (1934), based on the premise that although society was blind to the possibilities of science and technology, science was equally a blind force in society.

Marking the transition to a differentiated postmodern model of science in society, Huxley's important essay "Science and Its Relation to Social Needs," published in Jeans and others' *Scientific Progress* (1936), represents science as a matrix of diverse qualities and social interconnections. Although Huxley has not abandoned the Marxist model and critique of capitalism, his interpretation of science in society depicts the workings of class and power dispersed across a heterogeneous array of interacting social and cultural factors. Symptomatic of the conceptual upheaval in the science of the decade, Huxley's representation of science's social role is an uncomfortable mix of biological-organismic and technological-mechanical metaphors. Similarly, the ambiguity and contradictions that accompanied scientists' social self-reflexiveness are illustrated when Huxley leans away from a purely science-centered ideology and presents science as a mere tool for society's use, then adds, however, that science is the only reliable tool for social management and progress.

Science, Society, and Language

The wave of interest in his *Tractatus Logico-Philosophicus* (1922) and his connections with Bertrand Russell and the Bloomsbury group ensured that Wittgenstein's later language theory was taken up rapidly in intellectual and literary circles. Scientists were no exceptions to this vogue. Illustrating the point that popular discourse is a primary vehicle for transmitting intellectual innovation, as early as 1930 Hogben had set about popularizing a theory of science-as-language that was clearly indebted to Wittgenstein's philosophy. In *The Nature of Living Matter* (1930), Hogben redefined science in linguistic terms.

Already in the *Tractatus* Wittgenstein had dispensed with the sciences' claims to knowing and explaining an external nature, writing instead of different systems of description that comprise "the edifice of science." Hogben followed a similar line of interpretation when he spelled out what would survive today as the credo of much work in literature and science: "The important thing about the world construction of science is not its externality but its communicability" (Hogben, *Nature* 261). Further, Hogben's conflation of the social, material and symbolic in the form of "socialised reality" prefigures key elements of recent discourse theory (Hogben, *Nature* 262). Hogben later expanded his analysis of science as language to add a historical dimension to the role of metaphor, depicting science as an evolving structure of metaphors.

From the outset Hogben addressed the question of popularization in terms of translation between systems of **symbolism**: "Because common language and the language of science are not the same thing, there can never be a plain answer for the plain question of the man in the crowd. There can only be a familiar one" (Hogben, *Nature* 18). Hogben was also acutely aware of the dangers of the internal linguistic specialization and fragmentation of science itself. As Wittgenstein in his lectures at Cambridge from 1930 onward began to elaborate on his theory of culture as an assemblage of distinct systems of symbolism—"grammars," or "language games"—so Hogben's popular translation of that theory in terms of the relations between ordinary and specialist languages assumed a more clearly sociological shape.

Breaking society into fragments that nonetheless interact in myriad microscopic ways, Wittgenstein's and Hogben's models represent a historically significant conflation of mechanical and organismic concepts. From a present-day standpoint, Hogben's most important innovation was his wedding of Wittgensteinian theory to socialist-democratic principles; thus, in a move remarkably similar to that taken in recent post-Marxist theory of postmodern culture he set out to bring a greater particularity and differentiation to the concept of social class. For instance, according to Hogben, modern technologies had bred a new and disproportionately powerful social class of skilled administrators.

In "Mathematics, the Mirror of Civilization," the opening chapter of *Mathematics for the Million*, Hogben entertainingly illustrates historical instances of the linguistic exclusion of the common person from useful specialist knowledge; at its base is Hogben's strong commitment to the role that popularization can play in freeing the nonspecialist from economic tyranny allied with the exclusiveness and secretiveness of the expert. To Hogben, knowledge of mathematics—"the grammar of size and order" (Hogben, *Mathematics* 20)—is as vital to individual survival and social progress as a command of the conventions of ordinary language. Hogben's desideratum "freedom of discourse" was based on his understanding of the relations of knowledge and power; thus he advocated the "democratization of mathematics" to halt the historical process whereby the "grammar of numbers was chained down to commercial uses before people could foresee the vast variety of ways in which it was about to invade man's social life" (Hogben, *Mathematics* 20, 21).

Hogben's vigorous pragmatist demystification of the sciences spells out an **analogy** remarkably similar to sociologist **Bruno Latour's** model, in his polemical-theoretical work *We Have Never Been Modern* (1993), of concealed "networks" that tie science together with **politics** and culture—excepting that Hogben's model provides a crucial role for popularization. As Hogben explains, scientific knowledge has become a secret of the "priest in the temple," and the role of popularization is to bring science back to the nonscientists "outside the temple" by "tracing out the subterranean channel which connects the temple with the river of man's social experience" (Hogben, *Mathematics* 25).

In *The Two Cultures*, Snow asserted that the literary "culture" lagged far behind the social transformation wrought by the twentieth-century technological-scientific revolution. He later returned to explain that cultural lag in terms of the gap between science's symbolic language and literary language, between the "logic" of technology and the "logic" of everyday language. That is why, according to Snow, the industrial-scientific revolution has not found its way into the popular **imagination**. Snow's linguistically atomized model of science, technology, and society has its roots in the transition to postmodern ideology (*see* Politics and Ideology) and cultural critique during the popular scientific revolution of the 1930s.

References

Hogben, Lancelot. *Mathematics for the Million: A Popular Self Educator.* 2nd rev. ed. Primers for the Age of Plenty. 1936. London: Allen and Unwin, 1960.

———. *The Nature of Living Matter.* London: Kegan Paul, Trench, Trubner, 1930.

Kuznick, Peter J. *Beyond the Laboratory: Scientists as Political Activists in 1930s America.* Chicago: U of Chicago P, 1987.

McGucken, William. *Scientists, Society, and State: The Social Relations of Science Movement in Great Britain 1931–1947.* Columbus: Ohio State UP, 1984.

Russell, Doug. "Popularization and the Challenge to Science-Centrism in the 1930s." *The Literature of Science: Perspectives on Popular Scientific Writing.* Ed. and Intro. Murdo William McRae. Athens: U of Georgia P, 1993. 37–53.

Doug Russell

Scientists' Perspectives (in/on LS). Most typically (before the emergence of LS as a recognizable quasi-discipline), concerned with securing a measure of cultural status for science (especially in education), in the face of the overwhelming dominance of literature as the embodiment of **culture**. The first conspicuous scientist to speak out on this theme was **Thomas Henry Huxley**, in 1880; nearly eighty years later **C.P. Snow's** famous lecture and subsequent book on the **two cultures** demonstrated perhaps more than anything how little had changed in the intervening period. Both scientists were promptly challenged, most notably by **Matthew Arnold** and F.R. Leavis, respectively, who perceived them (more justifiably in Huxley's case than Snow's) as aiming for superiority, not just equality.

From the 1960s on, as the role of science in society became ever more pervasive, critics of all sorts began to turn their attention to the connections between science and traditionally humanistic fields—a development anticipated by Snow. But it was some time before scientists took much notice of these new activities. Of course, a number already participated in them: those practicing scientists who span the two cultures divide to work in one or more literary forms such as **fiction**, **essays**, or **poetry**. Some prominent examples in recent years include Primo Levi, **Lewis Thomas, Stephen Jay Gould, Roald Hoffmann, Carl Djerassi, Alan Lightman,** among others.

With LS activities now sufficiently visible to constitute a recognizable discipline, scientists have reacted to it in quite different ways. Probably a large majority of scientists have not reacted at all: Most do not know what LS is about or even that it exists. This is not necessarily a sign of rejection of Snow's call for communication between the two cultures. Even among those scientists who would favor moves in the direction of unification of knowledge (what

Edward O. Wilson has recently described as "consilience"), most find that a scientific career easily consumes all the time one allows it to.

But scientists do comprise (and have from the beginning) a small but enthusiastic group within the LS community. Often they have been driven by the urge to connect their own vocational and avocational interests. Such moves were relatively unproblematic in the earlier days of LS, when it was principally concerned with exploring the assimilation and exploitation of scientific ideas by writers and literary scholars ("**science in literature**"). Scientists interested in the development of ideas within their own disciplines became intrigued with the possibility of pursuing the interdisciplinary migration of those ideas into the nontechnical sphere. Such a program demands little, if any, introspection as to the nature of the scientific endeavor itself and hence is almost totally unthreatening.

More recently, some scientists have begun to come to LS from an interest in **history of science**, recognizing that forms of textual analysis brought to bear in recovering and interpreting the past are not significantly different from those of literary studies. This often broadens into a general interest in scientific **rhetoric**, with the role of metaphor, both within science and as a bridging mechanism between scientific and literary spheres, constituting a particularly prevalent theme. **Representation** and visual imagery comprise another important area of overlapping interests.

The Society for Literature and Science (SLS) has become a prime locus for much of this work of convergence; but even within its (mostly friendly) confines there is a significant degree of residual caution and even suspicion. In this territory science and literature have much more equitable standing, and its exploration may well imply a substantial degree of rethinking of *both* domains. Some scientists find such an exercise invigorating and gratifying, as it broadens and enriches their understanding of their primary field. That reaction is far from universal, however. Confrontations have arisen in which scientist participants express their concerns about inadequate attention to correct scientific usages, overemployment of arcane jargon, and some degree of devaluation of the scientific enterprise, on the part of their nonscientist colleagues. Attempts to defuse these by recognizing mutual misunderstandings about goals and methods have generally been somewhat (but only somewhat) successful.

On the other side of the coin, another group of scientists—probably no larger but certainly more vocal—amplifies the latter concerns into a stance of strong opposition to LS, or at least to that segment of LS that they characterize as postmodernism. A major objection is that the scientific content of this type of effort is generally so vague—or just incorrect—that the work contributes nothing to understanding either the science or literature. Authors incorporate elements of science that they understand poorly and tie them to their literary subjects by means of loose **analogies** and fuzzy metaphors. In this view the motivation is mainly to impress the reader with the author's erudition and perhaps to import a degree of reverence often granted to scientific knowledge into their own pronouncements. Such maneuvers are successful only because their readers have even less scientific awareness than the authors.

As a self-described "experimental" test of this opinion, physicist Alan Sokal constructed a mock postmodernist study of quantum gravity, deliberately made as outrageous and impenetrable as possible, but replete with many references to "authentic" work on related topics, and submitted it to the journal *Social Text* to see whether the parody would be unmasked. It was not, and the article was duly published—ironically, in a special issue (1996) entitled "The Science Wars" (*See* Science/Culture Wars). That issue was intended to consist of responses to the attacks by scientists on this body of literary work as well as the social constructivist school of science studies; but the Sokal article and its aftermath constitute the loudest salvo in the science wars to date.

Some of the critics, most notably Paul Gross and Norman Levitt in their book *Higher Superstition* (1994), complain not just of pretentiousness but of outright hostility. Since a substantial fraction of postmodernist work is perceived as denying the possibility of rigorous knowledge, then insofar as its practitioners address scientific issues, they appear to be trying to debunk scientists' conceptions of what the scientific endeavor is all about—a self-image that few scientists would be willing to compromise to any serious degree—and thereby undermining public confidence in science. Not surprisingly, these critics have called for scientists to become aware of, and to actively resist, such movements.

At the present time the science wars are rhetorically intense but relatively limited in consequences, although each side regularly blames the other for casualties, both specific (e.g., academic firings and nonhirings) and general (e.g., unfavorable public image of science, dismal state of scientific education). Still, as noted above, most scientists remain on the sidelines, largely through lack of awareness. It remains to be seen how these diverse and often conflicting trends will evolve and which side will be more successful at enlisting the support of the so-far silent majority of scientists.

References

Snow, C.P. *Public Affairs*. New York: Scribner's, 1971.
Sokal, A., and J. Bricmont. *Fashionable Nonsense: Postmodern Intellectuals' Abuse of Science*. New York: St. Martin's, 1998.

Jay A. Labinger

Scriblerus, Martinus. The persona adopted by a collection of early-eighteenth-century satirists (including Dr. John Arbuthnot, John Gay, **Alexander Pope**, and **Jonathan Swift**) to ridicule abuses in learning. The various **satires** on contemporary science produced by this group include *The Memoirs of Martinus Scriblerus* (pub. 1741), *An Essay Concerning the Origin of the Sciences* (c. 1727–1732), "A True and Faithful Narrative of What Lately Passed in London" (c. 1739), and *Three Hours after a Marriage* (1717). Topics satirized include anatomy, **astronomy**, geology, and **medicine**.

Richard Nash

Selzer, Richard (1928–　). American **physician-writer** noted for weaving his personal experiences as a surgeon into unique literary metaphor. In **essay** collections, such as *Mortal Lessons: Notes on the Art of Surgery* (1976), Selzer explores issues of illness and death by dissecting corresponding viewpoints of both **physician** and patient. More than simple medical discourse, Selzer's works deftly combine scientific knowledge with metaphorical language to capture the essence of the human condition within constraints of infirmity and mortality. His works blend **realism** and metaphor in striking portrayals of humans seeking to maintain their individuality and autonomy as they transcend restrictive afflictions.

Robert J. Bonk

Semiotics. The science of signs, describing any systems of differential significations without positive value. One of the most important theoretical approaches in LS. Charles Sanders Peirce (1839–1914) formalized semiotics, but Ferdinand de Saussure's (1857–1913) linguistic model remains dominant. Literary texts are exemplary signifying complexes, but semiotics considers all cultural practices as sign systems. Science and literature are included as branches in the general theory of semiotics.

Charles A. Baldwin

Serres, Michel (1930–　). French philosopher, historian of science, author of *The Parasite* (1980) and five works combining cultural studies with **thermodynamics** and **cybernetics** under the shared title *Hermès* (1968). Serres weaves into a singular interdisciplinary discourse sets of concepts specific to various domains of the sciences, the humanities, and philosophy. Reconnecting classical Greek thought with French classical and **Enlightenment** literatures, historically situated scientific events, the development of mathematics, and modern cultural phenomena, his earlier works are grafted on concepts of communication **theory**. His more recent cultural studies are primarily marked by aspects of **complexity** theories and nonlinear dynamics: *Statues* (1987), *Le Tiers-Instruit* (1991), *Les cinq sens* (1985), *La Légende des anges* (1993).

Maria L. Assad

Shadwell, Thomas (1642–1692). English playwright whose comedy *The Virtuoso* (1676) (*see* Virtuoso) satirizes seventeenth-century science. Through the character of Sir Nicholas Gimcrack, Shadwell mocks the apparently farfetched experimental work of pioneering scientists such as **Robert Hooke** and **Robert Boyle**. His play demonstrates a trust in the self-evident truth of the senses rather than in emergent scientific methodologies.

Anne Bratach Matthews

Shakespeare, William (1564–1616). Dramatist, actor, and entrepreneur of the Elizabethan and Jacobean theater. Shakespeare's **drama** challenged the early modern desire for a more productive and descriptive form of scientific learning. This often took the form of a radical questioning of the relationship between the Real (or the natural) and the artificial or ideological. Shakespeare used the metaphor of the theater to question the status of everything outside the fictionality of his **representations**. In other plays, he offered a critique of the humanist expectation of rational certainty by providing and validating an alternative **epistemology** of superstition and magic.

Diana B. Altegoer

Shaw, George Bernard (1856–1950). Irish essayist, playwright, and Fabian socialist, Shaw drew on Friedrich Nietzsche and Arthur Schopenhauer to critique the absence of will in Darwinian evolutionary mechanism (*see* Darwin; Darwinism; Evolutionary Theory), most fully in *Back to Methuselah* (1918–1920). He supported the antivivisectionist movement, criticizing animal experimentation in *The Doctor's Dilemma* (1906). His satiric view of scientific surety gave him repute as a critic of contemporary science. Shaw nevertheless advocated scientific **realism** in literature, particularly in his writings on **Émile Zola** and Henrik Ibsen.

Reference

Holroyd, Michael. *Bernard Shaw*. 4 vols. New York: Random House, 1988–1992.

Alison E. Bright

Shelley, Mary Wollstonecraft (1797–1851). Author of *Frankenstein: or, the Modern Prometheus* (1818). Written in 1816 when she was eighteen, the work earned her lasting fame. Her protagonist, Victor **Frankenstein**, has become the dominant archetype of the scientist in twentieth-century **fiction** and **film**, his name synonymous with any experiment out of control. *Frankenstein* retains its mythical power because, unlike its precursors, the Faust story, the Golem legend, and the Prometheus myth, it offered the first truly secular treatment of the great aspirations and fears of humanity, replacing eschatological punishment with scientific **determinism**.

In *Frankenstein*, the pursuit of science is most obviously associated with the desire for power, especially power over Nature and the limitations of the human condition. Thus Shelley, like virtually all the English Romantic writers (though not the German Romantics) (*see* Romanticism), constructs a view of science standing in opposition to Nature and to a whole cluster of Nature correlatives— the natural affections, human relationships, fertility, beauty, health, and morality. Estranged from Nature, postponing his marriage and rebuffing family and friends, Frankenstein denies inherent, organic order and aspires to create life by cobbling his creature together from disparate dead components. Hence the Monster, constructed like a machine, formed part of the ongoing debate on **mechanism. Descartes's** and La Mettrie's ideas of the assemblage of component parts is brilliantly parodied in Frankenstein's collection of assorted bones and muscles from graves and charnel houses. The Monster is thus both an *alter ego* and a substitute for the natural child he has denied existence by deferring his marriage.

The importance of Frankenstein as an enduring commentary on science is multiple. As a character, he is not only the arrogant overreacher determined to transcend human limitations and emulate the Creator; he is also the heir of Baconian (*see* Bacon) optimism, believing that everything can ultimately be known and that knowledge will inevitably be for society's good. He accepts the reductionist and mechanistic premises of eighteenth-century **physics** and **chemistry**, applying them to living beings. However, the being he creates is not merely the sum of its inanimate parts but a recreation of Frankenstein's own unconscious desires. Shelley thus reaffirms the Romantic view of the unconscious as more powerful than the rational mind.

Shelley presents Frankenstein's obsessive pursuit of scientific knowledge as unnatural, motivated by a desire for power and fame and achieved at the cost of physical and emotional well-being. Frankenstein's rejection of his creature, which precipitates the sequence of disasters, has been interpreted as the irresponsibility of scientists in not foreseeing or being accountable for the consequences of their research. This recurrent pattern of apparent success followed by unforeseen and uncontrollable consequences obtains because science always operates in advance of the ethical discourse and hence the moral preparedness of society.

Recent feminist criticism of *Frankenstein* has focused on the role of Elizabeth and of Mary Shelley herself, as commentary on the exclusion of women and feminine values by an overintellectualized practice of science, and Marilyn Butler has researched the contemporary medical relevance of the story. Shelley's later novel, *The Last Man* (1826), prompted by the cholera epidemic of the 1820s and her reading of Cousin de Grandville's *Le Dernier Homme* (1805), describes the lonely survival of Lionel Verney after plague has ravaged Europe in the twenty-first century. It is among the first explorations of a future society and the possible extinction of humanity.

References

Baldick, Chris. *In Frankenstein's Shadow: Myth, Monstrosity and Nineteenth-Century Writing*. Oxford: Clarendon, 1990.

Bennett, Betty T., and Charles E. Robinson, eds. *The Mary Shelley Reader*. New York and Oxford: Oxford UP, 1990.

Butler, Marilyn. "Introduction." *Frankenstein*. Ed. Marilyn Butler. London: Pickering and Chatto, 1993.

Cantor, Paul A. *Creature and Creator: Myth-making and English Romanticism*. Cambridge: Cambridge UP, 1984.

Levine, George, and U.C. Knoepflmacher, eds. *The Endurance of Frankenstein: Essays on Mary Shelley's Novel*. Berkeley: U of California P, 1979.

Tropp, Martin. *Mary Shelley's Monster: The Story of Frankenstein*. Boston: Houghton Mifflin, 1977.

Roslynn D. Haynes

Shelley, Percy Bysshe (1792–1822). British Romantic poet, avid in the study of sciences from his schooldays on. Shelley began as a materialist with **chemistry** as a model of **objectivity** but soon followed his early interest in **electricity** to antimaterialist conclusions, as reflected in the conclusion to *Prometheus Unbound* (1820). *Queen Mab* (1813) pleads for a unified **astronomy**, as later interest in microscopy would suggest a unity of atoms and microbes. *Alastor* (1816) and *Prometheus Unbound* reflect a detailed awareness of vulcanism (*see* Volcanoes).

William Crisman

Shute, Nevil (1899–1960). Nom de plume of Nevil Shute Norway, author of best-selling novel *On the Beach* (1954) and twenty-two other works of **fiction** and nonfiction. Born and educated in England, he studied engineering (*see* Engineer(s)/Engineering) at Oxford University and worked as a stress analyst on R-100, a large British airship built in competition with government-sponsored R-101, which crashed soon after completion. He discussed these activities in his only nonfiction work, *Slide Rule* (1957). Shute was a key figure in establishing Airspeed Ltd, an aircraft manufacturing firm, prior to World War II. His early novels were written in a John Buchan espionage vein, but he soon switched to novels about the use and impact of aviation (*see* Aeronautics/Aviation). After World War II, Shute's novels became increasingly focused on social issues, especially the impact of **technology**. He gained fame with *No Highway* (1948), a novel about an engineer testing modern commercial aircraft, which was made into a film starring James Stewart and Marlene Dietrich. Unhappy with British governmental policies, Shute moved with his family to **Australia** in the 1950s. The immensely popular *On the Beach* recounts the end of human life on the planet resulting from radiation sickness due to fallout from World War III. Perhaps no mid-twentieth-century author was so successful at presenting the impact of modern technology (especially in the form of aircraft) on the social welfare of the human race. Shute remains underappreciated for the degree of social concern found in his mature novels.

David Kirk Vaughan

Sidney, Philip (1554–1586). Poet and essayist, best known for the *Arcadia* (1590), *Defence of Poetry* (1595), and *Astrophil and Stella* (1591). Sidney domesticated continental literary forms such as the sonnet sequence and the pastoral romance as well as formulating England's first "apology" for the philosophical importance of **poetry**. The humanist Sidney, in the *Defence*, argues that the poet is identical to the astronomer, geometrician, and natural philosopher in having the works of nature as the principal object.

Diana B. Altegoer

Sinclair, Upton (1878–1968). Author of *The Jungle* (1906), a socialist novel of the Chicago meatpacking industry that led to unprecedented public health legislation. In his major novels, which include *King Coal* (1917) and *Oil!* (1927), Sinclair describes how capitalism incorporates scientific processes as industrial systems. Sinclair's naturalistic style and optimistic narrative resolutions reflect the "science" of dialectical materialism.

Nicholas Spencer

Smiley, Jane (1949–   ). American writer. Her contemporary revisioning of **Shakespeare's** *King Lear* (1605–1606) set in an Iowa farming community, *A Thousand Acres* (1991), foregrounds the constitutive role of metaphor in science. The novel probes the environmental and health consequences of the metaphorical link between women and nature in scientific discourse and dramatizes the toxic legacy of mechanistic conceptions of nature and the Baconian (*see* Bacon) faith in the limitless profitability of technologically manipulating nature. Smiley's *Moo* (1995), an acerbic portrait of a land grant university, explores the roles that institutional **politics** and corporate influence play in shaping knowledge claims and critiques the ethics of animal experimentation.

Desiree Hellegers

Smollett, Tobias (1721–1771). Scottish-born English novelist. Smollett drew on his medical apprenticeship to lend verisimilitude to his **fiction**. In *The Adventures of Roderick Random* (1748), the eponymous hero serves, as Smollett had, as surgeon's mate aboard a squalid warship bound for Cartagena, Colombia. Smollett also used his medical knowledge to illustrate the psychology (*see* Anthropology/Psychology/Sociology) of the patient. In the epistolary *Expedition of Humphrey Clinker* (1771), Matthew Bramble complains of his symptoms in letters to his physician. **Laurence Sterne** parodies Smollett as Smelfungus in *A Sentimental Journey* (1768).

Anne Bratach Matthews

Snow, C[harles] P[ercy] (1905–1980). British physicist, government official, and writer famous for coining the phrase "**the two cultures**" to describe the intellectual and professional schism between **experimental science** and literary **art**. Snow's novel *The Search* (1934) and several novels in his long *Strangers and Brothers* sequence, initiated in 1940, deal intimately with the scientific life and manners. In both his professional life and substantial body of writing, Snow stands as a unique bridge between the scientific and the literary intellectual traditions.

Robert C. Goldbort

Snyder, Gary (1930–   ). Pulitzer Prize–winning poet and essayist. Snyder integrates ecological concepts into social, spiritual, and aesthetic perspectives and finds them compatible with Native American and Buddhist traditions. Snyder draws upon the writing of such distinguished ecologists as Eugene Odum, Howard T. Odum, and Ramon Margalef. For them, and for Snyder, nature's unity is most clearly seen in the flow of **energy** through ecological systems, through "networks" and "loops." Snyder has steeped himself in ecological thought because, as he says, "far-out scientific knowledge and the poetic imagination are related forces" and the "ecological sciences are laying out (implicitly) a spiritual dimension" (*Old Ways* 63). His other works include *Earth House Hold* (1969) and *No Nature: New and Selected Poems* (1992).

References

McClintock, James I. "Gary Snyder: Posthumanist." *Nature's Kindred Spirits: Aldo Leopold, Joseph Wood Krutch, Edward Abbey, Annie Dillard, and Gary Snyder.* Madison: U of Wisconsin P, 1994.
Snyder, Gary. *The Old Ways: Six Essays.* San Francisco: City Lights Books, 1977.
———. *The Real Work: Interviews & Talks 1974–1979.* Ed. William Scott McLean. New York: New Directions, 1980.

James I. McClintock

Social Darwinism. A social and political ideology (*see* Politics and Ideology) in which competitive struggle in the natural order is taken as a model for social interaction. The catchphrases most commonly associated with the ideology are the "struggle for existence" and "survival of the fittest." The latter phrase was coined by **Herbert Spencer** and adopted by **Charles Darwin** to describe the process of natural selection: a process through which heritable variations in physical and mental traits result in differential reproductive success. Social Darwinism has often been used to explain or justify elitism within and among social groups. Elites are believed to gain power and monopolize resources because they are stronger, more intelligent, more courageous, and have greater initiative. When applied to individuals within a social group, social Darwinism has often been associated with laissez-faire capitalism. When applied to interaction among social groups, it has been associated with racism, imperialism, and genocide. Regarding policies of social welfare as obstacles to natural selection, social Darwinists have often advocated eugenics and have been particularly concerned to discourage **reproduction** among people with heritable physical or mental defects.

Social Darwinism was a main feature in the Darwinian influence on naturalist philosophers and literary authors. **Jack London** and Friedrich Nietzsche offer signal instances of writers who identify struggle and domination as central characteristics of social interaction. Since Nietzsche is a primary source for Michel Foucault and other poststructuralist theorists, social Darwinism enters indirectly but importantly into the theories of "power" that preoccupy current ideological critics.

Many Darwinians, from **T.H. Huxley** to the present, have opposed social Darwinism by simply repudiating biological **determinism** within the ethical sphere. Others, including Darwin, have argued that social sympathy is itself an evolved and adaptive human trait. Still others, seeking to avoid the political stigmas attached to social Darwinism, have argued that Darwinians should take account only of species-typical traits and treat all heritable variations as of negligible consequence.

References

Hawkins, Mike. *Social Darwinism in European and American Thought, 1860–1945*. Cambridge: Cambridge UP, 1997.
Hofstadter, Richard. *Social Darwinism in American Thought*. Philadelphia: U of Pennsylvania P, 1944.

Joseph Carroll

Social Ecology. Branch of ecophilosophy predicated on the belief that all ecological problems are social problems. Social ecology's primary architect is Murray Bookchin (author of, inter alia, *The Ecology of Freedom*, 1982; *Remaking Society: Pathways to A Green Future*, 1990; and, with Dave Foreman, *Defending the Earth: A Dialogue between Murray Bookchin & Dave Foreman*, 1991). Social ecology declares human society a natural by-product of evolution rather than an artificial constructed threat to the "natural world." The movement is largely homocentric; ecosystemic health forms a necessary by-product of social justice.

Discarding traditional oppositions between capitalism and socialism, social ecologists recommend an agrarian "eco-anarchism," stressing decentralized forms of production and food cultivation tailored to the carrying capacities of particular bioregions. Social ecology's relationship to other factions within environmentalism is often strained due to its deemphasis of such traditional environmental themes as wilderness preservation.

Reference

Gorz, Andre. *Ecology as Politics*. Trans. Patsy Vigderman and Jonathan Cloud. Boston: South End, 1980.

David N. Cassuto

Sociobiology. Study of the evolution of social behavior of animals, including humans. **Edward O. Wilson's** *Sociobiology* (1975) presented evolutionary explanations of altruism that initiated a controversy with **Stephen J. Gould** and others and received enormous media attention. Critics have analyzed metaphors such as selfishness, entrepreneurship, and rape in sociobiological writings. Sociobiology has entered literature in such works as John Gardner's *October Light* (1976).

Val Dusek

Sociology. *See* **Anthropology/Psychology/Sociology**.

Somerville, Mary Fairfax Greig (1780–1872). Scottish-born scientific and technical writer, highly regarded as a scientific authority during the mid-nineteenth century. Somerville's writing combines clear presentation of complex and weighty scientific concepts with a demonstration of the power of science to stimulate the **imagination**. Her writing has a painterly quality (perhaps owing to her skills as a painter); in it, science becomes a way of seeing the world that is grounded in, but superior to, ordinary experience. She is particularly skillful at evoking the scientific sublime.

Somerville's major works span the range from the highly esoteric to the more easily grasped. In *Mechanism of the Heavens* (1831), a translation of Laplace's *Méchanique Céleste*, and *On the Connexion of the Physical Sciences* (1834), an extended literature review synthesizing historical and recent scientific discoveries, Somerville conveys science both as exact calculation and as elevated meditation and, in that sense, carries on the tradition of the scientific poets of the eighteenth century (as described by **William Powell Jones**). Her later works, *Physical Geography* (1948) and *On Molecular and Microscopic Science* (1869), deal with less abstruse subjects and offer evidence of her strong descriptive skills and link her to the **nature writing** traditions of the later nineteenth century.

References

Neeley, Kathryn A. "Woman as Mediatrix: Women as Writers on Science and Technology in the Eighteenth and Nineteenth Centuries." *IEEE Transactions on Professional Communication* 35.4 (1988): 208–16.

Patterson, Elizabeth C. *Mary Somerville and the Cultivation of Science, 1815–1840.* Boston: Kluwer, 1983.

Kathryn A. Neeley

Space Travel. A journey beyond the bounds of the earth's atmosphere; for most of human history, only a fantasy, becoming a technological reality in the mid- to late twentieth century. The literary **imagination** has traveled through space since ancient times. **Marjorie Nicolson** cataloged a wide variety of early "voyages" to the moon (**Lucian, Kepler, Wilkins, Blake**, et al.). Early **science fiction** stories already displaced their narratives in **time** and space (**Verne, H.G. Wells**). Astronauts' biographies and autobiographies and popular documentaries and **films** valorize the human impetus to explore the "final frontier" and represent the technological challenges of space travel as the epitome of human individual and cooperative achievement (*Moon Launch, Apollo 13, Space Cowboys*). **Diane Ackerman's** *The Planets: A Cosmic Pastoral* (1976) offers a verse "travelogue" through the solar system, enabling her readers to experience, poetically, the local sights unique to each planet. Critiques of space travel often cite the economic costs at the expense of local social programs and the privileging of American views of space as a capitalistic resource. Buck Rogers, the various *Star Trek* series, *2001: A Space Odyssey*, David Bowie's rock **music** persona, Major Tom (from the album *Space Oddity*, 1970), and *E.T.* are but a handful of the myriad ways space travel and space travelers have been incorporated into and represented within popular culture.

Pamela Gossin

Spencer, Herbert (1820–1903). English philosopher who fostered the acceptance of evolution (*see* Evolutionary Theory), coined the phrase "survival of the fittest," and promoted **social Darwinism**. He was the first to espouse evolution as a cosmic process, applying it to all spheres of existence. His works, particularly *First Principles* (1862), influenced writers in England, the United States, France, and Russia.

Reference

Kennedy, James G. *Herbert Spencer*. Twayne's English Authors Series. Boston: G.K. Hall, 1978.

Heather V. Armstrong

Spenser, Edmund (1552–1599). Author of *Shepherd's Calender* (1579), *Faerie Queene* (1590; 1596), *Amoretti* and *Epithalamion* (1595), and shorter poems. In the *Faerie Queene*, Spenser used traditional forms of Homeric and Vergilian (*see* Homer; Vergil) epic to promote a nationalistic portrait of Elizabethan **culture**. By manipulating figural tropes of vision such as mirrors, lenses, and paintings, he followed the humanists by radically reconfiguring the philosophical perception of the Real by foregrounding the linguistic and the ideological.

Reference

Greenblatt, Stephen. *Renaissance Self-Fashioning: From More to Shakespeare*. Chicago: U of Chicago P, 1980.

Diana B. Altegoer

Sprat, Thomas (1635–1713). First historian of, and spokesperson for, London's **Royal Society**. Sprat's *History of The Royal Society of London, for the Improving of Natural Knowledge* (1667) promulgated a modern scientific **rhetoric**, inspired by **Francis Bacon**, for communicating scientific knowledge using a plain style of prose. This new rhetoric is symbolized by the *History*'s widely quoted line that scientists should communicate "so many things, almost in an equal number of words."

Robert C. Goldbort

Spy Novel. A narrative enactment of (1) **information theory**, which holds that any message can be encoded to resist distortion, and (2) systems theory, which holds that healthy systems depend on equitable distribution of information. Though they have ancient roots, spy novels arose to dramatize organized espionage designed to steal or protect nineteenth-century proprietary information, a category soon transformed by industrialization and ideology to include technologies identified with nations. One type of spy novel assumes that a shadow economy of clandestine information transfer realigns markets and **cultures**. Here spies blunt political advantage, undermine technological supremacy, or disrupt international balances of power. A second type enshrines fears that surveillance enables governments or businesses to control individuals. Here covert research neutralizes secrets and exposes abuses of authority in order to destroy conspiracies. Because characters mimic scientific method in their investigations, the genre formulas have influenced major writers such as **Pynchon** and **Borges**.

Reference

Slade, Joseph W. "Technology and the Espionage Novel." *Literature and Technology*. Ed. Mark Greenberg and Lance Schachterle. Bethlehem, PA: Lehigh UP, 1992. 225–52.

Joseph W. Slade

Stein, Gertrude (1874–1946). The twentieth century's preeminent "experimental" writer. She had a thorough training in **experimental science** that included three years in physiological psychology at Harvard, a summer at Woods Hole, and more than four years at the Johns Hopkins Medical School (already the leading medical school in the United States when she arrived several years after it opened). Students of Stein's career, such as Lisa Ruddick, Clive Bush, and Tim Armstrong, have tended to place greater emphasis on her Harvard years, when she studied with **William James** and Hugo Münsterberg, than on her work at medical school, where she conducted extensive neuroanatomical research in the decade after the articulation of the neuron doctrine. Nevertheless, as Meyer argues, Stein's experience at Johns Hopkins proved critical for her subsequent literary innovations.

Reference

Meyer, Steven. *Irresistible Dictation: Gertrude Stein and the Correlations of Writing and Science*. Stanford, CA: Stanford UP, 1999.

Steven Meyer

Steinbeck, John (1902–1968). American author who set many of his novels in Salinas Valley, California, spawning the term "Steinbeck Country." He also immortalized the run-down, fish-processing section of Monterey in *Cannery Row* (1945) and *Sweet Thursday* (1954). Steinbeck was also an accomplished amateur marine biologist and an avid proponent of his own "phalanx" **theory** of the human condition. His biological interests are well displayed in *The Log from the Sea of Cortez* (1941) and *Cannery Row*, while his phalanx theory (individuals form part of a larger organism and groups are more than the sum of their parts) is most evident in *In Dubious Battle* (1936) and portions of *The Grapes of Wrath* (1939). In this latter work, his descriptions of the ecological ravages of the Dust Bowl and its concomitant human tolls on migrant workers in California helped spur landmark protections for both the land and those who work upon it. After its publication, Steinbeck endured a campaign of innuendo designed to malign his credibility as a writer and the verisimilitude of the novel. Neither succeeded and his career continued to flourish. In 1962, Steinbeck was awarded the Nobel Prize for Literature.

David N. Cassuto

Stendhal [Beyle, Henri] (1783–1842). French novelist of the Romantic period, author of *Le Rouge et le Noir* (The Red and the Black, 1831) and *La Chartreuse de Parme* (The Charterhouse of Parma, 1839). His novels are discursive spaces in which initial strategies, deterministically calculated by the hero's energetic ambitions, evolve along recursive feedback loops and unforeseen bifurcations. These are intersections of **chaos** and order that prevent closure of the text and render its discursive process analogous to nonlinear dynamical systems.

Maria L. Assad

Stephenson, Neal (1959–   ). American writer who has achieved cult status, especially among fans of **science fiction** and "techie" **culture.** *Zodiac: The Eco Thriller* (1988) combined high-tech monkey-wrenching with **detective fiction**. Stephenson's groundbreaking **cyberpunk** novel *Snow Crash* (1992) presents a vision of the deterioration of postmodern civilization, juxtaposing **virtual reality**, Sumerian myth, and information **technology** with **computer** hacking and viruses. *Cryptonomicon* (1999) has rivaled the buzz created a quarter century ago by **Pynchon's** *Gravity's Rainbow* as a "must-read" novel. Here Stephenson creates a massive (over 900-page) puzzle of a text, recounting a tale of World War II cryptography replete with mathematical games and problems.

Pamela Gossin

Sterling, Bruce (1954–   ). Author of **cyberpunk science fiction**, editor of its first manifesto (*Mirrorshades*, 1986), and coauthor (with **William Gibson**) of *The Difference Engine* (1990), an alternative history linking **chaos theory** and **cybernetics**. His recent **fictions** *Heavy Weather* (1994) and *Holy Fire* (1996) explore the production of posthuman identities by global technosciences.

Reference

Porush, David. "Prigogine, Chaos and Contemporary SF." *Science-Fiction Studies* 18.3 (1991): 367–86.

Noel Gough

Sterne, Laurence (1713–1768). British novelist and clergyman. Sterne's writings properly belong to a tradition of learned wit, reaching back through **Swift, Burton**, and **More**. *Tristram Shandy* (1760–1767), in particular, at once draws on the scientific advancements of the day (particularly the Newtonian [*see* Newtonianism] **philosophy**, theories of madness, and contemporary **medicine** and obstetrics), while at the same time flouting the method and system of the new science with an enthusiastic style of exuberant wit: "I begin with writing the first sentence—and trusting to Almighty God for the second" (vol. 8, ch. 1).

Reference

DePorte, Michael V. *Nightmares and Hobbyhorses: Swift, Sterne, and Augustan Ideas of Madness*. San Marino: Huntington Library, 1974.

Richard Nash

Stevens, Wallace (1879–1955). American poet. Science, for Stevens, is part of the "pressure of reality" characteristic of the modern age, and as such it is to be resisted by **poetry**. This is hardly surprising, since his aesthetic is an attempt to hold the material world at arm's length through the power of language. In Thomas E. Walsh's *Concordance to the Poetry of Wallace Stevens* (1963), there are two references to the word "science" and two also to "scientist" but hundreds to "**space**" and "**time**." Stevens's interest in science is essentially philosophical. For Stevens, a world not animated by a human idea is hardly a world at all but an instance of "mere being." Stevens's most extended response to science occurs in "A Collect of Philosophy" in *Opus Posthumous* (1989).

Reference

Wilde, Dana. "Wallace Stevens, Modern Physics, and Wholeness." *The Wallace Stevens Journal* 20.1 (1996): 3–26.

Joseph Duemer

Stevenson, Robert Louis (1850–1894). English writer, greatly interested in contemporary psychology (*see* Anthropology/Psychology/Sociology), theories of dualism, and the Doppelgänger, who studied engineering (*see* Engineer(s)/ Engineering) and law before turning to literature. His only work of **science fiction**, *The Strange Case of Dr Jekyll and Mr. Hyde* (1886), a pre-Freudian study of ego and libido, is based on the mechanistic premise that even moral character might be changed by material (in this case, chemical) means. Predating the advent of personality drugs and lobotomies, the story is usually considered a parable about human nature and the splitting of personality into distinguishable but inseparable components. However, the clear parallels between Dr. Jekyll and **Mary Shelley's** character **Frankenstein** indicate Stevenson's intentional censure of **scientism** and complacent utopianism. The idealistic **physician** Dr. Jekyll believes he can improve human nature by excising the evil part of his personality, and like Frankenstein's, his experiment is technically a brilliant success; but he ignores the evil residing unalloyed in the by-product of his experiment, Mr. Hyde. The inescapable duality of Jekyll and Hyde is thus a metaphor not only for the nature of Man but for the nature of science. G.K. Chesterton, a trenchant critic of **H.G. Wells's utopias**, pointed out the major irony of the story: "The real stab of the story is not in the discovery that one

man is two men, but in the discovery that two men are one man. . . . The point
. . . is not that a man *can* cut himself off from his conscience, but that he cannot"
(Chesterton 72–73).

References

Chesterton, G.K. *Robert Louis Stevenson*. London: Hodder and Stoughton, 1927.
Sanford, John A. *The Strange Trial of Mr. Hyde: a New Look at the Nature of Human Evil*. San Francisco: Harper and Row, 1987.
Strathdee, R.B. "Robert Louis Stevenson as a Scientist." *Aberdeen University Review* 36 (1956): 268–75.

Roslynn D. Haynes

Stoker, Bram (1847–1912). Dublin-born theatrical manager and author of popular horror **fiction**. Educated in science at Trinity College, Stoker is best known for his novel *Dracula* (1897), which features blood transfusions, discussion of blood as a carrier of identity, and the victory of two scientific men (Dr. Seward and Dr. Van Helsing) against a **supernatural** horror.

Reference

Leatherdale, Clive. *Dracula: The Novel and the Legend*. Wellingborough, England: Aquarian, 1985.

Alison E. Bright

Strange Attractors. A region representing the equilibrium point of the behavior of a system. This pattern can be represented in phase space as a basin of attraction, a kind of magnet that draws the phase space to a recognizable shape. Until Edward N. Lorenz discovered a new kind of attractor, it was thought that either a system would generate a fixed-point, limit-cycle, or torus attractor, or it was truly random and could be described by no attractor at all. In other words, dynamical systems were thought to be either predictable or random. This belief was rattled when studying fluid flows in the attempt to understand the seemingly unpredictable behavior of the weather. Lorenz revived Poincaré's three-body problem by devising a simple system consisting of just three degrees freedom. Despite the prosaic nature of Lorenz's system, it generated a rather bizarre attractor. It is neither a point nor a cycle but a set of points whose dimensionality is fractional; that is, it is a **fractal** with a dimension between 0 and 1. And although when represented visually the double spiral of the Lorenz attractor appears to be a hauntingly beautiful set of butterfly wings or owl eyes, it is neither a stable structure nor simply subject to purely random fluctuations.

Like the Lorenz attractor, chaotic attractors are strange because they can generate recognizable shapes while never returning to a point that they previously occupied in phase space. Strange attractors are able to fulfill simultaneously two seemingly contradictory requirements—those of infinity and those of Procrustes—because they are fractal. They can squeeze an infinitely long line into a finite space by piling layer upon layer of detail at different scales, and they are self-similar since their fractal depth tends to uncover microstructures that repeat the general shape of the system's macrostructure.

Reference

Hawkins, Harriet. *Strange Attractors: Literature, Culture and Chaos Theory.* New York: Prentice-Hall, 1995.

Alex Argyros

Structuralism/Poststructuralism. Methods of textual analysis that have been of major intellectual import since the 1960s. Structuralism, largely developed from Ferdinand de Saussure's *Course in General Linguistics* (1906–1911), is a synchronic linguistic analysis of the sign and its two component parts, signifier and signified: The signifier is the linguistic or textual indicator, while the signified is the referent denoted by the signifier. The relationship between signifier and signified is entirely arbitrary; the two are linked only by the systems of signification that organize language. The interplay of *langue* (the systems of linguistic rules) and *parole* (actual individual utterances) enable the production of meaning and, more broadly, the organization of **reality**. Structuralism was also extended by theorists such as anthropologist Claude Levi-Strauss, whose interpretation of texts and institutions would prove valuable to many anthropologists of science and **medicine**.

Many later theorists saw the often binary or deterministic predilections of structuralist thought as impediments. While not necessarily intellectually unified, poststructuralists did generally reject the concept of an underlying structure of meaning. Signifiers could not be traced back to one stable signified but could only refer to a web of other signifiers. Two poststructuralist theorists are most influential for LS. First, in his writings on deconstruction, Jacques Derrida used the term *différance* to indicate the fundamental difference and deferral of language, suggesting that the ultimate delivery of meaning was always postponed. One can find traces of deconstructive theory in writers ranging from **Bruno Latour** to **Donna Haraway**. Second, Michel Foucault's analyses of the means by which discourses both allow and deny certain meanings are generally considered poststructuralist hallmarks, and his conception of power and knowledge undergirds much current work in cultural studies of science.

Chris Amirault

Strugatsky, Arkady and Boris (1925–1991; 1933–   ). Coauthors of the most popular and critically acclaimed Soviet **science fiction**. The Strugatskys' novels provided a highly informed and entertaining model of the intersection between science, society (*see* Scientists in/and Society), and ethics in the late Soviet Union (*see* Russia and the Former Soviet Union). In over thirty novels and short story collections, they satirized communist bureaucracy and Soviet-style bourgeois complacency and charged the creative scientist with the task of carrying humanistic values into the degraded present and imagined future.

Reference

Howell, Yvonne. *Apocalyptic Realism: The Science Fiction of Arkady and Boris Stru-gatsky*. New York: Peter Lang, 1994.

Yvonne Howell

Supernatural. Above or beyond the ordinary course of nature. The very term presupposes a boundary between nature and supernature and a dualism of matter and spirit; what is meant by the "supernatural," then, is dependent upon the model of nature by which it is defined. For instance, the "natural magic" studied by the Renaissance magus cannot (strictly speaking) be considered supernatural (although it is spiritual): If a spiritual power is envisaged as "working *through*" rather than "interfering *with*" nature, the antithesis between nature and super-nature disappears (Brooke 36). Although the rise of the "new science" in the seventeenth century is rightly associated with the "decline of magic" and the mechanization and "disenchantment" of the world, the supernatural—in the sense of providential intervention (including miracles) in the workings of the laws of nature—maintained a significant role in science until the early eighteenth century. Isaac Newton (*see* Newtonianism) insisted that divine activity continued within a mechanical context: God not only had imparted motion to matter but also actively adjusted his creation.

The presence of the "supernatural" within a providentialist context shared by both literature and science may be seen in such figures as **Shakespeare's** learned magus Prospero in *The Tempest* (1611) and **Milton's** archangel Raphael who offers Adam supernatural instruction about Creation in *Paradise Lost* (1667; 1674). By the late eighteenth and early nineteenth centuries, the supernatural had largely been "naturalized": (1) by viewing spirit as immanent in nature (as in German *naturphilosophie*) and (2) by internalizing supernatural experience, rendering it psychological. On the other hand, the Gothic (*see* Gothicism) novel and the Victorian ghost story (especially when they feature scientist protagonists) may be seen as antimaterialist critiques of the mechanistic **determinism** associated with contemporary science.

References

Brooke, John Hedley. *Science and Religion: Some Historical Perspectives*. Cambridge: Cambridge UP, 1991.
Carter, Margaret L. *Specter or Delusion? The Supernatural in Gothic Fiction*. Ann Arbor: UMI Research, 1987.
Reed, John R. *Victorian Conventions*. Athens: Ohio UP, 1975.

Lisa Zeitz

Suzuki, David (1936–   ). Noted Canadian geneticist and internationally prominent popularizer and critic of the sciences' roles in environmental and social issues. Suzuki has reached a wide audience as host of the television series *The Nature of Things* (since 1979, Canadian Broadcasting Corporation) and as author of a broad range of popular scientific writing (*see* Popularization; Public Science Writing; Scientist As Author). The important study *Genethics: The Ethics of Engineering Life* (1989) combines the **rhetorics** of expositor and critic and vividly illustrates the role of metaphor in explaining the complexities of molecular **genetics**. Latter-day "lay sermons," his public lectures—for example, "How Much Time Do We Have Left?"—mix rhetorical figures and tropes of ecological crisis and cure. In weekly newspaper articles, collected in *Time to Change* (1993), Suzuki attempts to represent a comprehensive ecological worldview in language that exceeds common environmental rhetoric; there, as in *Wisdom of the Elders* (1992), he incorporates aboriginal understandings of nature and critiques prevalent scientific and economic models.

References

Suzuki, David. "How Much Time Do We Have Left?" UWA Extension. Nedlands, West Australia: U of Western Australia, Nov. 20, 1993.
———. *Metamorphosis: Stages in a Life*. Toronto: Stoddart, 1987.

Doug Russell

Swift, Jonathan (1667–1745). Dean of St. Patrick's, Dublin; satirist. The lion's share of Scriblerian satires on "the new science" are generally credited to Dr. Arbuthnot, an opinion supported in part by Swift's letter to the doctor, which reads in part: "I could put together, and lard, and strike out well enough, but all that relates to the sciences must be from you." In part, Swift may be encouraging Arbuthnot to take a more active role in the composition, for certainly Swift took an active interest in the subject. Beyond the more ephemeral productions of the Scriblerians that satirize scientific projectors and medical quacks, Swift's most important epistemological **satires** often focus to good effect on the self-deluding capacity of many experimentalists. The entirety of *Gulliver's Travels* (1726) lampoons the popular travel literature of the time that Swift read with interest, while at the same time fashioning from that parody an imaginative narrative that constitutes an early contribution to **science fiction**. Particularly in the third voyage, where Gulliver visits the Flying Island of Laputa, the allusions to contemporary science and particular experiments recorded in the *Philosophical Transactions* of the **Royal Society** reveal an engaged interest in scientific discovery alongside a deeply held skepticism about the limits of scientific explanation. Swift's long-standing objection to Enthusiast belief in occult mysteries lent itself to witty attacks on **astrology** (*The Bickerstaff Papers*, 1708) and **alchemy** (*Tale of a Tub*, 1704), while at the same time prompting him to advocate a clear, forceful prose style associated with **Thomas Sprat** and the Royal Society. If, in these respects, Swift was allied with the new science's attack on superstitious mystery, he remained equally skeptical of the danger posed by a reductive recourse to scientific system: "[N]ew Systems of Nature were but new Fashions, which would vary in every Age; and even those who pretend to demonstrate them from Mathematical Principles, would flourish but a short Period of Time, and be out of Vogue when that was determined" (*Gulliver's Travels*, III, ch. 8).

Richard Nash

Swinburne, Algernon Charles (1837–1909). English poet and iconoclast. Leaving Oxford University without a degree in 1861, Swinburne immersed himself in London Bohemian life. In poems like "The Triumph of Time" (1866), "Anactoria" (1866), and "Hertha" (1871), Swinburne exploited classical legend and myth to evoke a conspicuously non-Christian **cosmos** of physical growth, decay, and animal sense. His **poetry**, saturated with images of pagan religiosity, sustained sensualism, and **naturalism**, reflects the 1860s ferment over the nature of man and religious experience, brought on by the great flood of anthropological and evolutionary literature originating in the diverse experiences of empire. With his close friend **Richard Burton**, Swinburne was a member of the Anthropological Society of London.

James G. Paradis

Symbolism. A style in Western literature, visual **art**, **music**, and emotional expression following the *Decadence* in France in the mid-1880s. Reacting to mid-century **realism** and **naturalism** and **scientism** (scientific **positivism**), Symbolism substituted symbols for intended objects and projected an invisible alternate world for them. Superseded by **Modernism** after 1900, the movement lasted longest in Russia. Best-known self-identified Symbolists include poets **Stéphane Mallarmé**, Alexander Blok, and Stefan George, painter Odilon Redon, and the playwright Maurice Maeterlinck, whose *Pelleas et Melisande* was set to music by Sibelius, Debussy, Faure, and Schoenberg.

References

Balakian, Anna, ed. *The Symbolist Movement in the Literature of European Languages*. Budapest: Akademiai Kiado, 1982; Philadelphia: John Benjamins, 1984.
Goldwater, Robert. *Symbolism*. New York: Harper, 1979.

William R. Everdell

Symbolist Movement. Primarily an artistic movement, begun in France in the latter part of the nineteenth century (1885–1895), although the poetry of **Charles Baudelaire** is also representative. In opposition to the scientific **positivism** of the day the Symbolists believed that **truth** only could be found through a natural approach that emphasized a subjective aesthetic (*see* Art and Aesthetics) to counter the deceptions of the realm of the senses. The techniques of writing employed by the Symbolists were harshly criticized in the early twentieth century by the Russian Formalists who countered the Symbolist movement by calling for a return to a scientific investigation of language and literature reminiscent of the positivists.

Shelly Jarrett Bromberg

T

Talbot, Michael (1953–1992). American novelist and nonfiction writer who wrote about the paranormal and produced **popularizations** of natural science. In *Mysticism and the New Physics* (1981), *Beyond the Quantum* (1986), and *The Holographic Universe* (1991), he links scientific ideas to philosophical and religious thought in a manner that resembles the works of **Fritjof Capra** and **Gary Zukav**.

June Deery

Technical Writing. A profession, an academic specialty, and a utilitarian mode of writing rooted largely in the rhetorical conventions of the modern scientific plain style. As a profession, technical writing is practiced by those trained on the job and/or in college courses and programs. Technical writers work in diverse settings, including law, government, industry, science, and education, and in such capacities as grant writing, software documentation, editing, and consulting. Scholars study technical writing using various approaches drawing from such areas as **rhetoric** and composition, literary theory, cognitive linguistics and discourse analysis, history of ideas, organizational **psychology**, **computer** theory, sociology of knowledge, cultural and gender studies, and **philosophy**. The field has its own professional organizations, conferences, periodicals, and **Internet** discussion groups.

Technical writing textbooks identify a broad purview of application for the field, from writing for the work world to writing for the sciences, **engineering**, and other "technical" professions, such as **medicine** and law. Regardless of its realm of practice or its content, technical writing has common features of format and design, such as its organizational and graphical elements, intended to maximize textual readability and functionality. There is also a shared expectation that technical writers prepare and communicate information ethically and responsibly, guided by the highest personal and professional standards of conduct, intellectual honesty, and truthfulness. Definitions of technical writing, while diverse, tend to share certain fundamental assumptions. In both process and product, technical writing is a form of **information** technology, to be practiced and studied as such. It is writing for practical purposes, from letters to manuals, conveying unambiguous meanings in language that is plain, accessible, and functional. The simple, direct, objective, and codified language of technical writing is diametrically opposed in sense and sensibility to the personal, playful, and emotive language of imaginative literature. **Fiction** is everything technical writing is not supposed to be. The contrasting rhetorical qualities of technical and literary writing express the historical tension between two "opposed" intellectual traditions, between **C.P. Snow's** two polarized cultures, two different ways of experiencing and knowing the world.

Important connections nonetheless do exist between technical writing and imaginative literature. Scientific and technological ideas have a historical presence in **poetry**, **drama**, and fiction worldwide, from **Ben Jonson's** "moon voyage" drama and magnification in **Swift's** *Gulliver's Travels* to **biotechnology** in **Mary Shelley's** *Frankenstein* (1818) and **Karel Capek's** *R.U.R.* (1923); and from the twentieth century's age of **science fiction** to transdisciplinarian and integrative forms like the poetry of physiologist **Miroslav Holub**, the personal narratives of anthropologist **Loren Eiseley**, and the factualistic fiction of chemist **Carl Djerassi**. Literary expressions of technological and scientific themata in our **culture** integrate and transcend the rhetorical purposes of, and challenge the perceived intellectual boundaries between, technical and literary texts. Reciprocally, narrative forms of technical writing like **scientific articles**, accident reports, and patients' records may be seen as having literary elements (characters, themes, plots, conflict)—and as plausible stories the validity and truth-value of which, like imaginative literature, often remains to be time-tested and proven. Technical and scientific writing also depends in critical ways upon metaphoric and figurative language, basic qualities of fiction and poetry.

References

Anderson, Paul V., R. John Brockmann, and Carolyn R. Miller, eds. *New Essays in Technical and Scientific Communication: Research, Theory, Practice.* New York: Baywood, 1983.

Fearing, Bertie E., and W. Keats Sparrow, eds. *Technical Writing: Theory and Practice.* New York: MLA, 1989.

Robert C. Goldbort

Technicians/Technician–Hero. **Engineers** and technical experts who, as characters and protagonists, are often portrayed negatively in literature. Most nineteenth-century writers generally criticized technicians as the instigators and sustainers of the negative effects of the **Industrial Revolution**. The work of **Edgar Allan Poe**, for instance, is fraught with harshness, his technicians existing merely to refine instruments of torture. Such portrayals are ameliorated, somewhat, insofar as the technician becomes a figure of pathos, run to ruin by trade unions and bosses alike, as exemplified by Stephen Blackpool in **Dickens's** *Hard Times* (1854). With the advent of **science fiction**, however, the technician emerged as an unapologetically heroic figure. From **Jules Verne's** Nemo (and company!) to **Robert Heinlein's** Blind Singer of the Spaceways, the technician has increasingly come to reflect an unalloyed delight in scientific and technical proficiency.

Michael B. McDonald

Technology. At the simplest level, defined as instrumentality, as in older anthropological definitions of humans as tool-using animals. Of the tools that humans employ, language—a system of symbols or **representations**—is the most primal. The ability to create specialized languages, from ethnic tongues to mathematics, makes possible the rise of all other human technologies. Because words can be decoupled from the things they represent, they can be independently combined and recombined to form new constructions that persist as long as they can be reproduced. Literary genres began quite literally as oral technologies: Poets, for example, "invented" rhyme and meter as mnemonic devices to assist imperfect memory in the recall of **information**.

Oral recitation matured into literature with the advent of secondary technologies such as writing and printing. The materialization of oral symbols by means of writing serves two functions, according to Jack Goody (*The Domestication of the Savage Mind*, 1977). Writing stores information in a more permanent, reproducible form than speech, and it displays the codes of language, a function that permits visual inspection and increased manipulation. It is no accident that the first product of the **Industrial Revolution**—the mass production of identical components—was the book. The printing press revolutionized the social, economic, and political organization of national states and, according to James Beniger (*The Control Revolution: Technological and Economic Origins of the Information Society*, 1986), led directly to sophisticated, continuous, interactive mass programming of the citizens in industrialized cultures. Moreover, mass reproduction of text generated **complexity** at the levels required to institutionalize science as skepticism and literature as imaginative symbol-making and generated as well ancillary technologies for training citizens to use them. Becoming literate—learning to write and to read messages—requires a period of education not necessary for, say, a medium such as **television**, whose pictures may or may not be worth a thousand words. Children understand the messages of television without external instruction, while twelve grades of schooling are scarcely sufficient for expertise in written codes. Oral, script, print, and electronic media are all conduits for stories that serve as sources of cultural **energy**. On the one hand, stories replicate formulas and themes in order to bind, stabilize, and reinforce social systems. On the other, they introduce novelty that can alter and refresh those systems. As entertainment or as "serious" narrative, literary discourse orders, preserves, and extends accumulated experience.

At another level, technology refers to "invention," the devising and construction of artifacts. Like other inventions, literary works are products of **imagination** and thus subject to Aristotelian (*see* Aristotle) definitions of technology as a "reasoned capacity to make." As **James Joyce** acknowledged by naming a favorite character Daedalus, writers are **engineers** of language and fabricators of artifice. Article I of the Constitution of the United States awards writers and inventors, and only those citizens, the privilege of profiting from intellectual property. Despite such Jeffersonian conflations of literature and technology, Romantic writers elevated the cachet of literary pursuits to distinguish them from the vernacular work of artisans, just as scientists often subordinated technology to the status of "applied science." Many Americans still equate technology with a "know-how" or "craft" associated with lower-class manual labor. Terms such as *artisan, technician, mechanic,* or *inventor* suggest the tinkering of amateurs whose untutored, undisciplined insight is somehow less rigorous than the pursuit of "pure" scientific knowledge or less inspired than the creation of a poem or novel. Class aside, neither writers nor scientists can avoid working with their hands. Authors must write or type to produce traditional narratives or manipulate programs to produce **hypertexts**. Similarly, the more advanced the science, the more elaborate the experimental equipment that the scientists must deploy. Relentless commodification of the artifacts of science and of literature has further eroded cultural and class distinctions. Commercial viability increasingly governs invention in all sectors, as an information economy determines value in terms of copyright and **patent** rather than in measures of immediate practicality or even long-term utility.

Metaphor, sometimes perceived as a literary device, helps humans construe technology, and in a sense metaphors can themselves operate as technologies of connection evoked by specific innovations. J. David Bolter notes that historians commonly refer to the ages of bronze or iron, navigation or exploration, and so on: metaphors that influence the ways in which humans conceptualize themselves and their cultures (*Turing's Man: Western Culture in the Computer Age,* 1984). The dominance of potter's wheels and weaver's spindles in the ancient world led classical poets and dramatists to represent the **cosmos** as a wheel of fortune and human life as a skein of thread woven by the Fates. Much later, physicists, philosophers, and writers found in navigation and watchmaking the clockwork metaphors to visualize and rationalize Newtonian mechanics, American democracy, and the novel of manners. More recently, the steam engine seemed to explain the human condition as one of mechanized routine, anonymous conformity, and industrial exploitation, while its boiler, drive-train, and flywheel governor gave **Freud** the parts for a psyche composed of id, ego, and superego. Digital media of the postindustrial period, however, have recast labor as information processing. Now "technology" refers not so often to machines as to ways in which we categorize, arrange, and stratify data. The Dewey Decimal System is a technology, as are corporate bureaucracies invented to process information. Modern metaphor holds that humans process information as their principal activity, as do the genetic, immune, and nervous systems that program and maintain organic activity through control and feedback. Study of the grammar and syntax of DNA has transformed molecular **biology** into a branch of linguistics and made organic processes themselves into narratives.

It is helpful to distinguish between hardware and software; popular parlance puts technology in the first category, literature in the second. Even so, both are aggregates of organized information, says Edwin Layton ("Technology as Knowledge"), and literature is one of the means by which we store information. A hammer, an aircraft, a library, a television, a medical procedure, a fertilizer, a naval maneuver, a bibliography, or an **Internet** embody knowledge and expertise gleaned from generations of design and experimentation, just as stories, novels, poems, plays, and computer narratives embody artistic templates and cultural transmissions crafted by centuries of organizational trial and error. In this regard, technology connects the physical world of matter and energy and their natural ordering as information, and the social world of humans who purposively organize structures for production, distribution, and consumption of materials and information.

Calling everything technology can erase all distinctions among human structures of information, however, leaving writers with no place to stand. Thanks to technologies of production and marketing, literature and literary criticism are now industrialized sectors of the economy, almost as much so as science. Scientists routinely separate investigation from implementation to avoid responsibility for the consequences of their discoveries (as in denying that their efforts necessarily produce weapons, for instance). Similarly, writers have traditionally distanced themselves from agency and have been largely successful in setting an agenda that depicts technology as subject rather than performance. That posture will become more difficult as texts become interactive and as writers create stories that will become the spines of **virtual reality** scenario. Even so, as Wylie Sypher (*Literature and Technology: The Alien Vision*, 1968) has pointed out, writers have reserved the right to define technology as they wish, often so that they can treat it as an Other (*see* Alterity). Bruce Mazlish ("The Fourth Discontinuity") rejects the characterization of technology as alien, arguing that humans' reluctance to accept their creations as extensions of themselves has set the stage for an overdue cultural shift as profound as the Copernican, Darwinian, and Freudian revolutions.

Thus far, only **science fiction** endorses the moral and metaphysical kinship of humans and their technologies that Mazlish postulates. Perceptions of technology have shaped science fiction and "thrillers" since the age of **Jules Verne** and **Wilkie Collins**, of course, but have also helped bring espionage, business, and children's genres into being, say the essayists in *Literature and Technology* (edited by Mark Greenberg and Lance Schachterle, 1992). Mainstream writers tend to cast technology as material culture, industrialization, or systemic **rationality** in an effort to identify cultural dynamics or to speculate on the effects of artifice on individual consciousnesses. Leo Marx (*Machine in the Garden*,

1964) argues that literary treatments of technology vary with a culture's history and social imperatives. In Marx's reading, just as the "dark satanic mills" of European novels give way to ambiguous **Frankenstein** once industrialization lost some of its darkness, so the machine invading the **garden** of a fictional American Eden eventually yields to the unstable "middle **landscape**" of a still largely agrarian nineteenth-century democracy convinced that it could control technology. Marshall McLuhan's literary criticism led to his assertion (in *Understanding Media: The Extensions of Man*, 1964) that technology is not merely a mediation of the world; for humans, technology *is* the world. Today writers as divergent as **Pynchon, Borges, Calvino**, and a host of authors of divergent nationalities make similar assumptions, a circumstance that has stimulated **gender**, ethnic, and cultural studies of fiction. Some deplore large-scale technology that despoils **environments**, undermines democratic governance, and oppresses individuals; others acknowledge the sublimity of invention; and still others, most notably **cyberpunk** writers, accept artifice as a neutral given.

References

Layton, Edwin. "Technology as Knowledge." *Technology and Culture* 15 (1974): 33–42.

Mazlish, Bruce. "The Fourth Discontinuity." *Technology and Culture: An Anthology*. Ed. Melvin Kranzberg and William Davenport. New York: New American Library, 1972. 216–32.

Joseph W. Slade

Telephone. Invention (*see* Inventor(s)) made by Alexander Graham Bell in 1876 to transmit the human voice. Originally dubbed the "speaking telegraph," Bell's device was improved upon by **Thomas Edison**, Emile Berliner, and others, and the **patent** rights to practical innovations were litigated for decades by the Bell Company (later AT&T) and Western Union. Edison reportedly invented the telephonic salutation "Hello?" which succeeded against Bell's "Ahoy!" as the device achieved a linguistic as well as a sociotechnic familiarity. **Mark Twain** early satirized patterns of telephonic speech in humorous sketches like "A Telephonic Conversation" (1880), and his *A Connecticut Yankee in King Arthur's Court* has a child named Hello-Central (1889). Despite Twain's precocity in owning a home phone, the primary application of the telephone remained business communication for many years. Not until the 1930s did the telephone industry fully reorient its sales strategy to identify the phone as an instrument of sociality.

Reference

Fischer, Claude S. *America Calling: A Social History of the Telephone to 1940*. Berkeley: U of California P, 1992.

Lisa Gitelman

Telescope. The most important investigative tool in **astronomy**. The optical properties of these instruments were well known to medieval and Arab scientists, as well as to early Italian spectacle makers. The first known telescope is associated with a Dutch lens grinder named Hans Lippershey who, in 1608, attempted to **patent** the device brought about by an accidental alignment of two lenses of opposite curvature and differing focal length. In 1609, **Galileo Galilei** constructed a simple instrument consisting of two lenses mounted in a tube (whose length was the difference between the focal lengths of the two lenses) and used this device for astronomical observations. The first modern refracting instrument was devised by the German astronomer **Johannes Kepler**, who was trying to improve on the Galilean telescope. Christian Huygens tried to minimize the aberrations and defects of image formation of earlier instruments by creating long aerial telescopes whereby the objective lense was mounted on a pole and connected to the eyepiece by only a taut wire. The first crude model of the reflecting telescope was developed by Sir Isaac Newton (*see* Newtonianism). In the seventeenth century, the instrument changed Western notions of size, distances, and relationships between celestial and terrestrial bodies. **Milton** in *Paradise Lost* used Galileo's discoveries of sun and moon spots to anatomize forbidden knowledge, while Francis Godwin (*Man in the Moone*, 1638), Cyrano De Bergerac (*Histoire comique ou Voyage dans la Lune*, 1650), **Margaret Cavendish** (*The Blazing World*, 1666) and **Fontenelle** (*Conversations upon the Plurality of Worlds*, 1686) were using fiction to speculate about life on the moon.

References

Biagioli, Mario. *Galileo, Courtier: The Practice of Science in the Culture of Absolutism.* Chicago: U of Chicago P, 1993.
Nicolson, Marjorie Hope. *Voyages to the Moon.* New York: MacMillan Co, 1948.
Van Helden, Albert. *Measuring the Universe: Cosmic Dimensions from Aristarchus to Halley.* Chicago: U of Chicago P, 1985.

Diana B. Altegoer

Television. The twentieth century's principal storytelling medium whose visuality has undermined the authority of print. Decades of programming have altered how literature and especially science are represented and consumed by creating a discourse that appropriates artifacts of the **two cultures** as entertainment. In translating science into an accessible public commodity, television demystifies **laboratories**, alters professional hierarchies by celebrating selected specialties and individuals, and adopts social science methodology to set agendas. The resulting stereotypes, some borrowed from literature, make visible issues of class, **gender**, and ethnicity, while television's juxtaposition of images, attenuation of **space** and **time**, and self-reflexivity shape postmodern critiques of narrative.

Joseph W. Slade

Tennyson, Alfred (1809–1892). English Poet Laureate. His interest in science stemmed from his observations of nature while he was a boy in Lincolnshire and became a major component of his **poetry**, establishing a vital tension with his Christian beliefs and enabling him to put human affairs in perspective as a small part of the **drama** of the universe. He realized that "Nature, red in tooth and claw" did not share human values and could ask of human life, "What is it all but a trouble of ants in the gleam of a million million of suns?" Tennyson had a special interest in **astronomy**. He was a friend of the leading astronomer Sir Norman Lockyer, made observations with him, and had a **telescope** of his own. Many of his poems reflect a strong sense of the majesty of the heavens, of "star and system rolling past." His major poem *In Memoriam* (1850) draws imagery from such diverse fields as geology, embryology, anatomy, and astronomy, but his knowledge of science intensified the conflict between rational and religious belief that characterized Victorian intellectual life. Tennyson fully approved the contributions science made to social and material **progress** and recognized its disclosure of principles of development similar to evolutionary ideas, but he also felt the threat they offered to Christianity and spiritual life. In the late poem "Parnassus" (1889), Astronomy and Geology are "terrible Muses" who challenge traditional poetry. *In Memoriam* asks: "Let Science prove we are, and then / What matters science unto men—?" It matters little, Tennyson concludes, because it cannot impart the spiritual strength offered by religious beliefs.

Reference

Millhauser, M. *Fire and Ice: The Influence of Science on Tennyson's Poetry*. Lincoln, England: Tennyson Research Center, 1971.

Jacob Korg

Theory. Derived from the Greek verb *theorein*, to observe; a coherent set of principles by which we seek to understand phenomena and their relation to each other. Theory is "organized" observation of the elements that compose reality; it is an activity shared by the sciences, the **arts**, **philosophy**, and generally any organized intellectual pursuit. It is common, constitutive ground for the most diverse human activities.

Embedded in the organization of observations, however, is the necessary tendency to form models of sets of observed data. A model is the communicative expression of the organizing process, on the one hand, and the **representation** of reality as the ordered outcome of an observation or contemplation, on the other. It is on the level of model constructions that the diversity of the domains of knowledge first crystallized. When humans create models, they add their individual perception to the data gathered from a particular part of reality. Consequently, the organization of observations varies with the tendencies, preferences, rejections, and talents of the individual observer. Knowledge is ordered according to philosophical, artistic, scientific, and sociological theories and other sets of principles.

The modern era is a period in Western episteme marked by a relentlessly increasing separation of theoretical domains and their growing alienation in relation to each other. Organized observations are no longer understood by all; frequently and often inexorably, they turn into arcane mental constructs intelligible only for the initiated. Today, we find this state of intellectual compartmentalization most natural. Our educational institutions with their growing number of specialized programs testify to the inevitability of the dysfunctional family of human thought, as knowledge multiplies into ever more refined stages whose sum total overtaxes individual intellectual capacity for absorption and retention.

Literature, science, and their often adversary relationship reflect this epistemic dilemma perfectly. Looking for theoretical approaches to overcome it is not a search for **scientific models** in order to create "better" literary understanding, or for literary models that will "humanize" what is perceived to be the cold objectivity or moral neutrality of scientific pursuit. Rather, the aim is to define a theory that offers an organized observation on the hybrid domain of "literature and science." Some understand it as a simple set of interdisciplinary rules and judge its chances for success or failure according to primarily academic cooperative efforts. For others, however, it means a promising but very complex set of principles that may succeed in spanning the gap between the humanities and the sciences. In either case, the stance of the observer is assumed to be in one of the two domains, with "feelers" going out to the other. Whether these are critical assessments of the opposite domain or, on the contrary, elements on loan from the other to establish more effective models in one's own domain is of little importance in describing such a position of "double vision."

A truly unified theoretical approach to literature and science constitutes an organized observation of the "and" whose copulative function both separates and joins the domains of knowledge targeted by the epistemologically wedded formulation of "literature and science." We are not simplistically proposing a "theory of the AND" but rather the most common coordinating conjunction for linguistic constructs as an initial model to underscore the universality as well as the critically problematic nature of the theoretical approach we are attempting to outline.

Philosophers of science and literary theoreticians who participate in this debate focus on the "and" and explain it as a bridge between their respective domain and the one "on the other side." Precursors for these issues were Henri Bergson, Alfred North Whitehead, Walter Benjamin, and others who reflected on models for synthesized systems but were often misunderstood as thinkers of retrograde romanticized thought systems. Bergson, for example, is slowly being rediscovered for the depth of his insight into theoretical approaches to science and philosophy. More recent contributors to the debate over the forms of such theoretical work, and who have had a significant impact, are Paul Ricoeur, Gilles

Deleuze, Ilya Prigogine, Isabelle Stengers, N. Katherine Hayles, **Michel Serres**, and **Bruno Latour**, to name only a few. Others are currently working on these issues and lend a powerful voice to the debate. A good example of a coherent portrait of the "and" is the collection of studies *One Culture: Essays in Science and Literature* (1987), edited by George Levine, who characterizes the writings of his collaborators as "proliferations" of questions and analyses swirling around the "and." His introductory essay is itself a demonstration of the coordinating link as a model for a "field" concept with fluid boundaries rather than for a linear reduction to a univocal idea. What unites these discourses is an earnest attempt to span the gap between scientific and literary/philosophical pursuits and to call the possible results the bridge that renders the far side intellectually visible to one's own side.

To delineate the **complexity** of the "and" and endow its space with meaningful modes of rapprochement, interdisciplinary researchers are wary of models that are uniquely marked by their origins and therefore proceed exclusively from either a scientific or a humanities/literary point of view. At these ends of the theoretical spectrum, the difficulties of attaining working models for a truly interdisciplinary discourse are evident: Attempts, for instance, to apply rigorously scientific or mathematical formulas to a literary text or even a sentence, have proven extremely frustrating and have not produced models that convince both the scientist/mathematician and the linguist or literary theoretician.

More promising are approaches based on the premise that the sciences and the humanities manifest their output through *discourse*. Laws of **physics**, for instance, express the coherence of natural phenomena; however, no matter how objective their logical construct, these expressions are realized through the scientist's discourse, parts of which consist of strictly mathematical equations that model the physical laws. Similarly, discourse is the principal material with which the humanities construct their models.

"Discourse" is therefore a common means to analyze the formalistic "and" and fill it with enough content to satisfy those who seek a more holistic relationship between science *and* literature. Such theoretical approaches are therefore numerous and especially welcomed by the humanists who feel at home on the theoretical and logical terrain discourse offers up for building bridges between science and literature or other cultural activity. The fine and varied nuances of this debate are often fortuitously revealed by the simple fact that much of it is presented in collections of essays that, together, run the gamut of the entire discursive spectrum.

Together, these efforts form what is sometimes referred to as a philosophy of science. It is when the debate reaches the point where science, like literature, is discussed as a product of cultural conditioning, or as a discourse within a cultural content with a corresponding set of metaphors, that the two sides often lose sight of each other and are no longer speaking a common language. A theory for a common approach is then unattainable. What remains always undeniable is the existence of genuine differences, or the perception of inherent different spheres of action and responsibility, between the two domains: clarity and log-ical rigor for the sciences, interpretative competence and aesthetic and ethical power on the side of the humanities. This difference is historically reflected in the dominance of one domain over the other during a particular historical era. The onset of modernity in sixteenth-century Europe may be equated with a transfer of this dominant power. Before, it was the worldview of a scholastic philosophy deeply imbued with theological dogma, aided by such arts of per-suasion as **rhetoric** and grammar (i.e., discourse), that explained reality and claimed guardianship of the **truth**. Activities related to observation or experi-mentation, and in particular conclusions drawn from such pursuits, were subject to absolutely binding approval or rejection by the combined authority of the moral powers of church and state. In the wake of the events of the sixteenth century, scientific activity slowly but definitively began to shed notions of magic or Mephistophelian collusion and took possession of objective truth and logical clarity. Today, scientific discourse is dominant and often plays the role of arbiter for the truth.

This may explain why many scientists do not share the ease with which humanists place the approach of the two domains within a common cultural conditioning for either of their discourses. Scientists base their authoritative discourse on the factual evidence attained through objective observation and logical deduction. Conceding that their discourse may be influenced by cultural habits and therefore to be shared with other domains, they nonetheless conceive of the authority behind their models and scientific expressions as untouchable and outside any debate other than scientific verification.

Many researchers see therefore more promise for an effective approach be-tween literature and science in another development. It has to do with what Robert J. Scholnick calls "permeable boundaries" in his introductory article to a collection of contributions by leading thinkers on the conditions for a theory of "literature and science." Summarizing the undercurrent that sweeps through these essays, he distinguishes "reality" from "systems of explanation" that, though each on its own ground, work in complementary fashion to cover all of reality (5). His observations echo N. Katherine Hayles's many critical commen-taries on the fluid boundaries of different systems of representation and how "coupling mechanisms" across the synapse can produce changes in the "cultural matrix" as a whole (Scholnick 15). More recently, Hayles searches for a "com-mon ground" in light of radical shifts representation itself has undergone. "In-teractivity" and "positionality" are key terms with which she formulates a common ground for claims of "consistency" made for scientific and literary/cultural models alike. By foregoing "the claim of truth," representation is able to observe "constraints" set by reality that define the limits within which rep-resentation(s) can be constructed according to "consistent" perceptions of a given cultural context.

Representative models have now arrived at a confluence of basic concepts that offers new possibilities for an effective synapsis. Aided by precursory research in **thermodynamics** and Henri Poincaré's studies of mathematical non-linearity, science and mathematics are confronting the coexistence of **determinism** and **randomness** in the systems they investigate. Scientific objectivity and mathematical rigor are severely tested; nonlinear dynamical systems theory, **complexity** theory, and **fractal** geometry are systemic responses to what has essentially become an epistemological dilemma. Some scientists even speculate about metaphysical or mythical aspects of the emerging concepts at the heart of these theories. They mirror much of the literary and philosophical developments of the last fifty years that have witnessed the total eclipse of positivist thought and the relativization of traditional value systems. The profusion of philosophical, linguistic, and literary theories in recent decades is indicative of a need, on the part of the humanities as well, to come to terms with an epistemological configuration where **chaos** and order are intertwined. It is therefore on the foundation of a profound philosophical "urgency" that the sciences and the humanities find common ground.

The popularity of chaos theory, as complex dynamical systems theory is also known, is the source of great excitement for those who seek interdisciplinary connections between literature and science and of cautious skepticism for others who see the terminology and concepts of chaos theory (ab)used in an often superficial, faddish, and sometimes poorly defined manner. In order to clarify the scope of the debate and safeguard the epistemological integrity of chaos theory as a valid link between literature and science, researchers who are knowledgeable in both the sciences and the humanities are therefore trying to identify—and limit—the parallels, juxtapositions, equivalences, and inherent differences, with which nonlinear complex dynamics fills the synaptic "and." Although the scientific terminology is the strategy for such an interdisciplinary discourse, it cannot be considered as dominant, since its elements themselves are highly metaphorical, often "poetic" or artistic, and reflect the difficulty of no longer being able to create models with purely objective or numerical expressions. Fuzzy logic, **strange attractors**, simulation, the butterfly effect, and "chaos" itself beg to be exploited through their many connotations by discourses in literature, philosophy, or the social sciences. It is imperative, however, that the concepts subtending these terms be used in a fashion that is not merely scientific but profoundly philosophical and an epistemological challenge for the humanities as well as the sciences and mathematics.

Backed by research data concerning the simultaneous evolution of chaos theory in the sciences and the humanities, Peter Weingart and Sabine Maasen attempt to summarize the common epistemological ground on which chaos theory can figure as the link between science and literature. Recognizing the proliferation of chaos theory as a working strategy for current research in many domains, they propose chaos and metaphor as two distinct epistemological "units" whose behavior, however, is equivalent. Positing chaos not "merely metaphorically" but "as a metaphor" in and of itself, they consider its interdisciplinary use as a valid *translation* of chaos theory's "rigorous mathematics into other realms characterized by nonlinear dynamics" (474). Their proposal constitutes a synaptic theory of "literature and science" and offers an interesting aspect for the question whether chaos theory should remain a strictly mathematical application, serve as a model, or be used only in a metaphorical sense.

The debate over the extent and validity of a commonly shared interdisciplinary discourse, drawing its intellectual inspiration from science and literature equally, is perhaps best served by keeping in mind that whatever epistemological ground fits best or is "consistent" with a given cultural context (Hayles) is the one most likely to succeed in endowing the "and" with a valid content. Nonlinear complex dynamics appears today to provide a consistent model for domains of intellectual pursuit on both sides of the "gap," as Weingart and Maasen point out. Moreover, it may well go beyond its usefulness as a tool for observation and transcend continuing debates over the degree and validity of literal or metaphorical transcriptions of its underlying concepts. To borrow from H.W. Brand, who speculates on the usefulness but also the risks of chaos theory and fractals for historical analyses, nonlinear dynamics and its basic concepts of nonclosure contribute above all to the insight that there is "no one way of viewing or describing" and analyzing complex systems in any domain of our episteme. If we understand any synaptic theory of the "and" from this perspective, chaos theory may effectively serve as the fluid field of "observation" and "contemplation" that will never allow the gap between science and literature to be cemented in dominant formulae but only to be continually renewed with flexible "consistencies."

References

Argyros, Alexander J. *A Blessed Rage for Order: Deconstruction, Evolution, and Chaos.* Ann Arbor: U of Michigan P, 1991.

Brand, H.W. "Fractal History." *Diplomatic History* 1 (Fall 1992): 495–510.

Coveney, Peter, and Roger Highfield. *Frontiers of Complexity: The Search for Order in a Chaotic World.* New York: Fawcett Columbine Book, 1995.

Hayles, N. Katherine. *Chaos Bound: Orderly Disorder in Contemporary Literature and Science.* Ithaca, NY: Cornell UP, 1990.

———. "Nature and the Disorder of History." *Reinventing Nature?: Responses to Postmodern Deconstruction.* Ed. Michael E. Soulé and Gary Lease. Washington: Island, 1995.

Scholnick, Robert J., ed. *American Literature and Science.* Lexington: UP of Kentucky, 1992.

Tabbi, Joseph, and Michael Wutz, eds. *Reading Matters: Narratives in the New Media Ecology.* Ithaca, NY: Cornell UP, 1997.

Weingart, Peter, and Sabine Maasen. "The Order of Meaning: The Career of Chaos as a Metaphor." *Configurations* 5.3 (1997): 463–520.

Weissert, Thomas P. "Dynamical Discourse Theory." *Time and Society* 4 (1995): 111–33.

Maria L. Assad

Thermodynamics. Originating in the mid-nineteenth century, the branch of science that describes the transfer and interconversion of **energy**, associated with the names of Robert Mayer, Hermann von Helmholtz, Rudolf Clausius, and William Thomson (Lord Kelvin), who formulated its first (conservation of energy) and second (spontaneous **entropy** increase) laws. Walther Nernst's third law (zero entropy at absolute zero) came a half century later. Before assuming quantitative guise the first and second laws were enunciated qualitatively, as formalizations of common experience, particularly the impossibility of creating perpetual motion machines. The first thermodynamicist *avant la lettre* was Sadi Carnot; after rediscovering Carnot's rare book (1824) on the efficiency of steam engines, Thomson realized its "remarkable consequences," which he expressed in the form of a prediction about the "heat death" of the universe. Extrapolating from the second law, Thomson concluded that the present climate of the earth, so conducive to human existence, was only an interlude; from an intolerably hot past the earth would eventually reach a state of life-destroying cold. **Algernon Swinburne's** *The Garden of Prosperine* (1866) closes by portraying a universe at this ineluctable end point. **Darwin's** theory of evolution (*see* Evolutionary Theory) appeared soon after the heat death **hypothesis**; each individually and especially the two in juxtaposition unleashed a torrent of cosmological and theological speculation. **Henry Adams** drew explicitly on the second law and the metaphors associated with it—degradation, dissipation—for his pessimistic view of the future. Oswald Spengler saw even more apocalyptic implications, linking the second law with Teutonic myths of the "Twilight of the Gods." The heat death was primarily a nineteenth-century preoccupation; in the twentieth the concept of entropy replaced it as a cultural and scientific metaphor.

Reference

Brantlinger, Patrick. *Energy and Entropy: Science and Culture in Victorian Britain.* Bloomington: Indiana UP, 1989.

Stephen J. Weininger

Thomas, Lewis (1913–1993). American **physician-writer** whose popular essays reflect his philosophical view of organicism, the integration of humans into a harmonious biosphere. In contrast to **mechanism**, Lewis's writings portray the earth and its inhabitants as a holistic organism; thus, humans should strive for harmony and symbiosis, as exemplified in nature. Despite focusing on difficult scientific topics, Lewis successfully captures the interest of lay audiences through the brevity and lucidity of his essays. *The Lives of a Cell* (1974), perhaps his most notable work, often merits inclusion in reading lists for both science and humanity courses.

Robert J. Bonk

Thompson, Francis (1859–1907). A religious poet of great originality who had an interest in **astronomy**. Much of Thompson's celestial imagery combines accurate astronomical knowledge with mysticism. In his most famous poem, "The Hound of Heaven" (1893), the poet, as a sinner, is pursued by a divine hunting hound. The image reappears in "Orient Ode," as the planets are seen as hounds "Lashed with terror, leashed with longing," aptly depicting the centrifugal and centripetal forces that determine their paths around the sun.

Reference

Boardman, Brigid. *Between Heaven and Charing Cross*. New Haven, CT: Yale UP, 1988.

Jacob Korg

Thomson, James (1700–1748). Scottish poet of *The Seasons* (1730), a highly influential sequence of "nature" poems, which utilized exacting observational detail and occasional anthropomorphic anecdote to carry the hopeful message of **natural theology**. In "A Poem Sacred to the Memory of Isaac Newton" (1727), he accurately versified the Newtonian (*see* Newtonianism) description of the rainbow, among his subject's other achievements in **physics** and **cosmology** (preempting **John Keats's** later complaint that such phenomena had been ruined for **poetry** by science).

Reference

McKillop, Alan Dugald. *The Background of Thomson's Seasons*. Rpt. Hamden: Archon, 1961.

Pamela Gossin

Thoreau, Henry David (1817–1862). American writer, philosopher, and natural historian. Author of *Walden* (1854) and *The Dispersion of Seeds*, a recently published unfinished manuscript expanding his 1860 essay "The Succession of Forest Trees." Though not a trained scientist, Thoreau possessed a keen sense of observation, a penchant for data collection and an interest in the relationships among plants, animals, and the **environment**. His ecological pursuits included limnology, plant succession, species distribution, and seed dispersal. Thoreau rejected the notion of a detached scientific attitude and instead viewed scientific study as consonant with his romantic engagement with nature.

Reference

Thoreau, Henry David. *Faith in a Seed: The Dispersion of Seeds and Other Late Natural History Writings*. Ed. Bradley Dean. Washington: Island-Shearwater Books, 1993.

Michael A. Bryson

Thought Experiments. Essentially **fictions** designed to substantiate—or subvert—concepts of nature untestable by laboratory procedures. Examples are James Clerk Maxwell's **hypothesis** of a molecule-sorting demon; **Albert Einstein's** of himself chasing a lightbeam; and Erwin Schrödinger's of a cat in a box (*see* Schrödinger's Cat), suspended between life and death at the emission of a radioactive particle. Thought experiments are heuristic narratives, like those **George Gamow** devised for his tales of Mr. Tompkins. Gamow asks us to "imagine other worlds" whose physical laws replicate physical laws in our world "but with different . . . values for the . . . constants determining the limits of applicability of the old concepts" (xv). He adopts the strategy of the thought experimenter, who situates us within events, enabling us to see nature through eyes other than our own. We perceive as the demon perceives, or as someone traveling at lightspeed, or as an observer inside the box. As we watch, a natural domain we thought we understood is transformed. Literary scholars have suggested that certain literary devices and forms may operate as the vehicles of "poetic" thought experiment, such as: extended metaphysical conceits, the philosophical long poem, the **experimental novel**, and realist and naturalist fictions.

References

Gamow, George. *Mr. Tompkins in Paperback.* Cambridge: Cambridge UP, 1965.
Sorenson, Roy A. *Thought Experiments.* New York: Oxford UP, 1992.

Barton Friedman

Time. May be variously understood as a concept, a physical or metaphysical entity, or mere signifier. Time stands at a complex, ambivalent nexus between literature and science. The division between the **two cultures** of the humanities and sciences is replicated in the mutual exclusion between aesthetic or philosophical interpretations of time and scientific analyses of time. A similar subdivision occurs with each **culture**: The formalist strand of literary aesthetics emphasizes the power of **art** to arrest time and hold it fixed, while several other approaches rather view literature as an expression of cultural process. Scientific analysis of time runs up against the "irreversibility paradox," which stems from the fact that many "fundamental laws" of **physics** are time-reversible, whereas **entropy** and observed experience point to an irreversible "arrow of time." This paradox has lost some of its hold on humanists, as many scientific fields of popular interest display an explicit emphasis on time, including **chaos** and **complexity** theory, **cosmology**, and (naturally) the life sciences.

Time is perhaps the most written about subject of the twentieth century. Debates over the philosophical implications of **relativity** theory alone have filled countless books and replicated anew the maddening but productive frictions between the two cultures. J.T. Fraser has developed a synthetic, interdisciplinary approach to time where an irresolvable conflict at one level necessitates the emergence of a level of higher complexity. Fraser correlates temporal levels to types of organization in the universe; his theoretical framework moves from the atemporal world of particles moving near light speed to the noetic level of consciousness and sociotemporal level of culture.

Time is easily viewed as a sort of unwieldy homonym that has irretrievably different meanings across different fields. As interdisciplinary research comes into its own, new debates may spawn productive dialogues.

Paul A. Harris

Time Travel. The ability to journey physically backward into history or forward into the future. Time travel fantasies developed in the nineteenth century under the influence of new concepts of space and **time** manifested not only in accelerated travel and communication but also in theories such as **Darwinism**. Early time travel reflects the age of the railway (Adelbert von Chamisso, "Das Dampfross," 1830) and the conflict between modernity and the past (**Mark Twain's** *A Connecticut Yankee*, 1889). The first time machine in **fiction** appears in Czech writer Jakub Arbes's "Newton's Brain" (1877). With **H.G. Wells's** *The Time Machine* (1895), the motif gains a popular appeal it has never lost again, as much of twentieth-century **science fiction** from **Philip K. Dick** and **Arthur C. Clarke** to Sever Gansovsky proves.

Reference

Nicholls, P., ed. *The Science in Science Fiction*. London: Michael Joseph, 1982.

Elmar Schenkel

Topography. The character and configuration of the land. The sense of place topography confers deeply affects literature. The term "regional literature" conveys the strong connection between the writer and the land, as well as the influence of region on literature. For example, the **fiction** of Flannery O'Connor and **William Faulkner** reflects a uniquely southern perspective, born of the distinctive personality of the land and its inhabitants. Similarly, Wallace Stegner and Gretel Ehrlich write of the West, and their works display a uniquely western topos.

Often, a writer will become so linked with a region that their identities merge. Faulkner's Yoknapatawpha county was his own invention, yet every year thousands of people journey to Oxford, Mississippi, to experience it. Much of northern California is known as "Steinbeck Country," and Garrison Keillor immortalized northern Minnesota in his imaginary town of Lake Wobegon. These links between writer and region would be impossible were it not for the distinctive and highly affecting topographies of the various regions.

References

Berry, Wendell. *The Unsettling of America*. San Francisco: Sierra Club, 1977.
Kolodny, Annette. *The Lay of the Land*. Chapel Hill: U of North Carolina P, 1975.

David N. Cassuto

Tragedy. Certainly the most famous definition is **Aristotle's**: "the imitation of an action that is serious and also, as having magnitude, complete in itself . . . with incidents arousing pity and fear, wherewith to accomplish its catharsis of such emotions" (*Poetics*, ch. 6). There are, of course, many others, including my own ideas that the notion of tragedy may be considered consonant with biological (*see* Biology) and evolutionary science (*see* Evolutionary Theory).

If we assume that the roots of tragedy (usually understood as a work of **drama** or **fiction**) lie in the experience of something we call the tragic, it is possible to postulate a **theory** of tragedy that derives from a fundamental conflict that arises in the human nervous system. There are many events that are typically labeled tragic, most of them having to do with death or loss. However, the basis of the tragic is the conflict felt by creatures who are able, because of their complex nervous systems, to entertain notions of infinity and yet who are in some way bounded by finite constraints. Simply, the tragic is the conflict between a longing for unboundedness and the awareness that it is necessary to adjust to a condition that is necessarily bounded.

When creatures attain a certain level of neural **complexity**, they become aware of the central facet of their finitude: their mortality. Simultaneously, they begin to imagine the world as it will be after their demise. From this realization, although clearly not simply in reaction to the knowledge of death, intricate brains begin to project themselves into all kinds of counterfactual realms: the afterlife, fictional worlds, transcendental dimensions, and so on. The neurological foundations of the tragic, and therefore of tragedy, lie in the irresolvable paradox between transcendence and finitude as it is perceived in the consciousness of self-reflexive, purposive, and mortal creatures such as us.

In general, I take foundation to mean something like epigenetic predisposition in the sociobiological sense. The question, then, is whether it is possible to locate in the biological realm a kind of epigenetic rule for the tragic. If we define the tragic as the unresolvable conflict between transcendence and finitude, or as the tendency of the human mind to project itself beyond temporal or physical constraints while periodically falling into awareness of its rootedness in the plodding rhythms of organic and inorganic matter, then the tragic can be said to be founded on the basic conflict that defines sexual **reproduction**: that genetic vitality comes at the price of death. The tragic, and its aesthetic **representation**, tragedy, are the complexification of the conflict between the fever of creativity brought about by genetic variation and the dull thud or welcome port of death into a tension so unbearable that most people and most societies develop elaborate ruses to disguise it.

Alex Argyros

Truth. In everyday parlance, something one either tells or fails to tell. In Mozart's *The Magic Flute*, the truth is what Pamina says you should always tell, even if there is a great risk involved. In a lot of contemporary literary **theory**, on the other hand, we are told that truth is a word that scientists and others sometimes use to glorify their own discourses or that truth is just powerful opinion.

When we turn to philosophical discussions of truth, we find that rather complex arguments surround its nature and role in semantics, **epistemology**, and metaphysics. These arguments can seem remote from the everyday and literary uses of "truth" but should not be ignored by anyone who wants to theorize about truth. The most traditional, and perhaps also the most intuitively appealing, idea of truth is the so-called correspondence theory, which describes truth as a re-lation of correspondence or adequation between mind and **reality**. Yet all three of its basic terms—"correspondence," "reality," and "mind"—require detailed explication if this intuition is to be developed into a genuine theory. What is the nature of the bearer of truth? Is it a proposition? An utterance? To what do these truth-bearers correspond? Facts? Situations? States of affairs? Is there re-ally one kind of thing to which all true beliefs correspond? And what is the property of "corresponding" to this item? Despair over the possibility of an-swering these metaphysical questions has motivated various alternative ap-proaches to truth, such as Charles Sanders Peirce's attempt to identify truth with verifiability: Truth is what the ideal community of observers will believe in the long run, or what an individual believes if he or she follows the right procedure for fixing belief. Yet there also seems to be a sense in which a belief could be true but unverified; and could not all of our evidence make a belief seem verified when in fact it is false? The pragmatic theory of truth, according to which true beliefs are those that successfully guide our actions, encounters a similar prob-lem, for we also want to recognize that faulty beliefs can play a role in actions that turn out to be successful.

Deflationary accounts of truth have gained prominence in twentieth-century **philosophy**. For example, Frank Ramsey's "redundancy" theory of truth tells us that "is true" does not assign any property to a belief or proposition: There is no semantic difference between "The proposition *that p* is true" and "*p*" *tout court*. Various counterexamples to that claim motivate the shift to an alternative deflationary account, for example, Paul Horwich's idea that the basic theory of truth contains nothing more than a potentially infinite list of equivalences of the form "The proposition *that p* is true if and only if *p*." This approach avoids some (but not all) of the problems that beset the rival, epistemic, and corre-spondence approaches. Yet one may wonder whether there is not a more sub-stantive notion of truth that still requires explication.

References

Davidson, Donald. "The Structure and Content of Truth." *Journal of Philosophy* 66 (1990): 279–328.
Horwich, Paul. *Truth*. Oxford: Blackwell, 1990.
Peirce, Charles Sanders. *Collected Papers*. Cambridge: Harvard UP, 1932.
Ramsey, Frank. "Facts and Propositions." *Proceedings of the Aristotelian Society* (Supp.) 7 (1927): 153–70.

Paisley Livingston

Turbulence. Irregular motions and currents, departures from smooth flow. When fluids are flowing smoothly, their motion is relatively predictable. For example, two bits of bark moving down a slow, smoothly flowing river will tend to maintain the same distance from each other for long periods, or if their distance diverges, it will do so linearly. However, as the river's pace increases, especially if it must flow around an obstacle such as a boulder, smooth flow is replaced by a wild crash of different motions: swirling eddies, whirlpools, undertow, and collisions of conflicting currents. In such a state of turbulence, the **complexity** of the trajectories will make the distance between the two pieces of bark change unpredictably. They will approach and diverge from each other discontinuously, rendering impossible any projection of their future paths.

Although the jury is still out at this point, many theorists argue that turbulence in fluid dynamics will eventually be understood in terms of **chaos theory**. Some claim that like other chaotic systems a fluid on the way to turbulence undergoes a sudden transition that is best understood as a cascade of period doublings. Still others maintain that it will be possible to postulate **strange attractors** for turbulent flows.

Alex Argyros

Twain, Mark (1835–1910). Pseudonym of Samuel Langhorne Clemens, American novelist and humorist. From his early years in his brother's print shop, Twain involved himself with the materiality of communication, with how things end up on the page as well as what things say. This double interest characterized his career as a writer and publisher and as a modern consumer, hapless capitalist, and amateur **inventor**. In novels like *A Connecticut Yankee in King Arthur's Court* (1889), *The Gilded Age* (1873), and *The American Claimant* (1892), Twain addressed the potentially transformative role of **technology**. In the farcical character of Colonel Sellers, denizen of the New York stage as well as two novels, he created a bilious avatar of all things technological. Nor was Colonel Sellers the only enthusiast: While he was writing *Connecticut Yankee*, Twain invested more and more money and hope in a complicated typesetting machine being developed by James Paige. It was a timely idea but a boondoggle investment, and it ultimately left him bankrupt, as simpler linotype and monotype typesetting machines seized the day. Twain experimented with genre and with the literary accoutrements of American regionalism; but he experimented in other ways, too. He obtained three U.S. **patents**—one for an "adjustable strap" for clothing, another for a historical board game, and the third for a "self-pasting" scrapbook or album with gummed pages. None of them did well, though the scrapbook turned a profit for a while. Meanwhile, he was an early and avid consumer of technical products. He had one of the first home **telephones**, one of the first Remington **typewriters**, and he experimented eagerly with a stylographic pen, a dictation **phonograph**, and a new engraving process. All of these material means of communication fed his **art** and composed his identity.

Lisa Gitelman

Two Cultures Debate. One of the seminal controversies of Anglo-American letters, centered on the comparative merits of literature and science as pathways to knowledge, truth, social justice, and moral vision. This centuries-old exchange between apologists of literature and the sciences plays a constitutive role in LS, as the terms and topics of the issues shift with the growth of science and **technology** and the development of literature and criticism. The most contentious episode of the controversy occurred at Cambridge University in the late 1950s and early 1960s between **Charles Percy Snow** and his literary antagonist Frank Raymond Leavis. Snow and Leavis—and hundreds if not thousands of their commentators from all over the world—wrangled over the proposition that scientists and literary intellectuals belong to opposing "cultures" with conflicting views on a great range of intellectual, social, and moral questions. This mid-century conflict has roots in the Baconian (*see* Bacon) critique, outlined in the *Advancement of Learning* (1605), which contrasted the classical knowledge of the Schoolmen with the new knowledge of a brotherhood of natural philosophers, methodically building upon their own experiences. A succession of more or less related debates in the seventeenth through nineteenth centuries, mainly in England, pitting ancient against modern learning and literature against science, has worked the dualisms of the original Baconian statement. As revived by Snow and Leavis, in the post–World War II setting of the vastly expanded institutional and industrial support for the sciences and applied sciences, the conflict raised urgent moral issues for writers and academics on both sides of the divide.

Snow's Position

In his Rede Lecture *The Two Cultures and the Scientific Revolution*, delivered at Cambridge University on May 7, 1959, C.P. Snow, British novelist and ex-scientific researcher, makes the provocative claim that Western intellectuals have become divided into "two cultures." Expanding a short opinion piece he had written a few years earlier for *The New Statesman and Nation*, Snow argues in imagery borrowed from the Cold War that crucial institutions of the West in government, industry, and education have become populated by two camps of silently contending intellectuals: "Literary intellectuals at one pole—at the other scientists, and as the most representative, the physical scientists. Between the two a gulf of mutual incomprehension—sometimes (particularly among the young) hostility and dislike, but most of all lack of understanding" (Snow 4). Scientists, who "have the future in their bones," view their literary colleagues with a sense of puzzlement, even contempt; literary intellectuals, "wishing the future did not exist," regard their scientific counterparts with deep distrust. In Snow's view, this cultural dualism, which is thoroughly entrenched in Western intellectual circles, leads to stultifying narrowness and rigidity on both sides and hampers the West in its efforts to become a competent, modern society that can compete in the international theater of modern states.

Few in Snow's considerable lecture and reading audiences could quibble with his argument that literary (not to mention other) intellectuals are deficient in the sciences and that scientists are often narrow specialists. Nor would many deny that, as **T.H. Huxley** and **Matthew Arnold** had agreed a century before in their own debate over literature and science, science is a great imaginative realm. But Snow sought redress for what he perceived was the entrenched and immoral attitude of superiority of the literary elite. World War II had changed the intellectual **landscape** by giving unprecedented momentum to the research output of major English and American universities and producing an immense cadre of practicing scientists and applied research specialists. Snow's insights drew on his personal experiences, especially in the 1940s, as technical director in the Wartime Ministry of Labour and, after World War II, as director for Scientific Personnel in the English Electric Company, where he had interviewed and recruited thousands of scientists and **engineers** to staff key projects in England and America (including the development of radar and the atomic bomb). Out of these experiences, he constructed the moral conflicts that define his two cultures, conflicts that often propel the action of his novels—for example, *The Masters* (1951) and *The Affair* (1960). The university was the natural locus of Snow's contending fictional elites: traditionalists, whose identities are bound up with the past glories of classical **culture**, and progressives, who see themselves as builders of modern institutions appropriate to the age of science. Snow's fictional world thus blended well with the arguments of his two cultures formulation.

But as Snow now generalized in his Rede Lecture about real rather than fictional elites, his word "culture," offered as a way of characterizing these elites, became difficult to distinguish from stereotype. The two cultures tensions that helped Snow create a distinctive fictional world of contending academic hierarchies is not so convincing as an account of how an entire living culture really works. Suspension of disbelief, routinely extended to the fictionist, is not granted to the social polemicist. Speaking confidently as scientist and novelist of the innermost thoughts of the two camps, Snow took his insider insights as evidence that two cultures actually do exist. In his Rede Lecture, he defined culture as a set of "common attitudes, common standards and patterns of behaviour, common approaches and assumptions," acquired largely, we must assume, during a university education. We are not told what culture, if any, the untrained occupy; nor do we know what culture all the postgraduates occupied before they acquired their opposing cultures at university; nor do we know what culture their spouses and children occupy. Such "cultures," which may be little more than the stereotypes of biased observers, fail to account for the spectrum of individuals participating in culture "as a whole way of life" (to use Raymond Williams's phrase). Snow's definition of "culture," in short, does not stand up to scrutiny.

Despite his credentials as both science researcher and novelist, Snow makes little effort to hide his bias. He valorizes scientists as rational, moral citizens and indicts literary intellectuals as self-indulgent and morally irresponsible. **T.S. Eliot**, the "archetypal" literary intellectual, is a self-pitying defeatist whose meager hope is to prepare the way for a new Kyd or a new Greene. In contrast, Snow's **Rutherford**, the "archetypal" scientist, confidently trumpets, "This is the heroic age of science!" When an unnamed "scientist of distinction" declares to Snow, "Yeats, Pound, Wyndham Lewis, nine out of ten of those who have dominated the literary sensibility in our time—weren't they not only politically silly, but politically wicked? Didn't the influence of all they represent bring Auschwitz that much nearer?" Snow declines to "defend the indefensible." Scientific culture, in contrast, has the "soundest group of intellectuals: There is a moral component right in the grain of science itself." Science has become privileged discourse: It cannot be science if it is not moral.

There is humor in Snow's blunt stereotyping of the modern literary elite and their nineteenth-century predecessors as progress-loathing "natural luddites" fighting social justice. However, the caricature, sustained and intolerant, was ill-calculated to solve the problems Snow thought he was addressing, and scores of artists and humanists took offense at Snow's sweeping dismissal of the introspective and aesthetic responses of certain artists to the growth of the industrial state. Moreover, in presenting his two cultures formulation as something to be transcended, Snow framed the contrast as part of a dialectical process. The once dominant "literary" culture is seen to be poised, as primitive cultures are poised, for displacement by the more vigorous, moral, and competent culture of muscular Rutherfordian science. Striving for moral high ground, Snow's expansive technological triumphalism glossed over the fact that the twentieth century's two world wars had assumed a vastness and virulence made possible by the very same enabling technologies to which Snow now appealed for world social amelioration. Seeking to discredit what he saw as the literary intellectual's complacent suspicion of technological development, Snow reduced the consciences of literary visionaries like Eliot, **Joyce**, **Yeats**, and Lawrence to irrelevant static amid the social and political aspirations of rising world nations. Snow thus took up a didactic position on **art** itself, the element of his Rede Lecture that has most alienated his critics. Art, he holds, should both reflect the social realities of a society structured upon a scientific foundation and serve the social aspirations of the masses. This social entailment of art, which vigorously opposes aesthetic freedom as mere anti-egalitarian indulgence, is in keeping with the socialist **realism** that in Snow's Rede Lecture merits the highest praise.

Responses to Snow

Although there were many responses, both favorable and critical, to Snow's brief 1956 two cultures essay and the much more ambitious 1959 Rede Lecture, that of the Cambridge literary critic F.R. Leavis was by far the most famous, not to mention notorious. In his Richmond Lecture, "Two Cultures? The Significance of C.P. Snow," delivered at Downing College, Cambridge, in February 1962 and published in the *Spectator* the following month, Leavis yoked a hasty critique of Snow's social vision of literature with a blistering, absurdly personal attack on Snow. This attack had the self-righteous energy of **Alexander Pope** excoriating the poetasters, Grub Street hacks, and new philosophers in the "Dunciad," without a hint of Pope's transcendent wit. Blunt, vitriolic, and remorselessly personal, Leavis sought to undermine Snow's authority by demolishing his claims as a novelist, an attack as superficial as Snow's own facile dismissal of writers like Eliot and Lawrence. Snow, Leavis declares, "is utterly without a glimmer of what creative literature is, or why it matters." Leavis's rebuttal offers Snow's own work as primary evidence of modern moral and cultural decline. Not only did Snow's analysis rest on sweeping stereotypes, but it was repetitious, empty, and structured on bald cliché. "Snow's pompous phrases give us the central and supreme instance of what I have called 'basic cliché.' He takes over inertly—takes over as self-evident simple clarity—the characteristic and disastrous confusion of the civilisation he is offering to instruct." For Leavis, Snow's view that the advancement of science and technology is the social hope of the world's masses summons the authority of science to misdirect us toward short-term material pursuits—pursuits that subordinate the spiritual needs of the individual to the theoretical needs of an abstract social class for higher standards of material well-being. Thus, Leavis finds in Snow the very face of the technocratic, industrialist menace that D.H. Lawrence had found oppressive.

Leavis's irascible response drew as much attention to the excess of his voice as to the issues of his critique. The Richmond Lecture had an "impermissible tone," observed Lionel Trilling in his *Commentary* essay "Science, Literature, and Culture: A Comment on the Leavis-Snow Controversy" (1962). Trilling's classic essay, which is so penetrating an assessment of the controversy as to be worth considering part three of the exchange, puts the debate into the historical context of past controversies, especially that between Thomas Henry Huxley and Matthew Arnold in the 1880s. For Huxley and Arnold, the question was one of whether a scientific or literary education was the better preparation for living in a contemporary culture, which both men assumed was a single entity. Part of the acrimony in the Leavis-Snow debate, Trilling suggested, arose from its fraternal nature. Both men had come from the provincial British middle class; both men had the earnest, confrontational personalities of Cromwellian Roundheads; both men were holding forth on their home ground of Cambridge. Both men, Trilling continued, "set too much store by the idea of culture as category of thought," their "cultures" being more the "life-styles" of certain elites than truly representative bodies of citizenry. Leavis himself, Trilling noted, had little sympathy with the modern writers targeted by Snow and could not, in good faith, go to their defenses. Trilling objected strongly also to Snow's vague generalization that Western society in all its institutional vastness and **complexity** was somehow managed by literary culture—a thought Trilling called "bewildering." Snow, he concluded, had the mistaken desire to reduce the complex political circumstances of well-intentioned scientists, struggling with the inertia or bad will of governments, to a simple formula of the "good culture of science" fighting the "bad culture of literature."

In addition to Trilling's response, many other major commentaries appeared, including **Aldous Huxley's** *Science and Literature* (1963), which explored the different roles and performances of language in the sciences and literary arts. Huxley concluded that modern science had produced a new window on the natural world upon which literature was partly built and argued that such material offered both challenge and opportunity to art. Snow himself added to the commentary in his "The Two Cultures: A Second Look" (1964), in which he likened himself to the Sorcerer's Apprentice for having begun a discussion that could not find closure. Feeling defensive about his use of the word "culture," he restated his argument that in the technical sense of an anthropologist a culture referred to a group of people linked by common habits, assumptions, and way of life. It did not occur to him that an anthropologist, a scientist, and a humanist driving through Cambridge, typed lectures in briefcases, to catch the ten o'clock train to London, shared **environment**, assumptions, and way of life in more profound ways than they might be divided by any devotion to their particular fields. Snow also revised his idea of two "polar" cultures by surmising that a "third culture" might possibly be taking shape in the social sciences. This idea of a third intellectual perspective is the subject of Wolf Lepenies's weighty study *Between Literature and Science: The Rise of Sociology* (1985). Lepenies, who has little interest in inducting sociologists into a third "culture," traces the development of the social sciences to the territorial scrapping between scientific and literary intellectuals in the nineteenth century, especially the debate between Huxley and Arnold. Some of these same issues are expanded upon in T.W. Heyck's *The Transformation of Intellectual Life in Victorian England* (1982) and Isaiah Berlin's "The Divorce between the Sciences and Humanities" in *Against the Current* (1977).

It is possible to see the more recent controversy among contemporary literary theorists, social constructivists, and antiobscurantist defenders of science as a continuation of the literature and science controversy. This new phase of the controversy concerns a body of works by historians and sociologists of science, as well as literary theorists and cultural critics—works such as Steven Shapin and Simon Schaffer's *Leviathan and the Air-Pump* (1985) and Andrew Ross's *Strange Weather: Culture, Science and Technology in the Age of Limits* (1991). These writers, among other things, examine scientific material in the contexts of various critical approaches toward history, society, literature, and culture. One strong reaction against this diverse science commentary is found in Paul Gross and Norman Levitt's *Higher Superstition: The Academic Left and Its Quarrels with Science*, 1994), a volume that places itself in the tradition of Snow's Rede Lecture. Gross and Levitt undertake to expose, from an **Enlightenment** rationalist's point of view, what they see as the dangerous relativistic and scientifically inaccurate thinking in contemporary postmodern, feminist, and social constructivist works by writers as diverse as Steven Shapin and Simon Schaffer, Evelyn Fox Keller, Michel Foucault, Jacques Derrida, Stanley Aronowitz, **Donna Haraway**, Carolyn Merchant, Sandra Harding, Jeremy Rifkin, Andrew Ross, N. Katherine Hayles, Larry Kramer and **Bruno Latour**. Sorting these authors into various leftist "anti-science" conspiracies that threaten the hard-earned and, one gathers, imperiled rationalism of the West, Gross and Levitt are especially worried about the threat to the independence and **objectivity** of modern science.

Although not without insight in identifying legitimate issues of debate in science studies and literary and cultural criticism, Gross and Levitt's dire warnings of the oncoming "sleep of reason" are hard to accept at face value (see also M. Norton Wise's response). Moreover, their claim that humanists and sociologists alike take pleasure in vandalizing "the mighty principality of the exact sciences" for mere academic plunder and egotism follows the familiar "us versus them" formula that has been typical of the science and literature controversy.

References

Cornelius, David K., and Edwin St. Vincent, eds. *Cultures in Conflict: Perspectives on the Snow-Leavis Controversy*. Chicago: Scott, Foresman, 1964.

De la Mothe, John. *C.P. Snow and the Struggle of Modernity*. Austin: U of Texas P, 1992.

Leavis, Frank Raymond. "Two Cultures? The Significance of C.P. Snow." 1962. Reprinted in F.R. Leavis, *Nor Shall My Sword: Discourses on Pluralism, Compassion and Social Hope*. London: Chatto and Windus, 1972.

Snow, Charles Percy. *The Two Cultures and the Scientific Revolution*. Introduced by Stefan Collini. 1959. Cambridge: Cambridge UP, 1993.

Snow, Philip, et al. "Symposium: The Two Cultures Revisited." *Cambridge Review* 108 (1987): 3–14.

Trilling, Lionel. "The Leavis-Snow Controversy." *Beyond Culture: Essays on Literature and Learning*. 1963. New York: Harcourt, 1965.

Wise, Norton M. "The Enemy Without and the Enemy Within." *Isis* 87 (1996): 323–27.

James G. Paradis

Typewriter. Mechanical writing instrument. The first commercial, type-bar model was perfected by Christopher Latham Sholes and marketed by the Remington Company, a maker of guns and sewing machines, in 1874. The application of machinery to authorship proved attractive to writers like **Mark Twain**, who briefly used an early Remington, and to Friedrich Nietzsche, who briefly used a machine made by Malling Hansen of Denmark. Twain's *Life on the Mississippi* (1883) is purported to be the first book submitted to its publishers as a typed manuscript. Early fictional **representations** of the typewriter include **Arthur Conan Doyle's** "A Case of Identity" (1891) and O. Henry's "Springtime a la Carte" (1904). Later authors came to acknowledge an affinity between mechanically producing a text and creatively composing it. **Henry James**, who dictated to a secretary, wrote of the stimulating "**music**" of the Remington, while **Ezra Pound** and later-twentieth-century authors counted the machine as a kind of muse.

References

Current, Richard N. *The Typewriter and the Men Who Made It*. Urbana: U of Illinois P, 1954.

Kenner, Hugh. *The Mechanic Muse*. New York: Oxford UP, 1987.

Lisa Gitelman

U

Unamuno y Jugo, Miguel de (1864–1936). One of the most important Spanish writers of the early twentieth century. He was deeply influenced by **Spencer** and **Darwin**. References to Claude Bernard, Ernst Haeckel, Henri Poincaré, and Pierre Berthelot abound in his writing. His novel *Love and Education* (1902) is a **satire** of **positivism** and the futility of bringing up children according to scientific theories.

Rafael Chabrán

Uncertainty Principle. The statement that it is impossible to have full knowledge of any physical system, derived from **quantum physics** by **Werner Heisenberg** in 1927. In classical **physics**, both the position and momentum of a particle can in principle be known with perfect accuracy. In quantum physics, a particle is also a wave that has extension in space. The momentum or the location of the wave-particle can be found exactly only if the complementary quantity is completely unknown, and it is impossible to simultaneously measure both to arbitrary accuracy. Another interpretation of the principle has it that a measurement disturbs a system sufficiently to change the quantity under measurement. The quantum uncertainties in position and momentum are extremely small. Hence the bizarre implications of the principle appear only on the subatomic scale, such as the fact that particles tunnel through walls. Its philosophical implications, however, profoundly affect our view of physical reality and have long been debated. Literary scholars, too, have explored the concept in their studies of such writers as **James Joyce**, **Thomas Pynchon**, and **Virginia Woolf**, among others.

References

Davies, P.C.W., and J.R. Brown. *The Ghost in the Atom: A Discussion of the Mysteries of Quantum Physics*. New York: Cambridge UP, 1986.

von Baeyer, Hans Christian. *Taming the Atom: The Emergence of the Visible Microworld.* New York: Random House, 1992.

Sidney Perkowitz

United States (LS in). A field of study whose dimensions have fluctuated since the 1950s, when scholars such as **Loren Eiseley**, **Marjorie Hope Nicolson**, Elizabeth Eisenstein, Gerald Holton, Leo Marx, Max Black, and **Gregory Bateson** first hybridized these disciplines. The Modern Language Association created a division of Literature and Science as early as 1939, but efforts to structure the field date from the 1982 Conference on Science, Technology, and Literature at Long Island University, whose papers were published as *Beyond the Two Cultures* (edited by Slade and Lee). Three years later, veterans of that meeting formed the Society for Literature and Science (SLS), which has since held annual conferences to discuss intersections among various sciences and clusters of disciplines in the humanities, the social sciences, and **medicine**. Scholarly articles and book reviews now appear in the SLS journal *Configurations* but also in periodicals sponsored by the Society for the History of Technology, the Society for Literature and Medicine, the History of Science Society, the Society for Social Studies of Science, and other academic organizations. Several economic and academic factors account for the hundreds of articles and books cataloged in annual American bibliographies of literature and science.

Both literature and science are engines of a postindustrial economy whose capital is **information**. Tightened control of intellectual property, the multiplication of channels, and the consolidation of worldwide communication infrastructures have stimulated the reexamination of print, visual, and electronic media, their content, and their audiences. At the same time, the information economy has foregrounded issues such as **gender**, ethnicity, and age because it seeks to bolster information consumption through widened markets of women, minorities, and other groups, to enlist those groups as information workers, and to lower the unit costs of information through mass production and reduced wages for middle-class information processors. Digitization in particular creates new patterns of consumption in markets for news, entertainment, education, and proprietary data but also exposes the similarities of tropes, metaphors, and other narrative structures in all kinds of messages. Given those trends, literary analysis deals with scientific narratives as readily as with classic literary genres, even at the high speeds at which commodification and delivery occur. Viewed from an economic perspective, literature and science as a field of study is a response to the merging of scientific and humanistic discourses into a single data stream that can be distributed globally.

Global information imperatives aside, exploring affinities between literature and science honors a historically American conviction that intellectual endeavor is seamless. Whereas colonial thinkers such as **Thomas Jefferson** gave equal weight to literature and science, twentieth-century Americans grant greater authority to artifacts of science. During the nineteenth century the major sciences professionalized themselves by developing specialized vocabularies, adopting and standardizing methods of investigation, and closing their doors to laymen, despite efforts by Transcendentalists, popularizers, and educators to keep them open. Tracing the factors that have over time ranked literature below science in the United States would note the long delay in copyright legislation that made domestic imaginative writing profitable only after 1891, the industrialization (*see* Industrial Revolution; Industry) that commercialized products of the **laboratory** more rapidly than those of the pen, the growth of public health initiatives and military budgets, and the funding of the space program, the Human Genome Project, and other "big" public programs that dramatized and enhanced science. Calling the field "literature and science" rather than "humanities and science" or "science and literature" indicates the resolve of literary scholars to recapture credibility by expanding the domain of literature.

American scholars so far have adopted two broad approaches: The first treats literature and science as **representations** of experience; the second treats both as performance. Ironically for the study of literature and science in the United States, the first approach has been strongly influenced by language-based French theories that destabilize all disciplines by treating their products as texts. Taking as one starting point *The Structure of Scientific Revolutions* (1962; 1970), in which Thomas Kuhn (*see* Revolutions) argues that paradigms and languages govern perception and interpretation, **poststructuralism** asserts that language ultimately refers back to itself. According to this view, linguistic self-reflexivity fixes the norms of all disciplines, prescribes objects and processes of investigation, influences the processing of data, and shapes to an extent the conclusions. This linguistic turn also leads to claims that researchers and artists alike "read" events and data and that lab notes, grant proposals, **scientific articles**, and **museum** exhibits are just as susceptible as poems and novels to linguistic and rhetorical analysis.

Scientists counter observations that language is duplicitous and **objectivity** a fiction by asserting that mathematics is not a culturally variable language (gender and ethnicity have little to do with the value of *pi*) and that the scientist's aspiration to neutrality may be sincere. Even so, many scientists acknowledge beauty, originality, and creativity (*see* Imagination and Creativity) as affinities common to literature and science while they dismiss poststructuralist excess. Alan Sokal and Jean Bricmont (*Fashionable Nonsense: Postmodern Intellectuals' Abuse of Science*, 1998), for example, attack Jacques Lacan, Jean Baudrillard, and other academics and New Age enthusiasts for misreadings of science. Such controversy is often trivial: Humanists ignorant of science characterize scientists as positivists, that is, those who believe that political and social forces do not influence experiments; scientists ignorant of a wider humanism think of humanists as social constructionists, that is, those who believe that there is no reality beyond representation. If some humanists insist that logic and skepticism reinforce oppressive social systems, some scientists hold that deconstructing all narratives in terms of social programming demeans ideas. According to the latter argument, poststructuralist emulations of science treat "meaning" as a function of Foucauldian behaviorism. Some literary scholars, persuaded by such criticism that the Second Law of Thermodynamics (once famously called by **C.P. Snow** the only scientific principle with which humanists were familiar) applies to closed poststructuralist systems, have turned to the parodoxes of **energy** and information explored by physicists and chemists to escape epistemological cul de sacs, a strategy detailed by Susan Strehle in *Fiction in the Quantum Universe* (1992). N. Katherine Hayles's *The Cosmic Web: Scientific Field Models and Literary Strategies in the Twentieth Century* (1984) and other bold interdisciplinary works attempt to extend the insights offered by **chaos theory** and other challenges to the Second Law to literature and culture at large.

A second approach concerns how humans *experience* the world and its investigation by literature and science. Thus far, few practicing authors of imaginative literature and few experimental scientists have joined literary and cultural critics or historians, philosophers, and popularizers of science in exploring the junctures of literature and science, a circumstance that has favored the study of textuality at the expense of performance, agency, and audience. Considered as text, a scientific calling is as much a construct as a literary genre, or, for that matter, any other mediated representation. As *performed*, however, literature and science remain mysterious, remote from second-order analysis. Following Joshua Meyrowitz's observation in *No Sense of Place: The Impact of Electronic Media on Social Behavior* (1985) that analyzing texts for clues is like trying to understand the industrial era by studying the colors of the first textiles to come out of English mills, some scholars examine instead the *technologies* of literature and science. Writing—imaginative, journalistic, or scientific—is not a discipline but a technology or a craft, an obvious bridge between disciplines and as much a performance as the "doing" of an experiment that is also "written up" for publication. The essayists of *The Literature of Science: Perspectives on Popular Scientific Writing* (edited by Murdo William McRae, 1993) note that scientists write to add to knowledge, to amuse, to make money, to secure funding, to voice ethical or moral concerns, to correct mistakes, but also to satisfy traditionally literary impulses: the need to confess doubt, to heal a damaged psyche, or to realize personal ambitions.

Scientists point out that writing is not the only means by which science and literature manifest themselves, that disciplines are processes of apprenticeship and evolution as much as successions of finished texts. Practitioners who attend interdisciplinary meetings hold poster sessions—rather than read papers—in which they demonstrate that experiments and theories emerge through action, vary orally and mathematically, and embody intellectual tools not easily categorized. Gradually more conversant with the diversity of sciences, literary critics are moving away from the Second Law to **biology's** Gaia Hypothesis, which foregrounds the processes of life as agency and actuality. Equally exciting is **information theory**, a series of theorems devoted to the coding of messages as functions of efficiency, integrity, and **complexity** without reference to cultural constraints. Organic and informational metaphors illuminate writing as a process in William Paulson's *The Noise of Culture: Literary Texts in a World of Information* (1988) and promise reconciliation between sociobiologists and humanists in **Edward O. Wilson's** *Consilience: The Unity of Knowledge* (1998).

Competing agendas will doubtless continue to shape the convergence of literature and science as ways of knowing, as strategies of interpretation, as bodies of knowledge, as forms of discourse, as messages between senders and receivers, as sociopolitical categories, as commercial enterprises, and as historical processes. So vast a field, constantly revised by emergent sciences and literary ingenuity, has room for serendipity and novelty. American scholars assume that disciplines are institutions arranged in cultural hierarchies of authority, prestige, and power but also communities of individuals. And that is surely the case with this new discipline, a subculture in formation, whose current ethnographers, biographers, philosophers, historians, and critics will give way to next-generation counterparts who will study the dynamics of this one.

References

Cohen, L. Bernard. *Science and the Founding Fathers: Science in the Political Thought of Thomas Jefferson, Benjamin Franklin, John Adams, and James Madison.* New York: Norton, 1995.
Holton, Gerald, ed. *Science and Culture.* Boston: Beacon, 1965.
Slade, Joseph W., and Judith Yaross Lee, eds. *Beyond the Two Cultures: Essays on Science, Technology, and Literature.* Ames: U of Iowa P, 1990.

Joseph W. Slade

Updike, John (1932–   ). Author of *Roger's Version* (1986), a novel that discusses **evolutionary theory** and particle **physics**: A **computer science** student attempts to prove the existence of God mathematically. Updike writes about neutrinos in the poem "Cosmic Gall" (1960) and **cosmology** in the novel *Toward the End of Time* (1997).

Elizabeth J. Donaldson

Utopias. Narrative (or less frequently, nonnarrative) accounts of particular, ideal, or alternative societies. The term derives from Sir Thomas More's narrative *Utopia* (1516), whose title combines the Greek "ou," meaning nonexistent, and "topos," meaning place, to signify "no place." Although scholars further distinguish between "eutopia" (good place) and "**dystopia**" (bad place), the more general term "utopia" is frequently used to describe a positive state, and "dystopia" is reserved for negative pictures. Utopias usually take the form of a realistic novel or traveler's tale set in a place distant in **time** or space from the author's own society.

In addition to More, commonly cited works in the Anglo-American canon are **Plato's** *Republic* (fourth c. B.C.E.), **Francis Bacon's** *New Atlantis* (1627), Edward Bellamy's *Looking Backward* (1888), **William Morris's** *News from Nowhere* (1891), **H.G. Wells's** *A Modern Utopia* (1905), as well as satiric forms such as **Swift's** *Gulliver's Travels* and **Samuel Butler's** *Erewhon* (1872). In mid-twentieth-century Europe the dystopian form became prominent with Evgenii Zamiatin's *We* (1920–1921), **Aldous Huxley's** *Brave New World* (1932), and **George Orwell's** *1984* (1949). From the 1970s until the present feminist writers have embraced the form in order to explore alternatives to patriarchy; for example, **Margaret Atwood, Ursula K. Le Guin, Marge Piercy**, and Joanna Russ.

From Plato onwards, scientific and mathematical thinking have been important elements in utopian designs, both as social activities and as models for reorganizing entire human cultures. Authors have regarded **technology** as a natural, as opposed to a **supernatural**, means for achieving a better life. The utopian form has encouraged writers to extrapolate scientific and technological developments to examine their future social consequences. Most early authors like Francis Bacon were wholly enthusiastic about science and **technology** improving the human condition. While this tradition continues, twentieth-century writers like Zamiatin and Huxley have also criticized the application of scientific thinking to social organization due to its totalizing and reductive tendencies.

References

Donawerth, Jane L., and Carol Kolmerten, eds. *Utopian and Science Fiction by Women.* Syracuse: Syracuse UP, 1994.
Krishan, Kumar. *Utopia and Anti-Utopia in Modern Times.* Oxford: Blackwell, 1987.
Levitas, Ruth. *The Concept of Utopia.* Syracuse: Syracuse UP, 1990.
Moylan, Tom. *Demand the Impossible: Science Fiction and the Utopian Imagination.* New York: Methuen, 1986.

June Deery

V

Varela, Francisco J. (1946–2001). Chilean-born, Harvard-educated cognitive neuroscientist who, with Humberto Maturana and Ricardo Uribe, coined the term **autopoiesis** in 1974. In recent works, such as *The Embodied Mind* (1991, with Evan Thompson and Eleanor Rosch) and *The Tree of Knowledge* (1992, with Maturana), he extended his "neurophenomenological" approach to account for "the structure of human experience" generally and, by implication, the structure of literary experience.

Reference

Varela, Francisco J. "Neurophenomenology: A Methodological Remedy for the Hard Problem." *Explaining Consciousness—The "Hard Problem."* Ed. Jonathan Shear. Cambridge: MIT P, 1997. 337–57.

Steven Meyer

Vergil (Publius Vergilius Maro) (70–19 B.C.E.). Perhaps the most famous Roman poet and author of the *Georgics*, a four-book didactic poem ostensibly on the subject of farming. Although the work harkens back to the poetic **natural philosophy** of **Lucretius** and Hellenistic didacticism, the *Georgics* complies with Augustan ideology by celebrating rural traditions that contribute to the myth of Italian unity.

Jacqui Sadashige

Vernadsky, Vladimir Ivanovich (1863–1945). Author of the concept of the **nöosphere**, whose pioneering investigations of biogeochemical cycles in nature and seminal contributions to Russian history and philosophy of science continue to shape ecological and intellectual discourse in post-Soviet cultural revival. His international reputation was established during his lifetime by his empirical investigations of the interrelatedness of organic and inorganic matter, which led him to found in consecutive order the fields of genetic mineralogy, geochemistry, and biogeochemistry (Borisov, Perchonok, Roginsky 434). This fundamentally ecological view of the biosphere's dynamic composition was extended by his humanistic interest in the history of knowledge to posit the existence of the nöosphere—a stage in the evolution of the biosphere during which conscious human activity (reason) constitutes the most powerful geological (i.e., formative) force shaping the earth's organic envelope. Vernadsky's ideas combine the empirical approach (and optimism) of Soviet science with a refusal to acknowledge any possibility of ultimate or universal knowledge about nature. Thus, it is no coincidence that Vernadsky's voluminous suppressed writings on the history and philosophy of science were rediscovered in the relative intellectual freedom after 1956 with the same excitement that accompanied the discovery of Bakhtin's "dialogism" in the humanities.

References

Bailes, Kendall. *Science and Russian Culture in an Age of Revolutions: V.I. Vernadsky and His Scientific School, 1863–1945*. Bloomington: Indiana UP, 1990.

Borisov, V.M., F.F. Perchonok, and A.B. Roginsky. "Community as the Source of Vernadsky's Concept of Nöosphere." *Configurations* 1.3 (Fall 1993): 415–38.

Yvonne Howell

Verne, Jules (1828–1905). French novelist often called the father of **science fiction**. During his lifetime he produced over sixty novels. His understanding of the scientific frontiers of the day produced classics of literature that presaged developments and discoveries over a century later. One of the most salient examples of Verne's predictive powers is found in *Paris au XXe Siècle* (Paris in the Twentieth Century, 1863), originally rejected by his publisher as too fantastic. Rediscovered and published only in 1994 an overwhelming majority of the futuristic details described in the novel have been realized in this century including the electric chair and email.

Shelly Jarrett Bromberg

Vico, Giambattista (1668–1744). Neapolitan professor of **rhetoric**. He wrote the final version of his most seminal work *La scienza nuova* in 1744. In this treatise on the origins, growth, and cycling of human history, Vico points to **poetry** as the most sublime linguistic expression of **truth**. *Poeisis*, or "making," underlies his "verum ipsum factum" principle, which explains the making of human interactions, **culture**, and institutions. In taking a stand against **Descartes's** geometric method and **epistemology**, Vico claims myth and **imagination** as the universals that inform knowledge. Only through "conoscenza" (recognition) of our origins and these principles can we begin to make and understand "scienza."

Reference

Mazzotta, Giuseppe. *The New Map of the World: The Poetic Philosophy of Giambattista Vico.* Princeton, NJ: Princeton UP, 1999.

Arielle Saiber

Virtual Reality and Artificial Intelligence. Computer-generated simulations aimed at representing, respectively, the functions of the human body (in a simulated **environment**) and the human brain. Although the technologies themselves are products of different generations of the computer age, the narratives through which we perceive virtual reality and artificial intelligence function (and fail to function) in similar ways. In each case, the mind/body split gets reimprinted upon computer culture, although in different ways.

Artificial intelligence, which owes its genealogy to the late work of Alan Turing, among others, is an attempt to model at least some human thought processes using alternatively "top-down" or "bottom-up" (emergent) organizational mathematics. Turing, a British mathematician working on first-generation computers (UNIVAC and ENIAC) in the post–World War II United States, posited a thought experiment later known as the "Turing Test," in which he proposed that, given a blind set of questions and asked to answer them, any computer whose responses could not be distinguished from a human's should be considered "intelligent." This test went on to become the standard by which we measure "intelligence" in computers.

Virtual reality, a more recent development, represents the culmination of a cluster of visualization and forced-feedback computer technologies and allows for proprioceptive immersion in a "seamless" artificial environment. A key concept in the genesis of virtual reality is Norbert Wiener's foundational work on feedback control (*Cybernetics*, 1947), in which he presents a mathematicized model of the body as a series of "feedback loops"—recursive informational processes by which the body regulates its functions. In this model "outputs" are fed back into the brain's "input" system to maintain equilibrium. Virtual reality uses feedback control to determine the position and functioning of the body in a simulated space.

Both artificial intelligence and virtual reality insist, directly (systems theory) or indirectly (mathematical theories of emergence), on the ultimate "computability" of the brain and body. This transcendent narrative carries on the tradition of **Descartes's** "mind/body dualism." In particular, both technologies depend heavily on the notion of the computable brain, in what **Donna Haraway** calls the "translation of the world into a problem of coding." In more traditional behaviorist models of human cognition, the common computer/brain metaphor works both ways: The computer is like a brain and the brain is like a computer. However, in artificial intelligence, the metaphor only works one way: The brain is an organic machine and as such can be successfully stimulated by a computer. Similarly, environments and bodies in virtual reality are expressed solely as the mathematical model of a brain's sensory inputs, suggesting the illusion of absolute computability.

The key crossover between these seemingly disparate disciplines is what gets "left out" of each process. Both virtual reality and artificial intelligence attempt to offer mathematicized solutions to the problem of embodiment (*see* Corporeality/Body)—virtual reality by "resurfacing" or coding the body into digital format, and artificial intelligence by leaving it out altogether. This process reifies intelligence as superior to and separate from embodied experience. In many ways, artificial intelligence is not so much an attempt to copy a human as much as it is an attempt to answer the question, Is it possible to "think" without a body? Similarly, virtual reality is an attempt to abstract the user from his or her own body and provide alternatively an omniscient, "bodiless" perspective or a resurfaced virtual body that is incapable of physical harm. Thus both artificial intelligence and virtual reality are at root metaphysical abstractions; what gets excluded in each case is the body. One of the more popular and extreme examples of this tendency can be found in the work of Marvin Minsky, in which the dream of ultimate abstraction is dependent on the achievement of the computability of a new, machinic embodiment—"uploading" human consciousness into computer networks.

Perhaps predictably, the reason these technologies have disappointed or failed to live up to the expectations of their users is that the narrative of computability constantly runs up against the real-time problems of trying to separate the mind from the body, or even to simulate the workings of a small portion of the behavior of mind or body. As an attempt to model sensory inputs, virtual reality nevertheless relies heavily on relatively simple visualization devices, often at the expense of other forms of perception. Even when confined to visual simulations, practical virtual reality remains clunky and unconvincing because of the problem of bandwidth—the amount and rate of data needed to simulate objects in real time. Unsuccessful for the most part in real-time gaming and simulation (even military flight/tank simulators mostly still consist of closed rooms that represent their simulated environments through physical modeling, rather than computer immersion), virtual reality's dream of a completely immersive simulated world remains confined to Hollywood executives.

Despite the failure of virtual reality and artificial intelligence to live up to the transcendent narratives from which they are historically derived, some more recent applications of both technologies have garnered considerable success, perhaps due to the acknowledgment that such narratives are no longer useful. While early, **science fiction** visions of artificial intelligence's ability to achieve cognition or even sentience have proven optimistic, more recent (and more successful) artificial intelligence research has limited itself to one function of "mind"—pattern perception, motion tracking, or story generation. Phoebe Sengers and Michael Mateas, for example, have suggested that artificial intelligence be investigated as "narrative intelligence"—local, limited, and discursively constructed. Similarly, the most promising recent applications of virtual reality have been medical technologies—for example, forced-feedback machines for teleoperation of surgical procedures. None of these applications of virtual reality or artificial intelligence pretend to access the same narrative of total machinic transcendence so ubiquitous in popular cultural **representations**. Ultimately, the best uses for these technologies remain limited to specific fields such as **medicine**, rather than acceding to the more grandiose narratives of the human triumph over "nature," the body, or cognition.

References

Haraway, Donna. *Simians, Cyborgs, and Women: The Reinvention of Nature*. New York: Routledge, 1991.

Markley, Robert, ed. *Virtual Realities and Their Discontents*. Johns Hopkins UP, 1996.

Rotman, Brian. *Ad Infinitum—The Ghost in Turing's Machine: Taking God Out of Mathematics and Putting the Body Back In: An Essay in Corporeal Semiotics*. Stanford, CA: Stanford UP, 1993.

Sengers, Phoebe, and Michael Mateas, eds. *Narrative Intelligence*. Advances in Consciousness Series. Amsterdam and Philadelphia: John Benjamins, in press.

Woolley, Benjamin. *Virtual Worlds: A Journey in Hype and HyperReality*. London: Blackwell, 1992.

Helen J. Burgess

Virtuoso. Formed the rank-and-file clientele upon which the early **Royal Society**, a voluntary institution, depended. The Society's scientific program was under pressure to conform itself (often reluctantly) to the dilettantish aims of the virtuosi, which frequently included the investigation of exotic phenomena and the collection of artificial curiosities. Men of letters such as **Cowley**, Evelyn, and **Dryden** considered themselves "virtuosi," and **Boyle** called his own treatise on science and **religion** *The Christian Virtuoso* (1690). In 1676, **Thomas Shadwell** published a play entitled *The Virtuoso*, which was a comedy intended to satirize scientists in general and in particular those of the Royal Society who followed **Bacon** in taking all knowledge to be their province.

Reference

Shapiro, Barbara, and R.G. Frank, Jr. *English Scientific Virtuosi in the Sixteenth and Seventeenth Centuries*. Los Angeles: William Andrews Clark Memorial Library, 1979.

Diana B. Altegoer

Visualization. In common usage, the formation of mental images of what is not actually present, be it real object or abstract idea, essential to poetic imagery, scientific thought, and other forms of mental activity. **Albert Einstein** first formulated the **theory** of **relativity** through visualization (which he called a *Gedankenexperiment*, or **thought experiment**); in his mind's eye, he saw himself riding on a light wave while looking across to an accompanying wave. In contemporary scientific usage, visualization also means the use of **computer-**

generated images to display mathematical results, data, or natural processes in comprehensible form. In one recent example, scientists used a supercomputer to solve the intricate equations that describe the behavior of a thunderstorm and to show the result as an animated picture on a monitor screen. **Art** and **technology** work together to produce scientific visualizations that display visual **representations** of quantitative information, as in the use of a range of colors to show different temperatures during heat transfer within the sun, three-dimensional medical imaging, and animations of data gathered by instruments during planetary fly-bys and modeling of the distribution of charged particles in the ionosphere.

Sidney Perkowitz and Pamela Gossin

Vitruvius, Marcus Pollio (first century B.C.E). Roman architect and **engineer** and author of *De architectura libri decem* (Ten Books on Architecture), one of the most influential books surviving from classical antiquity and an important source for the history of **art**, science, and **technology**. Vitruvius covers subjects ranging from construction techniques to acoustics, aesthetic theory, and the education of architects. He gained much of his influence through two leading figures of the Italian Renaissance, Leone Battista Alberti (1404–1472) and Andrea Palladio (1518–1580), who promulgated the "Vitruvian aesthetic," the idea that the proportions of the universe and the human body furnish an aesthetic ideal that can be applied to the design of structures. A number of writers, including **Ben Jonson**, **Dryden**, and **Pope**, extended this aesthetic to **poetry**, so that architecture became a model for design for poems and orations as well as for buildings.

References

Erskine-Hill, Howard. "Heirs of Vitruvius: Pope and the Idea of Architecture." *The Art of Alexander Pope*. Ed. H. Erskine-Hill and A. Smith. New York: Barnes and Noble, 1979. 144–56.

Johnson, A.W. *Ben Jonson: Poetry and Architecture*. Oxford: Clarendon, 1994.

Kathryn A. Neeley

Volcanoes. The emergence of hot gases and rock through cracks in the earth's crust, forming a molten mountain. Volcanoes appear in literature as early as **Homer's** *Odyssey*, if one accepts the common **theory** that the Cyclops is a personification of Mount Etna. The earliest literal description of an erupting Etna in **poetry** is by Pindar (c. 500 B.C.E.). The philosopher Empedocles (c. 480 B.C.E.), who wrote verses now lost, lived near the summit for a time and was first to study Etna in detail. **Lucretius** and **Ovid** both mentioned Etna in major poems of the first century B.C.E. "Aetna," an anonymous work in Latin hexameters once attributed to **Vergil**, is a thoroughly scientific poem on volcanic action as it was understood in the first century A.D. Vergil's description of Etna in the *Aeneid* is quoted in "Thule, the Period of Cosmography," a Renaissance madrigal from around 1600 that includes eruptions by Hecla (in Iceland) and Fogo (in the Cape Verde Islands) as well. Holderlin's never-completed drama *Empedolklus* (1790s) and **Matthew Arnold's** "Empedocles on Etna" (1852) also utilize Vergil. The Phlegraean Fields, a recently active volcanic area near Naples, influenced other parts of Vergil's *Aeneid*. Monte Nuovo formed there overnight in 1538 and is well documented in contemporary accounts. A more famous eruption account is Pliny the Younger's of Vesuvius (and the death of his uncle) in A.D. 79. **Bulwer-Lytton's** novel *The Last Days of Pompeii* (1834) and the many **film** versions of it, not to mention Pompeii itself, have maintained the reputation of Vesuvius as the most famous volcano in the world. Numerous literary works set in **Italy** during the eighteenth and nineteenth centuries make use of it, and there is a prodigious pictorial record as well. After years of frequent activity (1631 ff.), Vesuvius has been dormant since 1944. The eruptions of Tamboro in 1815 and of Krakatoa in 1883 (both Indonesian) each had some literary influence, and volcanic imagery has been popular with many writers.

References

Altick, Richard D. "Four Victorian Poets and an Exploding Island." *Victorian Studies* 3 (1959): 249–60.
Leppmann, Wolfgang. *Pompeii in Fact and Fiction*. London: Elek, 1968.
Matthews, G.M. "A Volcano's Voice in Shelley." *ELH* 24 (1957): 191–228.

Dennis R. Dean

Voltaire (Arouet, François-Marie) (1694–1778). French writer, philosopher, historiographer, and leading figure of the **Enlightenment**. Although Voltaire began his career intent on perfecting French **poetry** and **drama**, his youthful experience as an exile in England convinced him that some of the most compelling ideas were emanating from science and **philosophy** and that the duty of the contemporary man of letters was to disseminate those ideas with style and clarity. Those principles informed Voltaire's *Lettres philosophiques* (Letters Concerning the English Nation, 1734), where he celebrated the English people's religious toleration, political and economic freedom, and high esteem for thinkers like Isaac Newton (*see* Newtonianism), whom Voltaire revered as a founder of experimental philosophy.

Soon thereafter, Voltaire summarized Newtonian **physics** in the *Eléments de la philosophie de Newton* (1738), aiming both to combat **René Descartes's** philosophy and to acquaint the French public with Newton's **optics** and principle of gravitational attraction. He wrote this work while living in semiretirement at Cirey, when his intense intellectual curiosity prompted him to undertake experiments in science as well as in playwriting and stage production.

Voltaire's massive correspondence and many polemical works show that he kept abreast of an impressive number of scientific and philosophical authors. He was also a guiding spirit behind the *Encyclopédie* but wrote only a few, cautious articles for that project. Voltaire is best known today for philosophical tales like *Candide* (1759), a tragicomic **satire** of novelistic conventions in which Gottfried Wilhelm Leibniz's system of optimism is ripped to shreds (along with countless fictional bodies) under the onslaught of such real-life calamities as syphilis, war, and the Spanish Inquisition.

Reference

Besterman, Theodore. *Voltaire*. New York: Harcourt, Brace, and World, 1969.

Anne C. Vila

Vonnegut, Kurt, Jr. (1922–   ). American novelist, humorist, and social commentator. Since 1952, when *Player Piano*, his first novel, was published, he has used his **fiction** as a form of social critique—specifically, as the means of conducting a skeptical social analysis of the role of science and **technology** in Western culture generally and in American culture in particular. Vonnegut comes by some of his perceptions of that role firsthand. He was, for three years (1948–1951), a publicist for the General Electric Corporation, a company that for some time claimed that "**progress** is our most important product." His brother Bernard, an atmospheric scientist, was also on staff at GE, where he was a colleague of the physicist Irving Langmuir, among others.

Vonnegut's skeptical viewpoint owes a good deal to his education. He flunked out of Cornell (in residence, 1940–1943), where he had gone at his father's urging to pursue a career in science, like his brother. He subsequently flunked out of a wartime military intensive engineering (*see* Engineer(s)/Engineering) training program. Despite not having taken a bachelor's degree, Vonnegut embarked upon graduate training as an anthropologist while a GI Bill student at the University of Chicago (1946–1948). Although his thesis proposals were consistently rejected, he received his M.A. belatedly in 1971, his novel *Cat's Cradle* (1963) having been accepted as his thesis.

Vonnegut uses an anthropological point of view to examine the disparity between the narratives we invoke to construct ourselves as a cultural entity and the lived social reality that those narratives inscribe and enable. *Player Piano*, for example, is an almost prescient look at the effect of automation and a mass-consumption market economy on cultural autonomy and self-esteem. It begs the question of whether labor-saving devices actually make life better, as the government-industrial combine of the novel say they do, by enhancing that life's material basis, or whether those devices diminish the quality of life by subverting and, ultimately, by demeaning the dignity of human labor, especially creative and artisanal labor. *Cat's Cradle* subjects the scientific "innocence" of one Felix Hoenikker, who is modeled on Langmuir and who, like Langmuir, is one of the "fathers" of the A-Bomb, to a scathing critique for its failure to account for the social consequences of his discoveries and their applications. The world of *Cat's Cradle* ends not in fire, but in ice, when Hoenikker's last discovery, "ice-nine," infects the waters of the world, freezing them, all that is in them, and all that comes in contact with them, instantly. In *Galapagos* (1985),

Vonnegut reprises a different doomsday scenario, caused by artificial scarcity and greed masquerading as business acumen. The upshot of this ending is to demonstrate most pointedly that the laws of evolution still apply and that our inheritors will not be those who extend the mental dexterity of the human brain and the manual dexterity of the opposable thumb but rather those whose sleek, furry bodies, webbed extremities, and bullet heads make them better suited to swim among the Galapagos islands and catch the fish that are the staple of their diet.

Vonnegut's most famous novel is *Slaughterhouse Five* (1969). In it, he builds on his experience as a prisoner of war held in Dresden during the Allied fire-bombing of that city to present a simultaneously sad and funny meditation on our sense of human contingency and the terrible atrocities committed in the name of those causes—just and unjust alike—that we understand as calling for swift and decisive action. As for life in the universe, Vonnegut opines, it exists in more diversity and variety than we are capable of perceiving or imagining. As for death, "so it goes" is the phrase of acknowledgment that valorizes death as both inevitable and part of a process that human beings grasp but dimly. The only truly terrible acts are those we commit in ignorance of this **reality** and in the name of some higher reality we invoke by way of self-justification.

References

Allen, William Rodney. *Understanding Kurt Vonnegut.* Columbia: U of South Carolina P, 1991.

Leeds, Marc. *The Vonnegut Encyclopedia: An Authorized Compendium.* Westport, CT: Greenwood, 1995.

Merrill, Robert. *Critical Essays on Kurt Vonnegut.* Boston: G.K. Hall, 1990.

Mustazza, Leonard. *The Critical Response to Kurt Vonnegut.* Westport, CT: Greenwood, 1994.

Stuart Peterfreund

W

War Technology. The instruments, **information**, weapons, and machinery used to conduct warfare. Whereas close-combat technologies have dominated much war writing, the distancing effect and increased autonomy of war technologies have impacted techniques of **representation** in texts like Stephen Crane's *The Red Badge of Courage* (1895), Ernst Jünger's *In Stahlgewittern* (1922), **Thomas Pynchon's** *Gravity's Rainbow* (1973), and Jean Baudrillard's *The Gulf War Did Not Take Place* (1995).

Nicholas Spencer

Water. Biologically critical resource and preeminent commodity that has played a crucial role in the development of human **culture** and civilization. The ancient Nile civilizations, Chinese dynasties, Mayan civilizations, and others were dominated by elite groups capable of building and affording water delivery **mechanisms**. That process continues. In the United States, for example, the settlement of the American West grew from the Myth of the **Garden**, which posited that "rain would follow the plow." The ecological and literary ramifications of water's ascendancy took shape in and are reflected by the regional literature.

Reference

Worster, Donald. *Rivers of Empire: Water, Aridity and the Growth of the American West.* New York: Pantheon, 1985.

David N. Cassuto

Watson, James Dewey (1928–   ). American molecular biologist, research administrator. Watson's best-seller *The Double Helix: A Personal Account of the Discovery of the Structure of DNA* (1968) first revealed scientific competition and motives to many nonscientists. Many scientists deplored its candor. It has been analyzed as a folktale in which crystallographer Rosalind Franklin was a wicked witch and Linus Pauling was a distant wizard. Feminist critics have emphasized the extent of Watson's sexism both with respect to Franklin and the general rejection of women scientists.

Reference

The Double Helix: Text, Commentary, Reviews, Original Papers. Norton Critical Ed. Ed.
    Gunther S. Stent. New York: Norton, 1980.

Val Dusek

Wells, H[erbert] G[eorge] (1866–1946). English novelist. Along with **Jules Verne**, considered to be a founding father of **science fiction**. A prolific writer now best remembered for his so-called scientific romances. In these, Wells described technological feats still outside science's reach: best exemplified by *The Time Machine* (1895), *The Island of Dr Moreau* (1896), *The Invisible Man* (1897), *The War of the Worlds* (1898), and *The First Men in the Moon* (1901). Wells also constructed **utopias** that feature futuristic **technology**; for example, *When the Sleeper Wakes* (1899), *A Modern Utopia* (1905), *Men Like Gods* (1923), and *The Shape of Things to Come* (1933).

Wells studied at London's Normal School of Science (now Imperial College) where he was greatly influenced by **Darwinism** and its great promulgator, **T.H. Huxley**. After college, Wells worked briefly as a science tutor and published a **biology** textbook. Later he collaborated with **Julian Huxley** and his son, G.P. Wells, to produce an encyclopedic **popularization** of biology entitled *The Science of Life* (1929–1930). At the end of his career, he was awarded a D.Sc. by London University for a thesis written when he was seventy-six years old.

However, it was as a novelist and essayist that Wells chiefly made his mark, though, not surprisingly, science and its role in society (*see* Scientists in/and Society) is a major theme in this writing. Wells's scientific romances are often admired for domesticating the impossible, for rendering scientific extrapolations plausible as well as exciting. His aim was not always accurate prediction, and he knew his romances were not always scientifically possible. But he did have a real desire to inform and interest readers in science and in science's imaginative possibilities and often grounded his fantasies in sound scientific principles. Though it is difficult to generalize, Wells's attitude to science and technology was that both had great potential for good or evil. Both placed tremendous power in human hands and therefore needed careful consideration.

References

Haynes, Roslynn D. *H.G. Wells: Discoverer of the Future.* New York: New York UP,
    1980.
Huntington, John. *The Logic of Fantasy: H.G. Wells and Science Fiction.* New York:
    Columbia UP, 1982.

June Deery

Werner, Abraham Gottlob (1749–1817). Renowned teacher of earth sciences at the mining academy of Freiberg, near Dresden. He was the author of influential geological theory in which major rock types comprising much of the earth's surface were held to have been laid down uniquely in successive stages of withdrawal (Primary, Secondary, Transitional, Volcanic, Alluvial) by a once global ocean. Granite, he taught, was the oldest rock and had been deposited from water before the advent of life on earth; it therefore contained no fossils. Volcanic agencies were for him late, local, and relatively insignificant. Werner asserted, on inadequate evidence, that the sequence of rock layers adjacent to Freiberg was valid worldwide. His various theories were refuted within his lifetime, often by his own students, some of whom he had made into superb field geologists (without being one himself). He is best known to literary scholars for his profound influence on **Goethe** and **Novalis**, both of whom studied under him. **Coleridge** and **Carlyle**, among other British writers, were familiar with his theories. There are many literary references to the ongoing dispute (1802–1817) in Edinburgh between his partisans and those of the local geologist **James Hutton**, whose views eventually prevailed.

References

Dean, Dennis R. *James Hutton and the History of Geology.* Ithaca: Cornell UP, 1992.
Ospovat, Alexander M. "The Work and Influence of Abraham Gottlob Werner: A Reevaluation." *Actes du XIIIE Congres International d'Histoire des Sciences* [for 1971] 8 (1974): 123–30.

Dennis R. Dean

Wharton, Edith [Newbold Jones] (1862–1937). American novelist. Her correspondence, autobiography, and **fiction** attest to her intense interest in evolution (*see* Evolutionary Theory). Conflating scientific methodology and narrative strategies, she offers instructive examples to counter those popular beliefs associated with biological **determinism**. Her stories "Angel at the Grave" (1901) and "Descent of Man" (1904) address Darwinian (*see* Darwinism) issues of sexual selection and examine popular **representations** of scientists and their theories. Her novels *The Age of Innocence* (1920) and *The House of Mirth* (1905) explore notions of hybridization and transplantation.

References

Schrieber, MarySuzanne. "Darwin, Wharton, and 'The Descent of Man' ": Blueprints of American Society." *Studies in American Fiction* 17 (1980): 31–38.
Singley, Carol. *Matters of Mind and Spirit.* New York: Cambridge UP, 1995.

Sandra J. Chrystal

Whewell, William (1794–1866). Referred to variously as "polymath," "omniscientist," and "metascientific critic." Whewell produced accomplishments so wide-ranging that they defy **classification**. Whewell was a fellow and later Master (1841–1866) of Trinity College, Cambridge, and authored over 125 publications on subjects ranging from theology to **engineering**. Much of his career was devoted to establishing the intellectual, cultural, and moral value of science. His *History of the Inductive Sciences* (1837) helped establish the synthetic narrative **history of science** as a distinctive literary form. It exemplifies the rich use of metaphor and theatrical quality that characterize much of his writing. He coined a number of important scientific terms, including the term "scientist," translated **poetry**, and wrote some verse of his own. In *Gentlemen of Science*, he is referred to as "the Great Roman Candle of Science and Literature" (Morrell and Thackray 428), an epithet that captures his personality, his encyclopedic scholarly interests, and his legacy in the language and literature of science.

Whewell advanced a conception of science that sought to associate it with feeling and **imagination**. Although he was an ardent advocate of science, Whewell believed in a comprehensive education, which links knowledge of the past (classical authors) to questions of the present and future (mathematics and science). Both his scholarly accomplishments and his **philosophy** of education demonstrate the range and importance of interdisciplinary studies of literature and science.

References

Fisch, Menachem, and Simon Schaffer. *William Whewell: A Composite Portrait*. Oxford: Clarendon, 1991.

Morrell, Jack, and Arnold Thackray. *Gentlemen of Science: The Early Years of the British Association for the Advancement of Science*. Oxford: Clarendon, 1981.

Yeo, Richard. *Defining Science: William Whewell, Natural Knowledge, and Public Debate in Early Victorian Britain*. Cambridge: Cambridge UP, 1993.

Kathryn A. Neeley

White, Gilbert (1720–1793). Natural historian, disciple of such predecessors in **natural history** (and **natural theology**) as **John Ray** and **William Derham**. White was the author of several texts—most notably, the *Natural History of Selborne* (1789), the most popular work of natural history before **Darwin's** *Origin of Species*. Darwin, in fact, refers admiringly to White's study of the earthworm in his own work.

White attended school at Farnham and Basingstoke, then took his baccalaureate at Oriel College, Oxford, becoming a fellow of Oriel in 1743. He returned to his native region in 1761, as curate of Faringdon, only two miles from Selborne, the village of his birth and of his grandfather's parish. There, White lovingly studied the flora, fauna, geology, and **meteorology** of his native ground. In 1784, upon the death of the incumbent, White became curate of Selborne.

The distillation of White's studies is to be found in the *Natural History of Selborne*, an epistolary text in which White shares the specifics of the region, in the context of his reading in and study of natural history, with correspondents

Thomas Pennant and Daines Barrington. In addition to demonstrating a thoroughgoing knowledge of the discourse of natural history, White embellishes his text with copious allusions to the poets—most particularly to **Vergil** and **Milton**. The final letters of White's text, which deal with some twenty or more years of apocalyptic weather, suggest that the larger frame for his natural history is the Judeo-Christian theodicy, as this is brought into the study of natural history by the likes of Thomas Burnet in his *Sacred Theory of the Earth* (1690–1691).

References

Foster, Paul. *Gilbert White and His Records: A Scientific Biography*. London: Christopher Helm, 1988.
Mabey, Richard. *Gilbert White: A Biography of the Author of the Natural History of Selborne*. London: Century, 1986.
White, Gilbert. *Gilbert White's Journals*. Cambridge: MIT, 1971.

Stuart Peterfreund

Whitman, Walt (1819–1892). American poet, author of *Leaves of Grass*, which appeared in nine distinct editions during his lifetime. In the preface to the first edition (1855), Whitman characterized scientists as "the lawgivers of poets" whose "construction underlies the structure of every perfect poem." His understanding and use of contemporary science and **technology** has attracted diverse critical attention. The psychiatrist Richard M. Bucke, author of *Cosmic Consciousness* (1901), proposed that "the whole modern theory of evolution seem[s] to have been present . . . in his mind from the first." Scholnick has traced Whitman's understanding of evolution (*see* Evolutionary Theory) in relation to the scientific popularizer Edward L. Youmans. In *Walt Whitman and Sir William Osler* (1995), Philip W. Leon contextualizes Osler's 1919 reminiscence of his years as Whitman's **physician**.

Reference

Scholnick, Robert J. " 'The Password Primeval': Whitman's Use of Science in 'Song of Myself.' " *Studies in the American Renaissance*. Ed. Joel Myerson. Charlottesville: UP of Virginia, 1986.

Steven Meyer

Wilde, Oscar (1854–1900). Dublin-born writer known for his wit and **art** criticism as well as **fiction**. Wilde studied under **John Ruskin** and Walter Pater, combining interest in the arts with study of scientific **philosophy**. The latter informs Wilde's use of biological metaphor, particularly evident in *The Portrait of Dorian Gray* (1891). This work also contains the character of Lord Henry, a Faustian amateur naturalist. Positivist leanings in Wilde's worldview appear in such **essays** as "The Soul of Man under Socialism" (1891).

Reference

Foster, John Wilson. "Against Nature? Science and Oscar Wilde." *University of Toronto Quarterly* 63 (Winter 1993–1994): 328–45.

Alison E. Bright

Wilkins, John (1614–1672). Divine, linguist, Fellow of the **Royal Society**. The center of the Wadham College (Oxford) scientific circle in the 1650s, Wilkins was one of the founders of the Royal Society, a leading latitudinarian (liberal Anglican) spokesperson for the harmony of science and **religion**, and an important promoter of **natural philosophy** (his *Discourse Concerning a New Planet* [1640] popularized heliocentric **astronomy**). In *The Discovery of a World in the Moone* (1638) he argued that the moon was habitable, suggested (in the 1640 edition) the possibility of lunar travel and colonization, and "established the conventions" of the literary moon voyage "for more than a century" (Nicolson 94). Robert Paltock's romance *Peter Wilkins* (1751) pays eponymous homage. Wilkins is perhaps best known as a linguistic reformer and "chief source of the Royal Society doctrines about language and style" (Aarsleff 5)—doctrines satirized by **Jonathan Swift** in the School of Languages in *Gulliver's Travels*. In his pioneering *Essay Towards a Real Character and a Philosophical Language* (1668), Wilkins proposed an important (but ultimately unsuccessful) artificial universal language scheme that offered a "scientific" ideographic sign system in which characters would "signifie *things*, and not *words*" (Wilkins 21) and thereby (it was hoped) precisely mirror the natural order.

References

Aarsleff, Hans. "John Wilkins (1614–1672): A Sketch of His Life and Work." *John Wilkins and 17th-Century British Linguistics*. Ed. Joseph L. Subbiondo. Amsterdam: John Benjamins, 1992. 3–41.

Nicolson, Marjorie Hope. *Voyages to the Moon*. 1948. New York: Macmillan, 1960.

Shapiro, Barbara J. *John Wilkins, 1614–1672: An Intellectual Biography*. Berkeley: U of California P, 1969.

Slaughter, Mary M. *Universal Languages and Scientific Taxonomy in the Seventeenth Century*. Cambridge: Cambridge UP, 1982.

Wilkins, John. *An Essay Towards a Real Character, and a Philosophical Language*. Menston, England: Scolar P, 1968.

Lisa Zeitz

Williams, William Carlos (1883–1963). **Physician** and poet, author of many works thematizing science, such as "St. Francis Einstein of the Daffodils" (1921) and *The Embodiment of Knowledge* (1928–1930). In the latter work Williams proposed that **poetry** "be defined not by its superficial features [such as prosody] but by its character as an effect related to science, . . . by **physics** and not grammar." He also insisted—following Whitehead, whom he first read in 1927—that much of science was "a lie," consisting of abstractions falsely treated as actualities. Critics have traced the relations between Williams's poetry and modern **technology**. Hugh Crawford has argued for the importance of Williams's medical training and practice in his conception of writing.

Reference

Crawford, Hugh T. *Modernism, Medicine and William Carlos Williams*. Norman: U of Oklahoma P, 1993.

Steven Meyer

Wilson, Edward O. (1929–   ). World-renowned American biologist noted for his theories and work in **sociobiology**, human nature, social insects, **biodiversity**, and environmentalism. His work has won numerous scientific and literary awards, including the National Medal of Science, Audubon Medal, and two Pulitzer Prizes. He emerged as a leading expert and advocate-at-large for the preservation of biological diversity in the 1980s. "The one process now going on that will take millions of years to correct is the loss of genetic and species diversity," Wilson wrote in 1980. "This is the folly our descendants are least likely to forgive us" (qtd. in *Naturalist* 355).

Earning a doctorate in **biology** from Harvard in 1955, Wilson has taught there ever since. He became widely known in 1975 with the publication of *Sociobiology: The New Synthesis*. Arguing that human nature was, in part, genetically determined, Wilson sparked off debate among experts on evolutionary biology that continues into the 1990s. Wilson followed this book with *The Insects* in 1977 (he is an ant biologist, by training) and the Pulitzer Prize–winning *On Human Nature* in 1978.

In the 1970 and 1980s, while continuing his research on insect societies to the functioning of world's ecosystems, Wilson became convinced that an ecological crisis was forming as humans destroyed tropical habitats at alarming rates. Wilson's scientific realization prompted him to become an environmental "activist," along with other prominent biologists like Norman Myers and Paul Ehrlich (*Naturalist* 358). As a biodiversity advocate, Wilson published *Biophilia* in 1984, edited *BioDiversity* in 1988, and wrote the best-selling *The Diversity of Life* in 1992. These works combined scientific data with a potent **conservation** message of the ethical and ecological imperative of preserving the world's dwindling biodiversity and ecosystems.

An eloquent and forceful advocate for biodiversity conservation, Wilson's expertise has been sought out by environmental organizations and governments around the world. In 1996 *Time* magazine picked Wilson as one of the twenty-five most influential Americans, dubbing him "an ecological Paul Revere." Continuing his passionate and reasoned defense of nature, Wilson's most recent works include *In Search of Nature* (1996) and *Consilience: The Unity of Knowledge* (1998).

References

Kinch, John A. "Edward O. Wilson." *Newsmakers* 4(1994): 533–37.
Wilson, Edward O. *Naturalist*. Washington: Island, 1995.

John A. Kinch

Wollstonecraft, Mary (1759–1797). British feminist whose political views were informed by science. Her conversations with Dr. Richard Price, a Presbyterian clergyman and scientist, and with James Sowerby, a naturalist, shaped her subsequent writing. *Vindication of the Rights of Woman* (1792) investigates the influence of the **environment** on the individual, argues that both women and men are born with the facility to learn, and concludes that improved education of women would benefit society. The text anticipates later psychological reflections on sexual selection, repression, and desire. She married William Godwin and died following the birth of her second daughter, **Mary Wollstonecraft Godwin Shelley**, the author of *Frankenstein*.

References

Kelly, Gary. *Revolutionary Feminism—The Mind and Career of Mary Wollstonecraft*. New York: St. Martin's, 1992.
Poovey, Mary. *The Proper Lady and the Woman Writer: Ideology in the Works of Mary Wollstonecraft, Mary Shelley, and Jane Austen*. Chicago: U of Chicago P, 1984.

Sandra J. Chrystal

Woolf, [Adeline] Virginia [née Stephen] (1882–1941). Author of several groundbreaking, stream-of-consciousness novels, most famously, *To the Lighthouse* (1927). Woolf brought techniques to her literary **problem solving** that mirror the activities of the scientist at work. She kept a diary that served the same purposes as scientists' notebooks: to record her observations and memorialize her literary **hypotheses** and **problem-solving** methods. Woolf also completed numerous short sketches—primarily unpublished during her lifetime—that she utilized as pilot studies to test the effectiveness of particular writing techniques. When Woolf wrote her first novel experimenting with the stream-of-consciousness style, *Jacob's Room* (1922), she envisioned it as resulting from three of her shorter sketches joining hands and dancing in unison. In these three sketches Woolf conducted experiments in unifying her **fiction** by means other than an omniscient narrator, the employment of alternative perspectives, and the poetic limitations of prose. That is, Woolf incorporated rhythms in the net of words she used to capture the mental and material lives of her characters relying, as poets do, on word meaning as well as cadence in her efforts to represent experience.

Like scientific experiments, Woolf's novel writing was guided by preconceived designs. For example, *The Waves* (1931) utilized a structure akin to the longitudinal design formulated by psychological researchers to study the universal features of human development. The mental development of this novel's six characters is depicted in episodes separated by italicized interludes, which reflect the intervening passage of **time**, and the universal features of human **psychology** are thus highlighted.

Reference

Woolf, Virginia. *A Writer's Diary*. San Diego, CA: Harcourt Brace, 1981.

Maria F. Ippolito

Wordsworth, William (1770–1850). Romantic poet of nature, who appears to be the English literary figure least sympathetic to science. "We murder to dissect," he famously exclaimed. But his **poetry** also articulates a dynamic nature congruent with some tendencies in contemporary science: "There is an active principle alive/In all things." This ambivalence reflects his attitude to the divergent practices of the **natural philosophy** of his day: the investigation of phenomena within a universalizing, teleological framework, and an alternative experimentation which excludes larger purposes, interrelationships, and beliefs. While this ambivalence surfaces throughout his lifetime, poems from two distinct periods of composition appropriate the discourses of specific scientific developments with which he had direct or indirect contact.

In the 1790s, Wordsworth made the acquaintance of **Coleridge's** network of scientific friends, most of whom were their neighbors in the West Country: Thomas Beddoes, John Thelwall, **Humphry Davy**, and **Erasmus Darwin**. These individuals, for a short time at least, concurred in an extreme version of an "active principle" theory, traces of which can be found in Wordsworth's poetry of 1797–1800.

According to this theory, the sun produces light, an active principle identical to or convertible into (atmospheric) **electricity** and/or depholgisticated air (i.e., oxygen). Plants photosynthesize sunlight into oxygen, which is then respired by animals. It circulates through the bloodstream to the brain where it is transmuted into a "nervous juice" with electrical properties. This product of nature—sunlight/electricity/oxygen—functions in humans as the **mechanism** of thought and will.

The connection between natural phenomena (sun, plants, air) and mental functions is extended into the moral dimension by means of nervous vibrations, progressing from physical pleasure to intellectual satisfaction to moral habits and spiritual insight, on the basis of David Hartley's associationism. In Wordsworth's "Tintern Abbey" and the 1799 *Prelude*, this nervous motion is translated into pulsation, "Felt in the blood and felt along the heart." Thus his most optimistic poetry draws on scientific confirmation that human beings will flourish in a natural **environment** which provides physical resources for intellectual and especially moral improvement. His **philosophy** of the One Life circulates a necessitarian discourse: Human beings are ontologically homogeneous with "the life of things" they inuit.

This is, however, tantamount to pantheism, from which Wordsworth began to withdraw into a more orthodox dualism of mind and matter after 1805. His poetry continued to represent nature as a positive influence and a beneficial environment, but humans were no longer integrated into its physical processes.

However, a second network of scientific contacts coalesced around Trinity

College, Cambridge, after Wordworth's brother became Master in 1820, including the geologists, Adam Sedgwick and **William Whewell**. Despite the sarcasm directed at the collector of discrete samples ("he who with pocket hammer smites the edge/Of luckless rock"), Wordsworth shared these geologists' larger view. They accept that nature—the earth, landscape, human life—suffers change and loss, decay and decline, in the confidence that these represent stages in a progressive, ordered unity. Poet and scientists alike sought universal laws—moral as well as physical—which confirmed the Divine Plan, explicitly the subject of *The Excursion.*

Thus Wordsworth is not only the poet of nature but the poet of natural philosophy: His early pantheism absorbed the active principles of contemporary **chemistry**, while his later writings echo a science which raise the mind in contemplation of God in his works.

References

Bate, Jonathan. *Romantic Ecology: Wordsworth and the Environmental Tradition.* London: Routledge, 1991.

Durrant, Geoffrey H. *Wordsworth and the Great System.* Cambridge: Cambridge UP, 1970.

Piper, Herbert W. *The Active Universe: Pantheism and the Concepts of the Imagination in the English Romantic Poets.* London: Athlone Press, 1962.

Thomas, W.K., and Warren U. Ober. *A Mind for Ever Voyaging: Wordsworth at Work Portraying Newton and Science.* Edmonton: U of Alberta P, 1989.

Wyatt, John. *Wordsworth and the Geologists.* Cambridge: Cambridge UP, 1995.

Jennifer FitzGerald

World Wide Web. Is a hypertextual (*see* Hypertext) communications service on the **Internet**. With the introduction of the graphical browser in 1993, the Web has redefined the Internet as a major cultural site for entertainment and business as well as scientific and academic communication.

Jay David Bolter

Writing across the Curriculum. A pedagogical movement aimed at increasing writing skills through a sense of active involvement in the subject matter. This movement, known in Britain as Language across the Curriculum, began with Elaine Maimon and others in the 1970s as a response to increasing public and professional demand for a higher standard of writing among students. It incorporates the use of cross-curricular material (i.e., sciences, humanities, economics, etc.) as a means to engage students personally in their work. Writing across the curriculum is process-based, making use of workshop exercises to help develop skills in organizational development, summary, and peer response and thereby building a solid foundation for final written drafts.

Helen J. Burgess

X–Z

X-ray. Electromagnetic radiation used for medical imaging. Discovered in 1895 by German scientist Wilhelm Roentgen, the X-ray captured the popular **imagination** at the same time that it transformed medical practice. It became newly possible to see the unseen. Too-persistent experimenters throughout Europe and the United States gave themselves radiation burns in their excited search for an effective X-ray imaging device. Spiritualists and psychical researchers meanwhile seized on the possibility that the device would capture ghostly forms. X-ray vision became a new, superheroic model of penetrating inspection. Some of the social and literary implications of the new phenomenon were explored by **Thomas Mann** in *The Magic Mountain* (*Der Zauberberg*, 1927). Mann's tubercular protagonist, Hans Castorp, treasures the chest X-ray of a woman patient at his sanitorium, while the technologically generated image offers him a powerfully contradictory blend of intimacy and alienation.

Lisa Gitelman

Yeats, William Butler (1865–1939). Irish poet, awarded a Nobel Prize in 1924, who professed to hate science "with a monkish hate" (*Autobiographies* 82). Despite a youthful flirtation with **Darwinism**, he conceded authority to science only in its occult forms: as images and ideas drawn from theosophy, **alchemy**, and **astrology**. He followed **Blake** in demonizing **Bacon**, Newton (*see* Newtonianism), and **Locke** in a poetic fragment published in 1928 ("Locke sank into a swoon . . ."). Conjuring truth from nothing asserts Yeats's distrust of scientific **empiricism**, especially its reliance on generalizability. "Two and two cannot be four, for nature has no two things alike" (*Essays* 443). This skepticism toward science sensitized Yeats to the epistemological tremors accompanying the emergence of **relativity** and quantum theory: "[I]n two or three generations," he wrote in 1937, "it will become generally known that the mechanical theory [by which he meant classical **physics**] has no reality" (*Essays* 518); and, like

Einstein, he discerned the capacity of scientists to rationalize away troublesome data.

Yeats wrote a play, *The Resurrection* (1931), dramatizing precisely this behavior. In it, Greek and Hebrew (bespeaking rationalism and empiricism) manufacture artifice after artifice to explain Christ's empty tomb, until, when finally He appears, their systems collapse before them. As this play suggests, Yeats was interested less in science than in its **epistemology**, in what evidence it might inadvertently provide that "natural and supernatural are knit together" (*Essays* 518). Eccentric, surely; but such ideas led him to perceptive intuitions about dilemmas with which scientists and philosophers still struggle.

References

Friedman, Barton R. "Yeatsian (Meta)physics: *The Resurrection* and the Irrational."
    Yeats: An Annual of Critical and Textual Studies 8(1990): 144–65.
Gorski, William T. *Yeats and Alchemy*. Albany: State U of New York P, 1996.
Olney, James. *The Rhizome and the Flower: The Perennial Philosophy—Yeats and Jung*.
    Berkeley: U of California P, 1980.
Yeats, William Butler. *Autobiographies*. London: Macmillan, 1926.
———. *Essays and Introductions*. New York: Macmillan, 1961.

Barton Friedman

Zola, Émile (1840–1902). French novelist, journalist, and critic whose fictional cycle *Les Rougon-Macquart* (1871–1893) exemplified the vogue of **naturalism** in nineteenth-century literature and **art**. Designed as a comprehensive natural and social history of a single extended family, this twenty-novel series was imbued with the period's reigning scientific ideas and cultural myths, including heredity and **thermodynamics**. Zola attempted to codify the methodology of the naturalist or **experimental novel** in his essay "Le Roman expérimental" (1880), where he argued that the experimental methods established by Claude Bernard for biomedical science could be directly transposed into literature. Zola also wrote "J'Accuse" (1898), a celebrated diatribe against the trial of Alfred Dreyfus, a Jewish military officer who was unjustly accused and convicted of treason and finally exonerated many years later.

Reference

Serres, Michel. *Feux et signaux de brume: Zola*. Paris: Grasset, 1975. Translated excerpt:
    "Language and Space: From Oedipus to Zola." *Hermès: Literature, Science, Philosophy*. Ed. Josué V. Harari and David F. Bell. Baltimore: Johns Hopkins UP,
    1982. 34–53.

Anne C. Vila

Zukav, Gary (19?–   ). Author of the scientific **popularization** *The Dancing Wu Li Masters: An Overview of the New Physics* (1979). In a similar manner to **Fritjof Capra**, Zukav argues that concepts in twentieth-century **physics** are to be found in ancient Eastern philosophies. His *The Seat of the Soul* (1989), a national best-seller about evolution (*see* Evolutionary Theory) and the soul, has reached a wide popular "New Age" audience, due in large part to being featured on the daytime talk show *Oprah.*

June Deery and Pamela Gossin

SELECTED BIBLIOGRAPHY

BIBLIOGRAPHIC NOTE

The standard bibliographic resource in LS studies is *The Relations of Literature and Science: An Annotated Bibliography of Scholarship, 1880–1980* (MLA, 1987), edited by Walter Schatzberg, Ronald A. Waite, and Jonathan K. Johnson. Annual bibliographies were published in *Symposium, Clio*, and *PSLS: The Publication of the Society for Literature and Science* and now appear in the Society's award-winning journal *Configurations: A Journal of Literature, Science and Technology* (1993–   ). Another journal of ongoing significance to LS is *Literature and Medicine* (vols. 1–   ), with the retrospective issue published in volume 10 (1991) of special interest.

Students of LS can find additional information about individual figures important to LS and pertinent contextual background on scientific and literary concepts and developments by consulting standard reference tools in their respective disciplines, such as the *MLA Bibliography*, the *Isis Cumulative Bibliography* and *Isis Critical Bibliographies* for the History of Science, the *Dictionary of Literary Biography*, the *Dictionary of Scientific Biography*, and the *Companion to the History of Modern Science* as well as the new *The Biographical Dictionary of Women in Science*, edited by Marilyn Ogilvie and Joy Dorothy Harvey (2 vols.).

SELECTED WORKS

The list below represents some of the texts that have been formative, transformative, and/or of ongoing, general interest to LS scholarship. The list is by no means exhaustive.

Amrine, Frederick, ed. *Literature and Science as Modes of Expression*. Boston Studies in the Philosophy of Science. Vol. 115. Dordrecht and Boston: Kluwer Academic Publishers, 1989.

Anderson, Wilda. *Between the Library and the Laboratory: The Language of Chemistry in Eighteenth-Century France*. Baltimore: Johns Hopkins UP, 1984.

Argyros, Alexander J. *A Blessed Rage for Order: Deconstruction, Evolution, and Chaos.* Ann Arbor: U of Michigan P, 1991.

Arnold, Matthew. "Literature and Science." *The Complete Prose Works of Matthew Arnold.* Vol. 10. Ed. R.H. Super. Ann Arbor: U of Michigan P, 1974.

Barricelli, Jean-Pierre, and Joseph Gibaldi, eds. *Interrelations of Literature.* New York: MLA, 1982.

Barthes, Roland. *Mythologies.* Trans. Jonathan Cape. New York: Hill and Wang, 1982.

Bazerman, Charles. *Shaping Written Knowledge: The Genre and Activity of the Experimental Article in Science.* Madison: U of Wisconsin P, 1988.

Beer, Gillian. *Darwin's Plots: Evolutionary Narratives in Darwin, George Eliot and Nineteenth-Century Fiction.* Boston/London: Routledge, 1983.

Bleier, Ruth, ed. *Feminist Approaches to Science.* Elmsford, NY: Pergamon, 1986.

Bohr, Niels. *The Philosophical Writings of Niels Bohr.* 3 vols. Woodbridge, CT: Ox Bow, 1987.

Bolter, Jay David, and Richard Grusin. *Remediation: Understanding New Media.* Cambridge: MIT P, 1998.

Bono, James. *The Word of God and the Languages of Man: Interpreting Nature in Early Modern Science and Medicine.* Madison: U of Wisconsin P, 1995.

Brantlinger, Patrick. *Energy and Entropy: Science and Culture in Victorian Britain.* Bloomington: Indiana UP, 1989.

Bronowski, Jacob. *Science and Human Values.* New York: Harper and Row, 1956.

Bush, Douglas. *Science and English Poetry: A Historical Sketch, 1590–1959.* Oxford: Oxford UP, 1950.

Catalá, Rafael. *Cienciapoesía.* Minneapolis: Prisma Institute, 1987.

Chomsky, Noam. *Language and Mind.* Enlarged ed. New York: Harcourt Brace Jovanovich, 1972.

Christie, John, and Sally Shuttleworth, eds. *Nature Transfigured: Science and Literature, 1700–1900.* Manchester: Manchester UP, 1989.

Coles, Robert. *The Call of Stories: Teaching and the Moral Imagination.* Boston: Houghton Mifflin, 1989.

Cunningham, Andrew, and Nicholas Jardine. *Romanticism and the Sciences.* Cambridge: Cambridge UP, 1990.

Dennett, Daniel C. *Consciousness Explained.* Boston: Little, Brown, 1991.

Derrida, Jacques. *Of Grammatology.* Trans. Gayatri Chakravorty Spivak. Baltimore: Johns Hopkins UP, 1976.

Dobbs, Betty Jo Teeter, and Margaret C. Jacob. *Newton and the Culture of Newtonianism.* Atlantic Highlands, NJ: Humanities, 1995.

Doyle, Richard. *On Beyond Living: Rhetorical Transformations of the Life Sciences.* Stanford, CA: Stanford UP, 1997.

Edelman, Gerald. *Bright Air, Brilliant Fire.* New York: Basic Books, 1992.

Foucault, Michel. *The Archaeology of Knowledge and the Discourse on Language.* Trans. A.M. Sheridan Smith. New York: Pantheon Books, 1972.

———. *The Order of Things: An Archaeology of the Human Sciences.* New York: Random House/Vintage Books, 1973.

Gleick, James. *Chaos: Making a New Science.* New York: Penguin Books, 1987.

Gossin, Pamela. *Thomas Hardy's Novel Universe: Astronomy and the Cosmic Heroines of His Major and Minor Fiction.* Aldershot, UK: Ashgate Publishing, expected 2003.

Gratzer, Walter. *A Literary Companion to Science*. New York: W.W. Norton, 1989.

Gross, Alan G. *The Rhetoric of Science*. Cambridge: Harvard UP, 1990.

Gross, Paul R., and Norman Levitt. *Higher Superstition: The Academic Left and Its Quarrels with Science*. Baltimore: Johns Hopkins UP, 1994.

Haraway, Donna. *Modest_Witness@Second_Millennium/FemaleMan©_Meets_Onco Mouse™, Feminism and Technoscience*. New York: Routledge, 1997.

———. *Primate Visions: Gender, Race, and Nature in the World of Modern Science*. New York: Routledge, 1989.

———. *Simians, Cyborgs, and Women: The Reinvention of Nature*. New York: Routledge, 1991.

Harding, Sandra. *The Science Question in Feminism*. Ithaca, NY: Cornell UP, 1986.

———. *Whose Science? Whose Knowledge? Thinking from Women's Lives*. Ithaca, NY: Cornell UP, 1991.

Hawkins, Anne Hunsaker. *Reconstructing Illness: Studies in Pathography*. West Lafayette, IN: Purdue UP, 1993.

Hawkins, Anne Hunsaker, and Marilyn Chandler McEntyre, eds. *Approaches to Teaching Literature and Medicine*. Options for Teaching. New York: MLA Publications, 2000.

Hawley, Judith, gen. ed. *Literature and Science, 1660–1834*. London: Pickering and Chatto, 2002.

Hayles, N. Katherine. *The Cosmic Web: Scientific Field Models and Literary Strategies in the Twentieth Century*. Ithaca, NY: Cornell UP, 1984.

———. *How We Became Posthuman: Virtual Bodies in Cybernetics, Literature, and Informatics*. Chicago: U of Chicago P, 1999.

———, ed. *Chaos and Order: Complex Dynamics in Literature and Science*. Chicago: U of Chicago P, 1991.

Haynes, Roslynn D. *From Faust to Strangelove: Representations of the Scientist in Western Literature*. Baltimore: Johns Hopkins UP, 1994.

Heath-Stubbs, John, and Phillips Salman, eds. *Poems of Science*. Harmondsworth, England: Penguin Books, 1984.

Heisenberg, Werner. *Physics and Beyond: Encounters and Conversations*. Trans. Arnold J. Pomerans. New York: Harper and Row, 1977.

———. *Physics and Philosophy: The Revolution in Modern Science*. New York: Harper and Row, 1958.

Henkin, Leo J. *Darwinism in the English Novel, 1860–1910: The Impact of Evolution on Victorian Fiction*. 1940. New York: Russell, 1963.

Hesse, Mary. *Models and Analogies in Science*. Notre Dame, IN: U of Notre Dame P, 1966.

Holton, Gerald, ed. *Science and Culture*. Boston: Beacon, 1965.

Hunter, Kathryn Montgomery. *Doctors' Stories: The Narrative Structure of Medical Knowledge*. Princeton, NJ: Princeton UP, 1991.

Huxley, Aldous. *Literature and Science*. New York: Harper and Row, 1963.

Huxley, Thomas. *Science and Culture*. New York: D. Appleton and Co., 1882.

———. *Science and Education*. New York: A.L. Fowle, 1880.

Jacob, Margaret. *The Cultural Meaning of the Scientific Revolution*. New York: Knopf, 1988.

———. *The Newtonians and the English Revolution, 1689–1720*. Ithaca, NY: Cornell UP, 1976.

Jones, Richard Foster. *Ancients and Moderns*. New York: Dover, 1961.

Jones, William Powell. *The Rhetoric of Science: A Study of Scientific Ideas and Imagery in Eighteenth-Century English Poetry*. Berkeley: U of California P, 1966.

Jordanova, Ludmilla. *Sexual Visions: Images of Gender in Science and Medicine between the Eighteenth and Twentieth Centuries*. Madison: U of Wisconsin P, 1989.

———, ed. *Languages of Nature: Critical Essays on Science and Literature*. London: Free Association Books, 1986.

Joyce, Michael. *Of Two Minds: Hypertext Pedagogy and Poetics*. Ann Arbor: U of Michigan P, 1995.

Keller, Evelyn Fox. *Refiguring Life: Metaphors of Twentiety-century Biology*. New York: Columbia UP, 1995.

———. *Reflections on Gender and Science*. New Haven, CT: Yale UP, 1985.

Knorr-Cetina, Karin. *Epistemic Cultures: How the Sciences Make Knowledge*. Cambridge: Harvard UP, 1999.

Kroeber, Karl. *Ecological Literary Criticism: Romantic Imagining and the Biology of Mind*. New York: Columbia UP, 1994.

Kruger, Steven F. *AIDS Narratives: Gender and Sexuality, Fiction, and Science*. (Gender and Genre in Literature). New York: Garland, 1996.

Kuhn, Thomas S. *The Copernican Revolution: Planetary Cosmology in the Development of Western Thought*. 2nd ed. New York: Vintage, 1959.

———. *The Essential Tension: Selected Studies in Scientific Tradition and Change*. Chicago: U of Chicago P, 1977.

———. *The Structure of Scientific Revolutions*. 2nd ed., rev. Chicago: U of Chicago P, 1970.

Landow, George. *Hypertext 2.0: The Convergence of Contemporary Critical Theory and Technology*. Baltimore: Johns Hopkins UP, 1997.

Latour, Bruno, and Steve Woolgar. *Laboratory Life: The Construction of Scientific Facts*. 2nd ed. Princeton, NJ: Princeton UP, 1986.

———. *Science in Action: How to Follow Scientists and Engineers through Society*. 1987. Cambridge: Harvard UP, 1988.

———. *We Have Never Been Modern*. Trans. Catherine Porter. Cambridge: Harvard UP, 1993.

Levere, Trevor H. *Poetry Realized in Nature: Samuel Taylor Coleridge and Early Nineteenth-Century Science*. Cambridge: Cambridge UP, 1981.

Levine, George. *Darwin and the Novelists: Patterns of Science in Victorian Fiction*. Cambridge: Harvard UP, 1988.

———, ed. *One Culture: Essays in Science and Literature*. Madison: U of Wisconsin P, 1987.

———, ed. *Realism and Representation: Essays on the Problem of Realism in Relation to Science, Literature, and Culture*. Madison: U of Wisconsin P, 1993.

Levine, George, and U.C. Knoepflmacher, eds. *The Endurance of Frankenstein: Essays on Mary Shelley's Novel*. Berkeley and Los Angeles: U of California P, 1979.

Livingston, Paisley. *Literary Knowledge: Humanistic Inquiry and the Philosophy of Science*. Ithaca, NY: Cornell UP, 1988.

Locke, David. *Science as Writing*. New Haven, CT: Yale UP, 1992.

Mandelbrot, Benoit. *The Fractal Geometry of Nature*. New York: Freeman, 1977.

Markley, Robert. *Fallen Languages: Crises of Representation in Newtonian England, 1660–1740*. Ithaca, NY: Cornell UP, 1993.

Maturana, Humberto, and Francisco Varela. *Autopoiesis and Cognition*. Dordrecht: D. Reidel, 1980.

Medawar, Peter. "Science and Literature." *Pluto's Republic: Incorporating the Art of the Soluble and Induction and Intuition*. Oxford: Oxford UP, 1982. 42–61.

Merchant, Carolyn. *The Death of Nature: Women, Ecology, and the Scientific Revolution*. New York: Harper and Row, 1980.

Morton, Peter. *The Vital Science: Biology and the Literary Imagination, 1860–1900*. London: George Allen and Unwin, 1984.

Myers, Greg. *Writing Biology: Texts in the Social Construction of Scientific Knowledge*. Madison: U of Wisconsin P, 1990.

Nicolson, Marjorie Hope. *The Breaking of the Circle: Studies in the Effect of the "New Science" upon Seventeenth-Century Poetry*. Rev. ed. New York: Columbia UP, 1960.

———. *Newton Demands the Muse: Newton's "Opticks" and the Eighteenth-Century Poets*. Princeton, NJ: Princeton UP, 1946.

———. *Science and Imagination*. Ithaca, NY: Great Seal Books, 1956.

Paradis, James, and Thomas Postlewait, eds. *Victorian Science and Victorian Values: Literary Perspectives*. 1981. New Brunswick, NJ: Rutgers UP, 1985.

Paulson, William. *The Noise of Culture: Literary Texts in a World of Information*. Ithaca, NY: Cornell UP, 1988.

Peterfreund, Stuart, ed. *Literature and Science: Theory and Practice*. Boston: Northeastern UP, 1990.

Philmus, Robert M. *Into the Unknown: The Evolution of Science Fiction from Francis Godwin to H.G. Wells*. Berkeley and Los Angeles: U of California P, 1970.

Porush, David. *The Soft Machine: Cybernetic Fiction*. New York: Methuen, 1985.

Prigogine, Ilya, and Isabelle Stengers. *La Nouvelle Alliance: Métamorphose de la science*. Paris: Gallimard, 1979.

———. *Order out of Chaos: Man's New Dialogue with Nature*. New York: Bantam, 1984.

Rorty, Richard. *Philosophy and the Mirror of Nature*. Princeton, NJ: Princeton UP, 1979.

Ross, Andrew, ed. *Social Text*, nos. 46–47 (1996).

Rousseau, G.S. "Literature and Science: The State of the Field." *Isis* 69 (1978): 583–91.

———, ed. "Science and the Imagination." *Annals of Scholarship: Metastudies of the Humanities and Social Sciences* 4. 1 (1986).

———. Special issue. *University of Hartford: Studies in Literature* 19. 1 (1987).

Schiebinger, Londa. *The Mind Has No Sex?: Women in the Origins of Modern Science*. Cambridge: Harvard UP, 1989.

———. *Nature's Body: Gender in the Making of Modern Science*. Boston: Beacon, 1993.

Scholnick, Robert J., ed. *American Literature and Science*. Lexington: UP of Kentucky, 1992.

Serres, Michel. *Hermès: Literature, Science, Philosophy*. Ed. and Trans. Josué Harari and David F. Bell. Baltimore: Johns Hopkins UP, 1982.

Shaffer, Elinor, ed. *The Third Culture: Literature and Science*. Series of European Cultures: Studies in Literature and the Arts. Berlin and New York: Walter DeGruyter, 1998.

Shapin, Steven. *A Social History of Truth: Civility and Science in Seventeenth-Century England*. Chicago: U of Chicago P, 1994.

Shapin, Steven, and Simon Schaffer. *Leviathan and the Air-Pump: Hobbes, Boyle, and the Experimental Life*. Princeton, NJ: Princeton UP, 1985.

Shapiro, Barbara J. *Probability and Certainty in Seventeenth-Century England: A Study of the Relationships between Natural Science, Religion, History, Law, and Literature.* Princeton, NJ: Princeton UP, 1983.

Shinn, Terry, and Richard Whitley, eds. *Expository Science: Forms and Functions of Popularisation.* Dordrecht: Reidel, 1985.

Slade, Joseph W., and Judith Yaross Lee, eds. *Beyond the Two Cultures: Essays on Science, Technology, and Literature.* Ames: U of Iowa P, 1990.

Snow, Charles Percy. *The Two Cultures and the Scientific Revolution.* Introduced by Stefan Collini. 1959. Cambridge: Cambridge UP, 1993.

Sokal, A., and J. Bricmont. *Fashionable Nonsense: Postmodern Intellectuals' Abuse of Science.* New York: St. Martin's, 1998.

Sontag, Susan. *Illness as Metaphor.* New York: Random House, 1977.

Stent, Gunther S., ed. *The Double Helix: Text, Commentary, Reviews, Original Papers.* Norton Critical ed. New York: Norton, 1980.

Watson, James. *The Double Helix: A Personal Account of the Discovery of the Structure of DNA.* New York: Atheneum, 1968.

Wheaton, Bruce R. *The Tiger and the Shark: Empirical Roots of Wave-Particle Dualism.* Cambridge: Cambridge UP, 1983.

Young, Robert M. *Darwin's Metaphor: Nature's Place in Victorian Culture.* Cambridge: Cambridge UP, 1985.

INDEX

EDITOR'S NOTE:

A fuller list of names and titles will be posted at: **www.utdallas.edu/psgossin**
Boldface page numbers refer to main entries in the Encyclopedia.

Koch, Robert, 283; curve, snowflake, 159–60

Koestler, Arthur, **221–22**

Koran, 108

Korea, culture, 287

Koyré, Alexandre, 68–69, 414

Kress, Nancy, **222**

Kristeva, Julia, 10, 178

Kroeber, Karl, 120, 307–308

Krutch, Joseph Wood, **222,** 306

Kuberski, Philip, 219–20, 281

Kubrick, Stanley, 80, 154, 230

Kuhn, Thomas S., 194, 409; critique, 351; literary influence, 271–72; LS studies, 256–57, 482; popular science, 353; science studies, 414; scientific progress, 361. *See also* Revolutions/Crises/Paradigms/Kuhn

Kushner, Tony, 8–9, 114

Labor, 94, 158, 249–50, 290, 457, 493

Laboratory(ies), 94, **223**, 244, 274, 326, 460, 468; literature, 384, 388, 420; report(s), 353, 419, 482; science, 354, 427. *See also* Latour, Bruno

Lacan, Jacques, 10, 162, 482

Lafayette College, 261

Lamadrid, Enrique, 63, 190

Lamarck, Jean Baptiste, 45, 58–59, 71, 303

La Mettrie, Julien Offroy de, 244, 437

Land, 33–35; inhabitants, 35; ownership, 34; 445, 479; surveyors, 242

Land ethic, 45, 226–27

Landscape architecture, 25

Landscapes, 35, 67, 157, 211–13, **224,** 225, 251, 459; art, 296; description, 299; garden, 165; Greek, 292; literature, 263, 296, 354; painters, 263

Language, 10, 26, 47, 72; anthropomorphic, 60; complex use of, 13–20, 225–26, 228–29; culture, 198, 355–56, 432; Darwinian, 100, 280; denotative, 244, 332; evocative, 192; experimental, literary, 42, 215, 317; expertise, 82; fiction, 225, 356, 363; games, 432; gender, 167, 178; historians, 371; interdisciplinary, 254, 332, 463, 477;

knowledge, 60; limits, 80; literature, general, 230, 238, 240, 244, 255, 258, 455; medicine, 164, 278; metalanguage, 74; paralanguage, 14–16, 18; poetic, 344–47; poetry, scientific, 107, 175, 344, 346, 390; poststructuralism and, 482; power of, 447; primitive, 360, 402; psychology, 161–62, 228; race, 290; religion, 238, 374–75; science, 153, 163, 181, 205, 397, 419, 453; scientific, 43, 163, 255, 346, 369; style, "plain," 243, 392; technology, 456–57; terminology, 74; theory, 270, 378, 384, 386, 388, 427–29, 431–33, 482; universal, 243, 500; verbalism, 287; verbal skills, 81

Languages, 297, 300, 482; English, 316; European, 187; Russian, 262; Spanish, 188; Welsh, 213

Lapidary Lore, **224**

Laplace, Pierre-Simon, 22, 88, 250, 303, 307, 344, 443

Larsen, Kevin, 187, 313

Lassus, Bernard, **225**

Latham, Philip (pseudonym, Robert Shirley Richardson), 388

Latin, 326, 491

Latin America, 187, 189, 267, 269, 313

Latour, Bruno, xxi, 69, 119, 140, 152, **225**, 256, 280, 374, 432, 449, 463, 478; *Laboratory Life* (with Woolgar), 225

Lavoisier, Antoine-Laurent, 244, 359–60

Law, 196, 241, 394; astronomy, cosmology, 221, 281; divine, 32, 39, 91, 241, 308, 375; evolutionary, 46, 92, 494; gravitation, 176, 244, 410; literature, 76, 244, 252, 345, 447; mechanics, 231; metaphor, 91; physics, 187, 244, 273, 337–38, 421, 463; natural, 40, 86, 241, 305, 359, 375, 450; scientific, 40, 52, 454; universal, 273, 305, 504

Lawrence, D. H., 15, 208, 285, 476–77

Learning, 327, 384, 435

Leavis, Frank Raymond, xviii–xix, 322, 429, 433, 474, 476–77

Lecture(s), 313, 321, 392, 430, 432, 433, 412, 474–76; Davy, Humphry, 102; general audiences, 352–53, 361, 425,

Workshop for Potential Literature, 316. *See also* Writers

World(s), 173, 181, 483; economy, 368; imagined, 84, 152, 159, 403; world-making, 54; World Mind, 235; texts, as, 23, 219

World view(s), 186, 197, 199, 481; ecological, 102, 218, 225, 300; literature, authorial, 215, 255; science, 89, 105, 199, 381, 401, 412, 478; unified, 415

World War, 78. *See also* War; War Technology

World War I, 4, 78, 197, 218, 271–72, 412, 476. *See also* War; War Technology

World War II , 4, 78, 154, 193–94, 215; literature, 229, 231–32, 413, 446, 439; science, 78, 151, 310, 338, 340, 488, 474–76. *See also* War; War Technology

World Wide Web, 85, 86, 96–97, 201–203, 209–10, 257, 353, **504**

Wren, Christopher, 391–92

Wright brothers, Wilbur and Orville, 4

Wright, Richard, 368

Writers, 15–16, 18, 81, 320, 333, 373, 387, 456; alcohol, 9; Canada, 33; land, 479; language, 457; power, 350; reader, 294; reformist, 106; science, 192, 419, 491; workshops, 37, 213–14

Writing, 80–83, 237, 243, 370, 404, 483–84; ecology, 62; instrument, 479; medi-cal, 274; medieval, 239; painterly, 443; science, 419; scientists, 417; supernatural, 102; teaching, 229, 261; techniques, 502, 504; technology(ies), 65, 201–202, 456, 483; written language, 296

Writing Across the Curriculum, **504**

Xenophobia, 8–9

X-ray, 249, 368, 426, **505**

Yeats, William Butler, 9, 31, 206, 211, 281, 301, 476, **505–506**

Youmans, Edward Livingston, 353, 499

Young, Robert M., 361–62

Young, Thomas, 127–28, 314

Zamiatin, Evgenii, (Zamyatin, Evgeny), 115, 393, 485

Zeno, 235, 358; Zeno of Citium, 236

Zimbabwe, 5

Zodiac, 27–28, 298

Zola, Émile, 67, 81, 105, 318, **506**; evolutionary theory, 144; experimental novel, 145; literature, 152, 249, 252, 304, 319, 437; philosophy of LS, 328–29. Works: *Rougon-Macquart, Les,* 152

Zoology, 35, 175, 235, 289, 293, 302, 304, 353. *See also* Animals; Biology/Zoology

Zukav, Gary, 340, 454, **506–507**

Zulu, 5

ABOUT THE CONTRIBUTORS

YVES ABRIOUX, Département de Médiation culturelle, Université Paris III

DIANA B. ALTEGOER, Department of English, Old Dominion University

CHRIS AMIRAULT, Director, Institute for Elementary and Secondary Education, Brown University

LUIS O. ARATA, Department of Fine Arts, Languages & Philosophy, Quinnipiac University

ALEX ARGYROS, School of Arts and Humanities, University of Texas, Dallas

HEATHER V. ARMSTRONG, English Department, Drew University

MARIA L. ASSAD, Department of Modern and Classical Languages, State University College, Buffalo

CHARLES A. BALDWIN, Director, Center for Literary Computing, West Virginia University

LINDA S. BERGMANN, Department of English, Purdue University

STEPHEN D. BERNSTEIN, Department of English, University of Michigan, Flint

JAY DAVID BOLTER, Literature, Communications and Culture, Georgia Institute of Technology

ROBERT J. BONK, Communications, Department of Humanities, Widener University

ALISON E. BRIGHT, English Department, Drew University

SHELLY JARRETT BROMBERG, Department of Spanish and Portuguese, Miami University (Ohio)

J. ANDREW BROWN, Department of Romance Languages and Literatures, Washington University, St. Louis

MICHAEL A. BRYSON, Humanities, Evelyn T. Stone University College, Roosevelt University

RALPH W. BUECHLER, Department of Foreign Languages, University of Nevada, Las Vegas

HELEN J. BURGESS, Department of English, West Virginia University

JOSEPH CARROLL, English Department, University of Missouri, St. Louis

DAVID N. CASSUTO, Independent Scholar; Attorney, Coblentz, Patch, Duffy and Bass, San Francisco, CA

LEONARD CASSUTO, Department of English, Fordham University

RAFAEL CATALÁ, The Ometeca Institute, New Brunswick, NJ

RAFAEL CHABRÁN, Associate Dean for Academic Advisement and First Year Experience and Professor of Spanish, Whittier College

SANDRA J. CHRYSTAL, Communications, Marshall School of Business, Department of Business, University of Southern California

WILLIAM CRISMAN, English, Comparative Literature and German, Pennsylvania State University, Altoona

MARIAN ELIZABETH CROWE, Program of Liberal Studies, University of Notre Dame

MICHAEL J. CROWE, Program of Liberal Studies, University of Notre Dame

DENNIS DANIELSON, Department of English, University of British Columbia

DENNIS R. DEAN, Emeritus Professor, Evanston, IL

JUNE DEERY, Department of Literature, Rensselaer Polytechnic Institute

RAYMOND F. DOLLE, Department of English, Indiana State University

ELIZABETH J. DONALDSON, Department of English and Philosophy, Stephen F. Austin State University

JOSEPH DUEMER, Liberal Studies, Clarkson University

VAL DUSEK, Department of Philosophy, University of New Hampshire

WILLIAM R. EVERDELL, St. Ann's School, Brooklyn, NY

JENNIFER FITZGERALD, School of English, Queen's University, Belfast

BARTON FRIEDMAN, Emeritus Professor of English, Cleveland State University

LISA GITELMAN, Program in Media Studies, Catholic University

ROBERT C. GOLDBORT, Department of English, Indiana State University

PAMELA GOSSIN, History of Science and Literary Studies, School of Arts and Humanities, University of Texas, Dallas

NOEL GOUGH, Director, Deakin Centre for Education and Change, Deakin University, Australia

JOSEPH C. GROSECLOSE, Department of English, University of Arkansas, Little Rock

MARC HAIRSTON, William B. Hanson Center for Space Sciences, University of Texas, Dallas

PAUL A. HARRIS, Department of English, Loyola Marymount University

ANNE HUNSAKER HAWKINS, Department of Humanities, Pennsylvania State University College of Medicine

ROSLYNN D. HAYNES, School of English, University of New South Wales, Australia

LIAM F. HEANEY, Belfast, Northern Ireland

DESIREE HELLEGERS, English Department, Washington State University

YVONNE HOWELL, Department of Modern Languages and Literature, University of Richmond

MARIA F. IPPOLITO, Department of Psychology, University of Alaska, Anchorage

DOUGLAS KELLY, Emeritus Professor, Department of French and Italian, University of Wisconsin, Madison

JOHN A. KINCH, Executive Editor, *LSA Magazine*, University of Michigan

JACOB KORG, Emeritus Professor, English Department, University of Washington

JAY A. LABINGER, Administrator, Beckman Institute, California Institute of Technology

JUDITH YAROSS LEE, Co-Director, Central Region Humanities Center, and Professor, Rhetoric Program, School of Interpersonal Communication, Ohio University

MARY LIBERTIN, Department of English, Shippensburg University of Pennsylvania

PAISLEY LIVINGSTON, Department of English, McGill University

JORDAN MARCHÉ, Department of Astronomy, University of Wisconsin, Madison

ROBERT MARKLEY, Department of English, West Virginia University

ANNE BRATACH MATTHEWS, Department of English, Lane Community College, Jackson, TN

JAMES I. MCCLINTOCK, Emeritus Professor, Department of English, Michigan State University

MICHAEL B. MCDONALD, Department of English, Foreign Language, and Speech, Lane Community College, Eugene, OR

MURDO WILLIAM MCRAE, Department of English, Tennessee Technological University

STEVEN MEYER, Department of English, Washington University

RICHARD NASH, Department of English, Indiana University

KATHRYN A. NEELEY, Division of Technology, Culture, and Communication, University of Virginia

JAISHREE K. ODIN, Liberal Studies Program, University of Hawaii, Manoa

JOANN PALMERI, Independent Scholar, Norman, OK

JAMES G. PARADIS, Head, Program in Writing and Humanistic Studies, Massachusetts Institute of Technology

SIDNEY PERKOWITZ, Department of Physics, Emory University

STUART PETERFREUND, Graduate Director, Department of English, Northeastern University

ROD PHILLIPS, Writing and American Culture, James Madison College, Michigan State University

FERNANDO POYATOS, University of New Brunswick; Algeciras, Cadiz, Spain

DALE J. PRATT, Department of Spanish and Comparative Literature, Brigham Young University

DOUG RUSSELL, Deputy Head, School of Communication and Cultural Studies, Curtin University of Technology, Perth, Western Australia

JACQUI SADASHIGE, Department of Classical Studies, University of Pennsylvania

ARIELLE SAIBER, Assistant Professor of Italian, Bowdoin College

LANCE SCHACHTERLE, Assistant Provost for Academic Affairs, Worcester Polytechnic Institute

ELMAR SCHENKEL, Chair of British Literature, Institut fuer Anglistik, Universität Leipzig

JOSEPH W. SLADE, Co-Director, Central Region Humanities Center, and Professor, School of Telecommunications, Ohio University

NICHOLAS SPENCER, Department of English, University of Nebraska, Lincoln

SHARON STOCKTON, Department of English, Dickinson College

KRISTINE SWENSON, Department of English, University of Missouri, Rolla

FREDERICK TURNER, School of Arts and Humanities, University of Texas, Dallas

DAVID KIRK VAUGHAN, Head, Business Communication, Sultan Qaboos University, Oman

ANNE C. VILA, Department of French and Italian, University of Wisconsin, Madison

LAURA DASSOW WALLS, Department of English, Lafayette College

STEPHEN J. WEININGER, Department of Chemistry & Biochemistry, Worcester Polytechnic Institute

FRED D. WHITE, Department of English, Santa Clara University

PHILIP K. WILSON, History of Medicine, Department of Humanities, Pennsylvania State College of Medicine

ROBERT M. YOUNG, Professor Emeritus, Centre for Psychotherapeutic Studies, University of Sheffield

LISA ZEITZ, Chair of Undergraduate Studies, English Department, University College, University of Western Ontario